1982 ANNUAL EDUCATIONAL CONFERENCE PROCEEDINGS:
Focus on Education

Volume Twenty-Four

This book consists of edited texts of speakers' presentations at the Annual Educational Conference of the International Foundation of Employee Benefit Plans held October 15-20, 1982 in Montreal, Quebec, Canada.

Becky A. Wright, Editor

1982 ANNUAL EDUCATIONAL CONFERENCE PROCEEDINGS:
Focus on Education

Volume Twenty-Four

Montreal, Quebec, Canada

international foundation of employee benefit plans
18700 WEST BLUEMOUND ROAD • P.O. BOX 69 • BROOKFIELD, WISCONSIN 53005 • PHONE 414 786-6700

ANNUAL CONFERENCE PROCEEDINGS SERIES

1956 Workshop	Chicago	Out of Print
1957 Workshop	Denver	Out of Print
1960 Workshop	Miami	Out of Print
1961 Workshop	Philadelphia	Out of Print
1962 Workshop	Denver	Out of Print
1963 Workshop	Miami	Out of Print
1964 Conference	New York	Available
1965 Conference	San Francisco	Available
1966 Conference	Montreal	Out of Print
1967 Conference	Miami Beach	Available
1968 Conference	San Francisco	Available
1969 Conference	New York	Available
1970 Conference	Honolulu	Available
1971 Conference	Miami Beach	Available
1972 Conference	San Diego	Available
1973 Conference	San Francisco	Available
1974 Conference	Toronto	Available
1975 Conference	Honolulu	Available
1976 Conference	Miami Beach	Available
1977 Conference	San Francisco	Available
1978 Conference	Atlanta	Available
1979 Conference	New York	Available
1980 Conference	Honolulu	Available
1981 Conference	Acapulco	Available
1982 Conference	Montreal	Available

The opinions expressed in this book are those of the authors. The International Foundation of Employee Benefit Plans disclaims responsibility for views expressed and statements made in books published by the Foundation.

Copies of this book may be obtained from the Publications Department, International Foundation of Employee Benefit Plans, 18700 West Bluemound Road, P.O. Box 69, Brookfield, Wisconsin 53005

Payment must accompany order:

   $20.00 each for Foundation members

   $35.00 each for Nonmembers

©*1983 International Foundation of Employee Benefit Plans, Inc.*
ISBN 0-89154-201-9
Printed in the United States of America

9.5M-783

*The Board of Directors
of the International Foundation of Employee Benefit Plans,
on behalf of the entire membership,
wishes to express its gratitude
to the many persons
who contributed so generously
to the 1982 Annual Educational Conference
and to this volume of proceedings*

Officers and Directors — 1982

Officers

Wesley G. Jeltema
*President and
Chairman of the Board*

Edward D. Zacharko
President-Elect

Frank Parker
Secretary

Henry S. Hunt
Treasurer

Willard J. Carlson
Past Chairman

John L. Watts
Past Chairman

Lee R. Polacheck
Executive Vice President

Leonard Zarzynski
*Vice President of
Finance and Administration
Assistant Treasurer*

Voting Directors

John W. Bernard

Bernard Handel

Kenneth J. Brown

Jack T. Hayes

James D. Compton

Larry Hilaire

D. Richard Dobie

Lee F. Jost

Warren Driver

James Kemp

Raymond F. Gabel

Advisory Directors

 Vincent E. Kommer, Sr.
 Michael J. Riley
 Eugene B. Burroughs
 Daniel S. Kampel

 David M. LaPlante
 Donald H. Rowcliffe, Jr.
 William J. Chadwick
 Robert B. Lashly

 Sheldon P. Lewis
 William J. Taylor
 John J. Coury, Jr.
 Kenneth M. McCaffree

 H. Clay McCulloh
 Gerry V. Thibault
 Jeffrey R. Fuller
 Albert Morrison, Jr.

 Joseph E. Mastrangelo
 Wendell W. Young, III
 Martin J. Gallagher
 John S. Perreca

 Marc Gertner

President's Introduction

The 1982 Annual Educational Conference was a most successful event in a most successful year for the International Foundation of Employee Benefit Plans.

In quantity and in quality, from beginning to end, the program of sessions and activities was true to the conference theme—"Focus on Education." The more than three days of speeches, panel discussions and workshops added up to a virtual outpouring of information and enlightenment relating to the effective management of employee benefit plans. The trustees, administrators and advisors who attended could not help but go home armed with new ideas and greater insight to apply in operations of the plans they serve.

Problems and concerns were many for the employee benefits industry in the United States in 1982. Some were familiar, carried over in the category of unfinished business and wanting attention and resolution; others were of more recent vintage, testing anew the resourcefulness of trustees and plan professionals. In pointed and positive fashion, the Annual Conference attempted to address them.

At the forefront in everyone's mind in 1982 was the nation's economy. Coping with the recession—with countless variations on the theme—was a subject throughout the conference. Closely akin, sound and prudent investment of benefit plan assets was an area of considerable dialog—buoyed yet puzzled a bit by the then-new and uncharted stock market upsurge. Federal legislation—that passed and that proposed—along with the myriad administrative rulings and court decisions affecting benefit plans—occupied many a session's agenda. A pervading concern for those in the health and welfare plan area was strategies for containment of hospital-medical costs—on the rise at a disturbing pace despite significant reduction in the general inflation rate. And, as always, much time was given to changes in the mechanics and details involved in benefit plans' day-to-day business.

Preparing for the Annual Conference is a formidable task, and there are many who deserve a word of thanks and recognition for their contributions to its success. For the Board of Directors and the entire Foundation membership, I wish to extend sincere appreciation to the Educational Program Committee and other committees, to the many speakers and panelists and to the headquarters staff. The considerable contributions of time and effort by all resulted in a well-organized and well-executed program.

The 28th Annual Educational Conference was exemplary of the Foundation's constant striving in fulfillment of its educational mission. To the extent that the conference and our many other institutes and seminars help in that aim, so then do the published proceedings of those educational programs. It is our wish and our intent that this volume from the 1982 conference serve as a valued and widely used source of information.

Wesley G. Jeltema
President and
Chairman of the Board
1982

Contents

CHAPTER 1	THE LEGAL–LEGISLATIVE ENVIRONMENT		
	Current PBGC Legislative and Regulatory Developments	Edwin M. Jones	3
	Prohibited Transaction Exemptions—1982	Stephen A. Weinstein	13
	Suspension of Pension Benefits	Katherine A. Hesse, CEBS	17
	Confidentiality of Information and Plan Records	Margery Sinder Friedman	23
	Considerations of Post-MPPAA Benefit Improvements	Carolyn D. Gentile	41
	Legal Odds and Ends	Michael C. Greenfield and Lee Elberts	46
	Collecting Withdrawal Liability	Timothy P. O'Reilly	49
	Marital Property Interests in Retirement Benefits: Treatment on Divorce	Virginia L. Gibson and Charles A. Storke	56
	The Legal Right to Die	David L. Rider and Maria F. Melchiori	72
CHAPTER 2	WHAT COMES NEXT?		
	New Trends in Forecasting the Future of Pension Plans	John S. Perreca	85
	Employee Benefits: A Transformation	Dallas L. Salisbury	90
	U.S. Monetary Policy: Looking Forward	Beryl W. Sprinkel, Ph.D., CFA	95
	Computers With Human Characteristics—Threshold to the Future	Earl C. Joseph	100
CHAPTER 3	TOPICS IN PLAN ADMINISTRATION		
	The Role of a Trustee in a Collectively Bargained Pension Trust	E. Calvin Golumbic	115
	An Auditor Looks at Monitoring Cash Flow	Gilbert K. Reeves, CPA	117
	Techniques for Monitoring Cash Flow	Edward F. Zimmerman, Jr., CLU, FLMI	130
	Administrative Considerations in Establishing Voluntary and Deductible Employee Contributions to Multiemployer Defined Contribution Plans	Bernard Handel, CPA, CEBS	135

	Fiduciary Responsibility and Prohibited Transactions: 1982 Update	William J. Chadwick and Lawrence J. Hass	141
	Trustees' Personal Liability Under ERISA and the Importance of Proper "Defensive" Documentation—The Fabled "Paper Trail"	Richard J. Davis, Jr.	151
	Fiduciary Liability Insurance— What the Policies Cover and What They Don't	Warren H. Saltzman	154
	Fiduciary Liability Insurance— Its Place in the Insurance Program of a Multiemployer Fund and How to Buy the Cover	Stephen Horn, II, CPCU	158
	Collecting Withdrawal Liability	Robert A. DeCori	163
	Trustees' Responsibilities for Collection of Employer Contributions	Michael J. Carroll	168
	Attitudes and Approaches of Trustees Toward MPPAA	Marc Gertner	175
	The Actuarial Effects of MPPAA on Benefit Improvements	Russell W. Thurau	181
	The Trustee Examines Special Problems	David W. Silverman	185
	Trustee Education and Expenses for Educational Programs	Robert W. Ridley	192
	Policy Manuals	Leo A. Majich	197
	We Had a Barbecue and Nobody Came Except the Fire Department	Sheldon P. Lewis, CPA	202
	CEBS: A View From the Center of the Action	Joseph M. Courtney, CEBS	207
CHAPTER 4	PROFESSIONAL SERVICES		
	The Role of the Plan Professional	Donald A. Smart	211
	The Trustees' Duty to Monitor and Evaluate Professional Advisors	Geoffrey V. White	214
	The Board of Trustees and Its Counsel: A Question of Professional Responsibility	Bernard M. Baum	223
	You and Your Investment Manager	Gary P. Brinson, CFA	227
	Evaluating Your Investment Manager	Bonnie R. Cohen	230
CHAPTER 5	INVESTMENTS		
	An Investment Strategy for the 1980s	Martin D. Sass	239
	Spectrum of Investments: 1977-1982	Eugene B. Burroughs, CFA	244
	The Evolving Role of Labor in Pension Fund Investment	Jack Sheinkman	256

	Tying Defined Contribution Plans to Investment Earnings	Jon S. Brightman, CPCU, CFA	262
	Solving Investment Problems for Small Funds	F. Gilbert Bickel, III, CEBS	269
	Fixed Income Alternatives	George J. Collins	272
	Options for Employee Benefit Funds	Herbert B. Soroca	284
	Investing in Real Estate	Vincent F. Martin, Jr.	287
CHAPTER 6	COST CONTAINMENT: ISSUES AND STRATEGIES		
	Medical Care in the '80s	Larry M. Fisher	297
	Cost Containment Through Plan Design	Glen Slaughter	314
	A Business Perspective on the Management of Health Care Costs	Edgar G. Davis	317
	Cost Containment Through Health Education and Welfare Programs	Charles J. Mazza, CEBS	321
	A Major Innovation in Controlling Prescription Costs	Frederick Klein	335
CHAPTER 7	U.S./CANADIAN RELATIONS		
	Canadian–American Relations: A Canadian Perspective, or a Latent Continentalist Comes Out of the Closet	John Crispo, Ph.D.	343
	U.S./Canadian Reciprocity	William A. Rivers	347
CHAPTER 8	BENEFIT PLAN DESIGN OPTIONS		
	Flexible Benefits for Multiemployer Plans	William R. Breher	355
	Employee Assistance Programs for Alcohol and Drug Abuse	Denis Stallings, PE	364
	Dental Insurance: Goals, Plan Design, Choosing an Administrator and the Role of Dental Consultants	Robert J. Leaf, D.M.D.	370
	Prepaid Legal Plans: Structure and Implementation	William M. Kirschner	379
	Prepaid Legal Services as an Employee Benefit	Alec M. Schwartz	386
	Legal Service Plans: Legal Basis, Legal Developments	Cheryl Denney White	394
CHAPTER 9	ALTERNATIVES IN HEALTH CARE		
	Alternative Health Care Delivery Systems	James F. Doherty	401
	Labor's Involvement in Health Care Coalitions	Karen Ignagni	405

	Encouraging Hospital Involvement in Health Care Coalitions	Richard L. Epstein	408
	Health Care Coalitions: A Perspective From the Medical Profession	James S. Todd, M.D.	410
CHAPTER 10	RETIREMENT		
	Pre-Retirement Preparation Assistance	Todd Aldrich	415
	Retirement Counseling: Necessity or Frill?	R. George Martorana	422
	Funding Retirees' Health and Welfare Benefits	Steven A. Harrold, FSA	428
	Work: The Fourth Leg of Retirement	Matthew M. Lind, Ph.D.	440
	Myths and Realities of the Older Worker	Marilyn S. Albert, Ph.D.	445
	Communication With Retirees	Donald H. Rowcliffe, Jr., CPA	453
CHAPTER 11	COMMUNICATION PROGRAMS		
	Developing Communication Material	Joseph A. Brislin	459
	Understanding Production	Edward M. Finkelstein	466

CHAPTER 1

The Legal-Legislative Environment

Edwin M. Jones

Executive Director
Pension Benefit Guaranty Corporation
Washington, D.C.

Stephen A. Weinstein

Attorney
Gorsuch, Kirgis, Campbell, Walker & Grover
Denver, Colorado

Katherine A. Hesse, CEBS

Attorney
Murphy, Lamere and Murphy
Braintree, Massachusetts

Margery Sinder Friedman

Associate Attorney
Morgan, Lewis & Bockius
Washington, D.C.

Carolyn D. Gentile

Administrator/Special Counsel
Seafarers International Union and Related Funds
Brooklyn, New York

Michael C. Greenfield

Director
Asher, Goodstein, Pavalon, Gittler,
Greenfield & Segall, Ltd.
Chicago, Illinois

Lee Elberts

Associate
Asher, Goodstein, Pavalon, Gittler,
Greenfield & Segall, Ltd.
Chicago, Illinois

Timothy P. O'Reilly

Partner
Morgan, Lewis & Bockius
Philadelphia, Pennsylvania

Virginia L. Gibson

Associate
Pillsbury, Madison & Sutro
San Francisco, California

Charles A. Storke

Partner
Pillsbury, Madison & Sutro
San Francisco, California

David L. Rider

Member
Rider, Drake, Sommers & Loeb, P.C.
Newburgh, New York

Maria F. Melchiori

Associate
Rider, Drake, Sommers and Loeb, P.C.
Newburgh, New York

Current PBGC Legislative and Regulatory Developments

BY EDWIN M. JONES

I APPRECIATE the opportunity given to me by the International Foundation to discuss current regulations and developments affecting the Pension Benefit Guaranty Corporation (PBGC or the Corporation). First, let me note that there are many of you who work and live a good distance from Washington, D.C. Having been in that category for many years myself, I know it is often helpful to have the name of a person in Washington whom you can call from time to time for answers to questions or to get some kind of direction on a specific issue. If there is any way I can guide you on an issue relating to an area of PBGC authority or responsibility, feel free to call or write me. If I can't answer your question or resolve your problem, maybe I can at least set you in the right direction.

When Congress enacted ERISA in 1974, its intent was to protect the retirement benefits earned by millions of American workers. In a number of cases over the years, workers had reached retirement age only to learn that their pension income would be far less than what they expected; at times, their pensions were even nonexistent.

Title IV of the 1974 ERISA legislation established the PBGC to act as the government's insurer of basic pension plan benefits in the event that a defined benefit plan, if terminated, could not meet its benefit obligations. At that time, the concept of pension insurance was new in this country and, as a result, Congress had little guidance in formulating the program. Nevertheless, the insurance program was implemented and has worked well to date. The PBGC has assets of about $700 million and is paying out over $100 million annually in benefits to about 50,000 people. These benefits might never have been received had there not been a PBGC. There are another 50,000 workers who have deferred benefit rights guaranteed by the PBGC, which will be paid in the future.

From a broader perspective, the insurance program protects approximately 33 million people who are participants of defined benefit plans. This number accounts for about one-third of the American workforce. Of that total workforce, 14% is

Mr. Jones is executive director of the Pension Benefit Guaranty Corporation, a self-funding government corporation created by the Employee Retirement Income Security Act of 1974, which insures the pension benefits of 35 million workers in defined benefit pension plans. Mr. Jones was previously a partner in the lawfirm of Lane & Mittendorf and before that a partner of Shea & Gould, specializing in legal, insurance and investment problems under ERISA. Mr. Jones also has a background in the insurance industry and was a lawyer and officer of the New York Life Insurance Company for 20 years. He is a member of the Association of Life Insurance Counsel. In the financial area, he has been the president of a private investment company for a long period. Mr. Jones is chairman of the New York Area Committee on Employee Benefits of the American Bar Association's Tax Section. He is chairman of the New York State Bar Association's Joint Committee of Lawyers and Accountants and a past chairman of that association's Taxation Section. He is a Phi Beta Kappa graduate of Yale University and has a law degree and a master's of laws in taxation from the New York University School of Law.

over 55 years of age and 17% is between the ages of 45-55. These people are beginning to think more seriously about their retirement needs. The two segments combined also account for approximately one-third of the American workforce—people at or very near retirement age.

What do all these numbers mean to PBGC? What legislative and regulatory responsibilities do we have in providing insurance for an increasing number of retirees in defined benefit plans? In broad terms, the Congress requires that the PBGC do at least three things:

- *Encourage* the maintenance of defined benefit pension plans.
- *Assure* that the promised benefits can be paid to covered workers.
- *Charge* the lowest possible premiums but, at the same time, make sure that the plan remains financially sound.

Our job has not been easy as the number of terminations and benefit claims has increased in recent years, particularly during the last six months. I will discuss current developments in the single employer insurance program and the multi-employer program.

Single Employer Insurance Program and Required Premium Increase

In May 1982, the PBGC requested Congress to authorize a $6 premium per person per year, effective January 1, 1983 to help offset the costs of the increased number of claims in the single employer insurance program. It was then thought that about $85 million in claims would be made against the PBGC during its 1982 fiscal year. This sum reflected the average 9% annual increase that the Corporation had experienced over its years of existence. Average claims had been $62 million in the years 1978-81 and $25 million in 1975-77. However, the 9% increase proved to be far short of the mark.

On the day after I became executive director of PBGC, Braniff Airways filed for bankruptcy and subsequently terminated its four pension plans. Not long after, we received terminations from several firms, including White Farms, Rath Packing, Johnson Steel and several smaller plans. As a result, the earlier projected fiscal year 1982 claims figure of $85 million will probably exceed $200 million as of the end of fiscal year 1983.

Looking forward to the next five years, net claims against the system are projected to average about $100 million per year, or about $500 million during the next five years. This figure reflects a projected 9% a year increase in claims from 1981 levels. To finance those claims, we need to increase our present single employer $2.60 premium to $6.

If Congress does not act in time to make the increase effective on January 1, the $6 figure would have to be revised upward by about $1. Moreover, the $500 million does not include any figures for unprecedentedly large cases, such as is possible if the International Harvester plans are terminated. Recent figures indicate that termination of International Harvester's hourly and salaried plans could result in claims against the agency of $600-$800 million. If that termination were to occur, the $6 premium would not be enough to fund these claims on a sound insurance company concept. Each $500 million of additional claims received ratably over a five year period requires a minimum $3 premium increase for five years. Thus, a premium of at least $9-$11 would be needed if we were to fund additional plan liabilities of $600-$800 million over a five year period.

The second problem faced by the PBGC is its present deficit. Most insurance companies have a surplus over claim reserve of 7-15%. PBGC not only does not have a surplus, it has a deficit of approximately $350 million. Under typical state insurance regulatory principles, the Corporation would be classified as technically insolvent. Of course, we have assets of about $800 million and obviously have enough to pay our annual cash payment commitments of over $100 million for a certain amount of time. Therefore, there is no cause for immediate concern that guaranteed payments will cease. Benefit payments will continue, but we are falling short of running a truly sound insurance system unless we can get our assets up to the proper level.

The deficit was projected earlier to reach about $235 million by the end of the calendar year. Because of the recent large number of case terminations, this figure will probably be closer to $350 million. We have calculated that a $2 premium increase would enable us to pay off the $235 million deficit over the next five years. (With a $350 million deficit figure, the $2 should be increased to over $3.) Thus, we are asking Congress to permit a premium increase to $6 per participant per year in single employer plans—$3 for projected claims of $100 million, $2 to eliminate a $235 million deficit and $1 to cover administrative costs.

The PBGC's board of directors, composed of Labor Secretary Donovan as chairman, Treasury Secretary Regan and Commerce Secretary Baldrige, has not yet concluded that we must ask for more than $6. We have been trying to operate under the Congressional mandate to keep the premium at the lowest possible level. This premium is paid by employers, and we don't want to increase the load being carried by them prematurely.

In asking Congress for a $6 premium, the PBGC's board has had the endorsement of the Reagan Administration. This Administration is fully cognizant of the need for protecting pension benefits of American workers and for getting the PBGC insurance system on a strong financial basis, consistent with sound insurance company principles. To that end the PBGC has spent, and will continue to spend, much time and effort in giving facts to Congressional committees and in seeking the support of business, industry and labor.

In addition to the premium increase, Congress has before it legislation proposed by the Administration that would close certain loopholes that have posed a financial drain for the single employer program. This legislation complicates the picture. A brief summary of these legislative changes and their status follows.

Status of Single Employer Legislation

Changing the "Trigger"

One proposed amendment is to change the event that triggers insurance coverage from termination of a sponsor's plan to liquidation of the sponsoring company. This change would require a company, so long as it remains in business, to remain responsible for continuing to fund the unfunded vested benefits by making contributions to that plan over 15 years. The plan's vesting and accruals would be frozen. Its obligations would be reduced and the PBGC's insurance program would not take over unless the company was completely liquidated. Thus, an insurable event involving the PBGC would arise only if and when a company became completely liquidated. This amendment would close off the opportunity under current law for an ongoing company with low net worth to terminate its pension plan and dump its unfunded plan liabilities on the PBGC's insurance system, while continuing to do business as usual.

Changing PBGC's Creditor Status

Two other areas would change the status of employer liability claim to that of general creditor status and impose contingent liability on a plan sponsor that transfers unfunded plan liabilities to another company.

As to general creditor status, the policy position of the Administration, enunciated in November 1981 by William Niskanen, a member of the Council of Economic Advisors, is that the PBGC's claim against the employer should have the status of a general creditor and be for the entire amount of unfunded liability assumed by the PBGC under this insurance program. This situation would contrast with current law, in which PBGC has a priority claim equal to 30% of the net worth of the employer.

The PBGC has endeavored to secure the agreement of interested business and labor groups to the incorporation of that concept into the law. Business groups have responded with universal objection. They contend that, if the PBGC's claim were to have general creditor status without a net worth limitation, the ability of business to obtain credit would be adversely affected, the cost of borrowing would be unnecessarily increased and the adoption and maintenance of defined benefit plans would be discouraged.

After lengthy discussions with industry and labor groups, it has become clear that considerable diminution in the coverage scope of general creditor status is needed if the Administration is to obtain any significant business support for that concept. One alternative would be to permit the PBGC's claim to have general creditor status only if the funding status of the plan does not meet certain tests at the time of plan termination. In short, if the tests were met, PBGC's claims would have subordinated status. This possibility has considerable business support.

One test would require a plan to be 80% funded for vested benefits as of the date that its sponsoring employer enters a bankruptcy proceeding and to be 70% funded for vested benefits for the two prior plan years. In the case of new plans, this test would be phased in over eight years. Under a second test, PBGC's claim would have general creditor status, regardless of funding status, if the employer has been granted a funding waiver in the three preceding plan years. Other broad exceptions have been fashioned for small business that would exempt 98% of small business plans from general creditor scope. As an alternative measure of PBGC's claim, the PBGC could elect to seek 30% of the net worth of the employer, as under current law, and forgo any claims based on general creditor status.

Secondary Liability

A second important change under the proposed legislation being discussed would impose secondary liability on a plan sponsor that transfers unfunded liabilities to another employer. Current law presents a potentially attractive incentive for larger companies to spin off or sell losing operations, together with their associated pension liabilities, to a weaker company. Then, the transferee terminates the pension plans at a time when 30% of the net worth of the transferee is small or nothing. The plan's unfunded liabilities are then transferred to the PBGC.

One such case involved the sale by International Harvester of its Wisconsin Steel Division to a small company. The sale was completely leveraged and the loan was underwritten by the Economic Development Corporation. The company which purchased Wisconsin Steel went bankrupt within three years after the purchase and the PBGC had to pick up the pension plan and incur unfunded vested liabilities to the extent guaranteed. PBGC's loss for that plan alone is estimated to be in excess of $25 million.

The proposal of the Administration, enunciated in November 1981, to impose such contingent liability broadly has met with heavy resistance from the large and small business community. Discussions with such groups have developed modifications, which have considerable business support. However, the Administration has not yet expressed agreement with them.

Safe Harbor Tests

Under such modifications, transferor liability would be imposed only if the purchasing company is not able to meet certain safe harbor tests. If any one of the safe harbor tests is met, the transferor would never be liable for any underfunding under any circumstances.

The safe harbor tests would enable business to determine at the time of a proposed transfer transaction whether secondary liability is a potential risk to the seller, thus facilitating the normal operations of business. One safe harbor resulting in no possibility of transfer liability would exist if the level of net operating income of the transferee is three times the plan's unfunded vested liabilities for three years—in other words an income to liabilities coverage ratio of three to one. Another safe harbor test is the existence of factors that illustrate that the transferee is financially stronger than the transferor, to be promulgated in regulations of the PBGC. A third safe harbor test would be the existence of unfunded vested liabilities of less than $350,000 at the time of the transfer. All alternative legislative proposals currently under discussion are proceeding on the assumption that there will be no cutback in the level of guaranteed benefits.

There remains much to be done before any of these proposed changes receive the support necessary to secure their enactment. The overall view among legislators seems to be that a consensus of large and small business and of labor interests must exist before any legislative changes will be achieved, including the premium increase. Even with such a consensus there is no certainty that Administration approval of the consensus will be given. Without such approval, successful legislation is unlikely.

Multiemployer Plans Insurance Program Legislative Developments

Also of great importance and facing criticism and problems is the multiemployer insurance program, as enacted by the Multiemployer Pension Plan Amendments Act of 1980. That act is presently subject to considerable litigation contesting its constitutionality. There are about 120 cases pending in various federal courts around the country. All of the cases decided thus far have upheld the legislation on constitutional grounds, except for two decisions in one California court. To understand the present difficulties and criticism in light of the universal approval of that act in 1980 by all business and labor groups and only one dissenting vote in the House of Representatives, a brief comment on the law as it stood before the 1980 act is necessary.

Under the 1974 act (ERISA), an employer could withdraw from a multiemployer plan without further financial obligations to the plan, even if the withdrawing employer left behind vested benefits payable to its employees that had not been funded by its contributions. Remaining employers were then left with the responsibility for funding those benefits, as well as the benefits of their own employees. The only liability imposed on a withdrawing employer under prior law was liability to the Pension Benefit Guaranty Corporation in the event of plan termination within five years after the employer's withdrawal—and then only if the employer had contributed to the plan within the five plan years preceding termination.

The termination liability provisions and the absence of liability for withdrawal had the effect of encouraging employers to withdraw from multiemployer plans at the first sign of plan financial difficulties. By withdrawing early, employers could shift the funding burden to other employers and evade liability completely if the plan continued for five years and later terminated. This action could heavily penalize employers who remain in the plan, or impose liability on the PBGC insurance system for guaranteed benefits—a large portion of which might be attributable to benefits for employees of still viable employers who earlier pulled out of the plan without liability for the cost of such benefits.

Out of this basic problem of who should ultimately be responsible for the cost of plan benefits, and how the cost should be equitably shared, came the Multiemployer Pension Plan Amendments Act of 1980. PBGC, Congress and diverse groups representing plans, employers and unions wrestled with these issues during the development of that legislation. Concerns then and now centered on the Congressionally accepted policy of assuring payment of pension benefits earned by workers, and who would pay the cost of such protection. The concept of withdrawal liability, although troubling to many Congressmen, businessmen and labor groups, was nevertheless broadly supported in 1980 as necessary to assure continuation of multiemployer plans as viable retirement income vehicles and to assure a fiscally sound multiemployer termination insurance program at a reasonable cost.

Problems

It is now over two years since MPPAA was enacted. During that period much concern has been raised by employers, union legislators and others over the potentially adverse effects of the withdrawal liability provisions. Among these concerns are:

- Will withdrawal liability have a "chilling" effect on the long run viability of multiemployer pension plans by discouraging new entrants or discouraging expansion of operations by existing contributors because of unknown amounts of liabilities they may be assuming?
- Are other aspects of labor relations being adversely affected to an unacceptable degree?
- Will withdrawal liability be a constant source of conflict between labor and employers? There have already been a number of arbitration cases on disputes between management and labor trustees over benefit increases, with management trustees seeking to limit increases that would result in higher withdrawal liability.
- Are employers being treated inequitably? Significant facts existing at time of their withdrawal, when the amount of their withdrawal liability is fixed, often change as time passes for a wide variety of reasons, e.g., earnings increases or decreases, changes in interest assumptions or turnover and mortality rates.
- Will withdrawal liability have a negative impact on normal business operations by impeding sales of businesses, causing employers to continue unprofitable businesses or adversely affecting an employer's ability to secure financing?
- Does withdrawal liability impact the estates of deceased employers too harshly?

On the other hand, a case can be made for the view sponsored by many that the act is beginning to have its intended effect. Employers are more aware of the benefit structure in multiemployer plans than they were before enactment of MPPAA and of their responsibility for properly funding plan benefits accruing to their own employees during the period of their participation in the plan. From much correspondence that I have seen, it appears that many of the existing complaints stem from the fact that employers either were not aware that MPPAA impaired withdrawal liability when it was passed or did not recognize its implications until much later, often not until withdrawal liability was actually assessed.

Solutions

Well, what is to be done now? The central issue is still whether employers who do not withdraw from a multiemployer plan (the "stayers") should bear the brunt of paying for unfunded liabilities attributable to employees of employers who leave the plan (the "leavers") or whether such leavers should bear the cost of the unfunded liabilities attributable to the leavers' employees. What solutions are possible?

Many groups have made various legislative proposals to deal with these concerns. For example, the American Trucking Association and the Teamsters union have developed a legislative proposal jointly, as have various construction industry employer associations such as the Associated Specialty Contractors. The major focus of the ATA-Teamsters current proposal is to exempt employers in the trucking industry and employees contributing to trucking industry plans from withdrawal liability. The proposal would also expand PBGC's authority to grant "construction type" exemption to other industries. It would give PBGC the authority to approve the elimination of withdrawal liability for financially sound plans. Under the proposal, transportation industry plans would be subject to a rule similar to the construction rule in current law, i.e., a withdrawal does not occur if an employer discontinues operations in an area.

The proposals of other construction industry associations focus on reducing an employer's exposure to withdrawal liability by prohibiting increases in benefits that will raise unfunded vested benefits, unless the plan is "well-funded." Also, these proposals would exempt employers from liability for "involuntary" cessations of contributions, such as loss of a contract or because of a natural disaster, such as fire, which destroys the employer's facility.

A recently formed coalition group of food, printing industry and contractor associations has

caused a bill to be introduced in Congress that has the following initial elements:
- Prohibition of retrospective benefit increases or of granting past service credit unless the ratio of plan assets to vested benefits is at certain levels:
  1. 0.7 to 1, or 70% funded during the first five years after enactment of a new law
  2. 0.9 to 1, or 90% funded in subsequent years. Full notification to participants of plan amendments that increase benefits or grant past service credits and of methods of calculating assets and benefit values.
- PBGC would be given authority to grant variances from the 70% or 90% tests for limited periods.
- Any increases in benefits in violation of specified principles would be void.
- A basic premium of $1.40 per participant per year would be reduced by 35% if the plan is 90% funded, increased by 50% if the plan is 50-70% funded and tripled if the plan is less than 50% funded.
- If the plan is terminated, continued funding requirements would be cut back to PBGC-guaranteed levels.
- An employer can sell his company's assets, and not be stuck with contingent withdrawal liability (1) if the buyer's contribution base is at least 85% of the seller's contribution base, (2) if the purchaser provides a letter of credit equal to the seller's contributions for the year before sale or (3) if, during the next five years, the employer withdraws from a plan or fails to make a contribution when due.
- Seller has secondary liability if the purchaser withdraws and doesn't pay his withdrawal liability, phased down by 20% per year.
- Seller is excused from withdrawal liability if buyer's net worth exceeds the seller's withdrawal liability and the buyer's contribution requirement is equal to 85% of the seller's.
- No withdrawal liability if plan is fully funded at time of withdrawal
- PBGC rates must be used in calculating values, unless an actuary certifies that they are not appropriate.
- No withdrawal liability if sale or liquidation occurs within one year of the death of a sole proprietor actively engaged in business, on the death of a partner or shareholder actively engaged in the business or if a natural disaster caused cessation of business
- No withdrawal liability if employer loses a service contract or lease and has to close operations
- No withdrawal liability if government action causes cessation of the business
- If there is a dispute about amounts, no payment due until arbitration decision is reached
- Each employer must be given, free of charge, information on his withdrawal.
- Withdrawal is curtailed if there is a decertification of the union, a change in unions or a cessation of union representation or an agreement concerning a withdrawal. Then, if participants of employers in old plan transfer to a new plan, a proper amount of assets must also be transferred; withdrawal liability of the old plan would be offset by any withdrawal liability incurred by employer under the new plan.
- No withdrawal liability if withdrawal occurred before September 26, 1980, the enactment date of MPPAA.

Although groups such as the ATA, Teamsters and the Associated Specialty Contractors are urging legislative changes, the National Coordinating Committee for Multiemployer Plans has thus far maintained that it would be premature to amend the act. The Coordinating Committee maintains that there is sufficient flexibility under current law to deal with those concerns. Section 42-3(f), for example, allows nonconstruction and entertainment industry plans to adopt construction and entertainment type rules, subject to PBGC approval.

Regulatory and Related Developments

Special Withdrawal Rules

In this connection, in March 1982 we issued a regulation on procedures for applying for PBGC approval of special withdrawal rules. To date, we have received seven applications for special withdrawal rules. No withdrawal liability would be imposed on withdrawing employers. The test for granting this approval would depend on whether the industry seeking to adopt special amendments and rules has characteristics which show that the amendments and rules would be clearly "appropriate" and not pose a "significant risk to the PBGC."

The factors considered by the PBGC in determining "appropriateness" and "risk" include, but are not limited to:
- The extent to which cessations of the operations by employers in the covered industry have an adverse effect on the plan's contribution base
- The nature of employment in the industry
- The volatility of covered employment

- The current financial health of the plan and the impact that the special rules might have on the health of the plan.

In applying those factors we are looking to extend the special liabilities rules to plans that want to adopt them, which are not threatened by the withdrawal of one or more employers. I would hope that this action helps to provide an atmosphere where multiemployer plans can operate more effectively to provide benefit security to their participants. We're working to do that within a framework that will provide the benefit protection intended by the law.

In connection with these rules, seven applications are under consideration by the PBGC:

1. *International Longshoremen's and Warehousemen's Union Pacific Maritime Association Pension Fund*—19,500 participants and 110 employers
2. *International Ladies Garment Workers Union National Retirement Fund*—380,000 participants and 8,000 employers
3. *Division 1181 Amalgamated Transit Union— New York Employees Pension Fund*—4,700 participants and 84 employers
4. *Western Growers Pension Plan A*—10,000 participants and 160 employers
5. *Southern California Rock Products and Ready Mixed Concrete Industries Operating Engineer Employees Retirement Plan*—1,900 participants and 34 employers
6. *Southern California Rock Products and Ready Mixed Concrete Industries Teamster Employee Retirement Plan*—3,000 participants and 28 employers
7. *Southern California Rock Products and Ready Mixed Concrete Industries Machinist and Laborer Employees Retirement Plan*—300 participants and nine employers.

We are well along in the process of assembling the information necessary for the publication of a Notice of Pendency in the *Federal Register* on some of these applications, giving interested parties time to comment on the application.

Regulations

Regulations fall into two major categories. Some lessen statutory requirements (thereby lowering costs to the public and minimizing the burden on plans and plan sponsors) or reallocate costs imposed by the statute. Others implement statutory requirements designed to clarify ambiguous language and lessen the probability of disputes, litigation and public confusion. Examples of the first category are the issuance of a joint form (Form 5310) by the PBGC and the Internal Revenue Service (IRS) and amendments to the PBGC's Notice of Intent to Terminate regulation, 29 CFR Part 2616.

The Notice of Intent to Terminate regulation applies only to single employer plans; it will provide plan administrators with simplified procedures and a basic form for notifying the PBGC of plan terminations. Use of the new procedures will eliminate duplicative filing requirements now in existence for both the PBGC and IRS and is expected to reduce costs and administrative burdens connected with plan terminations.

Another regulation that may lessen the burden on plan administrators relates to reporting and notification rules. Section 4043 of ERISA sets forth several types of events with respect to which plan administrators must notify the PBGC and authorize the PBGC to waive the 30 day notification requirement for any of those events. The MPPAA amended Section 4065 of ERISA to authorize PBGC to waive the requirement that a list of reportable events be included in the annual report filed with the PBGC. In addition, MPPAA establishes separate reporting and notification requirements for multiemployer plans. Accordingly, the PBGC is amending its reportable events regulation, 29 CFR Part 2615, to further delete unnecessary reporting requirements for both single employer and multiemployer plans. The PBGC expects to issue a proposed rule early in 1983.

Another example of administrative relief relates to the sale of asset provisions in Section 4204 of ERISA. The PBGC has granted several individual variances from the purchaser's bond/escrow and the sale of contract requirements. It has also recently issued a class variance from those requirements for sales that occurred prior to January 1, 1981. The regulation to be issued under ERISA Section 4204(a)(1)(B) and (C) will assist employers who engage in sales of assets in structuring those transactions to avoid any immediate liability for seller's withdrawal from a multiemployer plan. Further, by waiving the requirement that the purchaser post a bond or establish an escrow account, the regulation frees up funds that the purchaser may use for other purposes.

Of 26 requests for exemption in fiscal year 1982, ten have been granted, seven were withdrawn or mooted by a class variance and nine cases were pending at year-end. Furthermore, we are developing a regulation that will waive those requirements for sales by *de minimis* contributors or to purchasers whose financial strength exceeds certain threshold levels.

The regulation to be issued under ERISA Section 4204(a)(1)(B) and (C) will assist employers who engage in sales of assets in structuring those transactions to avoid any immediate liability for the seller's withdrawal from a multiemployer plan. Further, by waiving the requirement that the purchaser post a bond or establish an escrow account, the regulation frees up funds that the purchaser may use for other purposes.

Another rule, falling in the category of clarification and avoidance of disputes, will set forth rules for valuing group insurance contracts as plan assets for single employer plans. This rule is necessary to provide uniform standards for plan administrators and employers to use in valuing insurance contracts. It will enable plans that are funded through insurance contracts to have appropriate guidance on how their assets should be treated in the plan termination context. This regulation is expected to alleviate time-consuming delays caused by uncertainty about how this commonly used plan funding vehicle should be valued.

Another regulation designed to lessen disputes relates to rules for recovery of benefit overpayments and early benefit reduction. It is designed (a) to reduce benefit overpayments made to plan participants after the date of plan termination, by requiring plan administrators to reduce benefit payments to the estimated level of Title IV benefits payable; (b) to define the circumstances under which the PBGC will recover overpayments from plan participants; and (c) to describe the methods by which the PBGC will recover overpayments. The proposed regulation, which applies only to single employer plans, is needed to establish rules and procedures for the prompt reduction of benefits after the date of plan termination. It will minimize overpayments to participants and establish a formal procedure for PBGC recovery of overpayments to participants.

In the same category are the rules governing the arbitration of disputes concerning employer liability. ERISA Section 4221 provides that any dispute between an employer and the sponsor of a multiemployer plan regarding the determination of the employer's withdrawal liability to the plan shall be resolved through arbitration.

Section 4221(a)(2) of ERISA provides that an arbitration proceeding under this section shall be conducted "in accordance with fair and equitable procedures" prescribed by the PBGC.

Other regulations of importance to be completed include:

Definition of Building and Construction Industry: Section 4203(b) of ERISA contains special withdrawal rules applicable to the building and construction industry. ERISA does not, however, contain a definition of the term "building and construction industry," nor does it define two other terms critical to the special rules: "primarily" and "substantially." This regulation would provide those definitions. Because there are conflicting views among the public about the need for this regulation, and because of the difficulty in developing appropriate definitions of these terms, PBGC has issued an advance notice of proposed rulemaking on this matter. After reviewing the comments received in response to the advance notice, PBGC will determine whether to proceed with a regulation.

Multiemployer Mergers and Transfers: This regulation was published in proposed form in December 1981. Comments were received and are being integrated, where appropriate, into a final regulation that is expected to be issued in the near future. The primary purpose of this regulation is to establish safe harbors for plans engaging in mergers and transfers, so that they can determine beforehand whether the transaction will satisfy the requirements of ERISA, as specified in Section 4231. I expect that this regulation will provide greater insight for employers in assessing their financial position at any given time.

Interest on Delinquent Withdrawal Liability Payments: Section 4219(c) of ERISA provides for interest on overdue withdrawal liability payments. Interest is to be "charged at rates based on prevailing market rates for comparable obligations, in accordance with regulations prescribed by" PBGC. The regulation will define what types of obligations are "comparable obligations."

Notice of Benefit Suspensions in Plans Terminated by Mass Withdrawal: Section 4281 of the act requires sponsors of terminated mass withdrawal plans to reduce and suspend benefits under certain conditions. PBGC is required by that section to prescribe, by regulation, notice requirements that assure that plan participants and beneficiaries receive adequate notice of benefit suspension. The notice will require that plan participants, particularly those in pay status, receive advance notice of benefit reductions or suspensions, without imposing excessive burdens and costs on plans. The cost of the notice will come from plan assets, and we do not want to drain those assets unnecessarily.

Supplemental Guarantee Program: Section 4022(g) of ERISA requires PBGC to establish a program to guarantee certain benefits that are not guaranteed under the basic multiemployer program because of the 75% and $20 limits. The supplemental program will be voluntary. To qualify, a plan will have to meet certain requirements to support the contention that it is financially sound.

Notice of Plan Insolvency: Section 4245 of the act requires plans in reorganization to provide notice to PBGC, sponsoring employers, unions and plan participants of possible plan insolvency. The new regulation will set the time limits for filing the required notices, as well as the information to be filed with those notices.

Abatement of Complete Withdrawal Liability: Section 4207 of ERISA requires the PBGC to establish rules for reducing or waiving the liability of an employer who has completely withdrawn from a multiemployer plan and subsequently resumes covered operations or renews the obligation to contribute under the plan. This regulation will prescribe the circumstances under which an employer's liability will be reduced or waived and the rules for computing the employer's liability for a complete or partial withdrawal after it has reentered the plan. It will benefit multiemployer plans by encouraging some employers who have withdrawn from these plans to renew their participation in the plans. By the same token, these employers will benefit by having some or all of their withdrawal liability waived.

While the plans will incur the cost of forgoing collection of some of the withdrawal liability owed them, the assumption underlying this statutory provision is that these costs will be offset by the contributions employers will make to the plans after their reentry. PBGC is unable to quantify these benefits and costs because it cannot predict the number of employers who will avail themselves of this rule. PBGC may issue a notice of proposed rulemaking by March 31, 1983.

Waivers in Cases of Multiemployer Transfers to Single Employer Plans: Under Section 4232(c), a multiemployer plan that transfers liabilities to a single employer plan is contingently liable to PBGC, up to the amounts specified in Section 4232(c), if the single employer plan terminates within five years after the transfer. PBGC is authorized, however, to waive the contingent liability if it determines that its interests and the interests of plan participants and beneficiaries are adequately protected.

This regulation will provide procedures for applying to PBGC for a waiver and the standards under which waivers will be granted. It will benefit those multiemployer plans that will qualify for a waiver for their contingent liability. To date, PBGC has received three requests for waivers, involving potential maximum liabilities of approximately $1.2 million. PBGC is unable to predict how many more plans may apply for waivers once this regulation is issued. Insofar as the intended purpose of this regulation, there will be no costs associated with it. The contingent liability will be waived only in those situations where it is extremely unlikely that the liability would ever become an actual claim of PBGC against the multiemployer plan. PBGC may issue a notice of proposed rulemaking by June 30, 1983.

Valuation of Allocation of Unfunded Vested Liabilities to a Withdrawn Employer: Three of the four statutory methods for allocating a plan's unfunded vested benefits to a withdrawn employer generally reduce the amount of the unfunded vested benefits by the value of outstanding claims for withdrawal liability. Section 4001(a)(12) of ERISA provides that these claims are to be valued in accordance with PBGC regulations. This regulation will prescribe those valuation rules. Issuance of a notice of proposed rulemaking by June 30, 1983 is targeted.

Redetermination of Withdrawal Liability on Mass Withdrawal: The rules for determining an employer's withdrawal liability do not necessarily allocate a plan's total unfunded vested benefits, as a result of rules, such as the *de minimis* rule, that reduce or eliminate withdrawal liability. Therefore, if all or substantially all of the employers in a plan withdraw, there may be large unallocated amounts that would constitute a potential claim on the insurance system. To avoid this result, Section 4219(c)(1)(D) requires the determination or redetermination of withdrawal liability in order to fully allocate a plan's unfunded vested benefits, on either the termination of a plan through the withdrawal of every employer or the withdrawal of substantially all the employers pursuant to an agreement or arrangement to withdraw. The proposed regulation will set forth rules for implementing this requirement.

This regulation primarily benefits the multiemployer insurance program and the plans that are required to pay premiums under it. It will ensure that, in the event of a mass withdrawal or the withdrawal of substantially all employers, the employers remaining in the plan will not be left with more than their fair share of the plan's unfunded vested benefits. June 30, 1983 is the targeted date for issuance of a notice of proposed rulemaking.

Conclusion

I hope my comments provide you with a reasonable sense of developments taking place with regard to the PBGC. From a broader perspective, we are a small agency by federal government standards that has been doing its job for the past eight years without being involved in high visibility problems. Within the last two months the PBGC's request for a $6 premium has focused attention on us. This attention has been accentuated by the publicity given to termination of the plans of large companies such as Braniff Airways, by the AlloyTek and Facet Enterprise litigations and settlements, by discussions and litigation over the constitutionality of the Multiemployer Pension Plan Amendments Act of 1980 and by the overall concern about the increased number of plan terminations that are increasing the liabilities of PBGC sharply. In addition, the activity with respect to possible legislative changes has accelerated and attracted close analysis of the insurance program.

All of these matters are significant and impact on the security of our nation's pension system. The PBGC appears to be entering an era of greater visibility and maturity.

The PBGC was established by the Congress and signed into law by President Ford in 1974 to protect the retirement programs of the American workforce to the limit of the law. Today, there are 33 million people whose pensions are insured by us. Over 100,000 people are either receiving or are entitled to receive benefits in the future from the PBGC. That number is increasing.

People are concerned about what is going to happen to them financially when they retire. PBGC has a role in protecting the benefits of all workers covered by defined benefit pension plans. Business, labor and professional communities have come to recognize and better understand the problems that the agency has. We hope that they will support us in the basic philosophy that, as an insurance company, we should be financially funded in such a way that the working population will have no concern about receiving the benefits guaranteed by the PBGC under the country's private pension system.

Prohibited Transaction Exemptions—1982

BY STEPHEN A. WEINSTEIN

Mr. Weinstein is a member of the lawfirm of Gorsuch, Kirgis, Campbell, Walker and Grover in Denver. This firm represents approximately 50 Taft-Hartley trust funds. Mr. Weinstein received a B.A. degree from the University of Colorado, a J.D. from the University of Denver and an LL.M. in tax law from New York University. He is active in civic affairs and has spoken at previous Foundation educational meetings.

NOT UNLIKE past years, 1982 has seen the Department of Labor bombarded with applications for prohibited transaction exemptions. Apparently, the spread between exemption applications granted and those that have received adverse rulings is increasing.

Whether the Department of Labor is more lenient or more knowledgeable (and thus more practical) or whether plans and parties in interest are more aware of what constitutes a justifiable transaction is a question for debate. Nevertheless, the case exists that employers, plans, financial institutions and many participants in such plans are increasingly interrelated. In many instances, it seems that wherever an employee benefit plan looks, it runs into a "party in interest" and, therefore, many transactions are raised to prohibited status. This situation is becoming more of a problem as the economy causes more and more hardships. Plans are asking why they can't keep their funds at home and use them to create jobs versus giving such funds to investment consultants and/or institutions who may, in turn, take them out of state.

In addition, there are increasing numbers of prospective investments and business arrangements with parties in interest that present lucrative opportunities for the plans but still constitute prohibited transactions as compared to less lucrative opportunities with concerns that are not parties in interest. In addition to this morass, the Department of Labor states that, "A party in interest who enters into a transaction with a plan without first securing an exemption from the Department, does so at peril."

With this direct warning (especially since the Department of Labor does not look favorably on applications for retroactive exemptions) and in the interest of being prudent, it is wise to look before leaping, that is, apply before acting. Although it appears that the Department of Labor is taking a hard stand, in reality the Department is very responsive and helpful with respect to the granting of exemptions.

What Is a Prohibited Transaction?

In order to be aware of what constitutes an exemption from the prohibited transaction provisions, it is necessary to review these provisions.

A prohibited transaction is any direct or indirect transaction between a plan and a party in interest that constitutes:

- A sale, exchange or lease of property
- A loan of money or an extension of credit
- A furnishing of goods, services or facilities
- A transfer to, or use by or for the benefit of, a party in interest of the income or assets of the plan
- An act by a fiduciary whereby he deals with the income or assets of a plan in his own interest or for his own account
- A receipt of any consideration for his personal account by any disqualified person who is a fiduciary from any party dealing with the plan in connection with a transaction involving the income or assets of the plan.

What Constitutes an Exemption?

Because, in many instances, prohibited transactions are increasingly difficult to avoid; because it appears that plans and parties in interest are increasingly aware of the ramifications if they proceed with a prohibited transaction; and because the Department of Labor appears to be granting an increasing number of individual exemptions, it is prudent to be cognizant of what the Department expects and what traits are common or similar in these exemptions.

Over the past several years, as compared to the first few years preceding ERISA's enactment, certain exemption trends have become apparent. 1982 exemptions appear to be reinforcing these trends, but in a very liberal fashion. For example, in one case, a nonmultiemployer plan was granted permission to loan a principal employer one-third of the plan assets. In return for the loan, the plan received a personal guarantee of repayment from the trustees, who happened to be officers of the employer. It is important to note that the collateral involved in the transaction constituted 150% of the balance of the loan and that an independent fiduciary was involved.[1]

In cases involving the sale of property to various parties in interest, of which there were many, common characteristics were:
- The purchase prices were at fair market value.
- An independent institution appraised the property and monitored the terms and conditions.
- The transaction with the interested party could be justified.

An example of this situation is a case where there was no market for property that happened to be located adjacent to a party-in-interest's real estate and the party in interest needed to expand.[2]

There were circumstances common to many of the favorable applications involving loans:
- If a loan were to be made to a party in interest, it must have been justified and the recipient must have had sufficient reason for requesting the exemption. For example, in one case, in order to stay solvent and to continue to employ workers, an employer needed to purchase new equipment. It was, therefore, in the interests of the plan to grant such a loan.[3]
- Secondly, if a loan was requested, the recipient paid the current, if not a higher-than-current, interest rate on the amount. An example of such a rate would be 1/2% over prime.[4]
- Thirdly, that a loan was well-secured and that sufficient collateral was available in the event the terms of the transaction were not met. In addition, in most cases an independent financial institution was involved, which monitored the terms and conditions of the contract and often had the authority to enforce repayment.[5]
- Lastly, a major concern of the Department of Labor, and one that should be for the applicant, was the status of the plan itself. The protection of the interests of the plan, and in turn the plan's participants and beneficiaries, was critical in determining whether a transaction was to be exempted. This is not to say that, as long as the transaction proved to be advantageous to the plan, there was sufficient evidence to grant an exemption. However, transactions that do benefit the plans are definitely looked on more favorably than those that do not make their benefits clear.

Class Exemptions in 1982

Whereas in past years there were numerous class exemptions, this year there was only one—Prohibited Transaction Exemption 82-87. This class exemption is for transactions involving certain residential mortgage financing arrangements. It was promulgated in May of this year and alters dramatically the real estate investment options open to employee benefit plans for residential units. Hopefully, P.T.E. 82-87 will be the pattern for a class exemption involving the permanent financing of commercial property. Prior to the issuance of the class exemption, and excluding individual exemptions, any mortgage financing by a plan could violate almost all of the prohibited transaction provisions.

Specific Provisions

The prohibited transaction provisions would prevent a bank that has a preexisting relationship with a plan from arranging investment options for a fee, from selling loans to a plan or from approving loans to individuals who are beneficiaries of the plan, since they are parties in interest. In addition, any fee in exchange for a loan commitment between the plan and bank would be prohibited.

Any commitment by a plan to make loans or purchase mortgages that would in some manner be used to purchase property developed or built by a contributing employer could violate the prohibited transaction provisions. A direct or indirect loan by a plan to a purchaser of a home who is an employee of a contributing employer, a service

---

1. MIH Profit Sharing Plan; Marine and Industrial Hydraulics, Prohibited Transaction Exemption: 82-146. "PT Exemption Asked for Plan's Loan to Employer," *Pens. Plan Guide* (CCH) ¶23,608J (July 23, 1982); "PT Exemption Granted for Loan by Plan to Employer," *Pens. Plan Guide* (CCH) ¶23,611Q (Sept. 21, 1982).

2. Earth Consultants, Inc. Profit Sharing Plan, Prohibited Transaction Exemption: 82-108. "PT Exemption Sought for Plan's Sale of Real Property to Parties in Interest," *Pens. Plan Guide* (CCH) ¶23,600S (May 7, 1982); "PT Exemption Granted for Plan's Sale of Real Property to Parties in Interest," *Pens. Plan Guide* (CCH) ¶23,605B (July 6, 1982).

3. Nielsens Lithography Company Employees' Profit Sharing Retirement Plan, Prohibited Transaction Exemption: 82-95. "Exemption Sought to Allow Loan from Plan to Employer," *Pens. Plan Guide* (CCH) ¶23,598Z (April 9, 1982); "DOL Grants PT Exemption for Plan's Loan to Employer," *Pens. Plan Guide* (CCH) ¶23,602Z (June 8, 1982).

4. Nielsens.

5. Nielsens.

provider or related union could violate the prohibited transaction provisions. Servicing of loans and mortgages, etc., by a bank already servicing the plan could be considered a prohibited transaction. The list continues, making it appear futile for a plan to invest in home mortgage financing, even though the opportunities for rewards would very likely be significant.

What the Class Exemption Covers

In light of the increased demand for funds directed toward the development and purchase of homes; the lack of funds in the savings and loans, the traditional home mortgage lenders; and the fact that mortgage investments could provide employee benefit plans with lucrative opportunities, the Department of Labor responded positively to the applications requesting a class exemption. In essence, then, the following transactions are now covered by the class exemption for home financing by employee benefit plans.

Effective retroactively to January 1, 1975 an employee benefit plan may make whole mortgage loans on residential units pursuant to a commitment for a fee. The plan may also acquire such loans on an over-the-counter or immediate purchase basis without violating the prohibited transaction provisions.

In addition to direct and indirect mortgage financing arrangements, the exemption covers the purchase of participation interests in individual mortgage loans originated by third parties.

A loan participation would be an agreement involving the ownership in common of a mortgage loan by two or more plans. These agreements are similar to the larger scale selling of certificate interests in loan pools, which was granted an exemption by Prohibited Transaction Exemption 81-7. Such investment arrangements can result in greater protection for an investing plan since the risks are then shared. Plans may also sell, exchange or transfer said mortgages or participations as long as the entire interest is sold, exchanged or transferred.

Conditions to Be Met

Any of these agreements or transactions made either directly with purchasers or through financial institutions could have been, prior to the exemption, prohibited. The opportunities now available to plans to invest in the housing market, thus making homes available to their beneficiaries, and to have those investments backed in some cases by other investors, are a welcome change. Any transaction, however, must conform to the following conditions if it is to qualify under the exemption:

- The transaction must be written out and recorded, with all commitments in writing.
- The terms of any transaction must be as favorable to the plan as the terms of any agreement made with unrelated parties. In other words, if the transaction was to involve unrelated parties rather than parties in interest, the terms of the transaction from the plan's point of view must not only be comparable to terms with the unrelated party but must favor the interests of the plan.
- Any loan or participation interest acquired must be what the Department of Labor defines as "a recognized mortgage loan." This loan is the only type covered by the exemption. A recognized mortgage loan, being a first lien, must be made on a "residential dwelling unit." The loan at its origination must be eligible for purchase through an established program by the Federal Home Loan Mortgage Corporation, the Government National Mortgage Association or the Federal National Mortgage Association. Each agency has already established criteria, which change from time to time; therefore, the definition of a "recognized mortgage loan" will undoubtedly expand in the coming years to meet the marketplace.
- "Residential dwelling units" is an obtuse term that defines a home; such homes, however, may be one to four dwelling units, may be condominiums or may be cooperatives. Multiple rental housing is not as of yet included under the definition. In addition, the units need not be new, thus expanding the opportunities for purchasers who would prefer to purchase a preexisting home. Especially with today's market, this inclusion of old and new homes is beneficial to all parties.
- The mortgage loan must be originated by an "established mortgage lender," which not only includes savings and loans, banks and insurance companies but also includes mortgage bankers. To protect the plans, the "established mortgage lender" must have the approval to process home mortgages. This approval can either come under the National Housing Act, the Department of Housing and Urban Development or through state housing finance agencies.
- In addition, "no person who is a developer or a builder involved in the development or construction of the units, or a lender who is associated with the *construction* financing arrangement for the units, or who, at the time

the decision to purchase is made by the plan is the *owner* of a mortgage or a participation interest therein which is subsequently sold to the plan, *shall* have exercised any discretionary authority or control or rendered any investment advice that would make that person a fiduciary with respect to the plan's decision to purchase, or to commit to purchase, a mortgage loan or a participation interest therein or setting the terms thereof;" (P.T.E. 82-87) in short, no self-dealing.

If a plan purchases a participation interest in a mortgage loan, certain conditions must be met. It is imperative that in any transaction or agreement the terms of the agreement are in the interest of the participants in the plan. Their interests must not be subordinated to the interests of the other participants.

Any majority interest must be owned by independent parties and not controlled by the person selling the participation interest and servicing the mortgages. Any decision regarding foreclosure options must be directed by an independent entity and not by the seller or servicer.

Obviously, the Department wants the interests of the participants to be top priority. By not allowing certain biased parties to conduct these transactions, the hope is that decisions will be made objectively, based on facts and circumstances and not the individual desires of the parties involved.

The final condition required by the Department of Labor on all transactions after June 18, 1982 is the inclusion of a "qualified real estate manager." This entity is the fiduciary who shall make decisions on behalf of the plan concerning the purchase and sale of mortgage loans, participation interests or commitments to do so. This manager must be a financial institution or business organization, which in the normal course of business advises institutional investors on matters similar to those the plan is considering.

In addition, the qualified real estate manager must not be under the controlling influence of any party in interest. This is not to say that trustees may not render any advice or make their desires known; it is necessary for some direction to be given. Nevertheless, care should be taken to avoid unduly influencing the manager, thus compromising his objectivity and, in turn, the transaction's exempt status. Lastly, the qualified real estate manager must recognize its fiduciary position in writing.

Advantages to Plans

Despite the conditions imposed on an employee benefit plan considering investment in residential mortgage financing, the opportunities available in this area could be sizable. The exemption enables a plan to make investments that offer a favorable rate of return and excellent security. It provides individuals, both parties in interest and unrelated parties, with personal investment opportunities and allows the plan to keep its funds working in the geographical area where its beneficiaries reside.

The Department of Labor views any mortgage loan or program of loans as a plan investment and, therefore, the expectation is that the plan will profit. In light of the return that may be realized through this vehicle to plans, to financial institutions, to builders and to employees, the far-reaching effects of this exemption can just barely be determined and, therefore, should be explored further.

Conclusion

The Department of Labor appears to be more and more receptive to the prohibited transactions exemption requests that it has received to date. However, with the increasing number of employee benefit plans and with the increased magnitude of their assets, many transactions will undoubtedly come under very close scrutiny. The critics are not only the federal agencies but plan participants, who appear to be very interested in a plan's investment strategy. In addition, it is becoming increasingly difficult for certain plans to locate transactions that are not, in some manner, considered to be conducted with parties in interest. Therefore, it is imperative to keep abreast of not only what transactions may be prohibited, but also what may constitute or what in the near future may constitute a prohibited transaction exemption.

Suspension of Pension Benefits

BY KATHERINE A. HESSE, CEBS

Ms. Hesse is an attorney with Murphy, Lamere and Murphy in Braintree, Massachusetts, practicing general labor law and employee benefits law. She serves as counsel to the board of trustees of a number of Taft-Hartley pension and welfare funds. A member of the Massachusetts and the District of Columbia Bars, Ms. Hesse received her B.A. degree from Smith College and her J.D. degree from the Boston University School of Law. Ms. Hesse was a member of the charter class of the Certified Employee Benefit Specialists (CEBS) and serves on the International Society of Certified Employee Benefit Specialists (ISCEBS) Continuing Education Committee. She also serves on the American Bar Association's Administrative Law Section Committee on Labor and Employment Law.

SECTION 203 of ERISA provides that an employee's right to his normal retirement benefit is nonforfeitable on attainment of normal retirement age. One exception to this general rule appears in Section 203(a)(3)(B), which permits the suspension of pension benefits where a retired employee becomes reemployed. The statute and regulations define and strictly limit the range of circumstances in which a suspension of benefits is permitted. Section 203(a)(3)(B) of ERISA provides:

> A right to an accrued benefit derived from employer contributions shall not be treated as forfeitable solely because the plan provides that the payment of benefits is suspended for such period as the employee is employed, subsequent to the commencement of payment of such benefits—
>
> (i) in the case of a plan other than a multiemployer plan, by an employer who maintains the plan under which such benefits were being paid; and
>
> (ii) in the case of a multiemployer plan, in the same industry, in the same trade or craft, and the same geographic area covered by the plan, as when such benefits commenced.
>
> The Secretary shall prescribe such regulations as may be necessary to carry out the purposes of this subparagraph, including regulations with respect to the meaning of the term "employed."

The Department of Labor has now issued final regulations under Section 203. After repeated delays and amendments, Regulation 2530.203-3 entitled "Suspension of Pension Benefits Upon Reemployment of Retirees" became effective January 1, 1982.[1]

If a plan contains or contemplates the inclusion of a provision for suspension of benefits, it must adhere to the Labor Department's regulations. The regulations impose strict limitations on what types of reemployment may cause a suspension of pension benefits, and they outline specific procedures by which plans must provide for notification to employees, verification of reemployment and review of decisions to suspend benefits. Suspension of normal retirement benefits on reemployment that is not expressly permitted by Section 203(a)(3)(B) is unlawful, regardless of what the plan provides.

Scope of the Regulation

Section 203 of ERISA is designed to protect the plan participant's right to receive a normal retirement benefit or its actuarial equivalent. In general, the statute does not apply to early retirement benefits or disability benefits, unless the suspension of those benefits affects the integrity of the actuarial equivalent of the normal retirement benefit. Thus, a plan may suspend prenormal retirement benefits for any reemployment without regard to the provisions of Section 203(a)(3)(B), as long as the affected employee's benefits are actuarially recalculated to compensate for benefit payments withheld and as long as payment of the recalculated benefits begins no later than the normal retirement age. If the plan provides for disability benefits greater than normal retirement benefits, any portion that exceeds the normal amount may be suspended even after the normal retirement age (see 29 CFR Section 2530.203-3(a)).

Section 203(a)(3)(B) allows plans to suspend normal retirement benefits in certain circumstances. Subject to the restrictions imposed by the

---

1. For a full text of this regulation, see "Suspension of Pension Benefits Upon Reemployment of Retirees," 3 *Pens. Plan Guide* (CCH) ¶14,433 (Dec. 11, 1981).

regulations, the general rule is that plans may provide for the permanent withholding of benefits for each calendar month, or for each four or five week payroll period ending in a calendar month, during which an employee is employed in "Section 203(a)-(3)(B) service" (see the following section on the definition of "service").

Suspendible Amount

Only that portion of the benefits derived from employer contributions may be withheld. If an employee has made contributions, that portion of his pension paid for by his own contributions must be determined, and that amount must be paid to the employee regardless of any reemployment.

If a plan provides for life annuity type benefits (benefits payable on a monthly basis for life), then its suspension of benefits provision may allow the entire amount of a monthly benefit payment derived from employer contributions to be withheld for each month in which the employee engages in Section 203(a)(3)(B) service. If the plan provides for some other form of benefit payment, the plan, for each month the employee engages in such service, may withhold the lesser of (1) the actual amount paid or scheduled to be paid to the employee for such month (payments scheduled to be paid less frequently may be converted to monthly payments for purposes of this provision) or (2) the amount of benefits that would have been payable if the employee had been receiving monthly benefit payments since actual retirement based on a single life annuity commencing at actual retirement age.

Definition of "Service" Under Section 203(a)(3)(B)

Benefits may be suspended under Section 203(a)(3)(B) only if the retiree has engaged in "service" as defined in the statute and regulations. Service is defined as employment subsequent to the time that the payment of benefits commenced or would have commenced had he not remained in or returned to employment. A plan may suspend benefits only if the employee was engaged in such "service" at least 40 hours during the month (or during a four or five week payroll period) for which benefits are being suspended. This 40 hour minimum allows the retiree to supplement his pension income to some extent without being subject to forfeiture of benefits.

When the regulations were proposed initially, the Labor Department asked for comments regarding the 40 hour minimum service requirement. Generally, the comments were negative.

Some commentators objected to any minimum hour requirement, arguing that any employment should be sufficient for purposes of suspending benefits. Others urged the adoption of a lower minimum. A major factor cited to support a lower minimum was the added burden of "policing" reemployment by retirees. It would be expensive, if not impossible, for plans to monitor the employment activities of all retirees and keep records of the number of hours worked by each employee each month.

The Department determined that the 40 hour standard gives plans sufficient flexibility to encourage participants to self-police by reporting any post-retirement employment. Plans could, for instance, tailor incentives to encourage retirees to report employment. The Department also found that the number of retirees who subsequently return to work is so small that this situation would not place an undue burden on plan administrators. Finally, the Department also noted that the 40 hour standard represents roughly the amount of work a retiree could perform without exceeding the Social Security earnings limit, assuming a part-time hourly wage of approximately $10 per hour.

Some commentators suggested a monetary standard, instead of the hourly minimum. Some kinds of employment, especially seasonal business, might not be well-suited to the hourly standard. The Department responded that a monetary standard would be inconsistent with the purposes of Section 203(a)(3)(B). It would allow lower wage retirees to work many more hours than highly compensated retirees before reaching the earnings limitation. Also, it is unlikely that a monetary standard could accommodate the diverse populations that would be affected.

Within hours of service, the original regulations did not include payments to retirees for accrued vacation leave, sickpay, holidays and other such credits. Commentators suggested that administrative problems and inequities would result in cases where participants received payment from the employer other than for the "performance of duties." They argued that if payments for vacation, sick leave, holidays, military duty and other paid nonworking hours are made after retirement, the employee should not receive a pension in addition to that amount. The final regulations adopted these suggestions and simply cross-referenced the definition of "hour of service" to 29 CFR 2530.200 b-2(a)(1) and (2), which includes most types of paid nonworking hours for which credit is given. Thus, benefits may be suspended during months when such payments are made for accrued credits exceeding the 40 hour minimum.

Some plans use methods other than the computation of actual number of hours worked for computing benefits. Requiring these plans to use the "actual hours" method solely for the purpose of determining the suspendibility of benefits would impose a significant administrative burden on them. The Department therefore revised the original regulations to accommodate those plans that use alternative methods. The final regulations allow plans to suspend benefits if the employee receives payment for any hours of service performed on each of eight or more days (or separate work shifts) in a calendar month (or payroll period), provided that the plan has not determined or used the actual number of hours of service for any purpose with respect to that employee.

Plans Other Than Multiemployer Plans

The statute allows suspension of benefits by plans other than multiemployer plans only if the retiree is reemployed "by an employer who maintains the plan." Section 2530.210 of the regulations generally sets forth rules for determining the employer or employers who maintain a plan. The same rules would presumably apply under Section 2530.203-3, and, in fact, Section 2530.203-3(c) specifically refers to paragraphs (d) and (e) of 2530.210.

Commentators had suggested that the expansive definition in 2530.210 would severely limit the ability of retirees to find employment that would not result in suspension of benefits. As a result, the regulation was modified to apply only to those employers maintaining the plan at the time the benefits commenced or would have commenced. Also, it should be noted that the regulation does not require suspension of benefits under any circumstances, but merely describes circumstances under which such suspensions are permitted. Plans are free to provide more liberal rules regarding suspension.

Multiemployer Plans

For multiemployer plans, the statute allows suspension of benefits only where the participant is employed in:
A. An industry in which employees covered by the plan were employed and accrued benefits at the time the employee's benefits commenced or would have commenced, and
B. The same trade or craft (or related supervisory activities) in which the employee worked at any time under the plan, and
C. The geographic area covered by the plan at the time the employee's benefits commenced or would have commenced.

The Same Industry

The original proposed regulation defined "industry" as "the business activities of any employers maintaining the plan." Comments suggested that this statement might be interpreted to mean that the retiree must have returned to work for an employer contributing to the plan in order to be considered working in the same industry. The language was modified to read "business activities *of the types* engaged in by any employers maintaining the plan."

The Same Trade or Craft

The regulations define a trade or craft as
A. A skill or skills learned during a significant period of training or practice which is applicable in occupations in some industry, or
B. A skill or skills relating to selling, retaining, managerial, clerical or professional occupations, or
C. Supervisory activities relating to a skill or skills described in A or B.

For example, Joe Smith, an electrician, retires and then becomes reemployed as a foreman of electricians. Because "trade or craft" includes related supervisory activities, Joe has remained within his trade or craft.

Whether a particular job can be considered to be included in a trade or craft will be decided on a case by case basis using a functional analysis of the actual job duties, rather than the job title. A major criticism of the definition in the regulation was that it allowed a retiree to regain employment in the same industry, perhaps even for the same employer, as long as the new job involved different skills from those he acquired in his previous job. The Department declined to revise the requirement to allow benefits to be suspended if a retiree returned to employment in any trade or craft practiced by any participants in the plan. Thus, to constitute Section 203(a)(3)(B) service, the retiree's new job must involve skills he acquired from his work for a contributing employer. Whether the employment is in a union or nonunion job is irrelevant for suspension of benefits purposes.

The National Coordinating Committee for Multiemployer Plans had raised objections to the proposed regulations. It takes the position that plans covering an industry in a geographic area without distinction as to trade or craft should be deemed to cover all trades or crafts in that industry in that area and that plans covering a certain trade or craft without regard to industry should cover the trade or craft in all industries in the area. The regulations, however, did not adopt this view; instead, they require all three conditions (same industry, same trade or craft and same geographic area) to be satisfied before benefits can be suspended.

The Same Geographic Area

"Geographic area" is defined as the state or states in which contributions were made or required to be made, and the remainder of any Standard Metropolitan Statistical Area (SMSA) that falls in part within such state, determined as of the time benefits commenced or would have commenced (29 CFR Section 2530.203-3(c)(2)(iii)). For example, Bill Brown, a plumber, is covered by a multiemployer plan in Pennsylvania. All contributing employers to Bill's plan have always been located within Pennsylvania. Bill retires and moves to the neighboring State of New Jersey. If he resumes employment in Burlington, Camden or Gloucester Counties in New Jersey, he will be considered to be in the same geographic area, since they are within the Philadelphia SMSA. If he moved to Florida or Maine or even to certain other parts of New Jersey, however, he would not be in the same geographic area.

Before the regulations were formulated, the term "geographic area" was not always construed so strictly. In *Nichols v. Board of Trustees,* 1 EBC 1868 (D.D.C. 1979) (dictum), the United States District Court for the District of Columbia interpreted the statute as allowing retirees to work only in areas where they would not be in any conceivable competition with active members of the local union participating in the plan.

After the proposed regulations were issued, commentators suggested that the geographic area, at least for some plans, should be determined as "national" or "regional," based on a definition in the plan that would be consistent with the claimed jurisdiction of the participating union. This definition would allow plans that cover employees working throughout a broad geographic area to be recognized as regional or national plans, so that there would not have to be a contributing employer in every state within the region for Section 203(a)(3)-(B) to apply. The Department, however, declined to adopt any of the suggested changes; the original definition appears unchanged in the final regulation.

Continued Employment After Normal Retirement Age

Despite considerable controversy over the applicability of the regulations on suspension of pension benefits to employees who continue working past retirement age and do not begin receiving benefits, both the Internal Revenue Service and the Department of Labor are taking the position that the regulations do apply to such employees.[2] Thus, employees who continue to work beyond normal retirement age without beginning to receive their pension benefits must be given a suspension of benefits notice, unless their benefits will be actuarially recomputed so that there is no forfeiture of benefits.

According to the Labor Department's letter to Dr. David T. Livingston dated July 12, 1982, if benefits are suspended as a result of continued employment, the employee incurs a loss of the value of his accrued benefit unless an actuarial recalculation or some other form of compensation is made at the time he actually retires. A forfeiture occurs not because of any failure to accrue further benefits, but because of a loss of benefits already accrued.

If such an actuarial recalculation or other compensation is provided for in the plan, then the employee does not incur a forfeiture and the suspension of benefits is permitted until the employee's actual retirement date. If the plan does not provide for actuarial recalculation or other compensation, benefits still may be suspended subject to the requirements of Section 203(a)-(3)(B). In this situation, if the continued employment qualifies as Section 203(a)(3)(B) service, the plan may suspend benefits after notifying the employee of the intended suspension and resulting loss of value of his accrued benefits. The notice should conform to the requirements set forth in the regulation as discussed in the following section on notification.

Notification

During the first calendar month or payroll period in which a plan intends to withhold payments, it must notify the participant in writing that benefits are to be suspended. The notice must be sent either by personal delivery or first class mail. *No payments may be withheld until this notice is given.*

The notification provision, 29 CFR 2530.203-

---

2. See generally IRS Rev. Ruling 81-140 (5/11/81), IRS Information Letter to George S. Grubbs, Jr. (2/17/82) and DOL Information Letter to David T. Livingston (7/12/82).

3(b)(4), requires a plan to include the following within its notification of suspension: (1) the specific reasons why payments are being suspended, (2) a description of the plan's provisions regarding suspension of benefits, (3) a copy of the pertinent plan provisions, (4) a statement that the applicable Department of Labor regulations may be found in 29 CFR 2530.203-3, (5) the method available for obtaining review of the plan's decision to suspend benefits, (6) the procedure and forms (if any are required) for filing requests for benefit resumption on termination of employment and (7) the notification must include the periods of employment, suspendible amounts subject to offset and the manner in which the plan will offset the suspendible amounts, if there will be an offset of amounts already paid.

Several commentators argued that the summary plan description (SPD), which must be distributed to all plan participants and beneficiaries, provides adequate notice. In response, the Department added language to the regulation that provides that to the extent the SPD contains information substantially similar to that required by the regulation, notice of suspension may refer the employee to the relevant pages of the SPD for information about a particular time.

If a plan uses this alternative means of compliance, it must make sure to include in the notification a description of how the employee can obtain a copy of the SPD or relevant pages. It must also honor requests for referenced information within a reasonable period of time, not to exceed 30 days. Also note that in order to take advantage of certain presumptions regarding verification, the plan must (1) make sure that the summary plan description and any other communications relating to verification describe the plan's verification requirements and the presumptions and (2) furnish retirees with this information at least once every 12 months. Regardless of whether the trustees wish to use the SPD method of compliance with the notification requirements, they would be well-advised to include all of the relevant notification information within the SPD.

Verification

A plan may provide that an employee must notify the plan of any employment. The plan may also require the employee either to certify that he is unemployed or to provide factual information verifying that he is not performing Section 203(a)(3)(B) service. This information may be requested at reasonable intervals to ensure that no benefits are being paid to employed retirees.

Specific information or documents, such as tax withholding statements received by a retiree within a given period, may normally be required by the plan. The plan requests for information must be reasonable, however, and overbroad requests (e.g., for complete copies of all tax returns for the period) should be avoided.

The plan may withhold benefit payments if the requested verification information is not provided. Once the information is received, however, the plan must pay all amounts due the employee, including payments for the period after the request up until the receipt of the information (29 CFR 2530.203-3(b)(5)).

If benefits have been suspended because the employee has performed Section 203(a)(3)(B) service, the plan may condition the payment of future benefits on receipt of notice from the employee that he has ceased such service. The plan may also require verification of cessation of service.

If a plan adopts provisions requiring verification of employment status, it may also adopt the following presumptions that facilitate administration of its suspension of benefits provisions. If the trustees discover that a retiree is employed in Section 203(a)(3)(B) service and that the retiree has not complied with the plan's reporting requirements regarding such employment, the trustees may assume that the employee has exceeded 40 hours of work in that month.

In the building trades, a presumption may also be adopted that if an employee is discovered to be working at a construction site and if that employee has not complied with the plan's reporting requirements, the employee has been working for that employer at that site for as long as that employer has been performing work at that site. These presumptions are rebuttable by the retiree; if he can establish that he did not work the minimum of 40 hours during any one month, he may recover his benefit for that month. Also, the presumptions may only be used where it is reasonable to do so (29 CFR 2530.203-3(b)(7)).

The advantage of adopting these presumptions is that it allows the plan to withhold benefits in many cases without going through the process of investigating employment records to determine actual numbers of hours worked. It also encourages employees to comply with the notification and reporting requirements.

Any plan adopting these presumptions must make sure to describe its employment verification requirements and the nature and effect of such presumptions in the summary plan description and in any communication to plan participants that relates to verification requirements. Furthermore, retirees must be informed of the requirements and of the effects of failing to meet the requirements at least once a year.

Complete and detailed verification provisions in plans are essential for the effective operation of any benefit suspension provisions. Since the regulation allows plans to require verification of employment status, and since there are few workable alternatives for monitoring employment of retirees, plans should take care to formulate effective verification requirements.

Resumption of Payments

If benefits have been suspended under Section 203(a)(3)(B), payments must resume no later than the first day of the third calendar month after the month in which the employee last worked at least 40 hours. As noted previously, the plan may adopt any reasonable procedure requiring a retiree whose benefits have been suspended to notify the plan of cessation of employment. The waiting period does not begin until after the employee has complied with such procedure. All benefits due him from the date of actual cessation of service must be paid in the initial payment less any amounts subject to offset.

If an employee is paid benefits for one or more months before it is discovered that he has been employed in Section 203(a)(3)(B) service, the plan can recoup overpayments both from the initial payment due and by deducting up to 25% of any future month's pension payment (29 CFR 2530.203-3(b)(3)). Originally, the regulation had allowed plans simply to deduct 25% from monthly payments to be made.

Commentators objected to the 25% limit, pointing out that in the great majority of cases the plan will have paid benefits to retirees before discovering reemployment. The additional administrative costs involved with collecting overpayments were substantial, even without the 25% limit. Restricting the plan's ability to collect monies owed to it by imposing such a limit was unjustifiable, according to commentators.

The Department responded by eliminating the 25% limit on the initial payment due. In the Department's opinion, the benefits that a plan may now recoup from the initial payment with minimal processing costs should cover most overpayments.

The cost of calculating and recouping overpayments can be reduced and often avoided by implementing effective verification provisions in the plan. At least for a period after retirement, the plan could require verification by the retiree of his employment status regularly, as well as requiring the filing of a benefit resumption notice on cessation of employment. The plan would then be assured that if the retiree became employed, all or most overpayments could be recovered by withholding the initial payment on cessation of employment.

Review Procedure and Status Determination

If a plan provides for suspension of benefits, it must set up procedures whereby an employee may obtain a determination of whether the contemplated reemployment is of a type that could result in the suspension of benefits (29 CFR 2530.203-3(b)(6)). The plan must also include a procedure affording review of a decision to suspend benefits. This procedure, as well as the procedure for a status determination, may be in accordance with the plan's normal claims procedure.

Practical Considerations

If you wish to include a provision for suspension of benefits on a participant's reemployment or continued employment beyond normal retirement age, you should amend your plan to include:
- A provision permitting suspension of benefits and stating the circumstances that will cause such suspension
- A provision requiring verification of the retiree's employment status, including, if desired, the adoption of the presumptions discussed in this presentation's section on verification
- A procedure whereby an employee can obtain a status determination
- A procedure whereby review of a decision to suspend benefits can be obtained
- A provision requiring employees to file a benefit resumption notice.

You should also amend your summary plan description to advise participants of the plan provisions regarding suspension of benefits, making sure to include any provisions requiring verification and any presumptions adopted by the plan. Remember that if your plan has adopted any presumptions, retirees must also be furnished with this information regarding the plan's verification procedures and the nature and effect of such presumptions at least once every 12 months. All notices to plan participants relating to verification requirements must also include this information. Finally, you should set up procedures for distributing appropriate suspension notices both for those who continue to work past retirement age and for those who become reemployed after retirement.

Confidentiality of Information and Plan Records

BY MARGERY SINDER FRIEDMAN

ALTHOUGH CONFIDENTIALITY OF information in plan records includes all personal or private materials that may be contained in the records of an employee benefit plan, the focus here will be on the confidentiality of medical records maintained by plans, especially employee health benefit plans. This topic has become increasingly important in the last few years as society has come to recognize the importance of protecting individual privacy rights, particularly in the age of the computer.

If you had been attending the confidentiality session of the International Foundation's Annual Conference every year since it was first offered, you would have undoubtedly learned about the new statutes affecting privacy interests that pass state legislatures each year. You would have undoubtedly noticed that new practical problems confront plan administrators each year in this area, particularly as we increase the use of computers in plan administration and increase our monitoring of claims paid in an effort to contain health costs. This paper addresses both the legal and practical issues of confidentiality and privacy rights—whether there are laws prohibiting a plan from obtaining certain information about a participant or releasing it to third parties and what a plan can and should do in the course of its day-to-day administration to make sure it has the information it needs to verify a participant's eligibility for benefits, while not interfering unnecessarily with the participant's right to privacy.

General Legal Issues

To understand the legal requirements that may be applicable in this area, it is necessary to do a three part analysis, breaking down the laws into categories based on who or what is being regulated.

State Laws Affecting Employers

The first category is made up of state laws that cover employers and place restrictions on employers' rights to collect and use private medical information about their employees. These state laws do not directly affect employee benefit plans *per se*, but depending on the employer's involvement in plan administration—particularly with a plan that is not a jointly trusteed, Taft-Hartley plan—you may find a state court taking the position that some plan records are subject to the requirements of state laws.

Ms. Friedman is an associate attorney with Morgan, Lewis & Bockius in Washington, D.C., practicing general labor law, with a specialization in employee benefit law. She serves as a neutral counsel to the boards of trustees of several Taft-Hartley plans. Ms. Friedman is assistant editor for the International Foundation's Legal-Legislative Reporter *and "Washington Update." She received her B.A. degree from Case Western Reserve University and her J.D. degree, magna cum laude, from Georgetown University Law Center. She has spoken at previous International Foundation programs.*

Note that state statutes are not supposed to impact on employee benefit plans because federal law—ERISA—preempts the application of state laws to ERISA-covered plans. Nonetheless, you should be aware of the few privacy statutes out there on the books, if only to get an idea of the direction various legislatures are taking to protect privacy. If you are an employer, learn what requirements you are subject to and set up your plan administration, on an independent basis, to make sure plan records are separate and away from the impact of state law.

State Laws Affecting the Insurance Industry

The second category of laws affects the insurance industry and includes those state laws that control the collection, use and disclosure of information gathered by insurance companies and insurance agents. If yours is an insured employee benefit plan, the plan itself will not be affected by these state laws, but the insurer may well be. The laws may thus provide access to medical records by your plan participants and prevent disclosure of confidential information by the insurance companies.

State Laws Affecting Benefit Plans

The third and final category of laws concerns those directly affecting employee benefit plans. This category may be the simplest to cover because there are no laws right now that directly affect employee benefit plans and specifically address privacy issues. State laws are inapplicable in this area, because they are all preempted by ERISA. However, ERISA does not specifically address participants' privacy rights. The question becomes what, if any, impact ERISA's general fiduciary obligations have on trustees and plan administrators in the area of preserving the confidentiality of participants' medical records.

Laws Affecting Employers

Turning to the first category of privacy laws—those affecting employers—there are two types of legal restrictions on an employer's right to collect and use private employee information. On the one hand, the states can by statute require an employer to give its employees access to their personnel and medical records, for learning what is in their employers' files and correcting erroneous or misleading information. The second type of restriction that a state may impose on employers is a prohibition against employer release of certain confidential information without the affected employee's consent.

To give you an idea of how important it can be to employees that there be some limits on the employer's right to use and disseminate certain confidential information, and thus to give you an idea of what has been motivating state legislators to pass laws in this area, note the following article, which appeared in the May 11, 1982 issue of the *Wall Street Journal:*

> *Privacy Please! Some Insured Workers*
> *Pay for Their Mental Treatment*
>
> As many as 15 percent of patients in therapy don't use available health insurance to pay for it, the American Psychiatric Association estimates. Workers fear employers will learn of the treatment in processing claims. The fears can prove valid. One clerk quit her job after someone who saw such forms told her colleague she was being treated for schizophrenia.
>
> A personnel manager lectured a man he learned was getting psychotherapy for alcoholism; the crushed employee resumed drinking. Psychiatrists also suspect some people avoid treatment entirely because of similar confidentiality fears. The psychiatric group and insurers urge concerns to let employees file claim forms directly to carriers, rather than through personnel offices.
>
> Aetna Life and Casualty already sees "a massive trend" toward direct submission, because it both protects privacy and is more efficient.

This story highlights the concerns that many employees have about employers learning confidential medical information about them in the course of routine administration of employee benefit plans. However, only a few states give employees any protection, and in the area of medical records, the protections do not go very far.

There are privacy laws on the books in 33 states covering employer-maintained personnel records. However, only about ten of those state statutes cover employer-maintained medical records—those records with the most sensitive information contained in benefit plan files. Many statutes deal only with hiring and interview information, arrest records, lie detector test results, consumer reports and other general information which may be found in personnel files.

Employee Access to Employer Records

The statutes of six states afford employees a certain amount of access to their employer-held medical records (see Appendix A). These state laws vary greatly in the amount of access afforded to employees and in other protections given to them, including the right to correct erroneous information in employer files.

Connecticut seems to have the statute that is most protective of employee rights, and requires employers to permit employees to inspect their medical records in the employer's possession, including all work-related papers, documents and reports prepared by physicians, psychiatrists or psychologists. An employer is required to maintain these documents in its file for at least one year after termination of the employee's employment. Once an employee reviews the information contained in his employer's medical records, he can request the employer to correct or remove any information with which he disagrees, or if the employer refuses to do that, the employee can submit a written statement explaining his position, which will then be maintained as a part of the employer's medical records. The employee's statement would have to be included with the medical records when the employer transmits or discloses them to any third party. Finally, Connecticut requires employers to comply with employees' written requests for copies of medical records to be sent to their physicians.

Not all of the other state statutes afford employees the right to insert in their medical record files their own statements of disagreement with information contained in those files, and some of the states only permit employee access to the files under certain limited conditions. For example, the Rhode Island statute only refers to employee rights in the event that an application for employment is denied or employment is terminated because of an individual's health. In that case, the employer would be required to comply with the individual's written request to transfer copies of confidential health care information to the individual's physician. However there is no general access provision in the Rhode Island statute. Other states, such as Ohio and Wisconsin, have general access laws, but do not permit employees to correct their records or to insert their own statements explaining matters that they believe are inaccurately reflected in the records.

Employer Use and Disclosure of Records

Four state statutes impose some limits on an employer's right to use confidential employee medical information and to disclose it to third parties (see Appendix B). California has the statute that is most protective of employee privacy rights in this area. A California employer that receives medical information pertaining to its employees is required by state law to establish procedures that will ensure the confidentiality and protection of those records from unauthorized use and disclosure. Under the statute, "medical information" means any individually identifiable information in the possession of or derived from a provider of health care regarding a patient's medical history, mental or physical condition, or treatment. In general, an employer is not permitted to use, disclose, or permit its employees or agents to use or disclose this confidential medical information without the affected employee's specific authorization.

There are, however, certain exceptions to this statutory limit on a California employer's use of confidential medical information. Employers are permitted to use the information for administering and maintaining their employee benefit plans, in connection with their investigations of industrial accidents and illnesses and in connection with required disclosures to federal and state law enforcement and social service agencies. In addition, if an employee puts his medical condition in contention in a lawsuit, arbitration, grievance or other proceeding, the employer will be permitted to use the medical information it has in its possession. Note that violations of the California law can subject employers to punitive damages not to exceed $3,000, attorneys fees not to exceed $1,000 and the cost of litigating, all in addition to ordinary compensatory damages for the employee.

Connecticut also prohibits unauthorized disclosures of individually identifiable information contained in the medical records of any employee. Rhode Island requires employers to establish security procedures for protecting the confidentiality of health care information in employer files. North Carolina limits public access to confidential medical information of state employees, but does not put any limits on private employer disclosures of confidential employee medical information.

In New York, there is legislation pending that would affect employers that provide health care benefits to employees through insured, self-insured or other health care benefit plans. These employers would be required to adopt health care benefit claims administration procedures that would preclude their obtaining correspondence, claim forms, medical records or other pertinent reports of a personal or confidential nature concerning a participant's reasons for seeking treatment or a provider's diagnosis and description of treatment relating to a claim.[1]

This last state statute, which is pending in the New York legislature to amend the state's labor law, raises most clearly the issue of whether state statutes can have any effect on employee benefit plans that are already subject to the requirements of federal law under ERISA. The statute purports to require an employer that provides benefits through an employee benefit plan to set up procedures, presumably plan procedures, that will prevent the sharing of information between the plan and the employer.

However, when Congress passed ERISA in 1974 to regulate the entire area of employee benefit plans, it specifically provided in Section 514 that, with very limited exceptions, "any and all

---

1. N.Y.S.Res. 10262 (introduced May 26, 1982).

State laws insofar as they may now or hereafter relate to any employee benefit plan" are superseded and without any effect whatsoever. This provision is the legal doctrine of preemption, and we refer to ERISA as preempting any state law that on its face purports to impose requirements on employee benefit plans. Because this New York statute would, if passed, ostensibly require the plan to implement certain procedures to protect the privacy rights of the employees covered, it probably could not be enforced against the plan.

The New York law would be similar to some portions of the California statute not described previously. In addition to the specific rules relating to the use and disclosure of medical information by employers, the California law has rules relating to the disclosure of medical information by doctors and other providers and a section dealing with the use and disclosure of medical information by third-party administrators. In each case, the California statute purports to prohibit anyone connected with the providing of health care from releasing confidential medical information to third parties without first obtaining an authorization from the patient. However, the Department of Labor has said in an Advisory Opinion that it considers the California law preempted to the extent that it would require an employee benefit plan to abide by any of its terms.

The Dilemma

What we have, then, is a situation in which an employer may be required to comply with state law in preserving the confidentiality of medical records in its files on employees, but an employee benefit plan may not. The difficult question is, "How do you treat an employer that administers an employee benefit plan in-house, or that plays some role in the administration of a plan, such as a Taft-Hartley plan?" Do you decide that if the employer possesses medical records in its files, it is subject to the state law regardless of whether those records are really plan records? Do you look at the records and say that if, on the one hand, they are maintained as separate plan records, the employer has no obligation to comply with the state law, but if, on the other hand, the records are filed with regular employer records, they do come under the auspices of the state statute?

There have been no clear answers to these questions from the courts, but the doctrine of preemption dictates what the answers should be. If an employer receives confidential information in the course of administering a program for providing benefits to employees—such as regular health care benefits or disability benefits to retirees—then those records should be considered part of the records of an ERISA-covered employee benefit plan; any state statutes purporting to regulate the collection or use of those records should be considered preempted. This preemption would hold regardless of whether an employer is involved in the administration of a legally separate Taft-Hartley benefit plan or whether the employer is administering its own in-house plan, which has no separate board of trustees.

So far, there is no case law on this issue, although there are many decisions in which state laws imposing requirements on the contents and administration of employee benefit plans have been held to be preempted. On the other hand, if an employer receives confidential medical information in the ordinary course of business, but unrelated to the administration of an employee benefit plan, then that information should be subject to state law. This situation could occur when an employer requires applicants to submit to pre-employment physical examinations or provides a company physician to conduct periodic checkups of employees.

Laws Affecting Insurers

The second category of state laws affecting privacy interests is the state insurance laws that afford access to information held by insurers and impose limits on disclosure. The National Association of Insurance Commissioners drafted the Insurance Information and Privacy Protection Model Act, which has been enacted in nine states so far—Arizona, California, Connecticut, Georgia, Illinois, Montana, North Carolina, Oregon and Virginia (see Appendix C). In these states, the model act requires that if an insurance institution, agent or insurance support organization receives a written request from an insured individual, the individual must be given access within 30 days to recorded personal information about himself and given the identity of those persons to whom the information has been provided within the last two years. The model act permits individuals to request correction, amendment or deletion of information they consider to be incorrect, and the act prohibits insurers from disclosing personal information about individuals without written authorization. There are exceptions to the model act's limits on disclosure, and unauthorized disclosures are permitted to verify an individual's eligibility for benefits, to detect or prevent criminal activity or fraud and to comply with various law enforcement requirements.

Thus, if your employee benefit plan is an insured plan, your participants may well have certain privacy rights under the model act that can be pursued through the insurance company involved with the plan. What effect does ERISA preemption have on the model act? Probably very little. As explained earlier, ERISA supersedes all state laws that relate to employee benefit plans, but there is an exception for state insurance laws. There have been cases that have held that although a state insurance law may not impose requirements on plans themselves, it may impose requirements on the insurance companies with which the plans may want to do business.

Laws Affecting Benefit Plans

The third category of laws addressing privacy rights—those that concern employee benefit plans—is easy to describe because such laws don't exist. To the extent that any state legislature thinks it has passed a law that affects employee benefit plans, the law is preempted. That leaves federal law—and there is only ERISA, which does not address the issue of the confidentiality of plan records or the privacy rights of plan participants.

To the extent that federal law provides any privacy protections for participants in employee benefit plans, those protections would arise out of ERISA's general fiduciary obligation, applicable to plan trustees and administrators. ERISA Section 404(A)(1) provides that a fiduciary must discharge his plan duties solely in the interest of participants and beneficiaries and for the exclusive purpose of providing benefits and defraying reasonable expenses of plan administration. Under that standard, any action taken for the benefit of a contributing employer or a sponsoring union rather than the participants and beneficiaries could violate federal law.

Let us examine those situations in which a fund has a need for certain private, confidential information about a participant and see whether any restrictions apply by virtue of ERISA's fiduciary standard. One very basic example of a benefit plan's need to obtain medical information about a plan participant is the case of the plan needing to verify a participant's eligibility for a claimed benefit under the plan. If a participant requests reimbursement for a doctor's bill, the fund needs to verify that the participant did indeed receive services from the doctor and may even have to find out what the doctor's treatment was for, because the plan may not cover all possible medical conditions.

Similarly, a pension plan would need to be able to determine that a participant is completely and totally disabled, if that is a requirement for eligibility for a disability pension. If the disability pension is to continue for a lengthy period of time, the plan may need to require the participant to submit to periodic physical examinations to determine continued eligibility.

If a participant were to protest that the fund has no right to have him examined or learn confidential medical details about his condition, the simple answer would be that the plan has a fiduciary obligation not to pay benefits to anyone until a determination has been made that the participant deserves them. In this type of case, the fiduciary obligations of ERISA support a plan in demanding confidential information and even in requiring individuals to submit to further physical examinations, the results of which would be turned over to plan fiduciaries.

Some practical problems will undoubtedly arise when a plan attempts to collect confidential medical information about a participant. Many physicians and hospitals will demand to see a waiver signed by the plan participant indicating consent to release of the confidential information. The doctor may be attempting to comply with one of the state statutes on the subject and may require the plan to submit a waiver that meets the detailed requirements of the state law. Arguing that ERISA preempts the application of state laws to employee benefit plans will probably not, as a practical matter, convince anyone to release information without a waiver.

In addition, a doctor may demand a waiver because he feels bound by a physician-patient privilege or medical ethics that prohibit unauthorized disclosure of confidential information about a patient. Many states have passed statutes that provide that a physician may not testify in court concerning confidential information learned in the course of treating a patient. As an ethical matter, many physicians consider the privilege to extend to disclosures outside of the courtroom. In addition, the Hippocratic oath taken by physicians requires that patients' confidences be kept.

Thus, in administering your employee benefit plans, you are well-advised to include a standard waiver or some release language on your benefit claim forms. There is nothing objectionable about requiring a participant to consent to the release of medical information pertinent to his eligibility for a benefit before he receives the benefit provided. If this provision is a requirement of your plan, it should be spelled out in plan documents. Then, there is no question that the plan can force compliance before having to pay benefits out of fund assets.

The purpose of the waiver that you will have participants sign is twofold. First, the participant will be authorizing the plan to receive information concerning treatment of the participant by physicians and hospitals, clinics, etc. Second, the waiver should be used for the participant to authorize disclosure of the information by the plan to those entities to which the plan finds it necessary to make disclosures. For example, to coordinate benefits with other insurers, the plan may have to make disclosures of treatment for certain illnesses to other plans or insurance companies. To fully protect yourselves and your plan, the participant should be asked to authorize these disclosures even though the fact that you are coordinating benefits may be spelled out in detail in your plan documents.

Disclosure Problems

It is readily apparent that disclosure of confidential information to insurance companies for coordination of benefits has a legitimate basis and may be justified by plan trustees as proper exercises of their fiduciary responsibility to safeguard fund assets and assure that only proper benefits are paid. Other possible disclosures of confidential information about plan participants, however, raise serious questions of legitimacy and propriety. For example, it is not unusual for plan trustees to be confronted with requests by employers and unions for confidential medical information. Often, employers are interested in monitoring health care costs and may request information about benefits paid and types of claims. Supplying this information may well be a legitimate function, particularly where the parties are working together to monitor costs, and sufficient disclosures can be made without including private medical information about individual participants that should be kept confidential.

However, employers have also been known to ask for information about particular employees, for disciplinary or other purposes. In one instance that came to my attention recently, an employer requested a plan administrator to provide it with a list of all of the employees who had filed benefit claims for treatment for alcoholism. Apparently, the employer was concerned about alcoholism in its workforce and wanted to identify its problem employees. Unions have been known to request private medical information for internal union purposes, rather than for any purpose connected with the administration of the plan.

In these cases, a plan fiduciary has to ask himself whether he is acting solely in the interest of the plan's participants and beneficiaries if he turns private, individually identifiable medical information over to the employer and the union. It seems reasonable that a plan participant would have a legitimate expectation that plan fiduciaries will treat information about him as confidential and that they will not disclose that information to third parties except when necessary in the course of fund administration and when specifically authorized. Thus, if you are either a union or management trustee, you should not be turning over confidential information to third parties unless the participant has indicated his consent to disclosure. You should not be using confidential plan information obtained in the course of your plan duties for any purpose outside of plan administration.

Illustrative Cases

There are no cases on the privacy issue concerning employee benefit plans, although there is one case that may be interesting because it provides some analogous support for the argument that individually identifiable medical information cannot be turned over to an employer or the union. In *Horne v. Patton,* 287 So.2d 824 (Sup. Ct. Ala. 1973), the Supreme Court of Alabama considered the case of Mr. Horne, who was suing his physician, Dr. Patton, for an alleged breach of the doctor-patient relationship. Horne claimed that Dr. Patton disclosed certain information about him to his employer, despite his specific instructions to the doctor to keep all medical information confidential. The lower court had dismissed the case, but the Supreme Court of Alabama reversed and remanded the case for trial, noting that Horne had stated a valid claim.

Language in the court's opinion suggests that the court believed that doctors stand in a confidential or fiduciary capacity as to their patients, and owe them a duty of confidentiality, except where the supervening interests of society may intervene. Based on that reasoning, it does not take much imagination to argue that if a duty of confidentiality flows from a fiduciary relationship, then that duty may extend to other fiduciaries, such as plan trustees, when they acquire private medical information about plan participants.

The only cases other than those involving the physician-patient relationship that address the privacy interests of individuals in their medical records are described in Appendix D. For various reasons, these cases have little relevance to employee benefit plans, but they are interesting in that the courts are beginning to recognize an individual's right to confidentiality in his medical records, and it may be that these relatively recent court decisions are just the beginning of what will be an evolution of the law as it adjusts to the tremendous growth in data collection and the problems that this growth makes for employees and individuals covered by health care plans.

Interestingly enough, the few court decisions that have discussed the individual privacy interests at stake in a tug of war over medical records have not arisen in the context of an employee either attempting to obtain access to his records or attempting to prevent those records from being disclosed to a third party. Rather, in all of the cases noted, some entity has attempted to obtain confidential medical information from another entity, usually the employer, and the entity in possession of the medical records has sought to assert the individuals' interest in their privacy to prevent disclosure.

The first case was the United States Supreme Court's decision in *Whalen v. Roe,* 429 U.S. 589 (1977). This case did not involve an employment relationship, but it does represent the first time the highest court in this land has addressed the individual's right to privacy where his medical records are concerned, and the Court noted that this privacy right is protected by the Constitution. The case concerned a New York statute that required physicians to report the names and addresses of all patients for whom they prescribed certain drugs for which there was both a lawful and unlawful market—such drugs as methadone and amphetamines. The patients' names and addresses were to be recorded in a centralized computer file so that New York state officials could attempt to regulate the flow of dangerous drugs. A group of physicians challenged the law, claiming that it violated their privacy rights in maintaining their medical practices, and that it also violated the privacy rights of their patients, who would be deterred from seeking medical treatment out of fear that the fact that they were being prescribed certain drugs would be disclosed.

The Court recognized that an individual's interest in avoiding disclosure of certain personal matters, including certain private medical information, is within the "zone of privacy" protected by the Constitution. Further, the Court noted that it was "not unaware of the threat to privacy implicit in the accumulation of vast amounts of personal information in computerized data banks or other massive government files." Thus, the Court recognized the inherent privacy threat in the increasing use of computers in our lives, and particularly the accumulation of large amounts of confidential information in centralized data banks. However, the Court upheld the New York statute, noting the legitimate state interest in controlling dangerous drugs and pointing out that the statute contained various security provisions designed to prevent unwarranted disclosures of confidential information. The Court saw no reason why the security measures would not adequately protect the patients' privacy rights.

In the next few cases, the federal appeals courts were considering employer challenges to regulations promulgated by the Occupational Safety and Health Administration (OSHA) requiring employers to disclose information about employees exposed to various hazardous substances or workplace conditions. In all of the cases the court upheld the federal agencies'—OSHA and the National Institute on Occupational Safety and Health (NIOSH)—rights to receive the records, ruling that the societal interest in occupational safety and health outweighed the employees' privacy interests in their employers' medical records.

The United States Court of Appeals for the District of Columbia Circuit in *United Steel Workers of America v. Marshall,* 647 F.2d 1189 (D.C. Cir. 1980), said that in its opinion, to require the federal agencies "to obtain express permission for disclosure from each of millions of workers would create an unthinkable administrative burden and risk the health of workers who for unfortunate but understandable reasons might fear any disclosure of their health records." However, in both *United States v. Westinghouse Electric Corp.,* 638 F.2d 570 (3d Cir. 1980), and *General Motors Corp. v. Director of NIOSH,* 636 F.2d 163 (6th Cir. 1980), the courts erected some safeguards for protecting privacy interests. In *Westinghouse,* the Third Circuit Court of Appeals ruled that NIOSH should give prior notice to the affected employees in order to permit them to raise personal claims of privacy. The United States Court of Appeals for the Sixth Circuit in the *General Motors* case remanded the case to the trial court to fashion a protective order that would include safeguards against the improper disclosure of the confidential information by NIOSH. Nonetheless, both courts held that the federal interest in promoting workplace safety and health justified some intrusion in employee privacy.

Concerning the right of an entity other than a federal agency to receive employee medical records, the court in *United Steel Workers of America v. Marshall* ruled that the OSHA regulation should be construed to permit disclosure to the union of only limited information concerning employees who had been removed from exposure to lead in the workplace. This information should not include private details of the medical examinations that had formed the bases for the employee removals. The D.C. Circuit Court of Appeals explained that if the regulation had permitted the union to examine intimate results of physician examinations without the employees' permission, the regulation could well violate both the statute pursuant to which it had been promulgated and the United States Constitution.

The final set of cases also concerns the rights of a union to receive confidential medical information, this time in the context of collective bargaining, where a union claims that certain information is necessary for it to perform its duties as a collective bargaining representative. In each case, the employer refused to provide certain private information, claiming to protect the employees' privacy rights. In general, the National Labor Relations Board and the courts have held that employers must provide certain information to the union, which should not include individually identifiable medical data unless the affected employees authorize disclosure.

All of the cases noted demonstrate the increasing recognition by the courts of an individual's right to privacy where personal medical records are concerned. Nonetheless, they are not terribly useful in giving guidance to either employers or employee benefit plan administrators about their recordkeeping practices. The cases are concerned only with the employees' constitutional right to privacy and whether a particular state or federal law is impinging on that right.

However, you should be aware that constitutional issues simply do not arise in the context of the relationship between a private entity such as an employer or an employee benefit plan and employees or plan participants. The Constitution offers protection from certain state and federal government actions, but has no application in the world of private parties, except where an entity is acting pursuant to a state or federal law.

However, these cases are important for the reason that they evidence a general societal recognition that employees have a legitimate expectation of privacy in their medical records. The reasoning of the cases suggests that the prudent plan fiduciary should not disclose confidential medical information about a plan participant without the participant's specific authorization.

We have already addressed disclosures to other plans, insurance companies, the union and the employer, and the discussion extends to all other individuals or entities that may request information from the plan. You may get a request from a wife in a divorce proceeding seeking information about her husband's entitlement to pension benefits or life insurance benefits; you may get a request from a defendant being sued by a participant in a personal injury action; you may get a request from a banker who is reviewing a plan participant's mortgage application.

In cases such as these, unless disclosure has been authorized specifically by the participant, you should make the requester force you to supply the information in response to a valid subpoena. However, even in a case where your plan records are subpoenaed, you may want to object to the subpoena on the ground that individual privacy rights are at stake. This tactic probably would not be successful in the case of an individual seeking information about his or her spouse's entitlement to benefits, but there are occasions when individuals in litigation with employers decide that the fund office is the best source of information about various employees' benefits, salary levels and hours worked. If your fund is served with a subpoena in this type of situation, you may want to protect the privacy interests of your participants and avoid the burdensome task of compiling a great deal of information.

Which Information Should Be Available?

One final issue that you should consider in the administration of your plans is what information you will make available to plan participants on request. As you will note from a review of the state statutes described, some states do not require a medical provider to turn over medical records to a patient if he believes that the patient would be harmed by viewing his own records. In that situation, the employer or the medical provider is often permitted to turn over the records to a physician designated by the employee or patient. Thus, if you are going to turn over medical records to a plan participant, you would be well-advised to have him release the fund from any liability in connection with that disclosure.

In some situations, you may not have a choice about whether to turn over medical records. When an employee's claim for a benefit is denied, he has the right to appeal the denial and to review fund documents pertinent to the decision to deny benefits. In one recent case, *Freeman v. IBEW Local 613 Pension Fund,* 3 EBC 1865 (N.D.Ga. 1982), the United States District Court for the Northern District of Georgia ruled that participants whose disability pensions had been terminated had a right to review the medical records that formed the basis for the trustees' decision that they were no longer permanently and totally disabled. The trustees in that case had required all disability retirees to submit to physical examinations to determine whether they continued to be eligible for benefits. The court relied on the Labor Department's regulations regarding participants' rights in the claims appeal process.

Listed in Appendix E are some of the recommendations of the Privacy Protection Study Commission, which was established by Congress in the Privacy Act of 1974. The Privacy Act governs the disclosure of certain records maintained by federal government agencies; when Congress passed that legislation, it also established the commission to study privacy issues in the private sector.

In 1977, the commission published a 620 page report, devoting an entire chapter to the employment relationship—and a significant section of that chapter to employer medical records and medical record information. Its recommendations for employers maintaining employee medical records and administering employee benefit plans basically reflect the commission's view that government regulation in this area would be unwieldy and difficult of enforcement and that employer safeguards should be voluntarily undertaken.

The commission did not make recommendations for employee benefit plan administrators per se, but the recommendations for employers in the benefits area will give you some idea of what it considered important in terms of protecting employee privacy. The recommendations regarding medical records focused on five employee procedural rights:

- Notice—of type of information kept by the employer and how used
- Authorization—collection of information from third parties should require authorization
- Access—to information on file with the employer
- Correction—either contest and correct or add own statement
- Confidentiality—disclosure to third parties should require authorization.

In addition to these rights, Recommendations 28, 29, 30 and 31 (Appendix E) are aimed at protecting employee medical records from use in employment-related decisionmaking. The commission recommended that employers maintain medical records apart from other personnel records, and that they maintain medical records developed under employer health care programs apart from other employment-related medical records. The commission was concerned that if employees fear that their medical problems will be used against them by employers making decisions on promotions and layoffs, they will not submit medical claims for payment in situations where the employers have access to the claim files. Although these recommendations are not aimed at employee benefit plans specifically, you can certainly use them as guidance in developing a policy for preserving confidentiality in your own benefit plan records.

Conclusion

I think that you can rest assured, at least for the near future, that we will not see legislation specifically addressing privacy protection for employers or employee benefit plans. President Carter supported the voluntary approach to employee privacy that was recommended by the commission, and it is safe to say that under President Reagan, the chances for legislation designed to increase governmental regulation of the private sector are not great.

One piece of legislation, proposed each session in the House of Representatives and sponsored by Congressman Philip M. Crane (R-IL),[2] would prohibit all government agencies from inspecting or collecting medical and dental records of patients who do not receive assistance from the federal government for their treatment, such as Medicare. Congressman Crane is concerned about the collection of confidential medical information by government agencies, and presumably his bill would completely do away with all of the OSHA regulations enabling that agency to collect confidential information about employee exposure to toxic substances in the workplace. It would also do away with Internal Revenue Service and Department of Labor inspection of confidential medical records in the possession of employee benefit plans, pursuant to routine audits. However, government audits of employee benefit plans have typically focused on such things as trustee expenses—for example, expenses incurred in connection with an International Foundation Annual Conference—and it would probably be unusual for a government agent to ask a plan to make available records that would contain individually identifiable medical information.

---

2. H.R. 4966, introduced in the 97th Congress (November 13, 1981).

Appendix A

STATE STATUTES AFFORDING EMPLOYEE ACCESS TO EMPLOYER-HELD MEDICAL RECORDS

Connecticut—An employer must, within a reasonable time after receipt of a written request from an employee, permit an inspection of medical records pertaining to the employee in the employer's possession. Medical records, which include all papers, documents and reports prepared by a physician, psychiatrist or psychologist that are in the possession of the employer and are work-related (or upon which the employer relies to make any employment-related decision), must be kept for at least one year after termination of the employee's employment.

If employee disagrees with information contained in employer's medical records—and employer does not agree to remove or correct the information—the employee may submit a written statement explaining his position, which will be maintained as a part of the medical records. The employer must include such a statement with the medical records when transmitting or disclosing them to a third party. Employer must comply with the employee's written request for a copy of medical records to be provided to the employee's physician. A reasonable copying fee may be charged. Conn. Gen. Stat. Sect. 31-128.

Maine—On written request from an employee or former employee, an employer must provide an opportunity for individual (or his duly authorized representative) to review his personnel file. A personnel file includes reports relating to the employee's benefits and nonprivileged medical records or nurses' station notes relating to the employee, which the employer has in his possession. Noncompliance without good cause may result in a civil penalty of $25 for each day that a failure to afford review continues, up to a maximum penalty of $500. Me. Rev. Stat. Ann. tit. 26 Sect. 631.

Ohio—An employer or a physician, other health care professional, hospital or laboratory that contracts with the employer to provide medical information pertaining to employees must comply with written request of employee for a copy of any medical report. The statute covers medical reports arising from physical examinations by physicians or other health care professionals and hospital or laboratory tests that are required by the employer as a condition of employment or arising out of any injury or disease relating to employment.

If a physician concludes that presentation of all or any part of an employee's medical record directly to the employee will result in serious medical harm to him, physician may indicate this conclusion on the medical record, and a copy of the record will be given instead to a physician designated in writing by the employee. The employee may be charged the employer's cost of furnishing copies of the medical reports, but not more than 25¢ per page. Noncompliance under the law constitutes a minor misdemeanor for each violation. Ohio Rev. Code Ann. Sect. 4113.23.

Rhode Island—If an employer denies an employment application or terminates an individual's employment for health reasons, it must, on written request by the affected individual, transfer copies of all of the individual's confidential health care information in its possession to a physician designated by the individual. The employer may require payment of its actual cost of retrieval, duplication and forwarding prior to completing the transfer.

The individual or his authorized representative may request the employer to amend or expunge any part of the health care information he believes is in error, or request the addition of other recent relevant information. The employer must notify the health care provider who initially forwarded the information to it, and if the health care provider concurs with the individual's request, the employer must return the information to the provider for modification. The employer is not itself permitted to modify the health care information except on court order. However, an affected employee has the right to place into the file at his own cost a statement of his view concerning the correctness or relevance of existing information or the addition of new information. R.I. Gen. Laws Sect. 5-37.3-5.

Vermont—Public employees or their authorized representatives are permitted to inspect their personnel records, which include information relating to medical or psychological facts. Vt. Stat. Ann. tit.1 Sect. 317(b)(7).

Wisconsin—On the request of an employee, an employer must permit the employee to inspect any of his personal medical records in the employer's files. If the employer believes, however, that disclosure of an employee's medical records would have a detrimental effect on the employee, the records may be released to the employee's physician or through a physician designated by the employee, in which case the records may be released by the physician to the employee or the employee's immediate family. The employer may require an employee to make his request in writing. Wis. Stat. Sect. 103.13(1)-(6).

Appendix B

STATE STATUTES IMPOSING LIMITS ON EMPLOYER DISCLOSURE OF EMPLOYEE MEDICAL INFORMATION

California—An employer that receives medical information pertaining to its employees must establish appropriate procedures to ensure the confidentiality of that information and its protection from unauthorized use and disclosure. "Medical information" means any individually identifiable information in the possession of or derived from a provider of health care regarding a patient's medical history, mental or physical condition, or treatment.

An employer is not permitted to use, disclose or knowingly permit its employees or agents to use or disclose medical information that the employer possesses pertaining to an employee without the employee's (the patient's) written authorization. However, employers are permitted to use medical information for administering and maintaining employee benefit plans, including health care plans and plans for providing short term and long term disability income, workers' compensation and for determining eligibility for paid and unpaid leave from work for medical reasons.

Information may also be used in connection with investigations of industrial accidents and illnesses, in connection with disclosures to federal and state law enforcement authorities and social service agencies (where required by law) and in connection with lawsuits, arbitrations, grievances, or other proceedings in which employees have placed their medical histories and mental or physical conditions in issue. An employer is prohibited from discriminating against an employee for his refusal to sign an authorization releasing his medical information. An employer found to have violated the statute may be liable for compensatory damages, punitive damages not to exceed $3,000, attorneys' fees not to exceed $1,000 and the cost of litigation. Cal. Civ. Code Sect. 56.05, .20, .22-24, .30, .35. (West).

Connecticut—An employer is prohibited from disclosing individually identifiable information contained in the medical records of any employee without that employee's written authorization. Exceptions include disclosures made in response to an apparent medical emergency, to apprise an employee's physician of a medical condition of which the employee may not be aware and disclosures made pursuant to the terms of a collective bargaining agreement. An employer is required to inform the employee giving authorization of his or his physician's right of inspection and correction of the records, his right to withhold authorization and the effect of any withholding of authorization on him. Conn. Gen. Stat. Sect. 31-128f.

North Carolina—State laws permitting public access to state agency records and information do not permit access to insurance coverage and medical information of teachers and state employees received by insurers under contract with the state retirement system. All information relating to insurance coverage of state employees is confidential, regardless of whether a claim has been filed or approved. N.C. Gen. Stat. Sect. 135-37 (Supp. 1981).

Rhode Island—Third parties (including employers) receiving and retaining a patient's confidential health care information must establish certain security procedures, including limits on authorized access to personally identifiable confidential health care information to persons with a "need to know." Other employees may have access to information that does not contain information from which an individual can be identified. R.I. Gen. Laws Sect. 5-37.3-4(c)(1).

Appendix C

NATIONAL ASSOCIATION OF INSURANCE COMMISSIONERS' INSURANCE INFORMATION AND PRIVACY PROTECTION MODEL ACT

The model act was designed "to establish standards for the collection, use and disclosure of information gathered in connection with insurance transactions by insurance institutions, agents or insurance-support organizations...." On written request to the insurer, an individual must be afforded access (within 30 days) to recorded personal information about himself, and the identity of those persons to whom the personal information has been provided within the previous two years. The model act also enables individuals to request correction, amendment or deletion of recorded personal information. Limits are imposed on insurer disclosure of personal information without the written authorization of the affected individual. Unauthorized disclosures are permitted for various purposes, including to verify an individual's eligibility for benefits, to detect or prevent criminal activity or fraud and to comply with state insurance regulatory or other law enforcement requirements.

States that have enacted the model act:

State	Effective Date
Arizona	April 1, 1982
California	October 1, 1981
Connecticut	October 1, 1982
Georgia	January 1, 1984
Illinois	August 6, 1981
Montana	July 1, 1982
North Carolina	July 1, 1982
Oregon	January 1, 1983
Virginia	January 1, 1982

Nevada has adopted an enabling statute authorizing the Commissioner of Insurance to adopt the contents of the model act as a regulation; to date, the Commissioner of Insurance has taken no action. Bills similar to the model act are pending in New Jersey and New York.

Appendix D

JUDICIAL (AND FEDERAL AGENCY) RECOGNITION OF INDIVIDUAL PRIVACY INTEREST IN MEDICAL RECORDS

Release of Information Pursuant to Federal or State Law

Whalen v. Roe, 429 U.S. 589 (1977)

The United States Supreme Court upheld the constitutionality of a New York statute requiring physicians to report (for recordation in a centralized computer file) the names and addresses of all persons who are prescribed certain drugs for which there is both a lawful and an unlawful market (including methadone and amphetamines). Although recognizing that an individual interest in avoiding disclosure of certain personal matters (including medical information) is within the "zone of privacy" protected by the Constitution, the Court held that the New York statute constituted a rational attempt at controlling the distribution of dangerous drugs and did not impermissibly interfere with individual liberty or privacy. The Court stated that it was "not unaware of the threat to privacy implicit in the accumulation of vast amounts of personal information in computerized data banks or other massive government files"; however, it emphasized that the state statute included various security provisions designed to prevent the unwarranted disclosure of accumulated private data.

United Steel Workers of America v. Marshall, 647 F.2d 1189 (D.C. Cir. 1980)

A federal appeals court upheld a regulation promulgated by the Occupational Safety and Health Administration (OSHA) requiring employers to maintain a variety of health records on employees exposed to lead and to make the records available to OSHA, the National Institute for Occupational Safety and Health (NIOSH) and authorized employee representatives, including union officials. The court upheld OSHA's and NIOSH's unrestricted access to all records, but ruled that absent the employees' permission, the union could only receive limited information concerning employees removed from exposure to lead. This information could not include details of the medical examinations forming the bases for the removals. Relying on *Whalen v. Roe,* the court found that the government collection of confidential information in this case and the limited access to medical information provided to employee representatives did not constitute an unconstitutional invasion of workers' privacy rights.

United States v. Westinghouse Electric Corporation, 638 F.2d 570 (3d Cir. 1980)

A federal appeals court ruled that an employer was not justified in refusing to turn over medical records of all employees potentially affected by exposure to hexahydrophthalic anhydride in response to a subpoena from NIOSH. The court concluded that the societal interest in occupational safety and health justified NIOSH's intrusion into records and information normally considered private, but concluded that NIOSH should give prior notice to the employees whose medical records are sought in order to permit them to raise personal claims of privacy, if they desire.

General Motors Corp. v. Director of NIOSH, 636 F.2d 163 (6th Cir. 1980)

A federal appeals court enforced a NIOSH subpoena for the medical records for all employees working in the "wet rubber process" of an employer's plant. The company had taken the position that it would comply with the subpoena only if individual employees authorized the release of their records. Four hundred ninety individuals failed to execute releases, but the court found that NIOSH's legitimate interest in the information outweighed the employees' privacy interests in their records. The court remanded the case to the lower court to fashion a protective order including safeguards against the improper disclosure of the confidential information by NIOSH.

OSHA Rule Revisions

OSHA has proposed revisions to its access to employee exposure and medical records rules. The changes are designed to streamline the complexity of the present requirements and to lift some of the present burdens of compliance from employers.

Legislation

H.R. 4966, a bill "to provide for the confidentiality of medical and dental records of patients not receiving assistance from the federal government," was introduced by Congressman Philip M. Crane (R-IL) on November 13, 1981. The bill would prohibit federal agency access to any part of medical or dental records of patients whose medical or dental care was not, or will not be, provided or paid for by the federal government, unless the affected patient has authorized disclosure.

Release of Information Pursuant to Collective Bargaining Obligation

Detroit Edison Co. v. NLRB, 440 U.S. 301 (1979)

The United States Supreme Court upheld an employer's right to refuse to disclose individual employees' scores on psychological aptitude tests to assist the union in processing a grievance. Where the company had promised the employees that their scores would remain confidential, the Court noted that "the sensitivity of any human being to disclosure of information that may be taken to bear on his or her basic competence is sufficiently well known to be an appropriate subject to judicial notice."

Minnesota Mining & Manufacturing Co., 261 NLRB No. 2 (1982), and *Colgate-Palmolive Co.,* 261 NLRB No. 7 (1982)

The National Labor Relations Board ruled that an employer's duty to bargain under federal labor law requires it to disclose workforce medical information requested by a union, except that which contains individually identified medical data.

United Aircraft Corp., 192 NLRB 382 (1971), *modified on other grounds,* 534 F.2d 422 (2d Cir. 1975)

The National Labor Relations Board upheld a company's refusal to disclose to the union any employees' medical records (including physicians' reports) without their consent, unless records became relevant to a particular dispute.

Johns-Manville Sales Corp., 252 NLRB 368 (1980)

The National Labor Relations Board upheld a company's refusal to turn over to the union the names of employees who had been "red-tagged" because they had been partially disabled by pneumonococcus. The company had taken the position that the names of the employees who had been red-tagged, as distinguished from the number of red-tagged employees, were confidential medical records.

Relying on *Detroit Edison,* NLRB concluded that the confidentiality interest of the red-tagged employees outweighed the union's need to know their identities, but made it clear that the privilege to refuse to disclose requested information belonged not to the company but to the employees. NLRB emphasized that the company had supplied a number of employees with forms on which they could indicate whether they wished their names to be disclosed to the union, and in fact disclosed the names of those employees who consented.

Appendix E

REPORT OF THE PRIVACY PROTECTION STUDY COMMISSION, ESTABLISHED BY CONGRESS IN THE PRIVACY ACT OF 1974

Public Policy Objectives for Employers Maintaining Medical Records

- To minimize intrusiveness (relates to the collection of records)
- To maximize fairness (relates to the use of information in records)
- To create a legitimate, enforceable expectation of confidentiality (relates to the dissemination of information from employer records).

Recommendations of the Privacy Protection Study Commission

Recommendation (19)

That, upon request, an individual who is the subject of a medical record maintained by an employer, or another responsible person designated by the individual, be allowed to have access to that medical record, including an opportunity to see and copy it. The employer should be able to charge a reasonable fee (not to exceed the amount charged to third parties) for preparing and copying the record.

Recommendation (20)

That, upon request, an individual who is the subject of a medical-record information maintained by an employer be allowed to have access to that information either directly or through a licensed medical professional designated by the individual.

Recommendation (21)

That an employer that acts as a provider or administrator of an insurance plan, upon request by an applicant, employee, or former employee should:
  (a) inform the individual, after verifying his identity, whether it has any recorded information about him that pertains to the employee's insurance relationship with him;
  (b) permit the individual to see and copy any such recorded information, either in person or by mail; or
  (c) apprise the individual of the nature and substance of any such recorded information by telephone; and
  (d) permit the individual to use whichever of the methods of access provided in (b) and (c) he prefers.

The employer should be able to charge a reasonable copying fee for any copies provided to the individual. Any such recorded information should be made available to the individual, but need not contain the name or other identifying particulars of any source (other than an institutional source) of information in the record who has provided such information on the condition that his or her identity not be revealed, and need not reveal a confidential numerical code.

Recommendation (23)

That an employer establish a procedure whereby an individual who is the subject of a medical record maintained by the employer can request correction or amendment of the record. When the individual requests correction or amendment, the employer should, within a reasonable period of time, either:
  (a) make the correction or amendment requested, or
  (b) inform the individual of its refusal to do so, the reason for the refusal, and of the procedure, if any, for further review of the refusal.

In addition, if the employer decides that it will not correct or amend a record in accordance with the individual's request, the employer should permit the individual to file a concise statement of the reasons for the disagreement, and in any subsequent disclosure of the disputed information include a notation that the information is disputed and the statement of disagreement. In any such disclosure, the employer may also include a statement of the reasons for not making the requested correction or amendment.

Finally, when an employer corrects or amends a record pursuant to an individual's request, or accepts a notation of dispute and statement of disagreement, it should furnish the correction, amendment or statement of disagreement to any person specifically designated by the individual to whom the employer has previously disclosed the inaccurate, incomplete, or disputed information.

Recommendation (24)

That . . . when an individual who is the subject of medical-record information maintained by an employer requests correction or amendment of such information, the employer should:
- (a) disclose to the individual, or to a medical professional designated by him, the identity of the medical-care provider who was the source of the medical-record information;
- (b) make the correction or amendment request within a reasonable period of time, if the medical-care provider who was the source of the information agrees that it is inaccurate or incomplete; and
- (c) establish a procedure whereby an individual who is the subject of medical-record information maintained by an employer, and who believes that the information is incorrect or incomplete, would be provided an opportunity to present supplemental information of a limited nature for inclusion in the medical-record information maintained by the employer, provided that the source of the supplemental information is also included.

Recommendation (25)

That when an employer acts as a provider or administrator of an insurance plan, the employer should:
- (a) permit an individual to request correction or amendment of a record pertaining to him;
- (b) within a reasonable period of time, correct or amend (including supplement) any portion thereof which the individual reasonably believes is not accurate, timely, or complete;
- (c) furnish the correction or amendment to any person or organization specifically designated by the individual who may have, within two years prior thereto, received any such information; and, automatically, to any insurance-support organization whose primary source of information on individuals is insurance institutions when the support organization has systematically received any such information from the employer within the preceding seven years, unless the support organization no longer maintains the information, in which case, furnishing the correction or amendment would not be necessary; and, automatically, to any insurance-support organization that furnished the information corrected or amended; or
- (d) inform the individual of its refusal to correct or amend the record in accordance with his request and of the reason(s) for the refusal; and
  - (i) permit an individual who disagrees with the refusal to correct or amend the record to have placed on or with the record a concise statement setting forth the reasons for his disagreement;
  - (ii) in any subsequent disclosure outside the employing organization containing information about which the individual has filed a statement of dispute, clearly note any portion of the record which is disputed and provide a copy of the statement along with the information being disclosed; and

(iii) furnish the statement to any person or organization specifically designated by the individual who may have, within two years prior thereto, received any such information; and, automatically, to an insurance-support organization whose primary source of information on individuals is insurance institutions when the support organization has received any such information from the employer within the preceding seven years, unless the support organization no longer maintains the information, in which case, furnishing the statement would not be necessary; and, automatically, to any insurance-support organization that furnished the disputed information; and

(e) limit its reinvestigation of disputed information to those record items in dispute.

Recommendation (28)

That an employer that maintains an employment-related medical record about an individual assure that no diagnostic or treatment information in any such record is made available for use in any employment decision; and

Recommendation (29)

That an employer that provides a voluntary health-care program for its employees assure that any medical record generated by the program is maintained apart from any employment-related medical record and not used by any physician in advising on any employment-related decision or in making any employment-related decision without the express authorization of the individual to whom the record pertains.

Recommendation (30)

That an employer that provides life or health insurance as a service to its employees assure that individually identifiable insurance records are maintained separately from other records and not available for use in making employment decisions; and further

Recommendation (31)

That an employer that provides work-related insurance for employees, such as worker's compensation, voluntary sick pay, or short- or long-term disability insurance, assure that individually identifiable records pertaining to such insurance are available internally only to authorized recipients and on a need-to-know basis.

Recommendation (34)

That Congress direct the Department of Labor to review the extent to which medical records made to protect individuals exposed to hazardous environments or substances in the workplace are or may come to be used to discriminate against them in employment. This review should include an examination of the feasibility of:

(a) restricting the availability of records generated by medical examinations and tests conducted in accordance with OSHA requirements for use in making employment decisions; and

(b) establishing mechanisms to protect employees whose health has been affected by exposure to hazardous environments or substances from the economic consequences of employers' decisions concerning their employability.

Considerations of Post-MPPAA Benefit Improvements

BY CAROLYN D. GENTILE

WHEN THE Multiemployer Pension Plan Amendments Act of 1980 (MPPAA) went into effect, many questions arose concerning the meaning of the statute and its impact on multiemployer defined pension plans. Now that some time has passed since the passage of MPPAA and the initial confusion has abated, it is somewhat easier to examine the statute objectively and rationally discuss some of the changes that the new legislation has caused.

The greatest impact of MPPAA has been on those plans for which only contributions are negotiated. On the other hand, the plans that have had a bargaining history of the parties negotiating benefits are not as deeply affected, because it was always within the contemplation of the negotiators that the employers would be obligated to pay the cost of the benefits even though those costs might rise. On the contrary, when contributions only are negotiated, the employers believed that their obligation was limited to the agreed-on contribution rate.

Issues Raised

To more closely examine the issues raised by MPPAA, it is necessary first to categorize the questions based on the particular interests of the parties affected.

Since 1980, many contributing employers have been struck with the realization that they have a legal, enforceable obligation to multiemployer pension plans that can be calculated and reduced to a sum certain, i.e., their share of the plan's unfunded vested benefits. Up until the time that MPPAA was passed, aside from the amount that was contributed pursuant to the collective bargaining agreement, employers had no fixed dollar obligation and, therefore, little attention was paid to what was perceived as merely a potential liability.[1] Moreover, employers have been advised that a change in the plan's

Ms. Gentile, since 1978, has been administrator of several Taft-Hartley funds as well as special counsel to the Seafarers International Union. Previously, Ms. Gentile served as special counsel to these trust funds. Ms. Gentile serves as an arbitrator on labor and commercial panels of the American Arbitration Association. She is an adjunct professor at New York University School of Law and Fordham University School of Law, teaching courses on jointly administered employee benefit trust funds and internal union affairs, and is the chairwoman of the New York State Law Revision Commission. Ms. Gentile received her B.A. degree, magna cum laude, from Barnard College and her J.D. degree, cum laude, from New York University. Ms. Gentile is listed in Who's Who in American Women *and is a member of the National Association of Women Lawyers of the American, New York State and City of New York Bar Associations. She has participated in previous International Foundation educational programs.*

rules and regulations either raising benefit payment rates or liberalizing eligibility rules[2] will have an immediate cost impact on their liability because these changes will increase the unfunded vested benefits of the plan.

Naturally, one way to meet such cost increases is to raise future contribution rates. However, during the term of a collective bargaining agreement, contribution rates are fixed. Thus, any proposed change must occasion an inquiry about whether

---

1. Of course, Title IV of ERISA had imposed significant obligations on employers of terminated plans (ERISA §4062, 29 U.S.C. §1362), but absent termination only those employees who were "substantial," as defined by the act (ERISA §4001(a)(2), 29 U.S.C. §1301(a)(2)) had any responsibility (ERISA §4063, 29 U.S.C. §1363). However, such duties usually were not perceived to be of major and immediate significance.

2. Hereafter, when the term "benefit increases" is used, it is meant to include a liberalization of eligibility rules as well.

the plan itself has sufficient reserves to absorb such a rise in costs. For example, there may be plans that presently are fully funded or are close to being fully funded. A change in the rules may move the fund farther away from that fully funded status. Because of these questions, employers are more reluctant to agree to changes in the rules and regulations of the plan during the term of existing agreements.

On the other hand, the union is likely to perceive its position to be unaffected by MPPAA because trustees are required to act solely in the interests of participants and beneficiaries.[3] Consequently, if the pension fund has monies available that would permit an increase in benefits prior to MPPAA, then such increase should occur even after MPPAA. Of course, such benefit increases would have to be consistent with the prudence requirements of ERISA.[4] In addition, many unions would argue that it is the trustees' duty to determine benefit improvements even though such decisions may result in increases in employer liability to the plan. The trustees, after all, have the responsibility to represent the interests of participants and beneficiaries, not the viewpoints of the party that has appointed them. Such an argument is strongly supported by the United States Supreme Court decision in the *Amax Coal* case.[5]

As for trustees, in theory at least their conduct can be governed only by the legal obligations imposed on them by ERISA. Those standards mandate that trustees act solely in the interests of participants and beneficiaries,[6] that they act prudently,[7] that their actions be consistent with the plan documents,[8] and that they ensure that the plan meets the act's minimum funding requirements.[9]

MPPAA did not alter any of the fiduciary standards imposed by ERISA. Rather, MPPAA imposed additional duties on trustees, because they are requested to implement the mechanism created by MPPAA to collect a withdrawing employer's share of the plan's unfunded vested benefits.[10]

---

3. ERISA §404(a)(1), 29 U.S.C. §1104(a)(1).
4. ERISA §404(a)(1)(B), 29 U.S.C. §1104(a)(1)(B).
5. *NLRB v. Amax Coal Co.,* 2 EBC 1489 (U.S.Sup.Ct. 1981).
6. ERISA §404(a)(1), 29 U.S.C. §1104(a)(1).
7. ERISA §404(a)(1)(B), 29 U.S.C. §1104(a)(1)(B).
8. ERISA §404(a)(1)(D), 29 U.S.C. §1104(a)(1)(D).
9. ERISA §302(a)(1), 29 U.S.C. §1082(a)(1).
10. MPPAA did, however, shorten some of ERISA's funding provisions as they applied to multiemployer plans and made them consistent with those of single employer plans.

The last affected group are the participants of these plans who, in many cases, may be unaware of the developments in law that have occurred since 1980 and the potential impact of these developments on their plans. However, it is reasonable to assume that participants who are younger workers will continue to place little importance on pension benefits. In general, such benefits are considered to be of only future concern. On the other hand, older workers likely would want their benefits to be protected and increased as much as possible. Still, if they were asked, I am sure that they would not want such increases to jeopardize their chances of receiving benefits that they have already accrued.[11]

How to Proceed

Having defined the positions of the various players, there remains the question of whether trustees can increase benefits if such action would mean increasing the unfunded liabilities of the plan. Before any meaningful consideration can be given to a proposed benefit increase, the trustees, as before, must obtain as much information as possible about the impact of such a change on the plan's costs. These facts can be supplied only by the plan's actuary, who is the person most familiar with the structure and cash flow of the plan.

It is the actuary who can best determine if the proposed benefit increase would compromise the plan's funding policy, adversely affect the interests of employer contributors and/or unfavorably impact on the plan's ability to meet its obligations to the participants. Perhaps most significantly, the actuary is the best source of suggestions for alternative methods to accomplish benefit improvements without increasing the employers' obligations.

Next, the plan's legal counsel should be consulted to provide an analysis of the arbitral and judicial decisions that have been rendered on the issue. To date, there have been a number of decisions with conflicting results.

In *In re Labor Trustees and Management Trustees of the Bay Area Painters Pension Trust Fund,*[12] a pension benefit increase was opposed by the management trustees because of the fact that it would have created an additional $625,000 in unfunded vested liabilities. The management trustees argued that the proposal would:

---

11. If the proposals to provide for prospective benefit increases only become more prevalent and gain general acceptance, it can be argued that MPPAA has caused the interests of older workers to be sacrificed and that of younger workers to be promoted.
12. 2 EBC 1724, 353 (BNA) A-12 (June 15, 1981).

1. "Render the pension plan less sound."
2. "Create additional liabilities on employers which were not agreed to, citing the withdrawal liability created by MEPPAA."

The union trustees argued that the increase would be prudent and consistent with the trustees' duty to act in the sole interest of the plan's participants and beneficiaries. Moreover, they claimed that an increase in the unfunded vested liability would not put the trust in any danger of insolvency.

The arbitrator ruled in favor of the union trustees and stated that, "The purpose of the pension trust is to provide as much benefit to the participants as is possible with the contributions and assets available."

The arbitrator rejected the argument that the benefit increase would render the plan less sound:

It is not the function of the trust to achieve the maximum soundness possible, but instead, it is the function of the trust to pay the greatest amounts of benefits possible within the framework of reasonable soundness.

The decision also rejected the management trustees' concern that the benefit increase could increase any potential withdrawal liability:

If withdrawal liability has some impact on the ability of the trust to meet its obligations to participants and beneficiaries it ought to be considered by the Trustees and their advisors... If the withdrawal liability merely limits the employer from going non-union or from selling its business for as much as he feels it is worth, these types of considerations have no place in a funding policy discussion.

The arbitrator stressed the fact that the law required the trustees to act in the interests of the beneficiaries and not in the interests of their respective institutions. Although the trust agreement allowed plan actuaries to consider the circumstances of contributing employers, the arbitrator noted the actuary's statement that, "The funding policy of the plan would not be compromised by the increase."

The decision concludes by rejecting the contention that benefit increases must be accompanied by contributions sufficient to support them: "If employers want control over the creation of unfunded vested liability, then they must exercise this desire at the collective bargaining table."

In *Borden, Inc. v. United Dairy Workers Pension Program*,[13] the plaintiff-employer sought to enjoin the pension fund committee from increasing benefits and consequently the unfunded vested liability of the plan. The terms of the collective bargaining agreement, which were established prior to the enactment of MPPAA, required a certain contribution rate from signatory employers. The employer in this case argued that the recent amendments to ERISA altered its obligations under the collective bargaining agreement and would result in "Substantial unbargained for liability on its part." Thus, the employer sought to enjoin a benefit increase until it bargained with the union over it.

The court ruled in favor of the employer, holding that MPPAA imposes unbargained for liability on the employer, which was not contemplated by the parties during negotiations. Accordingly, the court stated that the fully funded status of the plan should not be altered:

Having achieved this potential (full funding), the court believes it should be impermissible for the committee to "regress" the status of the fund when to do so would impose unbargained for liability on the employer-plaintiff.

The court noted that it was not enjoining the proposed increase because it would result in an increase in the plan's unfunded status. Rather the decision

Simply stands for the proposition that such a change in status should be effected only after the employer has agreed to it, in light of the September, 1980 ERISA amendments.

In *In re Union Trustees of the Northern Texas Carpenters Pension Plan and Management Trustees of the Northern Texas Carpenters Pension Plan*,[14] the management trustees resisted a proposal by the union trustees to increase pension benefits for all years of service, which would include past service credits. Using the *Borden* rationale, the management trustees argued that the enactment of MPPAA during the term of the contract imposed new liabilities on contributing employers. The union trustees, relying on the *Bay Area* decision, claimed that, "Employers must exercise their desire to have control over the creation of unfunded vested liability at the collective bargaining table and not through their trustees." In addition, the plan's actuary stated that the plan could support the increase, notwithstanding the fact that the benefit increase would have resulted in a $5.3 million increase in its unfunded vested liability.

---

13. 2 EBC 1625 (E.D.Mich. 1981).

14. 376 (BNA) 99 (Dec. 1, 1981).

The arbitrator rejected the union trustees' proposal, citing several factors, including:

> The impact of the size of the increase in unfunded past service liability, the effect the increase would have on employer withdrawal liability, the special withdrawal rules under the Multi-Employer Plan Act for the construction industry, the volatility of withdrawal liability figures, the Borden decision, and the phrase in the *Bay Area* case that reads "Review the impact of the proposal and decide whether it hurts the trust more than it helps the beneficiaries."

These decisions reflect a desire to permit employer input on changes that occur after a contract is negotiated, especially when those changes result in major cost increases. Despite these few decisions, the law remains uncertain and no definite answer can be obtained from the usual legal sources.

Lacking clear legal rules, the next best source of guidelines is prior experience. It may seem many years ago, but when ERISA was first passed, there was much uncertainty. However, one thing was clear—compliance with the statute would impose major cost increases on pension plans. Yet, despite the rise in costs, benefit improvements continued. The concerns that exist today concerning escalation costs are no different from those that existed previously, with one exception. In 1976, employers were not aware of the immediate cost impact on them, but in 1982, not only are employers cognizant of the relationship that cost increases to the plan have to their company, but they can place a precise dollar figure on their obligation.

However, in 1982 as in 1976, the relationship of benefit changes to costs existed. Is the only difference then the quantifying of that relationship? Perhaps, then, the only reliable indication of the answer to the question of post-MPPAA benefit improvements lies in a reexamination of the cause of the problem—MPPAA itself.

MPPAA's thrust was remedial. It sought to correct a perceived evil—the continued employer withdrawals from multiemployer pension plans with financial immunity. If you examine the legislative history you discover the following:

> In the case of a financially troubled plan, termination liability creates an additional incentive for employers to withdraw early. In such a plan, contribution increases may be escalating so sharply that termination liability may prove cheaper than continuing the plan. Where active employees determine that benefits may be provided for them at considerably less cost than current contributions and are satisfied that vested benefits for retirees and others are virtually 100 percent covered by the guarantees, there is an incentive for the union to agree to terminate the plan. The result is to transfer the cost of providing benefits to the insurance system. The current termination insurance provisions of ERISA thus threaten the survival of multiemployer plans by exacerbating the problems of financially weak plans and encouraging employer withdrawals from and termination of plans in financial distress.[15]

Such an erosion of multiemployer plans was found by Congress to be dangerous; the process was placing too heavy a burden on the Pension Benefit Guaranty Corporation. Therefore, Congress tried to prevent a further deterioration of these plans by stopping employers from leaving them without paying their share of the plan's costs:

> The purpose is to relieve the funding burden on remaining employers and to eliminate the incentive to pull out of a plan which would result if liability were imposed only on a mass withdrawal of all employers.[16]

Thus, MPPAA was limited in its intended results. It was not designed to affect the manner in which benefits were determined. Certainly, MPPAA was not intended to freeze plan benefits as they existed prior to its passage, because such a result would not be in the best interests of pension plans or their beneficiaries.

Conclusion

Yet, even though MPPAA may not have been intended to make benefit changes more difficult, the statute is having that effect. There are, however, sound legal arguments to be made supporting benefit improvements despite increasing employer obligations, because the trustees' duty is to the participants. Moreover, trustees have the power and authority to change the plan benefits, provided their decisions are prudent and not arbitrary or capricious.[17]

Nevertheless, since drastic cost increases may present labor-management problems even though legally justifiable, perhaps the most appropriate

---

15. H.R. Rep. No. 96-869, 96th Cong. 2d Sess. (1980), reprinted in 1980 *U.S. Code Cong. & Ad. News* 2918, 2921-23.

16. *Id.* at 2935.

17. See, e.g., *Pete v. United Mine Workers of America Welfare and Retirement Fund,* 517 F.2d 1275 (D.C. Cir. 1975).

forum for resolution of these issues, on an immediate basis, is not the trustees' meeting room or the courts but the collective bargaining table. There the parties, with the aid of their advisors, can have an opportunity to more fully explore the various options available for reconciling the differences that the latest Congressional action affecting multiemployer pension plans has caused.

Legal Odds and Ends

BY MICHAEL C. GREENFIELD and
LEE ELBERTS

FICA/Sickpay

Recent amendments to the Social Security Act and the Internal Revenue Code provide that third-party payers of disability income benefits are liable for the employer's share of Social Security taxes (FICA), unless certain specified procedures are followed. These procedures include the giving of notice to the last employer of the fact that such sickness or accident benefits were paid. The Internal Revenue Service has issued a temporary regulation that resolved some of the problems created by the statute.

By way of background, if the trust fund were not to give the notice to the last employer and then paid the employer's share of FICA, the payment probably would be deemed to be a prohibited transaction in violation of ERISA Section 406(a)(1)(d). That section prohibits a fiduciary from engaging in a transaction that results in the payment of fund assets to a party in interest or for the benefit of party in interest. Nevertheless, despite the issuance of this temporary regulation, many multi-employer health and welfare funds have either found it difficult to comply with the notice requirements or desire to pay the employer's portion of the FICA tax.

In response to continued inquiries and, in particular, in response to a request from the National Coordinating Committee for Multiemployer Plans, the U.S. Department of Labor issued an Advisory Opinion indicating that under certain circumstances a multiemployer fund may pay the employer's portion of the FICA tax requirements. Contrary to what many people seem to believe, this opinion is not a blanket approval for trustees to pay the employer's portion of FICA. The trustees must first satisfy the requirements of the Advisory Opinion.

According to the Advisory Opinion, a fund must determine it to be "less costly and burdensome" to pay the employer's portion than to give the notice. The determination of whether such payments are less costly and burdensome is a factual one, which must be decided on a case by case basis, the Department said. Moreover, the determination must be reviewed by the trustees at reasonable intervals to

Mr. Greenfield is a director in the lawfirm of Asher, Goodstein, Pavalon, Gittler, Greenfield & Segall, Ltd. and has practiced law since 1957 as an attorney for numerous Taft-Hartley trust funds. He received his B.A. degree from the University of Illinois and his J.D. degree from Northwestern University. Mr. Greenfield is a past member of the Foundation's Advisory Directors, in addition to having been on the Attorneys, Constitution and By-laws, and 25th Anniversary Committees. Mr. Greenfield is also a past member of the Employer Liability Committee. He has spoken at many educational meetings and has written articles for the Digest. *He is currently a member of the Educational Program Committee and chairman of the American Arbitration Committee.*

Mr. Elberts is an associate in the lawfirm of Asher, Goodstein, Pavalon, Gittler, Greenfield and Segall, Ltd. He serves as counsel to several jointly trusteed health and welfare and pension trust funds. Mr. Elberts is a graduate of Loyola University of Chicago and received his J.D. degree from De Paul University.

prevent acts that may constitute prohibited transactions.

The Department's position will require trustees to make a factual determination of whether it is less costly and burdensome to the plan to pay the employer's portion than it would be to give the required notice to employers. This determination, we would urge, should be documented with the assistance of the fund's administrative manager and/or accountant.

The consequences for trustees who pay the employer's portion but fail to document their decision could be serious. Use of trust fund assets for the benefit of an employer constitutes a prohibited transaction and, therefore, is a breach of the trustees' fiduciary duty. A trustee who breaches his fiduciary duty may be held personally liable to make good to the plan any losses resulting from the breach. Consequently, it is important for the trustees to document their compliance with the "costs and burdens" test, or to decline to pay the employer's share of FICA.

There is also an additional requirement that must be satisfied by trustees who wish to pay the employer's portion of FICA. According to the Department, an employer trustee may not participate in a decision that relates to whether the fund should transfer its obligation for payment of FICA taxes to that trustee's employer or company. To do so, the Department said, would constitute a transaction in which the trustee is representing a party whose interests are adverse to the fund—a prohibited transaction in violation of ERISA Section 406(b)(2). Taking this reasoning to its logical (or illogical) conclusion, a fund would not be able to take advantage of the Advisory Opinion because all employer trustees would be violating Section 406-(b)(2) in approving payment of their employer's share of FICA.

A fund which is unable to document its compliance with the "costs and burdens" test may nevertheless accomplish the same objective if the employers and union agree to modify their collective bargaining agreement. This modification may be accomplished by providing that a small amount of the employer contribution required to be paid to the health and welfare fund will be allocated for payment of the employer's portion of the FICA tax.

This instance appears to be the first time that the Department of Labor has sanctioned what is otherwise a prohibited transaction because it is "cost justified."

MPPAA Arbitrations

In the first reported case under the mandatory arbitration provisions of the Multiemployer Pension Plan Amendments Act of 1980 (MPPAA), an arbitrator rendered an award in favor of the pension fund (*Penn Textile Corporation v. Textile Workers Pension Fund,* 3 EBC 1609 (June 11, 1982) (Malcolm L. Pritzker, Arb.)). Although several issues were raised in this arbitration, two are of particular significance to trustees.

First, the arbitrator found that an employer who seeks arbitration is not required to specify in its demand for arbitration every issue that it wants arbitrated. The arbitrator found that as long as the issue is one involving Sections 4201-4219 of ERISA, the fund must be prepared to defend and explain all calculations used to determine the amount of withdrawal liability, as long as it has been advised by the withdrawing employer that the amount of liability is in dispute.

Second, the withdrawing employer in this arbitration challenged the use of a 6% interest assumption to calculate an employer's withdrawal liability. The calculation of withdrawal liability is, typically, highly dependent on the investment yield or interest assumption used by the actuary. In this case, the withdrawal liability was $188,000 using a 6% assumption. If an 11% assumption had been used, the assessment would have been $50,000 less. Because it is so highly leveraged, the assumption used is a "target" for employers. An assessment is contested as being based on actuarial assumptions that are unreasonable in the aggregate.

Under ERISA, an assessment is presumed correct unless the employer shows by a preponderance of evidence that the actuarial assumptions used were, in the aggregate, unreasonable. The employer in this case argued that the PBGC has established an interest rate for termination of single employer plans that is now substantially in excess of 6%, that insurance carriers were using interest rate assumptions for the calculations of annuities considerably in excess of 6%, that the fund had actually earned 10% for the four years prior to withdrawal (and at the time of the arbitration was earning 8%) and that a large national actuarial firm was recommending to its client multiemployer funds that the funds use the PBGC single employer fund termination interest rate to calculate employer withdrawal liability.

The arbitrator stated that where actuaries differ, as they did in this case, the arbitrator must turn to information from other actuaries to resolve the conflict. Relying on statements by various actuaries, including actuaries from the PBGC, the arbitrator concluded that the majority of actuaries do not agree with the employer's view that the PBGC single employer plan termination interest rate should be used. The arbitrator said that the PBGC itself does not indicate that such an approach must be used.

The arbitrator went on to say that although the trustees could sell all of the stocks and bonds in the portfolio and invest all of the fund's money with insurance companies for a guaranteed rate of return in excess of 6%, this procedure would appear to run afoul of the diversification requirements of ERISA. He also noted that the fund actuary concluded that the fund's current rate of return of 8% did not justify an increase in the interest assumption used for the ongoing actuarial valuation. For these reasons, the arbitrator found that the employer did not show by a preponderance of the evidence that the fund's use of the 6% interest rate was unreasonable, in aggregate, in the calculation of withdrawal liability.

This decision is extremely important for multiemployer pension plans because, if it is followed, other employers may be more reluctant to go through the expense of arbitration. If they do, they stand a lesser chance of overturning the plan's assessment of withdrawal liability, at least on the issue of the interest rate assumption.

Suspension of Benefits

Section 203 of ERISA provides that an employee's right to benefits must be nonforfeitable at normal retirement age. The regulations require that a notice be given to a pensioner whose pension is suspended because he returns to work in what we generically refer to as "prohibited employment." Prohibited employment is defined as work in the same industry, same trade or craft and in the same geographical area covered by the plan when the pension began. The U.S. Department of Labor has now said that notice must also be given to employees who continue to work beyond normal retirement age and who have not even applied for a pension. The Department said that the purpose of the notice in such cases is not to inform the employee that his benefits will not commence immediately, but to inform him that he will incur a forfeiture of pension benefits, in that he will be receiving, after benefits commence, a benefit of lesser value than if he did not continue in employment.

Trustees have typically evidenced surprise when told that they must send such a notice to employees who continue to work after normal retirement age. They are understandably concerned that such a notice will make employees think that they are either being persuaded to retire or that their pension is in jeopardy. Imagine the reaction of a participant who continues to work after age 65, secure in the knowledge that he can quit at any time and get his pension. Then one day he opens his mail, only to be told that his pension benefits are being forfeited. Although one may attempt to draft the notice as innocuously as possible, the fact remains that it is difficult to tell someone that he is not entitled to a pension at a time when he never thought he was entitled to one. We suggest that the notice will only confuse, terrify or anger most employees, not inform them.

The consequences could be significant, however, if the notice requirement is not met. As an example, if an employee who is 65 and entitled to a pension of $500 per month for life were to continue to work until age 67, but is never given notice that his pension has been suspended, he will be deemed to have "forfeited" $12,000. His benefit will have to be actuarially recalculated when he retires to take into account the forfeiture. The $500 a month pension must be increased so that over the employee's life expectancy he will recoup the $12,000. For this reason, most advisors are encouraging plan administrators to comply strictly with the Department of Labor's interpretation of the suspension of benefits regulations.

Conclusion

The diverse topics discussed here indicate that the federal government will continue to play a prominent role in the operation and administration of employee benefit plans. The Advisory Opinion issued by the Department of Labor concerning the payment of FICA taxes on sickpay, however, may portend a more understanding attitude, by the Department of Labor at least, toward the problems of plan administrators.

Collecting Withdrawal Liability

BY TIMOTHY P. O'REILLY

MY TASK IS to analyze how a multiemployer pension fund can more effectively collect withdrawal liabilities. I have divided the analysis into five topics. The first topic for discussion concerns identifying, obtaining and keeping records needed to calculate an employer's withdrawal liability. The second topic includes an analysis of methods by which a fund can identify a withdrawal. The third topic focuses on the calculation of the lump sum withdrawal liability and the payment schedule. The fourth area of discussion considers the fund's communication with the employer. Last, but certainly not least, I will review the status of legal actions for the collection and enforcement of withdrawal liability. Within each of these five topics, I will concentrate on three areas: first, what a fund should do in advance of a withdrawal; second, special problems within the five topics that a fund and its various officers and consultants must be prepared to confront; and finally, the role of fund consultants with respect to the five topic areas.

As partner in the Philadelphia office of the law firm Morgan, Lewis & Bockius, Mr. O'Reilly serves as employer co-counsel to numerous multiemployer health and welfare and pension plans. Active in the employee benefits field for over 11 years, he is associate editor and program chairman for the ABA Labor Section Committee on the Development of the Law Under the National Labor Relations Act. Mr. O'Reilly earned his B.S. degree in business administration, cum laude, from Ohio State University, Columbus, and his J.D. degree from New York University School of Law, New York. He has spoken before organizations including the American Bar Association, American Management Association, Midwest Labor Law Conference, Association of Personnel Administrators, Pennsylvania Bar Institute, American Trucking Association and Pennsylvania Motor Carriers Association.

Building the Necessary Records for Calculating Liabilities

Developing Reliable Employer Histories

As a first step, the fund must anticipate the possibility that withdrawals will occur. Obviously, in a planning stage it is in the fund's best interest to establish a system of recordkeeping that will allow it to react quickly and with accurate information should a withdrawal take place. With respect to each employer, a fund must have reliable records that show the employer's total contribution, the contribution rate and the number of contribution rate units—for example, hours, days or months—for which that employer contributed to the fund. If the employer's contribution rate changes during a particular plan year, the date it changes must also be recorded.

One of the problems that has arisen in implementing this law is that many funds do not keep accurate records with respect to the base units for which an employer contributed to the fund. Consequently, many funds have been faced with the problem of trying to reconstruct such records after the fact. This situation has been particularly difficult in two situations: where the contribution rate varies by employer or where the rate changes during a plan year.

Certain options contained in the statute ease the burden of trying to re-create records. One example eases the burden of calculating liabilities for withdrawals occurring in the 1980 plan year. Many of the funds in which we participate have taken advantage of options contained in ERISA Sections 4211 and 4219, which permit using five years of contribution history in the allocation and payment schedule formulas. The number of years to be used in these formulas increases by one year for each plan year after 1980. Thus, these funds will eventually build a ten year history for each employer. Funds that have not adopted these options have until April 29, 1983 to do so without prior approval from the

Pension Benefit Guaranty Corporation (PBGC). Thereafter, any plan amendments to take advantage of these options will require approval by the PBGC.

Another practical problem in administering this law arises from application of ERISA Section 4217. This section provides that when applying the complete and partial withdrawal liability rules, and in allocating unfunded vested benefits among employers, contribution histories attributable to facilities closed prior to the effective date of ERISA are not to be taken into account. As a result, other contributors will shoulder a larger share of unfunded vested benefits if they withdraw from the plan. For example, if an employer operated five facilities between 1975 and 1978 and thereafter closed two of the facilities, ERISA Section 4217 requires the fund to exclude the contribution histories attributable to the two closed facilities. By excluding these contribution histories, the unfunded vested benefits allocated to other employers are affected.

Therefore, in several of these funds to which Morgan, Lewis & Bockius is co-counsel, in an effort to clean up all of the Section 4217 problems at one time and to avoid disputes arising from inaccurate information, it has been suggested that each contributing employer be furnished copies of its total contribution history, contribution rate history and contribution base unit history. In receiving this information, the employers are told that any disputes with respect to these records, including disputes arising from the application of ERISA Section 4217, must be made known to the fund within 30 days of the receipt of the histories and that objections not so raised are deemed waived. Although it is not certain that this approach will succeed in curing all employer objections, mailing employers copies of their histories should minimize future problems.

Finally, funds must develop reliable records that identify members of the same controlled group of trades or businesses, since such information is needed both in determining whether a complete or a partial withdrawal has occurred and in applying the *de minimis* rule. As most of you are aware, the Multiemployer Pension Plan Amendments Act (MPPAA) defines a contributing employer as any member of a controlled group of trades or businesses. Thus, a parent and subsidiary corporation or two subsidiary corporations of the same parent are considered to be the same employer. Therefore, it is extremely important that pension funds be able to identify members of the same controlled group of trades or businesses. In addition to using information available from library sources, a fund may be able to obtain such information directly from the employer by using a questionnaire, which will be discussed later.

Actuarial Data

I want to note in passing that certain actuarial data must be developed for each fund. Rather than go into this topic in detail, however, I shall defer to the actuaries for a definition of the exact records that must be kept.

Creating Contractual Obligations for the Employer

In building the necessary fund records, we have found it advantageous to amend pension plan documents to create legal rights under the pension plan itself—rights that are independent of those created by law. Ultimately, this amendment process could insulate plans against unfavorable changes in the law. Thus, if MPPAA is declared unconstitutional, pension funds that amend the plan to incorporate the concept of withdrawal liability will still be entitled to collect withdrawal liability. Other advantageous amendments include incorporation of allocation formulas, payment schedule formulas, obligations on the employer to notify the fund in the event of a withdrawal and obligations to pay attorneys fees, interest and liquidated damages. These examples are only a few of the obligations that can be created by amending the plan document.

As part and parcel to this amendment process, I heartily recommend having a separate participation agreement between the fund and each contributing employer. This participation agreement should bind the contributing employer to the decisions of the trustees and should authorize trustees to take any actions that are in the best interests of pension fund participants. In addition, such participation agreements should include obligations on the employer to notify the fund in the event of a withdrawal and to pay interest, liquidated damages and attorneys fees for the collection of either withdrawal liability payments or delinquent contributions.

As previously noted, I recommend imposing obligations on employers to notify the fund in the event of a withdrawal. The purpose of this recommendation is to permit the fund to argue that the statute of limitations is tolled if an employer fails to notify the fund of a withdrawal. Although there is no guarantee that courts will automatically toll statute of limitations where an employer fails to make such a modification, it cannot hurt to include such a requirement.

Role of Fund Consultants

In building the necessary records for a fund, each of the fund's consultants and trustees plays a special role. First, it is the fund administrator who will have primary responsibility for building and maintaining current and accurate records. This function involves the day-to-day supervision of the fund's operations and collection of needed information. It is the fund's actuary, however, who has the obligation of identifying the records that will be necessary for detecting withdrawals, allocating unfunded vested benefits and determining the payment schedule.

The fund accountant must verify the accuracy of these records at least annually. In addition, through the use of employer audits and spot checks, the fund accountant can aid in the collection of delinquencies and ensure the accuracy of fund records.

Fund counsel has the responsibility for suggesting amendments to the plan documents that will create rights under the plan. In addition, fund counsel is best able to develop the participation agreements to create rights under the plan and to impose obligations on employers to notify the fund in the event of a withdrawal.

Finally, the fund's trustees have the ultimate responsibility for assessment and collection of withdrawal liability payments. In performing this duty, the fund trustees must always remember that they are fiduciaries who must act in the best interest of the fund's beneficiaries.

Identification of Withdrawals

Sources of Information

The second step of the collection process is identifying the occurrence of withdrawals—both complete withdrawals and partial withdrawals. The statutory definition of complete withdrawals lists two operative facts that constitute such withdrawals: cessation of the obligation to contribute or cessation of all covered operations. In most instances, the occurrence of a complete withdrawal should not be difficult to identify because the fund will simply no longer receive contributions from a particular contributing employer. The identification of partial withdrawals, however, is much more elusive and brings home the importance of accurate recordkeeping, for here the definition potentially requires examination of contribution records dating back eight years.

For example, a partial withdrawal may be triggered by such events as subcontracting, transfers of work, decertifications or a decline of 70% in the number of contribution base units contributed for. The last definition requires comparing contribution data over a three consecutive year period with the same data relating to the immediately preceding five year period. Furthermore, by focusing on the controlled group of trades or businesses, what appears to be a complete withdrawal of a subsidiary may turn out to be only a partial withdrawal of the group. Therefore, it is essential for funds to develop all sources of information to which they are entitled by statute.

The first and most logical source of information is the monthly contribution report. Careful analysis of these reports, including contribution histories over periods of time, will permit the fund to detect both complete and partial withdrawals. In large funds, such reports can be entered into a computer database and the analysis can be done in more depth and more quickly.

The monthly contribution report provides what we call quantitative evidence. In addition, however, qualitative evidence is necessary before the fund can assess liability. The two best sources of such information appear to be the union representative and the use of annual questionnaires. Based on our experience, union representatives have a tremendous amount of knowledge about sales of corporations, sales of assets, strikes, layoffs, subcontracting, union decertifications and transfers of work. Therefore, it is incumbent on the funds to encourage reports by union representatives when they believe that an employer's obligation to contribute has ceased either completely or partially.

Another possible source of information is the annual questionnaire mentioned previously.

The Central States Teamsters Pension Fund developed a ten page questionnaire that it uses when an employer either stops making contributions to the Central States Fund or reduces its level of contributions. The questionnaire requires identification of members of the controlled group of trades or businesses and asks whether a sale of assets has occurred. If so, it asks whether the sale has been structured in accordance with ERISA Section 4204.

Much useful information is gathered by this questionnaire, and for that reason I have used a similar questionnaire on an annual basis for many funds. One difficulty in using it on an annual basis, however, is that once obtained, the information must be analyzed and withdrawal liability assessed if appropriate—or the statute of limitations for collection may begin to run. Nonetheless, we strongly recommend the use of a questionnaire *whenever* a withdrawal is suspected, and more frequently if the fund can afford to review the information generated.

Finally, I urge that the funds impose reporting obligations on participating employers. As already mentioned, this obligation may be imposed either through the use of participation agreements or by amending the pension plan.

Problems of Identification

I only want to mention in passing that there are different problems of identification, depending on whether the general rules apply, the construction and entertainment industry rules apply or the trucking industry rules apply. However, I do want to focus on certain common problems.

The first such problem involves reviewing sales of assets for compliance with the sale of asset rules provided by ERISA Section 4204. This task is extremely important and requires an analysis of the transaction by the fund's legal counsel. For example, the contract for sale must be analyzed carefully to determine whether the buyer has assumed the obligation to contribute to the fund for substantially the same number of base units for which the seller has contributed to the fund. In addition, the fund must be assured that certain bonds have been posted. The document must also be analyzed to determine whether the seller has remained secondarily liable. Finally, the legal relationship between the buyer and the seller must be analyzed to be sure that they are truly "unrelated" parties.

Sale of stock transactions must also be analyzed. Where a division of a corporation recently has been incorporated and then sold to another company, funds might consider whether the transaction has been structured with the principal purpose of evading or avoiding the payment of withdrawal liabilities.

ERISA Section 4212(c) provides that where a principal purpose of any transaction is to evade or avoid withdrawal liability, the transaction may be ignored and withdrawal liability may nonetheless be imposed. Therefore, it is incumbent on the fund and its attorneys to carefully review all transactions where the fund's ability to collect withdrawal liability is substantially diminished.

Finally, I will reiterate a point mentioned earlier: Before a fund can determine whether a withdrawal has occurred, the fund must be able to determine whether the employer is a member of a controlled group of trades or businesses and whether other members of that group continue to contribute to the fund.

The Role of Fund Consultants

Once again it is the fund administrator who has the day-to-day responsibility for detecting and identifying potential withdrawals. When a fund administrator obtains information that makes him suspicious, he should send a questionnaire to the employer and inquire if a withdrawal has occurred.

The fund's actuary and the fund's auditor are responsible for compiling records and establishing systems that will identify withdrawals. This task is particularly important with respect to the detection of partial withdrawals resulting from a 70% decline in the level of contribution base units.

The fund's counsel plays an extremely important role in the identification of withdrawals since, in most instances, this determination requires a legal opinion. Until the law settles out, fund attorneys and fund fiduciaries are well-advised to pursue all cases in which there is a reasonable argument that either a complete or partial withdrawal has occurred.

Six Year Statute of Limitations Under ERISA Section 4301(f)

As a final note to the topic of identifying withdrawals, I bring to your attention the fact that a six year statute of limitations applies to the detection of withdrawal liabilities. Section 4219, however, imposes on funds an obligation to notify employers of a withdrawal and of potential withdrawal liability as soon as practicable. In several of the funds to which our firm is counsel, withdrawing employers have argued that the funds are estopped from collecting withdrawal liabilities where they failed to notify such withdrawing employer until months after the withdrawal. Furthermore, it is in the funds' own best interest to identify withdrawals quickly and to collect withdrawal liability as soon as possible.

Calculating Withdrawal Liability

Having anticipated and identified withdrawals, the fund must move to collect the employer's share of the fund's unfunded vested benefits, i.e., withdrawal liability. The obvious first step in the collection process is the calculation of just how much the employer owes. ERISA provides several methods by which a fund may allocate unfunded vested benefits and it is up to the fund in the first instance to choose and apply one of those methods. The choice of methods, however, is made by the fund in its organization stage and after the identification has occurred, it is just a matter of applying the method to the data applicable to the employer. Based on my experience, the choice of methods is often dictated by the availability or, more accurately, unavailability of fund records. Because most funds did not keep individual employee histories by employer, it has been impossible to apply the attribution method. Funds that use the 20 pool/presumptive method do so because it is the method that the statute presumes to be applicable in the absence of an amendment.

One of the most hotly litigated issues at present is the choice of the interest assumptions used by the plan in valuing plan assets. The reason for the controversy is straightforward—the higher the interest rate assumed, the smaller the fund's unfunded vested benefits. Based on my observations, few funds have an interest rate assumption below 5%, and few funds have an interest rate assumption above 8%. However, an actuary should be consulted for a discussion of current factors.

As a result of the need to allocate the unfunded vested benefits of the plan, most funds have decided to have an annual actuarial study performed. I heartily recommend the use of annual actuarial studies for two reasons. First, they lead to better fund records and a better understanding of the forces affecting a pension plan. For example, in a declining industry, annual actuarial studies avoid the need to apply for waivers of the minimum funding standards. I also recommend the use of annual actuarial studies because I believe that the actuarial assumptions will be easier to defend in arbitrations arising under the statute. Although there have been few arbitrations to date, I expect that within the next year there will be numerous arbitrations; then everyone will have a better idea of how important annual actuarial studies are.

Finally, note that there are certain limitations on the amount of withdrawal liability in certain circumstances. These limitations are found in ERISA Section 4225 and apply in the event that an employer is insolvent or in the event of a bona fide sale of all or substantially all of the employer's assets.

Calculating a Payment Schedule

A fund has the obligation to calculate a payment schedule for each withdrawing employer. Under the general rule, the payment schedule is derived by multiplying the highest rate at which an employer contributed to a fund over ten years by the average number of base units in the three highest consecutive plan years out of the last ten plan years. However, many funds did not collect contribution base unit information and consequently do not have the information needed to make such calculations. Under an option available until 1985, some funds have opted to calculate payment schedules based on the average annual contributions made by a given employer in the highest three consecutive years in the last ten. Furthermore, adoption of this alternative method of calculation has the effect of removing the 20 year payment cap. In one fund to which our firm is co-counsel, elimination of the 20 year payment cap resulted in extending one employer's obligation to make withdrawal liability payments for a total of $49\frac{1}{2}$ years.

Role of Fund Consultants

Once again, it is the fund's administrator who has the day-to-day responsibility for overseeing the calculation of the lump sum liability and the payment schedule.

In many instances, the fund's actuary will be able to assist by setting up computer programs or by advising the fund administrator about how these two items are calculated. The fund's actuary, however, will have primary responsibility for calculating both the lump sum liability and the payment schedule. The actuary is the most likely person to be asked to testify in any arbitration that may ensue. Therefore, the fund's actuary must play an active role in calculating both the lump sum liability and the payment schedule.

Finally, the trustees have the ultimate responsibility for overseeing the entire calculation process and should review assessment letters before they are sent.

Communicating With the Employer

Investigating Transactions—The Questionnaire

As previously mentioned, the Central States Teamsters Pension Fund developed a questionnaire that is useful in the detection of withdrawals, the evaluation of transactions and the identification of possible sources of assets—including the identification of members of the controlled group of trades or businesses. I have already suggested that such a questionnaire may be tailored to fit the needs of a given fund and can be an extremely useful tool for communication with the employer.

Communicating Assessments and Pension Plan Amendments

The statute requires the funds to communicate to employers the adoption of plan amendments that affect withdrawal liabilities.

After determining that a withdrawal occurred and calculating the amount due and the payment schedule, the fund must make a demand for payment of the withdrawal liability that has been assessed. Such demand letters, as well as other routine letters, can be reduced to standard forms and placed on word processing equipment if available. These letters should state the lump sum liabilities that are due and the payment schedules, and should inform the employer that he has a right to request a review. In addition, I also recommend that funds develop standard form letters regarding withdrawal liability payment delinquencies and defaults. With respect to the delinquency notice, a letter should be sent whenever an employer has failed to make the payment within 60 days of its due date. This notice of delinquency triggers a second 60 day period. On expiration of this second period, an employer can be deemed to be in default. On default, the fund may require immediate payment of the entire amount plus accrued interest.

Developing a Procedure for Handling Employer Requests

The statute also affords employers the right to request certain information from the fund. This right includes a right to request general information and information that is unique to the employer. A fund may not charge an employer for the provision of general information. However, with respect to unique information, the fund may charge the requesting employer.

Another right provided employers by the act is the right to request a review of a fund's assessment of withdrawal liability. I strongly suggest that the funds take full advantage of notifying employers of their right to request this review, because such notification will be useful in limiting the scope of matters subject to arbitration under ERISA Section 4221.

Role of Fund Consultants

As previously noted, the fund administrator has the day-to-day responsibility for communicating with employers. These communications include assessment of withdrawal liabilities and sending notices of delinquencies and defaults. In addition, the fund administrator must handle employer requests for general and unique information and requests for review. In responding to such requests, the fund's actuary and the fund's counsel should play an active role, and I recommend that the fund actuary and fund counsel work closely together in developing the standard form letters just mentioned. In addition, the fund administrator should send to fund counsel copies of all letters, so that counsel has a complete file in the event that an employer seeks an order to temporarily restrain the fund's collection efforts.

Finally, the fund's trustees have ultimate responsibility for overseeing the entire matter. Therefore, they should approve all standard letters used by the fund and should be kept aware of all action on behalf of the fund for collecting withdrawal liability payments.

Collection and Enforcement

The Duty to Pay Withdrawal Liability Commencing No Later Than 60 Days From the Date of Demand

After it has been determined that a withdrawal occurred, the total amount due and the payment schedule have been calculated and a demand has been made for payment of the withdrawal liability assessed, the employer must begin making payments as outlined in the notice within 60 days. This obligation is not in any way diminished by the employer's request for information pursuant to ERISA Section 4219 or by initiation of arbitration pursuant to ERISA Section 4211.

A recent decision by the United States District Court for the Eastern District of Pennsylvania highlights the latter point. In *Commission Salesmen, Drivers and Helpers Union Local 187 Pension Fund v. Hertz Corporation,* F. Supp. (E.D.Pa. 1982), after withdrawing from the fund, Hertz was assessed substantial withdrawal liability payable in monthly installments. Hertz disputed its liability and refused to make monthly withdrawal liability payments. On behalf of the fund, our firm filed suit to compel payment of withdrawal liability installments. Hertz contended that no such suit could be maintained prior to completion of the arbitration procedure, although Hertz had not requested arbitration at the time the suit was commenced.

At oral argument, Hertz first indicated that it would request arbitration. Accordingly, the district court held that despite the pendency of the arbitration case, Hertz was required to begin making installment payments on its withdrawal liability no later than 60 days after the fund's demand. The court refused, however, to grant the fund's request for delinquency penalties including liquidated damages and attorneys fees, although the fund was awarded interest.

The decision in *Commission Salesmen, Drivers and Helpers Local 187 Pension Fund v. Hertz Corporation* makes it clear that the employer must make payments in accordance with the fund's demand until the arbitrator issues a final decision with respect to the issues submitted. This decision also makes clear that once arbitration is requested, a default cannot occur until after the arbitrator rules.

The Duty to Pay Withdrawal Liability After Arbitration

Once an arbitration decision has been issued, an employer's failure to make a payment within 60 days of receipt of a notice that such payment is delinquent constitutes default. On default, all monthly installments become immediately due and owing and the fund may sue for collection of such.

Furthermore, once an arbitration decision has been issued, there is no question that an employer making delinquent payments is liable for interest and liquidated damages under ERISA Section 4301. Furthermore, although the fund may be entitled to recover attorneys fees, such recovery is at the discretion of the court under Section 4301. However, if the fund contends the action to collect as being one for delinquent contributions, as permitted by Section 4221(d), it appears that the award of attorneys fees may be mandated by the interplay of Sections 515 and 502(g).

Role of Fund Consultants

Once withdrawal liability has been assessed against an employer, the matter becomes primarily one that should be handled by counsel. Nonetheless, the fund actuary, the fund administrator and the fund trustees may be called on to participate as witnesses in the arbitration as provided by ERISA Section 4221 and in any litigation that may ensue. In addition, fund counsel should be prepared to defend the fund against attempts to temporarily restrain the collection of withdrawal liability payments. Because such requests occur quickly, as noted before, fund counsel should be kept apprised of all efforts to collect withdrawal liability payments and must be prepared to respond quickly.

Constitutionality Issues

Finally, I will briefly discuss the status of current litigation challenging the constitutionality of MPPAA.

As you are undoubtedly aware, numerous employers faced with withdrawal liability assessments mandated by MPPAA have instituted actions seeking to restrain or enjoin collection of amounts assessed, claiming that the act is unconstitutional. Since decisions are being handed down every day and since many are not yet published, I will not comment on numbers beyond noting that it appears that the courts are about equally divided on the question of availability of such relief.

With respect to the substantive issue, i.e., whether the act is or is not constitutional, I am aware of only eight cases in which opinions have been handed down. Six of those opinions hold that the act is constitutional. The other two opinions held that it was unconstitutional to apply the act to a withdrawal that occurred prior to the act's passage but after its effective date. Again, I must note that this summary does not include decisions in which judges have ruled from the bench without opinion. It is obvious, however, that the question is far from being resolved with only district court opinions being handed down to date. By now, well over 100 suits have been filed and the final resolution awaits further litigation and/or legislation.

Acknowledgments

The author is grateful for the assistance of Steven H. Spencer and James F. Anderson, both associates at Morgan, Lewis & Bockius, Philadelphia, Pennsylvania.

Marital Property Interests in Retirement Benefits: Treatment on Divorce

BY VIRGINIA L. GIBSON and
CHARLES A. STORKE

General Characterization of Pension Rights

In the last decade, a judicial trend has developed toward recognition of certain retirement benefits in dividing property or making alimony awards in state divorce or dissolution actions. Although numerous states now assume that pension and retirement pay constitute property by holding they are or are not subject to division or award on divorce or dissolution, only half of the state courts have expressly addressed this threshold question.[1]

In holding that retirement benefits constitute property, substantially all courts have regarded the benefits as compensation for past services and not as a mere gratuity to the employee.[2] As stated by

Ms. Gibson is an associate with the San Francisco law-firm of Pillsbury, Madison & Sutro, specializing in employee benefits. Ms. Gibson, who graduated from the University of California at Berkeley and received her law degree from the University of California Hastings College of Law, is a former employee benefit and corporate trust banker.

Mr. Storke, a partner with Pillsbury, Madison & Sutro, specializes in all aspects of employee benefits, deferred compensation and taxation. He received his A.B. degree in history from the University of California at Santa Barbara and his J.D. degree from the University of California Hastings College of Law. Mr. Storke also has served as an instructor for the CEBS course of study and has participated in previous Foundation educational meetings.

---

1. For cases expressly stating that retirement benefits are marital property, see *Ex Parte Pedigo* (Ala. 1982) 413 So.2d 1157; *Monsma v. Monsma* (Alaska 1980) 618 P.2d 559; *Johnson v. Johnson* (1981) 131 Ariz. 38, 638 P.2d 705; *In re Marriage of Brown* (1976) 15 Cal.3d 838, 544 P.2d 561; *Robert v. Barbara* (Del. 1981) 434 A.2d 383; *Shill v. Shill* (1979) 100 Idaho 433, 599 P.2d 1004; *In re Marriage of Bodford* (1981) 94 Ill.App.3d 91, 418 N.E.2d 487; *Gronquist v. Gronquist* (1982) 7 Kan.App. 2d 583, 644 P.2d 583; *Light v. Light* (Ky.App. 1980) 559 S.W.2d 476; *T. L. James & Co., Inc. v. Montgomery* (La. 1976) 332 So.2d 834; *Ohm v. Ohm* (Md.App. 1981) 431 A.2d 1371; *Ripley v. Ripley* (1982) 112 Mich.App. 219, 315 N.W.2d 576; *In re Marriage of Laster* (Mont. 1982) 643 P.2d 597; *Copeland v. Copeland* (1978) 91 N.M. 409, 575 P.2d 99; *Kikkert v. Kikkert* (1981) 177 N.J.Super. 471, 427 A.2d 76; *Jolis v. Jolis* (N.Y. 1981) 446 N.Y.S.2d 138; *Ex Parte Burson* (Tex. 1981) 615 S.W.2d 192; *Englert v. Englert* (Utah 1978) 576 P.2d 1274; *Farver v. Department of Retirement Systems* (Wash. 1982) 644 P.2d 1149.

For cases expressly stating that retirement benefits are *not* marital property, see *Paulsen v. Paulsen* (Ark. 1980) 601 S.W.2d 873; *Ellis v. Ellis* (Colo. 1976) 552 P.2d 506; *Wilson v. Wilson* (Ind.App. 1980) 409 N.E.2d 1169; *Delay v. Delay* (Mo.App. 1981) 612 S.W.2d 391; *Baker v. Baker* (N.H. 1980) 421 A.2d 998; *Baker v. Baker* (Okla. 1975) 546 P.2d 1325; *Carter v. Carter* (S.C. 1982) 286 S.E.2d 139.

2. See, e.g., *Johnson v. Johnson* (1981) 131 Ariz. 38, 638 P.2d 705; *In re Marriage of Fithian* (1974) 10 Cal.3d

the Supreme Court of Texas in *Cearley v. Cearley* (Tex. 1976) 544 S.W.2d 661, ". . . (d)espite an earlier view that retirement and pension plans were gifts bestowed by benevolent employers on retiring employees, they are now regarded as a mode of employee compensation earned during a given period of employment."

Even those states holding that certain benefits are not divisible often require that they be taken into account by the court when making a division of marital property or in awarding alimony.[3] The law is far from settled, however, because the courts are divided over "what" retirement benefits should be recognized and subject to division or award.

Before reviewing the varied positions of the state courts, it is necessary to note that retirement and pension benefits generally fall within one of three classifications: (1) those that have matured (all conditions for payment have been satisfied) and are currently being paid to the retiree, (2) those that are vested (nonforfeitable) but payable on some future event such as retirement and (3) those that are not partially or wholly vested.[4]

Community Property States

Arizona, California, Idaho, Louisiana, Nevada, New Mexico, Texas and Washington are community property states, under the laws of which a court's determination that all or a portion of a spouse's retirement benefits constitute community property is tantamount to holding them divisible on dissolution of the marriage.

In California, for example, the personal property of individuals during marriage is either separate or community. Separate property includes all personal property that was owned before marriage or is acquired by gift or inheritance after marriage, along with the rents, issues and profits thereof.[5] Community property includes all personal property that is not separate property and that is acquired during the marriage while domiciled in California.[6] The respective interests of the husband and wife in community property during the marriage are present, existing and equal interests.[7]

In general, to the extent a pension benefit (1) represents a property right, (2) is attributable to the personal services of a California resident rendered during the marriage and while not living separate and apart from the nonemployee spouse and (3) has not been subject to a valid agreement or gift otherwise affecting its character,[8] it will be characterized as community property in California. The

---

592, 517 P.2d 449, *cert. denied* (1974) 419 U.S. 825, 95 S.Ct. 41; *Husband B. v. Wife B.* (Del.Super. 1978) 396 A.2d 169; *Shill v. Shill* (1979) 100 Idaho 433, 599 P.2d 1004; *In re Marriage of Papeck* (1981) 95 Ill.App.3d 624, 420 N.E.2d 528; *Light v. Light* (Ky.App. 1980) 599 S.W.2d 476; *T. L. James & Co., Inc. v. Montgomery* (La. 1976) 332 So.2d 834; *Ohm v. Ohm* (Md.App. 1981) 431 A.2d 1371; *Weir v. Weir* (1980) 173 N.J.Super. 130, 413 A.2d 638; *LeClert v. LeClert* (1969) 80 N.M. 235, 453 P.2d 755; *Rogers and Rogers* (1980) 45 Or.App. 885, 609 P.2d 877; *Wilder v. Wilder* (1975) 85 Wash.2d 364, 534 P.2d 1355.

3. See, e.g., *In re Marriage of Ellis* (Colo.App. 1975) 538 P.2d 1347; *Fugassi v. Fugassi* (Fla.App. 1976) 332 So.2d 695; *In re Marriage of Delgado* (Ind.App. 1982) 429 N.E.2d 1124; *In re Marriage of Schissel* (Iowa 1980) 292 N.W.2d 421; *Baker v. Baker* (N.H. 1980) 421 A.2d 998; *Elmwood v. Elmwood* (1978) 295 N.C. 168, 244 S.E.2d 668; *Ginn v. Ginn* (Ohio App. 1960) 175 N.E.2d 848; *Baker v. Baker* (Okla. 1975) 546 P.2d 1325.

4. For a discussion of these classifications, see *Johnson v. Johnson* (1981) 131 Ariz. 38, 638 P.2d 705; *In re Marriage of Brown* (1976) 15 Cal.3d 838, 544 P.2d 561; *Copeland v. Copeland* (1978) 91 N.M. 409, 575 P.2d 99.

5. California Civ. Code §§5107, 5108. Separate property also includes the earnings and accumulations of a spouse while living separate and apart from the other spouse (California Civ. Code §5118).

6. California Civ. Code §5110. On dissolution of marriage or at death, certain items of personal property that are separate property are characterized as so-called quasi-community property. In general, quasi-community property is all personal property, wherever located, that would have been community property if it had been acquired while the husband and wife had been domiciled in California (Civ. Code §4803, Prob. Code §201.5). On dissolution or at death, such quasi-community property is treated in the same manner as community property, with one major exception: The spouse not responsible for the acquisition of the quasi-community property has no power of testamentary disposition over such property (Prob. Code §201.5). Quasi-community property will not be discussed further here. However, on dissolution of marriage and at death, these special rules must be applied in determining the respective separate and community property interests in pensions under California law.

Under California law, a court cannot award any portion of one spouse's separate property nor more than one-half the value of the community property to the other spouse except in very unusual circumstances (see *Robinson v. Robinson* (1944) 65 Cal.App.2d 118, 150 P.2d 7; *Phillipson v. Board of Administration* (1970) 3 Cal.3d 32, 473 P.2d 765).

In other community property states, property acquired after the parties separate and up to the date of divorce may also be community property (e.g., Nevada Revised Statutes 123.220), and the court may award a portion of one spouse's separate property and more than one-half of the value of the community property to the other spouse using "equitable" principles (e.g., Revised Codes of Washington §28.08.10).

7. California Civ. Code §5105.

8. A husband or wife may alter the character of the property owned by either or both of them by agreement between them or by gift to the other, subject to general confidential relationship principles (California Civ. Code §5103).

theory behind this general characterization is that not only current earnings but also deferred income represent compensation for personal services rendered by the employee spouse during marriage.

Employee Contributions and Benefits in Pay Status

In all community property states, an employee's own nonforfeitable contributions and any matured retirement benefits in pay status are community property, to the extent earned during the marriage, subject to division on dissolution of the marriage.[9]

In *Farver v. Department of Retirement Systems* (Wash. 1982) 644 P.2d 1149, the Supreme Court of Washington explained the basis for this position:

> Pension and other retirement plans are unique property rights. They are in the nature of deferred compensation. As such they are not mere expectancies but are vested rights possessed by employees. [Citations omitted.]
>
> It is a fundamental principle of community property law that since both spouses participate in the community, both are entitled to share in its reward. [Citations omitted.]

The non-employee (non-member) spouse, then, has a property interest in the employee or participant spouse's retirement plan.

Further, the Supreme Court of Texas, in *Cearley v. Cearley* (Tex. 1976) 544 S.W.2d 661, said:

> It is now well established that matured private retirement, annuity, and pension benefits earned by either spouse during the marital relationship are part of the community estate and thus subject to division upon dissolution of the marriage.

Deferred Vested Retirement Benefits

Often an employee's right to benefits vests after a certain term of employment but will not mature, for example, until the employee (1) reaches a certain age or has completed a certain number of years of service, (2) retires or otherwise terminates employment and (3) makes application for benefits. In such a case, the employee has a deferred vested retirement benefit.

In all community property jurisdictions, deferred vested retirement benefits earned during the marriage by an employee who has not yet reached retirement age are subject to division on dissolution of the marriage.[10]

---

9. See, e.g., *Johnson v. Johnson* (1981) 131 Ariz. 38, 638 P.2d 705; *In re Marriage of Gillmore* (1981) 29 Cal.3d 418, 629 P.2d 1; *Guy v. Guy* (1977) 98 Idaho 205, 560 P.2d 876; *Sims v. Sims* (La. 1978) 358 So.2d 919; *Ellett v. Ellett* (Nev. 1978) 573 P.2d 1179; *Copeland v. Copeland* (1978) 91 N.M. 409, 575 P.2d 99; *Ex Parte Burson* (Tex. 1981) 615 S.W.2d 192; *Farver v. Department of Retirement Systems* (Wash. 1982) 644 P.2d 1149.

10. In *Johnson v. Johnson* (1981) 131 Ariz. 38, 638 P.2d 705, the Arizona Supreme Court said "... it is well settled in Arizona and elsewhere that pension rights, whether vested or nonvested, are community property insofar as the rights were acquired during marriage, and are subject to equitable division upon divorce."

The California Supreme Court, in *In re Marriage of Gillmore* (1981) 29 Cal.3d 418, 629 P.2d 1, recently reiterated its position that "[u]nder California law, retirement benefits earned by a spouse during marriage are community property, subject to equal division upon the dissolution of that marriage. (Citations omitted.) This is true whether the benefits are vested or nonvested, matured or immature."

In *Ramsey v. Ramsey* (1975) 96 Idaho 672, 535 P.2d 53, the Supreme Court of Idaho held that retirement benefits "... to the extent that such benefits have vested or accrued while the husband and wife are domiciliary in a community property state, are community property subject to division between the parties upon dissolution of the marriage."

The Supreme Court of Louisiana in *Sims v. Sims* (La. 1978) 358 So.2d 919, said that the courts in Louisiana "... have uniformly held that, at the dissolution of the community, the non-employed spouse is entitled to judgment recognizing that spouse's interest in proceeds from a retirement [plan], if and when they become payable...."

Based on *In re Marriage of Brown* (1976) 15 Cal.3d 838, 544 P.2d 561, the Supreme Court of Nevada, in *Ellett v. Ellett* (Nev. 1978) 573 P.2d 1179, found that a trial court's division of an employee spouse's nonvested retirement benefits was not in error, acknowledging the propriety of treating vested retirement benefits as community property divisible on dissolution of the marriage.

After noting the soundness of the judicial trend toward considering unmatured pension benefits as community property, the Supreme Court of New Mexico, in *Copeland v. Copeland* (1978) 91 N.M. 409, 575 P.2d 99, found vested retirement benefits to be property that is subject to division on dissolution.

Relying on the reasoning of *In re Marriage of Brown* (1976) 15 Cal.3d 838, 544 P.2d 561, the Texas Supreme Court held, in *Cearley v. Cearley* (Tex. 1976) 544 S.W.2d 661, that "[p]ension rights, whether or not vested, represent a property interest; to the extent that such rights derive from employment during coverture, they comprise a community asset subject to division in a dissolution proceeding."

In *DeRevere v. DeRevere* (1971) 5 Wash.App. 741, 491 P.2d 249, the employee had not yet reached retirement age at the time of divorce. The court held that "... even though it might appear that Mr. DeRevere's interest in the company retirement plan had not yet fully vested, such rights as he—and the community composed of himself and wife—did have at the time of the divorce were properly divisible as property by the court."

Nonvested Retirement Benefits

Although often couched in different terms, the courts of all of the community property states have held or strongly implied that retirement benefits earned during the marriage, even though not yet vested, constitute community property subject to division on dissolution of the marriage.

The Supreme Court of Arizona in *Johnson v. Johnson* (1981) 131 Ariz. 38, 638 P.2d 705, took the unequivocal position that "an employee, and thereby the community, does indeed acquire a property right in unvested pension benefits. . . . Thus, to the extent that such a property right is earned through community effort, it is properly divisible by the court upon dissolution of the marriage."

In California, the leading case of *In re Marriage of Brown* (1976) 15 Cal.3d 838, 544 P.2d 561 (sometimes hereinafter referred to as *Brown*), overruled and disapproved many of the earlier California cases by holding that pension benefits earned during the marriage, whether or not vested, are community property and divisible on dissolution. Prior to *Brown* only vested pension rights were subject to division in California.

In *Shill v. Shill* (1979) 100 Idaho 433, 599 P.2d 1004, the Supreme Court of Idaho overruled a trial court's division of the employee's contributions by holding that the nonemployee spouse was entitled to a portion of the pension comprised of both employee and employer contributions. The court said that "[a]lthough [the employee] could not draw a pension from the fund until he had completed twenty years of service as a fireman, the pension is not earned on the last day of the twentieth year of employment. The value of the pension at the end of twenty years of service is a form of deferred compensation which is attributable to the entire period in which it was accumulated. The portion of the pension rights earned during the marriage were contingent earnings which may or may not have matured into a vested right to draw pension benefits, but constitutes a contingent community property interest subject to consideration and division upon divorce."

The Louisiana Supreme Court has taken a similar stance, overruling inconsistent prior discussions, by holding in *Sims v. Sims* (La. 1978) 358 So.2d 919, and in *T. L. James & Co., Inc. v. Montgomery* (La. 1976) 332 So.2d 834, that "[w]hen acquired during the existence of a marriage, the right-to-share [in a retirement plan] is a community asset which, at the dissolution of the community, must be so classified—even though at the time acquired or at the time of dissolution of a community, the right has no marketable or other redeemable cash value, and even though the contractual right to receive money or other benefits is due in the future and is contingent upon the happening of an event at an uncertain time."

Citing *Brown* without discussion, the Supreme Court of Nevada, in *Ellett v. Ellett* (Nev. 1978) 573 P.2d 1179, upheld the propriety of the trial court's division of nonvested retirement benefits.

In *LeClert v. LeClert* (1969) 80 N.M. 235, 453 P.2d 755, the Supreme Court of New Mexico held that nonvested pension benefits were community property. The court stated that "[t]he courts today regard retirement plans and retirement pay as a mode of employee compensation. . . . That portion of the retirement pay which was earned during coverture became property of the community."

In *Cearley v. Cearley* (Tex. 1976) 544 S.W.2d 661, the Texas Supreme Court unequivocally adopted the *Brown* rule that all pension benefits earned during the marriage, whether or not vested, are divisible on dissolution of the marriage.

Lastly, in *Wilder v. Wilder* (1975) 85 Wash.2d 364, 534 P.2d 1355, the Supreme Court of Washington upheld an award of a portion of the nonvested retirement pay to the nonemployee spouse. Citing consistent Washington appellate court decisions, the court said that ". . . an employee has a vested right with respect to pension benefits from the date of his employment, where a pension plan is in effect and is part of the compensation he earns. . . ." In his concurring opinion, Associate Justice Utter put it another way:

> A community that is in existence at any time during the span in which an interest is being acquired in retirement pay, contributes to the value of that property and should receive recognition at least to the extent its contribution increased the value of the right to retired pay. Its contribution should create a recognizable property right of sufficient value for judicial recognition that must be disposed of on dissolution of the community.

Disability Retirement Benefits

Unlike retirement benefits based on length of service, disability retirement pay has not always been regarded as compensation for past services and the community property jurisdictions are split on whether such benefits may be divided on dissolution of the marriage.

In California, retirement benefits are not community property where retirement is on account of disability and occurs before the employee has earned a vested right to retire for longevity of service.[11] The Supreme Court of California contrasts disability retirement benefits, which it views as compensation for personal anguish and diminished ability to earn a living in the future, with regular retirement benefits, which are deferred compensation for past services. Where, however, an employee elects to receive disability retirement benefits but is also eligible to elect a regular pension benefit, the nonemployee spouse is entitled to his or her community property share of the benefits that would have been payable had the employee elected regular benefits:[12]

> We cannot permit the [participant's] election of a "disability" pension to defeat the community interest in his right to a pension based on longevity. In the first place, such a result would violate the settled principle that one spouse cannot, by invoking a condition wholly within his control, defeat the community interest of the other spouse.
>
> * * * * *
>
> In the second place, "only a portion of husband's pension benefit payments, though termed 'disability payments,' is property allocable to disability" (*In re Marriage of Stenquist* (1978) 21 Cal.3d 779, 582 P.2d 96).[13]

Moreover, where the participant retires on disability pension when he or she is ineligible (because of age or length of service) for early retirement, but he or she would have qualified for early retirement at a later date, the nonemployee spouse is entitled to his or her pro-rata share of the benefits that would have been payable at such later date had the employee elected regular benefits. However, he or she will have to wait until then to begin collecting that share.[14]

The Washington Court of Appeals, appearing to adopt the California rule, held in *Matter of Marriage of Huteson* (1980) 27 Wash.App. 539, 619 P.2d 991, that a fireman's disability pension was the separate property of the disabled spouse. The court explained that ". . . the most compelling argument favoring a separate property characterization is that disability payments acquired *before* the disabled spouse has earned a vested right to retirement benefits are designed to compensate solely for loss of future earnings" (emphasis added). However, the *Huteson* court goes on to qualify its position by approving the language in *In Re Marriage of Kittleson* (1978) 21 Wash.App. 344, 585 P.2d 167, where that court said that if the disability pension serves as a form of deferred compensation for past services or is taken in lieu of a vested retirement benefit, circumstances may call for a different characterization. The *Kittleson* court stated that "[a]n inflexible rule that required a disability pension to be classified as separate property would ignore the fact that some 'disability' pensions step into the place of a regular retirement pension . . . yet other awards are made for disability alone."

In contrast, Idaho and Texas treat disability benefits in the same manner as retirement benefits based on longevity.

In *Guy v. Guy* (1977) 98 Idaho 205, 560 P.2d 876, the Idaho Supreme Court held plan disability benefits to be community property subject to division on dissolution of the marriage. The court regarded the employee's future disability payments, though not of a retirement nature and subject to termination in the event his disability concluded, as emoluments of employment derived from community labors. The court expressly followed a "source of benefit" theory rather than the "purpose of payment" rationale of the California courts and said that "[t]he California cases enunciating [the purpose of payment] doctrine may be explained as a practical accommodation to the rigid rule in [California] that all community property must be equally divided. . . . By contrast, in Idaho, our courts have the equitable power and discretion to divide community property toward the end of achieving a just and equitable result."

Similarly in *Busby v. Busby* (Tex. 1970) 457 S.W.2d 551, the Texas Supreme Court held that disability retirement benefits based on service largely taking place during the marriage constitute community property. Although the employee tried to distinguish disability retirement from voluntary longevity retirement, the court said that its analysis of the two types of benefits "leads us to conclude that the rule applied in the voluntary retirement cases should be applied here."[15]

---

11. *In re Marriage of Jones* (1975) 13 Cal.3d 457, 531 P.2d 420; *In re Marriage of Loehr* (1975) 13 Cal.3d 465, 531 P.2d 425.

12. In neither *Jones* nor *Loehr* was the disabled employee vested or eligible to receive regular retirement benefits when the marriage was dissolved.

13. See also *In re Marriage of Milhan* (1980) 27 Cal.3d 765, 613 P.2d 812.

14. *In re Marriage of Samuels* (1979) 96 Cal.App.3d 122, 158 Cal.Rptr. 38.

---

15. Cf.: *Ex Parte Burson* (Tex. 1981) 615 S.W.2d 192 holding that Veterans Administration benefits, unlike disability benefits, are not divisible or assignable, as they are not property.

Currently, the Arizona appellate courts are split on the treatment of disability retirement benefits.

In *Flowers v. Flowers* (Ariz.App. 1978) 118 Ariz. 577, 578 P.2d 1006, the court stated "[a]lthough the California cases are persuasive, Arizona does not follow the rationale of the California rule as set forth in *Jones* with regard to personal injuries. Unlike California, in Arizona damage claims for personal injuries sustained by a spouse during marriage are community property, even if the payment of the damages are recovered after divorce. [Citations omitted.] We cannot rationally distinguish disability benefits from personal injury benefits. Therefore, . . . we hold that the disability benefits in this case are community property to be equitably distributed by the court at the time of the dissolution of the marriage."

But in *Luna v. Luna* (Ariz.App. 1980) 125 Ariz. 120, 608 P.2d 57, another Arizona appellate court, citing the California case *In re Marriage of Stenquist* (1978) 21 Cal.3d 779, 582 P.2d 96, awarded the employee, as his sole and separate property, that portion of his monthly benefit allocable solely to his disability. The court said "[t]his 'disability pay' does not serve as a form of deferred compensation for past services. The amount of the disability payments depends primarily on the existence and extent of the disability. These payments serve to compensate the disabled [employee] for the loss of his . . . pay caused by his early retirement and for his reduced ability to compete for . . . employment."

Benefits Regarded as Separate Property

In the absence of an express statutory provision to the contrary, in most community property states, although retirement benefits found to be community property are subject to division on dissolution of the marriage, benefits found to be the separate property of one spouse are not subject to division.[16] Without specifically addressing this issue, some California and Louisiana cases have implicitly taken this position by holding that certain disability and other retirement or pension benefits constitute separate property not subject to division.[17]

Texas courts have split on this point but the most recent case concludes that separate property retirement benefits are still divisible in some circumstances to effect a just and equitable property division.[18]

Similarly, by virtue of the express statutory language of Section 26.08.110 of the Revised Codes of Washington,[19] the Washington courts have taken the position that separate property retirement benefits are subject to equitable division between the spouses.[20]

Common-Law States With Equitable Division Statutes

Over 30 common-law (noncommunity property) states[21] have statutes generally requiring that upon divorce the court shall divide the marital property in an equitable manner.[22]

---

16. See, for example, the discussion of California community property law in the section under "General Characterization of Pension Rights" in the present paper.

17. See, e.g., *In re Marriage of Stenquist* (1978) 21 Cal.3d 779, 582 P.2d 96 (disability retirement benefits in excess of longevity retirement benefits); *In re Marriage of Jones* (1975) 13 Cal.3d 457, 531 P.2d 420 (disability retirement benefits payable before eligibility for longevity retirement benefits); *In re Marriage of Loehr* (1975) 13 Cal.3d 465, 531 P.2d 425 (disability retirement benefits payable before eligibility for longevity retirement benefits); *Roberts v. Roberts* (La.App. 1976) 325 So.2d 674 (state employee's retirement benefits based on employee's contributions to state employee's retirement system).

18. See, e.g., *Coote v. Coote* (Tex.Civ.App. 1980) 592 S.W.2d 52 (separate property benefits earned in noncommunity property state or foreign country divisible); *Spencer v. Spencer* (Tex.Civ.App. 1979) 589 S.W.2d 174 and *Campbell v. Campbell* (Tex.Civ.App. 1979) 586 S.W.2d 162 (§3.63 of Texas Family Code allows court to invade separate property when necessary to a just and fair division); *Eichelberger v. Eichelberger* (Tex.Civ. App. 1977) 557 S.W.2d 587 (retirement benefits earned before marriage divisible).
Cf.: *Eggemeyer v. Eggemeyer* (Tex. 1977) 554 S.W.2d 137 (§3.63 of Family Code does not authorize divestiture of separate realty and transfer of title thereto).

19. R.C.W. §28.08.110 provides in relevant part: . . . If the court determines that either party, or both, is entitled to a divorce or annulment, judgment shall be entered accordingly, granting the party in whose favor the court decides a decree of full and complete divorce or annulment, and making such disposition of the property of the parties, *either community or separate,* as shall appear just and equitable . . . (emphasis added).

20. See, e.g., *Morris v. Morris* (1966) 69 Wash.2d 506, 419 P.2d 129 (all property, including separate property retirement benefits, subject to equitable disposition); *Weiss v. Weiss* (1969) 75 Wash.2d 596, 452 P.2d 748 (irrespective of values placed on retirement benefits, court can effect any just and equitable division).

21. For example, Alaska, Arkansas, Colorado, Connecticut, Delaware, Hawaii, Illinois, Indiana, Iowa, Kansas, Kentucky, Maine, Maryland, Michigan, Minnesota, Missouri, Montana, Nebraska, New Hampshire, New Jersey, New York, North Dakota, Ohio, Oklahoma, Oregon, Pennsylvania, South Carolina, South Dakota, Tennessee, Utah, Vermont, Wisconsin and Wyoming.

22. See, e.g., paragraph 5.c. of Part B of §236 of the New York Domestic Relations Law, which provides: "Marital property shall be distributed equitably between the parties, considering the circumstances of the case and of the respective parties" (N.Y. Dom.Rel.Law §236 (McKinney)).

Employee Contributions and Retirement Benefits in Pay Status

As in community property states, equitable division jurisdictions uniformly hold that an employee's own contributions made during marriage to a retirement fund, and absolutely subject to withdrawal by the employee, are properly included in the marital assets that are subject to division or award on divorce of the parties.[23]

The equitable division states, however, take a variety of positions on whether matured noncontributory retirement benefits in pay status are subject to division on divorce. A majority of the jurisdictions clearly take such benefits into account in the division or award of marital property.[24] A minority of states, however, refuse to recognize retirement benefits as property divisible or awardable on divorce even though the benefits are currently being received, often basing their determination on whether the benefits have a present cash surrender value and whether they are forfeitable on death.[25] To minimize the harsh result of finding retirement benefits not to constitute divisible property, some of these states and certain of the other equitable division jurisdictions have held benefits in pay status to be an "economic resource" or "source of income" of the employee spouse to be considered in awarding *other* marital property or alimony to the nonemployee spouse.[26]

Deferred Vested Retirement Benefits

Approximately half of the equitable division jurisdictions [27] have squarely addressed this issue and clearly held deferred vested retirement bene-

---

23. See, e.g., *In re Marriage of Pope* (Colo.App. 1975) 544 P.2d 639; *Hutchins v. Hutchins* (1976) 71 Mich.App. 361, 248 N.W.2d 272; *Walker v. Walker* (Mo.App. 1982) 631 S.W.2d 68; *Levandowski v. Levandowski* (Mont. 1981) 630 P.2d 239; *Pellegrino v. Pellegrino* (1975) 134 N.J.Super. 512, 342 A.2d 226; *Minnis and Minnis* (1981) 54 Or.App. 70, 634 P.2d 259; *Schafer v. Schafer* (1960) 9 Wis.2d 502, 101 N.W.2d 780.

24. See, e.g., *Ex Parte Pedigo* (Ala. 1982) 413 So.2d 1157; *Monsma v. Monsma* (Alaska 1980) 618 P.2d 559; *Thompson v. Thompson* (Conn. 1981) 438 A.2d 839; *Robert v. Barbara* (Del. 1981) 434 A.2d 383; *Myung Sun Kim v. Soo Myung Kim* (Hawaii App. 1980) 618 P.2d 754; *In re Marriage of Bodford* (1981) 94 Ill.App.3d 91, 418 N.E.2d 487; *In re Marriage of Jones* (Iowa 1981) 309 N.W.2d 457; *Gronquist v. Gronquist* (1982) 7 Kan.App.2d 583, 644 P.2d 1365; *Foster v. Foster* (Ky.App. 1979) 589 S.W.2d 223; *Capron v. Capron* (Me. 1979) 403 A.2d 1217; *Ohm v. Ohm* (Md.App. 1981) 431 A.2d 1371; *Hutchins v. Hutchins* (1976) 71 Mich.App. 361, 248 N.W.2d 272; *Elliott v. Elliott* (Minn. 1978) 274 N.W.2d 75; *Hurtgen v. Hurtgen* (Mo.App. 1982) 635 S.W.2d 69; *In re Marriage of Miller* (Mont. 1980) 609 P.2d 1185; *Kullbom v. Kullbom* (1981) 209 Neb. 145, 306 N.W.2d 844; *Kruger v. Kruger* (1977) 73 N.J. 464, 375 A.2d 659; *Majauskas v. Majauskas* (N.Y. 1981) 110 Misc.2d 323, 441 N.Y.S.2d 900; *Franzke and Franzke* (1981) 292 Or. 110, 637 P.2d 595; *Englert v. Englert* (Utah 1978) 576 P.2d 1274.

25. The Arkansas Supreme Court refused to divide retirement benefits currently being paid in *Paulsen v. Paulsen* (Ark. 1980) 601 S.W.2d 873, because the monthly retirement pay "... is not a fixed and tangible asset such as a vested pension or profit-sharing plan that may be collected in a lump sum. Rather, it terminates at death and has no loan, surrender or redemption value."
In *In re Marriage of Camarata* (Colo.App. 1979) 602 P.2d 970, the court affirmed the trial court's ruling that noncontributory monthly retirement benefits were too speculative to be divided as marital property because they were "contingent on the employee spouse's survival and terminate upon his death."
To the same effect was the holding in *In re Marriage of Delgado* (Ind.App. 1982) 429 N.E.2d 1124, where the court said "... where the pension is not present or vested in that the retiree must survive in order to receive the next periodic payment and is not entitled to receive payment on demand, the pension is not marital property which can be divided or awarded to the other spouse...."
In accord is the holding in *Baker v. Baker* (N.H. 1980) 421 A.2d 998, where the Supreme Court of New Hampshire stated that certain monthly retirement pay lacked the following characteristics of property: cash surrender value, loan value, redemption value, lump sum value and value realizable after death. The court determined that, lacking these characteristics, the retirement pay was too difficult to equitably divide.

26. See, e.g., *Paulsen v. Paulsen* (Ark. 1980) 601 S.W.2d 873 (retirement pay as an economic circumstance to be considered in making just division of property and fixing alimony and child support); *In re Marriage of Ellis* (Colo.App. 1975) 538 P.2d 1347, *cert. granted* (Colo. 1976) 552 P.2d 506 (retirement pay as an economic resource to be considered in fixing alimony); *Fugassi v. Fugassi* (Fla.App. 1976) 332 So.2d 695 (alimony awarded out of retirement income); *Sadler v. Sadler* (Ind.App. 1981) 428 N.E.2d 1305 (consideration of retirement in distribution of other marital property); *Baker v. Baker* (N.H. 1980) 421 A.2d 998 (retirement pay as a relevant factor in making equitable support orders and property distributions); *Elmwood v. Elmwood* (1978) 295 N.C. 168, 244 S.E.2d 668 (garnishment of retirement pay for support upheld as retirement is a source of income); *Ginn v. Ginn* (Ohio App. 1960) 175 N.E.2d 848 (retirement pay as a source of income for award of alimony); *Baker v. Baker* (Okla. 1975) 546 P.2d 1325 (retirement pay considered in awarding alimony); *Carter v. Carter* (S.C. 1982) 286 S.E.2d 139 (retirement pay considered in determining alimony).
Cf.: *Daves v. Daves* (Tenn.App. 1978) 576 S.W.2d 4 (trial court did not err in failing to take into consideration retirement benefits and awarding a portion to wife since to do so would be to award alimony, which a Tennessee court may not do under current law).

27. Alaska, Delaware, Illinois, Iowa, Kentucky, Maryland, Michigan, Minnesota, Montana, Nebraska, New Jersey, New York, North Dakota, Oregon and Wisconsin.

fits to be marital property subject to equitable division on divorce.[28] In addition, a handful of other equitable division states,[29] although not having addressed the issue, have strongly implied that deferred vested retirement benefits are marital property that is subject to equitable distribution.[30] Of the remaining jurisdictions, most have required deferred vested retirement benefits to be taken into account (as an economic resource or source of income) in effecting an award of alimony or of *other* marital property to the nonemployee spouse.[31]

A less-than-contemporary approach to the treatment of deferred vested benefits is still maintained by the courts of Arkansas (where vested benefits are not deemed marital property unless, at the time of divorce, they are subject to unconditional withdrawal and/or distribution at the time of employment termination);[32] Colorado (where vested benefits are not deemed marital property unless, at the time of divorce, they are payable in a lump sum, have a cash surrender value or are subject to withdrawal);[33] Indiana (where vested benefits are not deemed marital property if, at the time of divorce, they are not unconditionally payable and are contingent on survival);[34] and Missouri (where vested benefits under a noncontributory defined benefit plan are not considered marital property if the employee must reach normal retirement age before the benefits mature or must take an actuarially reduced benefit at early age retirement).[35]

Nonvested Retirement Benefits

Unlike the community property jurisdictions, the majority of equitable division states have either refused to recognize nonvested retirement benefits as marital property[36] or have not yet addressed the issue.[37] To date, only about one-third of the equitable division jurisdictions[38] have held nonvested benefits to be divisible on divorce.[39] Most of these state courts have followed the reasoning of the California Supreme Court in *Brown*

---

28. See *Monsma v. Monsma* (Alaska 1980) 618 P.2d 559; *Husband B. v. Wife B.* (Del.Super. 1978) 396 A.2d 169; *In re Marriage of Hunt* (1979) 78 Ill.App.3d 653, 397 N.E.2d 511; *In re Marriage of Schissel* (Iowa 1980) 292 N.W.2d 421; *Combs v. Combs* (Ky.App. 1981) 622 S.W.2d 679; *Deering v. Deering* (Md.App. 1981) 437 A.2d 883; *Gibbons v. Gibbons* (1981) 105 Mich.App. 400, 306 N.W.2d 528; *Faus v. Faus* (Minn. 1982) 319 N.W.2d 408; *In re Marriage of Laster* (Mont. 1982) 643 P.2d 597; *Kullbom v. Kullbom* (1981) 209 Neb. 145, 306 N.W.2d 844; *Kikkert v. Kikkert* (1981) 177 N.J. Super. 471, 427 A.2d 76; *Jolis v. Jolis* (N.Y. 1981) 446 N.Y.S.2d 138; *Webber v. Webber* (N.D. 1981) 308 N.W.2d 548; *Franzke and Franzke* (1981) 292 Or. 110, 637 P.2d 595; *Selchert v. Selchert* (1979) 90 Wis.2d 1, 280 N.W.2d 293.
29. Alabama, Connecticut, Hawaii, Maine and Utah.
30. See *Ex Parte Pedigo* (Ala. 1982) 413 So.2d 1157 (retirement annuity earned through gainful employment of a spouse during marriage "should" be treated as marital property); *Thompson v. Thompson* (Conn. 1981) 438 A.2d 839 (unaccrued pension benefits may be considered in making property assignment orders); *Linson v. Linson* (Hawaii App. 1980) 618 P.2d 748 (nonvested pension part of "estate of parties" subject to division); *Capron v. Capron* (Me. 1979) 403 A.2d 1217 (employee's vested benefits awarded to him as "intangible property"); *Englert v. Englert* (Utah 1978) 576 P.2d 1274 (all retirement benefits are marital assets).
31. See, e.g., those cases listed in footnote 26.
32. See, e.g., *Paulsen v. Paulsen* (Ark. 1980) 601 S.W.2d 873; *Bachman v. Bachman* (Ark. 1981) 621 S.W.2d 701; *Knopf v. Knopf* (Ark. 1979) 576 S.W.2d 193.
33. See, e.g., *In re Marriage of Mitchell* (Colo. 1978) 579 P.2d 613; *In re Marriage of Camarata* (Colo.App. 1979) 602 P.2d 907; *In re Marriage of Pope* (Colo. App. 1975) 544 P.2d 639.

34. See, e.g., *In re Marriage of Delgado* (Ind.App. 1982) 429 N.E.2d 1124; *Wilson v. Wilson* (Ind.App. 1980) 409 N.E.2d 1169; *Hiscox v. Hiscox* (Ind.App. 1979) 385 N.E.2d 1166; *Savage v. Savage* (Ind.App. 1978) 374 N.E.2d 536.
35. See, e.g., *Smiley v. Smiley* (Mo.App. 1981) 623 S.W.2d 56; *Murphy v. Murphy* (Mo.App. 1981) 613 S.W.2d 450; *Delay v. Delay* (Mo.App. 1981) 612 S.W.2d 391; *In re Marriage of Biancardi* (Mo.App. 1980) 611 S.W.2d 250.
36. See, e.g., *Knopf v. Knopf* (Ark. 1979) 576 S.W.2d 193; *Ellis v. Ellis* (Colo. 1976) 552 P.2d 506; *Wilson v. Wilson* (Ind.App. 1980) 409 N.E.2d 1169; *Miller v. Miller* (1978) 83 Mich.App. 672, 269 N.W.2d 264 (unless benefits have reasonably ascertainable present value; but if contingent they may not be divided); *Faulkner and Faulkner* (Mo.App. 1979) 582 S.W.2d 292; *Baker v. Baker* (Okla. 1975) 546 P.2d 1325; *Carter v. Carter* (S.C. 1982) 286 S.E.2d 139.
37. No contemporary cases were found specifically addressing the issue of nonvested retirement benefits on divorce in the following jurisdictions: Alaska, Florida, Georgia, Iowa, Kansas, Maine, Massachusetts, Mississippi, New York, North Carolina, North Dakota, Ohio, Pennsylvania, Rhode Island, South Dakota, Tennessee, Utah, Vermont, Virginia, West Virginia and Wyoming.
38. Connecticut, Delaware, Hawaii, Illinois, Kentucky, Maryland, Montana, Nebraska, New Jersey, Oregon and Wisconsin.
39. See, e.g., *Thompson v. Thompson* (Conn. 1981) 438 A.2d 839; *Robert v. Barbara* (Del. 1981) 434 A.2d 383; *Linson v. Linson* (Hawaii App. 1980) 618 P.2d 748; *In re Marriage of Bodford* (1981) 94 Ill.App.3d 91, 418 N.E.2d 487; *Light v. Light* (Ky.App. 1980) 599 S.W.2d 476; *Ohm v. Ohm* (Md. App. 1981) 431 A.2d 1371; *In re Marriage of Laster* (Mont. 1982) 643 P.2d 597; *Kullbom v. Kullbom* (1981) 209 Neb. 145, 306 N.W.2d 844; *McGrew v. McGrew* (1977) 151 N.J.Super. 515, 377 A.2d 697; *Rogers and Rogers* (1980) 45 Or.App. 885, 609 P.2d 877; *Leighton v. Leighton* (1978) 81 Wis.2d 620, 261 N.W.2d 457.

and have held that pension rights earned during marriage, whether vested or nonvested, constitute marital property that is subject to equitable division on divorce.

Uniquely, the Nebraska and Wisconsin legislatures recently enacted express provisions regarding the treatment of retirement benefits on divorce:

Section 42-366(8) of the Nebraska Revised Statutes provides in relevant part:

> ... The court shall include as part of the marital estate, for purposes of the division of property at the time of dissolution, any pension plans, retirement plans, annuities, and other deferred compensation benefits owned by either party, *whether vested or not vested* (Neb. Rev.Stat. §42-366(8)) (emphasis added).

And Section 247.255 of the Wisconsin laws provides in relevant part:

> Upon every judgment of annulment, divorce or legal separation ... the court shall divide the property of the parties.... The court shall presume that all other property except inherited property is to be divided equally between the parties, but may alter this distribution without regard to marital misconduct after considering:
>
> * * * * *
>
> (9) Other economic circumstances of each party, including pension benefits, *vested or unvested,* and future interests (Wis.Stat. §247.255) (emphasis added).

Disability Retirement Benefits

There is little indication in equitable division states of the treatment of disability retirement benefits. However, those courts addressing the issue have, for the most part, held them to be divisible or to be taken into account on divorce,[40] usually because the particular jurisdiction deems personal injury[41] or workers' compensation[42] awards acquired during the marriage to be marital property.

Although Wisconsin has an express statutory requirement that retirement benefits be taken into consideration in equitably distributing the marital property,[43] the Wisconsin Supreme Court, in *Leighton v. Leighton* (1978) 81 Wis.2d 620, 261 N.W.2d 457, appeared to adopt the California position by holding that disability benefits were compensation for the impairment of the employee's body and that the trial court properly treated such benefits as income to the employee and not as a marital asset to be divided between the parties.

Methods of Division of Retirement Benefits

Division or Award on Dissolution or Divorce

In those states (community property and equitable division jurisdictions) that recognize retirement benefits as community or marital property subject to division or award on dissolution or divorce of the parties, several methods are used to implement an equal or equitable division.

The court can determine the portion of present or future retirement benefits earned during the marriage and award the nonemployee spouse one-half of such benefits if, as and when the employee retires (the so-called time rule).[44] Using the time rule, the community or marital interest in the benefits would be a fraction, the numerator of which is the length of the employee's service during the marriage and the denominator of which is the employee's total length of service. This fraction can then be applied to each benefit payment (lump sum or periodic) as it is made to determine the portion of the benefit earned during the marriage, and the nonemployee spouse paid his or her one-half interest therein.[45]

---

40. See, e.g., *DeMello v. DeMello* (Hawaii App. 1982) 646 P.2d 409; *In re Marriage of Smith* (1980) 84 Ill.App.3d 446, 405 N.E.2d 884; *Irwin v. Irwin* (Ind.App. 1980) 406 N.E.2d 317; *Karr v. Karr* (Mont. 1981) 628 P.2d 267; *Kruger v. Kruger* (1977) 73 N.J. 464, 375 A.2d 659; *Harmon v. Harmon* (1978) 161 N.J.Super. 206, 391 A.2d 552.

41. See, e.g., *In re Marriage of Smith* (1980) 84 Ill.App.3d 446, 405 N.E.2d 884; *Kruger v. Kruger* (1977) 73 N.J. 464, 375 A.2d 659; *Harmon v. Harmon* (1978) 161 N.J.Super. 206, 391 A.2d 552.

42. See, e.g., *DeMello v. DeMello* (Hawaii App. 1982) 646 P.2d 409; *In re Marriage of Thomas* (1980) 89 Ill.App.3d 81, 411 N.E.2d 552; *In re Marriage of Dettore* (1980) 86 Ill.App.3d 540, 408 N.E.2d 429; *Evans v. Evans* (1980) 98 Mich.App. 328, 296 N.W.2d 248.

43. See the previous discussion of Section 247.255 of the Wisconsin laws.

44. *In re Marriage of Brown* (1976) 15 Cal.3d 838, 544 P.2d 561; *In re Marriage of Judd* (1977) 68 Cal.App.3d 515, 137 Cal.Rptr. 318.

45. For cases applying and/or discussing the time rule or variations thereof see, e.g., *Johnson v. Johnson* (1981) 131 Ariz. 38, 638 P.2d 705; *In re Marriage of Brown* (1976) 15 Cal.3d 838, 544 P.2d 561; *In re Marriage of Judd* (1977) 68 Cal.App.3d 515, 137 Cal.Rptr. 318; *Robert v. Barbara* (Del. 1981) 434 A.2d 383; *Linson v. Linson* (Hawaii App. 1980) 618 P.2d 748; *Ramsey v. Ramsey* (1975) 96 Idaho 672, 535 P.2d 53; *In re Marriage of Hunt* (1979) 78 Ill.App.3d 653, 397 N.E.2d 511; *In re Marriage of Jones* (Iowa 1981) 309 N.W.2d 457; *Light v. Light* (Ky.App. 1980) 599 S.W.2d 476; *Sims v.*

Unless specifically precluded by the court,[46] this approach can be used whether or not the employee is vested or even if he or she has already retired. Unless the employee has already retired, the only element of the formula known when the marriage is dissolved is the numerator of the fraction (the employee's length of service during the marriage). The denominator (total length of service) and the amount of the monthly (or lump sum) benefit cannot be determined until the employee actually retires.

Under the time rule, although the *extent* of the community or marital interest is determined as of the date of separation or date of divorce (depending on the applicable state), the *value* of that interest usually is determined at actual retirement (i.e., the benefit factor(s) in effect at the time of retirement is applied to the pension credits earned during the marriage). In other words, the nonemployee spouse is entitled to increases in or accruals on his or her interest because of the delay in receiving that interest.[47]

A second method of dividing the benefits is to have an actuary place a present value on the retirement benefits earned during the marriage and award them all to the employee spouse and other marital property of equal value to the nonemployee spouse.[48]

If, at the time of the dissolution or divorce, the employee is not eligible to retire, the court may enter an order to become effective at the earliest possible date the employee could retire, requiring the *employee*[49] to begin paying the nonemployee spouse his or her pro-rata share of the benefits that the employee would have received had he or she elected to retire on the earliest possible date. This requires a determination of the monthly benefits the employee would have received had he or she retired at the time of trial and the application of a modified time rule to determine the nonemployee spouse's portion of those benefits.[50]

If a court does award the nonemployee spouse a share of future payments under the retirement plan, it may retain jurisdiction to supervise the implementation of the order when the employee retires.[51] Some courts, apparently under the misapprehension that if pension rights are not yet

---

Sims (La. 1978) 358 So.2d 919; *Ohm v. Ohm* (Md.App. 1981) 431 A.2d 1371; *Faus v. Faus* (Minn. 1982) 319 N.W.2d 408; *Kullbom v. Kullbom* (1981) 209 Neb. 145, 306 N.W.2d 844; *Kruger v. Kruger* (1977) 73 N.J. 464, 375 A.2d 659; *LeClert v. LeClert* (1969) 80 N.M. 235, 453 P.2d 755; *Majauskas v. Majauskas* (N.Y. 1981) 110 Misc.2d 323, 441 N.Y.S.2d 900; *Cearley v. Cearley* (Tex. 1976) 544 S.W.2d 661; *DeRevere v. DeRevere* (1971) 5 Wash.App. 741, 491 P.2d 249; *Bloomer v. Bloomer* (1978)) 84 Wis.2d 124, 267 N.W.2d 235.

46. See *Ramsey v. Ramsey* (1975) 96 Idaho 672, 535 P.2d 53 (where the Supreme Court of Idaho reversed a lower court's division of each monthly benefit payment and required a present value "cash out" of the nonemployee spouse's interest because "each spouse should have immediate control of his or her share of the community property . . ."); *Combs v. Combs* (Ky.App. 1981) 622 S.W.2d 679 (where, because of equitable considerations, the court required a "cash out" of the nonemployee's interest in the employee's benefits rather than an apportionment of the future benefits).

47. See, e.g., *In re Marriage of Stenquist* (1978) 21 Cal.3d 779, 528 P.2d 96; *Waite v. Waite* (1972) 6 Cal.3d 461, 99 Cal.Rptr. 325; *In re Marriage of Jones* (Iowa 1981) 309 N.W.2d 457; *Miller v. Miller* (La.App. 1981) 405 So.2d 564; *Faus v. Faus* (Minn. 1982) 319 N.W.2d 408; *Sprott v. Sprott* (Tex.App. 1978) 576 S.W.2d 653; *Majauskas v. Majauskas* (N.Y. 1981) 110 Misc.2d 323, 441 N.Y.S.2d 900.

48. For a discussion of the present value method, see *Johnson v. Johnson* (1981) 131 Ariz. 38, 638 P.2d 705;

Phillipson v. Board of Administration (1970) 3 Cal.3d 32, 473 P.2d 765; *Robert v. Barbara* (Del. 1981) 434 A.2d 383; *Shill v. Shill* (1979) 100 Idaho 433, 599 P.2d 1004; *Ohm v. Ohm* (Md.App. 1981) 431 A.2d 1371; *Copeland v. Copeland* (1978) 91 N.M. 409, 575 P.2d 99; *Cearley v. Cearley* (Tex. 1976) 544 S.W.2d 661; *DeRevere v. DeRevere* (1971) 5 Wash.App. 741, 491 P.2d 249; *Bloomer v. Bloomer* (1978) 84 Wis.2d 124, 267 N.W.2d 235.

For cases using this method see, e.g., *Myung Sun Kim v. Soo Myung Kim* (Hawaii App. 1980) 618 P.2d 754; *Ramsey v. Ramsey* (1975) 96 Idaho 672, 535 P.2d 53; *In re Marriage of Bodford* (1981) 94 Ill.App.3d 91, 418 N.E.2d 487; *In re Marriage of Schissel* (Iowa 1980) 292 N.W.2d 421; *Combs v. Combs* (Ky.App. 1981) 622 S.W.2d 679; *Kis v. Kis* (Mont. 1982) 639 P.2d 1151; *DiPietro v. DiPietro* (1982) 183 N.J.Super. 69, 443 A.2d 244; *Haguewood and Haguewood* (1981) 292 Or. 197, 638 P.2d 1135; *Pinkowski v. Pinkowski* (1975) 67 Wis.2d 176, 226 N.W.2d 518.

Cf.: *Sims v. Sims* (La. 1978) 358 So.2d 919, where the court awarded a portion of the employee's future benefits to the former spouse because "[u]ntil the employee is separated from the service, dies, retires or becomes disabled, no [present] value can be fixed upon his right to receive an annuity or upon lump-sum payments or other benefits to be paid on his account."

49. See *Monsanto Co. v. Ford* (E.D.Mo. 1981) 534 F. Supp. 51 (court cannot require the *plan* to make a premature distribution to a spouse of her interest).

Cf.: *In re Marriage of Luciano* (1980) 104 Cal.App. 3d 956, 164 Cal.Rptr. 93.

50. *In re Marriage of Gillmore* (1981) 29 Cal.3d 418, 629 P.2d 1; *In re Marriage of Luciano* (1980) 104 Cal.App.3d 956, 164 Cal.Rptr. 93; *In re Marriage of Martin* (1975) 50 Cal.App.3d 581, 123 Cal.Rptr. 634; *Wilder v. Wilder* (1975) 85 Wash.2d 364, 534 P.2d 1355.

51. For cases discussing reservation of jurisdiction over retirement benefits, see *Johnson v. Johnson* (1981) 131 Ariz. 38, 638 P.2d 705; *Robert v. Barbara* (Del. 1981) 434 A.2d 383; *Shill v. Shill* (1979) 100 Idaho 433, 599 P.2d 1004.

vested there is nothing to divide, will not determine the extent of the community interest at the time of divorce but will reserve jurisdiction to determine the community interest when the employee becomes vested or eligible for retirement.[52]

Division of Retirement Benefits at Death

Although not followed in most other jurisdictions,[53] in California the community interest of the nonemployee spouse in an employee's retirement benefits terminates with the death of the employee spouse or the nonemployee spouse, whichever occurs first. This "terminable interest" rule holds that the interest of the nonemployee spouse in the employee's retirement benefits cannot pass to his or her heirs.[54] This means that if the former spouse predeceases the employee, the employee is entitled to all pension payments accruing after the former spouse's death. The terminable interest rule also holds that the nonemployee spouse has no right to any benefits payable at or after the employee's death.[55] Although the rule seems unfair to the nonemployee spouse, the lower courts in California generally have considered bound to apply it by decisions of the California Supreme Court. That court has recognized that the terminable interest rule makes the nonemployee spouse's share of the total pension package less valuable actuarially than the employee's share, but has declined to overrule its earlier decisions.[56] The court has indicated that any inequity arising from the rule can be mitigated or offset:

> ... the [trial] court, if it sees fit, may compensate the spouse by an award of more than half the value of some other community asset (*Waite v. Waite* (1972) 6 Cal.3d 461, 492 P.2d 13).[57]

The terminable interest rule has been criticized by courts and commentators.[58] Particularly where the amount of the benefit depends on mandatory or optional employee contributions or the form of the benefit is subject to the employee's election, the rule's application (without a compensating adjustment) results in a transfer of community funds away from the nonemployee spouse, which conflicts with the general tenets of the community property system. Nevertheless, until the California Supreme Court decides to overrule its previous decisions, the lower courts will continue to enforce both aspects of the terminable interest rule, at least where the employee invokes it.[59]

Court Orders Against Pension Plans in Dissolutions and Divorces

No ERISA Preemption of State Marital Property Laws

Section 206(d)(1) of ERISA requires that "each pension plan shall provide that benefits provided under the plan may not be assigned or alienated."[60] Section 401(a)(13) of the Internal Revenue Code contains similar language.[61] The regula-

---

52. See, e.g., *In re Marriage of Carl* (1977) 67 Cal.App.3d 542, 136 Cal.Rptr. 703; *In re Marriage of Adams* (1976) 64 Cal.App.3d 181, 134 Cal.Rptr. 298.

53. See, e.g., *In re Marriage of Miller* (Mont. 1980) 609 P.2d 1185 (wife's heirs entitled to receive wife's share of benefits for as long as husband is living); *Farver v. Department of Retirement Systems* (Wash. 1982) 644 P.2d 1149 (wife's interest in husband's benefits subject to state statute governing descent and distribution of property).
Cf.: *Cullen v. Cullen* (Fla.App. 1982) 413 So.2d 1196 (where trial court awarded wife one-half of the husband's pension as alimony, which award terminated on death of husband); *Corrigan v. Corrigan* (1978) 160 N.J.Super. 400, 390 A.2d 141 (retirement plan death benefits not subject to equitable distribution).

54. *In re Marriage of Fithian* (1974) 10 Cal.3d 592, 517 P.2d 449; *Waite v. Waite* (1972) 6 Cal.3d 461, 99 Cal.Rptr. 325; *Estate of Allen* (1980) 108 Cal.App.3d 614, 166 Cal.Rptr. 653.

55. *Benson v. City of Los Angeles* (1963) 60 Cal.2d 355, 384 P.2d 649; *In re Marriage of Peterson* (1974) 41 Cal.App.3d 642, 115 Cal.Rptr. 184: "Reading the cases . . ., we are bound to hold that Elizabeth's entitlement in this case is limited to Roy's pension rights while he is living, and that she has no 'vested' interest in any amounts payable after his death, even though these amounts are part of the pension package purchased with community funds."

56. Not all courts have refused to recognize that the spouse has a community property interest in death benefits that are payable in a lump sum (*Patillo v. Norris* (1976) 65 Cal.App.3d 209, 135 Cal.Rptr. 210) or for a term certain (*In re Marriage of Mantor* (1980) 104 Cal.App.3d 981, 164 Cal.Rptr. 121). Neither case addressed the terminable interest rule issue however, and *Mantor* involved a voluntary agreement between the spouse and the employee.

57. *In re Marriage of Milhan* (1974) 13 Cal.3d 129, 528 P.2d 1145.

58. See *In re Marriage of Peterson* (1974) 41 Cal.App.3d 642, 115 Cal.Rptr. 184; Reppy, "Community and Separate Interests in Pensions and Social Security Benefits After *Marriage of Brown* and ERISA," 25 UCLA L.Rev. 417 (1978); Thiede, "The Community Property Interest of the Nonemployee Spouse in Private Employee Retirement Benefits," 9 USF L.Rev. 135 (1975).

59. Compare *Estate of Allen* (1980) 108 Cal.App.3d 614, 166 Cal.Rptr. 653 with *In re Marriage of Mantor* (1980) 104 Cal.App.3d 981, 164 Cal.Rptr. 121.

60. 29 U.S.C. §1056(d)(1).

61. IRC §401(a)(13).

tions under Code §401(a)(13) are more expansive and provide in part: "... benefits provided under the plan may not be anticipated, assigned (either at law or in equity), alienated or subject to attachment, garnishment, levy, execution or other legal or equitable process."[62] Section 514(a) of ERISA preempts "all state laws insofar as they may now or hereafter relate to any employee benefit plan."[63]

In the past several years both state and federal courts have been called on to determine, in various contexts, whether ERISA, in fact, preempts state marital property and/or child and spousal support laws and, therefore, whether ERISA's antialienation provision is to be construed literally. The federal courts have been split on these issues, but it appears that the debate over preemption ended in 1981 with the United States Supreme Court's refusal to grant *certiorari* in either *Carpenters Pension Trust, Etc. v. Kronschnabel* (9 Cir. 1980) 632 F.2d 745, *cert. denied* (1981) 453 U.S. 922, or *Stone v. Stone* (9 Cir. 1980) 632 F.2d 740, *cert. denied* (1981) 453 U.S. 932.

Community Property Preemption Cases

In 1979, a California intermediate appellate court held in *In re Marriage of Campa* (1979) 89 Cal.App.3d 113, 152 Cal.Rptr. 362, that ERISA does not preempt California community property laws and therefore does not prohibit the division of benefits earned during the marriage. The United States Supreme Court, without issuing any opinion, summarily dismissed the pension fund's appeal of that decision.[64]

The next year, the Ninth Circuit ruled in *Carpenters Pension Trust, Etc. v. Kronschnabel* (9 Cir. 1980) 632 F.2d 745, that the Supreme Court's summary dismissal of *In re Marriage of Campa* was a decision on the merits, binding on all lower courts, that ERISA does not preempt California community property laws. The Supreme Court refused to grant *certiorari*.[65]

Moreover, that same year, the Ninth Circuit held in *Stone v. Stone* (9 Cir. 1980) 632 F.2d 740, that a nonemployee spouse who was awarded part of an employee's pension in a California dissolution was a plan participant under ERISA §502(a)(1)(B). Therefore, she could bring an action in federal court against the plan to compel the plan to pay the nonemployee spouse her share of the benefits directly. Again, the Supreme Court refused to grant *certiorari*,[66] which suggests that, with regard to private plan benefits, it is perhaps satisfied with the result in *Campa*.[67]

Other cases indicating that the preemption defense no longer bars a spouse from reaching an employee's benefits are *Operating Engineers, Etc. v. Zamborsky* (9 Cir. 1981) 650 F.2d 196 (where the court affirmed the garnishment of a pensioner's interest in a plan to satisfy an alimony arrearage, finding an implied exception to ERISA's antialienation rule) and *Carpenters Pension Trust Fund v. Reyes* (9 Cir. 1982) 688 F.2d 671 (where the court held that a nonemployee spouse who is awarded part of the employee's benefits is a participant in the plan for the purpose of awarding attorneys fees under Section 502(g) of ERISA in connection with the plan's suit in federal court to enjoin the state order).

Separate Property Preemption Cases

Generally, the separate property state preemption cases are in accord with *Campa, Kronschnabel* and *Stone.*

The leading case of *American Tel. & Tel. Co. v. Merry* (2 Cir. 1979) 592 F.2d 118, involved enforcement of a Connecticut court order garnishing Merry's interest in the AT&T pension plan to satisfy arrearages in alimony and child support payments. The court found an implied exception to both the preemption clause and to the antiassignment provisions of ERISA where enforcement of state family support orders is concerned. In accord are the holdings in *Senco of Florida, Inc. v. Clark* (M.D.Fla. 1979) 473 F. Supp. 902 and *Cody v. Riecker* (2 Cir. 1979) 594 F.2d 314.

A contrary determination, however, was made by a district court in *General Motors Corp. v. Townsend* (E.D.Mich. 1976) 468 F. Supp. 466, where the court simply held that ERISA §206(d) precluded garnishment against the GM Stock Savings Plan. The former wife was seeking her interest in the plan granted in a divorce proceeding. This case is the only one reported conflicting with the *American Telephone* case in separate property states and it has been rejected by another federal court in the same district (*Central States, Southeast and Southwest Areas Pension Fund v. Parr* (E.D.Mich. 1979) 480 F. Supp. 924).

---

62. Treasury Reg. §1.401(a)-13(b)(1).
63. 29 U.S.C. §1144(a).
64. *In re Marriage of Campa* (1980) 444 U.S. 1028.
65. (1981) 453 U.S. 922.
66. (1981) 453 U.S. 932.
67. But see *Hisquierdo v. Hisquierdo* (1979) 439 U.S. 572, which held that the Railroad Retirement Act *does* preempt California community property law so as to preclude division of an employee's interest in railroad retirement benefits.

Military Retirement

Although the Supreme Court held in *McCarty v. McCarty* (1981) 453 U.S. 210, that federal law governing military retirement pay preempts California community property law, Congress has recently enacted the Former Spouse's Protection Amendment, subjecting military pensions to state marital property laws.[68] The amendment authorizes the states to determine whether military retirement is property subject to division on dissolution or divorce.

It provides for direct payment to the former spouse of alimony, child support or his or her marital property interest in the benefits. However, no direct payment to the former spouse of his or her marital property interest need be made by the military unless the parties were married at least ten years. There is no length of marriage requirement for direct payment of child or spousal support, but in no event may a former spouse receive more than 50% of disposable retirement pay. The payments cease when the military member dies, unless an earlier termination date is specified in the state court order. Courts may not order survivor benefit coverage, but the service member may voluntarily provide it. Divorces and dissolutions that became final after *McCarty* may be reconsidered pursuant to the amendment, but divorces that were final before *McCarty* may not.

Specific Orders Requiring Action of a Plan

In California and certain other jurisdictions, state law permits a retirement plan to be sued directly or joined as a party in a marital dissolution matter to enforce a court order awarding the nonemployee spouse an interest in the employee's retirement benefits.[69] For example, California Civil Code Section 4363 provides for the joinder of a pension plan as a party to the marriage dissolution proceeding so that it can be bound by any orders entered that affect the employee spouse's pension benefits and the nonemployee spouse's community interest in them.

Stone also, in effect, holds that the nonemployee spouse has federal law rights under ERISA §502 to enforce his or her rights directly against the plan. Furthermore, it appears that a plan is subject to the jurisdiction of, and can be required to honor an order of, a court sitting in another state, if the plan has sufficient "minimum contacts" in that state for the court to properly obtain personal jurisdiction over it. In *Varsic v. U.S. District Court* (9 Cir. 1979) 607 F.2d 245, the court held that a pension fund's receipt of employer contributions and provision of benefits to participants who had worked in covered employment in a particular state are sufficient minimum contacts to permit a court in that state to exercise jurisdiction over an out-of-state pension fund in a participant's suit for benefits. In the context of divorce and dissolution actions, this ruling means that the nonemployee spouse may join or bring an action against a plan in the state where the employee worked and earned his or her pension credits even though the plan is located or administered in another state.

In many cases in which pension plans are joined or sued directly, courts have ordered the plan, rather than the employee, to pay the former spouse's community property portion of pension benefits directly to the former spouse.[70] Such orders can be made whether or not the benefits are in pay status, although no court has yet ordered a plan to begin paying benefits to the nonemployee spouse before the employee retires and at least one court has specifically precluded it. In *Monsanto Co. v. Ford* (E.D.Mo. 1981), 534 F. Supp. 51, a former spouse had attempted in a state dissolution action to have a plan distribute her marital property interest therein at the time of dissolution even though benefits were not yet payable. The plan filed a declaratory relief action and the court held that:

> Rights and obligations upon employees and employers arising out of employee benefit plans are contractual in nature. [Citations omitted.] A court may not rewrite the contractual obligations of the parties by compelling the employer to make a premature distribution to an employee or his spouse of funds held for the benefit of the employees. Such an action would be dis-

---

68. Defense Authorization Act of 1983, 10 U.S.C. §1408.

69. See, e.g., *In re Marriage of Campa* (1979) 89 Cal.App.3d 113, 152 Cal.Rptr. 362; *In re Marriage of Johnston* (1978) 85 Cal.App.3d 900, 149 Cal.Rptr. 798; *Johns v. Retirement Fund Trust* (1978) 85 Cal.App.3d 511, 149 Cal.Rptr. 551; *Monsanto Co. v. Ford* (E.D.Mo. 1981) 534 F. Supp. 51; *General Dynamics Corp. v. Harris* (Tex.App. 1979) 581 S.W.2d 300; *Collida v. Collida* (Tex.App. 1977) 546 S.W.2d 708; *Dessommes v. Dessommes* (Tex.App. 1976) 543 S.W.2d 165.

---

70. See, e.g., *In re Marriage of Campa, supra; In re Marriage of Johnston, supra; Johns v. Retirement Fund Trust, supra; General Dynamics Corp. v. Harris, supra; Collida v. Collida, supra; Dessommes v. Dessommes, supra.*

criminatory as against other plan participants. Furthermore, to the extent benefits were paid in such a case to one group of participants, i.e. a divorced participant and his spouse, and not to other participants who continued to work and who were not divorced, an abuse of pension fund assets would occur which is potentially detrimental to all participants.

A court may also direct a plan to abide by future orders dividing plan benefits or requiring payment of the community or marital property share to the employee's former spouse.[71]

There is some authority that a court may also order a plan not to honor an employee's election concerning the *form* of the pension benefits. *In re Marriage of Lionberger* (1979) 97 Cal.App.3d 56, 158 Cal.Rptr. 535, *cert. denied* (1980) 446 U.S. 951 upheld a trial court's order precluding the plan from honoring any election by the employee to receive a joint and survivor annuity (for the benefit of a subsequent surviving spouse) because such an election would reduce the monthly income payable during the employee's life, thereby reducing the former spouse's court-awarded interest in the benefits. This holding is questionable because the court's order against the plan raises a potential conflict with the ERISA requirements that a plan offer its employees the option of selecting a qualified joint and survivor annuity.

In a similar vein, at least one court has ordered a plan to cancel a previously elected form of benefit, even though the employee has already retired and benefits are in pay status. In *Ball v. Revised Retirement Plan, Etc.* (D.Colo. 1981) 522 F. Supp. 718, the employee had retired and elected to receive his benefits in the form of a joint and survivor annuity with his then-spouse named as survivor. If he had not elected the joint and survivor annuity, he could have selected a life annuity, which would have provided him with 45% more benefits during his lifetime. Subsequent to his retirement, the parties signed a divorce settlement agreement under which the wife was released from further obligation to support her disabled husband, in exchange for assigning to him all of her present and future rights to any portion of his retirement benefits. Based on an ERISA preemption argument, the plan refused to cancel the joint and survivor annuity and pay the retiree from the date of divorce the additional 45% he would receive under a life annuity. The court held ". . . that *valid* domestic relations decrees authorizing the transfer of pension benefits in satisfaction of support obligations are implied exemptions to ERISA §§1144(a) [preemption clause], §1056(d)(1) [antiassignment provision]" (emphasis added).

The court in *Ball* did not address the significant issue of the impact on plan funding of changing the form of benefits already in pay status or the issue of the court rewriting the plan contract.[72]

In summary, federal law does not preclude enforcement of state court orders requiring retirement plans to pay directly to the nonemployee spouse his or her community or marital share of the employee's benefits if, as and when the employee receives benefit payments from the plan. The extent to which a state court can interfere in other aspects of plan administration remains unclear.

Plan Administration of Dissolution and Divorce Matters

Obligation of Plan Administrators to Provide Information to Nonemployee Spouses

As noted previously, *Stone* held that a nonemployee spouse is a participant in a plan under ERISA §502(a)(1)(B) for purposes of bringing suit against the plan, and *Reyes* held the nonemployee spouse to be a participant for the purpose of receiving attorneys fees in his or her action against a plan. In light of these holdings, a nonemployee spouse *may* be entitled to the same information to which a participant is entitled under ERISA §§104, 105 (i.e., summary plan description, annual reports and statement of accrued benefits). At least one court has held—without specifically relying on ERISA—that where a nonemployee spouse has been awarded a portion of the benefits, the plan owes the same duty of disclosure to the nonemployee spouse as it would to the employee spouse and must reply to a request for information within a reasonable time.[73]

Until a divorce action is filed, however, it is unlikely that a plan has a duty to disclose, without the employee's consent, benefit information to the nonemployee spouse. Moreover, such a practice

---

71. *Carpenters Pension Trust, Etc. v. Kronschnabel* (C.D.Cal. 1978) 460 F. Supp. 978, *affirmed* (9 Cir. 1980) 632 F.2d 745.

72. See *Monsanto Co. v. Ford* (E.D.Mo. 1981) 534 F. Supp. 51; *In re Marriage of Brown* (1976) 15 Cal. 3d 838, 544 P.2d 561; *Benson v. City of Los Angeles* (1963) 60 Cal.2d 355, 384 P.2d 649.

73. *Mendenco, Inc. v. Myklebust* (Tex. 1981) 615 S.W.2d 187.

may violate the employee's legitimate expectation of privacy. Once an action has been filed, however, the nonemployee spouse may obtain information through normal state law discovery proceedings (e.g., subpoena, interrogatories or written deposition). Once the nonemployee spouse has used an appropriate discovery process, the plan must provide the requested benefit information in a timely manner or risk contempt.

The plan administrator may be asked to provide the nonemployee spouse some or all of the following information: the date the employee first became covered by the plan and his or her past service date, if any; the number of years/months/units of credited service at date of separation, divorce or trial (whichever is applicable in the relevant state); if a defined contribution plan, the account balance as of date of separation, divorce or trial, current account balance, and the current contribution rate to the plan; if a defined benefit plan, the accrued benefit at date of separation, divorce or trial,[74] when it is normally payable, the earliest date it is payable and any early commencement actuarial reduction applicable, all based on the current version of the plan; whether the account balance or accrued benefit is vested and the current vested percentage, if any; whether the plan is a contributory or noncontributory; whether the benefit is currently in pay status and, if so, the amount and method of payment and the date of retirement or other termination of service; applicable current eligibility, break in service, vesting and early and normal retirement plan provisions; and a copy of the current plan and summary plan description.

Where the request is general in nature, the plan administrator should attempt to provide sufficient information for the parties and the court to arrive at an appropriate disposition of the marital interests in the employee's benefits. In any event, whatever information is given should be accurate. The plan administrator may want to develop a special form of letter to use when providing an employee or nonemployee spouse with benefit information for use in a divorce proceeding.

Administrative Problems

As more and more states exercise jurisdiction over pension plans in connection with domestic relations matters, plan administrators and their legal counsel will have to establish procedures designed to minimize a state divorce court's interference in plan administration and to protect the plan from having to pay the same benefit more than once or having to pay to the employee and former spouse combined more than the employee otherwise is entitled to. The prospect of a lawsuit against the plan by an individual such as a spouse or former spouse claiming an adverse interest to the participant or the participant's designated beneficiary is perhaps the more serious of the two challenges.[75]

Recognizing the need of plan administrators, trustees and insurers for some protection from liability when making benefit and related payments to those persons apparently entitled to them, certain states have enacted so-called facility of payment statutes.[76] For example, California Civil Code Section 5106 provides in relevant part:

§5106. Employee retirement, death, benefit or savings plan; payment or refund; discharge from adverse claims; notice of claim

(a) Notwithstanding the provisions of Sections 5105 and 5125, whenever payment or refund is made to a participant or his beneficiary or estate pursuant to a written employee benefit plan governed by the Employee Retirement Income Security Act of 1974 (P.L. 93-406), as amended, such payment or refund shall fully discharge the employer and any administrator, fiduciary or insurance company making such payment or refund from all adverse claims thereto unless, before such payment or refund is made, the administrator of such plan has received at its principal place of business within this state, written notice by or on be-

---

74. It should be unnecessary and, in fact, is undesirable for the plan administrator to have the plan's actuary provide either the employee or the nonemployee spouse with an estimate of the actuarial present value of the accrued benefits earned during the marriage. Providing such information can be costly to the plan, may not conform to state law rules for valuing pension rights in a divorce and can result in the plan's actuary being called to testify in the divorce action. The employee and nonemployee spouse should hire their own experts to estimate the actuarial present value of the employee's benefits.

75. For example, a former spouse claiming his or her court-awarded community or marital property interest or claiming his or her community or marital property interest on death of the employee as against a designated beneficiary or a present or other former spouse of the employee.

76. See, e.g., Arizona Revised Statutes §20-1125; California Civil Code §5106; Louisiana Revised Statutes §638; Nevada Revised Statutes §123.240; New Mexico Statutes Annotated §58-19-1; Texas Revised Civil Statutes, Art. 5221d; Washington Revised Code §49.64.030.

half of some other person that such other person claims to be entitled to such payment or refund or some part thereof. Nothing contained in this section shall affect any claim or right to any such payment or refund or part thereof as between all persons other than the employer and the fiduciary or insurance company making such payment or refund. The terms "participant," "beneficiary," "employee benefit plan," "employer," "fiduciary" and "administrator" shall have the same meaning as provided in Section 3 of the Employee Retirement Income Security Act of 1974 (P.L. 93-406), as amended.

In the absence of an express statutory provision facilitating payment of benefits, a plan administrator or trustee may protect the plan in several ways. Lack of notice of the adverse claim may provide the plan with some insulation from liability for the payment. Where the plan has received notice of an adverse claim, the plan may withhold or suspend payments to the employee until the matter is resolved, and/or the plan may interplead the funds with a court for a judicial determination of the rightful recipient.

In many cases, the employee's divorce will precede his actual retirement by many years. This situation will require the plan administrator to have the capability to "remember" when the employee applies for benefits that because of a prior court order or other notice of adverse claim, the case requires special handling. Accordingly, plan administrators should adapt or develop their recordkeeping systems to accommodate the additional obligations that these state court orders may impose. These obligations may include: withholding current benefit payments to the retired employee until the marital property issue is resolved; obtaining court approval before beginning benefit payments to the employee; notifying the nonemployee former spouse of the employee's application for benefits; monitoring employee elections under the plan to ensure compliance with any court-imposed restrictions; and issuance of two benefit checks instead of one. Finally, legal counsel should consider developing a standard form of court order acceptable to the plan that the parties can use in a divorce proceeding where state law authorizes the court to order a plan to make benefit payments directly to the nonemployee spouse when the employee retires.

Whatever administrative and legal procedures plan administrators decide to use in handling marital claims against the plan, the authors, after eight years of representing pension plans in such matters, have generally found the best approach is to remain neutral in the domestic conflict and, to the extent possible, cooperate with the parties.

The Legal Right to Die

BY DAVID L. RIDER and
MARIA F. MELCHIORI

Preface

In our ever-present struggle against death, modern medical science has created its own peculiar horror: "A technology that can sustain a human being in a permanent and irreversible coma for an indefinite period of time . . . 'the possibility of being maintained in limbo, in a sterile room, by machines controlled by strangers.'" [1]

This article is an informal encapsulation of a lecture given to an audience consisting mostly of labor and management benefit fund trustees and professional fund administrators at the 1982 Annual Conference. It presents an analysis of the individual's right to receive or refuse life-sustaining treatment and explores how a resolution of this controversial issue impacts on multiemployer benefit funds. [2]

TERMINATION OF THE life cycle presents an age-old problem that we as members of Western civilization have been uniquely unsuccessful in confronting and resolving. The problem has come to the forefront recently as a result of media coverage of stories involving the terminally ill patient whose family must seek court approval to "pull the plug," the defective newborn whose nourishment is withheld per parental instructions, the emotional polarization of "pro-choice" versus "right-to-life" groups respecting abortion matters and the execution of criminals via injection.

Mr. Rider is a member of the lawfirm of Rider, Drake, Sommers & Loeb, P.C. and is engaged in the general practice of law. His personal fields of specialization are corporate law, labor law, hospital and medical services delivery law, pension, profit-sharing and fringe benefit law, and he is counsel to the board of trustees of several multiemployer trust funds and tax-qualified charitable organizations. Mr. Rider has lectured on fringe benefit fund issues; administrative techniques and fiduciary responsibilities. He is admitted to the bars of all courts of record of the State of New York, United States Supreme Court, and the United States District Court for the Southern District of New York. He earned his B.A. degree at Cornell University and his LL.B. degree at Yale Law School.

Mrs. Melchiori is an associate with Rider, Drake, Sommers and Loeb, P.C. in the corporate law department. Prior to joining that firm, she was associated with the firm of Proskauer, Rose, Goetz & Mendelsohn. Mrs. Melchiori received a B.A., magna cum laude, from Hunter College of the City University of New York with departmental honors in psychology. She received a J.D. from the New York Law School and was awarded the Elsberg Prize in contract law. While attending law school, she served as Notes and Comments editor and Book Review editor of the Law Review. *Mrs. Melchiori is a member of the Tri-County Women's, Orange County and Newburgh City Bar Associations. She is admitted to the bars of all courts of record of the State of New York and to the United States District Court for the Southern and Eastern Districts of New York.*

---

1. *Eichner v. Dillon,* 73 A.D.2d 431, 447-48; 426 N.Y.S.2d 517, 531 (2d Dept. 1980), *modified sub nom. In re Storar,* 52 N.Y.2d 363; 420 N.E.2d 64; 438 N.Y.S.2d 266 (1981).

2. Employee benefit plans, in general, serve to protect the individual beneficiary from financial disaster resulting from a medical emergency and to provide for retirement needs and even death benefits to a participant's family. Sources of funds for the plans consist mostly of contributions from employers and employees. The trustees, or plan trust board, hold legal title to the fund and administer it for the benefit of the participants or beneficiaries. There are tax advantages to the plans and competitive advantages to the employers instituting them. They have been declared a proper subject for collective bargaining and are sought actively by labor unions.

At the other side of the spectrum, also on today's front pages, we are reading about the ability of science to prolong life—sometimes indefinitely—through organ transplants, the completely artificial heart and the use of respirators, kidney dialysis machines, chemotherapy and other drugs, etc. Life is being created and prolonged through artificial means, but not without enormous cost, both economic and emotional.[3]

These recent developments impact strongly on employee benefit plans because these plans frequently are unable to cover rising claim expenses brought about by ultrasophisticated treatments. In fact, carriers and their underwriting departments have labeled claims based on these extended treatment modalities "shock claims." By their very nature, they demand new measures of cost containment, especially in light of the fact that although contributions to the plans may be fixed contractually for specified periods of time, the cost of medical services reflects current inflation rates. In this regard, the combined advice of investment analysts, actuaries, medical plan specialists and lawyers provides the definitional parameters that determine the extent to which a certain benefit will or will not be a covered expense of a particular plan and whether certain illnesses resulting in shock claims will be fully or partially insured under that plan.

Clearly, welfare funds must now be reviewed to update and define terms such as "terminal illness," "life-sustaining treatment," "heroic measures" and "extraordinary care," and to analyze the objectives of the particular plan considering the resources available and where the most benefit can be provided.[4] Obviously, how a particular term is defined in a benefit plan impacts on the plan's cost and on what benefits it makes available to its participants.

These recent medical developments also have given rise to a myriad of questions and opinions from philosophical, religious and jurisprudential viewpoints regarding society's interest in preserving and protecting life and the individual's right to exercise some measure of control over all aspects of his existence.[5]

The law concerns itself with illness in general, and specifically the terminally ill, because it has been a given that illness almost always affects society at large through the physical infection of healthy populations. Society must impose guidelines and controls to contain the spread of disease. In primitive times, these controls may have been as simple as the bells that lepers were required to wear when they ventured outdoors.[6] In modern times, these controls bear labels like "quarantine," "isolation ward," "antiseptic," "sterile" and "public health laws." The government, however, does not have unbridled authority to impose these controls arbitrarily. The individual's right to privacy, i.e., the right to be free from bodily intrusion, intervenes and employee benefits plans—again—feel the impact.

The Right of Privacy

" 'No right is more sacred, or is more carefully guarded than the right of the individual to possess and control his own person.' "[7] In fact, Anglo-American common law starts from the fundamental legal proposition that the human body is the exclusive personal property of its possessor and is inviolate without his consent.[8] The actionable torts of assault and battery, for example, are based

---

3. See, e.g., Haney, "Medical Costs," *Poughkeepsie J.*, Oct. 11, 1982, at 1, col. 1. (Annual individual cost of kidney dialysis, $25,000; heart bypass surgery, $20,000; implanting a pacemaker, $18,000; total spent annually by Americans in health care, $287 billion.)

4. "Extraordinary care" has been defined as medical care employing support systems that do not result in any appreciable benefit to the patient and cause an unnecessary prolongation of the natural process of dying. *In re Fox*, 102 Misc. 2d, 184, 193; 423 N.Y.S.2d 580, 586-87 (Nassau Cty. 1979).

See also Nelson, "Doctors Debate Right to Stop 'Heroic' Effort to Keep Elderly Alive," *Wall St. J.*, Sept. 7, 1982, at 1, col. 2: "For a paralyzed stroke victim in her 80s, even an ordinary nasal feeding tube could be considered an 'extraordinary' measure that, by indefinitely sustaining life, merely prolongs suffering."

5. "The State has a legitimate interest in protecting the lives of its citizens. It may require that they submit to medical procedures in order to eliminate a health threat to the community. . . . It may, by statute, prohibit them from engaging in specified activities, including medical procedures which are inherently hazardous to their lives. . . ."

In re Storar, 52 N.Y.2d 363, 377; 420 N.E.2d 64, 71; 438 N.Y.S.2d 266, 273 (1981) (citations omitted).

6. The bells were used as a warning in lieu of the cry "unclean, unclean." Leviticus 13.

Thus, an individual cannot rightfully refuse vaccinations that, if not administered, might imperil the health of the community. Treatment for contagious diseases may be compulsory.

Compare *Application of President and Directors of Georgetown Coll.*, 331 F.2d 1000 (D.C.Cir. 1964) (mother of seven month old infant not allowed to abandon child; life-saving blood transfusion ordered) with *In re Osborne*, 294 A.2d 372 (D.C. 1972) *infra* note 21.

7. D. Meyers, *Medico-Legal Implications of Death and Dying* §10:1 (1981) (footnote omitted).

8. *Id.*

on the fundamental concept of human bodily integrity and the right to be free from nonconsensual touching.[9] Additionally, a constitutional right of privacy has been discerned within the penumbras of the Bill of Rights, specifically from the language in the First, Fourth, Fifth, Ninth and Fourteenth Amendments to the United States Constitution.[10]

The freedom to care for one's health and person falls within this constitutional right of privacy and, according to Justice Douglas, "has no more conspicuous place than in the physician/patient relationship."[11] Thus, engaging a physician does not confer "carte blanche" privileges to prescribe whatever treatment, surgery or therapy the doctor may see fit to order. Pursuant to the doctrine of "informed consent," physicians have an affirmative duty to reveal to the patient not only what his condition is, but how it should be treated and what the risks of the treatment will be. The patient, in turn, has a right to determine whether to consent to any treatment or procedure. In fact, absent consent, most medical service institutions and physicians will not treat patients.

The courts, in turn, have extended this right of privacy to encompass a patient's decision to decline life-sustaining medical treatment under certain circumstances.[12] Since these circumstances are not, however, very clear, when faced with making a life/death determination, the question becomes, "whose *role* is it anyway?" *not* "whose life is it anyway?"[13] Why is the question, "whose role"? It is because decisions concerning a patient's treatment are being made by the patient (if capable), the doctor, the family or a guardian and even the courts, through a "substituted judgment" approach, or any combination of the above. Meanwhile, the administrator of the benefit plan or welfare fund, which may be paying for the particular treatment that a patient wishes to decline or seeks to discontinue, is powerless to intervene if the plan has made no specific provision to deal with this set of circumstances.

Defining Death

Traditionally, "death" has been defined by physicians as "a total stoppage of the circulation of the blood, and a cessation of the animal and vital functions consequent thereon, such as respiration, pulsation, etc."[14] This reliance on a purely medical definition itself creates clerical and jurisprudential conflicts, as it forces members of those disciplines to work with certain fixed concepts. The "brain death" definition, which is today followed by most states and physicians, is "the irreversible cessation of all functions of the entire brain, including the brain stem."[15] This irreversible cessation of functions, however, does not occur simultaneously. The brain dies in stages. The brain stem, which controls the vegetative body functions—i.e., breathing, heart rate—is the last to cease functioning; however, the upper brain, that which controls the cognitive functions that make one conscious and aware and provides thought, memory, personality and intellect, dies first.[16]

Where a patient with a brain injury is kept alive long enough through modern resuscitative and supportive measures, there generally is a tendency to recover some function adequate for a vegetative existence. The classic example is Karen Ann Quinlan, who has been leading such an existence for the past seven years since her respirator was disconnected—an event that was expected to cause her death.[17] Furthermore, because "right-to-die" cases are not decided based on a quality-of-life standard, there is a very strong probability that such a patient will continue to "live" even though the continuation of life in such instance may very well be against the patient's wishes and those of his family and present tremendous monetary cost and emotional expense.[18]

---

9. See W. Prosser, *Law of Torts* §20 (4th ed. 1971).
10. *Roe v. Wade,* 410 U.S. 113, 152-54 (1973); *Griswold v. Connecticut,* 381 U.S. 479 (1965).
11. *Doe v. Bolton,* 410 U.S. 179, 219 (1973).
12. *Canterbury v. Spence,* 464 F.2d 772 (D.C.Cir.), *cert. denied,* 409 U.S. 1064 (1972).
13. B. Clark, *Whose Life Is It Anyway?* (1972).
14. *Black's Law Dictionary* 488 (rev. 4th ed. 1968).
15. Lasden, "Coming Out of Coma," *N.Y. Times,* June 27, 1982 (Magazine), at 31, col. 1. The "brain death" definition has been proposed by the Presidential Commission and has the backing of the American Medical Association and the American Bar Association. Brain death diagnoses, in summary, may be made where there is no response to intense stimuli, no movement or breathing, no reflexes and a flat EEG.
16. See D. Meyers, *Medico-Legal Implications of Death and Dying* §4:2 (1981).
17. *In re Quinlan,* 70 N.J. 10, 25; 355 A.2d 647, 656, *cert. denied sub nom. Garger v. New Jersey,* 429 U.S. 922 (1976).
18. *Superintendent of Belchertown v. Saikewicz,* 373 Mass. 729, 246-47; 370 N.E.2d 417, 428 (Hampshire 1977). (Court firmly rejects equating the value of life with any measure of its quality—i.e., an "impaired" life will receive as much protection as a healthy, normal life.)
See also *Berman v. Allan,* 80 N.J. 421, 429-30; 404 A.2d 8, 12-13 (1979). (In an action for "wrongful life," court refused to accept that a mongoloid child would have been better off had she never been born, noting that "[o]ne of the most deeply held beliefs of our society is that life—whether experienced with or without a major physical handicap—is more precious than nonlife.") (citations omitted.)

The Law

There is no constitutionally guaranteed "right to die."[19] All of us will, of course, with or without a constitutional right. The problem being addressed is societal interference with the process and how that interference impacts on benefit funds and fund beneficiaries. A fund may wish to provide for terminal care at home or at a hospice.[20] However, the patient making this election may need a court order to discontinue certain life-support equipment in order to effect the physical move, where his right to control this decision is challenged by society, by health care institutions and by the state.[21] Conduct resulting in a death, whether by commission or omission, implicates homicide statutes.[22] The interest of the state in preserving life, protecting innocent third parties (such as dependent children and incompetents) and maintaining the integrity of the medical profession[23] competes with the individual's choice to terminate life-saving treatment and will prove to be sufficiently compelling at times to override that choice.[24]

Consider, for example, the case of Abe Perlmutter, who in 1977, at age 73, lingered in a hospital bed afflicted with the immobilizing effects of Lou Gehrig's disease.[25] He breathed only with the aid of a respirator, and simple speech was an "extreme effort." His doctor had advised him that the condition was irreversible and that he would soon die. Without a respirator it was expected that he would die within an hour.[26] He remained, however, in full possession of his mental faculties—i.e., Abe Perlmutter was mentally and thus legally competent.[27] He and his family were in accord that the respirator be removed, and he even tried to remove it himself repeatedly, only to have the hospital staff reconnect it each time the alarm sounded.[28]

Having no choice, Perlmutter petitioned the Florida trial court, at a bedside hearing, for an order permitting the respirator to be removed, which the court granted. Nevertheless, an appeal was taken by the state, which took the position that its duty to preserve life overrode the choice made by Abe Perlmutter for himself and, further, that termination of the "supportive care" being given to him constituted "an unlawful killing of a human being" that would expose the hospital to civil and criminal liability.[29] On September 13, 1978 the appellate court affirmed the trial court's decision based on Perlmutter's constitutional right of privacy and subsequently denied a rehearing on the matter.

The state then petitioned for writ of *certiorari* to the Florida Supreme Court. Although Perlmutter died during the state supreme court proceedings, the decision of that court, issued on January 17, 1980, affirmed his right to have the respirator removed—almost three years after Abe Perlmutter first tried to disconnect himself from the respirator and after considerable emotional and monetary expense to his family.[30]

---

19. *John F. Kennedy Memorial Hospital v. Heston,* 58 N.J. 576, 580; 279 A.2d 670, 672 (1971).

20. Hospices may provide either inpatient facilities for the terminally ill or in-home services. Full medical coverage to hospice patients recently has been approved by Congress. *Evening News,* Sept. 13, 1982, at 6A, col. 1.

21. See notes 22-32 and accompanying text, *infra.*

22. In New York State, for example, deaths must be registered within 72 hours; the medical examiner's office or the county coroner investigates all deaths occurring without medical assistance. N.Y. Pub. Health L. §§4140-4143 (McKinney 1977).
See also *N.Y. Penal L.* §§120.30 and 120.35 (McKinney 1977) (Promoting a suicide attempt is classified as a felony).

23. Meyers points out that arguments respecting the ethical integrity of the medical profession are made by lawyers, as "[t]he ethical integrity of [that] profession is not affected where a competent adult rejects . . . even life-saving treatment." The physician's duty is to inform his patient about the outcome of the treatment and to abide by the patient's decision. D. Meyers, *Medico-Legal Implications of Death and Dying* §10:16 (1981).

24. See, e.g., *In re Osborne,* 294 A.2d 372 (D.C. 1972). In this instance, a Jehovah's Witness, a father, was permitted to refuse life-saving blood transfusions even where his minor children would lose their sole provider as a result of his death. The opinion, however, points out that the children would be provided for by relatives and would not become wards of the state.

25. *Satz v. Perlmutter,* 362 So.2d 160 (4th Dist. 1978), *aff'd,* 379 So.2d 359 (Fla. 1980).

---

26. *Satz v. Perlmutter,* 362 So.2d 160, 161 (4th Dis. 1978).

27. *Id.*

28. *Id.*

29. *Id.* at 162.
Justice Meade's opinion in *In re Fox,* 102 Misc. 2d 184, 205; 423 N.Y.S.2d 580, 594 (Nassau Cty. 1979), *modified,* 73 A.D.2d 431; 426 N.Y.S.2d 517 (2d Dept. 1980), *modified sub nom. In re Storar,* 52 N.Y.2d 363; 420 N.E.2d 64; 438 N.Y.S.2d 266 (1981), points out that suicide at common law required one to " 'purposefully set in motion a death-producing agent with the specified intent of effecting his own destruction, or, at least serious injury.' " (citing R. Byrn) Since a terminally ill patient lacks the specific intent to destroy himself through a "death-producing agent" over which he has no control, he cannot be found guilty of committing suicide. Furthermore, no criminal responsibility should attach to a person authorized to remove a respirator, for instance, since there is no suicide to "aid or abet." The patient and doctor in such an instance are merely letting nature take its course.

30. *Satz v. Perlmutter,* 379 So.2d 359, 361 (Fla. 1980).

The Florida Supreme Court, in rendering its decision, made a very important observation, noting that "the issue at bar, and all its ramifications, is 'fraught with complexity and encompasses the interests of the law, both civil and criminal, medical ethics and social morality; it is not one which is well-suited for resolution in an adversary proceeding.' "[31] In other words, this is not the type of decision that should be made through the judicial process but should be addressed by the legislature.[31a]

More recently in New York, on October 8, 1982, Peter Cinque, age 41, who required kidney dialysis treatments to live and whose legs had been amputated because of long term diabetes, requested that these treatments be discontinued to allow him to spend his last days at home. His family fully supported his decision. After being withdrawn from pain-killing drugs that might cloud his judgment, Peter Cinque signed forms refusing treatment.[32] The hospital, "[acting] in the best tradition of hospital-patient care," sought a court order to continue the treatments.[33] Mr. Cinque's family was in turn forced to seek an order directing the hospital to honor the patient's request.

On October 22, after two days of testimony that revealed "clear and convincing evidence beyond a reasonable doubt . . . that Peter Cinque made an informed and rational and knowing decision to forego dialysis treatment . . .," the hospital was ordered to discontinue the dialysis.[34] An hour later, Peter Cinque died. The hospital, through its attorney, has made it clear that whether the hospital will seek court orders countermanding a patient's direction to discontinue treatments will be decided on a case by case basis.[35]

The resulting picture is a distressing one indeed for individuals and society as a whole. Decisions in "right-to-die" cases are and continue to be rendered on a case by case basis. The result is substantial disparity among jurisdictions and sometimes within the same jurisdiction where the facts differ somewhat. This situation is best illustrated by an examination of some of the other leading cases.

The seminal case is *In re Quinlan.*[36] In April 1975, Karen Ann Quinlan, then age 21, lapsed into a coma as a result of respiratory arrest and required the use of a mechanical respirator to remain alive.[37] Her condition later became fetal-like, her body emaciated and grotesque.[38] Her father sought to be appointed guardian of her person, so that he could request on her behalf that the respirator be disconnected, a request that Karen was legally incompetent and physically incapable of making for herself.[39] This request was denied by the New Jersey Superior Court and an appeal was taken to the New Jersey Supreme Court. That court, relying on the constitutional right of privacy as the basis for withholding or withdrawing life support from a terminal patient, approved the appointment of Joseph Quinlan as Karen's guardian, and let the ultimate decision concerning Karen's treatment be made by her guardian, her family, her doctor and a hospital "ethics committee."[40]

---

31. *Id.* at 360.
31a. "Living will" legislation has failed to be enacted in the State of Florida.
32. Barron, "Diabetic Dies After L.I. Judge Stops His Life-Sustaining Care," *N.Y. Times,* Oct. 23, 1982, at 1, col. 2.
33. *Id.* at 10, col. 2. More likely, the hospital acted in the best tradition of safeguarding its own best interests.
34. *Id.* at 1, col. 3.
35. *Id.* at 10, col. 3. Judge Arthur Spatt, in his opinion, agrees that "[s]uch a decision must be evaluated and determined on a case to case basis, depending on the factual situation in each particular case." *In re Lydia E. Hall Hosp.,* No. 82-23730, *slip op.* at 10 (Nassau Cty. Oct. 22, 1982).
Interestingly, the cases do not address the issue of the institution's standing before the courts to request that treatment be continued. Discussions with attorneys participating in this area reveal that if both sides tried to litigate the standing issue, more precious time and money would be spent by the patient's family. In any event, the hospital may always allege that a member of the patient's family wishes to continue treatments. Therefore, the issue is overlooked while the more crucial emotional issue is litigated. Additionally, the patient's family must also deal with the publicity aspects of the case. The press, in its quest for access to all of the facts, will attempt to intrude into every aspect of the proceeding, including demanding access to bedside hearings. The pressures on the patient's family at such a time are, indeed, enormous.
36. 70 N.J. 10; 355 A.2d 647 (1976), *cert. denied sub nom. Garger v. New Jersey,* 429 U.S. 922 (1976).
37. *Id.* at 23; 355 A.2d 653-54.
38. *Id.;* 355 A.2d 655.
39. In the law, there is a presumption that an individual who is "under disability," i.e., under age or incompetent for some other reason, requires special protection and may have interests adverse to those of the person making a request on his behalf or seeking to administer his affairs. Accordingly, the court appoints a guardian *ad litem* to protect the interests of the minor or incompetent and whose duty is without conflict, his only charge being the best interests of his ward. In this instance, on receipt of the petition by Karen's father, the court appointed a guardian *ad litem* to represent Karen's interest, which was presumed to be possibly adverse to her father's interest.
40. *Id.* at 54-55; 355 A.2d 671-72.

Not all courts have followed the *Quinlan* approach, however. Massachusetts, for example, although it recognizes the constitutional right to privacy as the basis for a terminal patient's right to refuse treatment, at first required that decisions concerning the incompetent terminally ill be made through the adversary system, with the court substituting its judgment for that of the patient's after evaluating all the alternatives.[41] This "substituted judgment" approach as developed in *Saikewicz* called for a time-consuming and costly court procedure that effectively tied the doctors' hands pending judicial approval of decisions to remove life-saving treatment.[42]

In a subsequent Massachusetts case, *In re Dinnerstein,* the court clarified its requirement for mandatory judicial intervention.[43] The court explained that judicial approval is required when a measure of choice exists concerning the result of a certain treatment. For example, when the result of the treatment merely suspends the act of dying, no approval is required. However, when the treatment may result in a remission of symptoms permitting a return "towards a normal, functioning, integrated existence," judicial approval must be sought. Thus, where a patient suffers from an "unremitting, incurable, mortal illness," the decision to withhold treatment may be made by the doctor, the patient, if competent, or the family and the patient's guardian.[44] Two years later, another Massachusetts decision reaffirmed the need for judicial proceedings to make a final determination in cases involving the withdrawal of life-prolonging treatment, such as dialysis.[45]

It is the policy of our court system, under the doctrine of *stare decisis,* to report and to adhere to those principles of law in a given jurisdiction that apply to a certain state of facts and to apply them to all future cases that have substantially the same facts.[46] However, as stated by New York's Appellate Division in *Eichner v. Dillon,* this "venerable doctrine of *stare decisis* becomes ineffectual in that it suggests institutional reliance on old answers at a time where the questions themselves have passed beyond the imagination of the judicial sages who formulated the precedents."[47]

Eichner v. Dillon arose in October 1979, when Brother Joseph Fox, an 83 year old Roman Catholic priest, member of the Society of Mary and a teacher, suffered a cardiac arrest during surgery for a hernia. The resulting loss of oxygen to his brain caused him to fall into a permanent vegetative state that would eventually lead to his death.[48] In this instance, it was the hospital's refusal to turn off his life-support systems and let nature take its course that compelled his superior and close friend, Father Philip Eichner, to petition the court to appoint him "committee of the person and property of Brother Fox."[49]

Father Eichner's application was in the form of an "order to show cause" to be served on all interested parties requiring them to appear at a hearing to literally show cause to the court why an order should not be made permitting his appointment as guardian and authorizing the removal of the respirator. The application for the order was supported by the affidavits of three physicians and affidavits of the relatives of Brother Fox. A guardian *ad litem* for Brother Fox was immediately appointed by the judge and a hearing scheduled for the end of the following month.[50]

---

41. *Superintendent of Belchertown v. Saikewicz,* 373 Mass. 728; 370 N.E.2d 417 (1977). Saikewicz was a 67 year old severely retarded patient at a state mental health facility suffering from an incurable form of leukemia. His mental age was 2.5 years. The facility petitioned the court to appoint a guardian who could make decisions about his care. Treatment of the leukemia with chemotherapy was in question. After hearing recommendations from the hospital physicians and the guardian, it was ruled that treatment with chemotherapy drugs not be commenced in view of the patient's age, his failure to understand and the suffering caused by the treatments.

42. *Id.* at 755-59; 370 N.E.2d at 433-34.

43. 380 N.E.2d 134 (Norfolk 1978).

44. *Id.* at 138-39. Shirley Dinnerstein was a 67 year old widow rendered incompetent by Alzheimer's disease. Her children and doctor sought court approval to enter a lawful "no code" order in her chart. This order would effectively prevent any resuscitation attempts should cardiac or respiratory arrest occur. The court noted that such approval was unnecessary, holding that it is "peculiarly within the competence of the medical profession" to decide what is appropriate to "ease the imminent passing of an irreversibly terminally ill patient. . . ." *Id.* at 139.

---

45. *In re Spring,* 405 N.E.2d 115, 122 (Franklin 1980). Earle Spring, age 77, was suffering from end-stage kidney disease requiring dialysis. He was senile, resisted the treatments and required sedation. His wife and son requested that dialysis be discontinued, a decision that the Supreme Judicial Court affirmed and that could not have been delegated to any other body once presented to the court.

46. *Moore v. City of Albany,* 98 N.Y. 396, 410 (1885).

47. 73 A.D.2d 431, 447; 426 N.Y.S.2d 517, 531 (2d Dept. 1980), *modified sub nom. In re Storar,* 52 N.Y.2d 363; 420 N.E.2d 64; 438 N.Y.S.2d 266 (1981).

48. *In re Eichner,* 102 Misc. 2d 184, 187; 423 N.Y.S.2d 580, 583 (Nassau Cty. 1979).

49. *Id.*

50. *Id.* at 188; 423 N.Y.S.2d at 584. See also *supra* note 39.

At the hearing, Father Eichner and the guardian were each represented by counsel. The district attorney appeared representing the state's interest in preserving life. An intensive investigation followed; substantial testimony of the witnesses was taken and written briefs were submitted.[51] The trial court took careful note of all that transpired, including Brother Fox's participation in discussions with his students concerning the *Quinlan* case and his expressed desire not to be kept alive were he to find himself in such a situation. On December 6, 1979, the court rendered its decision appointing Father Eichner a committee on behalf of Brother Fox. It directed that, after notice to the district attorney and additional examinations of Brother Fox by four doctors—two chosen by Father Eichner and two by the district attorney—and determination that there was no medical possibility that Brother Fox would ever regain "any sapient or cognitive function or capacity," the respirator be removed.[52]

The district attorney appealed on the following grounds: (1) Absent specific legislative authority, the court had no power to order the withdrawal of the respirator. (2) Even if the court had such power, the incompetent patient has no such right. (3) Even if the incompetent had such a right, Brother Fox's prior expressions on the *Quinlan* matter were hearsay and accordingly inadmissible.[53] Meanwhile, Brother Fox died on January 24, 1980. Some two months later, the appellate division rendered its decision affirming the supreme court.

The appellate division decision recognized that the judicial process has generally deferred to the medical profession in establishing guidelines to these questions. Additionally, it pointed out that in making its determination, no distinction should be made between competent and incompetent patients, something with which the New York Court of Appeals later disagreed.[54] The court then went on to state that although it must rely on the medical profession in deciding the medical aspects of these problems, societal interests in these instances are so great that the courts have no choice but to intervene and examine each case on a patient by patient basis. It then proceeded to outline a six step procedure to be followed in these situations.[55]

Shortly after *Eichner,* the New York Appellate Division considered the matter of *Storar*.[56] John Storar, age 52 but with a mental age of one and one-half years, was suffering from cancer of the bladder, which had metastasized to other parts of his body.[57] He bled internally, and blood transfusions were necessary to prevent a speedy death as a

---

51. *Id.* at 188; 423 N.Y.S.2d at 587. As is customary in matters involving public interest groups, briefs were submitted by the New York State Right to Life Committee, Inc., the Human Life Amendment Group and the Catholic Lawyers Guild of the Diocese of Rockville Center supporting Father Eichner's position and reasoning that Brother Fox could be removed from the artificial life-support systems.

52. *Id.* at 213; 423 N.Y.S.2d at 599. The opinion noted, with interest, that no suicide was involved. Brother Fox had not intended to effect his own destruction nor had he set in motion his own death-producing agent. Removal of the respirator could therefore not constitute aiding and abetting suicide under New York's Penal Law. *Id.* at 205; 423 N.Y.S.2d at 594.

53. *Eichner v. Dillon,* 73 A.D.2d 431, 465-66; 426 N.Y.S.2d 517, 530-31 (2d Dept. 1980).

54. See *In re Storar,* 52 N.Y.2d 363; 420 N.E.2d 64; 438 N.Y.S.2d 266 (1981), a case with facts somewhat similar to those in *Quinlan* (see text accompanying notes 36-40, *supra*). One would think that two neighboring sophisticated Eastern states would be of similar minds in reaching a decision based on two similar fact patterns.

55. *Eichner v. Dillon,* 73 A.D.2d 431, 476-77; 426 N.Y.S.2d 517, 550 (2d Dept. 1980).

The six step procedure is:
1. Physician certifies patient is terminally ill; patient is in a coma and prospects of recovery of brain functions are remote.
2. Relative or interested person presents prognosis to hospital and a committee of three doctors confirms it.
3. Relative or interested person seeks court appointment as committee of the incompetent and permission to withdraw life-sustaining treatment.
4. The attorney general and the district attorney are notified so they may have doctors of their own choosing conduct an independent evaluation of the patient.
5. A guardian *ad litem* is appointed to represent the interests of the patient.
6. The court reviews the reports and issues an order.

Needless to say, the procedure is a cumbersome and time-consuming one, even though the parties may try to expedite it. The court also concluded that since this was a civil proceeding, Father Eichner did not need to establish beyond a reasonable doubt that Brother Fox would want the respirator removed.

However, since the interests at stake did not merely involve a sum of money, the burden of proof to be met by Father Eichner in establishing Brother Fox's desire to stop the extraordinary measures was a "clear and convincing standard"—i.e., he should establish, by a high probability, that Brother Fox would want the respirator to be removed.

56. 78 A.D.2d 1013; 434 N.Y.S.2d 46 (4th Dept. 1980), *rev'd.* 52 N.Y.2d 363; 420 N.E.2d 64; 438 N.Y.S.2d 266 (1981).

57. *In re Storar,* 52 N.Y.2d 363, 373; 420 N.E.2d 64, 68-69; 438 N.Y.S.2d 266, 270-72 (1981).

result of the loss of blood through the malignant lesions.

In July 1979 his mother and legal guardian, who had initially, with some misgivings, given her consent to the administration of blood transfusions, sought court approval to have them stopped, claiming that they caused her son great distress and only served to increase his sensitivity to pain. The institution where Storar lived, and which was acting as his doctor, sought to continue the transfusions and refused Mrs. Storar's request to the contrary.[58] Mrs. Storar submitted her request to the court. Four months later, the appellate division affirmed and authorized termination of the treatment.[59]

The story, however, does not end at the appellate division level. The *Eichner* and *Storar* decisions were further appealed to the New York Court of Appeals, which consolidated the matters.[60] Concerning both decisions, the court first noted that the United States Supreme Court has declined to consider the question of whether an individual's right to refuse life-saving treatment is guaranteed by the United States Constitution as an aspect of the right to privacy and its corollary, freedom from bodily intrusion.[61] However, the court found it unnecessary to address that issue, stressing that such a right is "adequately supported by common law principles."[62]

Additionally, the court rejected the district attorney's contention in *Eichner* that once a patient becomes incompetent, a third party cannot exercise this right on his behalf. It found that where there exists *"clear and convincing"* proof that the individual whose rights are being asserted by a third person has "expressed his views and concluded not to have his life prolonged by medical means if there were no hope of recovery," extraordinary life-sustaining treatments may be terminated.[63] Since Brother Fox had indeed expressed these views and reached that conclusion, the decision to remove the respirator was affirmed.

The court, on the other hand, reversed both lower courts in the *Storar* companion case, reasoning that since Storar had never been competent, and had never been able to express his views on the matter, no one's judgment—not even the court's—could be substituted in lieu of that of the patient's in making that final determination. It held that although a parent has the right to consent to medical treatment on behalf of a child, a parent or other duly appointed guardian may not deprive a child of life-saving treatment.[64]

The "clear and convincing" burden of proof that must be satisfied in New York concerning the incompetent's views on termination of extraordinary support is a difficult one to sustain. Furthermore, the expenses and legal fees incurred in such a situation become considerable, especially when the appellate process is invoked.[65] Guardians *ad litem* are entitled to be compensated.[66]

Interestingly, in *Wilmington Medical Center v. Severns,* a dispute arose as to what source would provide the $10,000 guardian *ad litem* fees: the decedent's estate or the state. Mrs. Severns, who was comatose as the result of an automobile accident, had expressed views contra the use of extraordinary life-sustaining measures. The state, on the other hand, opposed the removal of life support, which the family sought. Thus, in pursuing its interest in preserving life, it was the state that created the controversy necessitating the appointment of a guardian *ad litem*.[67]

The court, however, concluded that the guardian's right to compensation should not be determined by the position the guardian takes in the litigation. Furthermore, it ruled that, although a

---

58. *Id.* at 373-74; 420 N.E.2d at 69; 438 N.Y.S.2d at 271.
59. 78 A.D.2d 1013; 434 N.Y.S.2d 46, 47 (4th Dept. 1980) *(mem.).*
60. *In re Storar,* 52 N.Y.2d 363; 420 N.E.2d 64; 438 N.Y.S.2d 266 (1981). In both instances, the decisions appealed from favored the discontinuance of treatment. Likewise, in both instances, no family member appealed. Only the district attorney appealed.
61. *Id.* at 376-77; 420 N.E.2d at 70; 438 N.Y.S.2d at 272-73.
62. *Id.* at 377; 420 N.E.2d at 70; 430 N.Y.S.2d at 272.
63. *Id.* at 379; 420 N.E.2d at 72; 438 N.Y.S.2d at 274. The court noted that the procedure outlined at note 55, *supra,* was not necessary.

64. *Id.* at 380; 420 N.E.2d at 73; 438 N.Y.S.2d at 275-76. Yet, the *Quinlan* court permitted removal of her respirator even though Karen Ann had certainly never addressed the subject and was not competent to do so at the time. See notes 36-40 and accompanying text, *supra.* The Massachusetts courts, through their "substituted judgment" approach, would reach the same result. See *supra* notes 41-45 and accompanying text.
65. In addition to legal fees, these fees include the cost of court reporters and stenographers, transcripts, expert witnesses, clerical costs, filing fees and the like.
66. See, e.g., *N.Y. Surr. Ct. Proc. Act.* §405 (McKinney 1967).

Compensation of Guardian *ad litem:*
1. For services rendered a guardian *ad litem* shall receive reasonable compensation to be allowed by the Court payable from the estate or from the interest of the person under disability or from the interest of the person under disability or from both in such proportion as directed by the Court.

67. 433 A.2d 1047 (Del. 1981).

court could equitably assess guardian's fees from the state, if the state did not waive its sovereign immunity, it was an error to assess guardian's fees against it.[68]

Conclusion

The role of the benefit fund as a dominant health insurer of working people and their dependents must be reevaluated in light of the increasing numbers of shock claims stemming from protracted treatment of the terminally ill. The funds themselves can ill afford this increasing drain on their reserves, and their beneficiaries can ill afford the protracted costs of litigation, largely uninsured.

Petitioning the court in a guardianship proceeding involving the terminally ill or comatose vegetative patient to obtain an order to show cause as to why a certain treatment should not be continued requires retaining of legal counsel, securing of experts to testify and a willingness to compensate a court-appointed guardian *ad litem*. Transcripts of the proceedings are necessary. Whatever the outcome, the family is frequently confronted with prosecuting or defending subsequent appeals with their attendant costs.

True, this article addresses the exceptional situation. Traditionally, decisions in terminal illness situations have been made by doctors, patients (if competent) and relatives without court intervention where there is no dispute. However, as further gains are made in equipment that can sustain and prolong the life of the terminally ill, those diseases for which we have no cures will be responsible for an increasing number of our deaths. Likewise, senility will have a greater opportunity to afflict us.[69] As a result, the ability to give valid informed consents to medical procedures or to decline heroic life-saving efforts will be severely impacted.[70] Given the medical profession's seemingly natural reluctance to withhold such life-sustaining heroic measures without prior judicial approval, and absent clear legislative response, it would seem that many individuals confronted with this problem will be required to invoke the judicial process to effectuate their purposes.

Benefit funds must therefore, in their own interest, foster and make available to their constituents information concerning the individual's right to decide his course of treatment in the event he becomes incurably ill. Additionally, it makes basic economic sense for benefit funds to make available to their constituents the legal advice and support that an individual (whether on his own or through a guardian) electing to discontinue extraordinary life-support measures or choosing to die at home or at a hospice may require. One such partial solution is a "living will," a document that provides clear and convincing evidence of one's intention. One such suggested format follows:

> If at any time I should have an incurable injury, disease or illness certified to be a terminal condition by two physicians who have personally examined me, one of whom shall be my attending physician, and the physicians have determined that my death will occur whether or not life-sustaining procedures are utilized, and where the application of life-sustaining procedures would serve only to artificially prolong the dying process, I direct that such procedures be withheld or withdrawn, and that I be permitted to die naturally with only the administration of medication or the performance of any medical procedure deemed necessary to provide me with comfort and care.[71]

This document should be signed by the individual in the presence of at least two witnesses who can attest to the person's state of mind. It may be supplied to plan participants on a regular basis together with any donor or beneficiary cards used by the fund.

"Living will" legislation to date has been formally adopted in only 13 states and the District of Columbia.[72] Moreover, living wills may be binding or nonbinding, generally falling into three patterns according to the specific statute: (1) binding whenever executed as any other testamentary instrument; (2) binding if executed after terminal diagnosis; and (3) nonbinding, or advisory, in na-

---

68. *Id.* at 1050-51.

69. See Nelson, "Doctors Debate Right to Stop 'Heroic' Effort to Keep Elderly Alive," *Wall St. J.,* Sept. 7, 1982, at 1, col. 1: "The segment of the U.S. population 75 years old and older increased more than 37% during the 1970s and continues to be one of the fastest-growing segments."

70. "'Human society has never before faced the issue of so many people living for so long with such severe impairment.' [t]he burgeoning population of elderly, disabled patients strains limited medical resources." *Id.*

71. D. Meyers, *Medico-Legal Implications of Death and Dying* §16:8, n. 65 (1981).

72. Alabama, Arkansas, California, Delaware, Idaho, Kansas, Nevada, New Mexico, North Carolina, Oregon, Texas, Vermont and Washington. Telephone interview with Alice V. Mehling, Executive Director, Society for the Right to Die (Jan. 27, 1983).

ture.[73] This divergence of categories presents a problem for the individual who becomes incompetent before he is able to sign a living will, or who has signed a living will but must reexecute it to make it binding on the physician and yet is unable to do so because of incompetence. Thus, there is an obvious need for legislative uniformity to eliminate disparate results and uncertainty in this area.[74]

For the present, pending further legislative developments, enlightened funds should consider providing the technical support and legal advice necessary to give effect to the participants' expressed intent in instances of terminal illness.

Acknowledgment

The authors gratefully acknowledge the materials and suggestions of Alice V. Mehling, Executive Director, Society for the Right to Die, 250 West 57th Street, New York, NY 10107.

---

73. Freamon, "Death With Dignity Laws: A Plea for Uniform Legislation," *Seton Hall Legislative J.* 105, 123-33 (1982).

74. *Id.* at 133.

CHAPTER 2

What Comes Next?

John S. Perreca

Senior Vice President
Edward H. Friend & Co.
Washington, D.C.

Beryl W. Sprinkel, Ph.D., CFA

Under Secretary for Monetary Affairs
U.S. Department of the Treasury
Washington, D.C.

Dallas L. Salisbury

Executive Director
Employee Benefit Research Institute
Washington, D.C.

Earl C. Joseph

Futurist/President
Anticipatory Sciences, Inc.
Minneapolis, Minnesota

New Trends in Forecasting the Future of Pension Plans

BY JOHN S. PERRECA

RETIREMENT AS WE know it is changing. There are many reasons why. Several are explained here and advice is given on how you can protect yourself and your employees against what appears to be inevitable.

New trends are unfolding which impact on our ability to forecast the future of pension plans. Working men and women are changing their perception of and attitude toward retirement because of the impact of inflation, demographic changes and the shrinking labor pool, increasing life expectancy, the impact of government intrusion on their lives, their interest in the quality of life and dignity of work and the developing trend toward delayed retirement.

What will be the respective roles of Social Security, personal savings, defined benefit pension plans and defined contribution plans as these trends unfold? Can incentives for later retirement be provided within the system under which we operate so that these trends can be dealt with effectively and successfully by those of us who are here today? Can the short term solution allow us to leave a legacy to those who follow us—our children and, in particular, our grandchildren—so that they will not be left with the responsibility of taking care of us because we failed to take adequate care of ourselves?

Impact of Inflation

The impact of inflation has been the most dramatic of all these trends. Table I depicts the portion of one dollar's purchasing power that remains after retirement under various inflation scenarios. For example, if inflation was 6% per year, at the end of five years the purchasing power of your fixed pension benefit dollar would have been reduced to 75¢. If inflation were to remain at 6% after you were retired for ten years, your purchasing power would have eroded to only 56¢. After 15 years, your dollar would be worth only 42¢, after 20 years 31¢ and after 25 years only 23¢.

The longer you live after retirement (20 and 25 years or more for members of the uniformed services is not at all unusual) and the higher the rate of inflation, the more dramatically the purchasing

Mr. Perreca is senior vice president of Edward H. Friend & Company, Washington-based independent actuaries and employee benefit plan consultants. His responsibilities include advising corporate employers, state, county and municipal government officials, hospital, foundation and association executives, as well as Taft-Hartley trustees on the design, financing, implementation and administration of employee benefit programs. Mr. Perreca is a graduate of Allegheny College and has done graduate work at Ohio University and the University of Maryland. He is a frequent lecturer before professional and business groups and has authored articles for numerous employee benefit and public sector publications, including the International Foundation Digest and Employee Benefits Journal. Mr. Perreca has spoken at many International Foundation educational meetings. He is a former member and past chairman of the Public Employees Committee and is currently a member of the Foundation's Board of Directors and Actuaries Committee. He has taught Certified Employee Benefit Specialist (CEBS) courses on pension plans and Social Security at American University, as adjunct professor.

power of your pension benefits will fall off—to the point of perhaps not enabling you to maintain the standard of living to which you have grown accustomed. To demonstrate that probability I asked several hundred business and labor leaders, together with their legal, accounting, actuarial, investment and other advisors, in my address to them in Montreal on October 18, 1982, for a show of hands from those who thought they could retire today on 100% of their current earned income, subject themselves to that kind of erosion and feel

Table I

PORTION OF ONE DOLLAR'S PURCHASING POWER THAT REMAINS AFTER RETIREMENT UNDER VARIOUS INFLATION SCENARIOS

Number of Years After Retirement	If Annual Rate of Inflation Is			
	6%	12%	16%	20%
5	75¢	57¢	48¢	40¢
10	56	32	23	16
15	42	18	11	6
20	31	10	5	3
25	23	6	2	1

that they could continue to maintain themselves in the fashion to which they had grown accustomed. Not a single hand was raised!

Demographics

Demographic changes and the shrinking labor pool are other trends with which we must cope. Beginning around the year 2000, the baby boom of the 1940s and 1950s will become the retirement boom. The workforce will shrink as a result of the decreased fertility rate that began in the 1960s. Employers will find it difficult to replace and support retiring workers—this prediction notwithstanding today's temporary 10% unemployment rate.

Increasing Life Expectancy

The impact of increasing life expectancy is also having a profound effect. The impact of this trend will increase during the next 20 years. For example, at age 65, life expectancy has risen 12%—from 14.6 to 16.3 years—just during the last decade. As one senior citizen was heard to remark, "John, if I knew I'd live so long, I'd have taken better care of myself."

Government Intrusion

Increased government intrusion is another trend with which we must cope. TEFRA, the Tax Equity and Fiscal Responsibility Act, impacts on the design of pension plans in a variety of ways—most of which are restrictive. Consider the following six specific points:
- TEFRA reduces the dollar limit on what can be contributed (on a tax deductible basis) to defined contribution plans. Although this limit is directed to the highest paid employees, the impact of the "trickle-down" could result in lower paid personnel receiving proportionately less, rather than more, benefits as may have been envisioned by TEFRA's drafters.
- TEFRA reduces dollar benefits under defined benefit plans. These limits, too, may have their effects felt. Just as water does not run uphill, pension benefit limitations applicable to the highest paid may eventually have their impacts felt among the lowest paid. Few highly paid business owners will be found so generous as to provide proportionately more benefits for their rank and file.
- TEFRA requires defined benefit pension plans be subject to actuarial reductions if retirement is to occur between ages 55 and 62. It has not been uncommon, for example, for highly paid professionals to finance pension plans designed to provide them with 100% of pay beginning at age 55.
- TEFRA requires actuarial increases in pension benefits under defined benefit plans whose payments begin after age 65. The significance of this actuarial increase is that it ties in with Social Security and is the precursor of what will likely be a gradual postponement of retirement beyond the traditional retirement ages to which we have grown accustomed. However, such an adjustment probably will not be practical within most of our lifetimes.
- TEFRA eliminates future cost-of-living adjustments (COLAs) on maximum benefit limits under defined benefit and defined contribution plans until 1986, a direct attempt to curtail inflation by withholding that which contributes to it.
- TEFRA reduces the two plan dollar limit from the old 1.4 rule to 1.25 for defined contribution plans.

Delayed Retirement

In addition to this prodding by our government, delayed retirement may become a national goal, if not a national necessity. You will recall that the 1978 Age Discrimination in Employment Act (ADEA) amendment guarantees employees the right to work to age 70 before they have to retire; they can work even longer if their employer permits it. The recently concluded National Council of Aging study reported that 54% of the labor force age 55 and older would like some type of employment after retirement. Might it be appropriate,

Table II

SOCIAL SECURITY TAXES CONTINUE TO INCREASE DRAMATICALLY

Maximum Annual Tax

Year	Employer/Employee	Combined
1937	$ 30	$ 60
1950	45	90
1970	375	750
1979	1,404	2,808
1980	1,588	3,176
1981	1,975	3,950
1982	2,171	4,342
1983	2,392	4,784

then, for us to lend support to eliminating the age 70 mandatory retirement age?

Social Security and Savings

What will be the respective roles of Social Security, personal savings, defined benefit pension plans and defined contribution plans in light of these trends? Social Security will be curtailed. Personal savings will increase. Defined benefit pension plans will decline in popularity. Defined contribution plans will increase in popularity. Also, the frequency of post-retirement employment will increase.

With regard to Social Security, both employer and employee taxes will increase and benefits will continue to be curtailed prospectively—at least with respect to the automatic COLA. The normal retirement age will gradually be delayed beyond 65 to 68 or 70, and there will be changes in the earned offset arrangement, which will have the catalytic effect of increasing the incentive to work even after Social Security pension benefits commence.

Both the Social Security tax rate and the taxable wage base will be increased. Remember 1937—when the employee tax was $30 and the employer tax was $30, for a total of $60? Trace the dramatic increase in the required employer and employee tax for Social Security in Table II.

One of the most ludicrous and financially devastating of all Social Security provisions is the automatic cost-of-living adjustment. It will have to be reduced, if not eliminated, in the years ahead. This uncontrollable federal budget item *exacerbates* inflation instead of mollifying its impact. Social Security benefits are indexed upward because of inflation, causing higher FICA taxes, adding to employer costs and resulting in higher wage demands from workers. These increased costs cause increased prices for goods and services, which trigger another indexed increase in benefits so recipients will not feel the pinch of inflation, causing still higher FICA taxes ad nauseam! Indexation provides only a temporary palliative to some of us who are retired; eliminating the causes of inflation will be to our best advantage over the long term.

Changing Trends

A slowing trend is in evidence. Social Security dependents' benefits have already begun to be reduced. Smaller COLA benefit increases will be experienced before the end of this decade. There is consideration being given to taxing the employer-financed portion of Social Security benefits, something that is possible but not probable.

What is probable is that there will be a postponing of the normal retirement age under Social Security from 65 to 68 or 70. There is already a provision under Social Security for actuarial increases on the occasion of postponing the commencement of retirement benefits beyond age 65. As an additional incentive to delay one's retirement, this actuarial increase will likely be made more favorable to the covered worker.

Earned Income Offset

The earned income offset under Social Security needs to be changed if not eliminated. The Social Security Earnings Test adds the equivalent of a 50% tax on benefits with respect to earnings above $6,000. When you include the impact of FICA taxes and federal income tax on that which you earn in excess of $6,000 a year after retirement while collecting Social Security, you face an effective tax of up to 70% on those earnings in excess of $6,000 a year. Of what value is this disincentive to us to earn more than $6,000 a year after "retiring" under Social Security? With one dollar in Social Security benefits withheld for every two dollars of annual earnings above $6,000 until age 70, where is the incentive for post-retirement employment? If this test were eliminated, the Social Security benefits disbursed would probably be offset by the Social Security and general income taxes gained from the taxation of those who choose to work beyond 65 and eagerly earn more than $6,000 a year.

Increasing Personal Savings

Another trend is that personal savings are increasing. Personal savings will increase through

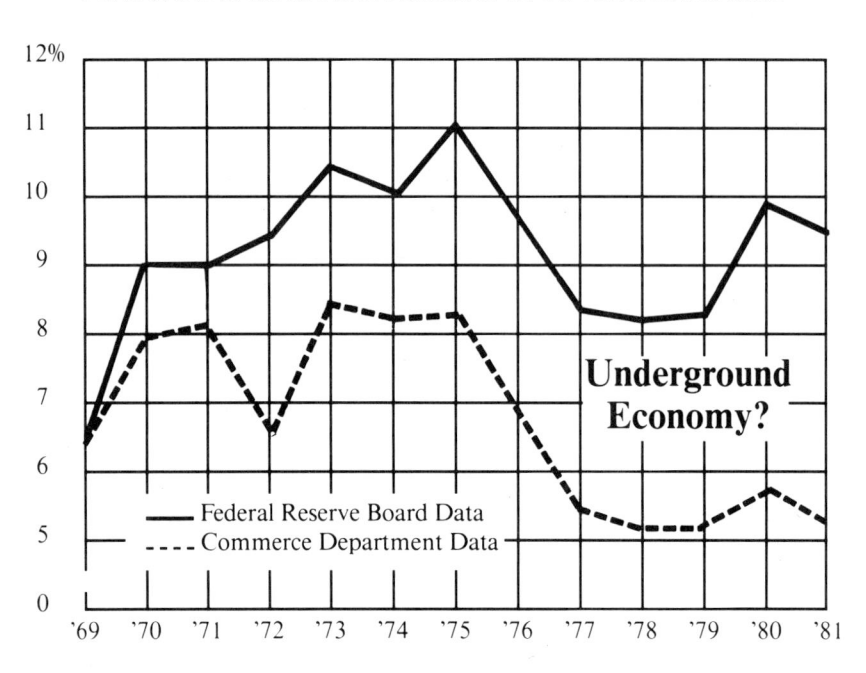

Figure 1

PERSONAL SAVING AS A PERCENT OF AFTERTAX INCOME

[Graph showing personal saving rates from '69 to '81, with Federal Reserve Board Data (solid line) and Commerce Department Data (dashed line). The gap between the two lines in later years is labeled "Underground Economy?"]

the use of such vehicles as individual tax-sheltered retirement accounts, the use of tax free municipal bond mutual funds and other arrangements. For example, the Uniform Gift to Minors Act is an arrangement under which you open up a savings account in your children's names, and let them earn the interest you would have earned had you kept the money in your own account. The interest income is charged to them instead of you. Because your children are not likely to have a big enough tax bite, they earn the interest from the savings account on a no tax or low tax basis.

Underground Economy

Less obvious are savings from income earned in our underground economy. Its existence is not limited to other nations. Figure 1 reveals the disparity in rates of personal saving as reported by the Commerce Department, which tracks savings accounts and related reportable transactions, and by the Federal Reserve Board, which monitors the money supply.[1]

Individual retirement accounts, or IRAs, are growing by leaps and bounds. The $2,000 individual deduction, the $2,250 deduction for you and your spouse or the $4,000 deduction if both of you are working is an attractive tax shelter. Tax savings under Keogh plans for sole proprietorships and partnerships, which before TEFRA had been limited when compared with what was available to corporate owners, are now almost on a par with the corporate sector.

Defined Benefit Pension Plans Losing Ground

Defined benefit pension plans are declining in popularity because fixed and predictable benefits are no longer crucial in retirement planning. With the shift away from a fixed retirement age, and because of the inflation-driven complexities involved in predicting a specific benefit capable of sustaining purchasing power after retirement, defined benefit plans have lost much of their luster. The impact of ERISA's 30% corporate net worth exposure has also had the effect of dissuading many employers from maintaining defined benefit plans. Even in the multiemployer area, we are painfully aware of the disinclination many employers have to being exposed to potentially large liabilities through their contributing to Taft-Hartley-negotiated cents per hour defined benefit pension plans.

---

1. Published with permission from Data Resources, Inc., 29 Hartwell Avenue, Lexington, MA 02173.

Defined Contribution Plans Advance

Defined contribution plans will continue to increase in popularity. They are immune to ERISA liability and can be designed to avoid a fixed cost. Defined contribution plans provide compatibility with the flexible and delayed retirement age that is emerging in our nation. On a personal basis, a defined contribution plan provides the employee with a distinguishable account balance—some comfort in these days of business and economic uncertainty. To many Americans, a bird in the hand is worth more than two in the bush, notwithstanding guarantees made by the Pension Benefit Guaranty Corporation.

Defined contribution plans also gain from the impact of productivity as an incentive through profit sharing. Remember, superior investment performance under a defined benefit plan reduces the employer's contribution, but under profit-sharing defined contribution plans employees gain from the impact of their productivity and of superior investment performance.

Post-Retirement Employment

Income supplementation through post-retirement employment is becoming widespread. It is emerging for several reasons, not the least significant of which is to protect against the impact of inflation. In addition, there is a growing concern on the part of many of us about established institutions on which we are unwilling to depend without caution. If you are free from doubt about the federal government (i.e., Social Security) taking good care of you, how would you like to be an American Indian?

Dignity of Work

In addition to improving the quality of life, another distinguishable trend is emerging as a phenomenon that many of us have ignored—a revival of the dignity of work. With growing medical evidence that people are as intellectually and functionally able at 75 and 80 as they are at 45 and 50, why should we be forced to retire? Someone who is old and sick is not sick because they are old; they are sick because they are sick.

Later Retirement

Can there be practical incentives for promoting later retirement? Yes, and some already exist. One of these incentives is the provision for accumulating additional credited service under defined benefit pension plans; another is the ability to continue to receive contributions to one's account and the investment earnings thereon under a defined contribution plan. A third incentive is to calculate defined pension benefits based on the likely higher final average earnings immediately preceding the postponed retirement date. A fourth is to provide actuarial increases for postponed retirement to reflect the then-shorter life expectancy at the later retirement age; this provision is already part of the Social Security system.

A lighter workload—fewer hours—is another way of accommodating the trend toward later retirement. Reassignment to less demanding responsibilities can also be helpful. Even changing careers, now seemingly a developing trend for some of us in our 40s and 50s, is often possible, reasonable, desirable and sometimes necessary.

Older workers taking longer vacations and tapering down their workload are other trends we will see. Finally, job sharing and part-time employment will increase in popularity. Job sharing by older and younger employees is unique in that it gives each more free time and is free of peer rivalry. Peer rivalry has been one of the problems in job sharing. However, if one is an experienced senior employee and the other an aspiring junior employee, the senior employee is not a threat to the junior employee and, in fact, can contribute to the junior's growth and maturity.

Finally, it is interesting to note that a growing number of major corporate employers are using their retired employees to temporarily fill positions of those people who are on vacation, out ill or are otherwise unavailable to work. The Traveler's Insurance Company, for example, has 60% of its temporary positions filled by retired personnel.

Conclusion

Today's older people have only two extreme choices—full-time work or full-time retirement. We must review and revise our private and public retirement policies. Even more important than oil, a national resource not to be wasted is our senior citizens—who have enormous knowledge, vast experience, considerable wisdom and mature judgment. The great American retirement dream, although not a broken promise, may be an elusive and perhaps undesirable goal for many of us. I'll leave it up to you to decide.

Employee Benefits: A Transformation

BY DALLAS L. SALISBURY

EMPLOYEE BENEFITS have entered an era of transformation. This transformation is principally represented by the increasing degree to which employee benefits have become important to corporate finance. Whether one looks at the role that employer stock owned by the employee benefit plans of Grumman Aircraft or Bendix has played in takeover battles, the role that benefits have played in "concession" negotiations in troubled industries or the way in which pension funding waivers have become a means of improving the financial health of troubled companies, we are increasingly aware of an era in which employee benefits and corporate survival are intertwined.

The result is that employee benefit issues are becoming a matter for the personal attention of the chief executive officer and the board of directors of the typical corporation. With growing impact on corporate flexibility and the "bottom line" that employee benefit decisions are having, a transformation has begun that will influence the corporate environment for decades to come.

An Environment of Change

This transformation is being driven by three principal factors: demographics, economics and government.

Demographics

A number of demographic trends are coming together in a way that will influence corporate human resource policies, workforce planning strategies, current workforce costs, the cost of maintaining a retiree population and the makeup of the balance sheet of the corporation. These trends appear irreversible. Human life expectancy at birth has been on the rise throughout this century. Average expected years of life have risen from 50 in 1910 to 60 in 1935, to 70 in 1960 and are expected to reach 80 by the middle of the next century. Since these estimates are based on present medical technology, there is a prospect that they will prove to have been conservative estimates should medical advances continue. In any case, they will mean continually increasing costs and challenges for employers and employees.

Longer life expectancy, the baby boom of the '50s and the baby bust of the late '60s are having a

Mr. Salisbury is executive director of the Employee Benefit Research Institute, based in Washington, D.C., a "think tank" dedicated to increasing knowledge and understanding of employee benefits. Prior to joining EBRI, Mr. Salisbury served as assistant executive director for policy planning of the Pension Benefit Guaranty Corporation (PBGC); assistant administrator for policy and research of the pension and welfare benefit programs, U.S. Department of Labor; and assistant director of the Office of Policy and Planning, U.S. Department of Justice, in addition to other positions. Before joining the federal government, Mr. Salisbury held public and private sector positions in the State of Washington. Mr. Salisbury attended the University of Washington and the Maxwell Graduate School in Syracuse, New York. He is a frequent author and speaker on employee benefit topics. Mr. Salisbury is currently a member of the Foundation's Government Affairs/Industry Relations Committee.

significant effect on the age structure of the workforce. Contrary to the implications of many recent popular reports, the retired population is actually growing very little in percentage terms. In fact, it is the 25-44 age group that will expand from 47% of the population to 61% of the population by 1990. Not until early in the next century will the retiree population begin to grow significantly as a proportion of the total population. For the private and public sectors, this statistic means that we may be in the final decade of opportunity for solving the many financing and balancing problems of our health and retirement income programs. The prospects for intergenerational conflict will grow greater as we move beyond 1990.

During the 1970s, another fundamental change took place in the demographics of the American population. Traditional households—those with a breadwinning husband, a wife who worked at home and two children—have declined to 7-15% of all American households. By 1980, over 64% of households had two wage earners present. This change has affected American worker attitudes and behavior, in addition to the availability of labor.

Among the behavioral changes we have seen are a movement of women out of the home and into the workplace, a movement from a focus on childbearing and child rearing to that of the working nonmother or the working mother, a movement from a tradition of marriage stability to the accepted practice of increasing rates of divorce, a movement from the traditional family of husband and wife to exceptionally high rates of single parent households and, finally, an attitudinal shift of passive dependency on the part of the workforce to an increasing insistence on independence and participation in corporate decisionmaking.

These changes will impact the American workplace fundamentally as the baby boom and baby bust populations mature. A dramatic drop in the average annual growth in the labor force will be the result of fewer new entrants in the wake of the baby boom and the fact that we are approaching a point of saturation of female labor force participation. By the latter part of the current decade, annual labor force growth is projected to be in the range of 0.92% per year, compared to a 1965-70 rate of 2.14% per year. For corporations, this percentage will mean an increasingly tightened employment market in the years ahead and a bidding up of the cost of highly trained workers. At the same time, it may move organizations to change their basic human resource and employee benefit strategies from encouraging individuals to retire to finding new ways of keeping people in the workforce longer.

Economics

Economic conditions have changed along with the changing demographics of America. The troubled economy of the last several years has led to frequent review of the American tax system and its role in achieving economic performance. Inflation has driven the economy and has distorted many traditional economic behavioral patterns. The challenge of dealing with changing rates of inflation in the future affects employee benefit programs and every other aspect of corporate business management.

Economic changes brought about by an interdependent world economy are raising fundamental questions about the industrial structure of the United States. Already, change has taken place with growth of the service and trade sectors of the American economy.

Economics has also had a major influence on another basic economic problem: productivity. For many segments of American business, the challenge is to restructure and reconceptualize. Employee benefit programs will play a crucial role in determining the effectiveness of those restructuring efforts and may be invaluable tools in that process.

Demographic and economic trends of recent years have contributed to the steady rise of benefit costs. All factors indicate that this rise will continue during the 1980s, putting increased pressure on the corporate bottom line. At the same time, employee groups will be pressured to cost share, to make tradeoffs and to forego further liberalizations of employee benefit programs. With the cost of employee benefits as a percent of total compensation now representing as much as 40% in some businesses, there is a question as to how much higher it can go.

For the first time, the government is looking critically at fringe benefit cost growth, because it lowers government revenues. Whether through the creation of new plans, the expansion of existing plans or the rising costs of currently promised benefits, the effect is to have an increasing portion of total compensation escape both the federal income tax and the Social Security payroll tax.

Government

Many of the demographic trends of recent years have fed into and influenced the structure and nature of our economy. Government and economics have also become increasingly inseparable. As the international trade environment tightens and worldwide production sharing becomes more common, the government role in economic planning is bound to grow.

The government will also affect the economics of American business through ongoing adjustments to our system of taxation, continuing pressure on expenditure levels at all levels of government, structural changes in Social Security and entitlement programs, and other specialized legislation and regulation. Action will focus increasingly on employee benefits and how much flexibility a corporation, or collective bargaining parties, will have in determining what this component of total compensation will represent.

Government decisions will be driven by a concern over revenue. Ten years ago the concept of "tax expenditures" and "tax subsidies" was one which was argued regularly in the halls of Congress. Now, its existence is accepted by both political parties. Therefore, perceived "tax subsidies" increasingly will help the government justify a focus on areas in which it wishes to concentrate tax reform and legislative activity.

Additionally, this concern over revenue will lead to a focus on the effective reduction of FICA taxes created by fringe benefit growth. The prospects for further restricting tax benefits to the corporation and qualified employee benefit programs will increase. Government estimates for fiscal year 1983 of "tax subsidies," as calculated by the Office of Management and Budget, make the "why" clear. For fiscal year 1983, employer pensions will reduce government revenues by $37.9 billion; IRA and Keogh contributions will reduce them by at least $5.8 billion. Government revenues will be reduced by life insurance premiums by $2.5 billion and by health insurance expenses by $21.5 billion.

Growth in nonstatutory employee benefits as a percent of total compensation from 5.4% in 1951 to 16.3% in 1981 indicates why there is growing concern over their exclusion from Social Security payroll taxes. The *1982 Trustees Report of the Social Security Administration* projects that nonstatutory benefits will reach 39.3% of total compensation by the middle part of the next century. This projection means that during the years in which Social Security will be undergoing its greatest financial strains, a great deal of revenue could be gained by broadening the base of FICA taxation to include a portion of employee benefit expenditures. Such a proposal is now being considered by the National Commission on Social Security Reform and some members of the Congress.

Government decisions regarding employee benefits and other aspects of taxation are also influenced by several beliefs. These beliefs can be summarized as including the belief that benefits favor the rich through discrimination, that benefits are subsidized by the tax system, that benefits undermine the financial stability of the Social Security program, and that pension receipts are low and remaining stable and, therefore, private pensions cannot be relied on to complement Social Security.

These beliefs have led to a continuing government interest in leveling benefits and in providing for nondiscrimination on a broadly defined basis. In the most recent tax bill, TEFRA, these concerns fueled changes regarding maximum benefit limits for pensions, maximum contribution limits for pensions and rules for the integration of pensions with Social Security, as well as the creation of top-heavy rules to tighten vesting provisions and a requirement that minimum benefits be provided. Legislation pending before the Congress would take these objectives and extend them through mandatory portability, an extension of survivor benefits on a mandatory basis and increased taxation of employee benefits. Additionally, as Congressional and public discussion of a flat rate income tax accelerates, this idea must be looked at in terms of its potential consequence for employee benefits.

Legislation

Legislation now before Congress and expected to be enacted during 1983 or 1984 will tie employee benefits increasingly to corporate survival. For example, changes in the plan termination insurance program would effectively eliminate the ability of a plan sponsor to voluntarily terminate his pension plan. At the same time, liability to the Pension Benefit Guaranty Corporation would increase from a maximum 30% of net worth to an obligation to fund all pension liabilities as long as the business is an ongoing concern. Further, in the event of corporate bankruptcy, the Pension Benefit Guaranty Corporation would have the status of a general creditor. These changes would serve to limit corporate flexibility and the flexibility of bargaining parties and would make decisions related to pension programs a central aspect of corporate financial planning.

Legislation to extend ERISA style provisions to public employee pensions could have side effects for private plan sponsors. It would undoubtedly run up the cost of public pension plans and therefore increase state and local taxation in order to maintain current service levels and to pay for pensions.

Numerous proposals now pending before the Congress would affect the flexibility and capability of plan sponsors to invest pension plan assets. Two central issues are of primary importance: first, proposals to mandate that a given percentage of pension assets be invested in particular segments of the economy; second, that plan participants be given a key role in the management and control of pension assets. Both of these changes would have a direct effect on the risk-to-return calculation in determining the appropriateness of pension plan sponsorship.

All of these perspective federal legislative changes would cause the financial cost attached to the sponsorship of employee benefit programs to grow significantly. Issues related to unfunded pension liabilities would become an increasingly important factor in every aspect of corporate financial decisionmaking. Changes in the Pension Benefit Guaranty Corporation's program would significantly increase the importance of unfunded pension liabilities to merger, acquisition and spinoff decisions. Also, the continuing growth of pension assets guarantees that special attention from special interest groups and public policymakers will not be avoided.

The government also has a broad range of legislative proposals under consideration that will have an effect on employee benefit programs and their expense to the corporation. Social Security changes could result in increases in the payroll tax rate and the period of time that employers are responsible for providing benefits to retired individuals. Continued discussion of health care competition and national health insurance highlights another potential area of continued corporate exposure. Continued attention to the Age Discrimination in Employment Act and total removal of the mandatory retirement age could affect the human resource and workforce planning strategies of corporations and the cost of their employee benefit programs.

Social Security

Fundamental changes in Social Security are not likely. Instead, tradition-bound changes and benefit adjustments are likely to be the order of the day. Such changes might include raising the normal retirement age, reducing early retirement benefits, tightening eligibility for ancillary benefits, reducing benefit indexing, increasing the income level provided by supplemental security income, eliminating benefit deductibility or increasingly taxing employee benefits and expenditures for employee benefits. In all of these cases, the expense of maintaining present employee benefit programs would increase.

Social Security changes raise many design questions that will have to be dealt with at the highest management levels. Each issue will have major implications for cost. Should the basic orientation in the design of employee benefit programs be one of maintaining levels of compensation or simply meeting basic needs? Will companies be able to maintain policies that include setting a target date for retirement or will total flexibility become the order of the day? Will corporations continue to find it beneficial to consider Social Security in setting retirement income goals and the benefit structures of their own retirement income programs, or should Social Security be ignored? To what degree should corporations by design attempt to coordinate their own medical programs with provisions by the government? To what degree can an employer afford, given human resource and workforce planning needs, to support Social Security incentives intended by the government or will corporations be left with no choice but to counter them? Finally, to what degree will employee benefits integrate with workforce planning strategies in the future and with the maintenance of acceptable levels of productivity? Naturally, these questions are of equal relevance to employees and employer representatives.

Social Security continues to be supported by a dedicated payroll tax. The business community traditionally has supported the payroll tax as the exclusive funding agent and argued vehemently against the introduction of general revenues. Unions traditionally have argued that general revenue money should be used. In both cases, the positions were supported by a belief that the payroll tax creates "fiscal discipline" within the program and holds down benefits. Since research indicates that the higher Social Security benefits go, the more employer-provided pensions are crowded out, there is reason to be concerned about benefit levels.

The ground surrounding the payroll tax versus general revenue issue may, however, be shifting. First, the Congressional Budget Office points out that we are facing federal budget deficits in each of the next several years in excess of $100 billion. Second, the payroll tax has allowed the American public to view Social Security as an earned right, including full indexation. Since Social Security is a pay-as-you-go intergenerational transfer program, no guarantee beyond good will is actually present. Are we at a point when both the public interest and fiscal prudence would argue for shifting a portion of Social Security financing to general revenues? Are we at the point where general revenue financing would offer the greatest guarantee of fiscal prudence? Employers, workers, interest groups and public decisionmakers should focus on this funding question sooner, rather than later. There is evidence that some traditional advocates of general revenues are abandoning that position.

The government activity just reviewed will lead to increased difficulty in plan design, disruption of retirement planning, a greater range in retirement ages, an increasing disincentive to integrate private programs with government-sponsored programs, pressures for bigger private benefits in all employee benefit areas, pressure for increased pre-Social Security benefit subsidies and an increasing likelihood of higher rates of disability claims. The bottom line implications lead to a reasonable expectation that total employee benefit costs as a percent of payroll will continue to climb, and that there will be built-in escalation in benefit programs to respond to government changes, including a great deal of direct and indirect cost shifting. Increased attention will be focused on the rates of return investment managers are achieving with their pension portfolios, which will become a central point in the debate over management and control of pension assets: Should the employer, the employee or both share in control? These changes will lead to a shift in liabilities. Promises made will be promises kept, even if the price is bankruptcy.

Influence on Directions

Demographic, economic and government policy trends currently combine to move us in the direction of mandatory versus voluntary provision of coverage. The most recent example of this trend is the TEFRA requirement that employers continue to provide full medical coverage for employees working beyond the age of 65. Also, we see a movement toward socially dictated rather than privately determined employee benefit programs—for example, TEFRA's provision for minimum benefit provision in "top-heavy" pension plans. There is an increasing movement in the direction of universal provision of any benefit rather than allowing selective use for specific human resources or management. For example, TEFRA extended to group term life insurance the same nondiscrimination criteria now found in other areas of the law.

These factors limit the flexibility of management and reduce the relative advantages to the employee of employer provision. As a result, we will see a movement toward provision by the individual rather than the employer. Concurrently, there will be continued growth in defined contribution pension plans. Reliance on defined benefit programs will decrease. TEFRA, ERTA and ERISA have moved us in this direction and, pending government legislative proposals, will have the effect of pushing us even further that way.

These provision changes, it is interesting to note, tend to support behavior changes brought on by the demographic and economic trends. Greater individuality and independence, however, simultaneously shift an increasing amount of risk for long term economic well-being to the individual. One must be concerned about the ultimate result of this shift, if the risk proves harsh and poverty rates rise.

Increasingly, public policy decisionmakers will focus on all sources of economic security, whether provided by the government, the employer or the individual. Integrated analysis of Social Security, personal savings and investments, needs-related public programs, income from employment, family transfers and retirement plans will become a part of the analytic process for decisionmaking. Such a comprehensive and integrated assessment of economic security and well-being will provide a basis for controlling the combined public and private sector costs of employee benefit programs. This control will help to assure government survival, individual economic survival and the survival of a free enterprise economy.

Surviving the Transformation

Government involvement in employee benefits will grow continuously during the 1980s and 1990s; the role of government in determining the structure of American corporations and institutions will grow as well. Government will influence the corporate bottom line and the prospects of corporate survival.

The external challenge will be to work to structure the debate and the possible solutions. The internal challenge will be to anticipate, plan and reconceptualize. Take the initiative in recognizing the importance of government involvement with employee benefits and the effect on your ability to control your destiny.

Rene Dubos once noted that "crises are practically always a source of enrichment and of renewal because they encourage the search for new solutions." We now find the government faced with a crisis in Social Security, in total government expenditures, in adjusting to a new international order and in rebuilding our economy. Our challenge is to help turn this period of crisis and transformation into a time of renewal and reward.

U.S. Monetary Policy: Looking Forward

BY BERYL W. SPRINKEL, Ph.D., CFA

REASONABLE AND INTELLIGENT people always seem to disagree about religion, politics and the economic situation. So I am sure that there is a wide variety of opinion among readers of this presentation about the economic events of the past year. However, I suspect that investors are more interested in a preview of upcoming events than in a recitation of the past.

We believe that we are on the verge of—if not already into—a solid recovery. Contrary to many of the pundits of the press, I am convinced that the upturn is looking more probable and more imminent with each passing day. The index of leading indicators has risen four out of the last five months. The turnaround in real Gross National Product (GNP), which began with modest positive growth in the second quarter, will give us even stronger growth later this year. Interest rates are down dramatically, and the stock market has moved up over 225 points in the past two months. Investors do not move into the market this way unless they perceive economic progress in the future.

There are reasons to believe that this recovery will not just consist of another inflationary burst of activity, but will lead to sustained, noninflationary growth.

There are obviously a multitude of factors—some domestic, some international—that will have an impact on the investment climate in the future. I will concentrate most heavily on the domestic monetary situation and make a few brief remarks, at the end, about the current international financial environment.

Domestic Economic Policy

I have been speaking out now for some time, emphasizing that prudent, noninflationary monetary policy is absolutely necessary to controlling inflation and reducing interest rates. Since last year, inflation has dropped dramatically. So far this year, the Consumer Price Index (CPI) has risen at an annual rate of 5.4%—nearly half the rate of inflation that had occurred in the six month period ending last September.

Interest rates, after hanging higher and longer than most of us anticipated, have declined sub-

Dr. Sprinkel was confirmed March 30, 1981 by the United States Senate as Under Secretary of the Treasury for Monetary Affairs. In this capacity, he is responsible for formulating and implementing U.S. international financial policies, developing U.S. policy toward the international financial institutions such as the World Bank and the International Monetary Fund, financing and managing the federal debt, establishing Treasury financial policies and coordinating between Administration economic policies and the monetary policies of the Federal Reserve system. Dr. Sprinkel previously served as executive vice president and economist at the Harris Trust and Savings Bank in Chicago, Illinois and as consultant to various government agencies and Congressional committees. Before joining Harris, he taught economics and finance at the University of Chicago and the University of Missouri School of Business and Public Administration. Author of two books and co-author of a third, he also has written numerous articles. Dr. Sprinkel received his B.S. degree in public administration from the University of Missouri, his M.B.A. degree from the University of Chicago and his Ph.D. degree in economics and finance from the University of Chicago. He is a chartered financial analyst and holds an honorary Doctor of Humane Letters degree from De Paul University and an honorary Doctor of Laws degree from St. Michael's College.

stantially in recent months. A year ago the prime rate was 19½%; today it is 12%. The average rate for three month Treasury bills auctioned during this August was 660 basis points lower than for last August, and they have declined further since. The problems and complaints about continued high interest rates aside, that is a very remarkable drop in rates. Among other things, of course, interest rates reflect the underlying perception of the prospects of future inflation.

In the past year, the Federal Reserve has persevered in its policy to reduce the rate of money growth to a noninflationary rate. Money growth over the past year has averaged 5-5½%, in sharp contrast to the 7.8% average for the four years from 1976 to 1980. This success in bringing down money growth is reflected in declining inflation and interest rates. Continued noninflationary monetary policy is a prerequisite to continued and permanent progress toward both price stability and further declines in interest rates.

The record of the 1970s clearly shows that faster money growth did not "buy" us lasting increases in production and employment. To the contrary, the lasting effects of excessive money growth—accelerating inflation, escalating interest rates and a deterioration of the incentives to save and invest—are powerful and pervasive *deterrents* to sustained growth. Sustainable economic expansion requires a financial system based on a reliable dollar, and that means monetary discipline.

Despite clear evidence that using inflationary money growth is a shortsighted policy, there are currently many voices calling on the Fed to do just that. Also, many people interpret recent events as a sign that such a shift occurred in recent weeks. Let me assure you that the Reagan Administration remains committed to a policy of noninflationary monetary growth. We support completely the policy of steady reduction in the *trend* of money growth. We believe that the Federal Reserve's announced monetary targets are appropriate to that goal and are confident that it will persist in its efforts toward *long term* monetary control.

A reacceleration of money growth that persists for several months would have disastrous effects on our long run goal of price stability and permanently lower interest rates. It would greatly reduce the potential for future output and employment growth and would be an engraved invitation to our third recession in as many years.

In a recent speech before the Business Council in Hot Springs, Chairman Volcker pointed to two near-term events that probably are going to distort the M1 numbers for the next few weeks. The first factor is the movement of billions of dollars out of all-savers accounts and into other forms of financial instruments. The second factor is the initiation of the newly legalized bank certificates. What these distortions mean is that it might be more difficult to interpret movements in the M1 aggregate over the next several weeks. What they do *not* mean is that the Administration has in any way changed the importance it places on achieving its long stated goal of moderate, stable growth in the money supply.

Factors such as short run shifts in velocity, a precautionary buildup of NOW accounts or financial innovations are not adequate explanations for prolonged periods of off-target money growth. Such developments may lead to short term blips in the money supply, but they cannot result in longer term changes in money growth without accommodating actions by the Federal Reserve. The Fed does not intend to sacrifice monetary control just because of current technical factors. I believe it will stick to moderate money growth and let the "Ms" sort themselves out.

Some may contend that the price we have paid for progress on inflation has been too great. There is, of course, no question that the price we have paid—in terms of lost jobs and output—has been significant. I do not wish to understate the hardship that has been imposed on many sectors of the economy and on individual firms and workers. But people who conclude that the cure has been worse than the disease are greatly underestimating, or incompletely recognizing, the true costs that continued inflation itself imposes on an economy.

Many of the chronic problems that have added to our economic troubles—lagging productivity, a low savings rate, the problems of the thrift industry—can, in fundamental ways, be attributed to inflation. Currently several factors, including indications of a rising savings rate and improving productivity, are signs that the insidious and pervasive effects of a decade of accelerating inflation are finally being reversed.

The length and depth of the current recession provide a valuable lesson for the American public. The recession illustrates an important principle: Once inflation and inflationary expectations become embedded, returning an economy to a noninflationary path is an extremely difficult and costly task. As West German Chancellor Helmut Schmidt once said, "Inflation is like toothpaste—once you get it out of the tube, it's very difficult to put it back."

It is certainly an overstatement to say that this recession was caused by anti-inflationary monetary policy; but it *is* true that reversing the trend of accelerating money growth of the past decade and a half has contributed to the economic slowdown. That is the inevitable result of the collision between inflationary behavior—automatic price increases, rising wage costs, high interest rates, etc.—and a monetary policy that does not provide sufficient money to finance continued inflation, that is, noninflationary money growth. This unavoidable adjustment period is necessary until inflationary expectations abate and the public's behavior ceases to be based on the presumption that inflation will continue into the future as it has in the past, the transition from an inflationary to a noninflationary economy. Once expectations adjust, current money growth rates, as represented by the Federal Reserve's money growth targets for 1982 and 1983, are sufficient to finance expanding economic activity.

The severity of the recession we have experienced is, of course, partially attributable to long term structural problems in some key industries, such as automobiles and steel. However, the severity of the recession also illustrates the intransigence of inflation and inflationary expectations. With inflation and inflationary expectations deeply entrenched in an economy, the downward adjustment of price expectations is slower and therefore the period of adjustment to a noninflationary economy is prolonged. The depressive effect on economic activity of the transition from inflationary money growth to noninflationary monetary policy is stronger.

The cost of the transition has been raised, however, by persistent uncertainty in credit markets. A contributory factor is the fact that the Federal Reserve has not achieved a steady and predictable deceleration of money growth. Instead, the overall decline in the rate of money growth that has occurred over the past year and a half has been accomplished by long periods of near-zero money growth, followed by periods of extremely rapid growth. The average of these feast/famine periods has been an overall deceleration of money growth. But with this stop and go pattern, following on the heels of more than a decade of generally inflationary money growth, enormous skepticism remains that money growth will be maintained at a noninflationary rate over the long run. Unfortunately, that skepticism is reinforced every time the Federal Reserve allows money to expand at a rapid rate for a period of several months or quarters.

No doubt, that skepticism has also been nurtured by the developments in the budget process over the past years. Prospects for continued growth of government spending do not enhance the credibility of an anti-inflationary policy.

Research at the Treasury Department shows that the *quarterly* variability of money growth has added, conservatively estimated, two to three percentage points to the level of interest rates over the last two years. In addition, volatile money growth induces similar volatility in interest rates. For precisely this reason, we have repeatedly urged the Federal Reserve to provide for more stable and predictable money growth, as it adheres to its long run policy of reducing the trend rate of growth.

Do we conclude from this experience that restoring price stability is not worth the cost? Of course not. The severity of this recession should lead us *not* to the conclusion that the process of restoring price stability is *too* costly, but that it is *so* costly that we cannot afford to go through it again. Thus, I do not conclude as some do that we need to have the Federal Reserve open the floodgates and revert to the inflationary policies of the past. To the contrary, we have no rational choice other than to persevere and reap the benefits of lower inflation: lower interest rates and higher real economic growth.

One of the important effects of this change from an inflationary economy as it goes through the process of disinflation is the impact on relative prices of real and financial assets. In periods of increasing inflation, real assets—houses, land, gold, antiques—provide investors with the greatest expected real rate of return. In periods of declining inflation, financial assets—stocks, bonds, bank accounts, money market funds—provide the greatest expected real rate of return.

During much of the last decade, as inflation rose rapidly, investors realized that they received their best expected rate of return on real assets and transferred their money accordingly. The prices of those real assets went up. The prices went down on the assets they sold to make those purchases—stocks and bonds.

We are now in a period of decelerating inflation. We are experiencing the reverse of the previously mentioned process: Investors have begun to sell their real assets and put their money into financial assets. It is not an accident that, in recent months, the prices of houses and gold have come down, while bond prices and, more recently, the Dow Jones index have risen.

I'm not saying that everyone is selling houses and rugs to buy stocks and bonds, but there is some of that going on. In a $4 trillion economy, which we are on the verge of having, a shift of one or two or three percentage points puts tens of billions of dollars into the economy in the form of expanded potential credit. Thanks to declining inflation, that phenomenon is already happening, and additional credit needed for economic expansion is forming rapidly.

This expanded credit availability results in downward pressure on interest rates, and we are quite confident that this downward pressure will overwhelm the budget deficit in its upward pressure on the level of interest rates. Downward pressure will be enhanced by the Administration's tax cut, which will stimulate new private savings. Therefore, if monetary growth remains under control and inflationary expectations continue to abate, rising deficits will *not* be translated into rising interest rates.

This reasoning does not mean that deficits are good things; they are not. However, it *does* mean that it is *not* worthwhile to eliminate the deficit at all costs. We will *not* eliminate the deficit by increasing inflation, and we will *not* eliminate the deficit by increasing individual tax rates. The unfinished business of achieving a balanced budget will take longer because a succession of Democratic majorities in the Congress have geared the government to spend and spend. Speaking of legacies of the past, let me offer some observations on the unemployment situation.

In a recent address before the nation, President Reagan reminded us that unemployment cannot be solved without solving the things that caused it—the out-of-control government spending and the skyrocketing inflation and interest rates that led to unemployment in the first place. Unless you get to the root causes of the problem, which is exactly what our economic program is doing, you may be able to relieve the symptoms temporarily, but you will *never* cure the disease. The President also pointed out that, in the past, attempts were made at "quick fixes" that resulted in unemployment dipping for a short time, only to rise again to new highs. This pattern has persisted for a decade.

In 1968, for example, unemployment in the U.S. stood at 3.6%. In 1971, it shot up to 5.9%. Then it started coming down again, but instead of going all the way back to 3.6%, it bottomed out at 4.9%. In 1974, it started shooting up again, and the same thing happened; it bottomed out at a higher level than before. In other words, for all its short term ups and downs, the unemployment roller coaster was really an escalator, edging its way up the charts throughout the last decade. It is, without a doubt, inflation and the resulting high interest rates that are the real culprits behind this bad unemployment trend. It is those menacing root causes that this Administration is finally getting under control.

The unemployment rate dramatizes, as no other figure can, the gradual decline of our industrial strength in the latter part of the 1970s. The impact of inflation, foreign competition, excessive regulation and government spending have all come home to roost. This situation underscores the task we faced at the beginning of this Administration and the one we face today. That challenge is to help strengthen the basic fiber of our economy, the underpinnings of the free enterprise system that will adjust to changing conditions.

This task is not a short term one involving quick fixes. It is a problem that requires a long term commitment. We are determined to reverse the policies of the past that created this problem and to help develop a steadily growing economy that will put people back to work.

International Economic Policy

This Administration is convinced that the objectives of growth, employment and stability can be attained through economic policy discipline and reliance on market forces, both domestically and internationally. Our goals for the rest of the world are the same as our goals for the United States: a reduction in inflation and an increase in real economic growth.

There have been many comments lately about the "instability" of the international economic system and the need for governments to intervene in various ways to restore stability. Our view is that there is nothing inherently wrong with the current international economic system. What is causing instability in the international economy is the lack of discipline and lack of convergence in the domestic economic policies of the countries that make up this system. The only international remedy is sound domestic policies that foster noninflationary growth through monetary and fiscal discipline and greater reliance on market forces.

The Versailles Summit in June 1982 and the World Bank/IMF Annual Meetings in Toronto in September 1982 made progress on these points. We also intend to continue to press these points at the GATT ministerial in November.

One of the most important achievements of the Versailles Summit was an agreement by the leaders of the seven participating nations to a program of closer cooperation in pursuing economic policies. This U.S. proposal was aimed at greater convergence of the medium term economic policies of the major trading nations intended to achieve lower inflation, higher employment and renewed economic growth. We are hopeful that this proposal will help us achieve greater currency stability, internally and externally. There have been several meetings to follow up, and the results are promising.

In Toronto, we expressed the very clear sentiments of this Administration that economic problems are not solved by throwing money at them. We encouraged the IMF to continue its emphasis on conditionality regarding balance-of-payments loans. It is those IMF conditions that will help recipient countries get their own economic houses in order. We also suggested the establishment of a new special borrowing arrangement in the IMF, which would be in place in the event there were any major threats to the international monetary system.

We have also applied these same free market policies to the multilateral development banks, or MDBs, as they're called in Washington. Shortly after I came to the Treasury, I initiated a study to learn why some countries grow and others do not. We determined that it was not the level of aid that was important, but rather the *domestic* economic policies that those countries were pursuing. We have been struggling for 21 months to get fiscal and monetary discipline at home, and we are encouraging countries abroad to go through an adjustment process also. Around the world, many countries are making these changes—not because *we* think it's a good idea, but because without the right kind of domestic policies, they find their sources of international credit drying up.

Conclusion

Either at home or abroad, the application of discipline and a reliance on market forces can have only one possible long term outcome: a stable, prosperous economy, characterized by high growth, low inflation, low unemployment and low interest rates. We've made a lot of the difficult changes and suffered a lot of the pain. I believe the worst is behind us.

William James once wrote, "A great many people think they are thinking when they are merely rearranging their prejudices." Those of you who are in positions of leadership in industry can play a very valuable role by speaking out and by helping to keep attention focused both on the facts and on the fundamental issues.

We need your interest and your support.

We now have—at long last—a President courageous enough to do the right thing for the country and for the long run, even if it means a short term sacrifice.

We have gone over some tough terrain during the last year and a half. But the only way around a problem is through it. It was essential that this Administration move boldly to shift this economy from a high inflation/high interest rate basis to a low inflation/low interest rate basis.

We have made tremendous progress to date. We are going to stay the course, and we are going to see a lot more progress ahead. We are going to see the beginning of a long period of sustained, non-inflationary economic growth.

Computers With Human Characteristics — Threshold to the Future

BY EARL C. JOSEPH

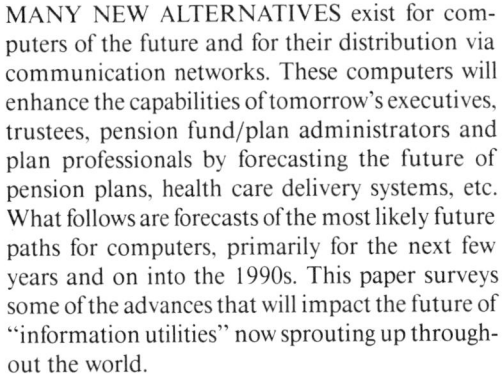

MANY NEW ALTERNATIVES exist for computers of the future and for their distribution via communication networks. These computers will enhance the capabilities of tomorrow's executives, trustees, pension fund/plan administrators and plan professionals by forecasting the future of pension plans, health care delivery systems, etc. What follows are forecasts of the most likely future paths for computers, primarily for the next few years and on into the 1990s. This paper surveys some of the advances that will impact the future of "information utilities" now sprouting up throughout the world.

The thrust of this article is to highlight forecasts of some of the many alternatives just now becoming visible that employee benefit executives (whether trustees, professional advisors, administrators or service providers) might expect to deal with in the long range future.

There have been many breakthroughs in the understanding of how the human brain works, but more so in the last decade than in all prior history. This new knowledge is now aiding in the design and implementation of artificially intelligent (AI) computer programs and personal computers, especially in the areas of inference reasoning and the development of computer systems with "expertise" concerning certain subjects. As a result, we are poised at the beginning of a major technology transfer to microcomputers with AI characteristics that will perform functions heretofore performable only by human minds. AI inference machines probably will be in general use in this decade.

Further, the rapidly evolving "silicon revolution" is producing a continuing list of new electronic and computer technology advances that will have continued widespread application in personal computers. "Smart machines" that are already impacting office systems—for example, in VDU (video desktop unit) word processors—usually have embedded microcomputers, sensors and actuators that give these machines adaptability and functions well in advance of their "dumb" forerunners. Now we are at the brink of embedding artificially intelligent "expert" systems into office automation machinery.

Mr. Joseph joined the staff of Sperry Univac over 30 years ago and has served in capacities including systems manager and project manager. He has directed, managed and performed the systems design, logic design, programming and applications of several computers and currently researches the future and advises management at all levels on future technology and alternative futures for Univac and society. He is president of Anticipatory Sciences, Inc. of Minneapolis. Mr. Joseph obtained a mathematics degree at the University of Minnesota. He holds three computer patents, is one of the creators of ethnotronic science, is a creator of a language to describe alternative futures, is the system architect of five major computer systems, has co-authored over 30 books and published over 150 papers. He is a founder, current director and past president of the Minnesota Futurists, as well as being a member of several other engineering and scientific organizations. Mr. Joseph, an advisory editor for Futurics *journal and the editor of* Future Trends *and* Systems Trends, *has lectured and conducted courses internationally at all educational levels. He also writes his own weekly column for the* Minneapolis Star, *"Alternative Futures."*

The last decade has been unusually fruitful in technology advances for almost all areas of computing. Heading the list are the rapid advances in silicon microchips and in microcomputers and their software. However, distributed data processing (DDP) also is high on the list. For the 1980s, DDP is pointing toward some fundamentally different directions, which give rise to insights on the future of information utilities (similar to today's energy utilities)—especially knowledge inference processing utilities.

Further, the smoke from the fires of new and yet-to-emerge technological advances is not expected to decline in the coming decades. In fact, technology advances can be expected to occur even faster, popping up many new alternatives for future information and knowledge inference processing systems.

Personal Computer Trends

This section is about both near-term and long range personal computer trends being developed in various computer manufacturer laboratories. It will steer clear of the type of information concerning the future that one could obtain by visiting a local computer store. Now that we are well into the 1980s, it's cogent to ask what new computer developments we should expect for the remainder of this decade and on into the next.

Are dramatic breakthroughs or turning points forecastable, or will the decade see only continued, rapid, evolutionary developments?

Microchip hardware components, computers, memory and software have been moving into the future along multiple trend paths. Some of these trends are taking off in new directions, whereas others currently are merging.

Computer hardware component technology has evolved over the last 20 years to ever-higher levels of integration. Soon chip components will advance into mixed technology, silicon (and other hardware type) microchips that combine digital and analog circuitry. Contained within the same component chips could be digital logic, memory, communications circuits, signal processing, sensor circuits, interface logic, data converters, display elements, voice synthesis, voice recognition and much more. A new set of basic components will exist to smarten up most personal computers, mainframes and communications subsystems in the future, thus closer entwining the computer with communications and forcing more changes, more uses and more distribution.

Microchips will continue to become denser, moving from LSI (Large Scale Integration) into and beyond VLSI (Very Large Scale Integration) circuit components, with upwards of tens of thousands of circuits, to VHSIC (Very High Speed Integrated Circuits), with hundreds of thousands of circuits, to ULSI (Ultra Large Scale Integration), with more than a million circuits, before 1990 to wafer-multichip systems components. As circuit integration levels increase, larger and larger (in capability, but not necessarily much larger physically) computers will be integrated as single microchip components, thus allowing "component computers." Increasingly, such component computers will become the primary type of computer embedded in machines—personal computers and much more. Thus, future computer systems and machines (noncomputer) will become "smart" via embedding component computers.

Next, multiple computers will be placed into single microchip components and later on into wafers—as "component computer systems." Large, step-function (as opposed to incremental) increases in microchip circuit density also spawn step-function increases in computer capability, usually without step-function increases in cost. This trend allows future personal microcomputers and chip component computers to reach mini and maxicomputer capabilities, at personal computer price levels. It may eventually lead to the possible future takeover of microcomputers or their merger with larger computers, especially as computers transform into and beyond supermicros, using VHSIC and ULSI hardware.

What is happening is that mainframe and embedded computers are in transition from: (1) a collection of boxes, to (2) a computer in a single box, to (3) a computer on a board, to (4) a computer integrated onto a chip component, to (5) becoming microcomputers. They are being further distributed as components/nodes in communication and control networks.

A similar trend is occurring with computer *systems* (collections of computers). The transition that computer systems are undergoing is again along multiple paths, from (1) centralized and decentralized collections of boxes, to (2) computer systems integrated within a box for both centralized and distributed applications, (3) distributed/ embedded board and chip level computers integrated as a computer system via denser bus networks and, later, (4) computer systems (collections of computers) integrated on single wafers and/or single large chips.

Near-term future trends in the classical larger scale computers are thus tending toward multiple directions, including: architecture managed through databases; advanced distributed data processor systems; higher levels of circuit integration; multimicroprocessor architectures; network configurations; considerably smarter, friendlier and easier-to-use data processing systems; more fault-tolerance logic and architectures; knowledge-based systems; integrated smart memory systems; more (artificial) intelligence; and component computers. For the longer range, the macro, mini and microcomputers' boundaries thus become increasingly blurred, as do the boundaries among data processing, software, knowledge processing and communications. In fact, all could merge in the far future.

This potential merging does not imply a single or standard embodiment or type of computers, or even a continuation of the "general purpose" class of computers. In fact, the most likely longer range future tends toward a multiplicity of special application types for computers. This alternative primarily is a result of the higher level of hardware integration trends that are making such types of mass-produced specialized or custom systems economically feasible.

Further, as next generation "calculators" become more complex and sophisticated, at least one trend should be toward smart "people-amplifier" devices—electronic "assistants." This category of future "computers" or smart distributed micro/personal computers includes: portable or wearable smart pilot machines, management machines, financial machines, programmer machines, banker machines, doctor machines, auditor machines, health machines, politician machines, systems design machines, accountant machines, secretary machines, writer machines (the list goes on and on, encompassing most professions).

As large capacity (but not physically large) memory components are added to these smart people-amplifier machines, together with direct communications links, these machines become "information appliance" personal computers. Most forecasts predict the turning point toward information appliances, allowing paperless systems and offices to become feasible, soon after the mid-1980s.

As society begins to apply and distribute these future calculator-spawned intelligent "computer appliances" massively, the need for bigger and smarter distributed data processors and memory also increases. Additionally, the need for more data communications (bussing) to link little data processors with other little ones and with the big ones will grow—requiring more high-speed data links and a movement toward optical fiber networks.

Eventually, such computerized and distributed information appliances could well make the physical office obsolete by allowing it to be portable (worn, carried or embedded in other machines). Obviously, such a future could allow the productivity of people and energy to be increased greatly. One way energy productivity could be increased is by substituting information appliances and data communications for travel and buildings (substituting for their construction costs in energy and materials, and the energy that would otherwise be needed to heat, cool, maintain and travel to them). Sometime toward the end of the 1980s or early in the 1990s, such distributed information appliances, together with their associated knowledge banks, should cost less than what it now costs for what we spend for energy to travel to and from the office.

Obviously such a trend, reducing the need for and making obsolete some geographically located office buildings—and paper—will have drastic, revolutionary and lasting future impacts on business and society. However, this trend only occurs if society opts to go in such a direction. Certainly, some will choose this more economical route in the farther future—especially when the energy crisis hits us again.

"Current awareness" is also being added to computer systems—communication subsystems with embedded computers, sensors and actuators (e.g., voice synthesis). For example, smart instruments for jet cockpits are being developed, which make pilots aware of abnormalities via voice output. This development is one way that jets are becoming more convivial (easier to use and friendlier). Another mode includes embedding component level "computers" between the interface of the machine (or at subsystem) and the human. This category of smart systems typically makes human operators aware of when to do something or to assist by "telling" how to apply the machine or subsystem. Additional microcomputers are being attached, embedded or integrated in systems like personal computers to do one or more of the following:

- Accelerator functions, e.g., to speed up certain functions and calculations
- To add special features/functions, e.g., ADA language capability or certain embedded special purpose applications such as telecommunications or signal processing
- To add fault-tolerance features, i.e., fail soft/safe/operational
- To field update the system, e.g., technology insertion
- To make the system more efficient and easier to apply.

Microsensors are also being added to computers. As more microcomputers are distributed and networked, collections of computer-based subsystems are cooperating at considerably higher levels.

Computers, communications and management functions are merging also. Data communication and distributed computer networking are becoming more and more crucial to most businesses and to the nation's economic well-being.

Impact of the New Technology

Many systems currently in use, even though they have been in use for a long time, could still be used a decade or more into the future. Some computers currently in use will even be in use beyond the year 2000. But revolutionary, alternative computers will also be added in the 1980s, to cohabitate with such an extended present. Some of the new component computers/systems will be attached to make the older systems smarter and more intelligent, i.e., to update the older systems piecemeal with new hardware as we now do with software.

In the early years of data processing, in the late 1950s and early 1960s, as technology advanced enough to allow a factor of two improvement in computer cost performance, designers and computer manufacturers introduced totally new computer systems into the marketplace. In the 1970s, even though innovations were coming faster, it took at least a factor of four improvement before a new system was born. Now, we expect innovations to occur even faster. Because of recent developments, however, we can forecast that new systems probably won't impact the marketplace until upwards to a factor of ten (and probably a lot more) in cost performance improvement can be designed into a system. This situation, of course, means that when a switch is made, it is apt to be bigger and, thus, have a bigger impact. However, manufacturers are expected to continue the practice of incremental evolution within each generation of computer systems.

Advances in technology force new computer developments, but the faster technological advances occur, the slower they seem to be integrated in systems and/or computers. For example, in the 1960s and 1970s (and forecasted for the 1980s), the leading edge functional capability of silicon microchip components doubled each year (in terms of the equivalent number of logic gates). This innovation, technological advance, doubling per year curve (a thousandfold increase in capabilities per decade) is the "Gordon Moore Curve." However, these advances were integrated into real systems at a rate closer to a hundredfold increase in component capability per decade, per type of technology (MOS, BIPOLAR, CMOS, etc.).

In the 1960s, manufacturers reacted to the new technology with new memory components each year (e.g., the 128 bit chip, followed by the 256 bit chip, then the 512 bit chip and, by the end of the decade, the 1024 bit or 1K chip). In the 1970s, manufacturers "batched" the advances, coming out with new memory microchips every few years (i.e., the 4K, 8K and 16K bit memory components). Now, there are some signs that the batching process could move to every three to five years. Therefore, when the advances are implemented, a bigger step-function change occurs, rather than small incremental changes. In either case, the same basic long term trend path is traversed.

In the far past of the 1950s and early 1960s, new maxicomputer generations occurred every six years. Now, the gap between maxicomputer generations has about tripled, whereas, in the microcomputer world, new generations of personal computers are occurring at a much faster clip, with a new generation appearing every few years. But how long will this pace continue?

There are many reasons for batching innovations over longer periods before making a step-function jump to capitalize on evolutionary trend advances in technology. One obvious reason for such a leveling or binding force is the high startup costs of changing to a new technology. The second reason goes hand in hand with the growth in the level of circuit integration. Higher levels of integration offer more alternative functions that can be cast as single components. Further, this increase in diversity increases the number of opportunities and the number of similar systems that emerge. Therefore, the higher the integration level, the more opportunities—and the longer it takes to use up the opportunities once a manufacturer or a nation chooses a technology level (e.g., VLSI or VHSIC at 10,000 circuits or at 100,000 circuits, etc.) as a standard.

In the meantime, a competitor (or another nation) can step in during the technology leveling period and leap ahead. The longer the stretch-out before making the next step-function advance, the easier it is (and the more impact the move has) for competitors to leap ahead. Of course, later on, the impacted manufacturer can leapfrog ahead again, long before the competition can get out of their binding force. Thus, the more rapid and higher the technology advances are, the more the opportunities pile up, but the more vulnerable the players (manufacturers and nations alike) become. In such a future technological environment, how can any single manufacturer stay at the leading edge throughout even a decade? Of course, for personal computer users, this competitive environment means continued price drops.

Implications of the New Technology

There are some straightforward reasons why computers and data processing are so important today and will continue to be in the future. First of all, our society is moving into the information age. Personal computers and computer networks increase the productivity of information activities—it's as simple as that. The smarter and more intelligent computers become through technological advances, the more productivity is raised.

Thus, a new breed of computers and computer management is needed and growing. Computer management is becoming more and more concerned with the role and function of information as it applies to their organization, rather than just the tools of information delivery, in order to increase productivity. Thus, distributed computers are moving computer management roles away from just managing the "processing tools" toward managing total information resources and services. As hardware integration increases, together with tumbling hardware costs, more software is cast into the hardware. Today, this trend of merging software into hardware is beginning to develop and is gaining speed. Before the end of this decade, some forecasters believe that more software for personal computers will be "hard" rather than "soft." Taken as whole, even for the short range, these trends allow for the long term future reality of going beyond science fiction—allowing "Star Trek"-like computers and steps toward (artificial intelligence) "inference engine" type computers.

Rapid technological change always has been the norm in the computer field and, recently, in the communications field. In the past, technology-driven change has forced an increasing diversity. From the foregoing, we now see that the same trends are forcing the merger of some of this diversity. However, most watchers of the future of computers see this merger as a way toward a new form of diversity. The most likely form that such future splintering, now forecastable, will take is along "smart"/"intelligent" vs. "dumb" computer lines, and along application lines. However, whichever multiple directions the computer and communication fields take into the future, there should be little doubt that these developments will penetrate deeper into society, providing new opportunities and causing considerable change and impact.

Artificial Intelligence

Artificial intelligence (AI), a relatively new technology, is now rapidly advancing beyond the research stage into practical use. In recent years, AI has been moving toward the practical use of expert systems, knowledge-based systems and inference processing systems. In most cases, practical AI is used in people-amplifier appliances or tools. Thus, future scientists, executives and managers, as well as most professionals, clericals and technical people in business and society will reap the benefits of almost 30 years of AI research.

Heuristics

What is an expert artificial intelligence system? Today, it is a computer system consisting of a set of AI programs that uses a stored knowledge base, inference procedures and logic rules to solve problems. Artificial intelligence research is a subfield of computer science that investigates the imitation of human processes (within computer systems). These AI processes are called "heuristics." Heuristics include learning, symbolic reasoning, logic, inductive discovery and reasoning, deductive analysis, problem solving, educated guessing and other intelligent processes including machine representation of knowledge for use in inference tasks. AI assumes that such heuristic knowledge is of equal or greater importance than factual knowledge. For AI purposes, heuristics are assumed to be the process defined as "expertise"—i.e., what "experts" do.

Heuristics go beyond the use of just logical, procedure-oriented strings of instructions operating on streams of data, or on databases—the programs that occur in standard computer systems. Simply, AI heuristics imitate the human brain, especially the heuristic processes for discovering how to solve a problem (or diagnose) and to assist in decisionmaking tasks. AI expert systems also are known as knowledge information processing systems. Their growth is spawning "knowledge engineering" as a new profession for computer scientists and programmers.

Conventional information processing computer systems execute a string of instructions (the program) as it streams from memory to process and transform data. In knowledge processing computer systems, layered over the conventional information processing system, tree strings of knowledge inference procedures working on data, heuristic rules and question answers are executed from and on information in memory. Expert systems thread through their knowledge bases via "If-Then-And" heuristic rules—that is, the contents of knowledge bases in expert systems are the recodification of knowledge into If-Then-And logic. Generation of knowledge bases using If-Then-And-Else rules is akin to programming, but without procedure-oriented statements and instructions.

AI heuristics include logical inference procedures that allow semantic access to knowledge bases that use AI processes for making "expert" judgments. AI expert systems capture and store the known expertise of a field. They translate such knowledge via AI programs and hardware that offer intelligent assistance to a practitioner in that field, i.e., providing "expertise" and using AI heuristics to interpret it. Expert personal computer systems can assist executives in becoming more expert.

AI heuristics with knowledge bases also can be embedded in common machines to make them more intelligent and more functional. Such AI intelligent and robotic-like machines also can be tied together in data communication networks to allow the growth of cooperative networks of distributed intelligent machines—considerably smarter than distributed data processing (DDP) systems.

Thus, an expert system uses AI inference coupled with a knowledge base to assist in solving problems and making decisions and judgments or for creating, discovering, synthesizing or inventing something—especially opportunities. Distributed cooperative and intelligent machine networks, coupled with microsensors, perform complete tasks that heretofore were performable only by groups of humans. Expert systems allow the tackling of problems that are difficult enough to require solutions that go beyond simple arithmetic or logic and require heuristics of significant power for approaching what heretofore required human "experts" for their solution. The knowledge and AI heuristic processes necessary to perform at such an expert level, plus the AI inference algorithms used, can be viewed in the AI expert system as a model of the collective expertise of the best human expert practitioners in that field.

Knowledge, once captured in such a fashion in an AI expert system, would also allow a nonexpert to apply such expert knowledge and the heuristics to nearly match and often exceed the average unaided human expert in that field. Further, AI expert systems and their knowledge bases can be constantly updated as society gains new knowledge—the "education" of expert systems continues via the updating of their knowledge base.

Knowledge Bases

A knowledge base is an electronic computer memory containing "expert knowledge" in the form of information and heuristics (logic rules) that normally would be used by human experts for whatever an expert does. The process of building a knowledge base for use with an AI expert system requires the compilation of an extremely "factual" taxonomy (body of information) of the specialized field of desired expertise—and the heuristics for the application of that information. Such knowledge-based taxonomies turn out to be far more understandable and accurate, and therefore more useful, than today's manuals and textbooks. Knowledge bases for expert management systems would contain taxonomies of strategic and tactical algorithms for decisionmaking, planning, control, communication and more.

Today, expert systems are computer programs employing artificial intelligence operations using knowledge bases for advising people (in an expert fashion) during the process of doing something—for example, assisting the average person to perform as an expert or for assisting decisionmaking, or inventing.

Tools and Appliances

The information age is upon us; over half of the U.S. work population now works at an information-related job. Therefore, we must expect new tools and appliances to be developed for amplifying what we do in this new age.

When we were in the agricultural age, tools of automation like the multiple gang plow, reaper, combine, manure spreader and irrigation machine hit the scene to amplify farm workers and the output of farmers. These mechanical people-amplifiers drastically raised the productivity of farmers via automation without computers. The result was a shift from over 90% of Americans working directly on the farm a few hundred years ago to less than 3% of our population working directly on the farm today.

In the industrial age, a recent age that for the U.S. already belongs to our past heritage, automation tools for raising the productivity of people (lathes, welding machines, riveters, punch presses, milling machines, numerically computer-controlled machines and, later, robots) were introduced. They altered the infrastructure of our society by molding it from the agricultural age into the industrial age. The result brought the number of people working directly in the factory from over 50%, at the height of our industrial age, to the present period with only 17% of the U.S. workforce working in the factory. This percentage is expected to fall rapidly in the eighties as new robotic automation technology wends its way into future factories.

Now, part of the world is entering into a new age, the information age. New tools and new appliances are coming into use, amplifying what society does. Usually in offices they amplify our ability to handle information and knowledge and open the door to greater information access. These new tools also are finding application both for raising the productivity of people outside of the offices and for the use of information everywhere—including in the home and factory and for leisure time activities.

Information age automation tools and appliances for raising the productivity of people start with computers. This tool emerged from the industrial age while speeding its demise. It also helped create the new age of information dimensions. Computers, word processors and the like, as they are forecasted to evolve into future information technology, portend to provide future business, education, government, professions, offices, farmers, industry, managers, politicians and institutions with increasing information access. They will provide expanding techniques and methods to help sense, measure, acquire, store, process, manipulate, associate, retrieve, disseminate, communicate and apply information, and will assist in turning information into knowledge applicable at the time it is needed.

The Transition

As one might expect, the transition into a new age is not easy—especially without the existence of social institutions necessary for the new age that is developing. For example, few nations as yet have either a Department of Knowledge or a Department of Computers. Nor are the architectures for the new machines, tools, appliances or systems for the information age as yet completely formulated or structured. Rather they come to us from the industrial age, and are thus largely cast in the image of the needs of that previous age.

Future AI Alternatives

In forecasting the future of AI expert systems, there are a number of obvious and expanding application areas. Perhaps at the top of the list for the course of future events for the 1980s are AI advice-giving systems. Already, expert system programs exist or are on computer-aided design (CAD) screens, for medical diagnosis, architectural design, the design of very large scale integrated silicon circuits, molecular generic design, programming, office management decisionmaking, factory management, home advice (e.g., financial, garden, lawn, repairs) and much more. Now being designed are expert management systems, expert programmer systems, etc. For example, envision how your profession would be enhanced and changed with an expert personal computer system.

Besides consulting, AI expert systems also can assist in the creative, management, design and other invention arts, as well as give diagnostic and prescriptive advice. They can take part in a dialogue, giving recommendations for real-time tasks at hand. Such dialogues involve the AI expert system threading itself through its knowledge base via "If-Then-And" heuristic rules together with the human whom it is advising. Some additional near-term uses and markets involve configuration management; robotics; assessment and planning; forecasting; intelligent agent functions; office automation; image, signal and voice interpretation; and education and training.

Future expert systems, in the form of "people-amplifiers" (future remote screen and keyboard computers, terminals or handheld computers) will present factual data or information, and advise or give opinions based on the "AI knowledge" contained in their knowledge bases. Further, and importantly, an expert system will backtrack to tell the logical process that it went through and recall the information it used to arrive at its "expert" advice or opinion.

The knowledge base of an expert system consists of "facts" and heuristics. The "facts" constitute a taxonomy of knowledge (information), similar to the information that a human expert would use for whatever expert task such an expert would be performing, codified by "If-Then-And" rules. But herein lies the stumbling block: What does an expert (human) do? Thus, it is no easy task to create a knowledge base that contains expert information and knowledge generally agreed on by experts in a field.

Further, not all expert knowledge is a set of "black and white" logic facts. Much expert knowledge is codifiable only as alternatives, possibles, guesses and opinions (i.e., as fuzzy heuristics). Heuristics, thus, consist of rules of good judgment, fuzzy knowledge and rules of plausible reasoning, as well as hard and fast logical reasoning, rules of good guessing and the like that are characteristic of expert level decisionmaking. Therefore, the performance level of an AI expert system is primarily a function of the size and capacity of the knowledge base, the quality of its contained expert information, the level of expertise and diversity of experts polled for forming the knowledge base, the completeness of its taxonomy, and the number and characteristics of its stored or programmed artificial intelligent heuristics (inference rules and procedures). Today, we are just at the ground floor of creating a variety of knowledge bases. The future will see this variety grow and the knowledge base contents evolve with considerable recodified knowledge.

There should be little doubt that, in the future, as AI expert systems evolve to become more expert, executives will possess very powerful people-amplifying tools to assist them, via personal computers netted with others, in almost any task tackled.

In fact, because a knowledge base arranges knowledge in a somewhat procedural fashion, as does a computer program, it will be more complete, correct and comprehensible than the typical textbook or manual. Experience with current expert systems shows that, when compared with traditional sources of knowledge (books, tapes, people, classrooms, etc.), present and future knowledge-based systems are (or can become) ten to 1,000 times more complete, precise, correct and comprehensible.

Perhaps more importantly, as stated earlier, AI expert systems allow knowledge application and amplification in the real-time of human decision-making and actions to amplify the management process. The expanded use of expert systems can thus be forecasted to impact distributed computer system development in the following directions: (1) more conviviality (more easily used, friendly and helpful interface functions); (2) more portability for real-time use by managers, technicals and professionals; (3) more inference and knowledge processing engines embedded for creating robotic-like machines and intelligent networks; (4) a growth in the number, quality and completeness of knowledge bases; and (5) widening applicability and diversity of expert systems.

Is There an AI Expert System in Your Future?

We can now forecast a positive "yes" to this question. Recently, two expert systems have reached the "champion" level—DENDRAL and MACSYMA. DENDRAL is a knowledge-based expert AI system for solving a class of symbolic chemistry problems. It is the culmination of 16 years of AI research and experimentation at Stanford University. It has reached such a level that there exists no other knowledgeable method (human or machine) for doing a subfield of chemistry symbolically. MACSYMA is a knowledge-based expert AI system for solving symbolic general math equations and systems of equations. MACSYMA solves symbolic algebraic equations (A + B = C) and performs differential and integral calculus. It also has reached the champion level, wherein no better means (tool) exists (human or machine) for performing general mathematics.

In the 1950s and '60s, mathematicians were impacted by large scale computers that allowed them to do mathematics which previously was impossible. In the 1970s, mathematicians were impacted with second generation "smart mathematician machines"—this time it was the handheld electronic calculator and microcomputers. Now, with AI, mathematicians are being impacted and amplified with third generation systems.

In development are numerous AI knowledge-based expert systems that soon could reach "champion" level status. Included in this growing list are AI knowledge-based expert systems for such applications as air traffic control, computer configuration, VLSI design, crisis management, computer-aided design and computer maintenance. Because of these recent AI breakthroughs, you should expect funding for AI research to be expanded significantly by government, industry and academia in the coming years.

However, the biggest recently announced development in AI comes from the Japanese. In October 1981, the Japanese announced their thinking relative to fifth generation computers for the 1990s: They are to be knowledge inference processing systems. Briefly, the AI computer system thrust that the Japanese recently have committed to develop includes a knowledge base management system, an intelligent interface system, a problem-solving inference system, a large knowledge base, a relational algebra machine, an intelligent programming system, an intelligent VLSI CAD development system and a collection of innovative non-von Neuman mechanisms and processors. Further, the expected speed ranges up to 1,000 *mega-LIPS* (logic inference processing steps); one LIP equals approximately 1,000 information processing steps). This upper computational speed range is close to executing the equivalent of a trillion instructions per second! Additionally, future AI architectures research will spawn many types of AI machines, most with less-than-maximum capability.

The Japanese goal recognizes that knowledge and information will soon be elevated to the level of a basic human need—as basic as food—and in so doing, recognizes that they must create a new industry and new machines. Their current plan is to leap far ahead of the rest of the world and to lead the world in AI machines. They have initiated this effort. Again the Japanese have set an advanced technology target for us to shoot at and perhaps go beyond in the next decade.

The future of AI includes widening application; rapid growth in usage; growth in AI application programs for assisting most scientific, engineering and management disciplines; development of new inference engine computers; and the development, growth, evolution and acquisition of knowledge bases. Further, AI expert personal computers and networks will transform future
- Offices, factories, schools, farms and homes
- Professions
- Arts
- Governments.

Is a Robot Simulator in Your Future?

As we cross the threshold into the postindustrial society via the information age, science and technology are undergoing major metamorphoses. On one side there is the pragmatic framing of new clusters of specialized knowledge fields. Ample examples are blossoming and growing explosively—computer and information sciences, cybernetics, the new genetics, etc., although the emphasis is often more on a branching into subdisciplines or on a growth of interdisciplinary and cross-disciplinary fields. On the other side are multidisciplinary holistic fields such as the general system sciences, the anticipatory sciences and the assessment sciences. Thus, there is a splintering toward deeper specialization as well as trends toward the unification and synthesis of knowledge.

On closer examination, what seems to be emerging is a mosaic or panorama of a vast amount of accumulated information—as well as immense growth in the need, amount and use of information—that requires new tools like advanced computers to be handled. For the computer to be a useful assistant to executives, or for any discipline, efforts are required to reduce this vast growth of detail into something digestible. Therefore, the trend is to squeeze individual discipline areas into specific frames or models. Such reductions are marked by their integrative nature through the universal language of knowledge bases and/or modeling disciplines that are fast taking over the role heretofore played by mathematics. The computer enters the picture as the tool allowing such real world models to be simulated.

Through computer simulation, scientific experimentation occurs and becomes possible without attendant, cumbersome, laboratory equipment and procedures. That is, through AI modeling and simulation, it is now possible for executives and scientists to "play" serious experimental and mathematical "games" with the object of their decision-making or research, via the computer. This accomplishment is possible for the manager or scientist without the need to learn sophisticated management science, laboratory techniques or mathematics. In other words, the detailed mathematical and discipline-oriented experimental skills and procedures are embedded within the knowledge-based computerized model.

Such "robot simulators" allow, for example, the scientist to concentrate on the science being investigated rather than being buried within the mathematics and discipline "crafts" needed to perform the desired experiment. However, the manager or scientist must first learn his or her field and also the computer simulation/modeling language. Robot simulator assistants now increasingly do for the scientist what the calculator does for the average person; they remove the need to perform bulky, precise and rote skill functions, allowing the researcher to get more quickly and easily to the core matters of science—the search for and acquisition of new knowledge.

With robot simulators, the manager can ask questions of knowledge-based computer modeling and have simulated experiments performed that otherwise are nearly impossible or too time-consuming and costly. For example, the executive could ask the all-important question, "What happens if?" Then the computer gives an answer, after performing the simulated experiment, while the experimenter views the progress of the computerized experiment and intervenes when desired. Then the experimenter can ask the next question, "What happens if something else is done instead?" to arrive at a different comparable answer from the robot simulator. Through such interactive simulations, the researcher can get right into the experiment as a surrogate participant.

Next, envision future robot simulators in the form of advanced handheld calculators with voice dialoguing capabilities. Further, envision them in the form of a simulator for general decisionmaking, rather than for calculating. The utility of such future smart robot simulators for managers, politicians, voters and so forth becomes obvious when we think of them as people-amplifiers—or electronic assistants. Consider a robot simulation in the form of a smart doctor machine for enhancing an individual's health. One form might be worn as a watch in the future, so that it could constantly monitor the body's functioning. In this case, a constant simulation would be occurring, triggered by changes in sensed body measurements (temperature, blood/sugar ratio, pulse rate, etc.). One purpose of the real-time simulation would be to warn the individual of pending conditions that need attention before they build to proportions that could harm the individual's health. Later forms might even deliver the necessary counteraction to "repair" the system (for example, genetic splicing intervention to fix a malfunctioning gland) or to treat the symptom (e.g., automatic injection of insulin for the diabetic).

Office Automation = Office of the Future

The office of the future has started and its evolution is under way. This electronic office is the result of two basic forces for leveraging change. The first and most obvious change agent is the basic economic need to raise productivity in the office. The second force for change results from the meteoric rise of science- and technology-intensive electronics/computer/communications industries. Considerable technology is lurking in the labs about to come to the rescue by increasing the productivity of executives, professionals and clerks in offices. Thus, one most likely forecast, as the office evolves through and beyond the 1980s, is the expectation of wave after wave of new electronic office technology—and wave after wave of resultant change. Further, these changes in the office will splash over to change and restructure our total society.

Computers + communications + video + software = the office of the future. However, since each of these technologies is rapidly evolving and advancing, the office of the future is also constantly changing its character. Modern office automation started essentially with the introduction of screen (TV-like) and keyboard word processing (WP) hardware, which automated some secretarial and clerical functions. The addition of the microcomputer as an office appliance now is raising the productivity of professionals and some managers. New software for these systems is being introduced almost daily, which makes office automation equipment friendlier, easier to use and, therefore, more useful and more influential. Component microcomputers are being added to office machines like the typewriter to make them smarter.

One future history map for the office of the future consists of the following milestones in the wake of such waves of change: (1) minicomputer-based stand-alone word processors, (2) smart word processors (with embedded microcomputers), (3) communication WP networks, (4) marriage of WP with data processing, (5) wave after wave of office-oriented microcomputer software, (6) computer mail, (7) computer conferencing, (8) database computers, (9) voice-activated typewriters and video desk units (VDUs), (10) smart office machines (office machines with embedded microcomputers and electronic sensors/actuators, like typewriters that would accept voice dictation), (11) electronic file cabinets (VDUs with mass storage), (12) people-amplifier appliances (e.g., smart and expert manager machines), (13) smart offices (distributed, cooperative and communications networked/interconnected smart office machines), (14) information appliances (VDUs and people-amplifier appliances with lots of memory) or "paperless office" machines, (15) knowledge-based, expert, artificially intelligent office and people-amplifier machines, (16) "information utility" office services, (17) the "electronic briefcase," (18) the "electronic book," and (19) "component offices" (office functions on a silicon wafer for embedding into other machines).

Already milestone (8) is here. As can be read between the lines of the foregoing list, there should be no doubt that the office and society as a whole will undergo many radical changes in this decade.

A key phenomenon of our current age is the avalanche of technological advances leading us ever-faster into a new era—especially for the office. The postmodern age now at its beginnings is, to a great extent, a product of the application of new knowledge resulting in the creation of new technological opportunities—especially for the office. This growing stream of developing high tech trends is also fed by many negatively impacting socioeconomic events. That is, negative consequences of past human actions are causing societal reactions that push the search for solutions. In modern times, many, if not most, solutions end up pushing society toward more rapid adoption of new technology. In either case, society is tugged or spurred even faster into the developing new postindustrial age.

Personal Computer Utility Futures

Distributed data processing (DDP) is headed along many diverse paths—with many more expected to follow in the future. Such a rich variety in DDP offers users a broad tapestry of alternatives and many choices, even the choice of distributing personal computers in local area networks for assisting executives. Since so many alternatives exist for distributed computing, each path taken will impact the users, the office, management and society somewhat differently.

Some of these alternatives are: an extended and

evolved version of the present, smart machines containing embedded computers, distributed people-amplifier appliances (beyond the calculator), distributed information appliances for the emerging "information utility," distributed knowledge-based systems, distributed artificially intelligent expert systems, inexpensive microcomputer alternatives to DDP and distributed decision support systems. Symptomatic of the coming period will be waves of computer alternatives swishing us toward multiple futures for applying information and knowledge via information utilities, which will deliver information much like electrical energy and water are now delivered into homes, businesses and factories.

A major trend is toward smart DDP systems, which will incorporate the new engine of change: microcomputers. Microcomputers also are being embedded in all manner of machines for making the resulting devices increasingly "smarter," friendlier and easier to use. Increasingly, these smart machines are being linked through communications, allowing cooperative networks of smart machines to form a part of future information utilities.

What Is DDP?

When Edison invented the light bulb, some forecasted that society would need to be redesigned and rebuilt to accommodate his new invention. Envisioned were new homes, offices, schools and factories, wherein each was designed and built around a centralized hall. Fanning out from the hall would be rooms. These rooms would have windows, not necessarily for looking outside, but rather for looking into the centralized hall—in order that Edison's newly invented "artificial sun" could provide light for the rooms.

We, of course, now know that society did not adapt in this fashion to the light bulb via centralization. Architects distributed light bulbs, usually many to a room, and the artificial sunlight invention was adapted to the then-existing societal infrastructure.

For most of the first 25 years of the history of our computer industry, the opposite situation has largely occurred, wherein the computer was centralized, requiring society to adapt. Now with the current trends in DDP, the computer is adapting to society with the new thrust of distributing computer power, which started long ago but now is expected to become the norm. However, since we have for so long been in a centralized world of computers, considerable recasting of offices, institutions and organizations will need to occur to adapt them to fit into the distributed mold, away from "big computers." Earlier in the last decade DDP grew slowly, but now the trend is snowballing.

Currently, however, even when we distribute computer functions, we still carry the big computer thinking paradigms along with us into the organizations sharply honed by the recent past thrust for centralized functioning. However, with rapid transitions toward DDP, together with the DDP trends forecastable for the coming information era, efficiency is favoring an entirely new set of distributed paradigms—away from large, centralized systems toward small, personal computer, distributed systems.

This change started slowly with minicomputers and is now growing in a big way with microcomputers, which are forcing and requiring a new wave of organizational transformations. Such change is beginning to be especially noticeable in the emerging office of the future. The current convergence and integration of DDP (with word processing, management information systems, database systems, data communications, decision support systems, satellite communications, computer mail, computer conferencing, computer-aided design, computer-assisted instruction and much more) demand further adaptations, different office, home and school interactions and new forms of organizational restructuring. Such changes and transformations are likely to cohabitate with the old technologies, as distributed personal computers will with centralized large computer systems, during the transition. In fact, such cohabitations are also apt to exist even for the long range future.

There are many expected impacts resulting from future waves of DDP penetration and merger into society with communications and the office of the future. For example, the distribution of computing power transforms computer operations and creates "information resource management" for managing the total information system (including computers, mail, communications, copying, word processing, filing, library, etc.).

DDP expands access to information resources, giving more timely information and, at the same time, lowers the status of traditional power structures as they are more easily bypassed. Management's span of control is extended, requiring fewer middle managers in the loop. DDP promotes horizontal communications, thereby undermining hierarchical and centralized power organizations and exposing the real power structures.

While bypassing the formal organization, DDP grows a new organizational structure and new hierarchies. Further, DDP decentralizes responsibility and makes the total organization more accountable. It distributes authority and decisions, deemphasizes or bypasses centralized control and creates more autonomous suborganizations of functions.

DDP, through information utilities, can substitute for a great amount of travel, thus allowing for more timely meetings and the fostering of energy savings. Additionally, DDP allows for greater and more rapid organizational adaptation, faster transfers of knowledge and fewer middle organizational "filters"; it triggers cooperation. Therefore, DDP can influence the growth of organizations less vulnerable to crisis, more able to react to urgent situations and, thus, more capable of quick reaction to change, opportunities and challenges.

In the 1980s and beyond, the distribution of personal computers and microchip computers will cause future computers to be integrated into "things" (offices, machines, etc.) for information handling, control and the automation of new functions, thus affecting and transforming most aspects of societal functioning. As the distribution of computer functions wends its way deeper into future systems, society will be drastically altered, as will the machines, systems and people that are made smarter and more intelligent.

We are moving into the information age. In this new age, the use and need for information and knowledge become a basic need of society, as basic as food, shelter and security for the individual in our daily functioning. The distribution of computer power, via the growth of a new industry (the information utility), thus becomes a basic necessity for this emerging new age. However, the screen and keyboard word processing jargon of tomorrow may not refer to the smarter information processing computer systems to be developed in the 1980s as distributed computers, but rather as "distributed smart machines."

It can be concluded that, with the further distribution of computer power, intelligent systems will continue the trend toward productivity increases for a widening number of applications, eventually encompassing nearly every activity that people and institutions are engaged in. Further, from the foregoing discussion it is now clear that the future of distributed personal computing, now growing into a new information utility industry, consists of multifaceted trends, alternatives and directions—only a few of which have been outlined in this presentation.

Conclusion

For centuries, advances in scientific and technological areas have altered the context of life and the structure of society many times over. Now we are at the threshold of placing society's accumulated knowledge into artificially intelligent expert systems for amplifying what we do.

Human capabilities are extremely limited when unaided. In the past, mechanistic technological advances amplified human abilities for pounding, locomotion, lifting, toting, cutting, seeing, digging, hearing, resisting diseases, coping with weather, arithmetic operations and much more. We are now at a new technological threshold—entering a new era in which human powers for perceptual reasoning, decisionmaking, inventing, creating, thinking and other mental activities will be amplified. This new era results from our recent acquisition of the ability to construct artificially intelligent expert machines. For raising the productivity of the mind, such amplification is achieved by imitating the human brain's reasoning and other mental powers with computer technology, in the form of expert systems.

The result of recent advances in AI expert systems is about to put society at the brink of the massive application of artificial intelligence. As a result, a new era is opening that should totally change the character of society. Even though AI has been a subject of study and research within computer science for decades, few people are versed in what it is and what it will mean. With its recent breakthrough into practicality, executives and the world of personal computing are, at present, ill-prepared for early reaping of its full potential or the opportunities it affords. Nor are we prepared for the changes that AI must force as it goes into massive use. However, there should be little doubt that this AI breakthrough should grow explosively. AI will be in future personal computers and thereby drastically restructure tomorrow's computer networks, which will supply executives and society with knowledge to be used for amplifying and enhancing our activities.

CHAPTER 3

Topics in Plan Administration

E. Calvin Golumbic
Partner
Arent, Fox, Kintner, Plotkin & Kahn
Washington, D.C.

Gilbert K. Reeves, CPA
Partner
Thomas W. Havey & Company
Chicago, Illinois

Edward F. Zimmerman, Jr., CLU, FLMI
Vice President, Money Markets
Prudential Insurance Company of America
Newark, New Jersey

Bernard Handel, CPA, CEBS
President
The Handel Group, Inc.
Poughkeepsie, New York

William J. Chadwick
Partner
Paul, Hastings, Janofsky & Walker
Los Angeles, California

Lawrence J. Hass
Member
Groom and Nordberg, Chartered
Washington, D.C.

Richard J. Davis, Jr.
Senior Attorney
Davis, Frommer & Jesinger
Los Angeles, California

Warren H. Saltzman
President
Saltzman & Johnson Law Corporation
San Francisco, California

Stephen Horn, II, CPCU
Executive Vice President
Jones Horn Insurance Brokers
San Francisco, California

Robert A. DeCori
Vice President–Financial Operations
Kelly & Associates, Inc.
Chicago, Illinois

Michael J. Carroll
Member
Erskine & Tulley, P.C.
San Francisco, California

Marc Gertner
Partner
Shumaker, Loop & Kendrick
Toledo, Ohio

Russell W. Thurau
Principal and Vice President
Tillinghast, Nelson & Warren, Inc.
San Antonio, Texas

David W. Silverman
Partner
Granik, Silverman & Campbell
New City, New York

Robert W. Ridley
Partner
Forster, Gemmill & Farmer
Los Angeles, California

Leo A. Majich
Fund Manager
Operating Engineers Trust Funds
Pasadena, California

Sheldon P. Lewis, CPA
President
Benefit Administration Corporation
Fresno, California

Joseph M. Courtney, CEBS
Administrative Manager
Service Employees International Union
Local 36 Benefit Funds
Philadelphia, Pennsylvania

The Role of a Trustee in a Collectively Bargained Pension Trust

BY E. CALVIN GOLUMBIC

The Role of a Trustee Generally

Under general principles of equity, a trustee bears an unwavering duty of complete loyalty to the beneficiary of the trust. This loyalty is to the exclusion of the interests of all other parties, and the rule against divided loyalties is rigidly enforced.

The Role of a Collectively Bargained Pension Plan Trustee

Section 302(a) of the Taft-Hartley Act generally prohibits an employer from making payments to a union representative. Section 302(c)(5), however, allows an employer to contribute to an employee benefit trust that satisfies certain statutory requirements.
- The funds may only be used for payment of benefits for employees and their dependents.
- The basis for these payments must be laid out in a detailed written agreement between the union and the employer.
- The funds must be kept in a trust.
- The employees and employers must be equally represented in the administration of the trust.

Although Section 302(c)(5)(B) requires an equal balance between union and employer trustees, nothing in the language of the section reveals any Congressional intent that a trustee may administer a trust in the interest of the party that appointed him. Rather, the legislative history confirms that Section 302(c)(5) was designed to reinforce, not alter, the long established duties of trustees. Congress directed that collectively bargained pension trustees must administer their trusts for the sole and exclusive benefit of the employees and their families.

The Role of a Collectively Bargained Pension Plan Trustee Under ERISA

The Employee Retirement Income Security Act of 1974 (ERISA) essentially codified the strict fiduciary standards of a collectively bargained pension plan trustee. Section 404(a)(1) requires a

Mr. Golumbic is a partner in the lawfirm of Arent, Fox, Kintner, Plotkin & Kahn, Washington, D.C., where he specializes in ERISA litigation. He was formerly the general counsel for the United Mine Workers of America Health & Retirement Funds and, before that, the assistant general counsel in charge of litigation for the Pension Benefit Guaranty Corporation. In those positions, he was involved in over 100 pension cases, at least 20 of which were on appeal. In the last year, Mr. Golumbic briefed or argued three pension cases in the Supreme Court, Amax, Robinson *and* Kaiser Steel. *He also directed the briefing in* Nachman *and* A-T-O, *which are the cases primarily relied on by counsel and the courts in litigation involving the constitutionality of the withdrawal liability provisions in the Multiemployer Pension Plan Amendments Act of 1980.*

trustee to discharge his duties solely in the interest of the participants and beneficiaries. Section 406-(b)(2) declares that a trustee may not act on behalf of another party. Section 405(a) imposes a duty on each trustee to prevent the other trustees from breaching their fiduciary duties.

In short, the fiduciary provisions of ERISA were designed to ensure that trustees act for the sole benefit of a plan's participants—to prevent trustees from being placed in a position of dual loyalties and to impose on trustees an obligation to take affirmative action to prevent a violation of these responsibilities.

Collectively Bargained Pension Plan Trustees Are Appointed by the Union and Employers

Nevertheless, collectively bargained pension plan trustees are appointed by the union and the employers under Section 302(c)(5) of the Taft-Hartley Act. In fact, Congress has provided that labor and management shall each appoint the same number of representatives to serve as trustees of a collectively bargained plan. The equal representation requirement reflects the fact that management and labor trustees may have reasonably different views on policy matters involving the exercise of broad discretion. For example, if a collective bargaining agreement authorizes the trustees to establish the contribution rates on salvaged lumber, the management trustees will certainly support a lower rate than the union trustees.

If the same collective bargaining agreement also requires contributions on tons of lumber produced for use or for sale, the union may reasonably argue that tons produced include moisture in the lumber used or sold. Management, on the other hand, may legitimately argue that moisture is not lumber, even though it has not been removed prior to use or sale and, therefore, an allowance should be made for the content thereof in calculating contribution requirements.

If the collective bargaining agreement also authorizes the health plan to provide benefits to pensioners whose last signatory employer is out of business, the union and management trustees may disagree on the construction of the phrase "out of business." The union trustees may adopt a very liberal construction of the phrase "out of business," so that pensioners may receive health benefits when the last signatory employer is financially unable to provide them. The management trustees, on the other hand, may adopt a more conservative construction to protect the remaining signatory employers from the burden of assuming the health obligations of the financially unstable company. Therefore, the union trustee may conclude that a signatory employer is out of business because it no longer operates a lumber industry facility and the management trustee may conclude that the employer is not out of business, because it continues to operate outside the lumber industry.

There may even be a dispute about when an employee reaches age 55 and becomes eligible for an early retirement pension. The union trustee may argue that the pension plan provides that all ambiguities are to be resolved by state law and that the law provides that a person reaches his birthday, including his 55th, one day before. The management trustee, however, may argue that there is no ambiguity because the plan provides that an employee is eligible for an early retirement pension at age 55, and that means not one day before.

Notwithstanding the Fact That They Are Appointed by Management and Labor, Collectively Bargained Pension Plan Trustees Are Solely Responsible to Plan Participants

Even though management and labor trustees may have legitimate differences on policy matters involving areas of wide discretion, their sole duty is to plan participants. They are not representatives of the collective bargaining parties. Indeed, they may not have dual loyalties. They must, in short, overcome any loyalty to the interest of the parties that appointed them, where those interests are inconsistent with the interests of plan participants.

For example, even though the reduction of pension benefits during a strike would be unpopular, the union trustee must join with the industry trustee in doing so where the plan requires such reductions in the event that assets become insufficient. Even though a refusal to return mistaken contributions would be unpopular with the industry, the management trustee must join with the union trustee in that refusal if it is required by law. Lastly, even though the collective bargaining parties may desire to provide coverage for a particular class not already provided for in the plan, the management and labor trustees may not do so unless the plan is formally amended.

In discharging their duties to plan participants, management and labor trustees are bound by the terms of the collective bargaining agreement and the plans and trusts incorporated therein. They must, in short, follow these documents unless they are inconsistent with existing law.

An Auditor Looks at Monitoring Cash Flow

BY GILBERT K. REEVES, CPA

JUST TO BE SURE we're all thinking along the same lines, let's agree that by using the term "cash flow," we are referring to the flow of dollars created by employer contributions, dividends, interest, rents and proceeds of sales and, in the other direction, created by purchases of securities and payment of benefits, refunds and expenses.

Cash Flow—General Operations

Before concentrating on *investment* cash flow as a specific, let's discuss cash flow from general operations first. Whether you are dealing with a pension fund or a welfare fund, you, as trustees, must see to it that you always have enough money on hand to pay your bills. However, at the same time you must maximize your investment income by not allowing cash to lie idle.

Zero Balance Checking Accounts

In the case of a welfare fund, whether insured or self-funded, one way to allow your cash to remain active is to establish a zero balance checking account in the same bank in which you maintain a savings or investment account. Simply stated, you never have a balance in the checking account. Your money will stay invested and working for you until your checks arrive at the bank. Then, and only then, will the bank transfer from your savings or investment account the money necessary to cover the checks you issued. To illustrate, please look at the financial statement at the beginning of the Appendix. You will note that both the general checking account and claims checking account are overdrawn.

The general checking account overdraw represents all the checks written and outstanding per the fund records as of June 30, the fiscal year-end. By the same token, the claims account overdraw represents all claim checks issued and outstanding at year-end. In total, they represent a half million dollars still at work earning at a rate of 8.49% annually, rather than sitting idly in a checking account.

Lockbox for Employer Contributions

To maximize the input side of this operation, the trustees should adopt a lockbox approach for employer contributions. In this system, employers

Mr. Reeves is a partner in the firm of Thomas Havey & Company, certified public accountants, Chicago, which he joined in 1967. He now serves as auditor for welfare, pension and other employee benefit plans and advises boards of trustees and/or professional administrators in accounting systems and plan design. He also conducts specialized audits and feasibility studies on self-funding versus insurance plans for hospital benefits. Mr. Reeves received his B.A. degree from Augustana College and did postgraduate work at Northwestern University. He was an auditor with Arthur Andersen & Company, later doing professional consulting and administration work. He is a member of the ERISA Committee of the Illinois Society of Certified Public Accountants. Active in International Foundation affairs for many years, Mr. Reeves was formerly chairman of the Accountants Committee and a member of the Educational Program Committee. He is also a past member of the Employer Liability Study, CEBS, Corporate Study and Financial Review Committees, and is a former member of the Board of Directors.

send their periodic reports directly to the fund depository bank. Upon receipt, the bank puts the money to work in a money market account, a variable note account or some other short term investment. The fund's money, therefore, is put into the investment stream as quickly as possible with no delay caused by having the money first go to the administrative office.

In the case of a pension fund, this combination also can be used. Some funds transmit new money to their investment managers only once a month. In the interim, the money lies idle in a checking account. The cash flow can be improved by adopting the lockbox-zero balance approach.

Financial Statement Review

Before moving on, let's take another look at the financial statement in the Appendix. Remembering the concept of "getting it in as soon as possible and taking it out as late as possible," let's look at the other items on the financial statement. The textbook approach to cash flow analysis is probably not appropriate here, but good old common sense still applies.

A quick review of cash receivables and investments doesn't indicate any problems. But I do find one of the prepaid items posing a rather serious problem. You will note that administrative expenses were prepaid by over $100,000. I am sure that the contract administrators in the audience could present cogent arguments about why this procedure is all right, but from the basis of a cash flow analysis, it represents bad planning. This review is a good example of the sort that trustees should make on their operations just to be certain that they are making the best possible use of their money.

Cash Flow—Investment Accounts

Having agreed that we are going to get our money into the investment stream as quickly as possible and leave it in as long as possible, let's discuss how we should monitor the cash flows generated by the investment process. To state the obvious, cash flow through investment accounts begins with the first transfer of funds to your investing agent. From that point forward, somebody should be monitoring the daily activities of the investment agent. A little later I will discuss who that somebody might be.

Cash Held by Investing Agency

Remembering the basic objective of getting your cash flow into the investment stream as quickly as possible and leaving it there as long as possible, your investor must be charged with the responsibility of putting your money to work "upon receipt." It does no good for your investment program to have money sitting idle while your investor is waiting for a "good buy." Therefore, he should be accountable to you on a daily basis for all cash handled by him. As an aside, in many large funds the investor will buy ahead for his client in anticipation of a transfer of money.

For example, in the financial statement in the Appendix, you will note that the First National Bank has a $400,000 overdraw in the investment agency account. Obviously, you are making the best use of your money when you have it invested before you ever put it into the marketplace.

If you are paying your benefits directly out of your investment funds, again you want to be sure that the monies are not transferred out of the investment flow any sooner than necessary to cover the pension checks.

Daily Activities of Investing Agent

The most difficult part of your cash flow to monitor is day-to-day transactions in the security markets. There are four basic questions that should be answered: If it is a purchase, was your cost within the day's range? If it is a sale, was your security sold within the day's range? If it is a dividend cash or stock, was it received in the correct amount and on a timely basis? If it is a payment of interest, was it in the correct amount and on a timely basis?

What's the Problem?

At this point, you might be wondering if that sort of picky information is really material to the net outcome of your investment program. Let's take a look at the excerpts from an audit report in the Appendix. Looking at this page, you will note that the fund has investments in excess of $400 million. For report purposes it is broken down by class of investment and is further broken down by the various investment agencies. If you will then turn to Table I in the Appendix, you will note that the investment income is itemized. I am sure by this point you are wondering, "OK, what is the problem?" Given the condition of the marketplace at June 30, 1981, the fund seems to be doing reasonably well. I submit, however, that a delay of two days in the reinvestment of dividend or interests, or a purchase at a cost higher than the day's average, or a sale at a cost lower than the day's average could have a meaningful impact on the results of the fund. When you are dealing with these kinds of numbers, one-tenth of 1% can produce a meaningful amount of money.

For example, this fund had hard dollar investment income of $40 million, or approximately $108,000 a *day*. Now you can move the numbers around to fit the size of your own fund, but even an income of $400,000 works out to over $1,000 a day. A one day delay in reinvesting $1 million at 14% costs the fund $383. If that delay were from Friday to Monday, the loss becomes more than $1,000. If you reinvest that same $1 million six times in one year and are constantly late on a Friday-to-Monday basis, you will have lost $6,000 on that one investment alone.

By this time I hope I have you all convinced that this is a problem that requires your attention, and I hope that you are asking yourselves what you can do about it.

It is not my function as an auditor to provide my clients with that kind of service on other than an annual basis. But I know that there are companies in the performance measuring service field that do provide their clients with a quarterly report answering the four questions that I mentioned earlier. A sample of one such report in the Appendix explains their methodology. Also in the Appendix, Table II shows daily transactions and indicates by an asterisk those transactions that fall outside the daily range. Table III shows daily cash and weighted daily cash average. Table IV is the summary of the exceptions. Table V is a sample of a trade settlement report. Finally, Table VI is a sample of an income receipt report. All of these reports are sent to the investment agent involved, as well as to the board of trustees, who are given ten business days to come up with a reasonable answer for the exception.

In conclusion, I would urge you all to become familiar with the flow of your cash and to make use of the professional services available to you to monitor it.

Appendix

STATEMENT OF NET ASSETS AVAILABLE FOR BENEFITS
JUNE 30, 1980 AND 1979

	June 30, 1980	June 30, 1979
Assets		
Cash in Citizens National Bank		
General checking account (overdraft)	$ (73,713)	$ 6,513
Receivables:		
Employer contributions	939,341	870,834
Accrued interest on investments	216,400	169,563
Total receivables	1,155,741	1,040,397
Investments—at current value:		
Savings account—Citizens National Bank	1,479	550,197
Certificates of deposit	5,604,563	3,100,000
U.S. Treasury obligations	1,481,191	1,873,109
Fidelity Trust Account—Citizens National Bank (current yield—8.49%)	770,895	—
Total investments	7,858,128	5,523,306
Other assets:		
Prepaid administrative expenses	119,124	—
Prepaid fiduciary liability premium	3,641	3,487
Prepaid fidelity bond premium	1,361	2,220
Deposit with life insurance company	130,000	130,000
Total other assets	254,126	135,707
Total assets	9,194,282	6,705,923
Liabilities		
Claims checking account overdraft	408,761	214,997
Claims payable	1,019,113	604,233
Estimated incurred but unreported claims	1,909,887	2,131,000
Life insurance charges and benefits payable	103,138	186,878
Accounts payable	16,685	26,763
Total liabilities	3,457,584	3,163,871
Net assets available for benefits	$5,736,698	$3,542,052

Cash

    Cash accounts at year end were as follows:

Checking accounts:		
American National Bank and Trust Company		$ (169,365)
Investment agency accounts:		
American National Bank and Trust Company	$ 30,934	
First National Bank	(400,518)	
Manufacturers Hanover Trust Company	1	(369,583)
Savings accounts:		
American National Bank and Trust Company		
Escrow	110,146	
Savings	37,277	147,423
Total cash (overdraft)		$ (391,525)

AUDIT REPORT EXCERPT

Investments

Total investments, at fair value, increased $60,706,107 during the current year. Investments at June 30, 1981 and 1980 are shown below together with the percentage of each type of investment to the total investments:

	June 30, 1981 Amount	Percent	June 30, 1980 Amount	Percent
Corporate stocks	$125,230,578	26.69%	$ 86,596,303	21.20%
Bonds and notes	157,987,671	33.67	125,069,494	30.62
Bank pooled funds	76,051,999	16.21	45,925,128	11.24
The Equitable Life Assurance Society pension accounts	109,940,714	23.43	150,913,930	36.94
Total	$469,210,962	100.00%	$408,504,855	100.00%

Investments at June 30, 1981 and 1980 are shown below by investment agent together with the percentage of investments held by each investment agent to total investments:

	June 30, 1981 Amount	Percent	June 30, 1980 Amount	Percent
The Boston Company Institutional Investors, Inc.	$ 9,678,243	2.06%	$ —	— %
First National Bank	67,908,512	14.47	74,288,219	18.19
Fixed Income Advisory Company	41,898,071	8.93	26,729,678	6.54
Funds Advisory Company	68,506,038	14.60	41,877,278	10.25
National Investment Services	—	—	32,005,663	7.84
L. F. Rothschild, Unterberg, Towbin	51,410,253	10.96	33,080,429	8.10
Wall, Patterson, McGrew & Richards, Inc.	45,840,417	9.77	33,263,710	8.14
Weiss, Peck & Greer	42,498,235	9.06	16,345,948	4.00
Manufacturers Hanover Trust Company—Five Year Immunized Bond Fund	9,609,666	2.05	—	—
Manufacturers Hanover Trust Company—Seven Year Immunized Bond Fund	18,920,813	4.03	—	—
The Equitable Life Assurance Society	109,940,714	23.43	150,913,930	36.94
American National Bank	3,000,000	.64	—	—
Total	$469,210,962	100.00%	$408,504,855	100.00%

Table I

ANALYSIS OF NET INVESTMENT INCOME
YEAR ENDED JUNE 30, 1981

	Interest	Dividends	Increase (Decrease) in Fair Value of Investments Sold — Corporate Stocks	Bonds and Notes	The Equitable Life Assurance Society	Increase (Decrease) in Fair Value of Investments Held at Year End — Corporate Stocks	Bonds and Notes	The Equitable Life Assurance Society	Total	Less Investment Expenses	Net Investment Income
The Boston Company Institutional Investors, Inc.	$ 648,563	$ —	$ —	$(72,578)	$ —	$ —	$(545,821)	$ —	$ 30,164	$ 11,512	$ 18,652
First National Bank	8,717,869	—	—	(13,039,767)	—	—	(1,411,232)	—	(5,733,130)	120,167	(5,853,297)
Fixed Income Advisory Company	4,454,921	—	—	(1,174,578)	—	—	(3,333,258)	—	52,915	142,005	(194,920)
Funds Advisory Company	4,721,655	761,674	4,536,171	2,815	—	1,294,150	(195)	—	11,316,270	312,785	11,003,485
National Investment Services	126,673	43,600	—	312	—	—	—	—	170,585	19,010	151,575
L. F. Rothschild, Unterberg, Towbin	2,583,286	770,084	852,872	(623,217)	—	4,557,741	(2,395,949)	—	5,744,817	138,419	5,606,398
Wall, Patterson, McGrew & Richards, Inc.	982,492	731,002	1,871,776	—	—	3,837,507	—	—	7,422,777	154,477	7,268,300
Weiss, Peck and Greer	1,663,365	575,109	649,577	(83,485)	—	2,948,437	(1,112,901)	—	4,640,102	142,290	4,497,812
Manufacturers Hanover Trust Company:											
Five Year Immunized Bond Fund	527,892	—	—	(99,375)	—	—	(600,251)	—	(171,734)	9,961	(181,695)
Seven Year Immunized Bond Fund	1,549,963	—	—	(170,774)	—	—	(1,820,630)	—	(441,441)	19,667	(461,108)
The Equitable Life Assurance Society	8,835,474	1,673,493	—	—	13,236	—	—	(541,419)	9,980,784	349,272	9,631,512
American National Bank and Trust Company											
Variable notes and repurchase agreements	206,069	—	—	—	—	—	—	—	206,069	13,675	192,394
Escrow	5,539	—	—	—	—	—	—	—	5,539	—	5,539
Savings	1,475	—	—	—	—	—	—	—	1,475	—	1,475
New England Merchants Bank	1,524	—	—	—	—	—	—	—	1,524	—	1,524
Custodial fees:											
Bankers Trust Company	—	—	—	—	—	—	—	—	—	40,789	(40,789)
First National Bank	—	—	—	—	—	—	—	—	—	67,533	(67,533)
Total	$35,026,760	$4,554,962	$7,910,396	$(15,260,647)	$13,236	$12,637,835	$(11,220,237)	$(541,419)	$33,120,886	$1,541,562	$31,579,324

QUARTERLY CASH FLOW REPORT METHODOLOGY

Explanatory Notes and Discrepancies

Ending Assets

Prices provided by the Trustee for New York Stock Exchange (NYSE) securities are verified as the closing prices on the report date. If the price differs from the NYSE close it is marked by an asterisk (*). Similarly, prices provided for over-the-counter (OTC) securities are marked with an asterisk if they do not fall between the final bid/ask prices on the report date.

Security positions are listed on a settlement date basis. If the Trustee uses trade date accounting, showing positions which include unsettled trades, the positions and market values are adjusted to exclude the effects of the unsettled trades.

Reconciliation

The price per share of common and preferred stock trades are verified as being a legitimate trading price on the trade date. If the price is outside the range of the low and high prices of the day, the price is marked with an asterisk. On over-the-counter securities, the prices shown in the low and high columns are the final bid and ask quotations of the day and, as such, do not reflect the entire trading range.

If trade dates are not provided by the Trustee, the fifth delivery day prior to the cash flow date is assumed to be the trade date.

Cash received in lieu of a fractional share of stock is represented as a sale of the stock with the cash flow date employed as a trade date. The price per share of these sales will often be marked with an asterisk because they are set by the issuing corporation. Reinvestment of dividend income is represented as a purchase of shares with the cash flow date used as the trade date. Because the reinvestment is done at a predetermined price, the price per share will often be marked with an asterisk.

The prices of bonds are compared to those of similar quality bonds, using a yield-to-maturity analysis. All bond prices which are inconsistent are marked with an asterisk.

When settlement dates are not provided on bond transactions, cash flow dates appear as settlement dates in the report. The purchase/sale accrual date column shows the date through which interest was paid or received on the trade. The settlement date should be verified when it is different than the purchase/sale accrual date.

If the reconciliation of a security results in a position different than that given by the Trustee, the position calculated by the report will be printed and marked with an asterisk.

Daily Cash

If the cash balance of the final day of the audit period provided by the Trustee differs from the final cash balance calculated by the report, it is marked by an asterisk. The reversals column lists the extensions of trades which were reversed during the quarter. Both the initial trade and its reversal must occur during the quarter for the trade to appear in the Daily Cash section. These trades do not appear in the Reconciliation section.

Summaries

The Brokerage Summary includes all trades for which the Trustee provided the amount of commission paid. Each broker is shown with the number and dollar amount of the trade, the percentage of total trade dollars handled, the amount of commissions paid and the percentage of total commission dollars paid. The discount from pre-negotiated fee schedules and commission expressed in terms of cents per share is also listed. The broker identification number also appears in the Reconciliation section with the individual trades.

Three additional summaries are included in the discrepancies section.

The Settlement Summary lists all common and preferred stock trades which settled during the audit period. The trade date and cash flow date for each trade are shown. The number of days elapsed between the trade date and cash flow date is included, expressed in both business and actual days.

The Income Summary shows all dividend and interest payments. Amounts printed in the amount difference column indicate a discrepancy in income for the security. The days difference column records the number of days elapsed between the date receivable and date received, expressed in both business and actual days.

The Principal Payment Summary lists all of the principal payments received during the quarter. The difference between the date receivable and date received is shown in the days difference column, expressed in both business and actual days.

Table II
DECEMBER 31, 1981–MARCH 31, 1982
RECONCILIATION OF ASSETS, TRANSACTIONS AND OTHER CASH ITEMS

Common Stocks

NAME OF HOLDING	DATE	TYPE ENTRY (BROKER)	NUMBER SHARES	DAILY LOW	PRICE/ SHARE	DAILY HIGH	EXTENSION	MARKET POSITION	MARKET VALUE	ACCRUED INCOME
ALA MOANA HAWAII PPTYS	12/31/81	POS			18.875			31600.00	596450.	0.0
	3/31/82	POS			16.625			31600.00	525350.	0.0
ALLIED BANCSHARES INC	12/31/81	POS			32.875			0.0	0.	0.0
	1/12/82	PUR	500.00	29.00	29.250	29.25	14625.00	500.00	14625.	0.0
	1/13/82	PUR	400.00	29.50	29.625	29.75	11850.00	900.00	26663.	0.0
	1/18/82	PUR	3400.00	29.88	30.382*	30.13	103298.75	4300.00	130643.	0.0
	1/20/82	PUR	4900.00	29.50	29.583	29.75	144956.69	9200.00	272164.	0.0
	1/22/82	PUR	2600.00	29.13	29.000*	29.13	75400.00	11800.00	342200.	0.0
	1/25/82	PUR	2300.00	28.38	28.915*	28.63	66504.50	14100.00	407701.	0.0
	1/27/82	PUR	7000.00	28.25	28.250	28.50	197750.00	21100.00	596075.	0.0
	2/ 3/82	PUR	8300.00	28.75	29.250*	29.00	242775.00	29400.00	859950.	0.0
	2/ 8/82	PUR	4200.00	28.75	28.750	28.75	120750.00	33600.00	966000.	0.0
	2/10/82	PUR	1500.00	27.88	28.125	28.13	42187.50	35100.00	987188.	0.0
	3/ 1/82	X-DIV			0.200		7020.00			7020.00
	3/31/82	PAYDATE								
	3/31/82	REC-INC					7020.00			0.0
	3/31/82	POS	35100.00		25.375			35100.00	890663.	0.0
AMERICAN BRANDS INC	12/31/81	POS			36.750			16700.00	613725.	−731.24
	1/29/82	X-DIV			0.875		14612.50	16700.00		13881.26
	2/16/82	PAID-INT	900.00				−731.25			14612.51
	3/ 1/82	PAYDATE								
	3/ 1/82	REC-INC					14612.50			0.0
	3/31/82	POS	16700.00		40.375			16700.00	674263.	0.0
AMERICAN CAN CO	12/31/81	POS	35300.00		34.375			35300.00	1213437.	0.0
	1/11/82	X-DIV			0.725		25592.50	35300.00		25592.50
	2/ 9/82	SAL	16863.00	29.25	33.500*	29.88	564910.50	18437.00	617640.	25592.50
	2/25/82	PAYDATE					25592.50			
	2/25/82	REC-INC	35300.00							0.0
	2/26/82	SAL (38)	800.00	26.63	26.891	27.38	21432.08	17637.00	474276.	0.0
	3/ 1/82	SAL (38)	2300.00	25.75	26.535	26.88	60798.46	15337.00	406967.	0.0
	3/ 2/82	SAL (38)	3900.00	26.38	26.534	26.63	103089.12	11437.00	303469.	0.0
	3/ 3/82	SAL (38)	1700.00	25.75	26.219	26.50	44400.81	9737.00	255294.	0.0
	3/ 4/82	SAL (38)	9737.00	25.75	25.750	26.13	249745.69	0.0	0.	0.0
	3/31/82	POS			27.750			0.0		0.0
AMERICAN HOME PRODS CORP	12/31/81	POS	59400.00		36.500			59400.00	2168100.	0.0
	2/ 5/82	X-DIV			0.500		29700.00	59400.00		29700.00
	3/ 1/82	PAYDATE								
	3/ 1/82	REC-INC					29700.00			0.0
	3/31/82	POS	59400.00		34.625			59400.00	2056725.	0.0

1982 Annual Conference   125

Table III

DECEMBER 31, 1981 – MARCH 31, 1982
DAILY CASH BALANCE

DATE	ITEM	PURCHASES	SALES	INCOME	CONTRIB.	DISBURS.	REVERSALS	DAILY CASH BALANCE	AVERAGE CASH BALANCE
12/31/81	FORWARD							292645.	0.
1/ 4/82	COMMON STOCKS	0.	0.	67146.					
1/ 4/82	CASH EQUIVALENTS	171000.	130000.	159.					
1/ 4/82	TOTALS	171000.	130000.	67305.				318950.	299222.
1/ 5/82	COMMON STOCKS	201663.	0.	0.					
1/ 5/82	CASH EQUIVALENTS	104000.	0.	0.					
1/ 5/82	TOTALS	305663.	0.	0.				13287.	242035.
1/ 6/82	COMMON STOCKS	19548.	0.	0.					
1/ 6/82	CASH EQUIVALENTS	0.	20000.	0.					
1/ 6/82	TOTALS	19548.	20000.	0.				13739.	203986.
1/ 7/82	COMMON STOCKS	8748.	471046.	0.					
1/ 7/82	CASH EQUIVALENTS	475000.	0.	0.					
1/ 7/82	TOTALS	483748.	471046.	0.				1037.	174993.
1/ 8/82	COMMON STOCKS	44504.	0.	13522.					
1/ 8/82	CASH EQUIVALENTS	0.	32000.	0.					
1/ 8/82	TOTALS	44504.	32000.	13522.				2055.	153376.
1/11/82	COMMON STOCKS	218510.	471046.	0.					
1/11/82	CASH EQUIVALENTS	253000.	0.	0.					
1/11/82	TOTALS	471510.	471046.	0.				1590.	112064.
1/12/82	COMMON STOCKS	451994.	0.	0.					
1/12/82	CASH EQUIVALENTS	0.	452000.	0.					
1/12/82	TOTALS	451994.	452000.	0.				1596.	102858.
1/13/82	CASH EQUIVALENTS	0.	396000.	0.					
1/13/82	TOTALS	0.	396000.	0.				397596.	125531.
1/14/82	COMMON STOCKS	0.	1347108.	1086.					
1/14/82	CASH EQUIVALENTS	1348000.	0.	0.					
1/14/82	TOTALS	1348000.	1347108.	1086.				397790.	144978.
1/15/82	COMMON STOCKS	0.	931434.	0.					
1/15/82	CASH EQUIVALENTS	931000.	0.	0.					
1/15/82	TOTALS	931000.	931434.	0.				398225.	161861.
1/18/82	CASH EQUIVALENTS	0.	1000.	0.					
1/18/82	TOTALS	0.	1000.	0.				399225.	201310.
1/19/82	CASH EQUIVALENTS	0.	15000.	0.					
1/19/82	OTHER HOLDINGS	0.	1082.	104.					
1/19/82	TOTALS	0.	16082.	104.				415411.	212579.

Table IV

EXCEPTIONS

PAGE D	1	ALLIED BANCSHARES INC	
		1/18/82	PRICE PER SHARE OF $30.38 WAS OUTSIDE OTC RANGE ($29.88 TO $30.13) ON TRADE DATE.
		1/22/82	APPARENT NET TRADE. PRICE PER SHARE OF $29.00 WAS OUTSIDE OTC RANGE ($29.13 TO $29.13).
		1/25/82	APPARENT NET TRADE. PRICE PER SHARE OF $28.91 WAS OUTSIDE OTC RANGE ($28.38 TO $28.63).
		2/ 3/82	APPARENT NET TRADE. PRICE PER SHARE OF $29.25 WAS OUTSIDE OTC RANGE ($28.75 TO $29.00).
PAGE D	1	AMERICAN CAN CO	
		2/ 9/82	PRICE PER SHARE OF $33.50 WAS OUTSIDE NYSE RANGE ($29.25 TO $29.88) ON TRADE DATE.
PAGE D	2	BAKER INTL CORP	
		12/ 7/81	TRADE OCCURRED BEFORE THE START OF THE AUDIT PERIOD.
		12/ 7/81	PRICE PER SHARE OF $34.43 WAS OUTSIDE NYSE RANGE ($40.75 TO $42.00) ON TRADE DATE.
PAGE D	2	CENTRAL LA ELEC INC	
		2/23/82	PRICE PER SHARE OF $13.63 WAS OUTSIDE OTC RANGE ($13.75 TO $13.75) ON TRADE DATE.
PAGE D	2	CENTRAL LA ENERGY CORP	
		12/24/81	TRADE OCCURRED BEFORE THE START OF THE AUDIT PERIOD.
PAGE D	3	DAYTON PWR & LT CO	
		12/24/81	TRADE OCCURRED BEFORE THE START OF THE AUDIT PERIOD.
PAGE D	5	MCRAE CONS OIL & GAS INC	
		1/22/82	PRICE PER SHARE OF $16.53 WAS OUTSIDE OTC RANGE ($16.13 TO $16.38) ON TRADE DATE.
		1/27/82	PRICE PER SHARE OF $15.63 WAS OUTSIDE OTC RANGE ($15.50 TO $15.50) ON TRADE DATE.
		2/17/82	PRICE PER SHARE OF $13.25 WAS OUTSIDE OTC RANGE ($13.38 TO $13.63) ON TRADE DATE.
		3/ 9/82	PRICE PER SHARE OF $11.56 WAS OUTSIDE OTC RANGE ($11.75 TO $11.75) ON TRADE DATE.
PAGE D	6	NORTHWEST INDS INC	
		2/22/82	PRICE PER SHARE OF $75.00 WAS OUTSIDE NYSE RANGE ($60.13 TO $69.13) ON TRADE DATE.
PAGE D	7	ROLM CORP	
		12/30/81	TRADE OCCURRED BEFORE THE START OF THE AUDIT PERIOD.
PAGE E	6	***TOTAL PORTFOLIO***	
		3/31/82	TRUSTEE'S ENDING CASH BALANCE OF $0. VARIED FROM CALCULATED BALANCE OF $4.

Table V
DECEMBER 31, 1981–MARCH 31, 1982
TRADE SETTLEMENT REPORT

Common Stocks

SECURITY	TRADE TYPE	NUMBER SHARES	AMOUNT ($000)	TRADE DATE	CASH FLOW DATE	*DAYS DIFFERENCE* BUSINESS	ACTUAL
ALLIED BANCSHARES INC	PUR	500	14.6	1/12/82	1/21/82	7	9
	PUR	400	11.8	1/13/82	1/21/82	6	8
	PUR	3400	103.3	1/18/82	1/25/82	5	7
	PUR	4900	145.0	1/20/82	1/27/82	5	7
	PUR	2600	75.4	1/22/82	1/29/82	5	7
	PUR	2300	66.5	1/25/82	2/ 1/82	5	7
	PUR	7000	197.7	1/27/82	2/ 3/82	5	7
	PUR	8300	242.8	2/ 3/82	2/10/82	5	7
	PUR	4200	120.7	2/ 8/82	2/17/82	6	9
	PUR	1500	42.2	2/10/82	2/19/82	6	9
AMERICAN CAN CO	SALE	16863	564.9	2/ 9/82	2/18/82	6	9
	SALE	800	21.4	2/26/82	3/17/82	13	19
	SALE	2300	60.8	3/ 1/82	3/17/82	12	16
	SALE	3900	103.1	3/ 2/82	3/17/82	11	15
	SALE	1700	44.4	3/ 3/82	3/17/82	10	14
	SALE	9737	249.7	3/ 4/82	3/17/82	9	13
AMERICAN TEL & TELEG CO	PUR	11500	674.0	1/18/82	1/26/82	6	8
BAKER INTL CORP	SALE	3700	127.1	12/ 7/81	2/ 9/82	44	64
	SALE	1600	52.0	1/28/82	2/ 4/82	5	7
	SALE	5000	162.6	1/28/82	2/ 4/82	5	7
	SALE	2200	73.6	2/ 2/82	2/ 9/82	5	7
	SALE	3100	101.5	2/ 3/82	2/10/82	5	7
	SALE	800	26.3	2/ 4/82	2/11/82	5	7
	SALE	5900	194.5	2/ 5/82	2/16/82	6	11
CENTRAL LA ELEC INC	SALE	3100	43.0	2/18/82	2/25/82	5	7
	SALE	3100	42.2	2/23/82	3/ 2/82	5	7
	SALE	4700	64.0	2/24/82	3/ 3/82	5	7
	SALE	3278	45.1	2/25/82	3/ 4/82	5	7
CENTRAL LA ENERGY CORP	PUR	500	16.4	12/24/81	1/ 5/82	6	12
	PUR	5600	185.2	12/28/81	1/ 5/82	5	8
	PUR	600	19.5	12/29/81	1/ 6/82	5	8
	PUR	1300	44.5	12/31/81	1/ 8/82	5	8
	PUR	5400	185.9	1/ 4/82	1/11/82	5	7
	PUR	13200	452.0	1/ 5/82	1/12/82	5	7
	PUR	12400	397.8	1/ 6/82	2/ 1/82	18	26
COMMONWEALTH EDISON CO	SALE	20700	412.7	2/ 5/82	2/16/82	6	11
	SALE	6600	131.6	2/ 5/82	2/16/82	6	11

Table VI
DECEMBER 31, 1981–MARCH 31, 1982
INCOME RECEIPT REPORT

Common Stocks

SECURITY	AMOUNT RECEIVABLE	AMOUNT RECEIVED	AMOUNT DIFFERENCE	DATE RECEIVABLE	DATE RECEIVED	*DAYS DIFFERENCE* BUSINESS	ACTUAL
ALLIED BANCSHARES INC	7020.	7020.	0.	3/31/82	3/31/82	0	0
AMERICAN BRANDS INC	-731.	-731.	0.	12/31/81	2/16/82	31	47
AMERICAN CAN CO	14613.	14613.	0.	3/01/82	3/01/82	0	0
AMERICAN HOME PRODS CORP	25593.	25593.	0.	2/25/82	2/25/82	0	0
	29700.	29700.	0.	3/01/82	3/01/82	0	0
AMERICAN TEL & TELEG CO	31050.	31050.	0.	1/02/82	1/04/82	0	2
BAKER INTL CORP	1800.	1800.	0.	2/25/82	2/25/82	0	0
BRISTOL MYERS CO	11914.	11914.	0.	2/01/82	2/01/82	0	0
CAPITAL CITIES COMMUNICATNS	605.	605.	0.	2/01/82	2/01/82	0	0
CENTRAL LA ELEC INC	6097.	6097.	0.	2/15/82	2/16/82	0	1
CENTRAL LA ENERGY CORP	-4132.	0.	-4132.	12/31/81	—		
	13200.	13200.	0.	2/15/82	2/16/82	62	90
COMMONWEALTH EDISON CO	19110.	19110.	0.	2/01/82	2/01/82	0	1
CONTINENTAL ILL CORP	14250.	14250.	0.	2/01/82	2/01/82	0	0
CRUM & FORSTER	8241.	8241.	0.	3/10/82	3/10/82	0	0
DAYTON PWR & LT CO	18098.	18098.	0.	3/01/82	3/01/82	0	0
GANNETT INC DEL	7439.	7439.	0.	1/04/82	1/04/82	0	0
HARTE HANKS COMMUNICATIONS	4635.	4635.	0.	3/19/82	3/19/82	0	0
HOLIDAY INNS INC	6938.	6938.	0.	2/01/82	2/01/82	0	0
HOSPITAL CORP AMER	1513.	1513.	0.	2/01/82	2/01/82	0	0
ILLINOIS PWR CO	18228.	18228.	0.	2/01/82	2/01/82	0	0
INTERNATIONAL BUSINESS MACHS	14190.	14190.	0.	3/10/82	3/10/82	0	0
LITTON INDS INC	9029.	9029.	0.	1/01/82	1/04/82	0	3
MCDONALDS CORP	4425.	4425.	0.	3/02/82	3/02/82	0	0
MORRISON KNUDSEN INC	3548.	3548.	0.	1/04/82	1/04/82	0	0
NATIONAL MED CARE INC	4278.	4278.	0.	2/10/82	2/10/82	0	0
NORTHWEST INDS INC	16080.	16080.	0.	1/04/82	1/04/82	0	0
PHILIP MORRIS INC	9850.	9850.	0.	1/08/82	1/08/82	0	0
PROCTER & GAMBLE CO	13650.	13650.	0.	2/15/82	2/16/82	0	1
RANSBURG CORP	4088.	3672.	416.	1/08/82	1/08/82	0	0
	0.	416.	-416.	—	3/19/82		
REYNOLDS R J INDS INC	13510.	13510.	0.	3/05/82	3/05/82	0	0
SOUTHERN CALIF EDISON CO	16524.	16524.	0.	1/31/82	2/01/82	0	1
SOUTHLAND CORP	10672.	10672.	0.	3/22/82	3/22/82	0	0
STERLING DRUG INC	12225.	12225.	0.	3/01/82	3/01/82	0	0
SYNTEX CORP	6360.	6360.	0.	3/15/82	3/18/82	3	3

Techniques for Monitoring Cash Flow

BY EDWARD F. ZIMMERMAN, JR., CLU, FLMI

THE WAY I THINK of my, and your, job in watching over the cash investments of a fund unfolds itself into three general areas of interest:
1. Determination of what cash we have, where it is and the "availability" of that cash
2. The short term—or money market—investment process
3. Evaluating the effectiveness of the investment management.

Funds Flow Reporting: Whys and Wherefores

Obvious perhaps, but nevertheless sometimes overlooked or not given the attention it may deserve, is the time value of money—not that any of us are unaware of the long term value of prudent investment and accompanying returns to our portfolios. However, the costliness of missing out on the earnings of any available cash can be illustrated by a few examples. Although today's interest rates are relatively low at around 9%, a weekend's lost earnings on $1 million amount to $750. Thinking of this amount in terms of benefit or claim payments brings home the need to keep money working. If rates were to go back up to 15%, we'd be losing $1,250 if we lost a weekend. If one element could be described as "key" to this discussion, it's the need to avoid the waste of idle cash. It's vital to keep that money working at $200+ per day.

Some of the tools available to the money manager, or to you if you are in the direct control of funds, are worth knowing about.

First, you should be aware of bank account monitoring. Just as we each get a monthly bank statement to aid (or confuse, as the case may be) in the reconciliation of our personal funds flows, so too are most modern banks in a position to render *daily* statements of the flows of funds into and out of accounts. One statement that I'm familiar with is produced by the Morgan Guaranty Trust Company in New York, but its counterpart is available under various proprietary names from many other banks. One element of this type of report that is significantly different from our personal statements is the distinction made between available balances and ledger balances. A summary normally is reflected for both types. To the money manager, available funds are just what the name implies: funds that can be used for new investments. The ledger balance, on the other hand, may reflect some items credited to one's account that represent, for example, checks in the process of collection by the banks, which are not yet funds "available" for use.

When checks are deposited into your account, the ledger balance immediately rises, but that "available" balance will not be credited until your bank gets credit for them either through the Federal Reserve System or via a direct relationship with the bank the check was drawn on. Similarly, when disbursements are drawn against the account that available balance is there until the checks are presented for payment. The money manager needs to follow these flows carefully, recognizing for example that some charges are in immediately available funds but others will give him a day or two of extra use—and earning power.

Mr. Zimmerman, as vice president of money markets with Prudential Insurance Company of America, is responsible for the management of all short term investment funds of Prudential, its subsidiaries and its pension accounts, the latter comprising over $2 billion. Active in the employee benefits field for over 13 years, in multi-employer and in corporate areas, he previously worked with Prudential as associate treasurer with responsibilities for short term investment, cash management and banking. Mr. Zimmerman earned his bachelor's degree at the U.S. Naval Academy and his M.B.A. at Fairleigh Dickinson University. He is a chartered life underwriter and fellow of the Life Office Management Association.

A big advantage of this type of bank account reporting is its direct availability; it can usually be drawn electronically before the bank is otherwise open for business or telephone calls.

Meanwhile, to aid in the identification and reconciliation of the actual cash flows, the manager of a fund will have or should have set up a system to track the investment payments (dividends, interest, maturities) that are due into the fund from the various sources of investment. This tracking system will also be the mechanism used to follow for correct crediting of any items that do not get credited in a timely fashion.

For example, my company's securities accounting unit prepares listings of dividend and interest amounts due, on a daily basis. The data forming the basic files are the original transaction sheets for either stocks or bonds and, subsequently, the dividend reporting service of an organization such as Standard and Poor's. In many instances, the onus of timely crediting of dividends can be transferred to a custodian bank through pre-negotiated agreement. Any mechanical "glitches" in the process will then not affect the fund's actual availability of cash for investment. That is, as part of its overall custodial responsibility, the bank will give credit on the due date and undertake the collection themselves; on balance, we find this service valuable. When securities are deposited in the depository transfer corporation, this service is automatic.

The key emphasis from the money manager's viewpoint is to avoid instances of lost use of funds because of money that came into accounts without prompt knowledge and thus remained uninvested. Good working cash flow projections are vital.

Looked at from the perspective of short term investment, the manager of such funds has, then, a reasonable amount of information available to him. This information is available both in terms of current information on the cash available for investment at the moment and in terms of the flows to be expected from investment sources over a workable time horizon, e.g., a month or so in advance, in fairly precise form—and longer in broad terms. He must put this information together with knowledge of the fund's expected outflows to enable him to come to some conclusions about the degree of flexibility he has with respect to his investment maturity and marketability choices.

A high degree of communication between the manager and the sponsor is desirable to achieve best results. That is, the manager will have choices between long and short maturities and between relatively marketable and perhaps somewhat illiquid investments of equally sound credit worthiness. He can do a better job for the fund if his information flows are good. (Cash and equivalents are often lumped together on a balance sheet, which can be misleading if for some reason it is decided to spend or withdraw the money and it's found to be tied up in a short investment with the risk of loss on sale.)

Characteristics of the Portfolio— The Ground Rules

The sponsors of a fund have the right and the obligation to set the parameters within which the short term investment manager will work. Just as the trustees can satisfy themselves concerning the degree of care exercised by their manager in the investment function with respect to risk and aggressiveness for a stock or bond fund, so too there are aspects of a money market manager's job that can be delineated and then monitored.

What are some of the characteristics to be investigated? What are some of the questions one might ask to satisfy oneself that a high degree of professionalism is being exercised in the managing of such investments?

Scope

First, and fundamental to the short term investment function, is the scope of investment instruments used in the portfolio. The range is somewhat a measure of the degree of aggressiveness being followed, but not a complete measure—consideration of individual holdings is necessary to really discriminate about the degree of risk.

Although public knowledge of what's involved in money market investments has grown by leaps and bounds over the past several years—largely coincidental with the growth of money market mutual funds—sometimes the exact nature of the investment employed by such funds is assumed to be known, when in reality a little refresher wouldn't hurt. I'd like to comment briefly on some of the characteristics of the most frequent short term investments as an aid to any discussions that might be held with your money managers. The instruments used can be thought of as being in three principal categories: securities of the U.S. government and its agencies, banks and corporates.

Securities of the U.S. Government

The measuring stick of short term investments is the U.S. government's Treasury bill. The Treasury bill is the premier quality and major volume instrument, of course. Its quality is being sought after in today's marketplace—so much so that a three month bill now yields about 250 basis points (2½%) less than a prime quality corporate investment. Incidentally, everybody involved with fixed income investments, long term bonds or short term notes and bills is always talking about basis points when referring to rate or price movements. Don't let them confuse you: *A basis point is simply one one-hundredth of a percent,* so that the difference between 9% and 9½% is 50/100 or 50 basis points.

In recent years, this differential between Treasuries and corporates has usually been in the range of 50-150 basis points, so current investments in government issues constitute a significant yield loss: On a $1 million investment for one month, the current yield difference translates into more than $2,000 (which many investors gladly trade for the perceived safety). The marketability of Treasury bills is unequaled by any other instrument in the money market, which gives them a very strong advantage where liquidity is a vital factor.

Of somewhat less importance within the government securities area are the securities of the various agencies and instrumentalities of the U.S. government, such as federal home loan banks, federal farm credit banks, etc. They yield somewhat more than direct government issues and are normally quite comparable to prime corporate paper. Recently, however, they have benefited from the "flight to quality," and thus yield less than prime corporates on average.

Bank Instruments

Predominant in this category are certificates of deposit (CDs), one of the most widely traded money market securities. These securities are simply negotiable evidences of large deposits (over $100,000) placed with banks for a specific period of time, from two weeks to a year, sometimes longer.

The key thing I would recommend that you look at concerning the use of this type of obligation in money market portfolios is the selectivity capability of the manager. As you know, deposits up to $100,000 are insured by the Federal Deposit Insurance Corporation; notwithstanding, careful analysis of banks is important, especially when larger sums are involved. The money manager should be able to conduct a fundamental analysis of banks' financial data and should have the capacity to make distinctions in relative quality and value, including the ultimate distinction of avoiding those banks whose credit he deems unsound for the fund.

Somewhat as an aside, the money markets until relatively recently had been quite forgiving of errant performance on the part of banks; the more current attitude and continuing trend is to impose price and rate-paying distinctions on poor performers, when in days of yore not much effort was made to distinguish among banks of comparable size and presumed stature. This change in attitude has an implication to managers and sponsors alike. The real economic value of the CD of a bank that falls out of favor also falls; the ability to dispose of such a security carries a price penalty that should be avoided by careful analysis and selection in the first place. At least one major bank's obligations have shown a yield differential of a full percentage point and even more in recent weeks because of perceived problems. There are several financial services available to assist interested parties in data collection and analysis, in addition to the public availability of the financial reports of the institutions.

Corporate Sector

The third major category of money market investment, the corporate sector, primarily means "commercial paper" to a money market fund manager. This term denotes the unsecured obligations of corporate issuers, maturing in a period from one day to 270 days, with the most active market for issuance being in the 15-45 day area. Denominations range from $50,000 to many millions of dollars. The largest issuers in terms of volume are the large captive finance companies, such as General Motors Acceptance Corporation, that do their own marketing of paper. The greatest number of issuers is found in a virtual myriad of industrial, utility and financial company issuers marketed through dealers such as Goldman Sachs, A. G. Becker and several others.

Within the overall category of bank instruments, and to a much lesser extent the category of commercial paper, the question of international, or foreign, investment participation should be considered. The thoughtful use of specific foreign issues can contribute to a portfolio's performance without diminishing its quality.

What are foreign money market investments? If the location of the investment is outside the United States, it is defined foreign for that reason: Examples would be Eurodollar certificates of deposit, for which the principal market is London. The actual instrument is there; changes in ownership of the CDs and payments take place there, outside the U.S. Another of this type of foreign short term holding is that of Eurodollar time deposits: fixed term, nonnegotiable deposits. They may be booked in London or perhaps Canada, but more likely they are located in either Nassau or the Cayman Islands. Both domestic U.S. and foreign banks conduct such business through branches in such locations. It probably would not be prudent for many funds to participate exclusively in Euromarket instruments, but a modest level of holdings can be a reasonable diversification approach, adding to rather than sacrificing real fund quality.

The other significant type of foreign holding is that determined by the nationality of the issuer. The most visible of these issuers are the foreign banks that have established branches in this country, where they compete for deposits with U.S. banks and make loans to domestic borrowers. These are the so-called Yankee banks; their branches are subject to state and/or federal regulation and their CDs, bankers' acceptances and commercial paper are a growing element in money market portfolios. Here again, the question of selectivity should arise. Most of these banks are of world stature, no less worthy of consideration for a money market investment than many U.S. banks, but careful review and analysis of their financial performance should be undertaken by the money manager before committing any funds.

No foreign investment of either type should be considered without full consideration of at least two important factors that are characteristic:
- There may be an element of "sovereign risk." In any transaction subject to regulation by a foreign government, there is a possibility that restrictions could be imposed on repayment. If such restrictions are imposed, can the risk be quantified? If not, it is undesirable.
- There may be difficulty, or delay, in obtaining necessary information to evaluate the issuer. Without such information, another element of risk is introduced that may not be acceptable.

Before leaving this topic of money market instruments, I'd like to mention two terms that sometimes don't get clarified in comparing the quoted yield of one instrument against another. (Maybe that's because they don't hold much interest for anyone but a money manager, but I'll chance this explanation in the hope it may be helpful.)

First, Treasury bills, commercial paper and bankers' acceptances are conventionally quoted on a discount basis, i.e., the par amount payable at maturity is "discounted" back to a lesser amount required to be invested. Thus, a $100,000 one year bill quoted at 10% would cost approximately $90,000. Therefore, the effective, or comparable, CD yield would be 11+% ($10,000 earnings on $90,000 investment). This difference in quoting method obviously must be carefully considered or one ends up comparing apples to oranges.

A second important consideration for the money manager is the fact that the yield on all money market instruments is calculated using a 360 day year. Since a year usually has 365 days, the actual effective rate of money market holdings over a full year's time is higher than it looks, by a factor of 365/360. At 10%, this factor adds 14 basis points to the yield—10.14%—and can be a significant factor in comparing money market securities to bonds, for example.

Credit Quality

Among issuers, credit quality is monitored by several rating agencies: Moody's, Standard and Poor's, Fitch and Duff and Phelps, with the first two being the major factors in this field. Their rating systems employ grades of 1, 2 and 3 for what are defined as acceptable credit: A-1, 2 and 3 for Standard & Poor's; P-1, 2 and 3 for Moody's, both in descending order. In actuality, issuers graded "3" have little chance of active participation in the market, and those graded "2" have to pay a substantial premium for their borrowed money. A broad based investment manager will use in-house evaluation of credit worthiness of issuers, relying on the services primarily for date and supplementary information about the companies in addition to the fundamental financial reports.

Maturity Risk

Depending on the tolerable degree of exposure to the risk of value changes that occur when interest rates change, it is a good idea to have some limits in mind concerning what length of maturities to hold in a short term portfolio.

For example, if a security is held at 10% and rates increase to 15%, the effect on value is quite different for different maturities.
- Thirty Days to Maturity: The value would be about 99.6% of what it would be at 10%.
- One Year to Maturity: The value would be about 94.4% of what it would be at 10%.

This effect is important when you need to "cash in" a security, obviously: The damage done is nowhere near so great if it's necessary to liquidate the shorter holding. Not so obvious, perhaps, is the fact that there's a substantial risk of losing the opportunity to reinvest at the higher rates if the original holding is "locked in" for some reason—the nature of the investment or accounting constraints, for example.

Of course, the ability to perform in the positive sense will develop if the reverse case comes about; i.e., if rates drop from 10% to 5%; the manager can't be tied down too tightly if he's to attain the best performance possible. The point is that there can be some maturity ground within which the risk and opportunity are both acceptable. (Many money market funds set limits of no more than one year to maturity for individual holdings and no longer for a portfolio than 120 days on average.)

I've already commented on the need to differentiate among banks, in the explanation of certificates of deposit. In setting standards for acceptability, several approaches, or combinations of the different approaches, might be used.

- Size of the institution: Most money market funds use a criterion of over $1 billion in assets. The theory here is that the regulators would be more reluctant to let larger banks fail—not a comfortable determinant for investment.
- Availability of FDIC insurance; this factor is useful for investments that are kept under $100,000 per bank.
- Use of criteria as established by an objective rating service (there are several) to limit investments to banks in some upper proportion of those rated
- Independent financial analysis using measures of profitability, capitalization, liquidity and loan portfolio quality, etc.

How Does One Evaluate a Manager of Short Term Funds?

The simplest and most direct answer, in my viewpoint, is to look at the track record and proven credentials, and perhaps within a modest range of comparable performance, what the cost of the service will be. From this vantage point, the main concern then is where to look for a database against which to compare the investment services offered by any manager.

What I suggest is a three pronged approach to the process:

First, I'd encourage you to evaluate the knowledgeability, experience and training of the potential manager, including learning about the people assigned or to be assigned to the portfolio. What is the manager's depth of expertise in the field, to what kinds of support has he access? For example, what are his *credit evaluation* capabilities, what is the extent of his *economic and interest rate and trend analysis skills,* what kind of *reports* can he produce to keep you informed? (But not overwhelmed!) At minimum, a report showing the flows in and out of the account is necessary. The frequency can depend on the extent of activity of the fund.

A look at fees and costs makes sense. An example of a good place to look for comparative cost data is the *Lippert Analytical Distributors* publication (others exist). They produce a monthly service in which comparative cost data are displayed in many ways, for managers of every type of fund imaginable. For the money market fund, these costs should be examined in at least two ways. First, the size of fees charged as a proportion of earnings should be examined, since these fees impact you directly. The published data provide a measure of comparison against many publicly traded funds. The differences in such charges are by no means inconsequential. In a recent report I saw a range of 0.3-1.2% of net assets managed. If the gross earning rates on the funds were 9%, the fee range would constitute from 3-13% of those earnings. Second, another aspect reported on that is of some degree of interest is the overall expense rate of a particular fund, since it can affect the ultimate net return on the portfolio.

That brings us to the bottom line—net return on the funds. This figure gives you an idea of what to expect relative to other managers. Prior to the advent of money market mutual funds, there was little comparative work done in this area. Now, several reporting mechanisms exist: Donoghue's Money Fund Report (a private organization) and the Investment Company Institute (a trade organization) publish weekly information on the average yields and maturities of those funds. Another source is that of the Wiesenberger Investment Companies service, which produces a monthly report of performance and dividend information, as well as a comparison of the type of portfolio holdings employed. (Donoghue's does this, too.)

As a frame of reference, the average yield differential for the most recent seven day period between the most conservative type of money market funds (holding U.S. Treasury obligations only) and those funds very heavily into Euro- and nonprime commercial paper was 7.9% for the former to 10.5% for the latter. Given the available information, it should be practical to get your own manager or prospective manager to report on a comparable basis to enable you to arrive at informed judgments about the results you can expect.

Administrative Considerations in Establishing Voluntary and Deductible Employee Contributions to Multiemployer Defined Contribution Plans

BY BERNARD HANDEL, CPA, CEBS

THIS PAPER WILL review the administrative considerations and problems relating both to voluntary employee contributions and the new concept of deductible contributions. Before you attempt to institute these innovations, I recommend that you do not seek your administrator's advice. He may oppose the concept, since the institution of either a voluntary or deductible contribution arrangement through a multiemployer plan is administratively complex. Institution of such programs is feasible, but may be expensive and create an administrative burden.

Employee contributions to pension plans represent an opportunity provided by ERTA to multiemployer plans to benefit their participants. That opportunity must be balanced against the complexity resulting from instituting required substantial administrative procedures affecting the traditional operations of multiemployer plans.

Employer deduction and payment of the employees' contribution are painless methods to the worker. The worker agrees that a certain amount of money shall be deducted from pay, and that amount is contributed automatically by the employer. There may be problems with the $2,000 tax deductible limitation, which I will go into, but the payroll deduction facilitates employee participation and acquisition of the individual retirement account (IRA) tax advantage and tax shelter.

The employee also gains the benefit of dollar averaging by spreading out contributions throughout the year. He is not required to contribute a substantial amount of money on a given date to a bank, mutual fund or insurance company. He pays the money regularly as he works. The arrangement also establishes closer ties to the multiemployer plan. However, based on my firm's experience with respect to supplemental annuity plans, it may not always be in the best interest of the multiemployer plan to develop this more intimate relationship.

Mr. Handel is president of The Handel Group, Inc., an actuarial, consulting and administrative firm specializing in jointly managed trust funds, corporate plans and public employee plans. Mr. Handel graduated from City University of New York, is a certified public accountant and a Certified Employee Benefit Specialist. He has over 27 years' experience in the joint trust field. Mr. Handel is a member of the New York State Society of Certified Public Accountants, the American Pension Conference, the Board of Directors of the federally established Hudson Valley Health Systems Agency and the American Health Planning Association, among others. He is a member of the New York State Hospital Review and Planning Council, which regulates hospitals, nursing homes, etc. He has spoken at numerous Foundation and other educational meetings and written many articles in the employee benefit field, some of which have appeared in the Digest *and* Employee Benefits Journal. *Mr. Handel is chairman of the International Foundation's Health Care Committee, a member of the Educational Program Committee, Governing Council of the International Society of CEBS and a Voting Director of the Foundation. He previously served as chairman of the Consultants Committee.*

General Advantages

By contributing to his multiemployer plan, the employee may gain the "advantage" of plan investment advisor expertise. In many plans, however, employees are not impressed by a 5% or 6% investment return by the defined benefit plan, when compared to the well-advertised return of bank, mutual fund and insurance company IRAs. Unless segregated asset accounts are used for employee contributions, with higher investment gain, participants may question the value of the investment advisor expertise.

An advantage is the fact that under a multiemployer plan, there is a different restriction on pay-out dates, in that an IRA requires such pay-outs at age 70½. This age can be extended by a multiemployer plan for active employees, which may be significant to an older employee. There are also tax advantages in the multiemployer plan handling deductible contributions by avoiding the penalties for excess employee contributions to an individual retirement account. If a defined benefit plan is amended to provide for both a deductible and a voluntary contribution, excess contributions by the employee above the $2,000 IRA limit would be considered a voluntary contribution and not subject to penalty. There were some estate tax advantages that might benefit a small number of participants; however, TEFRA changes appear to modify this exclusion.

Multiemployer sponsorship of a deductible contribution plan may resolve participant confusion on electing to commence an IRA; perhaps that role is the most significant the multiemployer plan can perform. In my part of the country, there has been little participation by blue collar workers in IRAs. For one reason, many are unemployed. In addition, many employed workers do not participate because they do not understand the IRA concept. They are overwhelmed by the advertising they are exposed to, the salesmen coming to their doors and bank solicitation. Many who are participating are only transferring their money market certificates to an IRA account and gaining a tax deduction. If the pension plan were to sponsor a deductible contribution scheme, or only facilitate a payroll deduction for IRAs, it might help to motivate participation. In the long run, the IRA concept may produce viable assistance to the long term pension problems of many plans by providing a source of supplemental pensions, which will enable employees to actually retire. The retiree's income would consist of Social Security, pension and IRA distributions.

If the pension plan handles the deductible contribution, it will simplify an employee's thinking, recordkeeping and tax preparation. The worker will receive one report (annually) incorporating pension data, IRA status and voluntary contribution account (if any).

General Disadvantages

All these advantages must be balanced against the administrative complexity occurring when a plan establishes voluntary and/or deductible employee contributions. The plan documents probably will be amended. The administrator must arrange the payroll deduction and collection mechanisms, which can be a tremendous problem in a multiemployer plan. The summary plan description (SPD) must be amended, in understandable, everyday language, and explained to employees. The recordkeeping changes can be a substantial problem. The trustees may be required to segregate assets for the employee contributions and treat those differently from other fund assets, with similar segregation for investment and expense allocations.

Communication efforts will include explaining to participants how contributions will be invested. Plans will have to conform to some yet-to-be-released government regulation on reporting to plan participants.

Benefit options will be different for employee contributions. More people will be applying for benefits at different times under unusual conditions, as compared with a traditional pension plan. Termination problems may be unique. An obvious problem will be represented by an employee who contributes to the plan, stops working for the contributing employer and changes to another industry or trade. What will the plan do with his contributions? Will the plan order a rollover or termination?

Voluntary and deductible contributions are always fully vested. The employee is always entitled to that money. Will the plan enable the terminated worker to maintain an account for his individual contributions if he is no longer an employee of a participating employer? Many multiemployer plans will reject that concept and require lump sum distribution, which may cause difficulties.

There will be a high cost of administration resulting from deductible and/or voluntary contributions, which also will create considerable problems. Nonparticipating employees may react adversely if the resulting administrative costs are not allocated entirely to voluntary participants' accounts.

Starting the Plan

Payment Method

If a plan decides to sponsor employee contributions, it must determine whether to use voluntary or deductible participant payments, or both. The voluntary employee contribution allows an employee to contribute up to 10% of his gross salary earnings (included in the plan base of contributions) to a fully vested individual account, which with investment credits, he may withdraw at any time. The second concept is the new tax deductible contribution of up to $2,000 a year for an employee, authorized by ERTA. Most plans will not enable spousal IRAs under multiemployer plan sponsorship.

To commence the institution of either or both methods, the trustees and their advisors will be required to draft plan amendments, approve them, notify the participants in the normal manner of all plan amendments, file with the Internal Revenue Service and ascertain that all procedures conform with Internal Revenue rules. In addition, trustees are obligated to review the SPD, file with the government and give copies to participants. These plan descriptions must be written in understandable, everyday language—at which we are masters.

Collection

To commence the collection process, it is necessary to explain the entire procedure to employees and employers. Obviously, it is impossible either to require employees to contribute or employers to participate in the program. Even if certain employees volunteer to participate, the plan is faced with the problem of obtaining the support of their particular employers. If that hurdle is overcome, the next problem is arranging the payroll deduction.

These plans are voluntary, not compulsory. A payroll deduction cannot be a condition of employment. Participation is entirely optional with the employee in either or both of the voluntary or deductible methods.

The fund must obtain a payroll authorization, to be maintained on a current basis. The employee could terminate that authorization at will, subject to such mutually acceptable rules as adopted by the plan.

Communication

After arranging a payroll deduction and employer approval, the employer must communicate with the employees. For the deductible IRA contribution, the Department of Labor Advisory Opinion requires the employer to notify each employee that the arrangement is voluntary, that the employee does not have to participate and that other IRA alternatives are available. From a practical view, it appears prudent for the union and the employer to notify the employees of all the conditions stated in the Department of Labor Advisory Opinion, not just the ones previously stated: other plans available outside of this particular scheme, no legal or tax advice, etc.

Forms and Procedures

After arranging for the payroll deduction, and obtaining the authorization forms, the plan must revise collection reporting forms and procedures to provide for voluntary contributions by employees. There may be a problem with those plans that now collect welfare, pension and other fund contributions with one employer reporting form. In some funds, this change simply may require new columns for the voluntary and/or deductible contribution. There are other problems:

- If the employee only wishes deductible contribution up to $2,000 a year, the fund has to monitor his account to ascertain that he does not deduct more than $2,000 in each year.
- The employee may want to terminate contributions during the year.
- If an employee works for a number of employers (as in the construction industry), there may be a problem each year about when contributions cease for the deductible contribution portion.
- For those plans that use various methods of collection, voluntary contributions create unique problems. For example, "stamp" plans cannot deal with the incorporated optional method of employee contribution. Under "stamp" or "voucher" plans, the employer purchases stamps or vouchers from a bank or other source to represent employer contributions. If some employees were involved with self-contributions and others were not, the stamp concept would fail. The contribution of the employee by payroll deduction would have to be represented by a direct cash payment by the employer to supplement the stamp or voucher method.

When the fund receives voluntary contributions, such payments must be identified for each participant individually and individual accounts maintained as in a defined contribution plan. If the fund authorized both voluntary and deductible contributions, separate accounts would be required for each type of employee contribution.

Specific Administrative Problems

Collection Pressures

In voluntary formats, there is increased pressure on the trustees to obtain immediate collection from employers. Although participants may not be overly concerned with how promptly the employer pays welfare or pension contributions, they are extremely concerned that their personal contributions are paid currently. Participants expect the maximum credit on their accounts. By tying all employer and employee contributions together, the employee becomes an aggressive ally to the fund administrator in obtaining contributions. However, the increased interest of the employee may put a great deal of pressure on the fund office and union and cause poor public relations.

Notification

A problem that may develop is the need for the fund office to notify the employee monthly, or every time the employer contributes. In individual accounts, the employee may wish to be advised whenever a contribution is made. His neighbor using a bank IRA may receive regular statements showing contributions and monthly credits. The worker may demand the same thing from his plan office.

Late or Lost Payments

In addition to pressures, which may not exist in welfare and pension funds, on trustees to collect individual contributions, late or lost payments may cause difficulties. The employee may demand fairly prompt and timely credit for contributions made by payroll deduction and resulting investment credits. Who will be liable for the payment that gets "lost" and is never credited to an employee's account? There may be considerable controversies in this connection.

In similar situations in supplemental annuity plans, when the employer verifies that contributions were paid on time, the fund has provided investment credit retroactively to the employee. When insurance companies have handled payroll deduction plans for tax-sheltered annuities or for defined contribution accounts, such retroactive adjustment has been the rule, when there is proof that payment was made but was not promptly credited to the employee. In those situations of misplaced or lost payments, equity seems to support the employee receiving credit from the date the money should have been received.

Withdrawals

Withdrawals will be a great problem administratively. Voluntary contributions may be withdrawn at will, as fully vested, subject to plan rules. Deductible contributions are withdrawable subject to IRS tax regulations. The 100% fully vested status of these contributions may conflict with the basic retirement plan, under which none or only a portion of the employee's pension may be vested (if vested, the worker may only be entitled to a deferred vested pension and no immediate cash lump sum distribution).

In a deductible or voluntary contribution plan, there are other administrative problems relating to withdrawals. There is an IRA ban on penalty free withdrawals before age 59½. If a participant applies for a distribution at 59½, the plan can pay him his balances in the deductible contribution account and voluntary account (if any). However, the plan cannot pay any pension benefit, unless plan provisions permit, until normal or early retirement date.

Another unique difference in plan operations is the continuation of investment credit on individual accounts of participants after commencement of withdrawal. If the employee applies at age 59½ or later for his IRA money over a period of years or lifetime, the participant will continue to earn investment income on the unexpended balance of his account. Another administrative problem—not only determining investment credits on active participants but also continuing credit to those on withdrawal—will be created.

Tax reporting of withdrawals by multiemployer plans to participants are yet to be determined. At the minimum, annual reporting will be required for participants and to the government relating to contributions made, distributions, rollover treatment, etc. IRA withdrawals will be subject to withholding under the 1982 tax act.

If an employee terminates participation with respect to deductible contributions, the plan may or may not be able to mandate a rollover or distribution. A plan might have to retain an employee's account until he terminates voluntarily or withdraws his account. A policy decision would be required as to whether the plan would permit self-contributions after termination of employment.

Costs

Another problem is the high administrative cost of investment credits. It would be simple to credit all investment income once a year, determine the ratio of each participant's account to all accounts and allocate investment income on that basis after deducting expenses. This simple method favors the person with a money account at the end and penalizes the person who has regularly contributed during the year and who had an opening balance at the beginning of the year. Most participants desire monthly, quarterly or semiannual credits. In addition, participants are not enchanted when they are penalized by a substantial reduction in the cost basis of investments made by the fund. Although trustees and advisors may understand that bonds decline in value as interest rates rise, this concept is difficult to explain to participants. Participants are not pleased by substantial "temporary" reductions in investments, even if assured that fixed income investments, if held to maturity, will produce 100% of their value.

Accounting

A major variation from traditional fund administration is the separate accounting required for employee contributions. Defined benefit plans will find this requirement a major change. If plan administration is computerized for benefit accrual credits based on reported service, the program will be inadequate to establish and maintain individual account dollar credits for voluntary or deductible contributions, investment credits and pro-rata expenses.

The tax law also creates certain unique problems with respect to deductible contributions. If a multiemployer plan operates on a fiscal year basis, it cannot request or suggest that the employee adapt his tax year to the plan's fiscal year. Even if the plan uses a fiscal year (not calendar), it will be required to keep records on a calendar year basis for deductible contribution purposes. The plan can place plan limitations on deductible contributions. As an example, the plan could limit participant contributions to those received in 12 calendar months and not permit revocation or additional contributions after the end of the calendar year, irrespective of statutory tax laws. A plan could permit additional contributions in a lump sum by the employee if it did not interfere with the method of furnishing investment credit. It does not appear realistic to allow revocation of contribution by participants during the year, no matter how advantageous for tax purposes.

A Possible Solution

Asset segregation of deductible contributions—one solution is for the multiemployer plan to act solely as custodian, if it does not wish to be involved in handling all the administrative and investment problems of deductible contributions. The trustees could turn over all such contributions directly to a savings bank or investment firm, which keeps all the records for deductible contributions and handles investments. In such instances, the plan functions in assisting the employee to start an IRA and facilitates the payroll deduction, but does not handle accounting, administration and investments. This method might be an appropriate solution for many administrative problems.

Investments

If the pension fund itself directly handles employee contributions, segregated employee individual accounts are required. Special investment guidelines may be adopted for voluntary or deductible contributions. These guidelines may place a premium on the preservation of capital and emphasis on high fixed income using conservative strategies.

In establishing and maintaining payroll deduction voluntary or deductible contribution plans, trustees will be, in effect, competing with banks, insurance companies, investment houses, etc. They will be expected to produce an investment return that is competitive with those custodians. A major unfavorable variation in investment results may cause a loss of credibility by participants, which will extend to welfare and pension funds.

Some advisors recommend that trustees should not only help the participants get started in such contribution plans, but they also should let participants select their investment vehicle. I believe that this concept is not practical, would be extremely expensive in operation and probably tends to violate rules on the prohibition against investment in collectibles and other types of odd investments. If permitted under plan provisions, the trustees might be liable if they failed to effectuate employee choices. The trustees might think that the employee had picked a particularly poor investment, but be surcharged for not fulfilling their selection, no matter how infeasible.

Points to Remember

Each plan will attempt to allocate income and expenses to participant's accounts in the most efficient manner. Some will do it monthly, others quarterly or annually. Annual allocations are easiest but penalize the employee who pays contributions evenly during the year. A computer is indispensable for this function.

An equitable system is required to charge off investment and other expenses to each individual voluntary and deductible contribution account. Plans cannot perform these services as a favor for voluntary participants, with no charge for administrative expenses. The trustees would be exposed to charges by nonparticipants of being overly burdened with the expenses of handling the voluntary/deductible contributions. There is a fiduciary obligation to the participants of the base plan, who do not make voluntary contributions, as well as to those participants who are involved with such deductions.

Communications, as discussed, will be a formidable hurdle. Plans are required to keep participants informed in great detail about individual contributions, credits, expenses, withdrawals, account balances, options, etc.

Voluntary/deductible plans contain benefit options that are drastically different from conventional pension plans. The lump sum withdrawal may be unusual for most multiemployer plans, as would be rollovers. Employees may maintain more than one IRA and try to shift funds back and forth, which will cause administrative problems.

Withdrawal before age 59½ is subject to excise tax with respect to deductible contributions, but there is no similar penalty with respect to voluntary contributions. There is no excise tax on withdrawals resulting from death or disability.

Any administrative system with segregated accounting for individual accounts and required computerized programming for voluntary and/or deductible contributions is going to be expensive. There will be a high initial programming cost, as well as continued large administrative costs for accounting, computerization and communications.

Investment costs may be substantial if separate segregated investment pools are maintained with separate investment strategies and specific investment fees.

Professional services may be substantial in connection with setting up the voluntary/deductible contribution scheme.

Administrators of welfare and pension plans are now involved in the time-consuming problems of participants' divorce and matrimonial actions. Deductible and voluntary contributions are an even more fertile area for such problems.

Fiduciary liability insurance may increase for trustees involved in voluntary and deductible contributions. There may be more litigation than in the past.

Conclusion

It is interesting that, based on most surveys to date, there is very little interest from multiemployer plans in establishing voluntary and deductible contribution programs. With the exception of some multiemployer plans that already have thrift, savings or supplemental annuity plans, most are not getting involved with deductible or voluntary contribution concepts.

Voluntary contributions may be appropriate for existing defined contribution plans. In defined benefit plans, though, voluntary employee contributions may contradict the operating and administrative methodology. However, individual accounts fit with the defined contribution concept if the plan is willing to undertake the hazards. When defined contribution plans presently handle and carry individual accounts, they are in a position to take on the burden of voluntary and/or deductible contribution.

Trustees and advisors should consider whether a multiemployer plan should adapt to voluntary and deductible contributions. They must decide: Does the opportunity to serve participants really balance the high cost of administration and the problems that are created?

Fiduciary Responsibility and Prohibited Transactions: 1982 Update

BY WILLIAM J. CHADWICK and
LAWRENCE J. HASS

Mr. Chadwick is a partner with the lawfirm of Paul, Hastings, Janofsky & Walker in Los Angeles and Washington, D.C. Formerly, he served as administrator of Pension and Welfare Benefit Programs, U.S. Department of Labor. Prior to joining the Labor Department in 1975, Mr. Chadwick was attorney-advisor for Tax Policy, Office of the Tax Legislative Counsel, U.S. Department of Treasury. In both capacities, he was responsible for reviewing and approving many of the Labor and Treasury regulations that interpreted ERISA and the Code. While at the Treasury, he participated in the Congressional Conference Committee's consideration of ERISA. Mr. Chadwick is the author of the book entitled Regulation of Employee Benefits: ERISA and the Other Federal Laws, *co-author of the book entitled* The Annotated Fiduciary *and the author of several articles related to employee benefits, ERISA and taxation. He has spoken at numerous International Foundation and other educational meetings, been heard on* Foundation Forum *cassettes and contributed to the* Digest. *Mr. Chadwick currently serves on the Foundation's Board of Directors, Corporate Study Committee, Governmental Affairs/Industrial Relations Committee and formerly served on the Educational Program Committee.*

Mr. Hass is a member of the lawfirm of Groom and Nordberg, Chartered, of Washington, D.C. He was formerly the special assistant to the administrator, Pension and Welfare Benefit Programs, U.S. Department of Labor. Mr. Hass has also served as assistant counsel for fiduciary responsibility in the Plan Benefits Security Division, Office of the Solicitor, Department of Labor and acting special counsel in the Divisions of Corporate Regulation and Investment Management Regulation of the U.S. Securities and Exchange Commission. A graduate of the University of Pennsylvania and Brooklyn Law School, he is a member of the New York State and District of Columbia Bars. Mr. Hass is also a co-author of The Annotated Fiduciary *published by the International Foundation in 1978 and revised in 1980, and is a member of the Foundation's Academy of Employee Benefit Authors. He has spoken at several International Foundation educational meetings.*

THE FIDUCIARY RESPONSIBILITY and prohibited transaction provisions contained in the Employee Retirement Income Security Act of 1974 (ERISA) have had and will continue to have a significant impact on the administration and management of collectively bargained employee benefit plans. New developments occur in this area of the law every year. In the following discussion, we have sought to highlight some of the most significant developments, including court decisions and regulations, prohibited transaction class exemptions and Advisory Opinions issued by the U.S. Department of Labor. Several of the developments discussed are of particular importance in the administration and management of Taft-Hartley pension and welfare funds.

Plan Asset Regulations

Section 403(a) of ERISA requires, with certain exceptions, that all plan assets be held in trust by the trustees of the plan. An important factor in determining compliance with this requirement is the definition of the term "plan assets." The term "plan assets" is also important in the context of other fiduciary responsibility requirements. For example, the definition of the term "fiduciary" in Section 3(21) of ERISA includes people who are responsible for the management or disposition of plan assets. Thus, to determine who is a plan fiduciary, it must be determined who has responsibility or authority over plan assets. Also, the prohibited transaction restrictions of Section 406 of ERISA prohibit various types of transactions involving plan assets. Thus, a determination of whether assets involved in a transaction are "plan assets" is essential in the application of the prohibited transaction restrictions.

In the ordinary course of managing or administering a plan, the determination of what constitutes "plan assets" may not be difficult. For example, when a plan invests in common stocks, it is clear that the shares of stock acquired by the plan are plan assets, since the shares will be owned solely for the benefit of the plan. Similarly, if a plan purchases a building, it is clear that the building will be a plan asset because it will be held (in trust) for the sole benefit of the plan.

The determination of what constitutes a plan asset is more difficult, however, when a plan invests in various kinds of investment pools. For example, a plan trustee or sponsor may determine that it would be prudent to invest plan funds in a bank collective investment fund. These funds typically have many pension plans participating as investors and provide for the bank to manage the assets collectively by investing the assets of the fund primarily in specific types of investments, such as common stocks, bonds or real estate. Insurance companies provide similar investment facilities through their pooled separate accounts. Additionally, in recent years, there have developed in the real estate area a number of pooled investment vehicles, such as group trusts or limited partnerships, where a real estate asset manager will collectively invest the assets of several plans in real estate or mortgages.

It is clear in the case of, for example, a partnership, that when a plan acquires an interest in the partnership, the partnership interest will constitute a "plan asset." It is not clear, however, whether the underlying assets of the partnership—the real estate that the partnership owns, for example—would also be deemed to be assets of the partner/plan. If the underlying assets are treated as "plan assets," then the general partner—the person responsible for managing the assets of the partnership—would be an ERISA fiduciary with respect to the partner/plan. The real estate owned by the partnership might have to be held in trust under Section 403(a) of ERISA, and the investments made by the partnership would be subject to all of the prohibited transaction restrictions of Section 406 of ERISA. It is, therefore, in the investment pool area that the determination of what constitutes plan assets has been very difficult and understandably controversial.

In 1979, the Labor Department published proposed regulations that were intended to provide a detailed explanation and definition of the term "plan assets" and to apply the trust maintenance requirement of Section 403 of ERISA to various types of "plan asset" situations. The general rule of the 1979 proposed plan asset regulation was that all tangible and intangible property in which a plan has a beneficial ownership interest, direct or indirect, would constitute "plan assets." The proposed regulation also listed several exceptions to this general rule.

The proposed plan asset regulation generated numerous comments from the public. As a result, the Labor Department published a revised proposed regulation in 1980, modifying many of the positions taken in the earlier proposal. The 1980 proposal also resulted in a host of public comments; consequently, many aspects of the regulation are still unresolved. The Labor Department has indicated that it intends to publish another revised proposed regulation on this subject, again modifying positions previously taken; it now appears that the "plan assets" issue is not likely to be finally resolved for at least another year.

In May 1982, however, the Labor Department was able to deal with several issues in the plan assets area without finally resolving all of the issues previously raised. In this regard, the Department issued a partial final regulation dealing with three specific issues—whether assets of government-backed mortgage pools in which plans invest are plan assets, the use of nominees to hold title to plan assets and the application of the trust maintenance requirement to assets held in investment pools. This final regulation will ultimately be only one small part of the overall plan assets regulation, but it is nevertheless a very important part.

Government-Backed Mortgage Pools

The "plan assets" question has been raised with increasing frequency in the context of mortgage pools. Plans around the country, particularly plans in the building and construction trades, but also plans in other industries and trades and crafts, have been interested in investing in the mortgage market. One means of investing in mortgages is through mortgage pools. Briefly, a mortgage pool involves an entity, typically a trust, that acquires a diversified portfolio of notes secured by mortgages or deeds of trust. The trust that holds these mortgage notes then sells undivided interests in the portfolio, or "pool," of mortgages evidenced by mortgage pool certificates, which entitle the investors (a pension plan, for example) to receive a portion of the interest that is paid on the underlying mortgages and ultimately to share in the repayment of principal.

Plans are frequently interested in investing in mortgage pools because, among other things, a mortgage pool enables a plan to diversify its mortgage investments in numerous mortgages instead of investing in only a few mortgages or in participating interests in only a few mortgages.

Generally, there are three types of mortgage pools. One type is commonly referred to as governmental mortgage pools. One example of this type of pool is Government National Mortgage Association (or GNMA) mortgage pools, where, although the issuer of the certificate of interest is normally a private lender, the underlying mortgages in the pool are guaranteed with respect to payment of principal and interest by the Department of Housing and Urban Development or by the Veterans Administration. Thus, the risk of loss to investors in these pools is very small because the underlying mortgage obligations are backed by the full faith and credit of the United States government.

A second type of mortgage pool is the quasi-governmental mortgage pool. Examples of this type of pool are Federal National Mortgage Association (FNMA) mortgage pools and Federal Home Loan Mortgage Corporation mortgage pools. In these cases, the issuer of the certificate of interest in the pool is either FNMA or the Federal Home Loan Mortgage Corporation, but there are no express guarantees with respect to payments on the underlying mortgages in the pool. The issuer of the mortgage pool certificates is, however, a federally chartered corporation subject to supervision and, therefore, a form of indirect control, by the United States government. Thus, in evaluating the credit worthiness of the issuer of the pool certificates, the involvement of the U.S. government is important and should be noted.

The third type of mortgage pool is private mortgage pools, in which a private entity issues the pool certificates; the U.S. government does not provide any guarantees and is not otherwise involved. That is, in these cases the underlying mortgages are not insured by the federal government and the issuer is not a federally chartered corporation. The only type of guaranty or insurance with respect to these pools may be mortgage pool credit insurance, which insures holders of pool certificates against default on the underlying mortgages.

In its May 1982 final plan asset regulation, the Labor Department took the position that the assets of governmental pools (e.g., GNMA pools) and quasi-governmental pools (e.g., FNMA pools and pools where the certificates are issued by the Federal Home Loan Mortgage Corporation), in which pension plans are investors do not constitute "plan assets." Thus, when a pension plan purchases a GNMA or FNMA pool certificate of interest, only the certificate would constitute a plan asset. The underlying assets of the pool—the notes secured by mortgages or deeds of trust—would not constitute plan assets. Therefore, the assets of such pools would not have to be held in trust and the person who services the mortgages would not be a plan fiduciary.

This position applies only to governmental and quasi-governmental mortgage pools. The Labor Department has not yet formally taken a position with respect to private mortgage pools. By all indications, however, it appears that the Department is inclined to treat the assets of private mortgage pools in which plans invest as plan assets. In this regard, a final prohibited transaction class exemption, PTE 81-7, provides a broad exemption for pools of residential first mortgages, and a recently published proposed amendment to PTE 81-7 would extend the coverage of the exemption to pools containing residential second mortgages.

The issue of whether the assets in a mortgage pool are plan assets is, of course, important to the people who manage the pools. The resolution of this issue is essential to determining whether these people are subject to the ERISA prohibited transactions restrictions and the general fiduciary responsibility provisions of ERISA. This issue is also important, however, to plan sponsors, trustees and other plan decisionmakers in connection with their responsibilities and potential liabilities in the review and oversight of the plan's investment in a pool.

For example, if, as is commonly the case, the pool manager is compensated by retaining the difference between the amount of interest passed through to pool investors and the actual interest received on pool mortgages, the pool manager, as a fiduciary, might be deemed to be dealing with plan assets (the underlying mortgages) in his own interest. Such a situation would constitute a prohibited transaction and could ultimately lead to co-fiduciary liability for plan fiduciaries if they permit such compensation to be paid without an exemption. PTE 81-7 might provide an exemption for such compensation arrangements, if its conditions are met.

Nominees

The second issue dealt with in the May 1982 plan asset regulation relates primarily to plan investments in securities and real estate. When a plan buys shares of stock in the securities markets, the shares are plan assets and it is generally required under ERISA that the shares be held in trust by trustees of the plan. Customarily, however, when investors buy publicly traded securities through a brokerage firm, the share certificates are registered in the name of the brokerage firm (i.e., "street name") primarily to facilitate the future sale of the securities. The brokerage firm is, of course, required to indicate in its records the identity of the actual owner of the securities. Thus, when plans invest in securities, the share certificates may be registered in the name of a brokerage firm instead of in the name of the plan trustees.

Similarly, when a plan purchases real estate, it is very common for the plan to establish a corporation, wholly owned by the trustees of the plan, to take title to the real estate. This arrangement has many advantages, one of the most important being that it can limit the potential liability of the plan for, e.g., claims for personal injuries that may occur on the property. In such cases, it may be possible to limit the liability of the plan to the assets of the corporation.

In both instances, the issue is whether the plan assets—the securities or the real estate—are held in trust in compliance with ERISA. The Labor Department first focused on the "street name" issue in the 1979 plan asset regulation proposal, where it indicated that plans would not be permitted to hold stock in street name because of the ERISA trust requirement. The securities industry strongly opposed this position, primarily because it would have hampered one of the customary ways in which securities transactions are executed.

The Labor Department subsequently reconsidered its earlier position; in the May 1982 regulation, it stated that when a plan acquires publicly traded securities, such securities may be held in street name rather than in the name of the plan trustee. Under this regulation, however, the only persons who can be titleholders of securities for plans are registered broker-dealers, banks or SEC-registered clearing agencies. Further, plan fiduciaries, such as trustees, are cautioned in the regulation that when street name is used, care must be taken to safeguard the interests of the plan. In this regard, a plan fiduciary should consider the holder's financial condition, its procedures for safeguarding certificates, the holder's insurance coverage and possible better alternatives.

With respect to real estate investments, the May 1982 regulation states that real estate acquired by a plan may be held in the name of a corporation, provided that all of the outstanding shares of the corporation are owned by the trust.

Investment Pools

The last issue dealt with by the Labor Department in the May 1982 regulation involved the question of whether, when a plan invests in an investment pool, the assets of the pool must be held in trust (assuming that the assets of the pool are plan assets). For example, when a plan invests in a real estate limited partnership, and the partnership holds parcels of real estate, must the partnership in turn establish a trust to hold the parcels of real estate? In such a case, the May 1982 regulation provides that the partnership would not be required to establish a trust because the trustees of the plan are holding the plan's investment interest in trust, which is adequate to satisfy the ERISA trust maintenance requirement. Thus, pooled investment funds that are seeking plan investors are not under a restriction to do business in the form of a trust if other arrangements are more appropriate.

Transfer of Surplus Assets

ERISA Sections 403 and 404 require plan fiduciaries to act solely in the interest of participants and beneficiaries and for the exclusive purpose of providing benefits to participants and beneficiaries and defraying reasonable plan administrative costs. DOL Advisory Opinion 82-05A deals with the applicability of these requirements to a Taft-Hartley welfare plan that has surplus assets. In this case, the terms of a plan were modified so that salaried employees were excluded from continuing participation in the plan. As a result, the plan had surplus assets of approximately $1.1 million. At the same time, a related pension fund covering essentially the same employees had unfunded liabilities significantly in excess of $1.1 million. The plan administrator of both plans determined that it was appropriate to transfer the $1.1 million surplus from the welfare plan to the pension fund. As a result of the transfer of the surplus to the pension fund, each contributing employer in the pension fund would receive a pro-rata credit against its share of unfunded liability. Thus, if any employer withdrew from the pension fund, its withdrawal liability would be reduced by reason of the transfer.

Prior to making the transfer, the administrator of the plans requested that the Labor Department issue an Advisory Opinion that the proposed transfer would not violate the prohibited transaction restrictions in ERISA. The Labor Department's reply focused, however, not on the prohibited transaction provisions, but on Section 403(c) of ERISA, which prohibits the inurement of plan assets for the benefit of any contributing employer and provides that plan assets must be used for the exclusive purpose of providing benefits to participants and beneficiaries and defraying administrative costs.

The Department stated that the transfer of surplus assets from the welfare plan to the pension fund would be a violation of Section 403(c) of ERISA with respect to the welfare plan, since the assets of the plan would be used for the benefit of the employers contributing to the plans and not for the benefit of the individuals participating in the welfare plan. In addition, the Labor Department pointed out that the transfer might violate the basic fiduciary duties contained in Section 404 of ERISA, which require the plan fiduciaries of the welfare plan to act solely in the interest of participants or beneficiaries of that plan, as well as the prohibited transaction provisions contained in Section 406 of ERISA.

Participant-Directed Transfers of Assets

Some Taft-Hartley vacation plans permit plan participants to direct the payment of their account balances to third parties. These directions can raise questions under the fiduciary responsibility provisions of ERISA. For example, in a DOL information letter, Washington Service Bureau No. (WSB) 82-47, the question arose whether the assets of a Taft-Hartley vacation plan may be transferred pursuant to the directions of plan participants to the political action committee of the union that maintains the plan.

The plan involved in this case was established to pay vacation benefits to participants and beneficiaries. The trustees were considering a proposal to amend the plan to install a "checkoff" system whereby each participant could elect to assign some of his benefits to the political action committee of the union that maintained the plan.

The employer trustees were not in favor of this proposal and insisted that Labor Department approval be obtained before the proposal could be implemented. The Labor Department responded that the checkoff system would be acceptable if administered in compliance with Interpretative Bulletin 78-1 issued by the Department in 1978.

Interpretative Bulletin 78-1 provides that participants in a vacation plan may direct a portion of their vacation plan benefits to any third person without violating ERISA if three requirements are met. The first requirement is that the plan must expressly provide for the checkoff system. The second requirement is that the participant direction must be in writing and must specify the amount to be checked off and paid to the third party (the political action committee in this case). The third requirement is that the payment in each case cannot exceed the benefits then payable to the participant. If these three requirements are met, a checkoff system involving a vacation plan is permissible, even if the recipient is the union's political action committee.

Sickpay Withholding

One of the most important Advisory Opinions of 1982 was DOL Advisory Opinion 82-32A, which deals with the relatively new Internal Revenue Service requirements relating to sickpay withholding and reporting. Basically, the sickpay rules are: A third-party payer of sickpay, such as a multiemployer plan, must at the end of each year issue a statement informing the employer that a payment was made, to whom it was made and the amount of the payment. The employer receiving that information must include it on the Form W-2 that is sent to the employee shortly after the close of the taxable year and must ultimately report this information to the Internal Revenue Service, so that the IRS can collect federal income taxes on the sickpay. In addition to income taxes, FICA Social Security taxes apply to sickpay, and the multiemployer plan making the payment is treated as the employer for this purpose. Thus, the plan is required to pay the employer portion of FICA withholding and to withhold the employee portion.

These rules contain alternatives, however, that permit a plan to avoid paying the employer portion of the sickpay withholding. The plan must immediately notify the employer with respect to whom the payment will be made and provide the employer with the relevant information for reporting to the IRS and paying the employer portion of the FICA taxes.

In Advisory Opinion 82-32A, the Labor Department stated that a plan is permitted to use whichever alternative is least burdensome and least costly for the plan. This determination must be made by plan fiduciaries on a case by case basis and may result in different treatment for different contributing employers or groups of contributing employers.

The Labor Department also focused on a subsidiary, but important, issue concerning the role of the individual trustee in deciding which alternatives to choose. For example, if a trustee of a multiemployer plan is a vice president for industrial relations for a contributing employer and the plan is considering which sickpay method it should use—whether it should report and pay directly to the IRS or whether it should merely report to employers individually—AO 82-32A provides that the trustee may take part in a general discussion of the issues and vote on matters of general applicability. If, however, the issue relates to how his company will be treated, the trustee cannot take part in or vote on the matter. To do otherwise might constitute a conflict of interest prohibited under Section 406(b)(2) of ERISA.

Advisory Opinion 82-32A also states that a plan may not pay an employee's portion of withholding unless the payment is deducted from the employee's sickpay benefit. Alternatively, the plan may provide expressly (in writing) that the payment of withholding on sickpay benefits is in and of itself a benefit under the plan.

Return of Employer Contributions

Section 403(c) of ERISA provides, generally, that the assets of a plan may not be used for the benefit of an employer. It contains several exceptions, however. The first exception, set forth in Section 403(c)(2)(A), provides that the return of contributions to an employer is permitted under certain circumstances. When ERISA was first enacted, Section 403(c)(2)(A) permitted a return of contributions to an employer if two conditions were met. First, the contribution to the plan by the employer had to have been made by mistake of fact. Second, if the contribution was made by a mistake of fact, a return of the contribution could be made only within one year from the date the contribution was made.

This provision raised several difficult problems. First, the term "mistake of fact" was difficult to define. The courts generally held that where an employer made a mistaken contribution because it misunderstood the terms of the plan, the mistake was a mistake of law, not a mistake of fact, and a return of the contribution could not be made. Second, the one year return rule made returns impossible in many cases because the traditional audit procedures used by plans frequently could not locate mistaken contributions until much longer than one year after the contribution had been made.

Consequently, in connection with the 1980 amendments to ERISA relating to its multiemployer termination insurance provisions, changes were made in the return of contribution rules for multiemployer plans. The "mistake of fact" rule was amended to provide that a return of contributions is permissible if made by a mistake of fact or a mistake of law. Additionally, the one year return rule was changed to provide that a return of contributions is permitted within six months from the date the mistaken overpayment is discovered by the plan administrator. This change actually provides a much longer period for returns because the six month period begins to run on the date the plan administrator discovers the mistake, which could be several years after the contribution was actually made.

This discussion provides the background for several developments in 1982. The case of *Ethridge v. Masonry Contractors, Inc.,* No. C78-1724A (N.D. Ga. March 26, 1982) dealt with the interaction of the original return of contribution rule and the amended rule. In this case, a Taft-Hartley plan performed an audit of an employer in 1980 and found that the employer had made overpayments to the plan of $64,000 since 1976. When the employer learned of this finding, it demanded a return of its excess contributions. The employer claimed that the overpayment resulted from a mistake in its calculation of the contributions. The plan refused to return the contributions, claiming that the old rule precluding returns after one year from the date of contribution was applicable, and that the plan had not determined whether the overpayment was a mistake of fact or a mistake of law.

The court ruled in favor of the employer on the mistake of fact/mistake of law issue. The court stated the plan could not refuse to return a contribution to an employer on the grounds that the plan administrator had failed to make a decision on whether the mistake was one of fact or of law. In effect, the plan administrator is obligated to make that decision and if he fails to do so, it will be assumed that there was either a mistake of fact or a mistake of law, since either one will satisfy the statute, as amended.

The court also ruled that the 1980 amendments to Section 403(c)(2)(A) apply retroactively to January 1, 1975. Therefore, the old one year return rule did not apply. Rather, the new six months from the date of discovery rule applied; therefore, the requested return of contributions in this case was permitted because the claim was made within six months from the date that the plan administrator learned that there was an overpayment.

An interesting feature of this decision is the court's holding that the employer is entitled to a return of its contributions. Section 403(c)(2)(A) provides that a plan is *permitted* to return contributions if the requirements of the section are met. It does not, however, *require* a return.

Also relevant to this subject is a DOL information letter, WSB 82-28. This letter dealt with the issue of whether, in the case of a mistaken contribution, the employer is entitled to, or may receive at the discretion of the plan, interest on the mistaken contribution for the period of time that the plan held the funds. The Labor Department in WSB 82-28 very firmly took the position that no interest payment is permitted on mistaken contributions.

General Fiduciary Duties — Collection of Contributions and Disclosure

One of the key ERISA court decisions of 1982 was *Nichols v. Board of Trustees of the Asbestos Workers Local 24 Pension Plan,* No. 80-563 (D.D.C. July 19, 1982). This case presented two very important issues. The first issue focused on the extent of the duty of trustees of a Taft-Hartley pension plan to disclose certain items of information to participants and beneficiaries. The question raised was whether the trustees' duty is limited to the statutory disclosure obligations contained in Title I of ERISA and in the Internal Revenue Code, or whether trustees are required in certain cases to go beyond statutorily required disclosures. The second issue related to the trustees' obligation to collect employer contributions that are owing to the plan pursuant to reciprocity agreements that the plan has with other funds.

The *Nichols* case involved the Asbestos Workers Local 24 Pension Plan, Washington, D.C. All of the plaintiffs in the case were covered employees who had retired between the end of 1977 and the beginning of 1979. Prior to the retirement of the plaintiffs, the monthly benefit payable under the plan was $16.80 per year of credited service. At approximately the time the plaintiffs retired, the trustees adopted an amendment pursuant to which benefits were increased by $8, to $24.80, for all people who retired after October 1, 1977. All of the plaintiffs in this case retired after October 1, 1977 and began receiving monthly benefits based on $24.80 per year of credited service.

Approximately one and one-half years later, the trustees and the actuaries for the plan reviewed the financial condition of the plan carefully and recognized that the plan was in financial difficulty. Consequently, they determined that the plan would not be able to support the benefit rate of $24.80 per year of credited service. Thus, in an effort to restore the financial solvency of the plan, the trustees amended the plan to reduce the monthly benefit rate retroactively to $16.80, thereby retracting the $8 benefit increase that had previously been granted. Although this latest amendment was adopted retroactively, the trustees decided not to attempt to collect a refund of payments that had already been made to retirees.

Before the trustees could implement the $8 benefit reduction, they were required to file an application with the Internal Revenue Service and obtain IRS approval. In this regard, the Internal Revenue Code provides that a retroactive amendment that decreases accrued benefits cannot be adopted and implemented without the approval of the IRS. Accordingly, the trustees prepared an application for such approval and submitted the application to the IRS. Shortly after the submission of the application, the trustees published a notice in a local union newspaper indicating that benefits would be reduced and that an application for approval had been made to the IRS. The Internal Revenue Service subsequently approved the application for the retroactive benefit decrease and the benefit decrease was implemented.

The retirees who were affected by the benefit reduction brought suit against the trustees and the IRS alleging that the trustees had failed to notify the retirees in a timely manner that this action was going to be taken. The retirees claimed that, had they known in a timely manner that this application had been made to the IRS for approval of a reduction in their benefits, they could have brought relevant information to the attention of officials at the IRS. The retirees claimed that, as a result of having that information, the IRS would not have approved the application and benefits would not have been reduced.

On this issue, the court ruled in favor of the trustees, stating that the trustees had satisfied all of the statutory disclosure requirements contained in ERISA and that an additional disclosure obligation would not be implied except in egregious cases. This decision is consistent with other court decisions, such as *Hopkins v. FMC Corporation,* 535 F. Supp. 235 (W.D.N.C. March 25, 1982). In that case, the court ruled that if a plan has distributed a proper summary plan description to participants and beneficiaries, the plan sponsor is not required to provide an explanation of the plan to individual participants or to advise participants on the applicability of various plan provisions to their particular circumstances.

The retirees in the *Nichols* case also alleged that the trustees breached their fiduciary duties by not making appropriate efforts to collect contributions due pursuant to reciprocity agreements, and that the failure to make such efforts was a significant cause of the plan's financial difficulties. The trustees responded that the plan had reciprocity agreements with nine other jurisdictions. They had not found it possible to devise an effective means of determining when employees were working for an employer in another jurisdiction and, therefore, whether contributions to other plans are properly being remitted to the plan. The trustees indicated that, at the end of each year, the plan sends a contribution report to each participant, listing the employers from which the plan has received contributions on behalf of the participant and the amount received. Participants are requested to inform the plan if the report is incorrect or otherwise inconsistent with the contributions that the participant believes should have been made.

Based on these arguments, the court ruled that plan trustees have an obligation to attempt to collect contributions pursuant to reciprocity agreements. The court refused, however, to indicate what procedures would satisfy this obligation and did not impose any liability on the trustees in this case for failing to take appropriate actions.

Duties of Plan Counsel

A 1982 district court decision in *Washington-Baltimore Newspaper Guild v. The Washington Star Company,* No. 81-1980 (D.D.C. July 16, 1982), deals with the responsibilities of attorneys for an employee benefit plan. This case arose in connection with the closing of the *Washington Star* newspaper in Washington, D.C. and the termination of the pension plan maintained by the *Star.*

In 1976, the *Star,* as a result of collective bargaining, adopted a plan amendment that provided that in the event of the termination of the plan, assets in excess of liabilities would be distributed to the participants and beneficiaries of the plan. Approximately two weeks after the decision was made (in 1981) to close the *Star* and terminate the plan, however, another amendment was adopted that, in effect, reversed the 1976 amendment. The 1981 amendment provided that, in the event of plan termination (which had already been scheduled), any assets in excess of liabilities would be returned to the *Star.*

After the plan termination, the union that covered employees participating in the plan brought suit to challenge the 1981 amendment. As part of its challenge, the union attempted to introduce into evidence an affidavit of an attorney for the *Star* who also served as attorney for the plan in connection with the adoption of the 1976 plan amendment. The *Washington Star,* in defending the suit, attempted to assert attorney/client privilege in an effort to block the introduction of the affidavit into evidence. The *Star* claimed that the introduction of the affidavit would violate the confidentiality between the attorney and the *Washington Star,* which would be a violation of both the attorney/client privilege and the canon of ethics.

On the affidavit issue, the court ruled for the union on the grounds that when an attorney is advising plan trustees or the members of a plan's administrative committee, the attorney's client is the plan participants and beneficiaries, not the trustees or other plan fiduciaries. Accordingly, a trustee or other fiduciary cannot raise the attorney/client privilege to block an effort by participants and beneficiaries to assert claims. Fundamental to this decision is the proposition that a plan is an entity that is separate and distinct from the contributing employers or the local union whose members are participating in the plan, and that the trustees or other plan fiduciaries have an obligation to act solely in the interest of participants and beneficiaries of the plan. Further, an attorney who provides advice to plan fiduciaries is responsible to the participants and beneficiaries of the plan, not merely to the plan fiduciaries.

The court also stated that its conclusion applies even where, as here, the plan's attorney was also the attorney for the corporate plan sponsor. The court stated with regard to the dual role aspect of the case that the *Washington Star* could have had separate counsel from the plan's counsel. In this way, the *Star* could have asserted the attorney/client privilege with respect to advice it received from its counsel regarding plan matters.

Class Exemptions for Real Estate Transactions

In the first ten months of 1982, the Labor Department issued three administrative class exemptions in proposed or final form. Like statutory exemptions, class exemptions are exemptions that apply to any plan, party in interest or fiduciary who can satisfy the terms and conditions of the exemption. Two of the 1982 exemptions related to real estate mortgage loan investments by plans.

In January 1981, the Department issued PTE 81-7, a class exemption for transactions involving mortgage pools in which plans have invested. The exemption covers numerous transactions that customarily occur in the management of private mortgage pools. As issued in 1981, however, PTE 81-7 applied to pools that contain only first mortgage loans, not second mortgage loans. Further, it only covers investments in pools that have an existing portfolio of mortgage loans; it does not apply to forward commitment investments in pools, whereby a plan makes a commitment to invest in a pool that will be formed in the future. In addition, the 1981 exemption applied only to mortgages on residential single family properties.

In 1982, the Department proposed an amendment to PTE 81-7 that would change two of these rules. The proposed amendment would expand the exemption to cover pools containing second mortgages and to permit forward commitment investments in mortgage pools. Even as amended, however, the exemption would continue to apply only to pools of mortgage loans on residential single family properties.

The other important 1982 class exemption development in the real estate area was the issuance of PTE 82-87, a final exemption issued by the Labor Department to cover several prohibited transaction problems that may arise when plans make residential mortgage loan investments. This exemption is particularly useful for Taft-Hartley plans in the building and construction trades that decide to establish mortgage lending programs as a means of investing in the community where the plan is located.

One of the problems encountered in these cases is that a contributing employer may be the developer of property with respect to which the plan provides single family mortgage loan commitments. This problem is covered by PTE 82-87. The exemption is, however, extremely complicated and contains many conditions.

One important condition is that a plan's mortgage investment program (including the origination of loans), the decision to make mortgage investments and the servicing of the loans must be administered by qualified independent professionals. The exemption does not cover a program that is administered internally by the trustees or the staff of a plan. Also, as in the case of the mortgage pool exemption, PTE 82-87 is limited to residential properties; it does not cover commercial properties. Additionally, the exemption does not permit mortgage loans at below the prevailing interest rate. All loans must be at an interest rate that is the prevailing rate in the community at the time the loan is made.

Conflicts of Interest

An important 1982 court decision on fiduciary conflicts of interest was *Donovan v. Cunningham,* Civ. Action No. H-80-27 (S.D.Tex. May 21, 1982). Mr. Cunningham was chairman of the board, president and sole shareholder of a company. He decided to sell all of his shares in the company to an employee stock ownership plan (ESOP) maintained by the company. Toward that end, a valuation of the shares was obtained from an independent appraiser of $200/share, and the sale was consummated.

The Labor Department challenged the sale, however, on the grounds that the administrative committee of ESOP did not follow proper procedures in determining the fair market value of the stock and that more-than-adequate consideration was paid by the ESOP to Cunningham for the stock. In addition, since Cunningham was a party in interest with respect to the ESOP, the Department claimed that the transaction was a nonexempt prohibited transaction. Finally, the Department argued that the indemnification provisions contained in the plan and in separately executed documents were in violation of Section 410 of ERISA.

Although the court ruled in favor of Mr. Cunningham, the decision establishes a strict position on fiduciary conflicts of interest. In this regard, the court stated that where an individual both is in a corporate management position and serves as a fiduciary with respect to a plan maintained by the corporation, he may not discharge his corporate management role without considering the interests of the participants and beneficiaries of the plan.

This ruling could have broad impact, even in the case of Taft-Hartley plans. For example, if a person who serves as vice president for labor relations of an employer or a business agent for a local union is also a plan trustee, and he or she must make a decision on a particular corporate or union matter, this court decision might require the person to take into account, in making the decision, what the impact of the decision might be on plan participants and beneficiaries. Although this is a very broad application of the ERISA fiduciary responsibility provisions, it seems to be consistent with a series of court decisions, including the recent Supreme Court decision in the *AMAX Coal Co.* case.

Another feature of this case is that the Court indicated that a fiduciary may rely on the judgment of an independent appraiser in establishing the value of property. However, in relying on such a valuation, the fiduciary is obligated to take into account his own knowledge of factors that may affect the valuation.

Also note that, with respect to the prohibited transaction issues in this case, this Court (and a number of others) stated that a person seeking to rely on a statutory exemption from the prohibited transaction restrictions has the burden of proving that the exemption was available and that the conditions precedent to the availability of the exemption were satisfied.

With respect to the indemnification issue raised in this case, ERISA permits indemnification of fiduciaries by employers. However, it does not permit indemnification of fiduciaries by a plan because such indemnification is equivalent to an exculpatory clause, which is precluded by Section 410 of ERISA. In this case, the documents provided for indemnification of plan fiduciaries by the employer. However, inasmuch as the plan owned a 36% interest in the employer, the Court said that the indemnification was, in effect, an indemnification by the plan and, therefore, would be void under Section 410.

Plan Assets — Bank Deposits

The First Circuit Court of Appeals decision in *O'Toole v. Arlington Trust Company,* Nos. 81-1861 and 82-1042 (First Cir. June 29, 1982), deals with the issue of whether a bank that has received ordinary bank deposits from a plan becomes a fiduciary with respect to the monies deposited by the plan in the bank and, therefore, subject to the prohibited transaction restrictions of ERISA. In this case, funds were deposited in a bank by the trustees of a single employer plan. The trustees were also the officers of the employer corporation. The bank had previously made loans to the corporation, and when the corporation later encountered financial difficulties, the bank, in order to protect its loan positions, offset the plan deposits against the corporation's outstanding loans. The trustees brought suit against the bank for return of the bank deposits, alleging breach of fiduciary duty by the bank.

The court held, however, for the bank on the grounds that the bank was not a plan fiduciary merely by reason of receiving bank deposits. The court stated that the bank deposits did not give the bank any discretionary authority over plan assets and did not result in the bank providing investment advice to the trustees of the plan. It stated that the trustees retained full discretionary authority and control over the bank account. Although the court did not explain the rationale for its decision, it is apparent that the court considered a bank deposit as no more than a debtor/creditor relationship between the bank and the depositor plan. The plan made a deposit in the bank and the bank owes the amount of the deposit to the plan. Thus, the bank is, in effect, a debtor of the plan, but is not a fiduciary (or a party in interest) with respect to the plan.

Although not discussed by the court, it should be noted that the offset of the deposits against the loan balance was a prohibited transaction involving the employer and the plan, since the offset resulted in a use of plan assets for the benefit of the employer. Thus, by virtue of the decision in this case, the employer was, in effect, obligated to repay the loan in order to avoid engaging in a prohibited transaction and incurring prohibited transaction excise taxes.

Trustees' Personal Liability Under ERISA and the Importance of Proper "Defensive" Documentation—The Fabled "Paper Trail"

BY RICHARD J. DAVIS, JR.

THIS PRESENTATION may reflect a seemingly very cynical evaluation of the treatment of trust funds by American courts and governmental agencies. In truth, however, this presentation assumes that, with few exceptions, it will be the obligation of the trust fund to prove that the actions it takes are proper and justified.

As those trustees with any legal experience will immediately note, this assumption violates basic legal principles: The plaintiff or claimant has the "burden of proof." He or she ordinarily must prove that the action of the fund is improper or violates the law. However, the experience of many attorneys lately is that, regardless of principles, courts and governmental agencies are looking first to the trustees to account for their actions.

The "deep pocket" theory of liability is becoming a recognized fact of life in litigation: Some courts try to find some basis of liability against the defendant who can best afford to bear itself, or "pass-through" to others, the cost of liability. In trust cases, a court may find that, although the claimant did not actually qualify for benefits, the cost of those benefits to the trust is small compared with the fund's total assets, on the one hand; on the other hand, denial leaves the poor claimant with no benefits at all. As these benefits may be sought either by a claimant who has been injured or ill, or who is poor and retired, these persons present appealing plaintiffs. This factor might be cynically labeled the "widow/orphans corollary" of the deep pocket theory. The parallel concept at work among governmental agencies might best be characterized as the "Ralph Nader" school of regulatory review—"What have you to say in your defense of the following accusations made by your long-suffering, mistreated participants?"

In this kind of regulatory and litigation setting, the premise of this presentation is that "defensive documentation" may be the trustees' best hope of overcoming the very strong inclination to favor the position of claimants over that of trustees and the trusts they serve. This purpose may amount to combating a "worst case syndrome." I will leave

Mr. Davis is a senior attorney with the legal firm of Davis, Frommer & Jesinger in Los Angeles, San Jose and San Francisco. He has been active in the joint trust field for many years with major building trades labor organizations and Taft-Hartley trust funds in the Southwest as clients. Mr. Davis received his A.B. degree from the University of California at Berkeley and his J.D. degree from UCLA. He is a member of the Los Angeles County and American Bar Associations. Mr. Davis is also a member and past chairman of the Foundation's Attorneys Committee. He has spoken at previous Foundation educational programs.

that judgment to you trustees, whose experiences ultimately affect the judgment of your attorneys.

Sources of Trustee Liability Under ERISA, Joint and Individual

Section 409 of ERISA specifically imposes personal liability on "fiduciaries with respect to employee benefit plans" in the exercise of their responsibilities on behalf of the participants of the trust. This provision is one of the hinge pins of the regulatory scheme adopted by ERISA. Congress apparently believed (or was convinced) that the imposition of this personal liability would somehow assure that trustees would act only in the interests of participants.

In addition, Section 405 of ERISA adds to the direct liability of Section 409 an indirect source of potential liability described as "co-fiduciary liability," which may derive from the misconduct of other "fiduciaries." This section of ERISA imposes on trustees the additional responsibility of policing their fellow trustees and fiduciaries.

Delegation of Responsibilities

Section 409 of ERISA further defines the scope of fiduciary liability under ERISA by allowing a board of trustees to "delegate" fiduciary authority to specifically identified fiduciaries. But, does it reduce trustees' risk exposure?

Delegation under proper circumstances to identified fiduciaries *may* relieve other fiduciaries of potential liability over those delegated functions, but the remaining trustees must still exercise a supervisory responsibility over the fiduciaries who have been delegated those functions. Further, it may well be that the "delegatee fiduciary" assumes a higher potential liability for his conduct of trust functions, particularly if the delegated function corresponds to a professional discipline or responsibility. In any case, if the trustees are seeking to use delegation to allocate responsibilities and, perhaps, limit risk exposure, that program must be clearly reflected in the trust's minutes. In fact, a specific trust policy of delegation is advisable, setting forth the program to be followed by the trust.

The Several Distinct "Liabilities" Facing Trustees

In planning a program of creating and preserving proper documents—documents that serve the "defensive" purpose that fiduciaries may someday need, three kinds of liability, which must concern all fiduciaries, should be kept in mind:
- "Joint" liability, wherein the trustees as a board must defend themselves against attack from the outside
- "Individual" liability, wherein a single trustee seeks to avoid liability by segregating himself from other trustees
- "Individual" liability, wherein a single trustee seeks to defend attack from the remaining trustees.

Each of these potential liabilities imposes its own special needs for recordkeeping. Some basic records are common to all such liabilities.

Documents That Trustees Should Consider Their "Lifeblood"

Minutes of ALL meetings of the trustees, however small or informal, should be considered the first line of defense against any attack on the trustees. Too often, trustees take little care with the minutes. Minutes are often brief, without much detail of discussion of questions that arise. A brief case study of the value of minutes is in order.

When ERISA was adopted, an issue came up: Was every investment then in effect subject to review by ERISA standards? The theory that the DOL and the federal courts have developed is that "continuation" of an investment is an "action" by the trustees that may be reviewed at any time.

Prior investments may have been made for reasons that the current trustees do not now remember or understand. Yet, it may be the current trustees who must defend those investments. If the discussions that led to those investments are not carefully and completely preserved, investments made before the tenure of the current trustees may become a basis of liability for them.

For similar reasons, written reports submitted to the trustees or presented to trust meetings that may influence trustee policy should be preserved. Professionals and trustees who may be delegated special functions should be instructed to present written reports about significant issues for the trust. These reports, too, should be attached to the minutes.

Copies of all IRS qualification letters, Form 5500 filings, federal and state exempt organization tax returns and all fund audits, including compliance audits, should be kept easily available at the trust offices, for it is automatic that representatives of reviewing governmental agencies ask to see them. Any procedure to keep these materials at hand will save time and, perhaps, a more thorough review when "routine" visits from the DOL or IRS occur.

If the trustees have sought exemptions for any party-in-interest transactions, records of those transactions are a requisite of most exemptions and are a major item of review by the DOL and the IRS. The Department of Labor has displayed a paranoid interest in the expense reimbursement records of Taft-Hartley trusts, so trustees must consider such records as a vital part of their "paper trail."

As a final note about minutes, the importance of keeping complete minutes of ALL meetings must be emphasized. Often, subcommittees of the trustees may review certain specific subjects. Most trusts delegate functions in this way, even if informally. Unfortunately, that practice can be a problem. Such informal meetings may not produce minutes. Then, when the full board of trustees is presented with the subcommittee's recommendations and adopts them, the minutes not only may not reflect the trustees' full reasoning; they may inaccurately reflect hasty action by the full board on an important subject.

Individual Trustees' Rights and Interests in Minutes

Individual trustees may find themselves (rarely, I hope) in a situation in which they must attempt to set themselves apart from their colleagues. Although it may not be a pleasant experience for that trustee, what little opportunity ERISA allows a fiduciary to attempt to isolate himself from liability requires an "up front, public" break with the trust's other fiduciaries. However, with regard to a particular decision of the trust, few options exist to avoid "co-fiduciary liability." Each trustee who seeks to segregate himself from a decision taken by the board must make a clear, public record of his disagreement and his reasons for his opposition. The obvious place to make that record is in the trust minutes.

In the opinion of most attorneys, each trustee has an absolute right to place any vote or a statement of explanation of any vote in the minutes. Refusal of other fiduciaries to allow the dissenter to exercise that right leaves that trustee with no choice but to seek the aid of the Department of Labor or a federal court in his effort to isolate himself from liability.

The Department of Labor has developed a series of opinions to cover the situation in which an individual trustee may face what is described as a "divided loyalty" issue under ERISA Section 406 (b)2. Example: A trustee intends to bid on a job that will be paid for by the trust. Under Section 406(b)2, a fiduciary may not act for a trust when he may have any kind of contrary interest. The DOL opinions require the affected trustee(s) to abstain from participation in the decisionmaking process concerning that transaction. Such trustees should insist that their abstention is clearly recorded in the minutes of any meeting of the trust in which the transaction comes to a vote.

"Defensive Documentation"

Defensive documentation, whereby the trustees seek to establish, by specific procedures, methods to defend against possible claims to be made by participants, is not a practice for trustees to be ashamed about. Make certain that the lawyer who has "Exhibit A" in his pocket on the first day of trial is the trustees' counsel, not the opposition.

The happiest day of any litigant's life is that storied day in the courtroom when the judge asks, "Doesn't any of the parties have a document or a letter that answers the issue raised by this claim?" and it is *your attorney* who stands up to say, "It just so happens, Your Honor...." The contrary situation, where it is the *claimant's attorney* who stands up, is an event that is just as important to avoid.

The fund's recordkeeping processes should seek to avoid giving a potential litigant his lawyer's "Exhibit A," while striving, through the establishment of a systematic chain of internal forms, to produce documents that will serve as the trustees' lawyer's "Exhibit A" in as many situations as are foreseeable.

Even small items, such as phone calls and office visits for information, must be recorded systematically. It may be important to the trust to be able to establish that information was provided and what that information was. Unfortunately, the two most common allegations in ERISA litigation usually are:
- "I never received any letter or booklet from that fund, and every time I went down to its office no one would answer my questions."
- "I can't remember who I talked to at the fund when I went down to its office on the day I cannot now remember, but whichever person it was, he or she promised me that I would get a million dollars a year, at least."

Summary

Whether by making certain that the official documents of the trust properly reflect the decisions and the consideration of the trustees, or by making equally certain that there are records to reflect the contacts between interested persons and the trust and trustees, it is the firm, if cynical, view of this observer that trustees must be prepared to prove the proper execution of their duties when questioned. If they aren't, they will face the consequences of legal systems that are very likely to be inclined (if not biased) toward the interests of participants and beneficiaries, or toward the "disinterested" position taken "only to help the trustees" by federal administrative agencies.

Fiduciary Liability Insurance — What the Policies Cover and What They Don't

BY WARREN H. SALTZMAN

ALTHOUGH FIDUCIARY liability insurance was available before ERISA, few Taft-Hartley trusts purchased it. Governing trust agreements generally contained exculpatory clauses stating that the trustees would not be liable for any acts or omissions on their part unless dishonesty, bad faith or gross negligence was involved. Because of these exculpatory clauses and the fact that lawsuits seeking to establish trustees' personal liability were almost nonexistent, trustees who acted in good faith had minimal exposure to personal liability before ERISA.

But when ERISA was enacted, it became clear that legal actions against trustees for simply imprudent actions could be anticipated. Since Section 410(a) of ERISA voided exculpatory clauses, it became essential to have insurance against potential personal liability and legal defense costs if union and business representatives were to continue to serve as trustees. Since Section 302 of Taft-Hartley requires trust funds subject to that law to be administered by joint union-management boards, any impediment to attracting qualified trustees would have been a very serious matter indeed. Furthermore, since Section 408(c)(2) of ERISA also prohibited using trust assets to compensate most Taft-Hartley trustees, the cost of the insurance to the trustees had to be affordable to them or to the entities that appointed them.

Fortunately, Section 410(b) of ERISA stated that the voiding of exculpatory clauses under Section 410(c) did not prohibit trusts from purchasing insurance to protect the trust and the trustees or other fiduciaries. However, there was one significant exception—any policy purchased with trust assets would have to give a right of "recourse" to the insurance company, e.g., the right to recover any sums paid out by the insurer from any fiduciary whose breach of fiduciary obligations contributed to the loss. However, the insurance companies were willing to waive this right of recourse for payment of an additional premium. Although ERISA would not permit this additional premium to be paid from trust funds, it was made available at a very low cost

Mr. Saltzman is president of Saltzman & Johnson Law Corporation, specializing in Taft-Hartley trust funds in various industries. He received his B.A. degree from the University of California-Berkeley and LL.B. from the Yale Law School. He was a teaching fellow at Stanford Law School and taught trust law at Golden Gate University School of Law for several years. Mr. Saltzman has spoken at numerous International Foundation educational meetings. He is chairman of the Foundation's Attorneys Committee and a member of the Educational Program Committee.

(less than $30 annually per trustee), so that its cost presented no problem. (The low cost reflects the fact that the right of recourse would not be particularly valuable to the insurer because of the cost of enforcing the right and the fact that few Taft-Hartley trustees would have assets sufficient to justify those expenses.)

The net result, therefore, is that the protection that trustees used to have through exculpatory clauses at no expense to the trust is now obtained through fiduciary liability insurance at substantial expense to the trust. Of course, that insurance also gives the trusts themselves protection that they may find valuable—particularly protection against the high costs involved in the ever-increasing litigation that has followed the enactment of ERISA. Considering the cost of this insurance, it is important that those plans acquiring it clearly understand what it will do for them and what it will not do. This article will analyze typical policies from that standpoint.

Summary of Fiduciary Liability Insurance Policies

Following is a summary of the provisions found in most fiduciary liability policies:
1. *Insuring provision*—what acts or omissions are protected by the policy
2. *Losses covered*—what types of losses are covered
3. *Limits of liability*—the amount of insurance provided and any applicable deductibles
4. *Persons covered*—which individuals or companies are protected by the insurance
5. *Exclusions from coverage*—specific acts or omissions excluded from coverage, generally including:
   A. Benefit claims
   B. Fines, penalties and exemplary damages
   C. Intentional torts, dishonest or fraudulent conduct
   D. Bodily injury
   E. Failure to comply with laws protecting employees
   F. Failure to maintain adequate insurance
   G. Assumption of liabilities of others
   H. Obtaining personal profit or advantage
   I. Collection or return of contributions
   J. Potential losses known to the trustees at policy inception
   K. Violation of antidiscrimination laws.
6. *Notice requirements*
7. *Settlement of claims*
8. *Policy extension clause*
9. *Claims made extension clause*
10. *Right of subrogation*
11. *Right of recourse*
12. *Effect of other insurance.*

Each of these provisions will be discussed in order.

Insuring Provision

Although available policies use somewhat different words to describe the types of acts or omissions with respect to which they offer protection, the differences do not appear to be significant. All policies state that they will protect against alleged breaches of fiduciary duty, e.g., failures by the fiduciaries to carry out their responsibilities under ERISA.

Some of the policies specifically refer to administrative errors; the specificity is obviously useful, but any administrative error for which a fiduciary could be held personally liable would surely also be a breach of fiduciary duty.

All available policies are "claims made" policies, e.g., they apply only if a claim is made within the policy period. In other words, even if a breach of fiduciary responsibility occurs during the policy period, it is not covered unless a claim based on that breach is also made within the policy period, or such later period as may be permitted by the policy extension clause described later.

Losses Covered

The provisions describing the losses covered are—together with the exclusions—the most important to review. In particular, one should note whether and to what extent defense costs are covered, e.g., whether defense is provided if an exclusion applies or if no monetary damages are sought, as in a suit for declaratory relief.

Limits of Liability

The maximum amount of coverage provided will generally be described on the face page of the policy, but the policy should be reviewed to determine whether defense costs are included in the maximum or are in addition to it. Most policies also have a deductible, but it usually does not apply to defense costs. Additional defense limits may also be available for an extra premium.

Persons Covered

Current trustees are covered by all policies, as is the trust itself; prior trustees are also generally covered, whether or not they were covered while the policy was in effect. Fund employees are also covered and contract administrators are covered by most policies at little or no extra cost. Some carriers will also include the investment manager.

However, it is important to remember that since these are claims made policies, the trustees are protected only so long as coverage is continued. If a claim arises after the trust ceases to carry fiduciary liability insurance, there will be no protection except as may be provided by the policy extension clause described later.

Specific Exclusions

When reviewing the exclusion clause, it is important to determine whether defense coverage is also excluded. At least one commonly available policy specifically states that it will provide legal defense for excluded claims. Another policy reimburses the cost of legal defense for otherwise excluded benefit claims if the trust is *un*successful in its legal defense. Other policies are ambiguous on this point. If the policy is not clear, it is advisable to seek a clarification from the carrier or its agent concerning how the exclusions apply to defense claims. Additional comments on the typical exclusions follow.

Claims for Benefits

None of the policies will pay denied claims if the court finds that the participant was entitled to the benefit, although one policy will do so if "recovery for such benefits is based upon a [breach of fiduciary duty] and is payable as a personal obligation of the insured." The difficult question is whether this exclusion applies when the real issue is not a simple factual question, but rather the validity of a general plan rule whose adoption by the trustees is alleged to be arbitrary and capricious and thus a breach of their fiduciary responsibilities under Section 404(a) of ERISA or under Section 302 of Taft-Hartley.

Even though the plaintiff may be seeking payment of benefits in such cases, the author believes that fiduciary liability policies should be interpreted to require the insurer to provide the legal defense if the basic claim is for a breach of fiduciary responsibility in establishing improper rules; at least one commonly available policy so provides. There is reason to believe that whether the carrier will provide a defense in these cases may sometimes turn on the language used by plaintiff's attorney in bringing the lawsuit, e.g., whether the emphasis is on payment of the claim or on the trustees' breach of fiduciary responsibility. Since the main benefit to a trust fund in obtaining fiduciary liability insurance is the payment of its costs of litigation, and since litigation challenging the validity of plan rules is not uncommon, any ambiguity on this point should be clarified with the carrier if possible.

Fines, Penalties and Exemplary Damages

This type of loss is excluded by all major insurances.

Intentional Torts, Dishonest or Fraudulent Conduct

These types of losses and other intentional torts are also generally excluded because they are covered by other types of insurance, e.g., the legally required fidelity bond.

Bodily Injury

This type of loss is also generally excluded because it is covered by other types of insurance.

Failure to Comply With Laws Protecting Employees

Although this exclusion is also common, it would obviously apply only to a plan that hires its own employees rather than using a contract administrator.

Failure to Maintain Adequate Insurance

This common exclusion is presumably intended to prevent the trustees from relying on the fiduciary liability policy to avoid obtaining other appropriate insurance.

Assumption of Liabilities of Others

If the assumption of another's liabilities would be a breach of fiduciary responsibilities, query whether legal defense will be provided.

Obtaining Personal Profit or Advantage

The reason for this common exclusion is obvious.

Failure to Collect or Return Contributions

Some policies contain this exclusion, but the theory behind it is not completely clear to the author.

Acts Occurring Prior to the Policy Inception of Which the Trustees Had Knowledge

Since these are claims made policies, the carrier has a legitimate interest in knowing whether the trustees are aware of any possible outstanding claims before taking on the coverage. When switching carriers, one should ascertain whether the old carrier will have the responsibility under the policy extension clause described later or whether the new carrier will accept the risk.

Discrimination

One policy specifically excludes claims of discrimination under applicable antidiscrimination laws. In some cases, this exclusion can be of particular significance to a trust, particularly one that has its own employees. Discrimination suits can also arise against pension plans that use different actuarial tables for men and women.

Notice Requirements

All policies require prompt notice of the claim to be given to the insurance company. Notice should certainly be given as soon as litigation appears likely or when an attorney threatens litigation, but the necessity of giving notice of every protested claim denial is not so clear.

Settlement of Claims

All the policies contain provisions limiting the insured's right to settle the claim at the expense of the carrier.

Policy Extension Clause

These clauses enable the plan to obtain continuing protection after policy termination by notifying the carrier of any potential claims of which he may be aware, e.g., any denied claims on which the statute of limitations has not run out.

Claims Made Extension Clause

These clauses protect the insured if the carrier terminates. This clause enables the insured to assure continuation of coverage for a limited time for a higher premium.

Right of Subrogation

All policies contain subrogation clauses. They enable the carrier to step into the shoes of the plan with respect to any rights that the plan may have against some third party in connection with the loss.

Right of Recourse

This clause was discussed earlier in this article. It is generally made inapplicable through the purchase of a waiver.

Effect of Other Insurance

This clause may be of some significance where the trustees have other insurance that might be applicable, e.g., a case in which dishonesty (covered by the fidelity bond) is alleged, as well as breach of fiduciary responsibility.

Conclusion

In determining which policy to select, it is advisable to ask the broker for its experience with the various carriers when claims are filed—e.g., how strictly they interpret policy exclusions, whether they permit fund counsel to handle the defense, etc. Although most policy differences may appear slight, the attitude of the insurer when problems arise can magnify these differences significantly.

Fiduciary Liability Insurance— Its Place in the Insurance Program of a Multiemployer Fund and How to Buy the Cover

BY STEPHEN HORN, II, CPCU

ALTHOUGH FIDUCIARY LIABILITY insurance was available prior to the enactment of ERISA in 1974, most multiemployer funds did not carry the insurance because the individual trustees were not held liable for their acts in administering a plan except in extreme cases. However, under ERISA 409 any person who is a fiduciary is *personally liable* to make good to a plan any losses to the plan resulting from breach of fiduciary duty. The liability exists even if the trustee is acting honestly and in good faith.

Since no one, no matter how competent, can be certain a plan will be run without error, virtually all funds should carry this important form of insurance coverage. Administrative errors are inevitable, and decisions prudently reached on one date may turn into wrongful acts with the passage of time. Fortunately, the personal liability of trustees can be insured using a fiduciary liability policy, but the coverage must be purchased by a plan because an individual trustee wanting protection has no way of buying separate insurance to protect only himself or herself.

The insurance contract that protects the policyholder (a fund) and individual trustees (past, present and future) against claims for "breach of fiduciary duty" or "wrongful acts" may be called Trustee & Fiduciary Liability Insurance by Lloyd's of London, a Fiduciary Liability Policy by Chubb, Trustees Protective Liability Insurance by CNA, or Pension & Welfare Fund Fiduciary Responsibility Insurance by Aetna. These names are merely labels for similar policies used by the various underwriters of the coverage to differentiate their fiduciary liability policy from other kinds of insurance written by them.

No matter what it is called, the policy intent is to protect the fund and the trustees by paying the cost of defending claims, and if the fund is deemed responsible, to pay to claimants settlement amounts or court awards. The policies are by no means standard, and the wording of each is distinctly different from the others. The intent of all of the policies is similar, however, since the policies all cover the cost of defending against claims and pay losses awarded against the insured.

Mr. Horn, executive vice president of Jones Horn Insurance Brokers in San Francisco, has been active in the employee benefits field for over 18 years and deals with general insurance brokerage. As chartered property and casualty underwriter, he is past president of the Northern California Chapter, CPCU and is currently a member of the publications committee, Society of CPCU. Mr. Horn is past president of the Western Association of Insurance Brokers, is an associate in risk management and serves on the curriculum advisory committee of the Insurance Educational Association. He is an adjunct professor in insurance and risk management at Golden Gate University, San Francisco, and is author, reviewer and member of the advisory committee of the Insurance Institute of America Producer Program, a three semester program leading to an Accredited Advisor in Insurance designation. Mr. Horn additionally serves on the producer liaison committee of the California Department of Insurance. Educated at the University of California, Berkeley, he has spoken before professional groups including the Western Association of Insurance Brokers, the Society of CPCU, the San Francisco Insurance Women's Association and the Casualty Insurance Underwriters of San Francisco.

All of the available fiduciary liability policies

Figure

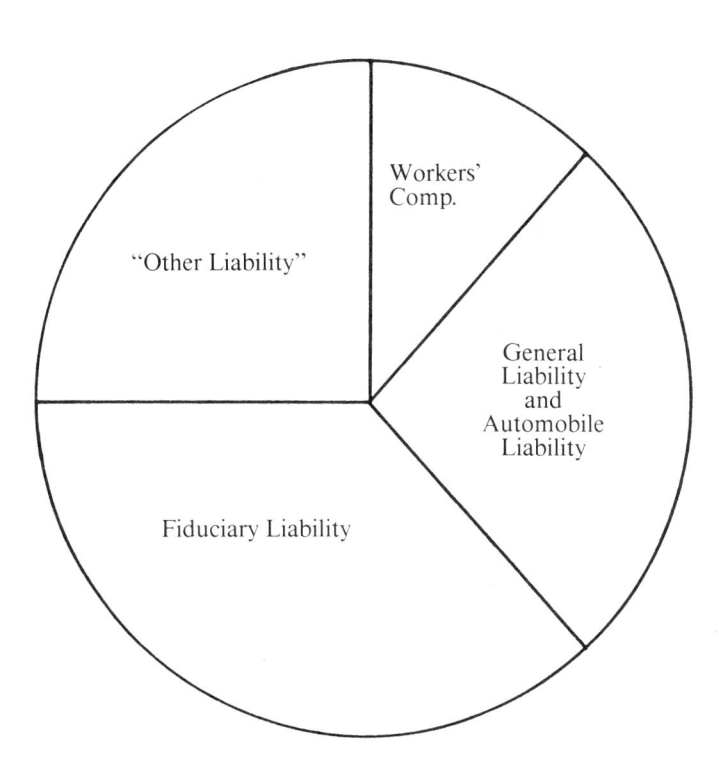

[Pie chart divided into four sections labeled: "Other Liability", Workers' Comp., General Liability and Automobile Liability, Fiduciary Liability]

are "claims made" policies, as opposed to the "occurrence" policies often found in other kinds of insurance policies. The difference is that the occurrence policies cover only losses that result from acts or omissions that take place during the policy period, no matter when the claim is first presented. For instance, automobile insurance is always provided on an occurrence basis, so a policy in force from January 1, 1982 to January 1, 1983 would cover claims arising from an accident on June 1, 1982, even if the lawsuit for damages was not filed until 1984. Fiduciary liability policies respond to claims first made during the policy period, no matter when they may have occurred. Thus, an investment decision made in 1975 that went sour in 1982, resulting in a lawsuit against the trustees for negligence in managing investments, would be covered by the policy in effect in 1982 when the claim was first made. A "claim" does not necessarily mean a lawsuit. It could be an administrative proceeding by the Department of Labor or other governmental agency, or it could be even the threat of a lawsuit.

Because of the "claims made" feature of fiduciary liability insurance, it is imperative that "prior acts" (that is acts that occurred before the policy period) are not excluded. It is also critical that coverage be continuous, even extending in some cases beyond the termination of a plan.

The fiduciary liability policy is but one form of liability insurance protection required by the average fund. The available kinds of insurance can be thought of as pieces of a pie that fit together to protect the trustees. Each policy intends to provide coverage for a particular exposure to loss resulting from claims made against the trust and/or the trustees individually. This concept is shown graphically in the figure.

The other liability policies carried by most funds should include:

Workers' Compensation Insurance. Technically, this insurance is not a liability policy, but it is included in this discussion because it protects the trust for legal obligations to employees for the costs of work-related injuries and illnesses. Each state labor code mandates benefits in that state, and in some states even unpaid trustees might be interpreted to be employees for the purposes of being eligible for workers' compensation benefits. Workers' compensation benefit payments are specifically excluded from the fiduciary liability policy.

General Liability and Automobile Liability In-

surance. Funds, like other financial entities, have responsibilities not only to employees, but also to members of the general public. Claims for bodily injury and property damage are covered by general liability and automobile liability policies. (If watercraft or aircraft were owned by a fund, additional coverage would be required for the liability exposures arising from them.) The typical comprehensive policy would cover a fund, and officers and employees while acting within the scope of their duties. The insurance should include personal injury (false arrest, detention or malicious prosecution, libel and slander, wrongful entry or eviction or other invasion of right of private occupancy, and humiliation). The policy should also be broadened by the use of the extended liability endorsement that adds additional protection. Coverage would normally be excluded for intentional acts of the "insured"; pollution unless sudden and accidental; liability assumed by the insured to purchase insurance; the exposures covered by the workers' compensation policy, Social Security or any similar plan; damage to the property or products of the insured (since these should be covered by the insured using property insurance); property of others in the care, custody or control of the insured; alienated premises; poor workmanship; product recall; fines, penalties and punitive damages.

Most funds have few general liability exposures unless they own real estate or other physical assets; however, it is important to have this protection because claims for bodily injury, personal injury and property damage are excluded from the fiduciary liability policy. For example, complaints of breach of fiduciary liability filed against funds often include an allegation of "emotional distress" by the claimant. Defense of such an allegation of bodily injury would be undertaken by the general liability insurer, not the fiduciary liability insurer.

Fiduciary Liability Insurance. For most funds, the fiduciary liability policy is the largest "piece of the pie" in terms of both the scope of protection and the cost. The coverage for breach of fiduciary duty is for the benefit of the insured fund, anyone for whom the insured is legally responsible and, by waiver of recourse, the trustees. Typical exclusions are acts known at the time of application for the insurance (which should have been presented to a previous insurer); dishonest, fraudulent or criminal acts (which should be covered by a fidelity bond); willful violations of statutes; failure to provide insurance; bodily injury, property damage, libel and slander (all of which can be insured by a general liability policy); exposures covered by the workers' compensation policy, Social Security or any similar plan. Certain claims for benefits are also often excluded.

A fiduciary bond is required of each fund by ERISA. This bond protects the plan participants against dishonest acts resulting in financial loss to the fund. This "honesty insurance" is often confused with the fiduciary liability insurance because of the similarity in name, but it should be noted that the exposure covered by this bond is excluded specifically from the fiduciary liability policy.

"Other Liability." Not all exposures to legal liability are insurable, and unless such claims as breach of contract or disputes about amounts owed are alleged to be breach of fiduciary duty, they will not be covered by any insurance at all. These and other uninsurable exposures are labeled in the figure as "other liability."

Buying Fiduciary Liability Insurance

How is fiduciary liability insurance marketed by insurers, agents and brokers? The coverage is specialized and not offered by most insurers. In fact, most of this coverage for multiemployer plans is underwritten by just four insurers—Aetna Casualty, Chubb, CNA and Lloyd's. Others, like Ulico and Transit Casualty, have recently entered the field, but there are very few sources for this insurance.

The insurance marketplace is highly fragmented, so before comment is made on how the coverage should be purchased, the sources of the insurance must be identified. Insurance companies are like manufacturers. Their product—protection—is distributed primarily by retailers who are agents or brokers. Legally, an agent represents the seller of insurance, whereas a broker represents the insurance buyer. A broker generally has access to more insurers than an agent, because the agent is limited to those insurers that authorize the agent to represent them. In specialty insurance fields like fiduciary liability, some of the insurers are represented by "wholesalers" who sell only to agents and brokers. Lloyd's and CNA are represented in this way by intermediaries for fiduciary liability.

The best approach to the insurers is through an independent insurance agent or broker who knows about fiduciary liability insurance and who has had experience in arranging insurance for trust funds. Agents and brokers who specialize in arranging insurance for multiemployer trust funds will be familiar with many of the particular needs of these funds and of the various options available for their coverage.

How are the policies to be compared? A detailed analysis of the wording of the available policies is beyond the scope of this paper, but it is important to note that they are not "standard" and that differences in wording do exist. It is also important to compare the insurance companies in the field for financial soundness and reputation for fair dealing.

Financial soundness is regulated by the various state departments of insurance, and the National Association of Insurance Commissioners has an early warning list of insurers in financial difficulty. The A. M. Best Company annually publishes policyholder ratings that indicate the financial position of each insurer in comparison with others based on averages within the insurance industry. These ratings range from C− (Fair) to A+ (Excellent). A second criterion is insurer size, and Best ranks companies using Roman numerals from Class I (the smallest) to Class XV (the largest). Thus, an insurance company that is large and financially sound would be rated as A+XV.

Lloyd's is not an insurance company and is not rated by the Best system. Yet it is one of the oldest and most respected of insurance organizations, dating from the 17th century. Lloyd's does not issue policies as a corporate organization, but its members underwrite as individuals under the supervision of a governing committee. There is a trust fund maintained in the United States that, as of December 31, 1980, was in excess of $3 billion; there is great confidence in the ability of the underwriters at Lloyd's to meet their obligations.

Reputation for fair dealing is more difficult to evaluate. Insurers, as large financial institutions, develop their own distinct personalities over time, but those underwriting fiduciary liability all have excellent reputations.

It is generally the agent or broker who designs the coverage for the fund, so it is important that the person selected to represent the fund in the insurance marketplace have experience with fiduciary liability coverage and in tailoring the available policies to meet the individual needs of a fund. Experienced agents and brokers will also be of assistance in administering the policy and in monitoring claims to see that reported losses receive the prompt attention of the insurer.

The cost of fiduciary liability insurance is a significant factor in evaluating which policy to buy. Most of those who buy the insurance think that the cost of the insurance is too high and, unfortunately, the insurance companies publish no statistics to justify their premiums. An agent or broker can get competitive bids for a fund from several of the leading underwriters. This process is not recommended each year, however, because it is important to establish a relationship with underwriters so that there is continuity of protection and cooperation between the fund and the insurance company personnel.

The basic policy price is based on the size of plan assets, the amount of annual contributions, the number of participants and the number of trustees. Underwriters also evaluate other factors like the quality of fund investments and the experience and reputation of the trustees and of the professionals retained by a fund. With these criteria in mind, the underwriter establishes a premium based on judgment of the risk of loss. Although there are different rating approaches that might favor one kind of a fund or another (for instance, an underwriter whose primary criterion is plan assets would have a lower premium for a health and welfare plan than for a pension plan covering the same number of participants), the final pricing is based on the judgment of the underwriter.

Waiver of recourse against the trustees is a separate endorsement that should be included on every policy to protect the individual trustees personally. The cost for this coverage has traditionally been $25 per trustee, and ERISA prohibits payment of this premium by the fund. The waiver premium must, therefore, be paid by the trustees or their sponsoring organization.

There are sometimes taxes and fees added to the premiums if the insurer is not "admitted" to do business in a particular state. Normally, compensation to the agent or broker is in the form of a commission included in the premium.

Preparing the Application for Coverage

Fiduciary liability insurance always requires a completed application for a quotation or policy issuance. A short form application is normally used for policy renewal. In completing the application, several areas are of particular importance.

Who should be covered? It is necessary to list each fund to be covered; new funds must be added to coverage when they are established. There are certain advantages to combining coverage for related funds in one policy, including the fact that each trustee who sits on multiple boards of trustees would only be charged one waiver of recourse premium. There may also be disadvantages, like the sharing of policy limits.

It has been customary for the contract administrator to be extended coverage under the policy without charge; however, other plan advisors like the legal counsel, the investment manager or the consultants normally rely on their own professional liability insurance.

Many funds have affiliated entities like joint apprenticeship committees, which may not be trusts, per se, but which should be extended coverage because they might invest in property or could be accused of engaging in prohibited transactions. Other outside entities occasionally require insurance. For instance, under Subsection 302(C) of the Labor-Management Relations Act, provision is made for arbitration when a fund board of trustees is deadlocked between the employee trustees and the employer trustees. An independent umpire brought in to break the deadlock may refuse to serve without fiduciary liability insurance.

In filling out the application, of course, it is necessary to pick a limit for the insurance, and a question which often arises is, "How much insurance should be purchased?" There are no published guidelines to assist trustees in picking limits of insurance, but it is important to consider defense costs as well as the maximum potential liability. Pension funds generally have greater exposure than health and welfare funds because of asset size and long term pension commitments. Coverage is available up to $25 million or more, if such limits are required. The policies are generally sold with a $1,000 deductible applying to loss, but not to defense costs. Aetna has recently eliminated the deductible provision entirely.

Every application asks about prior claims and about knowledge of future claims that might arise. Since the policies only cover claims first made during the policy term, it is important that no prior claims are left uncovered when switching insurers. It is recommended that counsel review the applications and perhaps suggest wording to minimize the effects of these questions. For example, what wording might be used to respond to the question, "Have any claims been made during the past year against the trust or any of the present trustees or, to the knowledge of the trust, against any past trustee for errors or omissions?" The answer might read, "In the course of the administration of the trust, claims have been and are made on a regular basis against the trust and granted or denied by the trustees. None of such claims have resulted in a court action against the trust or any of its trustees during the past year. The fund from time to time receives conflicting claims to benefits and in such cases interpleader proceedings have been necessary where the conflicting claimants have not resolved their disputes by agreement."

Finally, who should sign the application? The Aetna application merely calls for the "signature of applicant." CNA requires a "trustee or other fiduciary." The Chubb application states, "The person completing this application on behalf of all persons for whom coverage is requested affirms that all the information contained herein is complete and current to his/her knowledge." Lloyd's states, "I/We declare that, after inquiry, the above statements and particulars are trust, and I/we have not suppressed or mis-stated any material facts, and that I/we agree that this application shall be the basis of the contract with the underwriters."

Summary

The personal liability imposed by ERISA on individual trustees can be insured with a fiduciary liability policy. The coverage should be arranged through an expert insurance agent or broker with a company having the financial resources to honor its commitments. The applications for coverage should be completed meticulously and should be reviewed by legal counsel. The limit of insurance selected should be adequate to permit the trustees to sleep soundly at night.

Collecting Withdrawal Liability

BY ROBERT A. DeCORI

TO EFFECTIVELY DISCUSS this subject, one has to examine and review the entire procedure and system used in administering the Multiemployer Pension Plan Amendments Act of 1980 (MPPAA). The collection of the withdrawal liability, in essence, is the end result of the various procedures throughout the administration cycle. Many management trainees in various retail industries are surprised, upon graduation from college, to find themselves the first days on the job to be on the loading docks rather than in the office. The philosophy is simple: For one to control the merchandise at the end of the cycle, that is the retail sale and, hopefully, the generation of a profit, the merchandise must be controlled at the front end. If one loses control in the beginning (at the start), he is less apt to be effective in generating his end goal, profit. Collecting employer withdrawal liability is not dissimilar. With that perspective, let's address administrative aspects.

Allocation Method

The administrative impact of the Multiemployer Pension Plan Amendments Act of 1980 is unquestionably significant. MPPAA created a need for both vastly improved and additional data and new and expanded procedures. This need has to be met to assure proper administration of the withdrawal liability provisions under the act.

Regardless of the withdrawal allocation methods, selected additional "computerization" will be required. Essentially the act allows selection of the allocation method within two general types of allocation methods or the selection of a more "tailored" or custom design mode, which could be a combination of the two. The presumptive, two pool (modified presumptive) and one pool (rolling-five) methods fall under the aggregate umbrella. The second category is attribution, which can be either direct (pure) or modified. Aggregate methods essentially allocate the unfunded vested liability on the basis of employer contributions, whereas with an attribution method the employment history and resulting liability are determined by tracing this information on an employee basis for each withdrawn employer.

Obviously, without the need to track complete employment history, the aggregate allocation

Mr. DeCori is senior vice president of Kelly & Associates, Inc., Chicago, Illinois. Prior to his present position, he was the vice president of financial operations, encompassing both the financial and systems areas. Mr. DeCori received his B.S. degree with an accounting major from Bradley University. He has participated as a member in various American Management Association (AMA) activities, including the AMA Presidents Association. He is also a member of the Society of Professional Benefit Administrators and the Data Processing Managers Association. Mr. DeCori has spoken at previous Foundation educational meetings.

methods will have less administrative and cost impact than will the attribution modes. However, as indicated earlier, there still will be additional automation of data needed to administer the function regardless of the allocation method chosen. One of the higher cost, attribution methods or a combination of attribution and aggregate methods may be selected because it is better suited to the plan's needs. In this instance, startup costs may be higher and there may be high ongoing administrative costs, but the overall goals of the plan justify the selection of a more complex recordkeeping methodology.

Some plans have selected a combination of an aggregate and an attribution method. Obviously the data processing requirements in this instance would have to be comprehensive. The selection of a combination method can address the problem of the lack of accurate historical employment data per employee. It is generally considered cost and time prohibitive, if not outright impossible, to recreate or collect the historical employment data necessary for a pure attribution allocation method for a plan of any significant size or age. Therefore, by combining a presumptive method with an attribution method, the problem of incomplete historical data is addressed, yet the more equitable assignment of withdrawal liabilities (at least from a point in time forward) is also applied.

Recapping, there are many considerations in choosing a method to allocate liabilities to a withdrawing employer. The trustees' desire to protect the remaining employers and employees, the desire to assess liabilities on an equitable basis and the cost associated with administration of the methods chosen are three principal considerations. Depending on the method or combination of methods chosen, there is varying administrative impact, but the least complex method, in all likelihood, would require additional automation on one's existing recordkeeping system. Whether it requires a complete redesign and development of one's existing data processing system depends to what extent one's system was operating prior to MPPAA. Hopefully, limited modifications can be made to meet the additional administrative impact. It is questionable that the modifications will be limited if an attribution method is selected. Either way, there will be programming and systems changes.

Recordkeeping Systems

Taking a more specific look at the recordkeeping and procedural implementations of MPPAA, assume that there is "in place" a relatively efficient fund processing system (automated). In all likelihood, it is probably an online system or at least a comprehensive "batch" type data processing operation. In examining employer recordkeeping needs, there is a major shift in philosophy brought on by the enactment of MPPAA. Pre-MPPAA employer information was not consistently thought of as information that would be required to be kept on a permanent historical basis, or at least on an easily accessible permanent basis; MPPAA has changed that assumption. Employer record information retention not only has to be permanent, but it must be readily accessible. It is hard to imagine a recordkeeping system not being computerized with the information accessibility required under the act.

For the purposes of this presentation, let's assume that the administrator has the need for both aggregate and attribution withdrawal calculation techniques. In all likelihood, he suffers from incomplete historical data, which may bring about a combination of both methods. The system implemented or modified to administer MPPAA needs to track contributions made by each employer and contributions required of each employer. With the system tracking employer contributions paid, the denominator for all employers for that period can be determined. By the same tracking, the system can provide initial information to develop an employer's individual numerator. The initial tracking will indicate the amount (dollars and units) by period that the employer has paid and reported. By comparing (through the data processing system) this information to the prebillings (if used) or the prior month's individual payment history (hours/weeks), a delinquency or underreporting flag will appear if applicable. That flag could trigger a payroll audit.

In summation, at least the system can interface with payroll audits and delinquency subsystems (automated or manual) in arriving at contributions required. Optimally, if one were to implement a new fund processing system, an online, fully interactive delinquency tracking subsystem (payroll audits, correspondence, collection, attorney referral, etc.) would have a great deal of appeal. From the viewpoint of timeliness (communications/actions), it may be more of a necessity than just an attraction.

Additionally, the system should identify all employers that are within a common group. Depending on the definition of "common group" and the withdrawal liability method selected, at least some of this information will have to be retrieved and reconstructed. If the existing system does not retain historical contribution data, obviously a form of conversion effort will have to be undertaken. As indicated previously, an optimum system closely monitors delinquency records and payroll audits to determine contributions required (MPPAA) versus contributions paid. If that information is not available on one's present system, historical information can be collected from old "in-house" records, whether hard copy, microfilm/fiche, year-end computer tapes, employer confirmation letters or 5500 filings.

Enhanced computer application systems greatly ease the administrative effort in locating, identifying and flagging potential or actual employer withdrawals. The ability to use an online employer alpha search facility can readily bring forth an employer screen (an employee record on a CRT), which can provide critical information such as common group code, delinquency, billings and contribution history. Number of employers billed, number of employees paid for and number of hours paid for can also be tracked on an advanced system.

Identifying Withdrawing Employers

Communication

Since administrative systems are necessary to collect, record and maintain the required information at the employer level, quick identification of those employers who have ceased contributing should be available. Once nonpayment has been identified, the administrator can act. Communication is critical in effectively administering withdrawal liability. Notices to withdrawing employers, trustees, attorney, etc., are time-dependent. Failure to act in a timely manner will weaken the fund's position in assessing and collecting a withdrawal liability amount.

Worksheets and form letters are necessary for effective employer communication. This communication includes, but is not limited to, responses to request for liability information, notice and collection, calculation of withdrawal amount, payment schedule and requests for further information, including common ownership queries (controlled group).

Withdrawal Tests and Abatement Provisions

Partial withdrawal liability (which is not effective until 1983) would require additional tracking of total units on an employer basis or employer-controlled group basis. The test for a partial withdrawal is the reduction in an employer's contribution base. The test is applied by comparing an employer's contribution basis for a three year period to the level for the highest two years within the five year period preceding the test period. The act calls for a drop of 70% for three years in a row to bring about a partial withdrawal. The retail food industry may substitute a 35% threshold. In addition to the 70% (35%) or greater drop in an employer's contribution base, a partial withdrawal can occur in the following circumstances:

- A facility (formerly contributed on) that continues to operate is no longer covered by the plan.
- An employer that has been contributing under a particular collective bargaining agreement stops contributing and continues to work either there or at another location.

In the event of a subsequent increase in an applicable employer's contribution base, provisions to monitor possible abatement of a liability resulting from severe shrinkage as provided by MPPAA have significant administrative implication. The tests for partial withdrawal and any application of subsequent abatement provisions should be done on an annualized basis. As indicated earlier, an automated fund processing system will have to track and maintain units contributed on as well as cash history, on an employer level as well as common group/facility/collective bargaining unit identification. It is safe to say that without an effective systems approach (even though an associated startup cost is involved), effective administration of partial withdrawals will be extremely difficult and more costly over the long term.

Employee Census Data

Once again, as defined by the plan, employers who fall under common ownership have to be "grouped" together, as MPPAA looks at these employers as one employer. These various employers have to be identified with a common group code.

A strong trend demanding improved employee census data originated with the passage of ERISA. The need for complete and accurate census information hasn't been diminished with the passage of MPPAA; if anything, that need has increased. With the likelihood of the actuarial calculation of the unfunded vested benefit liability being challenged at various levels, inaccurate or incomplete data can have an effect on the calculations and subsequent actions. Accurate employee census information includes birth date, sex and, in many instances, initiation date and/or date of initial employment in the industry.

The ability to identify a break in service and indicate it in the record or have a system that can calculate the break "on the fly" is a plus. Hopefully, most systems are calculating future service properly, whereas greater efforts are generally required to attain correct past service information. Historically, with future service most systems (manual or automated) accumulated this information for the current year and an accumulated total for the previous years. This approach, for the most part, has been acceptable for actuarial purposes. With an attribution method for calculating withdrawal liability, accumulated totals for future service are not acceptable.

In the purest form of attribution, an individual employee's service has to be attributed to a given employer. If the employee is mobile, there is more than one employer during the year. Therefore, the service would be distributed or attributable to the applicable employers to the extent that the employee worked for each of them during the year. Some plans, rather than attempt to track it at such a low level, have elected to use the employer as of the year-end. That is, regardless of the number of employers the employee has worked for during the year, the service credits attributable will be applied to the employer of record at the end of the fiscal year.

This approach appears to minimize the amount of data processing effort that would be required under a pure attribution method, but it should be noted that to track on a yearly basis is not that much less of an effort than tracking on an individual monthly basis during the year, particularly prospectively. If an employee's employer and corresponding service credit are available on a yearly actuarial tape or other appropriate computer file, attribution can be applied on a historic basis (to the extent data are available). With that availability, selection of the employer as of year-end is probably logical. Whatever the logic, using well-designed and thought-out data processing systems can minimize the ongoing administrative burdens of an attribution selection. A similar, if less, effect occurs under an aggregate selection.

Certainly, the ability to collect ongoing employee census is easier than addressing census information needs for inactive employees. There are several approaches to improving inactive census data. Census information requests mailed out to former employers and/or the local union is one method. If addresses are available, direct mail requests to the individual can be used.

Comparison of census information on a health and welfare or similar fund to the information on a pension fund is an excellent vehicle to update individual records. This approach uses data processing with a minimal amount of "people interface" necessary, if the programming and "match up" is tight. A match up of the employee record to an international union tape is also a very effective path to more accurate census information.

As stated earlier, for each employee, the contributions made within any given plan year must be separated by the applicable participating employer. Likewise, the benefit credit earned by individual employees has to be allocated to the applicable participating employer for which he worked during the year. In all likelihood, the allocation will be based on the amount of work (hourly or monthly) with each employer. Correspondingly, benefit payments have to be tracked and separated by the employer for each employee. As for annual calculations, the vested benefit liabilities for each employer would be calculated under the attribution method based on the composite liabilities of the individual employees.

Summary

The ability to extract employee information or employer information readily is obviously a goal of any enhanced data processing system. The ability to extract an employee's payment history identifying by period the employer, the deposit date, the rate of contribution and the number of units is reassuring, particularly if online, to administrators. In essence, if the fund processing system generates critical information online, i.e., member employment history, employer payment history, etc., the capability to identify, track and calculate (to an extent) withdrawal liability should be a by-product of that system.

As indicated earlier, even with an advanced data processing system, MPPAA impacts administrative procedures. Individual store (employer) locations have to be tracked and a determination made as to a common group. Once determined, that information must be entered into the system. To determine common groups from a historic basis a review of old information is your starting point, but a system to determine new employers is necessary for the ongoing work of the administrator. Procedures to identify potential withdrawals also are necessary. Probably the first area to be alert to is delinquencies. Local unions can supply information, as well as newspaper articles, that will alert an administrator to a potential withdrawal. Timeliness is often critical with an employer going out of business.

Collection of the withdrawal liability and enforcement is the logical conclusion of any administrative system. Payment schedules, notices and payment tracking logically would be enhanced and monitored with a comprehensive data processing approach. This capability should be a natural offshoot of your employee benefit administration system.

This presentation does not attempt to detail every MPPAA-generated nuance and procedure and its related administrative impact. What it attempts to do is highlight the administrative requirements of the act and point to a systems solution.

The selection of the withdrawal liability method has significant administrative cost implications. Although the cost of administration is a consideration of the trustees in determining the withdrawal method, the overall goals of the plan should not be negated by a seemingly high administrative cost alone. In many instances, a high startup cost may actually reduce the ongoing administrative cost. Nevertheless the costs, startup and ongoing, must be justified by the end.

One should be aware that the complexities and the need for additional computerization are real. But with well-thought-out design and effective implementation, a flexible benefit administration system for fund processing, using online and possibly database techniques, can minimize the administrative impact of MPPAA.

Building the necessary records, implementing systems and procedures to identify withdrawals, supplying information for the calculation of the liability and generating necessary employer communications are preludes to collecting the liability. The fund administrator's role is critical in this endeavor and effective systems and procedures, both manual and automated, are a necessity.

Trustees' Responsibilities for Collection of Employer Contributions

BY MICHAEL J. CARROLL

EVERY DELINQUENT EMPLOYER should be treated as a business executive with a temporary financial problem that will be rectified as soon as possible. Treat such employers with courtesy and tact until you discover that they're not going to adhere to their obligation.

In discussing delinquencies, keep in mind that there are three types. One to two percent of all contributing employers are repeaters, who are consistently delinquent almost as a matter of policy. The second type of delinquency occurs when there is a mistake or a sudden cash squeeze. Obviously, this situation is entirely different from the first. In construction and other seasonal industries, sudden cash squeeze cases are becoming very big problems. The third type of delinquency is the business failure.

During the current recession, 500 employers per week are filing bankruptcy petitions, for a total of 24,000 bankruptcy petitions in 1982. In addition, 4,000 businesses are quietly folding their tents each week, simply going out of business after paying their bills. These businesses are mostly small scale enterprises: lumber yards, machine shops, retail stores—businesses with sales in the range of $100,000-$200,000 a year. These businesses are the heart of the typical multiemployer plan. These are the people who make up the substance and basis of many plans.

One final introductory note: Multiemployer plan trustees did not create this problem. Trustees are not responsible for the economy or for the business acumen of the employers contributing to the trust. Unfortunately, in many situations, the trust becomes the lender of last resort in bad times, in the sense that employers pay on a slower basis. Following are suggestions to rectify that situation.

The Trust Must Know Which Employers Have Contracts Requiring Contributions and Must Bill Them Promptly

Just within the last year, an employee in a single member bargaining unit in a retail store in San Francisco checked with the trust fund to see what his pension rights were after 13 years of employment. The trust fund had never heard of this gen-

Mr. Carroll is a member attorney with the San Francisco lawfirm of Erskine & Tulley, a professional corporation. During the past ten years he has specialized in the collection of delinquent employer contributions for the trucking, construction and printing industries, as well as numerous others. He earned his B.A. and J.D. degrees at the University of San Francisco and has spoken before other professional organizations, including previous Foundation educational meetings.

tleman. There had been a severe breakdown of proper management of the documents. The union was quite embarrassed. Fortunately, the case was settled with the assistance of the employer. The trust fund was completely unaware of the existence of the contract and of this individual. It is very important for the administrator to have some written evidence of the contract obligation to pay fringe benefits, which can only be accomplished if the trust rules compel the union to supply documentation.

These guidelines do not merely apply to the first contract document, which of course starts the monthly computer billing process. The administrator needs a copy of each successive contract, preferably a photocopy of the entire agreement. Even today, cases arise in which a seniority provision in another portion of the contract is being used to discriminate against certain employees. The administrator has to review the entire contract to determine whether it complies with the rules established by the board of trustees and the law.

In addition to a photocopy of the contract, the administrator should have an original of a subscriber of certification agreement. In this manner, the administrator has in his files a document actually signed by the employer and, in the ideal case, a certification that is also signed by the union, which states in effect: "These are the terms of our agreement as they affect your responsibility, and we intend to carry them out." It also binds the employer to the trust agreement and to the trust rules. You will find this document quite helpful if a legal proceeding becomes necessary.

Every Delinquency Must Be Pursued Vigorously

Followup is only going to be possible if the trustees have a set of rules, a pattern of conduct, that they require their administrator and their attorney to follow in every case. The existence of a set procedure does not mean that a $30,000 a month employer who is delinquent cannot be specially handled if a bankruptcy appears possible. It does mean that the $30,000 a month case and a $300 a month employer should proceed along a certain track in the delinquency procedure. All delinquencies should move at a predetermined pace through a series of letters, perhaps through personal contact or contact by the union, but eventually, at a predetermined date, to an attorney's office.

In smaller trust funds, where trustees actually know many of the employers, there will be pressure for special handling to slow down, or avoid the delinquency procedure. This pressure can be avoided if the board of trustees requires its attorney to submit a written opinion on the handling of all delinquencies. The attorney will, in all likelihood, tell you that you need a set of strict procedures to fulfill your fiduciary duties under ERISA. You, as a board of trustees, pass that set of procedures or rules to be followed in all cases. Thereafter, when approached by an employer for special treatment, the trustees can honestly say that their hands are tied.

If any special treatment is to be granted, it should be done only by the entire board of trustees. One recent court opinion involved an employer who was 22 months delinquent, yet the trust waited an additional year before filing suit. That is a terrible situation—one that can be avoided by following a set of delinquency rules.

Audits Must Be Used to Uncover Unknown Potential Trust Liabilities, and as a Deterrent to Underreporting

A trust fund without an auditing program is operating in the dark. It will eventually pay benefits to covered employees that it never knew existed. In addition, the trust exposes itself to potential litigation, sometimes class litigation, by beneficiaries who have not had contributions paid on their behalf.

Trustees' Duty to Preserve the Trust Assets Means the Delinquent Employer Should, to the Extent Possible, Bear All the Costs of Collection

Increased Administration Expense (Liquidated Damages)

This item is only fair to all of the other employers who are paying on time. In these economic times, should the trustees waive liquidated damages or interest?

Liquidated damages allow the trust to recover out-of-pocket expenses. Additional clerical help, correspondence, computer runs of delinquency lists, administrative time spent dealing with attorneys, time spent by clerical help appearing as witnesses in cases—all of these added costs should be covered by liquidated damages. A trust fund with no penalty provision not only fails to recoup these costs from the responsible party, but it also encourages consistent late payment of contributions. In a bankruptcy situation, the trust's priority position can be seriously jeopardized.

The largest multiemployer plan in the United States charges 20% liquidated damages. That fund also has an interest charge. Waivers are very rare with this trust. Usually a waiver of liquidated damages will be granted only for administrative error, such as a computer breakdown. Any error committed by the employer is not deemed a sufficient excuse.

Small trust funds should borrow some of these same hard and fast rules. Liquidated damages are their only effective tool to encourage timely payment. I don't believe in waivers of liquidated damages, even in these economic times. Instead, allow a payment schedule for the employer to pay off the liquidated damages over time. In that way, he's reminded every month of his obligation and how important it is to pay on time.

Lost Income or Interest

If trustees decide that a waiver of liquidated damages is appropriate in certain situations, the trust should at least collect interest if the employer is more than two months in arrears.

Attorneys Fees

Attorneys fees should be paid in every situation

in which the trust fund has had an attorney file a lawsuit and where there is a favorable result for the trust, either by bringing the case to trial or by a settlement of the action. Needless to say, a delinquent employer should pay all court costs.

Audit Fees

Audits are becoming very expensive. A typical three year audit costs $800-$1,700 in the construction industry. That sum does not include the auditor's appearance at the trial. The employer should be responsible for paying that fee in any case where the audit uncovers underreporting of more than 10%. Some trusts are even more stringent, requiring payment if the error was more than 5%.

Contract Terms Checklist

The language of your collective bargaining agreement should:

Clearly Describe the Bargaining Unit for Whom Contributions Are Due

This problem doesn't get much thought because many of the "covered work" clauses in collective bargaining agreements were drafted 30 years ago and remain virtually unchanged to this day. The bargaining parties should review the contract language and compare it with their experience and the experience that trust fund auditors are having out in the field. In many cases some changes are in order. Here are two examples:

One example would be the term "cleanup man." What in the world is a cleanup man? Where does he work? In some industries, auditors pick up cleanup men quite frequently. He looks like an apprentice to them. The employer frequently contends that his cleanup man never touches the tools of the trade and that he's actually a janitor. Sometimes the controversy involves a squabble over whether the cleanup man is in the shop or out in the field. The matter becomes very complicated. If cleanup men or janitors are a recurring problem in your industry, your attorney would appreciate it if you negotiate a clarification in the contract.

Another problem area is the subcontract clause. There have been a couple of recent changes in the law. The subcontract clause can be renegotiated to provide that contributions will be due on behalf of any employees working for a subcontractor whether or not the subcontractor is a signatory. A simple statement, which many contracts have, stating that subcontracts with nonunion employers are illegal will not suffice.

State the Duty to Pay a Contribution and Describe Clearly How the Amount Is Computed

State clearly how the contribution amount is computed. In one recent case, the employer had many employees working three week months. He thought that he was entitled to a $2,500 rebate on his contributions. Either he didn't read his contract, which could very well be the case, or the contract wasn't clear. Take a careful look at your language to see if it clearly states weekly, hourly and monthly rates. Also clarify any exceptions, such as jury duty. In another recent case, an employer sought over $60,000 of accumulated alleged credits because the employer mistakenly paid on jury duty over the years.

Try to iron out these problems by constant review of contract language. Prevent repetition of the same controversies. This language should not just be in the trust agreement or in a set of rules and regulations, even if they are printed on the reporting form. Restate the contract language in the collective bargaining agreement.

State When the Contribution Is Payable and When It Is Delinquent

International Foundation statistics indicate that 1-2% of your employers are going to be repeaters. If that is the case, all parties need a definite date distinguishing the delinquent employers from the nondelinquent employers.

Alert the Employer to the Consequences of a Delinquency

Some employer representatives like to avoid this issue. They prefer to keep the collective bargaining agreements short and leave the bad news to the trustees, i.e., the liquidated damage charge, the interest charge and the fact that the employers may have to pay audit fees. All of these obligations should be set out in the collective bargaining agreement. Admittedly, this method means a longer document, but it alerts the employer to his obligations.

Incorporate by Reference the Trust Agreement and Any Amendments

It is absolutely crucial that the labor agreement incorporate by reference the trust agreement and any amendments to that agreement. The trustees, as third-party beneficiaries to the contract, have certain rights to establish rules and regulations, and you want the employer to be bound by them in a clear manner.

Other Terms

Many contracts also contain some of the delinquency rules set forth in the next section.

Trust Delinquency Rules Checklist

A. State When the Contribution Is Payable

Should the employer post a copy of each paid reporting form in the workplace? Trustees have a duty to notify employees when the employer is not paying contributions, but this is difficult to do if an employee has never been reported. Posting of the reporting form is an effective tool. It's a representation by the employer that he's paid those contributions; he'd be hesitant to put it up there if he hadn't. However, it has another effect. It's a deterrent because unreported additional employees who may legitimately feel they're part of a bargaining unit discover that in the employer's opinion, at least thus far, they're not. Inquiries would then be made, and the problem of underreporting is handled quickly and without an audit.

B. State the Place Where Payment Is Due

This statement is important to the attorney because it establishes venue where the trust desires to sue, rather than where the employer is actually located.

C. State When the Contribution Is Delinquent

D. State the Consequences of a Delinquency

- Liquidated damages
- Interest
- Attorneys fees
- Court costs
- Audit costs.

All of these items should be in the trust agreement, even if they are in the contract.

E. Delegation of Right (but Not Necessarily Obligation) to Sue

If suit is filed in federal court, it can be filed in the name of the trust fund. In many state courts, the trust fund is still not considered a proper party.

F. Establish Venue Favorable to Trust

G. Establish Subcommittee With Power to Compromise and Settle Cases

Situations do arise where there may be legitimate areas of dispute with an employer and the trust's attorney believes that the collection case may be lost, e.g., when no witness is available to contradict facts important to the case. In situations like that, the attorney needs a little flexibility as the day of trial arrives. Quick decisions are not possible if your trust only meets quarterly. Therefore, delegate the right to make certain decisions about how the case is going to proceed to perhaps two trustees as a committee, in conjunction with your attorney.

H. Establish the Right to Audit Any Employer and Describe the Documents That Must Be Produced

Description of the documents to be produced is very important in all construction trades, because the auditor must review documents that the employer considers somewhat confidential, i.e., the cash receipts journal and canceled checks. Only in this way will he find out if there's a subcontractor who shouldn't be on the job. It's the only way to find out if the employer has made cash payments to individuals. The auditor must look at those documents, but some judges are hesitant to allow you to do that unless you have stated a contract right to do so somewhere in your paperwork. Therefore, be as specific as you possibly can in this area.

I. Cash Deposit or Surety Bond

There are certain optional rights that you may want to use when more than one delinquency occurs. Some trusts use a cash deposit or surety bond, and will impose it on an employer who is, for example, two months delinquent. This imposition is very difficult. If he can't pay the contribution that month, how will he secure the bond? However, it is a good idea to have a special provision for a contractor who comes from outside the area.

J. Automatic Audit of Books and Records

In the event of a delinquency, some trusts will impose an automatic audit of the books and records. I'm not in favor of this tactic for two reasons. First of all, it assumes that an employer having trouble paying his contribution is also cheating by underreporting, which is not necessarily the case. There isn't necessarily a direct relationship between delinquency and underreporting. The second kind of problem with this type of policy is that auditing costs, especially in times like these, can get completely out of hand.

K. Increase in Amount of Liquidated Damages Due

This new idea is being tried in my area in lieu of the surety bond. The concept is simply that if an employer has been delinquent two or three times within a 12 month period, liquidated damages are raised automatically from the usual 10-20%, and they're retroactive for the other delinquent months.

L. Mechanic's Lien Procedure for Construction Trades

Speed is essential in this area, not only in government jobs, but also in any case where notices of completion have been filed. Usually, when you find out that delinquent payments are related to a particular job, time is running out and you need an accelerated procedure. My suggestion is that you delegate the power to agree on a lien to the employer and union representatives in that particular area. It's a serious step, one you wouldn't want to take every day, so the trustees must establish overall guidelines.

M. Trustees' Contract and Delinquency Procedure

1. *Proof of the Contract Obligation Must Be Filed With the Administrator Before Contributions Are Accepted*

This area has already been covered somewhat. It is the only way you're going to cover your responsibility under the *Moglia* decision that there be a written contract. When the parties continue to bargain under the old agreement, you can continue to accept contributions; the failure to pay is an unfair labor practice. However, the trustees should keep track of the situation. If a new contract is presented to you, for example, six or nine months after the contract's expired, there should be an automatic system in your administrative office for followup.

2. *Establish a Startup Procedure— Including Review, Approval and Acceptance of the Contract Obligation*

This procedure will require someone on the administrative staff who's acquainted with the collective bargaining agreements and who will review them. It is absolutely crucial if you're going to anticipate problems, especially with regard to "me too's" executed by employers who are not members of the association.

3. *Establish in Advance What Circumstances Will Be Considered, if Any, for Liquidated Damages or Interest Waiver Request*

The trust's answer to this problem is going to decide, in effect, how long the trustee meetings are. If you wish, you can spend from three hours to a full day at a meeting agonizing over whether a waiver request should be granted just because the employer's bookkeeper was sick. Or, you can sit around holding up envelopes to the light to see if the stamp cancellation is actually the day the employer said it was. In any case, I don't consider this a valuable use of trustee time. Instead, have a set of rules that relieve you of this burden.

4. *State Precisely When a Delinquency Must Be Referred to an Outside Collection Specialist*

There should be an automatic procedure, e.g., when two months are delinquent, and the first day of the third month rolls around, the delinquency is referred out.

5. *Notice to Employees of Delinquency: How, When and by Whom*

Once an employer is perhaps four months behind, it is time for the administrator to notify the employees. Trustees should adopt some reasonable rules governing this situation.

6. *Establish a Contract Renewal Review System*

Administrative Office Action

Notices to the Employer About the Delinquency and Its Consequences

The Delinquency Letter

Keep the delinquency letter short and to the point, so that the message is seen before it hits the circular file. The message is simply this: "Where's the report? Where's the money? This is to alert you, Mr. Employer, that liquidated damages and interest are going to be due if your contribution is not paid within x days." In seasonal or construction trades, an employer often will have no employees. Give him a chance to tell the trust that he has no people currently working by providing a tear-off sheet at the bottom of the letter, which he can return to the trust with this information.

The Last Attempt to Get the Employer's Attention

Some experts say that buff or hot pink paper for your delinquent letters will get more attention. I think that either an employer has the money in his bank account or he doesn't. However, the next time your trust runs out of delinquency letter forms, change the color—it may work. There are other things that can be done in an attempt to get the employer's attention. One large trust fund uses a Mailgram and, apparently, it's very inexpensive when done by a direct computer tape. Another suggestion, if your trust is small enough, is telephone contact.

Pros and Cons of Allowing the Administrator to Make Payment Arrangements

- Good public relations and least expensive method
- Enforcement problems and loss of priority creditor position.

Evaluating an Employer's Proposal to Pay Delinquent Contributions on an Installment Basis

What Sort of Person Are You Dealing With?

It's not really just who the person is, it's when and who—because when and who equal desire and ability. When did he contact the trust? Did he contact the trust after the first letter? Did he contact the trust after litigation commenced? Did the employer wait until the attorney levied on his biggest asset or closed down his business for a day? When you were contacted is just as important as who contacted you. The earlier he contacted you, the more likely it is that he has a desire to handle the problem.

You, as trustees, must exercise that degree of common skill, common prudence and common caution that reasonable men exercise regarding their own property. In dealing with various employers, you're going to be making judgment calls. You have to rely on your judgment, your experience and, really, on all the documentation you can get your hands on. When an employer wants to make a payment schedule with you, the trustees' first question is, "Where is your profit and loss statement?" In many cases, the employer won't have one. However, you're going to have to try to get as much information as possible before you make a decision.

What Are the Employer's Chances of Continuing in Business?

What is his track record? What are his assets?

Why Is the Employer Delinquent?

There is a tremendous difference between a retroactive rate increase or a retroactive billing, over which there might have been an honest dispute, and an employer who has just been audited and revealed to be seriously underreporting. You will treat those two individuals differently when they request a payment schedule.

Is the Proposal Serious or an Attempt to Gain More Time?

This consideration is important. I recently did a levy on an account receivable—monies, in effect, owed for services rendered. It was a $50,000 levy and there had been no contact from the employer, through letters, litigation and right up through the levy stage. The employer discovered from the sheriff, as he's entitled to, that the trust had levied on his account receivable. He immediately wanted to make a payment arrangement for $1,000 a month. As a result of all the other factors involved, the trust decided to go through with the levy and collect the money in that fashion, because it appeared that this employer's financial situation, his lack of desire and all of the other elements of the case required that we proceed.

Can the Employer Stay Current in the Future?

This requirement should be an absolute quid pro quo to any arrangement. The trust can't allow the employer to use current contribution money to pay off the old obligation. You are not getting anywhere and you are not covering the liability.

What Security Does He Offer?

As I indicated before, a judgment is your first goal. However, if in addition to the judgment your attorney can negotiate any additional security, such as a note, or a uniform commercial security agreement, it should of course be taken.

How Long Does the Employer Want?

The original Department of Labor proposal was that if the trust entered into a payment schedule with an employer that was longer than 12 months it should be a prohibited transaction, but that was only a proposed regulation. Now trustees are simply required to be prudent. This area is difficult. I still believe that trying to keep a payment schedule under a year should be the trust's goal. There are always going to be exceptions, however, and I've encountered many of them.

Who Decides to Accept or Reject?

In the case of the levy on the $50,000 account receivable, a decision was needed very quickly on the employer's settlement proposal. Here the smaller committee, perhaps two trustees, becomes a valuable tool.

Conclusion

During the current economic climate, it is very important that multiemployer plan trustees adopt and apply a set of stringent rules and procedures to the delinquent employer problem. Failure to do so can mean serious losses to the trust in uncollected contributions, especially in light of the increasing resort of delinquent employers to the use of bankruptcy proceedings to continue operation.

Attitudes and Approaches of Trustees Toward MPPAA

BY MARC GERTNER

THE MULTIEMPLOYER Pension Plan Amendments Act of 1980 (MPPAA), P.L. 96-364, has provoked reaction on various fronts as its effects become more apparent. In the legislative area, Senator Hatch and others have introduced bills in Congress that would limit the scope of employer withdrawal liability by redesignating certain Taft-Hartley multiemployer plans as defined contribution plans, placing them beyond MPPAA's scope. At an April 1982 conference sponsored by the American Law Institute–American Bar Association, Henry Rose, general counsel of the Pension Benefit Guaranty Corporation (PBGC), noted that over 100 lawsuits had been filed by the end of March, with new cases arising at the rate of one or two a week.

The courts generally have been occupied with ruling on preliminary injunctions for collection of payments of employer withdrawal liability. Not all of the decisions have been consistent; yet, as a result of continued activity, a body of precedent is slowly building that will assist trustees in performing their fiduciary obligations. These are the trends on which I wish to update you.

Pre-MPPAA Guidelines

Courts have allowed trustees leeway in their decisionmaking for plans in their care unless the action taken is arbitrary, capricious, or an abuse of discretion (see, e.g., *Bueneman v. Central States, Southeast and Southwest Areas Pension Fund*, 572 F.2d 1208 (8th 1978)). Several ERISA cases, which are still viable even after the enactment of MPPAA, offer guidelines for trustees. In *Winpisinger v. Aurora Corp. of Ill.*, 456 F. Supp. 559 (N.D.Ohio 1978), for example, trustees of a pension plan called on a district court to determine whether a proposed amendment to the plan was lawful. The amendment under discussion purported to cancel past service credits for certain former employees (noncollective bargaining unit employees), while protecting the past service credits of bargaining unit employees. The court concluded that in offering such an amendment, the trustees had failed to discharge their fiduciary duties "solely in the inter-

Mr. Gertner is a partner in the lawfirm of Shumaker, Loop & Kendrick in Toledo. He is the responsible partner for all Taft-Hartley trust clients. Admitted to the bar in 1957, he is a member of the Toledo, Ohio and American Bar Associations and has been a lecturer on law at Toledo University Law School. He is a graduate of Harvard College and received his law degree from Ohio State University College of Law. Mr. Gertner has spoken before American Bar Association annual and sectional conferences; Pacific Coast, Arizona and Midwestern labor law conferences; national and regional conferences of the Financial Analysts Federation Practising Law Institute; and is co-author of the book, The Prudent Man. *Long active in Foundation activities, Mr. Gertner has been a frequent speaker or panelist at educational meetings and has contributed to the International Foundation's* Digest *and* Foundation Forum *cassette program. He is a former member of the Foundation's Board of Directors, Attorneys Committee, Employer Liability Study Committee, and Constitution and By-Laws Committee which he formerly chaired. He was also a member of the special committee that prepared the* Investment Policy Guidebook for Trustees.

est of the participants and beneficiaries" of the plan as ERISA required.

The trustees attempted to defend their action through an actuarial report stating that unfunded liability for the nonbargaining unit class of participants represented $2.6 million, against which only $1.2 million in contributions had been received. The trustees argued that imposing the burden of the unfunded liability of this group on all other covered employees in the plan would be unfair. The court rejected this argument, stating:

> This unfairness argument is selective. *The Trustees owed a duty of fairness to all*—not just to some—of the covered employees. Under the plan, they are required to exercise their discretion in a nondiscriminatory manner; and under ERISA they were required to conform to the Plan without preferences amongst either participants or beneficiaries. [Emphasis added.]

The court also commented that if forfeiture of past service credit were necessary in some circumstances to protect the fund, the "forfeiture must fall evenly on all participants in the fund." To do otherwise would violate Section 404(a)(1) of ERISA by virtue of not being an action solely in the interest of participants and beneficiaries.

In *Pierce v. NECA-IBEW Welfare Trust Fund,* 488 F.Supp. 559 (E.D.Tenn. 1978) *aff'd,* 620 F.2d 589 (6th Cir. 1980), *cert. den.* 101 S.Ct. 574 (1980), trustees amended a welfare plan by cutting off extended benefits to employees after 31 days beyond the date on which their employer's obligation to contribute to the plan terminated. Just as in *Winpisinger,* the trustees explained the basis for their decision to be the financial integrity of the trust fund. In *Pierce,* however, the court affirmed the trustees' action and recognized that they had no corrupt or improper motive, but rather were acting for the exclusive benefit of all the participants of the plan. Both cases illustrate the general rule that has emerged: As long as trustees decide and act solely in the interest of the plan participants and beneficiaries, and in an evenhanded manner, the courts will uphold decisions made within the limits of the trustees' discretionary authority. Now, however, MPPAA has complicated decisionmaking for plan trustees.

Impact of MPPAA

As you are aware, MPPAA inspired numerous immediate challenges to the assessment of employer withdrawal liability. Three decisions, one a district court opinion and the other two arbitrations, gave an early indication of how MPPAA would be variously interpreted when a contributing employer attacked the act's underlying concepts.

In *Borden, Inc. v. United Dairy Workers Pension Program,* 517 F. Supp. 1162 (E.D.Mich. 1981), a district court granted a preliminary injunction to a major contributing employer of a pension plan when the employer showed that a proposed benefit increase would throw the plan into an unfunded position and impose significant liability on the employer if it were to withdraw from the plan. The Michigan district court refused to allow the increase because it reasoned obligations of that sort should not be imposed without the employer's first being allowed to bargain on its own behalf.

This court is persuaded that the imposition of liability under the ERISA amendments does operate to impose on Borden unbargained for obligations and that this change in law was not one which could have been foreseen by the parties when entering into the collective bargaining agreements. Such obligations should not be imposed on a contracting party absent a meeting of the minds. The decision to grant the Committee unfettered authority to set the benefit factor under the conditions existing prior to September of 1980 should not be binding on the employer under the conditions existing today. 517 F. Supp. at 1166.

On the other hand, *Bay Area Painters Pension Trust Fund,* 2 EBC 1724 (June 15, 1981), raised important points on the same issue. The *Bay Area* case was an arbitration decision arising from a trustees' deadlock over a proposed increase in benefits. Actuaries had estimated that employer withdrawal liability attributable to the fund would increase an estimated $625,000 if the proposal were to pass.

Labor trustees argued that ERISA compelled them to act as fiduciaries rather than as representatives of the groups that had appointed them. The arbitrator agreed, and decided that any alleged harm to the contributing employers was not relevant unless that harm had a direct and immediate impact on the administration of the trust. He was influenced by the actuaries' opinion that the funding policy of the trust would not be altered and thus refused to consider the circumstances of the employers. He reasoned it was not the trust's function to achieve the maximum soundness possible but, rather, to pay the greatest amounts of benefits possible within the framework of reasonable soundness. In saying this, the arbitrator rejected the employer trustees' arguments that benefits should be only prospective in nature or, instead, should be offered to provide funding for vested liability.

The *Bay Area* decision expressed an interesting suggestion near the end of the opinion:

> . . . If the employers want control over the creation of unfunded vested liability, then they must exercise this desire at the collec-

tive bargaining table. During collective bargaining, there is no restriction [sic] on an employer representing its own interests as trustees are restricted in this Trust. If an employer does not want unfunded vested pension liability to increase, that employer should insist that such a provision be made a part of the collective bargaining agreement.... (2 EBC 1724 at 1735)

An argument is often made that it is not possible for employers to place any restriction on trustee powers over trust administration through collective bargaining. Typically, trusts do provide broad powers to the trustees and give them unlimited discretion in setting benefits for participants and beneficiaries and, therefore, it may be difficult for employers to include any provision within the collective bargaining agreement that might be seen as "hampering" the authority of the trustees.

Trustees have a primary duty to participants and beneficiaries under ERISA and furthermore the Taft-Hartley Act provides the trust funds are not to be used for the benefit of management or the union to the detriment of those for whom they were established (*Blankenship v. Boyle,* 329 F.Supp. 1089 (D.D.C. 1971) *stay den.* 447 F.2d 280 (D.C.Cir. 1971) *supp. dec.* 337 F. Supp. 296 (D. D.C. 1972), *aff'd, without opinion,* 511 F.2d 47 (D.C.Cir. 1975); *Donovan v. Bierwith,* 81 CV 3408, 2 EBC 2145 (E.D.N.Y. 1981)). Thus, if the plan and trust clearly provide that only the trustees will have the power to set benefit levels, it may seem initially that employers are helpless to stem increases that might "incidentally" add to unfunded vested benefit levels.

Moreover, as the other arbitration decision, *North Texas Carpenters Pension Plan,* 2 EBC 2313 (Dec. 1, 1981), reveals, a board of trustees may now have its own difficulties in acting unanimously on benefit level issues. In *North Texas,* when deadlock occurred, an arbitrator was called in to choose between two proposals designed to increase pension benefits. Under the proposal offered by the union trustees there were to be past service as well as future service credits, which would increase unfunded vested liability by $5.3 million or 95%. Under the management proposal there were to be future service credits only, with no significant increase in unfunded vested liability. Since both proposals were economically viable, the real difference was the relative impact upon employers' potential withdrawal liability. The arbitrator looked to the analyses in *Bay Area* and *Borden* among other points before voting to adopt the management trustees' proposal.

Ideally, arbitrators would not be needed to cast the tie-breaking vote in a deadlock over proposed benefit increases; ideally, such a stalemate would not arise. Yet, *North Texas* shows that the traditional "hands off" approach to trustees' authority may, of necessity, be undergoing modification.

There is an emerging argument that, given a proper interrelationship of the plan with the collective bargaining agreement, employers may place the issue of unfunded vested benefit levels on the bargaining agenda just as they do the issue of contribution levels. Another argument suggests that requiring both employers and the union to approve a plan amendment before benefits are increased can avoid being characterized as an improper displacement of employer interests over those of plan participants and beneficiaries.

United Mine Workers v. Robinson

A unanimous Supreme Court decision provides food for thought (*United Mine Workers v. Robinson,* 50 U.S. Law Week 4288 No. 81-61 (March 8, 1982)). In this case, the Supreme Court reversed a court of appeals decision that held that trustees could not rely on a labor contract provision that required them to allocate welfare benefits in a supposedly discriminatory manner.

The widows bringing this case argued that they were improperly discriminated against by the trustees who, they alleged, arbitrarily apportioned health benefits. Whereas the widows of retirees who had died before December 6, 1974 received an increase in health benefits by virtue of a 1974 collective bargaining agreement, widows of men eligible for retirement but still working at the time of their death before December 6, 1974 did not receive extra benefits. The purpose of the distinction and the history behind this particular collective bargaining agreement impressed the Court. Throughout their 1974 negotiations, the union attempted to "even out" an unequal situation existing between the two classes of widows; a widow of a miner eligible for a pension but still working at the time of his death was entitled to a death benefit $3,000 greater than a widow within the other class. This distinction was consciously bargained for.

The Supreme Court took a different view than did the court of appeals, which found the trustees allocated improperly, saying first that the provisions of the collective bargaining agreement did not violate federal law or policy. Footnote 2 of the opinion referred to the National Bituminous Coal Wage Agreement of 1950, which originally created the Welfare and Retirement Fund and specifically stated:

Subject to the stated purposes of this Fund, the Trustees shall have full authority, within the terms and provisions of the "Labor-Management Relations Act, 1947," and other applicable law, with respect to questions of coverage and eligibility, priorities among classes of benefits, amounts of benefits, methods of providing or arranging for provisions for benefits, investment of trust funds, and all other related matters.

The broad authority granted to trustees by this paragraph is typical of most trust agreements.

Footnote 13 of the Supreme Court opinion cites the language of the 1974 National Bituminous Coal Wage Agreement, which made pertinent language changes:

The Trustees are authorized, upon approval by the Employers and the Union, to make such changes in the Plans and Trusts hereunder as they may deem to be necessary or appropriate.

They are also authorized and directed, after adequate notice and consultation with the Employers and Union, to make such changes in the Plans and Trusts hereunder, including any retroactive modifications or amendments, which shall be necessary:

(a) to conform the terms of each Plan and Trust to the requirements of ERISA, or any other applicable federal law, and the regulations issued thereunder;

* * *

(b) to comply with all applicable court or government decisions or ruling.

National Bituminous Coal Wage Agreement of 1974, Art. XX, §(h)(5).

In reviewing this language, the Supreme Court found that the trustees did not have full authority to determine eligibility requirements and benefit levels since these were fixed by the 1974 labor contract provisions, which of themselves did not violate federal law or policy. The Supreme Court, in reversing this case, allowed the trustees protection against court review of their allocation decision, which had been based on the terms of the collective bargaining agreement.

If the *United Mine Workers* case, unanimously decided, emphasizes the importance of honoring bargaining language, even when that language seems to control the discretion of the trustees, it may indeed be possible to restrain trustees' authority over benefit increases when the effect on employers will be to increase their contingent liabilities.

Calculating Unfunded Liabilities Before MPPAA

Much of the current controversy exists because nontrustee parties are not familiar with the concepts and the terminology of actuarially designed defined benefit plans. Before MPPAA, most employers were concerned about the amortization period for unfunded vested benefits. Liabilities were first calculated by projecting the cost of funding a benefit level for all current plan participants who would actuarially be presumed to reach normal retirement date minus those plan participants who actuarially were presumed to drop out of the plan because of death, disability, or service termination. Next, the actuary would calculate how many years it would take to accumulate the cost of these benefits at current rates of contribution, based on the actuarial interest assumption. Typically, the amortization period was 20-35 years.

Although the concept troubled employers, when it was explained that the liability included benefits presumed to be earned in the future, the concern diminished somewhat. To add to the confusion, analogizing unfunded vested liability to a mortgage was often done. However, whereas most homeowners hope to pay off their mortgage loan eventually, most actuaries agreed that a plan should never pay off its unfunded liability.

Employer Withdrawal Liability

The enactment of MPPAA has brought into focus a new concept, "employer withdrawal liability," also generally not understood by employers. The relevant calculations under MPPAA are:

a. Current value of unfunded vested benefits
b. Current value of plan assets.

The difference of (a) less (b) is the plan's unfunded vested liability and is the base number (the denominator) on which all potential employer withdrawal liability is based. If, as is the case with some plans, (b) exceeds (a), there is no withdrawal liability.

MPPAA calculation differs fundamentally from the unfunded liability discussed previously, since a calculation usually made at the end of the plan year answers the question, "If the plan were to terminate today, what, if any, liability do employers have?" Only vested benefits earned to that date are included in the calculation, not benefits to be earned in the future, or contributions.

Because of the new concepts created by MPPAA regarding liability for unfunded vested benefits, employers may now expect more control over the number representing unfunded vested liability. It may well be that in future negotiations, employers will insist on some measure of involvement in order to regain control over their level of exposure. One of the more important cases wending its way through the courts has suggested that this outcome should be expected.

Peick v. PBGC

The first important case deciding the constitutional issues raised by MPPAA has already been thoroughly analyzed for you in a lengthy memorandum (*Peick v. PBGC*, 3 EBC 1377 (N.D.Ill., May 14, 1982)). The conclusions expressed by Judge Getzendanner were anticipated four days earlier by a district court judge in California, although without her complex supporting analysis (*Ells v. Construction Laborer's Pension Trust*, 3 EBC 1449 (C.D.Cal. May 10, 1982)).

You will recall that in *Peick* pension plan trustees and employer associations (along with the union, which was dismissed from the case) challenged MPPAA on a variety of issues. Relying on *Nachman Corp. v. PBGC*, 592 F.2d 947 (7th Cir. 1979), *aff'd*, 446 U.S. 359 (1980), for its analysis of when an act of Congress is rational, the district court found that based on reliance interests of the parties, prior federal regulation, equities, and MPPAA's "moderating features," it was not unconstitutional on its face.

Peick upheld MPPAA's constitutionality, but the court explained its decision in almost a reluctant fashion. After stating the equitable reasons for Congress' attempt to deter withdrawals from multiemployer plans, and discussing the options selected in detail, the court concluded:

> Congress thus spread the pain around. It chose a mix of options which it thought best responded to the problems it perceived. To be sure, its solution may not have been the wisest. Plaintiffs have so argued, and not without force. Moreover, sentiment already exists on Capitol Hill to amend MPPAA in significant ways. See *The Wall Street Journal*, March 5, 1982, at 40, col. 1. Yet all this is not my concern. My concern is only with the basic fairness of the choices Congress actually made in 1980. Plaintiffs have convinced me that withdrawal liability can be harsh and onerous in certain instances. However, after examining the statute as a whole and the context in which it operates, I cannot say that the "mere enactment" of MPPAA was unconstitutional. The basic structure of the statute is not so inequitable that a facial attack on its validity can succeed. 3 EBC 1377 at 1400.

One of the mitigating factors the court considered in reaching its conclusion corresponds with suggestions expressed in the *Borden* and *Bay Area* cases:

> ... at a subsequent round of bargaining, employers can insist that restrictions upon trustee behavior be written into the actual contract and declaration of trust establishing their plan. They can bargain for language forbidding future benefit improvements which increase the Plan's unfunded vested liability by more than a set amount or percentage. [Citations omitted] If these demands are accepted, the employers will clearly regain substantial control over their level of exposure. 3 EBC 1377 at 1396-97.

Bargaining and Employer Withdrawal Liability

Although this suggestion may be attractive, it is a novel, rather than a traditional, approach to the administration of Taft-Hartley trusts. Typically, trustees retained unfettered power over trust administration and trust administration was not a usual bargaining issue. MPPAA's enactment, as the *Peick* case carefully discusses, may change this particular rule.

Indeed, it is respectfully suggested that both labor and management have a legitimate concern that their plan be maintained within the bounds of manageable unfunded vested benefit levels. The only way existing companies may be willing to remain in the industry in the jurisdiction of the fund or new companies may be organized will be to have a pension plan without significant employer withdrawal liability.

To that end, it would not be improper for the representatives of labor and management to set forth in their collective bargaining agreement certain guidelines and goals, as an expression of their wishes. These suggestions could include that a one to one ratio of plan assets (at current market value) to unfunded vested benefits be maintained at all times, that any surplus be dedicated to past service increases, that new contributions be used to buy future service credits, etc. Other provisions may be adopted to allow the respective bargaining parties access to actuarial data and input before benefit revisions.

The ultimate authority and fiduciary responsibility remains with either the fiduciaries or named trustees of the plans, not with the union or association membership or with the respective bargaining committees; yet greater two way communications can and should be achieved. Presumably, the bargainers do not wish to take on fiduciary liability and responsibility under ERISA and, conversely, since the trustees have these liabilities and responsibilities, they must have the area and flexibility to fulfill them. The conflicts are more illusory than real and can be resolved through the good will of all parties.

Conclusion

MPPAA has withstood the first attacks on its constitutionality. Although an appeal to the United States Supreme Court will eventually be heard, the *Peick* decision has a great possibility of being affirmed. The post-*Peick* decisions generally continue to affirm the constitutionality of the act. The PBGC is working diligently to build a surrounding body of precedent. It is vigorously challenging all lawsuits filed before completing the statutorily prescribed arbitration proceedings. It is the duty of the withdrawn employer to continue contributions under the payment schedule pending resolution of all disputes. There are several pending arbitrations and suits challenging the employer withdrawal assumptions adopted by the trustees, which is a critical issue.

Notwithstanding the existent uncertainties, we have drawn several conclusions and we are advising our trustees to act accordingly. First, we believe MPPAA is here to stay. Therefore, we are going forward and implementing its various aspects. We have urged our trustees to act, and all have acted, to promulgate rules and regulations and/or amended pension plans to provide for:

- Acceptance of statutory *de minimis* rule
- Adoption of a prevailing rate of interest
- Adoption of a definition of a building and construction industry plan and ratification of the status of the plans as building and construction industry plans, where appropriate
- Adoption of employer withdrawal calculation assumptions
- Adoption of rules for handling reciprocity receipts as a part of employer contributions to determine the base
- Adoption of procedures to be used for arbitration proceedings
- Adoption of procedures for the assessment and collection of employer withdrawal liability
- Determining the period to be used to calculate the employer contribution base
- Other details of implementation.

Second, the trustees are working closely with the union, the association and the employers to gain the confidence and acceptance of the plan sponsors and thereby avoid plan sponsor interference and regulation of trustee discretionary conduct. The trustees have adopted operating procedures that require the plan's actuary to distribute all reports at least seven days before any meeting at which they will be discussed, a 30 day cooling off and communication period between recommended benefit improvements and action thereon and written disclosure of the impact of any proposed benefit increases on the amortization period, on unfunded vested benefits and on employer withdrawal liability, etc.

The Cassandras of doom and gloom predicted that ERISA would be the end of our Taft-Hartley plans and, later, that MPPAA was the death knell of the plans. They were wrong both times. With a recognition of the requirements of the law, with the requirements of named fiduciaries, the Taft-Hartley plans in Northwestern Ohio are alive and doing well. Yours can be also.

The Actuarial Effects of MPPAA on Benefit Improvements

BY RUSSELL W. THURAU

MY COMMENTS on the Multiemployer Pension Plan Amendments Act of 1980 (MPPAA) will be those of an actuary concerned with his responsibility to the trustees, to the plan and to the participants. First, I will compare three fairly distinct periods of benefit increases—the pre-ERISA period (prior to 1974), the post-ERISA to pre-MPPAA period (1974 to 1980) and the post-MPPAA period, since 1980.

We could characterize the pre-ERISA days as "the good old days." Our primary limiting factor was what IRS called a minimum contribution, which essentially was nothing more than whatever liabilities you had accrued that were not funded. You merely had to pay interest on that amount to prevent it from increasing plus the annual cost accruing for benefits being earned. That figure, then, was compared to actual contributions. This period was one in which the IRS was more concerned about people taking too large a deduction, rather than too small a deduction. IRS operated from the viewpoint that everybody was trying to defer paying taxes. With such a view, it was a watchdog on oversized deductions, but didn't care about too little being deducted.

Moving from 1974, when ERISA was passed, up to 1980 might be described as the "not too bad days." Essentially, ERISA tightened the funding period; the accrued liabilities had to have a fund period not to exceed 40 years now, instead of not being funded at all. Actuarial gains and losses were funded over 20 years. An organization called the Pension Benefit Guaranty Corporation was set up and warnings of possible regulations were given, none of which were too meaningful at the time. The limitations were not really very different from the pre-ERISA period.

The effects of going from no funding to 40 year funding, most plans were facing an increase requirement of less than 5% for required contributions. Also during this period, there were very rapidly increasing yields on the funds. For the first time, ERISA charged the actuary with making "his best estimate." In the continual actuarial war of conservatism vs. best estimate, combined with general rapidly increasing interest rates, many

Mr. Thurau, as vice president and principal of Tillinghast, Nelson & Warren, Inc., San Antonio, Texas, is primarily responsible for the firm's employee benefit consulting operations in the Southwest. He serves as actuary and consultant to pension and health and welfare plans in the multiemployer field, and is a consultant to corporate management in all areas of employee benefits. Active in the benefits field for over 22 years, Mr. Thurau is associate in the Society of Actuaries, member of the American Academy of Actuaries, fellow of the Conference of Actuaries in Public Service, an Enrolled Actuary and past president of the Actuaries Club of the Southwest. Mr. Thurau is currently a member of the Foundation's Consultants Committee. He is a graduate of Drake University, Des Moines, Iowa.

plans were also increasing their actuarial assumption about yield. Hence, funding requirements had very little effect on benefit increases.

In 1980 came MPPAA, and I would characterize this post-MPPAA period as the "not at all days." What brought about the change? A new player called unfunded vested benefits (UVBs) was brought into the game and became the dominant and controlling force in benefit increases.

Historically, then, during the pre-ERISA period, the IRS was controlling benefit increases and our concerns were long range. Even during the post-ERISA/pre-MPPAA period—when it came to benefit increases, the concerns were long range. However, during the present post-MPPAA period, we have a totally new game, with new rules and new players.

Actuarial Considerations

Unfunded vested benefits essentially are actuarial considerations. ERISA says that in the aggregate the assumptions must be reasonable, taking into account the experience of the fund and its expectations. It says that the combination must be the best estimate of anticipated experience.

The actuary as a fiduciary—what are his responsibilities? An actuary must act "solely in the interest of the participants and their beneficiaries." Note: ERISA says nothing about actuarial assumptions or fiduciary responsibilities regarding conservatism or margins.

What does MPPAA say regarding actuarial assumptions? Basically, it reiterates ERISA: It says that a plan may use its own actuarial assumptions as long as they are reasonable in the aggregate. It also says that PBGC may issue regulations, but to this point none have been issued. These assumptions are quite important. After all, who wants an unnecessarily conservative yield rate? Certainly the union does not, since it wants to negotiate benefit increases solely in the interest of the participants. Realistically, I can see no way that management would want a UVB.

In light of recently high yields and fixed income assets, here is an actual example of a fund with an average yield on existing investments of 13 1/2%—the asset side of the equation. The liabilities were discounted at a rate of 6% interest. Does that figure represent the best estimate? In light of current investments, one must be concerned—does the UVB actually exist?

Further assume that we have a 6% long range yield assumption and that we are grading down from 12% to 6% over ten years. In the interest of the required "best estimate," we'll then stay with the 6% for the long term. However, with respect to the yield on existing assets, where we would expect no less than 8%, we'll use an 8% assumption.

Translated to UVBs, what does this change in assumptions mean? In the case at hand, under what we'll call the "traditional determination," we had a $10 million present value of vested benefits, $8 million of assets and a $2 million UVB. If, however, we were to match up assets against liabilities more directly—8% on existing assets, 6% in the future—the value of the vested benefits now becomes $7.4 million against assets of $8 million. We have eliminated the UVB—in fact, we have a $600,000 negative UVB.

There are many variations of this approach, going from PBGC assumptions to many others. Stated another way, how real are your UVBs?

Arbitrations

Briefly, from the standpoint of the actuary there are two important cases in the area of benefit increases.

In the first case, the union was requesting a $10.50 benefit for all years of service; management was holding out for a $20 benefit covering future service only. A key point is that the actuaries representing both management and union agreed that the contribution rate would support a $10.50 benefit for all years of service; however, the $10.50 rate would increase the UVB by $5.3 million. By ERISA rules, the decision would be made in favor of the union position, according to the funding requirements and the fact that both parties agreed that the contributions would support the $10.50 benefit. However, the arbitrator held that it was a prudent exercise of fiduciary responsibility to adopt the proposal of the management trustees because there would be no increase in the UVB. When contributions were compared to actual cost over the long range, past service credits were rejected in favor of no increase in the UVB.

In the other case, the key issue was the challenge to a 6% yield assumption. The fund in the aggregate had no unfunded UVB but was using the direct attribution method of allocation, i.e., each employer picked up his own tab when it came to vested benefits. The arbitration held that the 6% interest rate assumption complied with MPPAA. The arbitration in these two cases went along the line of no increase in the UVB. Existence or avoidance of a UVB evidently outweighs long range cost considerations.

Investment Influence

Will MPPAA/UVB considerations ultimately dictate investment policy? Let me give you an example: A fund has a vested benefit of $95 million and assets of $30 million in equities, $30 million in bonds, $40 million in other fixed income. Therefore, it has 30% in what are called swinging assets (equities) out of $100 million and a negative unfunded vested benefit of $5 million.

Now, consider the following scenario. Equities decrease in value by one-third (an occurrence we've all seen) at the same time that other asset values go 25% higher. See what happened between the two years. Last year we had a vested benefit value of $95 million, assets of $100 million and a negative UVB of $5 million. However, because we had a swing in the equities, this year there is still only $100 million in assets, but the vested benefits have gone to $105 million. We've gone from a negative $5 million UVB to a positive UVB of $5 million. Will this situation not raise questions from the standpoint of the management, with trustees trying to explain why the fund went from no UVB to having a UVB? From the standpoint of the union members, the trustees will have to explain why there will be no benefit increases because the plan now has a UVB.

Can the same thing happen because of bond fluctuations? Possibly this situation could be circumvented by using a different asset valuation basis such as amortized values. Therefore, from a fixed income side there would not be the same potential fluctuations as with equities.

In summary, I see that it is very possible that in the long run MPPAA may have side effects on the selection of investments. It could lead to investment asset valuation methods that may be less sound than the ones that have been used up to the present.

Retirees' Equity

What about retirees' considerations? What should their equity be in light of recent inflation, which has produced higher yields on their assets and likewise has increased their needs? Stated another way, if retirees' assets (the assets derived on behalf of the retirees from their respective contributions) have enjoyed relatively high yields because of high inflation, what is the obligation—what is the responsibility—of the trustees to distribute part of that income back to them, in a time when they are severely strained by that inflation?

For example, in this particular fund we are examining, there is a retired life liability of $27.5 million, a yield assumption of 6% and a funding ratio for the overall plan of 94%. If we said that everybody—retiree and active—is equally funded, we would take $25.9 million of assets on behalf of the retirees; the required yield to fund retirees' benefits would be 7%. That is, if we earn 7% on retirees' assets, their benefits would be fully funded. If we actually earn 8%, we have 1% more than is required for them and we could give them a 6% benefit increase. Going on, if we earned 10%, we would have 3% more than the 7% that we need for full funding and we could give them 18% more than they are getting. If we have a 12% yield now, we are 5% over the required rate and could be giving the retirees a 30% increase, if we gave them the entire equity. The question is—what should be done with respect to retirees and what can we do because of UVB concerns? If benefit increases are deferred, the present retirees lose and future generations would gain. What is the balance between the generations?

Post-MPPAA Benefit Increase Practices

With respect to post-MPPAA benefit increases, the most restrictive that I've heard of is one fund where there was a 25¢ an hour contribution increase granted, no benefit increases granted and no benefit increases to be granted until the UVB was eliminated.

More predominantly, there have been no increases in existing UVBs but anything regarding future service that was actuarially sound was acceptable. This situation has led to an approach that's basically been updating past service out of actuarial gains. Benefits are also granted if there are any negative unfunded vested benefits, to the extent that the UVB returns to zero but never becomes positive.

For example, if we had a current benefit rate of $18 per year of service, assets of $49.1 million and vested benefits of $45.8 million as of June 30, 1982, we would have a $3.3 million negative UVB. July 1, if we made no benefit changes, the UVB would be the same and if we projected out for one year to the end of June 30, 1983, it would be $5.8 million negative. The key point to keep in mind is that the UVB is determined as of the last day of the plan year. Therefore, you could give an increase the first day of the plan year, in anticipation of gains that will arise for that year and have the UVB nonexistent by the end of the year. For example, if we went to a $19 benefit rate on July 1, we would have a negative UVB of $0.1 million; if we went to $20, we would have a positive UVB of $1.4 million, but the next point at which the UVB counts is the following June 30 of 1983. Then it would be negative by $400,000. Hence, we could move from an $18-$20 benefit rate and still have no positive UVB.

Another route that has been used has taken the form of an annual bonus—sometimes in the form of an extra month of payments to retirees. This method accomplishes three things: First, it helps meet the retirees' needs in a time of inflation; second, from the standpoint of equity during these periods of high inflation, there is an excess yield from "retiree assets" that now is being returned directly to the retirees in the form of benefits; and third, it has no substantial effect on the UVB. You grant the bonus and you pay it; the UVB is basically affected to the extent that assets have been used. However, it is important that this bonus is represented clearly as a one shot approach, with no guarantee regarding any future bonuses other than that the trustees will make periodic reviews.

Another development that we are starting to see where there are no unfunded vested benefits is that there is a push, generally by management trustees, to convert from defined benefit to defined contribution plans. In defined contribution plans, the contribution rate is negotiated much the same as under the traditional defined benefit plan. However, the *actual* benefit ultimately to be paid is the end result of the contributions paid directly on behalf of each participant and the investment return thereon. In other words, the participant shares totally in the investment performance.

It might be beneficial to examine for a moment the attributes of a defined contribution plan in the multiemployer area: These accounts are individual and per se would be contradictory to the basic total membership philosophy of unions. Since the individual member underwrites the investment gains or losses, control of the assets is very important, as is determining who has to answer to each member regarding investment performance. Since there is an allocation of actual contributions, to the new members and to the younger workers these plans might appear attractive; to the older workers, certainly they are not. Further, there is no predictability regarding what benefits anyone will have or their relationship to need. The benefits are totally a function of contributions and yield.

Beyond that problem, I suppose that my biggest concern is that most defined contributions pay off on termination of employment, not necessarily on retirement. In a time of need, if a person terminates, he can pick up his assets and leave. One must seriously evaluate what is going to be around when the individual comes to actual retirement. Don't think for a moment that the defined contribution plan is the answer. I see us going from defined benefit plans to defined contribution plans, which will then be cashed out. Members will come up with no retirement benefits, either facing Social Security or another plan of defined benefits. Are we not really just going in a circle?

Summary

In the past (pre-MPPAA), benefit increases have been less complicated than those we are facing at present. The game has changed by unfunded vested benefit concerns.

Particularly of concern are the needs of retirees. How can they be answered when the funds are being frozen with UVB considerations? As to the future, will we see UVB concern extending into the limitations of investments? Also, there is a push toward defined contribution plans. We must seriously question the accomplishments of MPPAA. However, before we jump to any conclusions regarding MPPAA, we must also consider the bureaucratic alternatives we might wind up with as a potential "cure."

The Trustee Examines Special Problems

BY DAVID W. SILVERMAN

THE DUTIES AND OBLIGATIONS of a trustee have, since the passage of ERISA and its amendments, greatly increased the need for knowledge on the part of the individual trustee in the field of trust fund administration and the legal requirements that affect the trust. The trustee in any jointly administered fund or in any single employer pension fund acquits his duties either consciously or unconsciously in a defensive manner by the creation of documentation to substantiate an opinion. The trustee is likewise surrounded by experts so that the decision arrived at can be substantiated by the expert within the framework or requirements imposed by law. I leave a short discussion of the experts or advisors who surround the trustees to later in this discussion, but point out to the trustees that their actions are subject to the scrutiny of not only the management contributors, but also the unions in their function of providing for the overall welfare of the union members.

Certainly, in today's legislative scene, statutes such as ERISA and the Multiemployer Pension Plan Amendments Act (MPPAA) impinge on the obligation of trustees. Additional government agencies have an increasing input into the operation of a pension or welfare trust fund. The effect of the Pension Benefit Guaranty Corporation and the statutory framework of present legislation, to the effect that a benefit promised will be a benefit delivered, adds to the trustees' responsibility in seeing that their actions fit into the broad legislative concept. As discussed later in this presentation, the participant, or the participant's beneficiary, is given wide powers to monitor the performance of the pension fund or the welfare fund, a power that was practically nonexistent prior to the passage of ERISA in 1974. The trustees, being aware of the divergent interests of management, unions, the Department of Labor, the Pension Benefit Guaranty Corporation and the participants, and knowing that their actions are subject to scrutiny within the wide legislative framework of what is reasonable and prudent under the circumstances, create with each decision the necessary paper backup to justify the action taken.

Mr. Silverman is a partner in the lawfirm of Granik, Silverman, Sandberg, Kirschner, Campbell & Nowicki. He is responsible for handling litigation for the firm's clients, which include public utilities, state insurance departments, insurance companies and banks. Mr. Silverman is serving as a management trustee on Local 363 International Brotherhood of Electrical Workers, Local 964 United Brotherhood of Carpenters and Local 29 Bricklayers, Masons, etc., trust funds. He also serves as counsel to various multiemployer funds and management associations. He received his B.S., LL.B. and LL.M. (taxation) degrees from New York University. Mr. Silverman has spoken at previous Foundation educational programs and currently serves on the Foundation's Attorneys Committee.

The Trust Fund's Expert Advisor

In listening to a discussion of special problems that trustees encounter, the initial reaction might be to question why a trustee, surrounded by experts, would have to be himself, or herself, knowledgeable. A discussion of litigation and decisions that have been flowing from the courts in ever-increasing numbers might very well tempt the trustee to bypass personal knowledge and acquaintance with the subject, based on the fact that the trust is paying a fair and adequate fee to the advisor. The simplistic answer is that the expert only advises and the trustee is primarily responsible for the decision. Every case discussed in this presentation results from the actions of trustees; presumably every action that resulted in an adverse decision to the trustees first obtained the imprimatur of approval by the trust fund's expert. The trustees are incapable of knowing the extent of their expert's expertise unless they, themselves, have knowledge sufficient to judge the expert.

There seems to be a growing trend, as exhibited in the *Donovan*[1] case, that trustees who engage in transactions making use of the trust funds are held not to the ordinary and reasonable care of trustees operating trust funds of similar size and scope, but to the accepted practices of a reasonable and competent expert in the field.

In the *Donovan* case, which involved a real estate loan for investment, the trustees were judged by the standards of a reasonably competent real estate lender; these real estate loans had to be performed in accordance with accepted lending practices. In an examination of the expert reports, by virtue of judicial hindsight, the court came to the conclusion that the expert report submitted to the trustees should not have been acted on by them because that report would not have been acted on favorably by a reasonably competent lender under similar circumstances. The fees that were paid to the preparer of the report were, likewise, held by judicial hindsight to be an imprudent amount, for the trustees paid far more than they should have.

Trustees, after electing to invest a portion of their fund into real estate, are held to the standards of real estate investors, not to those of laymen trustees advised by what they considered knowledgeable advisors. Therefore, the trust fund that believes it is in the best interests of all of the participants to become involved in real estate or other target investing must be doubly sure that the experts who surround the trustees are truly knowledgeable of investment practices in the field of the proposed loan.

As the court was quick to point out in the *Glaziers*[2] case, the mere fact that the plan trustees acted in the best interests of the plan, and that their sincerity and honesty were never questioned, was held by the court to be immaterial. The court explains that, although there is great flexibility in the prudent standard, it is not a refuge for fiduciaries who are not equipped to evaluate a complex investment. These trustees will be judged by the standards of others acting in a like capacity or similar manner, but the standard is that of the party who is involved in those large complex real estate transactions and not, as some trustees believe, that of the honest, simple, unassuming trustee.

The situation is not entirely bleak, in that if the trustees do avail themselves of legitimate expert advice and professional help, and if their motive or actions should be attacked by the Department of Labor, the trustees' ultimate victory, as pointed out in the *Cunningham*[3] case, may result in the reimbursement of the financial expense of defense under the Equal Access to Justice Act (28 U.S.C. 2412(d) 1 A).

The only way that the trustee can judge his professional advisors is to take his business and/or union training and apply that to the selection of an expert for the trust fund. People are constantly engaged in seeking the services of others who are expert in the solution of a specific problem. Whether it be for a supplier or for special construction problems, or for any field that impacts on the fund, labor-appointed or management-appointed trustees should use their own expertise, plus an increasing fund of knowledge, to make sure that the expert selected is an expert whose opinion, when accompanied by the paper trail of the trustee, justifies the decision made.

Special Problem—What the Trustee Should Be Familiar With When the Appointing Authorities Are Negotiating a New Labor-Management Agreement

The remaining portions of this discussion deal primarily with the Taft-Hartley Act, an act of Congress which legitimizes the various jointly administered trust funds. The Taft-Hartley Act was not repealed by ERISA or its amendments and still imposes legal requirements, as well as grants privileges, for the operation of trust funds. Trustees are prone to overlook the Taft-Hartley Act, but many of their actions are governed by it.

We assume that the trustees are informed that the labor-management agreement has come to an end, the parties have been unable to arrive at the terms and conditions of a new agreement and further that the basis of any jointly administered trust fund is an agreement, in writing, usually as a result of collective bargaining between the parties. Absent such agreement, any contribution to the trust fund would constitute a misdemeanor by the party making the payment and a misdemeanor by the party receiving the payment. Since the trust fund is established pursuant to Section 302(c) of the Labor-Management Relations Act (29 U.S.C.

---

1. *Donovan v. Mazzola,* 2 EBC 2115.
2. *Marshall v. Glass/Metal Assoc. & Glaziers,* 2 EBC 1006.
3. *Donovan v. Cunningham,* 3 EBC 1641, 388 *Pens. Rep.* (BNA) 538.

186(c)), the trustees might be advised that to accept any contributions would, of course, be improper.

However, negotiations are continuing; no impasse in collective bargaining has been reached and, as the courts have said in the *Producer's Dairy*[4] case, payments are to be continued by virtue of the expired written agreement. That being the case, it is perfectly lawful for the employer to continue the payment. Should the employer forget to contribute the payment, it might constitute an unfair labor practice because the employer is required to "maintain the status quo" for wages and working conditions. The obligation to maintain the status quo encompasses the obligation to continue making pension fund contributions. This obligation continues until negotiations reach an impasse. Under the circumstances, as long as the parties are bargaining, it is incumbent upon the trustees to see that the funds are contributed as per the agreement that has now expired. Any attempt to halt those payments while the employees are still at work immediately should prompt the trustees to determine that a payment is in default and make use of their reasonable, systematic and diligent procedure for collection of past due contributions.

It is recommended to trustees that they continue the collection of the amounts due the trust fund and follow their procedures until there is an impasse. An impasse can best be determined by parties to the collective bargaining agreement and not by the trustees. If any of the contributing parties should seek an injunction and, thereby, ask the court for an order to determine that there is an impasse, and if the injunction is granted, it will, of course, impact on the trustees. Its denial will likewise impact on the trustees. In the event that the union, as one of the negotiating parties, brings an unfair labor practice charge against an employer, the employer might very well defend on the ground that there is an impasse. That determination will impact on the trustees. Until such an impasse, however, or until the commencement of a strike or a lockout, it is recommended to the trustees that they consider the payments due.

Let us assume that the negotiations have now reached a point where there has been a withdrawal of labor, or where there has been a lockout, and under the circumstances a true impasse has arisen. The problem facing the trustees deals with what payments are now legitimate from the trust fund to the participants who are engaged in economic actions against the designating authority of half the trustees.

Trustees should be familiar with the general overall rules that bind employer and union under the National Labor Relations Act. The trustees do not have to become labor lawyers or experts in the National Labor Relations Act, but some of the guiding principles should be familiar. A trustee must be aware of the fact that an employer's conduct in failing to make benefit payments, or the performance of certain actions which are "inherently destructive" of important employee rights, constitutes unfair labor practices whether or not there is a legitimate business motive (*NLRB v. Great Dane Trailers, Inc.*, 388 U.S. 26).

Trustees should also be aware that some of the employer's actions might be "comparatively slight" as they affect employee rights and the failure to pay benefits. Under those circumstances, if the employer should show a competent business motive for the actions taken, it would not be violative of this nation's labor policy and an unfair labor practice (*NLRB v. Erie Resistor Corp.*, 373 U.S. 221). The second point that trustees should be familiar with concerns payments to a participant during a strike or lockout, which requires a determination of whether the payments are more closely akin to wages or more closely akin to benefits. Certainly, an employer is not required to finance the strike against itself and pay wages. On the other hand, an employer may not withhold payment of sums of money that are already earned or accrued benefits merely because the collective bargaining parties are at an impasse or strike (see *Wiegand v. NLRB*).[5] The trustees, therefore, must consider whether the benefit being sought is a wage or whether it is a benefit, so that the appropriate payment can either be made or denied.

It is fairly easy to delineate the guideposts between wages and benefits; it is far more difficult to determine under the facts and circumstances whether that payment being sought is a wage or benefit. The trustees, however, must be aware of the guideposts and go to their expert to determine wherein the requested payment falls.

Under certain circumstances, sickness and accident payments, payments made to those who are disabled and physically unable to continue with employment, have been determined to be benefits. The determination impacts on retirees, and continued payments of sickness and accident premiums on behalf of retirees have been directed in

---

4. *Producer's Dairy Co. v. Western Teamsters*, 2 EBC 1834; *Central States v. Hitching*, 472 F. Supp. 1243.

5. *Wiegand v. NLRB*, 2 EBC 1185.

such cases as in *Cadillac Malleable Iron Company*[6]; yet, a directly contrary result is found in *Metal Polishers Local 11 v. Kurz-Kasch, Inc.,* 3 EBC 1938. Each determination is based on the logical presentation of facts that justify the determination of wage or benefit. It is generally considered that vacation pay is a benefit that has been earned, but in the *Vesuvius Crucible Company*[7] case, it was held that, under the circumstances, vacation pay monies would have to await the entry into a new agreement by the bargaining parties. The important determination, however, is that the trustees act in accordance with their fiduciary duties and do what in their determination acquits these fiduciary duties. The trustees' actions should not be the subject of direction by the union (see *Jacob Transfers, Inc.,* 227 NLRB 1231), nor should the trustees allow their actions to be dictated by management.

The trustees have now reached that point where the bargaining parties have agreed on a new contract and the impasse is over. A question arises concerning which employer constitutes a signatory to a labor-management agreement. With respect to employer contributions from those who signed the contract, there is direct compliance with the Taft-Hartley Act for there exists an agreement in writing. Certainly, if a contributing employer has signed a new agreement and, as agreed, is bound by the terms that set forth the contributions and purposes thereof, the trustees merely file away a copy of the agreement.

The problem becomes more difficult when association bargaining has resulted in the association's signature to a signed labor-management agreement. Once again, the trustees must have some knowledge of the general principles of labor law, because it is imperative that their knowledge be used to determine who should be a contributing employer so that the necessary contributions can be made. Certainly, with respect to association bargaining, all those parties who agreed and assigned their bargaining rights to the association would be bound by the association's signature to the contract.

There may, however, be other employers who, in past years, have been involved in association bargaining. The general principle of law guiding the trustee is that the association member or, perhaps, even a former member, is bound by the agreement entered into unless there has been given to the union unequivocal, timely and adequate notice of the withdrawal of that employer from association bargaining. It is therefore possible that a contributing employer might have withdrawn from the association many years in the past but never given notice as required under the principles of labor law. That employer would still be bound by the new agreement and required to make the contributions. The requirement of the employer to make the contributions, though no longer a member of the association, has been discussed in the *Labbé*[8] case and, most recently, in the *Bonanno*[9] case.

Should a new agreement be signed, either by the individual employer signatories or by the association, and it comes to pass that there are still employers who are bound by neither general rule, it is wise that the trustees immediately consider whether that employer has withdrawn from the trust fund and that the appropriate remedies be taken to establish withdrawal liability.

Special Problem—
The Plan Participant as an Adversary

The trustees must be aware of what it is that makes the participant either a litigant or an adversary to the trust fund. A plan participant has been given great rights under ERISA and, from the increasing volume of litigation, it is evident that adversaries who are participants find no shortage of counsel to undertake their cause and that they make most dangerous opponents. The basic principle that a trustee follows is that he is forced by the limitation of funds to draw hard boundary lines. The participant who becomes an adversary is on the wrong side of the benefit line (*Reuda v. Seafarers International*).[10]

Recent litigation has established that, once again, the purpose of the plan is to provide benefits to as many of the members of the bargaining unit as is economically possible while protecting the financial stability of the plan. Recently, in *Elser v. IAM National Pension Fund,* a decision rendered by the Ninth Circuit in August of 1982, the court held that the cancellation of past service credits upon the decertification of the union as the bargaining agent could not result in the application of the plan's language of eliminating past service credit for those individuals. The court pointed out

---

6. *UAW v. Cadillac Malleable Iron Co.,* 3 EBC 1369.
7. *Vesuvius Crucible Co. v. NLRB,* 2 EBC 2218.
8. *Labbé v. Heroman,* 2 EBC 1901.
9. *Bonanno Linen Service v. NLRB,* 102 Sup. Ct. 720.
10. *Reuda v. Seafarers International,* 576 F.2 942.

that to cancel past service credits would be arbitrary and capricious. The arbitrary cancellation would allow those employees who had been participants for a shorter period of time to benefit, whereas those employees who were decertified having longer years of service would not be eligible. The court found no adverse effect to the plan could be shown by allowing the retention of the past service credits. The court disregarded the argument that those persons who had voted for the decertification must certainly have been knowledgeable of the effects of the decertification.

Correspondingly, the court has given great weight to the procedure followed by the trustees and the requirement that the trustees follow the procedure clearly defined in ERISA and regulations of the Department of Labor in denying a benefit to the participant. Recently, in *Freeman v. IBEW, Local 613* (3 EBC 1865), the court stated that if nothing more were involved other than its passing on the determination of the trustees about whether it was proper to cease paying benefits to those who were no longer, in the trustees' opinion, completely disabled, the court would have upheld the determination. The determination, however, was not upheld because the trustees, in arriving at that determination, failed to give a full and fair review; they prohibited the participant's examination of documents that they relied on for their decision; they did not review pertinent documents; they made the submission of the issues in writing impossible; and they did not give specific reasons for their denial of the benefit. The court held, therefore, that the manner in which the decision was made violated the requirements of ERISA and the regulations of the Department of Labor; therefore, the benefits could not be withdrawn.

To trustees, the principle of law they are facing is a simple one. The principle merely states that trustees, while passing upon benefits, are not antagonists against or advocates for the participant's interest. It is incumbent on the trustees to take the initiative and to cause any evidence, which must be reasonably available, to be developed. Trustees cannot rely in their determination on what is presented to them by a participant. The trustees, if they are aware of information, have an obligation to obtain all the information so that a full review is available. The trustees are not only required and have a responsibility to see that evidence is developed before a decision is made against the claim, but that the evidence is substantial evidence and includes all of that which was reasonably available even if it has to be obtained by the trustee; that is the message of the *Toland* case. To those who care to use the legal principles involved, the participant must be afforded not only procedural due process, but also substantive due process.

Since the trustees can only administer the fund when there are dollars and cents in the fund, they can, in the welfare field, change rules and regulations to preserve the fund for all, even though it might impact upon a participant who otherwise might be on the correct side of the benefit trust. This is the determination in the *Pierce*[11] case and the *Caudle v. UMW* case (523 F. Supp. 91). The courts have not yet reached the point where it would make the trustee take money from his own pocket to fund a welfare benefit, but the courts have had no hesitation in overseeing the activities of the trustee in accordance with the statute. The trustees are further required to keep a constant and knowledgeable check on their procedures and the manner of their administration, because the participants have the legal opportunity to seek injunctive relief against the trustees if the rules and regulations and manner of administration are not in the interests of the participant (*Lechner v. National Benefit Fund,*[12] *McGinnis v. Joyce,*[13] *Janowski v. Teamsters*[14]).

If the rules and regulations of the particular fund have placed the participant on the wrong side of the benefit line, the participant makes his claim in court by attacking the trust fund and the rules and regulations and claiming that the trustees' conduct was arbitrary and capricious. If, however, one is dealing with claims by those who do not even qualify as participants, or claims made by those who would like to participate in the trust fund, such a challenge is made under the Taft-Hartley Act, claiming a structural defect. The member of the bargaining unit attacks the validity of the fund, not its rules, regulations or method of operation.

The *Ponce*[15] case took the position pursuant to the Taft-Hartley Act that a structural defect is present (a defect that allows the court to exercise jurisdiction under the Taft-Hartley Act) when the plan excludes a sizable number of union members with no reasonable purpose behind their exclusion. An extremely high percentage of people who

---

11. *Pierce v. NECA-IBEW Fund,* 2 EBC 2470; *Toland v. McCarthy,* 2 EBC 2335.
12. *Lechner v. National Benefit Fund,* 2 EBC 1315.
13. *McGinnis v. Joyce,* 2 EBC 1485.
14. *Janowski v. Teamsters,* 3 EBC 1225.
15. *Ponce v. Construction Laborers,* 2 EBC 1777.

have contributions made on their behalf but who can never obtain a benefit leads a participant to claim a fundamental or structural defect of the plan. More recently, in *Miranda v. Audia*,[16] it was claimed that there was a structural defect by virtue of the fact that 96% of the people on whose behalf contributions were made could not qualify for the benefit. The court repeated the claim and pointed out that the trustees there were able to meet their burden of proof and show to the court's satisfaction that this great disparity had its legitimacy in the nature of the industry. It is an obligation of the trustees to show that their trust fund is for the sole and exclusive benefit of the participants and that their rules and regulations are not only fairly administered but that they were not created to undermine the basic proposition contained in the Taft-Hartley law that the trust fund should cover as many of the members of the bargaining unit as can be reasonably covered.

Special Problems—To What Extent Must the Trustees Monitor the Total Business Operations of the Contributing Employer?

The trustees are usually in possession not only of knowledge of the employers contributing to the trust fund, but also of those employers engaged in the same business who are not contributing to the trust funds. The basic consideration by the trustees is to what extent those who are not contributing to the trust fund should be legally required to do so. The information comes to the trustees from the participants, from the union-designated trustees, from management-designated trustees and, often, in the form of an audit. The trust fund's auditors uncover operations that have not resulted in contributions to the trust funds. If it should happen that the trust fund is given information or gains knowledge that an employer who is a signatory to a labor-management contract has been paying the employees in cash rather than making the contributions to the fund, the trustees would be required to have those contributions made to the fund even though it was a double payment on the part of the contributing employer (two *Audit Services* cases).[17]

The problem, however, becomes more difficult when a separate entity is set up; one entity that has the collective bargaining agreement and another entity that does not. Here, the trustees are required to search for elements of common control to see whether the nonsignatory entity is being used as a subterfuge in not making the payments. Once again, the guideposts are easily established, in that if an employer signs an agreement to make payment to the various trust funds as additional benefits to the people in the collective bargaining unit, the employer is required to live up to the terms and conditions of the agreement. The opposite guidepost is that any person is entitled to set up a business and, as long as his employees do not wish to be bound by any labor-management agreement, or wish to remain in a nonunion status, that is the privilege of the parties involved; the employer need not be subject to claims of trust funds set up by union and management employers.

The difficulty arises, however, when the second company (nonunion) is set up as a subterfuge to avoid the obligations contained in the first agreement (union). Here, one examines such aspects as the interrelation of operations, a common management, a centralized control, a common ownership and common control of critical matters at a policy level. If these factors indicate that the nonunion company is being used as a subterfuge, then it is incumbent upon the trustees to seek collection of contributions for the fund (*Soule Glass*).[18]

Many times companies are taken over by new management entities and, once again, the principle of law can easily be stated in that there should be no prohibition of one company taking over another company (omitting, of course, antitrust considerations). As the United States Supreme Court stated in the *Burns*[19] case, a potential employer may be willing to take over a moribund business only if he can make changes in corporate structure, composition of labor force, work location, task assignment and nature of supervision. Being saddled with an old contract may inhibit the transfer of capital. Once again, a question arises about the rights of those persons who are still employed by the company once the takeover has been completed. These considerations must include new or old labor contracts and the effect of the takeover on participants and on withdrawal liability. If the new company, however, is merely

---

16. *Miranda v. Audia,* 407 BNA 1181, 3 EBC 1847.
17. *Audit Services v. Rolfson,* 107 LRRM (BNA) 2586 9th Cir. 1981; same is *Audit Services, Inc. v. Stewart & Janes,* Sup. Ct. of Montana 662 P.2d 217, 327 *Pens. Rep.* (BNA) A17.

18. *Soule Glass & Glazing Co. v. NLRB,* U.S.C.A. 1st 91 L.C. 17,899.
19. *NLRB v. Burns International,* 406 U.S. 272; *Wiley v. Livingston,* 376 U.S. 543; *Carter v. CMTA Molders,* 489 F. Supp. 704; *Audit Services, Inc. v. Stewart & Janes,* (Montana) 662 P.2d 217; *Waggoner v. N.W. Excavating,* 2 EBC 1356.

the alter ego, as in the *Scott Printing Corporation*[20] case, then its purpose is to evade responsibility, and the trustees should take action accordingly.

In all circumstances, the limiting factor is the labor-management agreement entered by the bargaining parties, which acts as the parameters of action for the trustees. A labor agreement containing clauses to the effect that all work performed in the territorial jurisdiction will be performed by union labor and further provisions that any signatory to the labor-management agreement will not subcontract its work to anyone other than those having a signed agreement with the union or who will bear responsibility to the trust funds sets the parameter of the trustees' actions in collection from nonsignatories to the collective bargaining agreement. These clauses, with respect to the construction industry, have been upheld in the *Pacific Northwest*[21] case and the *Schriver*[22] case.

It is interesting to note that in the *Schriver* case, the court specifically pointed out: "It is through sub-contracting agreements that a union may guarantee payments to a particular established fund." The Court of Appeals for the District of Columbia has pointed out the advantage of such wide clauses in a construction industry contract to the trust fund. If the clause should be legal in the district wherein the trust fund operates, then the trustees would effectuate the clause by requiring that all contributions payable thereunder are in fact paid to the trust fund.

Not every circuit has joined with the District of Columbia and the Ninth Circuit with respect to the exemption in the construction industry from the Taft-Hartley Act's general prohibition against such clauses, and the trustees must be made aware of the parameters in the construction industry in other circuits. The trustees must also be aware of the type of agreements that have been entered into, generally termed "8F" agreements, and must have a fair working knowledge of at least the general principles enunciated by the National Labor Relations Board and the courts in the area of contributions to the trust fund (see *NLRB v. Haberman Construction,* 641 F.2d 351; *Metropolitan Detroit Bricklayers v. Hoetger,* 672 F.2d 580; and *Griffith Company v. NLRB,* 2 EBC 21 63).

Conclusion

The basic purpose of this discussion of special problems of trustees has been to alert the trustees once again that there are other statutes that impinge on the performance of their duties. I have, basically, spoken of the impact of the Taft-Hartley Act on the duties and obligations of the trustees. It can only be repeated that the trustees must be aware of the fact that there are such acts as the Taft-Hartley Act or the National Labor Relations Act and that, perhaps, some of the general principles that guide union and management under that act should be known to trustees. It may very well be that the oft-quoted expression about a little knowledge being dangerous is true. However, harkening back to my first point, a little knowledge may be better than none, provided there is the realization that trustees have a continuing responsibility to be knowledgeable.

---

20. *NLRB v. Scott Printing Corp.,* 6123 F.2d 783; *NLRB v. Blake Construction,* 92 L.C. 1834; *NLRB v. Bell Company,* 561 F.2d 1264; *Howard Johnson Co.,* 417 U.S. 259.

21. *Pacific N.W. Chapter AGC v. NLRB,* U.S.C.A. 9th 1980.

22. *Schriver v. NLRB,* 89 L.C. 25,494; *Griffith Co. v. NLRB, cert denied* #81-1485 (6/7/82) 2 EBC 2163. *Contra Metropolitan Detroit Bricklayers District Council v. J. E. Hodger & Co.,* 672 F.2d 580.

Trustee Education and Expenses for Educational Programs

BY ROBERT W. RIDLEY

EVEN THE MOST casual observer of the changing pension scene must be aware of the recent tendency on the part of the regulatory agencies to focus on alleged abuses on the "expense" side of the fiduciary's ledger as opposed to inadequate performance on the "income" side. This tendency has recently manifested itself in activities by the United States Department of Labor involving the filing of lawsuits or the mailing of precautionary letters to fiduciaries warning of the dire consequences of administrative contracts that are too rich or of junkets that go beyond the realm of reason and are luxurious to the point of opulence.

Although the investigative thrust of the Department of Labor has been aimed primarily at those fact situations that appear to be extreme, nevertheless, the whole question of reasonableness in the matter of fund expenses is of general concern to everyone in the benefit field—and is of particular concern to individual trustees who are themselves generating expenses by certain activities associated with their duties as fiduciaries.

Since the majority of questions and problems involving the reasonable nature of trustee expenses (and therefore their reimbursement) arise out of the attendance by individual trustees at educational meetings, we will focus on the question of trustee educational expenses, their reasonableness, their basic necessity and, finally, on specific questions relating to educational expenses.

The Basic Question

The basic question is whether it is proper to expend trust funds to educate trustees. The argument against such expenditures is that the mandate that requires trustees to discharge their duties with respect to a plan solely in the interests of participants and beneficiaries is an overriding, primary charge on those individuals who assume the burden of trusteeship. Trust funds are to provide benefits for participants and their beneficiaries, and expense items like air fare, conference registration fees, meals and lodging of trustees produce an outlay of funds obviously diverted to purposes other than benefits.

Mr. Ridley is a partner in the Los Angeles lawfirm of Forster, Gemmill & Farmer. A Loyola University School of Law graduate, he is a member of the California, American and Los Angeles Bar Associations. Mr. Ridley has lectured at the University of Southern California Tax Institute, the Hawaii Tax Institute, the Southern Federal Tax Institute, the American Law Institute–American Bar Association continuing education programs, California Continuing Education of the Bar programs and numerous International Foundation educational programs. He is active in several employee benefit-oriented organizations. He is a member of the International Foundation's Attorneys Committee.

Statutory Language

The counterargument is that the very section of ERISA that mandates that fiduciaries shall function for the exclusive purpose of providing benefits also includes in the exclusive purpose rule the purpose of defraying reasonable expenses of administering the plan. Thus, the law clearly contemplates that plan assets may be used for purposes other than the specific payment of dollar benefits to participants. It would seem that the use of the word "benefits" is a broad usage of the word encompassing the concept of "doing what is best," rather than the more rigid "dollar pay-out" concept.

The prudent man rule goes on to state that fiduciaries will function for these exclusive purposes with the "care, skill, prudence, and diligence under the circumstances then prevailing that a prudent man acting in a like capacity and familiar with such matters would use in the conduct of an enterprise of a like character and with like aims." Reading the prudent man rule makes one realize that there are probably a lot fewer people who possess all of these characteristics than there are positions that must be filled. The result is that the majority of individual trustees are intelligent people of good will who find themselves constantly striving to meet the standards established by ERISA. We are faced, not with a shortage of prudent and intelligent persons willing to undertake onerous tasks, but with a definite shortage of individuals who are "familiar with such matters" and with the conduct of enterprises of like character and with like aims. This statement is not an indictment of trustees; rather, it is a recognition of the complexity of the subject matter with which the trustees must be familiar.

ERISA 408(c) provides a specific exemption from the prohibited transaction at ERISA 406(a)(1) by allowing a fiduciary to receive "reimbursement of expenses properly and actually incurred, in the performance of his duties with the plan." The conclusion appears to be inescapable that as the trustees strive to attain the level of excellence demanded by the law, within reason, the cost of so striving may constitute an expense properly and actually incurred in connection with the performance of the trustees' duties with the plan.

ERISA Mandate

"Honorary" is a concept frequently used in our society. We confer honorary degrees. We defer to honorary titles and organizations award honorary membership. One thing that you will never see is an honorary trustee. Why? The very nature of the function of a fiduciary is that it is an active function. The trustee inquires, reviews, researches, probes, questions, considers and, most importantly, decides. I believe that the trustee's decisions should be intelligent ones.

When one looks at the very nature of the trustee role and couples that with the mandate of ERISA concerning the level at which the trustee is to function, it seems that the propriety of trustee educational expenses ceases to be the primary concern and that the real concern becomes a positive mandate that, within reason, a trustee must seek out beneficial educational experiences to become a better, more knowledgeable and more active trustee.

DOL Regulations

ERISA Section 408(c) requires that trustee expenses be properly and actually incurred in order to be reimbursed or prepaid. The Department of Labor has issued corresponding regulations at Regs. §2550.408(c)-2. These regulations not only preclude the payment of compensation to trustees from the trust, but go on to provide for specific rules regarding reimbursement or prepayment of expenses. In connection with advances for expenses, the regulations authorize such advances if the amount of the advances is reasonable with respect to the anticipated amount of direct expense and if the trustee accounts for the advance against the expense at the end of the period covered by the advance.

Although the regulations are relatively short, a good deal can be learned by a close look at them:

1. "Reasonableness" is judged on a per case basis.
2. "Indirect" expenses are not reimbursable. An indirect expense is one that the trust would have incurred had the trustee not performed the particular service, or an expense that represents an allocation of some part of the trustee's overhead costs. An example is the case of a trustee who has an office in his home and who attempts to charge the trust with an allocable portion of his overhead expenses. This is not, of course, a direct expense.
3. In connection with the matter of per diem advances, the original Department of Labor regulations (since superseded) specifically referred to per diem advances. The current regulations make no reference to them, and the conclusion I draw is that a per diem advance is acceptable so long as it is only an advance that must be accounted for, with any overage being repaid to the plan. Obviously, if expenses should exceed the per diem, additional reimbursement would have to be made if the expenses were otherwise proper. We feel the "true" per diem (no repayment, no accounting) is prohibited.
4. The regulations say that expenses that are reimbursable from multiple sources are not properly charged to the trust. The question not answered by the regulations is whether they are declaring invalid reimbursements by the trust in cases where the trustee could seek full or partial reimbursement from another source. Clearly, double reimbursement is improper. The question of available reimbursement from another source is one that would fall under that provision of the prudent man rule that requires that the trustee should defray the reasonable cost of

administration. This requirement and general principles of equity would seem to indicate that some sort of reasonable proration should be made.

What Is Proper, Actual and Reasonable?

Probably the major question raised by the regulations and by the law itself involves the determination of what is meant by an expense that is "properly and actually" incurred.

In considering the word "actually," we find that the dictionary says the word means "existing in fact or reality" or "not false or apparent." Translating this definition into our context, an example might be the case of a trustee who travels to the site of the educational meeting, attends the opening banquet, enjoys the buffet breakfast and then never attends a single session. It seems to us that, absent illness or some other good cause, the trustee has not actually incurred the expenses and so should not be reimbursed.

Obviously, the question of whether an expense is "proper" is far more complex. Again, looking at the dictionary we find that "proper" means "marked by suitability, rightness or appropriateness: fit." I like to think that this definition translates into the question, "Is the expense suitable—that is, is the expense inappropriate to the general purpose of the trust or is it one that is appropriate to the general purpose of the trust and to the interests of the beneficiaries?"

Beyond proper and actual, we also know that the expense must be reasonable. We thus are faced with the problem of applying the concepts of "reasonable," "proper" and "actual." We have categorized "actual" as fairly simple to determine, i.e., the particular service or commodity was, in fact, used by the trustee. "Reasonable" may well relate to the relative nature of the expense of the particular commodity or service, and it is not too difficult to conceive of satisfying this particular requirement. It is the concept of "proper" that appears to be a great equalizer and thus the most difficult to determine. Perhaps the following example will help:

> A trustee attends an educational meeting and resides at the headquarters hotel. The site of the meeting is a convention center approximately one mile from the hotel, and free shuttle bus service is provided. The trustee researches all of the available chartered limousine services and selects the best bargain from among the various services. The trustee actually uses the limousine service to travel to and from the convention center.

We think that the above example satisfies the "reasonable" standard on at least a relative basis. It certainly satisfies the "actual" standard. "Proper" is the concept that would clearly pass the limousine bill back to the trustee for payment.

Specific Problem Areas

Now that we have reviewed some of the principles that can be gleaned from the law and from the regulations concerning educational expenses of trustees and their reimbursement, let us look at some of the specific questions which should be considered in the day-to-day operation of benefit trusts.

1. *Provisions of the documents.* The trust document should be reviewed to make sure that it authorizes the method of reimbursement used by the trust.
2. *Appropriate educational experience.* If the expense is for education, it should be clear that education is aimed at benefiting plan participants. Not every course of study fits this requirement. For example, a trustee of a welfare fund probably should not be attending an educational meeting devoted to penalizing actuarial methods employed in pension funds.
3. *Number of meetings.* Frequency of educational meetings is a major question. One meeting per trustee per year is a rule adopted by some trusts, and we have no real argument with that; however, we feel that going beyond it is not necessarily unreasonable. Certainly, attendance by every trustee at every meeting probably would be improper. Consideration must be given to the total number of trustees, the size and complexity of the fund, the various programs offered by the fund and similar factors. It is most important that the consideration of these matters and their resolution be documented as part of the ongoing operation of the board of trustees.
4. *Travel expense.* Probably the greatest number of questions arise in connection with method and class of travel. The problem is exacerbated by the existence of incredibly complex and varying rate structures and bargain deals of the various airlines. Comparisons of various rates under circumstances of travel that comply with special bargain arrangements, and the comparison of those bargain arrangements with other such ar-

rangements, can be so complex as to go well beyond any rule of reason. With respect to travel by air, we generally recommend that trustees travel coach or, if the trustee wishes to travel first class, that the reimbursement be keyed to the coach fare.

Travel by automobile presents the question of whether the auto travel is undertaken by the trustee for the trustee's own convenience or whether it is the most reasonable way to move from the trustee's residence to the place of the meeting under the circumstances prevailing. We feel that it is reasonable to establish a reimbursement rate per mile without regard to such niceties as the precise type of car or the number of cylinders of the vehicle that the trustee drives. We then recommend measuring the multiple of the per mile reimbursement against the coach air fare and reimbursing the trustee for the lower dollar amount. Perhaps the best answer to all of the complex problems that arise in considering travel arrangements by trustees is to reiterate the principle that the rule of reason should prevail and that the real world probably lies midway between opulence and penury.

5. *Meals.* A trustee is entitled to reimbursement for reasonable cost of meals while attending educational programs. Problems revolving around food and drink inevitably raise the question of entertainment and whether entertainment is reimbursable. Although the majority of fact situations involving entertainment and its reimbursability generally prove to be improper from a reimbursement standpoint, we have seen many occasions where entertainment was legitimately incurred for a proper trust purpose and was thus reimbursable. On the question of trustee meals, the real world would seem to lie between gourmandizing and fast-food franchises.

6. *Loss of wages.* It is not an uncommon practice for a trustee who is unable to work because of attendance at educational meetings to be reimbursed by the trust for his loss of wages. Payment of compensation, as such, is specifically denounced by both the law and the regulations in cases in which the fiduciary is already compensated by an employer or a union. However, the question arises concerning whether reimbursement for lost wages is actually payment of compensation by the trust as contemplated by the statute. I believe that it is not, and I find support in a private letter ruling issued by the Department of Labor on March 17, 1976, addressing itself to this question in the context of an apprenticeship fund. The rationale of the private letter ruling is that the union trustees were individuals who were not receiving pay from employers during the time that they were away performing services for the plan, so that reimbursement received from the plan for wages not paid was permissible since the duality of sources of compensation did not exist. The same would not be true with respect to management trustees who continue to earn salary while away from work at educational meetings.

As a practical matter, elimination of reimbursement for lost wages for labor trustees would result in a major disruption of the functioning of most Taft-Hartley plans and would not, in my opinion, be in keeping with the intent of ERISA.

7. *Spouse expenses.* Except in very unusual situations, it is my opinion that the expenses of nontrustee spouses in attending educational meetings are not properly reimbursable by a trust.

8. *Location of meetings.* With regard to meeting location, the rule of reason would require that the meeting that is closest to the trustee's hometown should be attended, rather than the one that is a better vacation choice. This rule is, however, subject to exceptions. If it is important for a trustee to attend an educational meeting and the trustee lives in Tampa, there is nothing wrong with the trustee attending the meeting in Chicago, even though the same meeting was presented in Miami, if the trustee was simply unable to attend the Miami meeting because of legitimate schedule conflict.

9. *Substantiation of expenses.* Both for income tax and reimbursement purposes, trustees should be required to submit detailed statements of expenses to obtain reimbursement or to render an accounting.

10. *Feedback.* In a typical multiemployer trust, a small percentage of the total number of trustees will attend any given educational meeting. To derive the maximum benefit from these educational meetings, the trustees who attend the meeting should report back to the entire board not only for the

purpose of sharing educational experience but also to document the propriety of attendance at the meetings and the expenses incurred in connection therewith.

In sum, problems of trustee expenses are similar to other problems in the field of employee benefits. Their solution depends on the good will of dedicated individuals functioning in accordance with both the letter and spirit of the law.

Policy Manuals

BY LEO A. MAJICH

THE SUBJECT OF policy manuals appears to cause different reactions among the people who are involved in the development or use of such documents. Some people like them, while others don't; also, there are those who use policy as a "copout." How many times have you heard the statement, "Sorry, that's our policy"? A policy manual should be a set of rules designed to guide an organization in a consistent pattern of behavior.

Before getting into the subject of policy manuals, it would appear to be appropriate to define some terms. It is important to establish the differences among an "objective," a "procedure" and a "policy." Most of those terms tend to overlap and, without an understanding of what they mean, much unnecessary confusion is created.

- *Objective*—essentially a specific goal or aim. An objective is something to achieve. It is *what* you want done.
- *Procedure*—a process, method or manner of performing something. Well-defined procedures assist employees in the performance of their duties. A procedure describes *how* to do something.
- *Policy*—a basic framework of principles or rules to be used as a basis for decisionmaking. Policies usually supplement each other and tend to expedite decisionmaking. A policy is a guide to the achievement of an objective. It is the *why* behind the decisionmaking process.

Now that the terms have been defined, I believe it is equally important to set the framework within which policy manuals will be used or applied. Trust funds are of different sizes, with different administrative arrangements and different objectives. It is fair to say that all are essentially the same, but all have substantial differences. Many of the trust funds deal in small numbers, whereas others deal in very large numbers. Some trusts are contract administered, whereas others are self-administered. All of these factors have a bearing on whatever policy manual you intend to develop.

Background—A Working Trust Fund

It would be difficult to cover the matter in a general way and at the same time expect to provide meaningful information. Consequently, I will discuss what we do in our trust fund operation and try

Mr. Majich has been the administrator of the Operating Engineers Trust Funds (Southern California) since 1972. The four funds making up this group—pension, health and welfare, vacation–holiday and journeyman and apprentice training—cover about 25,000 employees in 12 Southern California counties and four Southern Nevada counties. Approximately 4,000 employers report to these funds. Between 1950 and 1971, Mr. Majich was a partner in a heavy engineering construction firm. During this time he was active in the Southern California Chapter of the Associated General Contractors. He was a member of numerous committees and, in 1966 and 1967, served as president of the chapter. During this period Mr. Majich also was a trustee on several employee benefit funds. He served with the 20th Air Force in the South Pacific during World War II. He was a member of the Los Angeles County Economy and Efficiency in Government Commission for five years. He currently serves as a member of the Los Angeles County Housing Development Advisory Council. Mr. Majich is a graduate of Loyola University (Los Angeles) with a degree in business administration and accounting. He served on the Industry Relations Committee of the International Foundation in 1977 and has participated in previous Foundation educational programs.

to provide you with the reasons why we do certain things. By giving you some of the background of our operation, I believe you will be able to understand why we rely on policy and procedure manuals. Without them, I am certain you will appreciate that we would be courting disaster with all of the operations and functions that we have to perform daily.

The Operating Engineers Trust Funds are self-administered and I am the salaried administrator.

The trust fund office is responsible for the administrative activities required on behalf of four trust funds—health and welfare, pension, vacation–holiday and training. The geographic area of our plan includes 12 Southern California counties and four Southern Nevada counties. That area, in excess of 90,000 square miles, has employers and participants throughout.

Administrative duties are performed through an administrative corporation. The directors of the corporation are also trustees. The administrative corporation employs all fund office personnel and performs all administrative duties based on written agreements between each trust and the corporation. The operating expenses of the corporation are funded by each trust on a pro-rata basis in accordance with the agreements in effect.

We have approximately 8,000 employers on our master file, of which approximately 4,000 are active at any given time. There are approximately 26,000 active participants, with over 10,000 retired members receiving benefits from the pension trust. Most readers will be aware of the requirements imposed by federal law regarding the retention of information on participants in the pension plan. We estimate that we have detailed history and information, accumulated since the inception of our plans, on over 300,000 individuals. We also keep, in current files in the health and welfare plan, history on over 120,000 individuals.

June 30 is the cutoff of the fiscal year for each of the trusts and the administrative corporation. During the year ending June 30, 1982, the administrative corporation received and processed total income on behalf of the four trusts in excess of $172 million. Pension benefits paid during the same year exceeded $53 million. The health and welfare fund paid out $44 million in claims. The vacation fund paid out over $18 million in benefits during the same year.

The health and welfare fund is self-insured and the administrative corporation provides a claims department to handle all the claims activity in-house. During the year just ended, over 490,000 medical and dental claims were processed by the fund office.

The pension fund has assets in excess of $450 million at this time.

Another function of the administrative office is the operation of a property management department. That department is responsible for the management of real estate owned by the pension trust. The real estate assets consist of office and commercial properties with a value in excess of $40 million. One of the properties is a 12 story office building on Wilshire Boulevard in Los Angeles. Another 12 story office building is under construction, which will cost approximately $30 million and will be another income-producing property for the trust beginning early in 1983.

Almost all of our activity is on a computer, which is essentially in-house with programming and system support provided by a service bureau.

We have procedure manuals for data processing, accounting, claims, pension and vacation–holiday activities. In addition, we have an extensive procedure manual for our employer department, which handles all collection matters. All of those procedure manuals have a direct relationship to the basic policy manuals that are in effect. They all tie together and are cross-referenced.

Policies

We can't possibly eliminate the human aspect in the functioning of an organization. There are those who insist that everything should be clearly defined, who want rigid policies. There are those who believe a more flexible approach is better in the long run. I subscribe to the flexible approach. I have never seen a policy that didn't have to be modified somewhere along the line because of a circumstance that no one anticipated.

I believe that policies can simplify decision-making throughout an organization. The framework of those policies, as well as the policies themselves, help develop guidelines for each member of the administrative office. The purpose of a policy manual should be to ensure that the organization will make steady and consistent progress toward its objectives. The policy manual should provide general decisions that can be used to handle recurrent events. All policies should be developed through discussion with key personnel in related areas of responsibility, so that everyone knows what to do.

The best description of a set of policies that I have seen was that of a group of mountain climbers holding on to the same rope. Being tied together, no one could get lost. They had to coordinate their activities or the rope got in the way.

In our operation we have two distinct sets of policies—administrative office policies and trustee policies. Most of our policies are written, or formal.

Administration

The setting of administrative policies is the primary function and responsibility of the administrator. Several principles apply.
- Identify the problem.
- Recognize the need for a policy.

- Assign the development of the policy language to those persons who know the problem.
- The statement should be definite, clear and understandable to everyone in the organization.
- The policies should be permanent, but they should not be inflexible.
- Avoid constantly changing policies.
- Try to anticipate as many conditions as possible that would limit the policies, so that they do not become confusing or meaningless.
- Do not prescribe detailed procedures unless that is absolutely necessary. The policy tells you why something is being done, not how.
- All policies should conform with federal and state law and be compatible with the rules and regulations of the trusts.
- Every policy should be reexamined periodically, because new laws or changed circumstances introduce new factors that require policy changes.
- Have a thorough knowledge of the operations and the effects of every policy on employees in all departments.
- Last, but not least, you must involve your legal counsel, auditor, insurance consultant and actuary. Many policies relate directly to their involvement with the daily operations of the trust fund office. Those individuals must be aware of administrative policies, as they implement established trustee policy. If you use a service bureau for computer processing, you must involve it also, to make sure that all activities function properly.

Whether you have an office of three or four people or an office that has 100 people, the use of policies—formal or informal—cannot be disregarded or ignored. Every decision should be made at the lowest possible level of supervisory authority; that level should be at the point where all relevant information comes together. A policy permits the delegation of authority and that delegation must include responsibility for the decision. The decisionmaker lives with the results of the decision, *good* or *bad*. There is no "buck-passing."

Examples

Our administrative office has a number of policies and a few examples can demonstrate their purpose. We do not use a "lock box" in our operation. All funds are remitted by employers directly to the trust fund office daily. Consequently, one of our objectives is to get those funds into the interest-bearing trust accounts immediately. Our policies for handling income from all sources permit us to process the income and make *daily* deposits into the respective trust accounts. There is a clearly defined policy designed to achieve the objective, i.e., to get the funds into the bank the day they are received.

We have over 10,000 retired engineers who expect to get their check on the first of each month. A policy is established to ensure that the checks are prepared, processed and mailed in sufficient time to have that check in the hands of the retired participant on the first of each month.

Everyone knows that the benefit booklet and summary plan description are supposed to explain benefit provisions understandably to all participants. I have struggled with that problem for years and I have yet to see anyone do the job so that everyone is satisfied. We deal with every level of education and with different backgrounds. I consider the task to be impossible but we never stop trying.

In that vein, we developed an administrative policy directed toward explaining the benefit provisions to the members. Several years ago we developed audiovisual programs for the health and welfare and pension plans. Meetings are held in the various districts of Local 12, which the members and their spouses are invited to attend. The program includes a slide presentation that explains the highlights of the plans. This presentation is followed by a question and answer session, during which my assistant and I explain some of the more complicated provisions. The sessions have helped us to modify our benefit booklet and summary plan description by revealing those areas that are difficult to understand.

One result of the meetings was a significant change in our daily office routine. After we had conducted several seminars, it was obvious that our office was not providing correct answers to questions from members regarding benefit provisions. It was apparent that a member or his wife could call our office and get an answer to a question from one person and a little later get a different answer to the same question from someone else.

Because of that problem, I developed a questionnaire using the basic information available in our benefit booklet and conducted a test for everyone in our claims department. I discovered that many of our people did not really understand all aspects of our plan and, more importantly, did not know how to respond properly.

To overcome that problem, we developed what we now call our Information Center. We have several people assigned to this unit, whose primary job is to answer all telephone calls to the claims department. They are prepared to answer general inquiries about the plans and to develop information if there is a complaint. That procedure has relieved most of our people in the claims department from answering the phone and at least we have consistent answers being given to similar questions. Policy requires that the Information Center refers specifically difficult problems to supervisory personnel. The Information Center is also the first phase of our training program for those who have the ability to move up to a claims examiner's position.

I have a personal policy about communicating with participants. I receive a copy of every letter, other than form letters, written in our office. That policy started several years ago when I realized how many of our employees could not spell. In other cases their grammar was terrible. As an example of peculiar communication, I use a letter written by one of our claims examiners years ago. The letter was attempting to explain a problem with a surgery claim. The sentence structure and punctuation were such that the letter was really saying that our member had operated on the surgeon.

I detest buzzwords. I do not permit our employees to use technical language that only another technician would understand. All employees in our office know that I read their letters and they know that they will hear from me about misspelled words, poor grammar or buzzwords.

The Fund and the Union

Another aspect of our policy involves the union. Typically, a member will see a business agent or officer of the union and invariably question him about a benefit provision or a particular personal problem with the fund office. Established policy requires all such inquiries to be referred to the fund office. Business agents are under orders from the officers of the union to avoid explaining benefit provisions or any other aspect of the operation of the plans. Obviously, there are Privacy Act restrictions regarding the release of information and our office does not release information to anyone without authority in writing from the participant.

Fortunately, the officers of the union who are also trustees are aware of the legal hazards and emphasize the policy that requires all responses regarding benefit provisions to be handled by the fund office. During the audiovisual seminars that I've already mentioned, we always explain the *why* of that policy to the members, who usually do not separate the trust funds from the union.

Trustee Policies

Trustee policies are a different matter, but have a direct bearing on the operation of all of the trusts. Many of the functions of the administrative office are directed by trustee policy, which is not necessarily part of the rules and regulations of any of the plans. One example is our written statement of investment policy for the pension trust. In that case, the trustees have a clearly defined policy that establishes the criteria for investments of all types and sets guidelines pertaining to the investments. That policy controls or directs the efforts of the investment advisors and others handling pension investments on behalf of the trustees. It also simplifies dealing with anyone proposing investments. No time need be wasted explaining investment policy—a copy of the document provides the criteria and so forth.

Other trustee policies deal with benefit provisions; an example is our policy regarding disability pensions. We will accept Social Security disability awards as evidence of total and permanent disability and we will award a pension based on that evidence. In cases where Social Security awards are not available, the trustees will accept conclusive medical evidence establishing total and permanent disability. Trustee policy in this regard has two aspects: (1) An applicant unable to establish evidence of disability at the time of application is provided additional medical examinations at trust expense. This provision includes mileage from the applicant's home to the doctor and back. (2) If the written medical reports are not conclusive, the applicant has the right to appear personally before the appeals committee; the trustees then make their decision based on personal observation of the individual along with the medical evidence provided. Those policies have a direct impact on the processing of disability application forms by the trust fund office.

Is a Policy Manual Always Necessary?

The basic question you have to ask yourself is whether you think it is necessary to have a policy manual in your operation. Until a few years ago, I never paid much attention to the matter because we had a significant number of trustees who had served on the trusts for many years. Six years ago, we had a change in union administration, which resulted in a substantial number of new trustees being appointed to the trusts. Fortunately, two of the union trustees had served in that capacity for many years and were aware of trust policies. However, during the same period a number of employer trustees retired from business or for personal reasons decided to resign as trustees.

It became evident very quickly that we had a job on our hands, because the new trustees were obviously unaware of trust policies and had to be "educated" about their intent and purpose. That statement in no way demeans new trustees. A trustee's job is difficult at best and a trust operation is not like any other business. What may be a normal decision in a commercial enterprise could be illegal or imprudent in a trust action.

Another important factor that affected trust policies was the passage of ERISA and the Multiemployer Pension Plan Amendments Act of 1980. Many of our policies had to be modified because of the new legislation.

I believe that it is good insurance to have a policy manual regardless of the size of your office. I am convinced that policy manuals make things work better. A payroll policy is especially important when you deal with employees in the fund office. Regardless of the size of your office you're exposed to charges of racial or sex bias, particularly when you have disputes over promotions or terminations of employment.

The other insurance factor in a policy manual is some semblance of a guarantee that all participants are being treated fairly and in a manner consistent with plan rules and regulations. You cannot have policies that create exceptions. Everyone must be treated the same. That is why I take the position that no policy should be so rigid or inflexible that it causes problems. You have to be able to roll with the punches and be able to accommodate situations that you did not anticipate. Once a policy is modified, everyone should be aware of the modification so that mistakes can be avoided.

Developing a Policy Manual

Assuming that some readers do not have a policy manual, I would expect that one question is, "How do I develop such a manual?" I don't believe that there are any set procedures regarding the development of a policy manual. Common sense dictates what you have to do; you must analyze your internal operations and develop manuals that will be used consistently and will serve a useful purpose. In the administration end of the operation, you obviously need payroll policies that include provisions regarding sick leave, vacation and so forth. In your accounting department you must have policies that provide clear audit trails for all funds received and disbursed.

Trustee policy was developed by reviewing all of the minutes of all of the trust meetings. We developed an index of all minutes cross-referenced by subject matter, which is maintained regularly. An extract of that index is a manual identifying trustee policy. Our trusts have been in operation since 1954 and we have a great deal of information maintained in three-ring binders. A review of your minutes should provide you with a picture of what trustee policy is on any aspect of the operation of a specific plan.

Conclusion

I would like to emphasize a few important points regarding policy manuals. Writing a policy is no substitute for getting the job done. A written policy is not an end in itself; it is a means to an end. It should be clearly stated so that it cannot be misinterpreted and should be generalized to the extent that it can anticipate events of any significance to your organization. Keep it simple, keep it clear and avoid the policy straitjacket.

We Had a Barbecue and Nobody Came Except the Fire Department

BY SHELDON P. LEWIS, CPA

Preface

Benefit Administration Corporation is a contract administrator in Fresno, California with a staff of approximately 65. At 6:00 a.m. on March 9, 1982, we were notified that our office was on fire. Smoke could be seen several blocks away as I rushed to the scene to find the fire department working to put out the fire.

The flames were extinguished relatively quickly, but not before the structure and contents were damaged to the tune of approximately $750,000—and we were out of business.

During the mopping-up process, the fire inspector stated without qualification that it was arson, that three fires were set in separate locations, and, most interestingly, that the person or persons responsible had turned off the burglar alarm and had entered with a key. Minor items were stolen but there was no attempt to make off with easily marketable equipment such as typewriters and printing calculators. At the time this paper was being written, a person charged with numerous burglaries in the area had been arraigned for the arson but had not yet been tried.

Since the fires were started with paper taken from desks (no flammable liquids were used), a minor amount of unknown claims in process were destroyed. Flames, but mostly smoke, destroyed all of the typewriters and printing calculators, several desks, chairs and filing cabinets, both copy machines, the check signing machine and the mailing machine. Also beyond repair was most of our computer equipment, including the disc drive, printer and all of our terminals. The central processing unit and tape drive were repairable.

All files, claim documents and blank claims checks—in other words *all* paper—were damaged by smoke but, generally speaking, ultimately usable. All furniture items not destroyed were damaged but repairable.

Although six days later we had found and moved into a temporary location with desks, chairs, typewriters, printing calculators, copy machine, mailing machine, file cabinets (all rented) and the beginnings of a telephone system, we had no operative computer and no files. It would be another three weeks before all of the ozone-treated and soot-removed files were on-site and something resembling normal operations was under way.

Mr. Lewis, president of Benefit Administration Corporation, has been a contract administrator for 29 years. His employee benefit experience covers a wide variety of trades, industries, and programs, private and governmental, with beneficiaries in all Western states. Mr. Lewis is a graduate of the California State University, Fresno and received an M.B.A. degree from Harvard Business School. Currently president-elect of the Fresno Chamber of Commerce, he has participated as a speaker, panelist or moderator at numerous International Foundation educational meetings and is a former member of the Foundation's Accountants, Administrators and Financial Review Committees. Mr. Lewis is presently a member of the Foundation's Board of Directors and CEBS Committee.

How Could This Disaster Happen?

We had a burglar alarm. A limited number of trusted and executive personnel, as well as janitorial personnel retained by our landlord, had the burglar alarm key.

Does one then come to the conclusion that a burglar alarm is useless? No, but I have certainly studied the different types of burglar alarms since March 9 and have concluded that burglar alarms are like all systems of internal control. There is no perfect solution but there are opportunities to reduce substantially the possibility of unauthorized intrusion, depending on the degree of effort and expense one wishes to expend.

There apparently are at least three types of key or lock arrangements. The oldest, sort of a round key, is what we had. After the fire, I discovered that this type of key has been around a long time and blanks are easy to get, thus making it relatively easy for a person fairly skilled in the art of locksmithing to duplicate any key. An example of a more recent type of key is called "Medico" (I have this on my house burglar alarm) and apparently the blanks are distributed on a very limited basis and require more skill and specialized equipment to duplicate. Nevertheless, even this type of key, like any key, can be reproduced.

The third type of lock arrangement is digital. Basically consisting of ten numerical keys, the good ones can be reprogrammed and are clearly better from a control point of view than either of the key arrangements.

I have concluded that the most secure limited entry system involves a supervised service. The alarm will be inoperative during the normal business hours on the normal business days. At any other time authorized personnel would have to telephone the burglar alarm service prior to entry, indicating the approximate time of entry and the code assigned to that individual. On entering the office, the individual would then have to telephone the service within a required period of time and state the length of time that he or she intended being in the office along with the assigned code. The individual would also have to set an open/close switch to verify his or her authorized presence.

Janitorial personnel would have a separate type of code and a limited access status based on the assigned times for such service. As often as necessary the janitorial codes (or anybody's code for that matter) could be changed.

The supervised service arrangement naturally costs more than the usual type of key burglar alarm, is more complicated and requires a certain degree of attention to reduce the probability of unauthorized entry. There is no doubt that when we move back to our permanent office we will use the supervised service arrangement.

A few words about fire or smoke alarms might be appropriate. In our situation the burglar alarm company called, not because the burglar alarm had been tripped in the normal fashion, but because the fire had shorted out the system. That did not make it a fire alarm. Had a heat-rising-activated system been installed, or even if there had been smoke detectors, the damage would have been vastly reduced. Apparently the system involving heat identification is the most desirable system because it requires a great deal less maintenance than the traditional smoke detectors. Certainly not all fires are caused by intruders and I am going to take a very long look at the use of a fire or smoke detector system prior to moving back into the reconstructed building.

It is easy to conclude that the degree of security is directly proportionate to the use of state-of-the-art methods to protect against disasters of all kinds. We are all in the risk business in one form or another. Certainly we should seriously consider a loss of great probability—namely the risk of loss from unlawful entry and fires.

What About Computer Data?

All of our discs (except the ones on the drive) and tapes were stored in our fireproof vault. All current data as well as source programs and working programs were in backup form, disc and tape as well as hard copy. Was this enough?

Certainly not. Although the fireproofing of the vault prevented loss from fire, the room was not smokeproof and it should be pointed out that one of the fires was set in the computer room.

Although our discs cleaned up quite well, the effort to extract the information caused us to lose the permanent use of most of the discs; some information was in fact lost and had to be re-created from other sources. This loss was covered by insurance, of course, but the effort required to extract data from the discs and to re-create them was time-consuming and delayed in some instances our return to a normal operation.

What can you do in a practical sense to ensure security of programs and data in case of a loss of computer hardware to a disaster such as the one we experienced? The hardware, of course, can be replaced relatively quickly or temporary arrangements can be made to use like equipment off premises.

Software is another question. Not only must source and operating programs be secure from destruction but also the vast amount of necessary information that is used in the payment of claims, the accumulation and maintenance of eligibility data and the vital information relating to pension history of all types must be transferred to duplicate media on a current basis and stored in a secure and accessible alternative space. It is not too difficult to transfer data to disc or tape storage, but the location and utility of secure and accessible alternative space can be a problem.

The ultimate place, of course, is the proverbial salt mine—but frankly, if nuclear destruction occurs, who cares about the payment of claims and pension history if the beneficiaries and administrators no longer exist? So what we are concerned about are the location and use of reasonably secure and available space for backup data. As in all aspects of control, there is a certain degree of cost/benefit relationship.

Backup data could conceivably be placed in a locked area within the same office. Availability is excellent and access can be controlled. Unfortunately, if a disaster (such as a fire) occurs, all could be lost depending on the nature of the fire and the quality of protection against flames.

Another alternative calls for the movement of the backup data on a daily basis to some other location with or without fire protection but definitely with a reasonable degree of security from unauthorized access. Excellent security can be provided by banks or savings and loan associations which have vaults of substantial size. It is not unreasonable to contemplate the possibility of an entity such as this, with whom the administrator maintains a substantial relationship, providing at no cost or at very reasonable cost, some space on a permanent basis if that space is readily available. However, only that data which need not be referred to currently could logically be placed under this type of security, since access based on the institution's opening and closing times and security provisions would be very limited.

Another appropriate type of secure and accessible storage space would be provided by a commercial safe deposit organization providing 24 hour access and security and the type of structural integrity that would provide the optimum in protection from unnatural disaster. Spaces of this nature are not cheap but, considering the risks and problems inherent in other alternatives, it is the type of expense that one can hardly afford to be without.

Although the selected location for storage of backup programs and data is important, it is less vital than the existence of a strictly adhered to program of off-site backup storage, wherever the location.

"I Don't Worry. I'm Adequately Insured."

It is easy for one who has suffered a major loss to bemoan the inadequacy of insurance. It is not the purpose here to lecture the reader about the exact kind and quantity of insurance to carry, but only to cause a certain amount of introspection and review of each individual situation. With this review, a conscious decision is made and then, if a claim of consequence occurs, let the chips fall where they may.

I believe that generally speaking the insurable risks of an administrator or a self-administered trust may be broken down into the following categories:

1. Insurance against the loss of hardware
2. Insurance to fund the cost of reconstruction of valuable papers and records
3. Insurance against the cost of temporary security of all documents, files and hardware at the time of the disaster
4. Insurance for the out-of-pocket costs incurred and not covered by any of the previous categories
5. Fidelity bonding
6. Professional liability (malpractice) coverage.

Professional liability and fidelity bonding are risk areas of great importance, especially for trust fund operations with great exposure to the disbursement of money and the commitment by employees to participants of eligibility verification and plan provisions. They are, however, subjects that deserve thorough review at another time. We shall review, however, the first four areas of risk.

Insurance Against the Loss of Hardware

Anybody who insures his furniture and equipment on a replacement value less depreciation has rocks in his head. It is practically a physical impossibility to go out and replace an office full of equipment and furniture on this basis with the proceeds that an insurance company would pay.

Since today it is more common to use full replacement insurance, one might imagine that this would create no problems in the case of a major loss. This assumption is only true if the insured carefully evaluates the actual replacement cost of all furniture and equipment each year. By actual evaluation I do not mean the mere use of an assumed inflation factor. Although some items, such as calculating equipment and certain computer hardware, actually cost less today than they did several years ago, this is definitely not true in the case of typewriters, desks, chairs, leasehold improvements and certain types of copying equipment.

The reason why this frequent evaluation of replacement costs is important is that insurance of this nature has a coinsurance factor, which states that the value of all insured articles on which a premium is paid must be within 90% of the actual replacement value or a portion of all losses must be borne by the insured.

Let us assume that the insurance premium was paid on a basis of an estimated replacement value of $300,000, that the actual replacement value of the equipment was $400,000, and that the loss was $250,000. The portion of the loss paid by the insurance company would be determined by taking 90% of the $400,000 inventory amount ($360,000) and dividing this into the amount of insurance carried ($300,000) yielding the percentage of the loss to be paid by the insurance company of 83.33%. Thus, approximately 16.7% of the $250,000 loss must be borne by the insured. This amounts to approximately $41,750.

Fortunately, this assumption is not a reflection of our actual experience because a reasonably current review of replacement cost factors occurred on an annual basis; nevertheless, one cannot be complacent about replacement cost insurance unless care is taken to review the realistic and actual possible expenses of replacement frequently.

One last comment in this area. It is not always possible or necessary to replace all furniture and equipment with the exactly identical articles. The definition used in the insurance policies is that the items replaced must be of "like kind and quality" as the articles damaged beyond repair. With the many changes in the state of the art in computer equipment and copying machines as examples, interesting questions can arise as to how to value the existing inventory.

For example, a copy machine which cost $20,000 five years ago might be replaced by the vendor with its "equivalent" costing twice that amount today, yet changes in technology and manufacturing expertise can provide a piece of equipment performing exactly the same function for half the original price. It is also common to find computer technology causing equipment purchased not too long ago to be replaced by much better equipment costing the same amount of money. How do you value your inventory, at the original cost considering the more productive equipment as the normal replacement or at a discounted cost for a used or rebuilt replica of the existing hardware?

These are all questions which must not only be evaluated when establishing the insurance limits before a disaster occurs but are also very germane in the valuation of the inventory and its replacement after the fact.

Insurance to Fund the Cost of Reconstruction of Valuable Papers and Records

Insurance for the cost of reproduction of "valuable papers" is a rather nebulous category of insurable risk. There is always the question of what are "valuable papers" and the type of expenditures one might experience to cause their replacement. Obvious expenses involve duplication of important hard copy documents, but most important in today's computer world is the cost of the recovery of data from damaged or partially damaged discs or tapes and the programs necessary to accomplish this recovery, as well as the costs of identifying and inputting from alternative sources data that have been lost for whatever reason as the result of the disaster.

Selecting the amount of such insurance is difficult, to say the least. Certainly the principal amount would depend on the quality of security for backup data and the frequency of transferring all information to this medium. In addition, one cannot ignore the type of hard copy information that is not on computer and would have to be reconstructed from a variety of sources in the case of destruction.

Selecting the amount of insurance in this category is much more difficult than for the replacement of furniture and equipment and a good deal of soul-searching is required. Probably the best thing to do is to estimate the amount of coverage one assumes is reasonable and then at least double it.

Insurance Against the Cost of Temporary Security of All Documents, Files and Hardware at the Time of the Disaster

In the ordinary course of daily activity there are normal working hours during which the usual complement of staff is present; at the end of the day, the office is locked up and possibly guarded by a burglar alarm, night watchman or other security methods.

Suddenly a disaster occurs and there is no ordinary working day with the usual complement of employees, in effect, guarding the premises and, because of the nature of the disaster, there may be no locked doors. This situation may occur for a period of days before all of the records, furniture and equipment can be removed from the premises. It is therefore important to review the terms of insurance coverage to make certain that the cost of a 24 hour a day guard is provided. In our case, it took six days before all records and equipment were removed from the premises and, fortunately, our insurance covered the cost of a round the clock guard.

Insurance for the Out-of-Pocket Costs Incurred Not Covered by Any of the Previous Categories

Also fortunately included in our insurance policy was a separate benefit paying for 100% of all costs involving cleanup of the premises after the fire. At the time of this writing, I have no idea as to the magnitude of this cost element but it can be fairly substantial.

Now we get to that catchall, the miscellaneous expense category, which is possibly the category of coverage least considered but immensely valuable. The cost of renting office furniture and equipment for the period of reconstruction and other temporary costs can be reasonably measured, but consider the loss of productive time.

Despite herculean efforts we lost, for all practical purposes, four weeks' work product, at least in the aspect of our services pertaining to the production of health and welfare claims. It does not take a great deal of imagination to estimate the cost of extra labor, overtime or the retention of a catch-up claims service to recognize the cost of one month of lost productive time.

This type of cost is not often contemplated in the evaluation of insurable risks that an office of this nature faces. Certainly we did not contemplate it and did not purchase a sufficient amount of this type of coverage. Needless to say, we will investigate its costs in the future evaluation of our insurance program.

Short Term Considerations

At the time of and immediately following the fire, there were many decisions that had to be made, actions of great importance to be taken and, above all, leadership to be exhibited.

First and foremost was the requirement to make certain that all records not destroyed had the maximum amount of security during their removal, storage and ultimate return. In this regard, the highest priorities were given to blank claims checks, computer discs and tapes, pension benefit printouts, primary accounting records, name and address files of all trustees and employee payroll records.

Number two on the list of immediate requirements was the telephoning of key trustees, informing them about the fire and asking them to notify plan participants that we would not be in telephone contact with anyone for a while and to understand our predicament. At the same time, we contacted the banks that were used by all employee benefit plans to inform them of the situation and, not knowing if any claims checks had been stolen, to request them to stop payment on any claims checks signed manually. (As it turned out, there were no forged checks.)

Key employees were given leadership roles immediately and performed them with dispatch. Communication with all employees was vital from a morale point of view and for their effectiveness in performing the numerous menial tasks required. Coincident efforts were made to locate adequate temporary space and the acquisition, either by immediate purchase or in most instances by short term rental, of furniture and equipment to fill that space.

Six days after the fire we had moved into our temporary location replete with all required office furniture and equipment. We had no files or operative computer but necessary wiring for the computer, as well as the special air conditioning required, had been installed. We even had the beginnings of a temporary telephone system; a comment about that might be appropriate.

Private telephone systems are generally cheaper than those provided by the Bell System. In addition, for taxable entities they provide the delightful temptation of investment credit on the corporation's income tax return because the systems are owned outright by the user. Ignoring these economic benefits, we opted for a somewhat elaborate Bell System installation because of the known reliability and promptness of Bell System service, since telephone communication is such a major part of the administration business.

We were not disappointed. The day we moved to our temporary headquarters a team of installers arrived, and at least one man was there for the three weeks necessary to complete the installation of our temporary system AT NO COST TO US. I shudder to think what would have happened if we relied on a private vendor without the personnel and facilities to draw on when our emergency installation was required.

Summary and Conclusions

Disasters of all types are usually considered to be something that always happen to somebody else. Since it happened to me, *it can happen to you.*

We are always overwhelmed with the day-to-day requirements of managing employee benefit plans. We deal in prudence and risks and all too often fail to take into consideration the risks inherent in our pursuit. Perhaps the recounting of this experience will cause all of you not to just contemplate your risk exposures for a moment or two but to keep them in mind and protect yourselves appropriately every day of the year.

CEBS: A View From the Center of the Action

BY JOSEPH M. COURTNEY, CEBS

SPEAKING OF THE value of the CEBS program is easy and difficult at the same time. Perhaps this dichotomy is understood best by administrators because of our role in the employee benefit field. From our vantage point we are exposed to all of the elements that make up the employee benefits. It is our function to unite these elements into the attainment of specific goals. As we observe the action around us, certain impressions might well be worth noting, particularly to those persons saddled with the ultimate responsibility, the trustees.

Practical Value

One cannot dismiss the importance of actuaries, attorneys, investment advisors, consultants, accountants and other professionals. Each performs a vital role without which the fund could not function properly. Benefit funds are very complex operations, subject to continual change. The latest change, The Tax Equity and Fiscal Responsibility Act of 1982, almost immediately sent the professionals back to the drawing board. Funds must be reexamined for compliance and certain changes may have to be made. You as a principal in your fund not only must know why amendments are necessary but must ensure that these changes do not distort the purpose for which your fund originally was created.

In today's world, benefit funds are associated with megadollars; they have become principal factors within the economy and a major component of our society. The emergence of social investing as a topical issue is a perfect example of a justification for the Certified Employee Benefit Specialist program in real terms. The raw materials of the issue are contained within the curriculum.

Other Values

It is difficult to describe the sometimes silent business dialogue that exists among professionals. By virtue of understanding each professional's role and how it serves your fund, you attain the perspective that permits your thoughts as a concerned party to be translated into the flow of the interaction between your advisors. Here again, the CEBS curriculum is on target.

There have been and will continue to be dynamic changes in the fabric of our society. One

Mr. Courtney is administrative manager of the Service Employees International Union Local 36 Benefit Funds. Active in the joint trust field for over 19 years, Mr. Courtney has served in various elected positions as an official of Asbestos Workers Local 14. Prior to assuming his current position, Mr. Courtney served as administrative manager of the multilocal Asbestos Workers Philadelphia Benefit Funds. He performs consulting services for various organizations. Mr. Courtney is a member of the Philadelphia Council AFL-CIO Health Care Cost Containment Committee and has served on its Institutional Review Board. He is a past president of the Delaware Valley Administrators Council. Mr. Courtney has completed the International Foundation/Wharton School Certified Employee Benefit Specialist program.

cannot overlook the fact that employee benefits are subject to these influences, too. If your fund is to continue providing meaningful benefits to your membership, then you must move into the interaction with your thoughts and direction. Participation in the CEBS program provides positive exposure to those areas that suggest a need for further understanding and education.

Conclusion

Looking back, it was inevitable that something be formulated to fill the existing educational vacuum in the employee benefit field. It is true that the evolution from modest beginnings to the present CEBS program was a long time coming. However, the Certified Employee Benefit Specialist program has stepped in to fill the void. By its very design, the program promises to grow with us into the future. That, I believe, will be the reason for its continuing existence and success.

CHAPTER 4

Professional Services

Donald A. Smart

Vice President
Deferred Compensation Administrators, Inc.
Madison, Wisconsin

Geoffrey V. White

Associate
Davis, Cowell & Bowe
San Francisco, California

Bernard M. Baum

Director
Baum, Sigman and Gold, Ltd.
Chicago, Illinois

Gary P. Brinson, CFA

Chief Investment Officer and
Senior Vice President
First National Bank of Chicago
Chicago, Illinois

Bonnie R. Cohen

Vice President of Finance and Administration
National Trust for Historic Preservation
Washington, D.C.

The Role of the Plan Professional

BY DONALD A. SMART

WHEN ONE TALKS about a "plan professional," he may be referring to a consultant, actuary, attorney, accountant, investment advisor, administrator or others. Depending on how responsibilities are assigned and how large the fund is, there are many legitimate roles for professionals to play in assisting plan trustees. Thus, when hiring professional assistance, the trustees must understand clearly what that professional will provide, how the person or firm will interact with trustees and other professionals and what qualifications are needed to do the job.

The Need for Communication

If there is a common thread that binds the various trustee-plan professional relationships, it is the singular need for good communication—both to be able to listen and to be able to be heard. Each relationship is different because it is affected by the personalities of the trustees, fund size, breadth of expertise or simply the way in which the fund evolved over time. Yet, the ability of trustees and advisors to communicate will be a major determinant of how successfully the plan is run.

Unfortunately, the way in which communication lines are established often does not allow for total effectiveness. Let me give you a few examples of all too typical situations. How many of you use your plan advisors as referees to mediate confrontational situations that arise between labor and management? How many of you, as trustees, insist on almost total servitude from your advisors? Since you are the boss, you will decide when they will speak and when they will be heard! How many trustees rely solely on advisors to make decisions for them? Essentially, in this case, plan advisors are asked to go beyond the role for which they were hired and perform the trustees' duties.

Do any of you meet with one advisor at a time? This type of meeting typically occurs in single employer plans and I think it limits the opportunity for better interchange and communication among the disciplines. It allows for gaps in responsibilities or duplication of effort. Meeting together allows one set of marching instructions to be given and less opportunity for misunderstanding.

Finally, regarding communication, there is another common situation in multiemployer funds

Mr. Smart is vice president of DCA, Inc., an actuarial, consulting and administrative firm based in Minneapolis. His responsibilities include advising clients on the design, investment and administration of employee benefit plans. Prior to joining DCA, he directed an extensive study of the Wisconsin State Investment Board, which examined investment policies for the state's public employee pension funds and how the funds could be invested locally without increasing the risk or reducing the return on those investments. Mr. Smart is a graduate of Lawrence University and received his M.B.A. from the University of Idaho. Mr. Smart serves on the International Foundation's Consultants Committee and is a founder and past chairman of the Madison Pension Council. He has addressed numerous groups and written several articles on the subjects of employee benefits and targeting investments.

that has both pluses and minuses. I refer to it as the "Greek god syndrome," where one advisor takes total control of the whole show. Often, this situation is good where there is a particular problem that is the legitimate concern of a particular discipline. However, it can be less than satisfactory when one advisor prevents other advisors from effective interchange with the trustees—when the "Greek god" starts to act as the go-between and interpreter for other advisors.

The Plan Administrator

Note that not every multiemployer plan uses a plan administrator. Sometimes this role is filled by the consultant and sometimes it is performed piecemeal by banks, attorneys, etc. The majority of multiemployer situations, however, do use an administrator and he often is the primary liaison with other professionals. As the primary liaison, he becomes the engineer who keeps the plan on track—the glue that holds all the pieces together.

Working on behalf of the trustees, the plan administrator coordinates each professional's role to assure that all aspects of the plan are run in an efficient and timely manner. He is looked to by the trustees as the source of general knowledge about events that can and do affect the plan. He is the recordkeeper and is expected to collect contributions, pay benefits, generally operate the funds and keep the various accounting records.

Importantly, he is responsible for coordinating the regular trustee meetings. Thus, it is his responsibility to contact the trustees and the plan professionals individually, so that all matters requiring discussion or action are raised in the meeting. It has been my experience that a good deal of the work, decisionmaking and matters facing the trustees can be discussed one on one prior to the meeting, so that "informed consensus" can be achieved at the meeting without unnecessary confrontation.

To perform as the nucleus in the maze of plan responsibilities and personal relationships requires a considerable degree of political skill. The plan administrator must make sure matters are dealt with accurately and efficiently in an air of cooperation vs. contention. The skill with which the plan administrator handles his role will be a direct function of his ability to relate with individual trustees and advisors.

I have witnessed situations in which the professional advisor—be it the plan administrator or someone else—was viewed with suspicion, simply because, philosophically, he was not attuned to the members of the plan he served. One example that comes to mind is the case in which an extremely conservative investment manager agreed to invest pension fund assets emphasizing certain social investments that had strong labor connotations. Philosophically, the investment manager could not have been further away from what he agreed to do. The hypocrisy of the exercise was not lost on the trustees; the investment manager, as a result, faced a considerable uphill battle to be viewed in a credible light. For the plan administrator, the better his feel for the business, the industry and, importantly, the participants themselves, the better he will be at his job.

The Consultant

Some would suggest that the consultant is better qualified to perform many of the tasks attributed previously to the plan administrator. Often, consultants are better qualified and individual roles and responsibilities change from plan to plan, depending on the expertise of various advisors as well as a host of special circumstances that might surround a particular plan.

I view the consultant's role as separate and distinct from that of the plan administrator. Although the plan administrator is primarily a coordinator and recordkeeper, the consultant is a man for all seasons. He is the pre-eminent innovator among the other professionals and, more than any other, he is an initiator rather than a reactor. Most professional advisors have clearly defined roles; however, the consultant's is less so. He needs to be the creative force, the quintessential problem solver in the realm of employee benefits. Thus, he may be called on to perform a multitude of tasks:

- Designing and drafting employee benefit plans
- Assisting in the selection of other professional advisors
- Monitoring investment performance
- Performing special feasibility studies on cost and use of facilities, services, benefits and trends
- Assisting in establishing procedures, training personnel, preparing manuals and administrative rulemaking
- Drafting communication materials for participants
- Negotiating with providers
- Being involved in collective bargaining matters.

Jealousies Among Professionals

Almost every professional has a degree of overlap in the services he provides. This overlap can be the catalyst for certain jealousies among advisors. The consultant works closely with virtually all other advisors and, as a result, probably has more opportunities than most for engaging these jealousies. He is in a position to provide administrative services and indeed may act as plan administrator. Some of the recordkeeping functions he performs might step on the accountant's toes. He often provides actuarial services; involvement in the design and drafting of retirement plans may irritate certain attorneys. If it is possible to distinguish the consultant from other plan advisors, it is in that he is hired more for his ability to provide direction as opposed to specific services.

Jealousies will, however, undoubtedly continue to increase as firms expand their services to protect, if not extend, their perceived markets. This phenomenon is already in evidence as accountants provide a wider range of recordkeeping services, attorneys expand their capabilities in design functions, bank trust departments begin to employ actuaries and so on down the list of plan professionals.

Conclusion

In fulfilling a role, few advisors come cheap and many trustees view a professional advisor as a necessary evil . . . but evil nonetheless. To more than a casual extent, the acceptance and appreciation of an advisor come from his fulfillment of the appointed role in a professional manner. Acceptance, if not appreciation, is an educational process, a process that is the responsibility of that very professional. This presentation began by emphasizing the value of communication. The professional must be a good communicator, but he must also be understood.

The trustee sits in judgment as the elected representative of his peers. Does his election connote omniscience in the field of employee benefits? Of course not; however, the role of the plan professional is to provide that trustee with a sufficient mantle of knowledge to fulfill his fiduciary duty. Events such as the new tax act (TEFRA), the needed revision of Social Security and the changing nature of labor-management relations are but a few of the coming events that will require a professional—that someone with the expertise, imagination and political savvy to meet the challenges of his role.

The Trustees' Duty to Monitor and Evaluate Professional Advisors

BY GEOFFREY V. WHITE

AS THE TITLE of this presentation suggests, one aspect of selection and monitoring advisors concerns the legal framework for delegating responsibilities to professionals in order to limit potential fiduciary liability. I shall discuss this legal framework in the first part of my remarks, although in my opinion it is not the most important aspect.

The Problem: Decisionmaking Procedures

The more important aspect involves the "management techniques," the procedures and controls that you as trustees can use to ensure that fund objectives are accomplished efficiently. The trustees' duties in selecting and monitoring professional advisors are part of the larger problem of establishing these effective decisionmaking procedures. Once those procedures are in place, concerns about legal liability become quite insignificant.

Certainly it is important to delegate fiduciary responsibility to advisors to assure that competent trustees serve without undue risks of liability. But it is not very helpful to design fund decisionmaking procedures on the basis of avoiding liability. There are two reasons. First, ERISA provides that the trustees' duty is to act solely in the interest of the participants and beneficiaries, not to maximize their own protection against liability regardless of efficiency and expense. Second, as a policy matter, a fund decisionmaking structure that is chiefly designed to limit liability leads to overuse of "experts," domination of plan policymaking by advisors and, ultimately, trustees' abdication of their role in establishing fund policy.

A better fund decisionmaking structure will orient you toward efficient administration, not toward escaping liability. Part of efficient administration, in my view, is the use of professionals (a) to assist the trustees in making informed and considered decisions with regard to fund operations, (b) to execute the policies that the trustees establish and (c) to bring problems back to the board with recommended measures to correct and refine those policies.

My approach to evaluating and monitoring ad-

Mr. White is a partner in the San Francisco lawfirm of Davis, Cowell & Bowe, which represents over 35 jointly trusteed labor-management, pension, welfare and apprenticeship funds. A graduate of Stanford University and Boalt Hall School of Law, Mr. White has been responsible primarily for ERISA and MPPAA compliance of the firm's trust fund clients.

visors, then, is to emphasize the use of a systematic decisionmaking procedure, rather than to suggest detailed criteria for particular advisors. If the trustees view decisionmaking as a *process,* and make systematic use of advisors, you will be able to justify and validate your decisions; thus, any liability problems will take care of themselves.

Legal Framework of Delegation

In the court decisions interpreting fiduciary responsibilities under ERISA, it has become increasingly clear that the trustee duty of prudence may require delegation of fiduciary responsibilities to advisors. There are two divergent trends in the decisions interpreting the standard of prudence: One trend uses the standard of a prudent expert; the other holds trustees to the standard of a prudent, experienced trustee. However, both trends may require the use of advisors to avoid trustee liability.

The first trend is the result of Department of Labor efforts to establish a prudent expert standard. For example, where the Department of Labor challenged real estate loans made with plan funds, several courts have held the trustees to a standard of care exercised by a person *in the business* of making such loans. Under this standard, if the trustees are not already experts in real estate transactions, they are effectively required to retain such an expert to avoid potential liability. Typical of this approach is *Donovan v. Mazzola,* 2 EBC 2115 (N.Cal. 1981), which I will discuss in more detail later.

The second trend, and in my opinion the better view of the law, is exemplified by *Fentron Industries, Inc. v. National Shopmen's Pension Fund,* 3 EBC 1323 (9th Cir. 1982). In that case, the court of appeals decided that the trustees could not be held personally liable as fiduciaries for actions in administering the plan that violated other provisions of ERISA. The court held that the fiduciary standards enacted by ERISA conform to those of the Taft-Hartley Act; trustees breach their fiduciary duty only when the action taken was in bad faith, without factual foundation or unsupported by substantial evidence.

This standard, which I have characterized as the experienced trustee standard, also may require the use of advisors where a prudent experienced trustee should know that the advisor could assist substantially in evaluating or executing matters of plan administration. In particular, I suggest that this application is true of the special trustee responsibility for investments and loans of plan assets. It may also be necessary in the areas of claims disputes, plan design, plan tax qualification and reporting and financial controls.

Under either standard of fiduciary responsibility, then, trustees may be required to make use of professional advisors, depending on the size and complexity of the fund, the reasonableness of expenses for such advice and the particular transaction involved. Obviously, the full array of advisors is not necessary for every step of a transaction, but consultation with advisors can be an effective measure in preventing trustee liability and assuring prudent decisionmaking.

If prudence tells you that you should delegate some fiduciary responsibilities to a professional, ERISA establishes the legal framework for doing so. Initially, your plan or trust document must authorize the delegation; trustees have the exclusive authority and responsibility for management and administration of the plan, unless the plan or trust document provides for delegation of these fiduciary responsibilities to others.

The manner of delegation depends on the type of fiduciary responsibility involved. The first type, as I mentioned earlier, is the special trustee responsibility for asset management. Under ERISA, this responsibility may only be delegated to a qualified investment manager who acknowledges fiduciary status in writing. Other fiduciary duties not involving asset management—that is, duties with any discretionary authority in the management or administration of the plan—can be delegated to any person, who then becomes a fiduciary with respect to those duties.

ERISA also permits the trustees to allocate fiduciary responsibilities among committees of trustees. Many of you may already have established such committees to review claims appeals, delinquency collection matters, withdrawal liability cases or plan investments. Not only does it help insulate other trustees from liability, but a committee structure can also enable the trustees to gain specialized experience, which will assist them in monitoring and evaluating the professional advisors involved in these areas.

Once the trustees have delegated a particular fiduciary responsibility, the focus of liability under ERISA shifts. No longer are the trustees liable for errors made by the professional advisor—unless they knowingly have participated in the breach or failed to remedy it. Rather, the trustees will be held liable only if they were imprudent in selecting, monitoring or retaining the advisor.

However, you should note that the trustees cannot escape liability simply by relying on the advice of a consultant or lawyer who would generally not be considered a fiduciary; you will be held legally responsible for your decisions based on that advice. Thus, you need to look just as closely when selecting and evaluating nonfiduciary advisors.

Recent Litigation

Two recent cases illustrate the problems and possible consequences of inadequate or improper use of professional advisors. One such case is the recent trial court decision in *Donovan v. Mazzola,* 2 EBC 2115 (N.Cal. 1981). The Department of Labor alleged that the trustees of a construction industry pension fund had been imprudent by (1) making a $1.5 million loan to a related labor-management convalescent fund operating a resort, (2) making a second $2.25 million loan to a real estate developer to construct a health spa and (3) paying $250,000 to a partner in the health spa venture for a feasibility study concerning development of property owned by the convalescent fund.

On the first charge, the trial court held that the trustees had been imprudent by failing to evaluate and monitor the loan the way a competent real estate lender would have; they failed to act as prudent experts. On the second charge, the trial court said that the trustees imprudently authorized the loan after relying on the developer's inaccurate feasibility study, without an independent review of the architectural plans and marketing prospects. On the third charge, the trial court found that the trustees had agreed to the developer's fee for the study without negotiation or inquiry on similar charges by others, without any bidding procedure and without independent expert advice. The court found that they had as a result paid several times what the study was worth.

In a similar case, *Marshall v. Glaziers Pension Plan,* 2 EBC 1006 (D.HI 1980), the trial court also applied a prudent expert standard in reviewing the trustees' proposed loan of approximately 23% of plan assets for a real estate construction project. The trustees had obtained legal, but not investment, advice about the loan and relied mainly on the developer's information without expert analysis. At the Department of Labor's request, the trial court issued a preliminary injunction against the loan.

There are several problem areas illustrated by these and similar cases. First, as I mentioned earlier, there is the risk that the court will apply the prudent expert standard in evaluating whether trustees have breached their fiduciary duty. Although the better view would be to hold trustees to the standard of a prudent experienced trustee, some courts may be persuaded that a stricter standard is more appropriate in evaluating the special responsibility that trustees have for asset management. As the court stated in the *Glaziers* case,

> While there is flexibility in the prudence standard, it is not a refuge for fiduciaries who are not equipped to evaluate a complex investment. If fiduciaries commit a pension plan's assets to investments which they do not fully understand, they will nonetheless be judged, as provided in the statute, according to the standards of others "acting in a like capacity and familiar with such matters."

Secondly, inadequate investigation by trustees, without independent professional advice and a review of alternatives, can be factors in establishing trustee imprudence if the transaction goes awry. This situation may be especially true if the trustees have failed to use a bidding procedure, with full analysis of written proposals and arm's length negotiation of fees.

Finally, after the transaction is under way, the trustees continue to be liable for a failure to monitor its progress and the application of plan funds by periodic reporting and financial controls.

Phases of Trustee Monitoring and Evaluation

Trustee monitoring and evaluation of professional advisors is a continuing process, which should be made an integral part of your plan's administrative structure. The essential phases of this process concern the selection, supervision and periodic performance evaluation of advisors.

The initial step, of course, in selecting advisors is to evaluate the needs of the plan and the capabilities of the various professionals. For example, a qualified independent accountant is required under ERISA to perform an annual audit of your plan. However, an accountant may also be important in performing a payroll audit to confirm that contributions are being properly paid, or a claims audit to monitor performance of your professional administrator. Similarly, an enrolled actuary is required under ERISA to perform the valuation for your pension plan, but the actuary can also assist you in plan design or, for self-funded welfare plans, in establishing the necessary level of reserves.

Professional consultants may be useful not only for specific transactions, such as developing a computer system or evaluating a new dental service plan, but also generally in plan design, negotiations with insurance companies and in the bidding and selection procedure for other advisors.

A lawyer is obviously an indispensable part of your plan's administrative structure! Naturally a lawyer is important in litigation, but is perhaps more important in preventing litigation: in resolving claims appeals and in negotiating and drafting contracts with service providers. As the cases I mentioned indicate, there may be serious dangers in simply accepting contracts proffered by service providers without such independent review. Lawyers may also be necessary, in cooperation with the plan actuary or consultant, in plan design, in preparation of the plan and trust documents and in tax qualification.

Once you have evaluated the plan's needs, you should consider whether to use bidding procedures to select an advisor. Bidding may not be required when the transaction is minor and the fees for services are small. But bidding procedures may be a critical part of the process of decision-making. It is often a mistake to rely on friendships with a particular service provider without testing the market by soliciting bids and negotiating an arm's length written agreement for services. The bidding procedure should also require disclosure of any relationships that the bidder may have to any trustees, other fund service providers or parties in interest. Full disclosure will help to eliminate conflicts of interest, possible prohibited transactions and any improper influence in the selection of professional advisors.

If you do solicit bids for a service contract, I suggest that you use written specifications, preferably prepared by your consultant or administrator. This procedure gives all of the bidders comprehensive data on the plan, helps to eliminate any inside information that one bidder may otherwise obtain and assures an adequate basis to compare the responses. The bid responses should also be in writing, to allow you to compare the details of the proposals and to serve as the basis for a later written contract.

Interviews with the bidders are often a helpful means of evaluation. Written responses can give you information about the fees and services proposed, but other factors cannot be evaluated without face-to-face communication. Professional services are personal in nature, and often the quality and effectiveness depend on the individuals involved. An interview procedure enables you to have some basis for comparing the experience, candor, reputation and personal philosophy of the professional advisors you are considering.

Regardless of the type of advisor you select, a written agreement can be very important, both from a legal standpoint and as a management device in evaluating and monitoring the advisor. From a legal point of view, ERISA provides that *all* payments to service providers are a prohibited transaction, except where trustees have contracted or made reasonable arrangements for necessary services and paid only reasonable compensation. This viewpoint implies that trustees should use a written contract for services wherever practicable. To show you that written agreements need not necessarily be long and detailed, I have included in Appendix A an accountant's engagement letter that is only a page and a half long. However, it does contain all the essential elements of the agreement, including detailed provisions for fees, coordination with other advisors, expected completion of the project and the final reports required. Lawyers' retainer agreements may be even shorter.

More importantly, a written agreement provides a clear statement of the duties and responsibilities of the trustees and the advisor, with benchmarks to evaluate the advisor's performance and guidelines for the advisor in planning and organizing services. The contract also establishes essential controls over such matters as fees, subcontracting or assignment of duties, reporting requirements and termination of services.

You should consider closely the structure of the contract's fee arrangement. Very often, contracts for administrative services will provide for payment of a flat dollar fee per month for all services. Such a fee structure may build in a conflict of interest, because any reduction in services directly operates to increase profits, and reports to the trustees may not be adequate to monitor the level of services. A variation of this fee structure may reimburse the contract administrator for direct charges and overhead, plus a fixed management fee. Under this arrangement, however, it is difficult to evaluate the reasonableness of charges for overhead and other indirect costs without an independent audit.

The approach I prefer is to reimburse the contract administrator for all direct charges, plus a fixed management fee that covers overhead *and* profit. This arrangement provides no incentive to reduce services, since these costs are fully reimbursed after a detailed report of all direct charges, and profit and overhead costs to the fund are fixed for the contract term.

A written contract can also establish important controls on fees for brokers and consultants. Even though Department of Labor regulations permit brokers/consultants to receive commissions for plan services, provided they make full written disclosure of the relationship, disclosure does not fully resolve the inherent conflict of interest. Increasingly, plans are attempting to control the fees paid to their advisors directly, either by requiring brokers to waive commissions and agree to a fixed fee paid by the trustees or requiring them to offset fees paid against commissions.

Your professional services contract can establish other important controls, depending on the particular transaction or advisor. Your investment management contract, for example, could contain not only a fee schedule, but also negotiated commissions for the manager's broker, as well as limitations on "soft dollar" research services provided by the broker. A contract can provide explicit standards of performance, such as acknowledgment of fiduciary status. It may contain requirements for reports and periodic review of performance. In addition, it should contain provisions for termination on short notice without penalty, for compliance with bonding and fiduciary liability insurance requirements, against assignment or subcontracting of services, for disclosures such as those required by Prohibited Transaction Exemption 77-9 and for ownership of materials or computer programs.

In short, a written agreement can provide

benchmarks, reports and procedures for review of the relationship with the advisor and can be essential in assigning responsibility for any problems that may develop.

Supervision

The trustees' supervisory responsibilities in monitoring professional advisors begin with establishing the governing fund policies. These policies are the "navigation aids" for both the board and staff, many of which are required by ERISA. You undoubtedly have a trust agreement and plan document or insurance policy, which establish the duties of the trustees and the eligibility and benefit rules for participants. You also have established a funding policy and investment guidelines for the investment manager and actuary. You probably also have procedures and guidelines for claims appeals, delinquency collections and review and arbitration of withdrawal liability, as well as an administrative policy manual that compiles other trustee decisions and resolutions. Only on the basis of these governing fund policies can the board and its advisors make consistent judgments concerning plan operations.

Within these governing fund policies, the trustees also need to establish systematic decisionmaking procedures. Such a procedure, in my view, has several distinct elements: the presentation of alternatives, a review of recommendations, the exercise of trustee judgment, detailed steps for implementation and regular reporting. I shall discuss each element in turn.

Alternatives

For trustees to control the decisionmaking process, it is essential that all information on alternatives be presented by the professional staff. If the board is presented with only two alternatives, one clearly correct and one impossible or implausible, then staff has made the decision simply by the manner in which the alternatives are presented. By requiring all alternatives to be presented, the board assures that it can consider the full range of options available.

Review of Recommendations

Advisors' recommendations also should not be accepted at face value. You should review the facts, methodology and alternatives discussed in their reports. You may also require status reports to be presented in a format established by the board itself. For example, in the sample investment management report included in Appendix B, you can see that the trustees of that particular fund did not simply accept the data presented by the investment manager, but instead tabulated all essential information on investment performance according to their own format. This format compares the investment manager's performance with the investment return that would have been received from a "risk free" investment over a similar period and computes the net yield on investments after deduction for investment management fees and commissions. As the courts have indicated, you should insist on sufficient information to understand the details of any substantial transaction and the available options. There is no such thing as a "dumb" question from a trustee: You properly demand that your advisors be able to explain and justify their recommendations to your satisfaction.

Although you should compare any recommendations with the fund objectives and policies to assure consistency and fairness, you should also apply your own judgment in making the final decision, recognizing that it is your experience and familiarity with the plan and the industry that are being asked for. It can be just as valid in determining the merits of a proposal as your advisors' expertise.

I hope that you will not stop at that point, but will go on to detail the steps necessary for implementation of your decision. As an advisor, I am uncomfortable with a general direction from a board of trustees to "take all steps necessary" to accomplish the particular objective. It fails to define my responsibility and the measures I am authorized to take. Part of the duty of trustees is to coordinate advisors and establish areas of responsibility in implementing the board's decisions. In addition, a plan of implementation will assure that the board thinks through the problem fully before committing substantial assets to a project and dedicates the resources necessary to achieving the objective desired.

Finally, the board must monitor the implementation of its directives. It is not enough to simply inquire at the regular trustee meeting, under the agenda item "other business," how things are going with the fund staff. The agenda is a terrific control device. The board should use this device to assure that decisions and problems are followed on a continuing basis; it should not let staff decide when items may be presented to the board. Your plan of implementation could also include specific reporting requirements by staff.

The professional administrator should assist the trustees in coordinating and monitoring the implementation of decisions. One method of doing so is for the administrator to send a memo to all staff summarizing the decisions taken at the prior trustee meeting and assigning responsibilities to staff for a report at the next trustee meeting. This procedure can help prevent staff misperceptions of trustee directives and the consequent failure to coordinate tasks.

Periodic Performance Evaluation

This area is always difficult for both advisors and trustees. The trustees may assume that their advisors are competent because they have a professional degree or that trustees without such a degree are unqualified to judge. A professional degree, however, is only one predictor of an advisor's ability to serve your fund; especially in the area of Taft-Hartley trusts, the advisor's experience is probably the best indicator of adequate performance. Trustees who are similarly experienced will therefore gain the ability to judge the qualifications and performance of their advisors.

The prerequisite for proper evaluation of professional staff is effective communication. Many times, trustees' rating of advisors is informal or confined to offhand comments away from the board meetings. The criteria for evaluation may be unspoken and thus different for each trustee. The result often is that trustees form a subjective judgment of a particular advisor based on "style" or personality, to the exclusion of objective factors based on the advisor's performance.

Informal evaluations also result in the advisor receiving inadequate feedback from the trustees on performance, with a consequent inability to confront problems, criticisms and rumors. The advisor may even be ignorant of problems and thus will make no effort to correct them.

Rather than grumbling informally about an advisor's performance, I hope you will be direct. If you confront the advisor with criticisms, both positive and negative, that are based on objective factors of performance, I believe you will find the advisor quick to correct mistakes and change the methods you find unsatisfactory. The advisor's ability to do so should be an important factor in your evaluation. Even matters as sensitive as professional fees can be resolved by approaching the matter directly. Believe it or not, the advisor may be most aware of ways in which professional services can be performed more economically or efficiently, once told of your requirements. Moreover, a direct approach to criticism and evaluation allows the advisor an opportunity to correct trustees' misperceptions and assures accuracy and fairness in your evaluation.

Direct performance review, however, requires methods of evaluation that avoid the appearance of an advisor being called on the carpet where this action is unwarranted. One such method is to establish regular periodic reviews for each advisor. I am not suggesting a laborious checklist approach, such as the kind used in standard personnel evaluations. What I am suggesting is the use of something like a management letter or annual report to the board from each advisor. This letter should be a brief report on the prior year's objectives relating to that advisor, any problems the advisor encountered in achieving those objectives and the advisor's recommendations or projections for the following year. Such a management letter or annual report by each advisor could be presented to the full board or reviewed by an executive committee of trustees to facilitate communication.

Some such reports are already familiar to you. Your investment manager will present at least an annual review of investment performance as part of the trustees' evaluation of the plan's funding policy. Similarly, your auditor may provide you with an annual management letter as part of your review of the fund's recordkeeping and financial controls.

It may be more difficult to establish regular review procedures with your plan consultant, actuary or lawyer, but such a "management letter" could be required as part of the regular contract renewal—or you could simply expand an existing report. Your lawyer, for example, already writes an annual letter to your fund accountant summarizing any material matters of litigation or claims against the fund that would affect its financial report. This kind of letter could be expanded to include not only current litigation, but also other legal problems such as compliance with new recordkeeping or reporting requirements, establishment of withdrawal liability procedures or patterns of claims appeals that indicate a need to modify the plan.

Other professional staff can also assist the trustees in evaluating an advisor's performance, just as they are useful in the bidding procedures for initial selection of staff. Again, I am not suggesting that advisors fill out checklists about each other. However, the board may properly consult with staff about problems that concern an advisor, especially where staff were involved in efforts to correct the problem before it reached the board level.

Generally speaking, professional advisors will help set goals for staff and coordinate their work to attain those goals; advisors help to ensure performance, rather than to formally evaluate other staff.

Nevertheless, where problems in an advisor's performance do arise, other staff may have to be involved in the monitoring process. Initially, staff will raise problems directly with the advisor for correction. If errors continue, or prevent other staff from doing their own job, advisors may be legally obligated as fiduciaries to bring the problems to the board of trustees to seek the board's authority in resolving the matter.

Certainly there is a possible conflict of interest in having staff participate in the evaluation process, where advisors may have other business relationships with each other that could detract from their loyalty and undivided fiduciary obligations to the trustees. I suggest, however, that the "management letter" approach, combined with consultation as needed with all staff, can help to minimize any such conflict by systematic reporting and disclosure of problems periodically.

Conclusion

I hope that some of the evaluation procedures and monitoring devices that I have suggested can help you make systematic use of advisors to improve your own decisionmaking as trustees. Once established, these procedures should help you handle the most complex transactions as trustees of prudence and experience.

Appendix A

ACCOUNTANT ENGAGEMENT LETTER[1]

Board of Trustees

Gentlemen:

In this letter we are setting forth our understanding of the arrangements that have been agreed upon for an examination of the financial statements of the _____ Fund as of and for the year ending _____, 19___.

We will examine the fund's financial statements and issue our report thereon as soon as reasonably possible after completion of our work. Our examination will be made in accordance with generally accepted auditing standards and will include such tests of the accounting records and such other auditing procedures as we consider necessary in the circumstances.

The objective of an audit examination is to form an opinion on whether the financial statements present fairly the financial position, results of operations and changes in financial position in conformity with generally accepted accounting principles consistently applied. Although an audit examination is planned to search for material errors or irregularities, their discovery cannot be assured because of inherent limitations in the auditing process.

We will also prepare the related Form 5500 and federal and state annual information returns for nonprofit organizations (Forms 990 and 199) required to be filed by the fund for the year stated above.

We understand that Mr. _____ and members of the accounting department staff will assist us to the extent practicable. They will provide us with detailed trial balances, supporting schedules and other information we deem necessary. A list of these schedules and other items of information will be furnished to him shortly after we begin our examination.

Our fee will be based upon the time required to complete the engagement, computed at the hourly rates specified in our letter to co-consultants dated _____, which rates ranged from a low of $18 per hour for clerical personnel to a high of $80 per hour for partners, but in any event will not exceed $18,500.

In addition, we would expect to be reimbursed for any out-of-pocket expenses incurred. Progress billings will be submitted biweekly as the work progresses and will be payable upon presentation.

We are pleased to have this opportunity to serve you.

If this letter correctly expresses your understanding of the terms of our engagement, please sign the enclosed copy where indicated and return it to us.

Sincerely,

_____

APPROVED:

By: _____   Title: _____   Date: _____

By: _____   Title: _____   Date: _____

---

1. This document is included for illustrative purposes only. It is not intended to be a model legal document.

Appendix B

FINANCIAL SUMMARY[1]
(Month Ending 7/30/82)

Investment Manager _____

1. Performance

		Month Ending 7/30/82	12/31/81 to date	Inception to date
a.	Beginning balance (market)	$39,226,832	$36,783,975	$34,609,412
b.	Total income received	204,570	2,609,621	10,898,152
	Dividends $ _____			
	Interest $204,570			
c.	Net contributions			
d.	Gain/(loss) in principal	1,173,913	1,211,719	(4,902,249)
	Ending balance (market)	$40,605,315	$40,605,315	$40,605,315
	Ending balance (cost)	$44,955,650	$44,955,650	$44,955,650

2. Fund management costs

   a. Pension trust fund cost

Commissions[2]		$ _____	$ _____	$ _____
Investment management fee		_____	24,674	_____
Total costs		$ _____	$ 24,674	$ _____

3. Portfolio return—actual % vs. standard %

   A. Actual % portfolio return

		6/30/82- 7/30/82	12/31/81 to date	Inception to date
1.	Income % return[3]	0.52%	7.09%	31.49 %
2.	Portfolio % return[4]	2.99%	3.29%	(14.16)%
	Total actual % return	3.51%	10.39%	17.33 %

   B. Portfolio % return standard—(Risk free return plus 100 basis points annually)

		6/30/82- 7/30/82	12/31/81 to date	Inception to date
1.	Three month Treasury bill[5] rate—average of monthly close	0.88%	7.11%	36.01%
2.	Risk adjustment factor— (100 basis points annually, i.e., 1.0%, or 0.25% per quarter)	0.08%	0.58%	2.83%
	Total portfolio return standard	0.96%	7.69%	38.84%

---

1. This document is included for illustrative purposes only. It is not intended to be a model legal document.
2. Actual commission paid plus net trade charge = (Cost of transaction as charged by broker, i.e., ⅛)
3. From Item No. 1=(b÷a)
4. From Item No. 1=(d÷a)
5. Quarter, year to date and inception to date data from *U.S. Financial Data—Federal Reserve Bank of St. Louis.*

The Board of Trustees and Its Counsel: A Question of Professional Responsibility

BY BERNARD M. BAUM

THE LAWYER WHO is asked to represent a multiemployer trust fund has myriad and serious responsibilities. Since the advent of ERISA, the role of fund counsel has been performed within the context of a new set of statutory and regulatory provisions. ERISA raised a number of interesting questions concerning the role of the lawyer. For example, some asked if counsel were a fiduciary. Although lawyers as a general rule responded with a loud "no," there were some who answered that question by saying that it depends on the activity of counsel. However, we will concentrate on those ethical and legal questions that fall under the aegis of counsel's professional responsibility in representing an employee benefit fund whose board of trustees is equally divided between management and labor trustees. We must begin with some fundamental questions.

Whom does counsel represent? From a legal point of view this question is simple to answer—the board of trustees. Rule 113 of the proposed model rules of professional conduct, which are awaiting approval by the American Bar Association, contains a section entitled "Organization as the Client" and states, in part: "A lawyer employed or retained to represent an organization represents the organization as distinct from its . . . officers, employees, members, or other constituencies."

However, before we discuss the application of this rule and possible conflicts of interest, let us review the primary functions of fund counsel. For simplification, fund counsel's role is generally divided into the following categories:
- Legal advisor
- Litigator.

Legal Advisor

In the first posture, as a legal advisor, counsel's role is quite broad. Counsel must advise the trustees of the requirements of applicable law, e.g., ERISA, LMRA and other federal or state laws. He or she is required to render legal opinions concerning many problems. Counsel is required to be present at meetings of the trustees and their committees. It is important for counsel to remember that he or she is not the plan consultant nor the investment manager. Counsel should also keep in mind that he or she is not a trustee.

Mr. Baum is a director of Baum, Sigman and Gold, Ltd., a Chicago lawfirm engaged primarily in the practice of labor-management and fringe benefit fund law. He has over 20 years' experience representing jointly trusteed plans, primarily in the building and construction industry. He is counsel for numerous multiemployer fringe benefit funds. Active in state and national bar associations, Mr. Baum is also an arbitrator and has decided numerous fringe benefit fund and labor-management disputes. He has written articles for the Chicago Bar Record *and the International Foundation* Digest *and has given presentations at several International Foundation meetings.*

Litigator

As a litigator, counsel's role breaks down into offense and defense.

Offense

Counsel must vigorously pursue and protect the legal rights of trustees. Counsel is often required, for example, to sue employers who are delinquent in the payment of fringe benefit contributions. Counsel may also be asked to sue plan participants who have been overpaid or who are guilty of making fraudulent claims. In addition, counsel may have to sue former plan employees or even individual trustees on behalf of the board of trustees where there is a question of whether these individuals have violated their fiduciary duty or committed some other unlawful or wrongful act.

Defense

Defensively, counsel may be required to defend the board of trustees against suits brought by unhappy participants whose claims have not been paid in part or in whole, or where there is a claim that an action of the board is contrary to plan documents or applicable law. Counsel may also be called on to defend the board of trustees against claims of a government agency that the trustees violated an applicable law. In those situations, there is a clear potential for conflicts of interest that could interfere with counsel's ability to perform his or her primary role of legal advisor or litigator.

Conflicts of Interest

There are those delicate problems that arise between the board of trustees and an individual trustee. For example, counsel may discover that an individual trustee has acted in a manner which is contrary to the interest of the trust fund or has violated his or her fiduciary duties. Does counsel have a duty to report such acts to the board of trustees? Paragraph 1.13 of the proposed model rules provides:

> If a lawyer for an organization knows that an officer, employee, or other person associated with the organization is engaged in action, intends to act, or refuses to act in a matter related to the representation that is a violation of a legal obligation to the organization, or a violation of law which reasonably might be imputed to the organization, and is likely to result in substantial injury to the organization, the lawyer shall proceed as is reasonably necessary in the best interest of the organization.

The rule then continues:

> In determining how to proceed, the lawyer shall give due consideration to the seriousness of the violation and its consequences, the scope and nature of the lawyer's representation, the responsibility in the organization, and the apparent motivation of the person involved, the policies of the organizations concerning such matters, and any other relevant considerations. . . . Any measures taken shall be designed to minimize disruption of the organization and the risk of revealing information relating to the representation to persons outside the organization.

In the case of actual "knowledge," it seems clear that the rule requires that counsel immediately advise the board of trustees. But, as in criminal law, actual knowledge is not so easily defined—nor is counsel's ultimate responsibility in such a situation.

There are many other instances in which possible conflicts of interest could arise. For example, assume that the board of trustees has an active delinquency program. In the course of enforcement of such a program, counsel is required to sue an employer who is also a client. The proposed rule clearly prohibits the representation of parties in contentious litigation whose rights and obligations are materially adverse. Rule 1.7 states, in part:

> RULE 1.7 Conflict of Interest: General Rule
> (a) A lawyer shall not represent a client if the lawyer's ability to consider, recommend or carry out a course of action on behalf of the client will be adversely affected by the lawyer's responsibilities to another client or to a third person, or by the lawyer's own interests.

Complicating the problem, assume that counsel who is engaged in the recovery of delinquent employer contributions for Fund A also represents Funds B and C. All three funds are maintaining simultaneous actions against the same employer for the recovery of contributions. The first question the counsel must answer is whether the representation of the three separate funds against the same defendant establishes a situation where their individual interests are materially adverse. If the employer's assets are sufficient to pay the claims of each fund, the possible conflict is substantially reduced, if not eliminated. The difficulty arises where there are insufficient funds to pay all such claims.

What happens when counsel, in representing Fund A in a delinquency action, gains knowledge that is important to Funds B and C, but may potentially be adverse to Fund A? In this case, let us assume counsel knows that the delinquent employer has limited resources and that unless he notifies Funds B and C immediately, Fund A will obtain a total recovery and other clients will recover nothing. Rule 1.7(b) of the model rules provides:

> When a lawyer's own interests or other responsibilities might adversely affect the representation of a client, the lawyer shall not represent the client unless:
> (1) the lawyer reasonably believes the other responsibilities or interests involved will not adversely affect the best interest of the client; and

(2) the client consents after disclosure. When representation of multiple clients in a single matter is undertaken, the disclosure shall include explanation of the implications of the common representation and the advantages and risks involved.

Rule 1.8(b) also establishes as one of the model rules a "prohibited transaction" that a lawyer shall not use information relating to the representation of a client to the disadvantage of a client unless the client consents after disclosure. Obviously, the application of these rules depends on the facts of a given case.

Another possible conflict may occur when the Department of Labor or other governmental agency is investigating a board of trustees for possible violations of ERISA. It is generally part of the "audit" or investigative procedure of the Department of Labor to request interviews with one or more of the trustees. Counsel may be placed in a very delicate position depending on the nature of the investigation. The difficulty arises because the Department of Labor may conclude that an individual trustee has engaged in a prohibited transaction, but not the board of trustees. In that case the individual trustee and the board of trustees are placed in adverse positions.

The safest policy for fund counsel has been to suggest to an individual trustee that he or she retain separate counsel who will advise as to the trustee's rights and obligations concerning such an interview. Patently, in the event an action is brought by an agency against a trustee, counsel for the board will not be able to provide representation, so counsel has the obligation to the individual trustee to advise him or her of the propriety of retaining separate legal counsel during the investigation.

Counsel also confronts a clear conflict of interest where there is a voting deadlock among the board of trustees. Section 302 of the Labor-Management Relations Act, as amended, provides that in the event there is a deadlock between employer and employee trustees, the separate groups are to select an impartial umpire to resolve the issues or an umpire will be appointed by the federal district court in the event the board cannot agree to select one.

These "deadlocks" are becoming more prevalent because of disputes between management and labor trustees over an increase in pension benefits and the effect on unfunded vested benefit liability. It is clear from the model rules that when such a dispute arises, counsel for the board of trustees cannot represent either group. Accordingly, when the deadlock occurs, it is incumbent upon counsel to advise the whole board, and each group, to retain separate counsel. In my experience, counsel must maintain an evenhanded approach; participation must be limited to providing each group with any evidence or documentation that is in the control of the board of trustees.

Example

The professional minefield that constantly confronts a lawyer who has a separate professional relationship with either a related employee or employer organization was highlighted in the recent arbitration decision involving the *Allied Food Workers Health and Welfare Fund.* In that case, there was a deadlock between employer and employee trustees over the retention of legal counsel who was also counsel for the union. The employer trustees sought to replace the fund counsel, arguing that the out-of-state attorney was costing the fund too much money. The arbitrator ruled that the attorney who also represented the union had to be replaced, even if it were necessary to look outside the geographical area. The arbitrator held that even though there was "absolutely no evidence" to suggest that the counsel ever used his position to influence a more favorable condition for the union, the potential for distrust of counsel's advice or a potential conflict of interest was sufficient to authorize counsel's termination.

The arbitrator's comments, in my opinion, were not warranted in light of the fact that the employer trustees never raised any questions concerning counsel's ability to represent the entire board adequately, but sought his termination solely on the ground of saving money by retaining local counsel. Since there was no issue of conflict of interest, the arbitrator appears to have exceeded his authority by basing his decision on a so-called potential that was not at issue.

The fact is that many multiemployer funds are represented by a lawyer who has a professional relationship with related employee or employer organizations. Yet, we very seldom hear of any dispute based on a real conflict of interest. The reason is simple; in most cases competent counsel will anticipate such a conflict and will take appropriate action to avoid the problem when it does occur. The arbitrator's decision in *Allied Food Workers Health and Welfare Fund* also assumes that counsel will not abide by the rules of the legal profession and will jeopardize his or her ability to continue practicing law.

Conclusion

Suffice it to say, counsel's ultimate professional and ethical responsibility is to the board of trustees. Any time counsel confronts a situation that establishes a potential or actual conflict of interest, he or she must act consistently with the rules governing the practice of law. The fact that so few disputes have arisen regarding representation by counsel in conflict-of-interest situations is the best evidence that the rules governing the practice of law are working and that they provide the required protection to the client—the board of trustees.

You and Your Investment Manager

BY GARY P. BRINSON, CFA

THERE IS PROBABLY no element of more vital importance to your success in the investment markets than *the nature of the relationship between you and your investment manager.* I want to share with you my thoughts from the perspective of an investment manager involved with client relationships for over 15 years.

When appropriately positioned, the nature of the client/investment manager relationship should be similar to that of any professional relationship such as the one you would have with a lawyer or doctor. The actions, qualifications and "language" of the investment professional are rigorous, demanding and at times complex. Therefore, as with a doctor, lawyer or accountant, you should carefully understand the advice and recommendations of your investment manager and ensure that they are implemented in a fashion designed to meet your objectives.

The best way to view the nature of the relationship with your investment manager is to keep in mind this profession's similarities to those of law and medicine while noting the similarities of this job to those that emphasize action and results—coaching football, for example. "Monday morning quarterbacking" is as prevalent in investment management as it is in football. But the focus must be on a review of the total game plan and not on short term results and random patterns of good or bad luck.

Defining the Playing Field

The first step in establishing your relationship with your investment manager is to define your

Mr. Brinson is senior vice president and chief investment officer in the Personal Banking and Trust Department of The First National Bank of Chicago. Mr. Brinson joined The First National Bank of Chicago in July 1979 as chief investment officer of the Trust Department. He had formerly served as president and chief operating officer of Travelers Investment Management Company in Hartford, Connecticut. He has made periodic contributions to investment journals and is a frequent lecturer at universities and professional investment forums. He received a B.A. degree in finance and accounting from Seattle University and an M.B.A. degree in finance from Washington State University. He is a chartered financial analyst and a member of the Chicago Society of Financial Analysts, American Finance Association, Financial Analysts Federation and the International Foundation's Corporate Investment Policy Guidebook–Ad Hoc Committee. He has participated in previous Foundation educational programs.

Figure 1

```
        ┌──────────────┐
        │  Investment  │
        │    Policy    │
        └──────────────┘
               ▲
       ┌───────┴───────┐
┌──────────────┐  ┌──────────────┐
│  Investment  │  │ Organization's│
│   Markets    │  │     Goals    │
└──────────────┘  └──────────────┘
```

goals clearly and then, working with the investment manager, explicitly set out your investment policy (Figure 1). Aspects of investment policy that should be considered are:
- Total return expectations
- Risk tolerances: portfolio
- Liquidity needs
- Income preferences
- Time horizon.

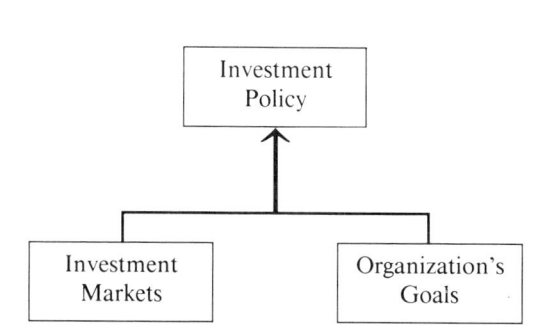

The next step is to install the structure for implementing that policy. In this regard, the client should determine what the investment management structure looks like and how it should function. In addition, the client must carefully specify who is going to make what decisions regarding asset areas eligible, asset allocation and asset selection.

When selecting a manager(s) you, as a client, should view the "opportunity set" of investment managers in terms of their personal style and characteristics. If you put together a multiple manager structure, pay close attention to how the styles of the individual managers fit together in an integrated "portfolio" of people and characteristics geared to your policy goals.

In that regard, it is critical that you avoid the fragmentation that results from a narrow focus on specialization. Total portfolio performance is a result of:
- Asset classes included and excluded
- Asset weights: policy and strategy
- Performance of markets
- Performance of individual managers.

On a long term basis, the vast majority of total return is determined by asset class selection and allocation. The performance of individual managers is not a large contributor. Overall, you should be sure to define who has control of the total portfolio and where the core management is positioned.

The next step after establishing the parameters of the general investment structure is to determine the specific policy statement for each manager. These individual policy statements will be derived from the overall policy statement for the total asset pool. All individual policy statements when summed across all managers should equal the overall policy. The goal is to ensure that the individual managers act in a manner consistent with the policy established for the entire pool of assets and to avoid having the actions of the individual managers determine the general policy.

Once policies have been established on both a "macro" and "micro" level, it is necessary to develop a benchmark portfolio. The key aspects of a benchmark portfolio are:
- Explicit representation of policy
- Passive
- Baseline for actual results.

A review of the roles of investment policy and the benchmark portfolio concept in the investment management process are seen in Figure 2.

Relationship Dynamics

In determining the dynamics of the relationship, clients must decide how active they or their consultants will be in terms of reviewing and monitoring the investment manager. This issue is important and should be resolved by a conscious decision. Such a decision can be the source of problems leading to poor performance; it also can contribute greatly to the future success of your investment performance. Traps to avoid are:

Figure 2

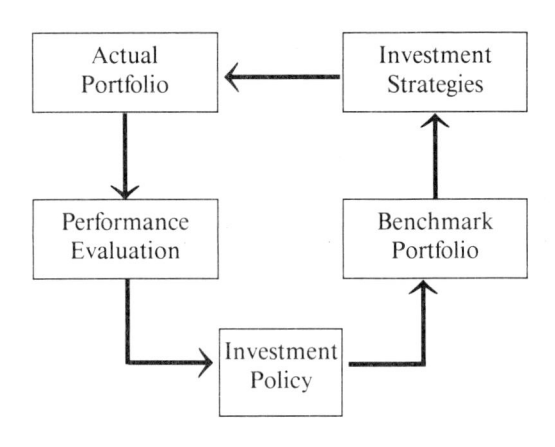

Actual Portfolio ← Investment Strategies
↓ ↑
Performance Evaluation → Benchmark Portfolio
↓ ↑
→ Investment Policy →

- Overemphasis on *short term* results
- Overemphasis on data and analysis
- Unsuitable to manager style
- Belief that past foretells future
- The rearview mirror syndrome.

A good way to monitor and stay in constructive communication with your investment manager is to review the portfolio periodically *relative* to the policy benchmark and to gain an understanding of where and why strategic deviations exist.

Monitoring Your Managers

To monitor your manager effectively, one of the first steps is to understand the critical components of the manager's organization:
- People
- Philosophy
- Decisionmaking process.

The "bottom line," so to speak, is of course performance results. The best structure for monitoring the performance of your manager effectively begins with establishing a benchmark for overall aspects of the portfolio, as discussed previously. Once the benchmark is established, the appropriate passive standard needs to be determined. Finally, the active manager comparison needs to be established.

Conclusion

It is important to summarize the main points I covered:
- The *human* relationship is the key. Trust your judgment, ride with it and beware of too many statistics on results or of casual interpretation of those statistics.
- Define a logical and workable playing field.

Remember, you set the policy; the manager implements it.
- Define performance benchmarks.
- Don't try to "overcontrol" investment management.

Investments is not a field suited to production line standards. It is a subtle professional challenge to let the relationship between you and your investment manager blossom in the fertile field of trust and understanding.

Evaluating Your Investment Manager

BY BONNIE R. COHEN

ESTABLISHING THE APPROPRIATE relationship with outside managers is an important part of the successful management of the investment process. Most of the pension literature focuses on subjects such as:
- Fiduciary responsibility
- Establishing investment goals
- The asset allocation mix.

Unfortunately, the problems with managers tend more often to be the less theoretical ones of miscommunication, misinterpretation and misunderstanding of expectations.

I know. I served as treasurer of a large pension fund with seven outside managers, as investment advisor to a large university endowment and currently as vice president for finance at a nonprofit institution with three outside managers. I know what it feels like to hire a stock manager and see the portfolio six months later 50% in cash while the market climbs 100 points, or see the portfolio 100% in cash as interest rates drop.

Managing managers is more than giving them money, receiving quarterly performance reports and paying high fees. Each year funds pay millions of dollars in investment fees. All too often what they pay for is inappropriate investment strategies, market tracking or poor rates of return.

To reduce conflict and disappointment, the administrators and trustees of pension plans must establish, from the beginning, strong, open communications with investment managers. Based on my experience, I will concentrate on steps I think can be taken to accomplish this goal. These steps may not assure your fund better-than-average performance; I can't guarantee that any more than your managers can, although they may promise it. However, improved communication will help to obtain each manager's best performance, and importantly, I think, permit you to limit the fund's losses. The basic steps which I plan to discuss are:
- Self-assessment
- A clear set of basic assumptions
- Routine manager monitoring that goes beyond performance tracking
- Carefully structured review meeting agendas.

Ms. Cohen, as vice president of finance and administration for the National Trust for Historic Preservation, is primarily responsible for the oversight of endowment investment strategy, as well as for outside investment managers and an operating budget of $15 million. Prior to joining her present organization, she was investment advisor for Stanford University Endowment and, prior to that, she served as treasurer for the United Mine Workers of America Funds. Ms. Cohen earned her B.A. degree in political science at Smith College, her Ed.M. degree at the Harvard Graduate School of Education and her M.B.A. degree at the Harvard Graduate School of Administration. She has previously spoken before the Institutional Investor Bond Conference Pension Roundtable.

Self-Assessment

There are three groups of players involved in the successful management of money—managers, plan administrators and trustees.

As trustees or administrators, too few of us stop and ask ourselves what we can and cannot do on our jobs, what skills and knowledge we do and do not have—in this case, what we do and do not know about investing, what we bring to the task and the kind and amount of outside help we will need. There is a *minimum* amount of knowledge we must, by definition, possess to do our jobs: We must know and understand what it means to be a fiduciary, must hold the interest of the beneficiaries paramount and must recognize and avoid conflict-of-interest situations.

Beyond that, as we assess our strengths, we must remember to begin with a critical appraisal

of the trustees. Trustees are too often neglected in our analysis. To the administrators, they're the named fiduciaries—it's their neck first; to the investment managers, too often they're viewed solely as the audience for slick slide shows. But what has their appointment brought to the plan and the investment process? Is it:
- Knowledge of the industry?
- Experience with the company and its markets?
- Familiarity with the beneficiary population?
- A background in investments?
- Legal expertise?
- Attitudes toward: risk? receiving information?
- Availability?

The trustees' knowledge of the beneficiaries and tolerance for credit and market risk will have an important impact on their relationship with a money manager. For example, trustees who are uncomfortable with illiquidity may never totally accept a real estate manager. Trustees who see themselves serving a mature, nearly retired population may have little tolerance for market volatility, regardless of theoretical arguments about long term rates of return.

Next, as an administrator, ask yourself and your staff the same questions. Determine how much time you have available to manage the funds and what experience and knowledge you bring to the job. Is this a full-time job or not? I have worked in situations with in-house professional staffs of five or six people devoted solely to the investment process; I also have worked in situations where there is no one on staff who is overseeing the investments on a full-time basis. This assessment allows you to determine how much and what kind of outside help you will need.

Too often in measuring our value, whether we are administrators or trustees, against that of outside investment managers, we overlook the fact that we are more expert than any outside manager or consultant in knowing the terms of the plan, the industry and the workers that the plan serves. We know if it is a rapidly expanding company with a plan serving a young population, where the main concerns are investing a high cash flow for the long term, or a plan in a mature or declining industry, where cash flow may be barely sufficient to cover benefits. We know if the plan depends on dividend and coupon income or whether total return is the main objective.

There are, of course, certain areas in which you will need outside consulting, regardless of the size and expertise of your staff (Figure 1). This figure does not represent the risk-return tradeoff; it is rather a more graphic way of viewing the decisions involved in hiring outside assistance. At a minimum, a plan needs actuaries, custodians and, I believe, an outside performance monitoring service to track performance. The spectrum of outside involvement then extends from that minimum level all the way to the extreme, where the assets are assigned to a named fiduciary such as a bank. Where a plan falls in that range at any time is a function of experience, resources and the trustees' comfort level. (Remember, the amount of outside expertise you require may change over time.)

A Clear Set of Basic Assumptions

After a realistic assessment of your strengths and weaknesses, clear and explicit agreement on certain basic assumptions is fundamental to maintaining a good working relationship with the investment manager. There are, at a minimum, six areas on which total agreement should be reached at the beginning:

- *The asset allocation strategy.* Administrators and trustees play a crucial, but often overlooked, role in determining investment performance of the fund by assigning the relative weights of stocks, bonds, cash, real estate and venture capital. The asset allocation strategy provides a broad framework within which to assign assets to your managers on a rational basis over time, and permits them to anticipate and plan for cash flow.
- *Acceptable risk levels,* including credit quality, volatility and liquidity. There is nothing quite as bad as discovering that you and your manager do not really understand each other on this point by watching him buy Braniff or International Harvester the day before bankruptcy is declared (based on his comfort level, not yours).
- *Cash flow characteristics.* The timing of the plan's income receipt and benefit dispersals, and the relationship of these factors, is crucial to investment performance. Successful investment strategies are based on a clear understanding of liquidity constraints. Overtime money needed in six months to pay benefits should not be placed in the stock market—no matter what your view of the market is—whereas money not required for ten years should be invested with an eye to maximizing the total return within the given constraints.
- *The discretion assigned to a manager.* Can your manager invest overseas? In private

Figure 1

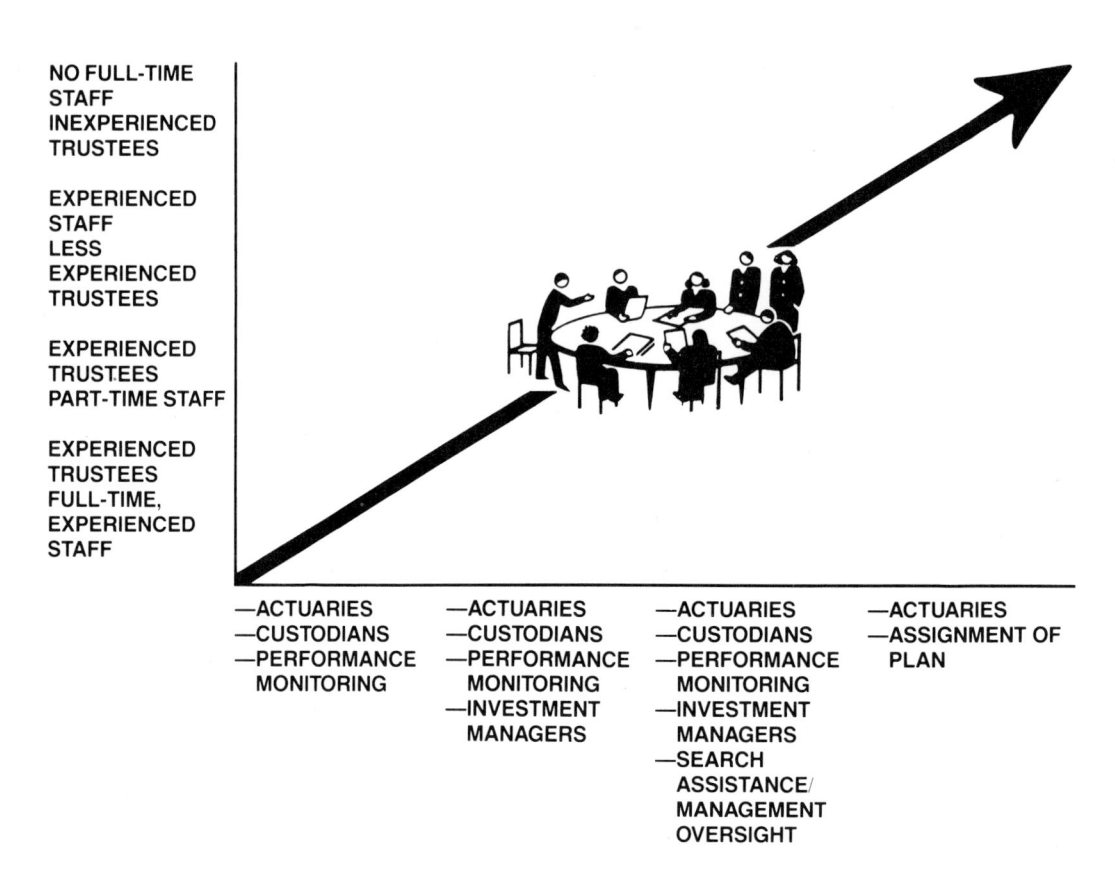

NO FULL-TIME
STAFF
INEXPERIENCED
TRUSTEES

EXPERIENCED
STAFF
LESS
EXPERIENCED
TRUSTEES

EXPERIENCED
TRUSTEES
PART-TIME STAFF

EXPERIENCED
TRUSTEES
FULL-TIME,
EXPERIENCED
STAFF

—ACTUARIES
—CUSTODIANS
—PERFORMANCE
 MONITORING

—ACTUARIES
—CUSTODIANS
—PERFORMANCE
 MONITORING
—INVESTMENT
 MANAGERS

—ACTUARIES
—CUSTODIANS
—PERFORMANCE
 MONITORING
—INVESTMENT
 MANAGERS
—SEARCH
 ASSISTANCE/
 MANAGEMENT
 OVERSIGHT

—ACTUARIES
—ASSIGNMENT OF
 PLAN

placements? In the bond market if he is stock manager? Does he have total control over the placement of trades? All of these points must be clear in advance or you'll be unhappy later.
- *The list of ineligible investments.* This point may not apply to all plans, but if, for example, South African companies, or companies that are openly antiunion or parties in interest are excluded from purchase, make this exclusion clear ahead of time.
- *Actuarial assumptions.* These assumptions are basic to all of your operations and need to be shared with your managers.

Monitoring Your Managers

Once the process of selecting the investment managers is complete, how do you ensure that you get the services you bargained for? A clear, systematic evaluation procedure that assesses performance against objective measures is the first step in the process of knowing the person you actually hired. The steps to establish this process include:

- Determining the *review cycle*
- Evaluating *absolute versus relative measures of return*
- Determining the *component parts of performance.*

Length of the Review Cycle

Most plans have an equity objective something like that of the Pension Benefit Guaranty Corporation: "Over a period of time to cover a complete market cycle (roughly three to five years), the performance objectives of the account, including the use of cash reserves, will be to outperform the S&P 500 market index, including income."

Although a market cycle seems to be the generally accepted length of time for review, its actual duration may be exceedingly long, and at some points appear infinite. Because your evaluation of the manager's work will also compare him or her with other managers who face similar market conditions, the duration of the cycle may not be as critical a boundary as it might first appear.

Figure 2

TREASURY BOND 8.25% OF MAY 5

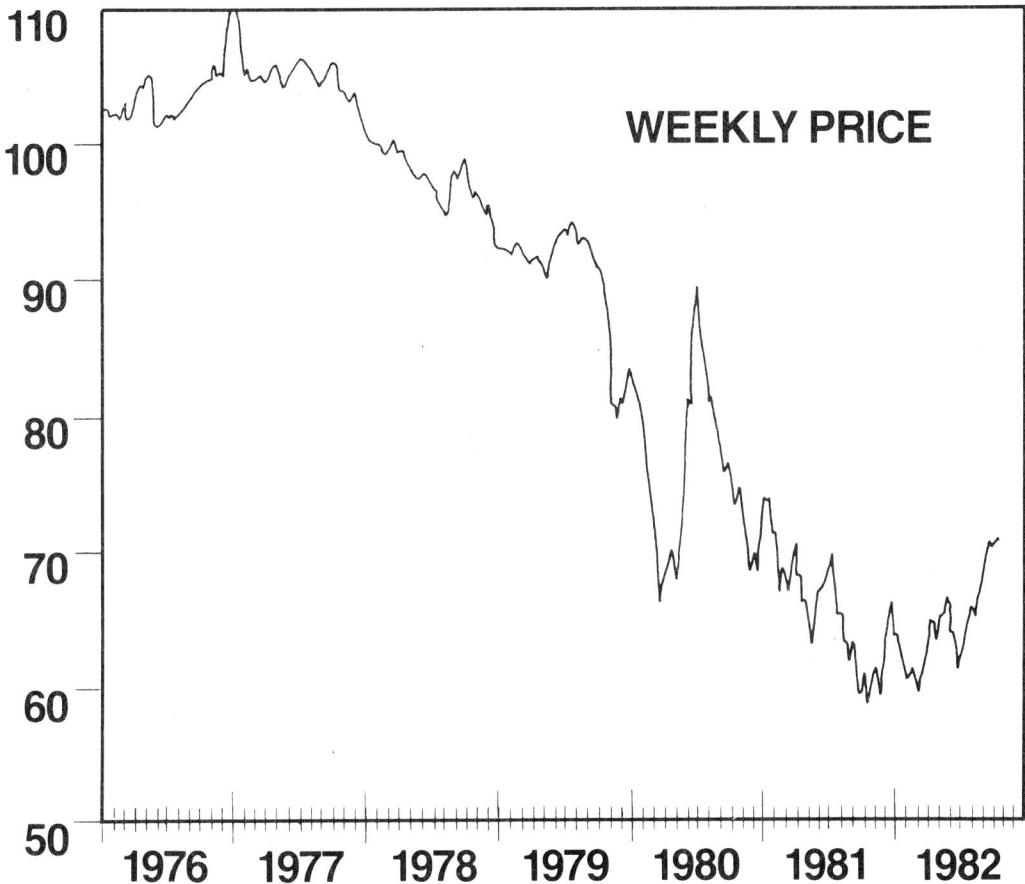

WEEKLY PRICE

In the example of the price of the Treasury 8.25% bond of May 5 (Figure 2), what would you define as the market cycle at the beginning, middle and end of 1980? When you hired a bond manager in 1976, did you have to wait until this year to evaluate him? It has always seemed to me that a market cycle can only be defined in hindsight. Although keeping in mind the concept of a "market cycle," you clearly would have wished to evaluate your manager against the more temporal signposts along the way—other bond managers, the 90 day Treasury rate.

Absolute Versus Relative Measures

Another easy trap for administrators and trustees to stumble into is establishing unrealistically high expectations for the fund's performance, particularly at the beginning. The inevitable disappointments then strain the relationship with the manager. It is important to be realistic, no matter what the manager has promised, rather than hoping for the highest ranking in some pension magazine's sweepstakes. The job of an administrator or trustee is to assure that the needs of the fund's beneficiaries are met over time.

Again, as with the review cycle, judgment is required. A combination of absolute and relative measures compared against each other should guide the review. The absolute measures, for example, can be your actuarial assumptions, whereas the relative measures are related to an index such as the S&P 500, the Salomon Brothers Intermediate Bond Index or the Consumer Price Index. However, whatever combination of absolute and relative measures you choose, they should be specified to the manager in writing at the beginning.

Evaluation of the Components of the Fund's Performance

If the portfolio return was an annualized 8%, did the market drop 5% or increase 25% over the same period? Was inflation 6% or 13%?

You are paying a management fee, presumably for value added. Over the review cycle, is this manager keeping pace with or outperforming the market? Outperformance should reflect selection skills. However, in evaluating the means of this performance, recognize that a portion of the manager's success or failure will be directly attributable to asset allocation decisions made by you. Did you increase your cash weighting from 10% to 30% this summer—as one major fund did—on the assumption that rates would continue to be high? Did you hold money back from the equity managers in June and July because the stock market looked so bad? Asset allocation decisions are probably the most critical determinants of fund performance.

Review Meeting Agendas

Review meetings serve as the stage on which our management of managers is most visibly played. For these meetings, perhaps the most important determinant of success is the attitude that administrators and trustees have. It is important that they control the meeting and not be controlled. Only by covering the issues and questions important to administrators and trustees are we serving the beneficiaries' interests.

The first step is to go over, in-house, the portfolio transactions since the last meeting—the major holdings initiated and sold and their performance. From this first review you develop the specific agenda. It is better if managers know in advance the topics to be covered. Ask the manager to stay within the confines of the outlined topics of the meeting. If he or one of the other members of the group diverts the presentation, bring it back to the issues at hand.

In particular, I recommend that you do not allow the meeting to be sidetracked with a lengthy discussion of the economy. We all know that tactic—the colorful charts, the bar graphs, the look into the future and the fancy suits. Use the meeting to pursue areas where you feel the manager may be weak and to gain a thorough understanding of how the manager makes decisions. Topics to cover in the meeting include:

Review of Stated Strategy

Don't dwell on the portion of the meeting in which the managers outline their strategies; however, it is important that all participants in the meeting start from a common level of understanding. The Delphic oracle is said to have pronounced "know thyself." In about 300 B.C., a scholar added that "In many ways the saying 'know thyself' is not well said. It is more practical to say 'know other people.'" Both parts of this adage apply to the process of the institutional management of money.

Strategy Implementation

If the manager has strayed from his agreed-upon discipline, you should determine why. Although there may be justification from the point of view of the overall economy, you must determine if your portfolio allocation and weighting can tolerate such a change, and whether the manager can handle this shift. Watch the trades in the portfolio over time and ask why specific trades were made. Watch for uncharacteristic moves, such as that of a small cap manager into IBM. These moves can undermine your fund's diversification and raise questions about the manager's integrity and/or understanding of his role.

To get a sense of how security selection or sell decisions are made, ask the manager to explain his rationale on several specific stock choices. The way in which the manager describes this will tell you a good deal about his ability to stick to his original plan. This is particularly important if you hire a manager for a specific market sector, such as growth stocks.

Performance: Past and Future

Check the portfolio's performance over time against your objectives, the market indexes and comparable strategies of other managers. Ask the managers briefly what they see happening in the next 12 months. What do they intend to do about it and why? Write these answers down. Just following up from one meeting to the next makes managers more careful in their management of your portfolio.

Unacceptable Surprises

Have there been any unacceptable surprises? Hopefully not, but if there have been, now is the time to discuss them. Why was International Harvester bought? Why was IBM sold at 65? Why is your stock portfolio 50% cash?

Management Problems

The purpose of asking about management problems—difficulties with the custodian, transfers, fails, uninvested cash, anything else—is to discover small problems before they become big ones.

Agenda Summary

An agenda that covers the following topics will give you a real insight into the management of your portfolio:
- Investment strategy
- Strategy implementation
- Performance
- Future actions
- Unacceptable surprises
- Management problems.

If you are unhappy after covering these areas, you must be prepared to criticize directly. Do not harbor dissatisfaction in silence. Secure satisfactory explanations or take appropriate action.

Performance Guideposts

If you feel that the portfolio is not performing as well as it should, and you are satisfied that neither the market conditions nor the allocations of assets are at fault, you should implement the following procedure:
1. Check turnover of securities in the portfolio. If it is low, your manager may be ignoring your portfolio; if it is high, he may be scrambling for another investment scheme or he may be "window dressing" the portfolio for the quarterly review.
2. Are the underlying assumptions and forecasts reasonable? Is your manager still going on an assumption of 8%, 9% or 10% inflation?
3. Is the manager really following through on his strategy? Are the responses to your questions on particular stock selections consistent and in keeping with the overall strategy?
4. Is the manager's specialty still viable? Is he beginning to drift from his specialty area?
5. How are similar managers faring? Are they doing significantly better or worse than your manager?
6. Has there been a change in key personnel at the management firm? The departure of your portfolio manager may adversely affect your fund's performance.
7. Size of asset base. For example, when you hired the manager, he was managing $120 million; now he is managing $1.2 billion. Can he do it?

If all of the answers to the questions above point to poor performance on the part of the manager, you probably want to ask yourself why you have not fired him.

Conclusion

Before wrapping up the review meeting, make sure you and the manager have a clear understanding of any changes—barring the unpredictable—in the management of the portfolio. This understanding is particularly important if you wish to change any of the variables affecting cash flow or asset allocation.

Finally, interaction with a manager over the course of a year teaches you a great deal about your own shortcomings and strengths. The process is a means of reviewing staff and trustee performance, as well as that of the managers.

CHAPTER 5

Investments

Martin D. Sass

Chairman and President
American Management Enterprises, Inc.
and M. D. Sass Investors Services, Inc.
New York, New York

Eugene B. Burroughs, CFA

Director, Investment Department
International Brotherhood of Teamsters,
Chauffeurs, Warehousemen & Helpers of America
Washington, D.C.

Jack Sheinkman

International Secretary-Treasurer
Amalgamated Clothing and
Textile Workers Union
New York, New York

Jon S. Brightman, CPCU, CFA

Vice President
Harris Trust and Savings Bank
Chicago, Illinois

F. Gilbert Bickel, III, CEBS

Director of Consulting Services
E. F. Hutton and Company, Inc.
St. Louis, Missouri

George J. Collins

Vice President and Director
T. Rowe Price Associates
Baltimore, Maryland

Herbert B. Soroca

Options Manager
L. F. Rothschild Asset Management
L. F. Rothschild, Unterberg, Towbin
New York, New York

Vincent F. Martin, Jr.

Managing Partner
Westmark Real Estate Investment Services
Los Angeles, California

An Investment Strategy for the 1980s

BY MARTIN D. SASS

THE YEAR 1982 is one of significant transition in terms of reversing the trends of accelerating inflation and interest rates that prevailed in the 1970s. This transition has significant economic and investment implications. In the current period of disinflation and declining interest rates, financial assets—notably stocks and bonds—will far outperform tangible assets (i.e., real estate, collectibles and natural resources), which were the primary investments of the 1970s. Borrowers who are paying record high "real" interest rates are now being penalized, as reflected in the record number of bankruptcies, and lenders or owners of bonds are being rewarded.

I have "hated" bonds for 18½ of my 20 years in the investment business because they represented "certificates of confiscation," as a result of their meager or negative real returns relative to inflation. However, from May 1981 to August this year I favored bonds over stocks because of the enormous "real" or inflation-adjusted returns offered with no risk of loss. In mid-August as interest rates declined further, common stocks developed a risk/reward ratio equally as attractive as bonds. P/E ratios and bond valuations are both benefiting from lower interest rates. Both common stocks and bonds should outperform inflation and money market instruments significantly over the next several years. Because I believe that the bulk of the drop in interest rates will take place by year's end, P/E ratios are not likely to expand much after this year. Once an economic recovery gets under way early in 1983 corporate earnings will rebound sharply, propelling further gains in equities, which will then outpace the total return on bonds.

With the caveat that forecasting financial markets makes weather forecasting respectable, I will discuss the implications of the changing economic environment on the outlook for the equity and bond markets.

Equity Market

On August 16, 1982 the Dow Jones Industrial Average hit 777, again successfully testing the high 700 area that we expected to prevail at the bottom of this market cycle. Since August 16, an explosive buying panic lifted the Dow Jones over 200 points on the highest volume in history. (This rally, how-

Mr. Sass is chairman and president of M. D. Sass Associates, Inc., an independent registered investment management firm specializing in Taft-Hartley union pension funds. He is also chairman and president of M. D. Sass Investors Services, Inc., which manages corporate employee benefit funds. Founded in 1972, both companies currently manage assets of approximately $480 million. Mr. Sass' previous experience includes serving as president of Neuwirth Management and Research Corp., as an officer of Argus Research Corp. and as founder of the Argus Special Situations Division. Mr. Sass is a member of the International Association of Financial Planners, the New York Society of Security Analysts and the Young Presidents' Organization. He received his B.S. degree in accounting from Brooklyn College, and completed graduate studies in finance and investments at City College of New York and the New York University Graduate School of Business.

ever, has not yet matched the gain in 1980 from 757 to 1000.) The five principal factors that have turned the equity investment climate positive are:

- Sharply lower interest rates, which increase stock valuations (by reducing the equity discount rate applied to earnings) and reduce the threat of further significant economic decline or of a credit crisis
- A 180 degree reversal to a positive interest rate scenario by the two remaining prominent interest rate bears, "Doctors Doom and Death"—Henry Kaufman and Albert Wojnilower
- Passage of the $98.3 billion three year tax increase on August 19. This increase was a necessary midcourse policy shift to permit the Federal Reserve to lower interest rates.

- Outlook for a bottoming in corporate profits—After an estimated 20% decline in 1982, I expect a sharp 25% recovery in 1983.
- Continued moderation of inflation. Inflation has plunged dramatically from a peak 18% in early 1980 to about 5% currently, which is resulting in the first year-to-year increase in real personal incomes ("buying power") since May 1978. With lower mortgage rates, energy costs and home prices, inflation will be surprisingly low for the next few months.

Is this the beginning of a bull market in equities or just a rally in a bear market? An unusual degree of skepticism is accompanying this rally. In a recent interview in *Barron's*, Joe Granville again stated, "Sell all stocks," and predicted that the Dow will plunge to between 550-650 by January 1983. I think he will be proven wrong! I believe that not only have the stock market's lows been seen, but that this is just the first stage of a new bull market in equities. Initially stock prices will expand because of higher price/earnings ratios. Further stock price gains will come from higher earnings in 1983 and beyond. To illustrate the potential of this market, the average trough-to-peak rise in the ten post-World War II bull markets has been 66% over 30 months' average duration. Notwithstanding my optimism, some pullbacks are inevitable; but don't be fooled by sharp market reactions—the "big picture" is that this is a major bull market.

Most people believe that the 1000 level will again prove to be an insurmountable level; bear in mind the market hit 1000 in 1966—16 years ago! I believe that before the end of this year (1982), the Dow Jones Industrial Index will exceed its all-time high of 1051.70 posted on January 11, 1973. Institutions will continue to dominate the first stage of the rally (because of widespread skepticism by individuals), which will be reflected in record trading volume in excess of 150 shares in a single day. Sometime after the major averages post new highs and the remaining skeptics get invested, some pullback or consolidation is likely.

As the bull market continues, I expect that market interest will broaden and that the other averages will catch up with the Dow. Substantial buying support will come on market weakness from "megadollar" institutions that are beginning to increase equity exposure now that investor psychology has turned strongly favorable.

The percentage of equities in 4,000 pension funds monitored by A. G. Becker dropped sharply to 49% on June 30, 1982 from 76% at the end of 1972. The equity percentage in Taft-Hartley and public employee funds is even lower. This trend will now at least partially be reversed. Further market support will come from individuals who missed this rally—Merrill Lynch reports that its retail cash and margin account customers have both been net sellers throughout this rally. Furthermore, short selling increased sharply to a record 140 million shares during the rally, money fund assets are still rising and margin debt is modest, all of which will lead to further buying power.

The greatest risk to my forecast of a continued bull market for stocks is a postponement in my forecast of an economic recovery early next year. Failure to reduce ballooning budget deficits running at a postwar record of almost 6% of GNP could forestall a recovery. Also, potential shocks will cause continued high volatility in the financial markets. My greatest concerns are the threat of further serious international upheavals in Poland and Latin America, risks of major loan losses in the domestic banking system and continued business failures. Concerns about a possible inflationary bailout of the banks and debtor countries have been reflected in the recent surge in the price of gold and an intensified "flight to quality" in both the stock and bond markets.

Bond Market Outlook

Most investors consider stock and bond market investment strategies to be entirely different. I believe that bonds and stocks are interrelated, since a precondition to higher stock prices is rising bond prices. Furthermore, effective equity and fixed income investment strategies call for similar buying and selling disciplines—both securities should be bought for selling to maximize risk-adjusted returns. Bonds actually have become about 20% more volatile than stocks since the Federal Reserve instituted its new monetarist operating policy in late 1979, which led to increasing variability in interest rates. This situation contrasts to the decade from 1969 to 1979 when stocks were twice as volatile as bonds. To achieve high risk-adjusted returns, you should set yield targets at which bonds should be bought and sold.

Simultaneous with the recent positive swing in stock market sentiment, the bond market also enjoyed an explosive breakout. Bond prices have risen 26-46% from their bottom about a year ago. Although the bulk of the decline in interest rates is now behind us, we expect interest rates to continue to be highly volatile with a downward sloping trading range. I expect a drop to approximately 9-10% for U.S. government bonds from peak levels of 15-16% in September 1981.

The recent breakout in bond prices came as the Federal Reserve eased rates aggressively, as exemplified by five consecutive half point cuts in the discount rate to the 9½% level (I expect further cuts after the November 1982 elections), a reduction in the federal funds rate of more than four percentage points and an expansion in nonborrowed bank reserves. The Fed recently abandoned its policy of trying to control the money supply and Chairman Volcker has stated publicly that he will ignore money supply growth over his targets temporarily. Instead, the Fed will focus on preventing a credit collapse and on stimulating economic recovery.

The trigger that caused the Federal Reserve bank to start to lower interest rates and add liquidity to the system was the bankruptcy of Drysdale Government Securities in June. The Fed accelerated its new accommodative stance after the Penn Square National Bank and Lombard-Wall bankruptcies, just in time to avert a serious credit collapse of the 1930s' variety. More recently, the Administration also moved quickly in the mammoth rescheduling of Mexican loans.

Also importantly aiding lower rates was the recent sharp deceleration in private business borrowings. Private sector borrowing is a key indicator to watch—if it rises again, interest rates will rebound, stock prices will weaken and the economic recovery will abort.

The yield curve has now moved to a sharply positive slope, up to five-seven year maturities for the first time in two years, which is causing an arbitrage between short and intermediate long term rates. The widening yield curve has been a key to the current market rally and has also accompanied market rises in 1970, 1974 and 1980. The five percentage point spread between long term government bonds and Treasury bills is pulling money out of short term liquid reserves and into the bond market. On balance, short term interest rates have dropped about 50% from their peak, which is about the same decline as in previous recessions.

Bond market sentiment was also aided by passage of the $98.6 billion tax increase over the next three years. Although almost everyone is opposed to the tax increase, as I stated before it represents an important "midcourse correction" in Administration policy from supply-side theory toward a more pragmatic approach to battling ballooning budget deficits. Furthermore, the tax increase was a necessary precondition for the Federal Reserve to moderate its previous tight monetary policy in the tug-of-war against the Administration's expansionary fiscal policy.

Although lower interest rates and the tax increase will help somewhat, swelling budget deficits estimated at $170 billion in fiscal 1983 (versus $111 billion in fiscal 1982) and rising to $250 billion in fiscal 1985 will forestall recovery and pose a significant ongoing challenge to the stock and bond markets. Unless Washington restrains ballooning budget deficits shortly after the November elections, the financial markets will be in for a setback. I suspect that the President's January budget message will call for reduced spending on entitlements and military spending costs and for new taxes to reduce the deficit.

Economic Outlook

The economy is still mired in a deep recession and unemployment is still rising. Unfortunately, many of the people laid off in the auto, steel, machinery and other basic industries are not ever likely to be called back to their jobs. (The steel industry is now operating at a mere 37% of capacity!) Incidentally, our unemployment rate of 10.1% in the United States (the highest since the 13% level reached in early 1941) seems modest next to unemployment in Canada, which has hit 12.2%, the highest since the 1930s. Recovery is still not visible, confounding most economists who expected the midyear tax cut and Social Security increase to be the miracle drug to spur economic recovery. Consumers have been increasing savings instead of going on the widely predicted spending spree. Real business capital spending will drop 9.5% in 1982, reflecting excess capacity. The meager growth reported in real GNP during the first half of 1982 reflected inventory adjustments, not true business growth.

Although forecasts of an impending depression are widespread, I believe that the stock market's reliable postwar record as a three to six month leading indicator of business recoveries will be maintained. The rally has already added about $200 billion to the net worth of the nation's approximately 32 million stockholders. As nominal interest rates fall further, we expect increased sales of consumer durables to lead to a sluggish economic recovery commencing early in 1983. The recovery will be subnormal, which will permit stable inflation and lower nominal interest rates. A more robust recovery would reignite inflation and interest rates. Mild economic growth will reflect restraints on fiscal and monetary policy, the lack of incentive for capital spending with capacity utilization at only 69% (versus 87% in 1979's first quarter), sluggish consumer spending and a lack of confidence with one in ten unemployed and high real mortgage and other consumer loan rates, which will deter borrowing and keep the dollar high. Corporate profits should expand at a much faster rate than the GNP next year, as profit margins are aided by increased productivity, lower unit labor and raw material costs (spot commodity prices plunged 22% since the peak in 1980), lower breakeven points because of plant closings and layoffs and the drop in interest rates (interest expense and amortization accounted for about 47% of net profits last year). Furthermore, unless Washington makes further budget cuts, the deficit will reach a $200 billion annual rate at the end of 1983, stalling further drops in long term interest rates and choking off the recovery.

On balance, I believe that nominal interest rates will continue to decline erratically, particularly since another round of spiraling inflation is unlikely in the dull economic environment we foresee. High real rates and competitive pressures will prevent a resurgence in most commodity prices that, coupled with expected improved productivity, will hold inflation in the 5-6% area for the next couple of years. Nominal interest rates are expected to continue to decline to cyclical lows of 6-7% for short term rates, compared with a peak 17% for 90 day Treasury bills on May 13, 1981. I expect a 9-10% range for long term Treasury bonds over the next year versus a peak of 15.2% on September 30, 1981. However, real (inflation-adjusted) interest rates will remain above historical levels as a result of fears of reflation and rising Treasury borrowings to finance the deficit.

Security Selection

The "easy" money already has been made in this recent explosive rally in the financial markets. Further attractive gains will be made, but the key to future successful investment results will depend more heavily on good security selection and on identification of the powerful investment themes that will benefit segments of the markets strongly. In 1981 we changed our strategy from inflation hedges to disinflation beneficiaries. Disinflation remains the single most dominant positive investment theme. U.S. Treasury and agency bonds and GNMA (Government National Mortgage Association) participation certificates remain attractive in this environment. However, I don't expect bond gains nearly to match those gains of the past year; they should now be bought and sold within predetermined yield ranges, rather than merely held to maturity.

Equities of financially strong companies with good unit growth and hidden stock strengths (un-recognized by investors) will prove very rewarding. Hidden strength stocks offer the greatest reward with relatively low risk because their stock prices do not reflect the companies' underlying strengths. Hidden strength stocks can be found in the following four areas—hidden assets, unexpected earnings breakouts, hidden sector participation and companies undergoing fundamental business changes.

With the entire Standard and Poor's 500 index still selling at about a 40% discount from the replacement value of their assets, there are numerous opportunities in companies with hidden assets. Even in a dull economy, careful investigation can uncover companies experiencing unexpected breakouts in earnings. Rapid unit growth can be found in the technology, health and defense electronics sectors and among companies benefiting from declining commodity costs. Special situations with hidden sector participations and companies undergoing a fundamental business change also provide sources of interesting investments.

Companies that previously benefited from inflation through product price increases, rather than through unit growth, i.e., oil and other commodity-related industries, remain unattractive. We continue to avoid most bank stocks because of the risk of loan losses. Capital goods stocks remain under pressure while capital spending plans are pared back as corporations reliquify their balance sheets. As the economic recovery is getting closer, selected depressed consumer cyclical growth stocks are becoming interesting investments.

Conclusion

Despite widespread anxiety and skepticism, we are in a major bull market for equities and bonds in an economy that is likely to be characterized by sluggish growth, improving productivity, stable inflation and further moderately declining interest rates. Whereas cash was king in 1981 and bonds were the best investment for the first seven months of 1982, at this juncture stocks and bonds are about equally attractive. Both stocks and bonds will, with good selectivity, provide superior risk-adjusted returns, well in excess of inflation, tangibles and money market instruments.

If your funds are still retaining heavy short term cash equivalent reserves, I suggest that you take advantage of market reactions to get more fully invested in stocks and high quality bonds and to reduce short term money market exposure. Previously, with a negative to flat yield curve and double-digit short term rates, investors could hold money market instruments comfortably. With the current positive sloping yield curve, you or your investment advisor will have to make the hard investment decisions in stocks and bonds to earn significant real returns for your pension fund beneficiaries.

Spectrum of Investments: 1977-1982

BY EUGENE B. BURROUGHS, CFA

THE PURPOSE OF this presentation is to offer insight into what different classes of investments can do for a portfolio, particularly in light of encouragement from Department of Labor (DOL) regulations to diversify. I don't need to remind you of the myriad of pressures that you have in your task of overseeing an employee benefit plan's investment portfolio today. There are the "prudent expert" demands of ERISA and its attendant fiduciary liability concerns. The participants in the plan and the contributing sponsors are holding you to acceptable performance results. You are concerned about how to balance off your management responsibilities, how much discretion to give your manager and all the problems related to diversification guidelines, etc. Nowadays, on top of all of these problems, you want to act responsibly and be able to sort out the conflicting demands of superior relative return versus vested interest and social investing advocates.

I am going to use a case study approach. This session was first presented at the Annual Conference in 1977. I looked at different classes of investments and their expected rates of return. I have looked at this portfolio at each subsequent Annual Conference since then. This year, then, is the fifth. Now we can compare what was *expected* in 1977 to what was *achieved* over the five years since.

This is no academic pie-in-the-sky exercise. It is a real live pension plan to which supervision is given—day by day. As you look down the highway of your investment objectives, it is always good to keep your eye on the rearview mirror. You must learn from the past as you face the future.

After we finish, you will have an appreciation of the value of diversification, particularly in a volatile economic environment. Looking at the past several years, when both the stock market and the bond market were so volatile, you can really appreciate the fact that your employee benefit plans should be more fully diversified. Certain classes of investments do well in an inflationary environment; others do well in disinflation. By having an appropriate mix in the portfolio, you should be able to achieve acceptable rates of return with limited portfolio variability from period to period, thereby producing the pension payment promise over the longer term.

Mr. Burroughs is the director of the Investment Department of the International Brotherhood of Teamsters, Chauffeurs, Warehousemen and Helpers of America. He is responsible for the research, development and implementation of investment policy in the administration of the International Union's operating monies and two related pension funds. A chartered financial analyst, he was appointed by President Ford to the Advisory Committee to the Pension Benefit Guaranty Corporation. He was a charter member of the Investment Policy Panel of the Advisory Committee of the Pension Benefit Guaranty Corporation and currently serves as chairman. He is a past president of the Washington Society of Investment Analysts and is an Advisory Director of the International Foundation of Employee Benefit Plans. He is also a member of the Financial Analysts Federation (FAF), the Institute of Chartered Financial Analysts and serves on the Board of Regents of the Financial Analysts Seminar, FAF. He has written articles for Pension World, Financial Planner, Employee Benefits Journal, Pensions & Investment Age *and* The Journal of Portfolio Management. *He currently serves on the Editorial Advisory Board of* Pension World *and speaks frequently at educational conferences.*

Appropriate Considerations

Starting on a basic level will be a review, but a review once a year is good for us. In fact, I am going to start with the Department of Labor's regulations, which came out several years ago. Fiduciaries who have been doing a good job for years have known the DOL's approach is essential to the decisionmaking process. The "new" definition of prudence by the DOL is really the old approach used by responsible fiduciaries prior to the scare response to ERISA when it was adopted in 1974.

I will then build on that basic approach to the development of a portfolio, using an actual portfolio. You will see the way it was postured in 1977, why it was postured that way, what it did—both bad and good—and what the economy's effect was on its results. Out of this exercise perhaps you can come to an appreciation of the economy's effect on these different classes of assets. Remember, you and your fellow fiduciaries are in the *risk management* business. The key decision to your fund is your *asset allocation* decision and your asset allocation decision is influenced by your outlook on *inflation, disinflation* and *deflation.*

I am going to end by putting my neck on the line regarding the various classes of investments that you might consider emphasizing or deemphasizing in your particular plan, depending on the plan's needs. Based on professional opinion, I will once again consider what returns can reasonably be expected from the pension portfolio, just as I did in 1977.

One principle included in the Department of Labor regulations is the encouragement to develop a systematic commonsense approach to solving your investment decision riddle. Whether it is a health and welfare fund, a large or small pension fund, a vacation plan, a dental plan or something else, you must undertake a step by step process.

This step by step process primarily involves the trustees, and includes the investment manager, the actuary, the consultant, the accountant—whomever you use in your decisionmaking process to attain your goal of producing rates of return that will help you meet the benefit payment promise. It has been estimated that more than half of future payments will come from investment return. This result comes from the productive power of compounding interest, the power of reinvestment of earnings.

The average pensioner-to-be is 42 years old; you have approximately 20 years to prepare for him. Your participants are looking to you to produce investment return.

The first place we have to look is at the plan itself. There is no one who knows the needs of the plan better than you. You know the industry and the companies. You know the mentality and the attitude of the participants. You know the membership. You are the one who has the basic understanding and you need to share this information with the investment manager.

In addition to knowledge of the plan, we need to have a knowledge of the portfolio. As you increase your knowledge of the portfolio—where it stands today and what you are trying to do with it—you and your fellow trustees will become more responsible clients. Unfortunately, many breakdowns in investment management relationships result from a lack of communication.

All of this activity is for the purpose of producing the future benefit promises.

Your Plan's Needs

What does your plan need?

Income Level

How much income does your particular plan need? Health and welfare plans and mature pension funds generally need a certain level of income.

Preserving Principal

Does your plan need to preserve principal value? In 1974 and 1975, unfortunately, if you had a portfolio that was very heavily oriented toward common stock, you could have been down 40% or 50% in principal value. The aberration was short term and the plan could have come back significantly since that period, so that event really made no long term impact on the fund. Conversely, a health and welfare plan that may have to pay out reserves over the next six months may have to put a lot of emphasis on the subject of preservation of principal value.

Liquidity

Liquidity relates to your need to provide adequate cash flow. Common stock of IBM in a health and welfare plan may be inappropriate. It is highly marketable, but if something occurred yesterday in the fortunes of IBM and the stock drops 5% or 10%, if you need cash to pay benefits, you will find the stock marketable but not "liquid." A price is paid for liquidity. Thus, it is important to provide only as much as is needed.

Management Assistance

Generally, an investment management decision is only as strong as its weakest link. Therefore, it is incumbent upon all co-fiduciaries to have a full understanding of what is really involved in the process. Otherwise, in a market like the one in 1981, someone may say, "Look, I don't want to touch bonds with a ten foot pole. Get them out of the portfolio." This action, of course, could be completely inappropriate for the long term needs of the fund. Someone needs to decide how much management assistance is available and needed.

Volatility

How much volatility (pain) can you really take? Remember that there is a price paid for stability. You can have stability. You can put all your money in certificates of deposit. But if the markets act efficiently, you will be rewarded for holding assets that have greater volatility and variability in value. If your planning horizon is long enough, you can include investments that fluctuate in value and earn a greater rate of return.

Simplicity

Simplicity in your program also is important—a cardinal rule, especially for funds with significant numbers of trustees. That isn't to say that the results from simple strategies cannot be profound. They can be. We are sometimes led by the investment management community to overly sophisticated programs that we don't fully understand, which can cause problems.

Annual Valuation

An annual valuation of your investments is extremely important. It was a good idea before ERISA and is now required by ERISA. There must be a periodic evaluation of your investments. Real estate is the toughest to value frequently and appraisals can be very expensive, which is why many plans go into real estate through commingled funds that value their portfolio on a unit value basis.

Preserving Purchasing Power

Last, but certainly not least, is the concern for the preservation of purchasing power of the plan. How can we keep these plans competitive with inflation? The record shows that most of our funds haven't even kept up with the drop in the purchasing power of the dollar. One issue that will surface repeatedly over the next three or four years is the subject of post-retirement indexing of benefit payments. With inflation the way it is, you somehow have to figure out ways to keep participants at least equal to the standard of living they had when they retired.

There are different ways to accomplish this goal. One is to tilt your pension fund toward those assets that have the potential for and probability of increasing in value over time. Great emphasis should be put on the goal of preserving the purchasing power of the accumulated assets.

All of this search mission to identify your plan's needs is for the purpose of defining the plan's objectives. The ultimate objective, of course, is to pay future benefit payments, but there are a host of policy and strategy objectives that must be attained before the future benefit payment promise is assured.

Investment Facts

We are encouraged by DOL regulations to seek out investment facts and the risks of ownership, as well as the characteristics of different classes of investments. The different classes of investments respond differently to economic events. For instance, during the last couple of years you've made lots of money by owning income-producing real estate. Why did that happen? Because real estate has a different personality than either stocks or bonds.

The first risk to consider is interest rate risk, commonly referred to as "market risk." When interest rates go up, the value of your fixed income securities drops. Thus, you suffer interest rate risk. The market of stocks itself suffers from interest rate risk because there is a discounting mechanism operative. As interest rates go up, a lot of money is attracted to fixed income securities. Where is it coming from? It is withdrawn from stock ownership that produces a discounted rate of return from the stock market that is competitive with returns from buying bonds.

If you have an active bond manager, who is turning over your portfolio three or four times a year, chances are he is trying to anticipate the changes in interest rates. If interest rates are expected to rise, he wants to have your portfolio in CDs to protect the principal. If interest rates are expected to fall, he will extend the maturities, riding the interest rate curve to increase principal value.

What about purchasing power risk? In just the five years that I have been making these presentations, inflation has averaged 9.7%. That means that a bond you paid $1,000 for in 1977 is now valued at about $600, in 1977 dollars. Next we must consider the potential for political or confiscation risk. In the event there is a nationalization of certain industries, the investors in those industries will be compromised.

Even if we are not yet at that point, we certainly should consider social change risk. The real question is, in fact, should you be an investor or a lender? Most of you are from middle America. As an investor group, you have preferred bonds. You had less than 40% of your money in common stock at the end of 1981. You've made a decision.

You've perceived that something is fundamentally wrong in this country. Risk is not being rewarded. Thus, you want to be a lender instead of an investor. You don't want to participate as an entrepreneur. Such a decision is partially in response to your evaluation of social change risk.

Finally, financial or business risk must be considered. Bonds are rated Aaa, Aa, etc.—Aaa indicating superior investment quality, A investment quality and Baa investment quality but containing elements of speculation. These ratings are measurements of financial risk. You might have a guideline for your investment manager requiring that all of your stocks meet certain investment criteria. The criteria assure a certain level of quality that all positions in the portfolio must meet.

Characteristics of Investments

In addition to the risks of ownership, we need to examine the characteristics of these investments. Their "personalities" are different.

For instance, each class of assets differs in marketability. Marketability is the degree to which you can easily sell, or buy, a particular security. Most pension funds could deemphasize marketability. For some reason, we have put a lot of value on marketability; unfortunately, there is a price. If you have a strong positive cash flow in your fund, you can most likely deemphasize marketability and pick up increased yield as a result. With health and welfare plans, marketability is extremely important. You may have to sell those reserves because of an unforeseen level of claims.

Stability is a characteristic of investments. Common stock, as a class, is very unstable. Which classes have elements of stability? Money market instruments, of course, are very stable. Real estate can be relatively stable if it is attractive income-producing property in a good location, with good tenants and negotiable leases.

Liquidity is a particular characteristic of the money market instruments because of their stability in value and their high marketability. Liquidity may be needed in the plan to assure short term cash flow needs or to create reserves while awaiting for attractive permanent investment opportunities to emerge.

Preservation of purchasing power is another characteristic. Many feel that common stock over time will be competitive with inflation rates. Over the longer term, common stock has been very competitive. Bonds have not kept pace with inflation. But the reinvestment of interest you receive in higher yielding bonds, over time, can produce a growing cash flow stream.

Growth in value is yet one more characteristic. Stocks have the potential for growth in value. The companies are reinvesting their earnings. They are taking advantage of strong research and development capabilities. They are compounding their resources over time, which results in growth in value. Real estate has shown us significant growth in value in the last few years.

With the different classes, you can emphasize those classes that have high current income. Our plans are tax exempt. Market research has indicated that by emphasizing current income you can achieve a higher total return over time.

Concerning ourselves with the benefit plan's needs and developing the portfolio are all for the purpose of producing the promised benefits. Those promises will only be fulfilled if we provide for adequate cash flow. This aspect is particularly important with a health and welfare plan that has a very short cycle in terms of using reserves for benefit payments. It is also very pertinent and relative if you have a mature pension fund. By that I mean a pension fund which has passed its accumulation phase and is in its termination phase. You are in the period where your benefit payments actually exceed the amount of contributions coming in. Therefore, the manager needs to know that you require cash from the investment program to pay benefits over the next year, or next two or three years. It's very, very important, the DOL says, that you provide adequate cash flow.

Diversify, diversify, diversify! The DOL reminds us that it is the protection of principal through diversification that is very important. Diversification is required by ERISA, but it really was the name of the game prior to ERISA. ERISA just called our attention to the importance of diversification. Plans that have been more fully diversified over the last ten year period have had positive rates of return exceeding inflation.

Classes of Investments

What is available to you among the classes of investments? We have the products of insurance companies, fixed income securities, equity securities and securities that have a combination of equity and fixed income characteristics. There are a lot more products for you now than just a few years ago. The toughest job you have is to separate the wheat from the chaff. Which ones are appropriate for *your* fund? This process is where your use of consultants is very important.

You can go the fully insured route through the purchase of annuity contracts, laying off the mortality and investment rate risk on the insurance company. You can use deposit administration contracts or separate accounts. The separate account is where the insurance company acts just like an investment manager or a bank. You are hiring the company just to manage investments for you.

Insurance companies are financial department stores. They manage real estate. They supervise private placement and, of course, many of you participate in guaranteed investment contracts. These companies are the ones where you can, for a fixed number of years, contract at a certain rate. The most significant feature is that at times they may guarantee the reinvestment rate. That's a very valuable feature.

Within fixed income investments we have money market instruments, bonds, mortgages, private placements, mutual funds and commingled accounts. Within equity investments, we have common stock, real estate ownership, index funds, mutual funds, commingled accounts and stock options—many alternatives for participation in the equity side of the business.

There comes a time when we have asked all the relevant questions, have, hopefully, increased our understanding of investment opportunities, and are thus ready to cooperate in building the diversified portfolio. Remember, each of us is in the risk management business. We're dealing with an uncertain future. What has significantly complicated the future is the impact that inflation has had on the securities markets. Will disinflation continue? Will it escalate into deflation? Will we return to the hyperinflationary environment of the last few years? This question is extremely important because it influences the way we should tilt our benefit plan portfolios.

The future costs of movements in levels of prices determine whether tangible assets or financial assets should be emphasized in the portfolio. Tangible assets are the so-called hard assets such as real estate, oil and gas, timber, precious metals, etc. Factors favorable to an increase in value in tangible assets are an escalating rate of inflation, rising taxes, increasing government regulation, political instability, an economy favoring consumption and fear of personal harm. Conversely, factors favorable to increasing values in financial assets are increasing confidence in money (i.e., declining inflation rate), reduced government intervention in the private sector, sustained economic growth, improving productivity, political stability and an economy favoring savings and investment.

From 1977 through 1981, we had rising inflation. What investments did well? As you would suspect, tangible assets did best: Farmland was up

Table I

COMPOUND ANNUAL RATES OF RETURN (6/1/77–5/31/82))

	Five Years (Annualized)	Rank
U.S. stamps	27%	1
Chinese ceramics	24%	2
U.S. coins	21%	3
Oil	21%	4
Gold	17%	5
Oriental rugs	17%	6
Diamonds	14%	7
Old Masters	14%	8
Farmland	11%	9
Housing	10%	10
Consumer Price Index	10%	11
Stocks	8%	12
Silver	6%	13
Foreign exchange	2%	14
Bonds	1%	15

Source: Salomon Bros., Inc.

9%; silver, housing and real estate did well; financial assets did poorly. What about from the beginning of 1981 through the present with disinflation? As you would suspect, bonds and commercial paper are doing well.

The ideal, of course, is a period of stable inflation. The record shows that in periods with stable inflation rates, the real rates of return on stock have been +13% and bonds have done well; of course, they are both financial assets. Conversely, the hard assets such as land and silver have not done all that well.

Looking back over the last five years (Table I), we can see that basically it was in a rising inflationary environment that the tangible assets did so much better than the financial assets. In fact, you can see, unfortunately, that the largest component of our portfolios, bonds, performed the very worst. Recently, however, there has been a big rise in bond portfolios. With the markets anticipating lower inflation—thus lower interest rates—bonds have been very productive. Who knows? Maybe five years from now, when you look at a similar chart, bonds will rank near the top instead of fifteenth.

A Representative Portfolio

Now, let's look at our representative portfolio (Table II). In our case study approach, we will

Table II

REPRESENTATIVE PORTFOLIO
MAY 1977
Yield (at cost)—5.5%

Fixed income—43%
    Bonds 54%
    GICs 24%
    Money market 17%
    Private placement fund 5%

Equity—57%
    Common stock
        Actively managed 44%
        Index fund 35%
    Real estate 21%

examine the past and prepare for the future. We have been reminded to diversify the portfolio, provide for cash flow and compare expected and realized returns. Having "appropriately considered" all the facts and circumstances, we must act.

The primary purpose for this case study is not that we might conclude that the investment decision process produced superior, acceptable or inferior rates of return over the five year period. The purpose for this case study is to see the value of diversification, particularly as this diversified portfolio was subjected to extreme movements in inflation rates, and to see the impact of those changing price levels on the valuation of the investments in the portfolio. In effect, we hope to learn from the past in order to position the portfolio successfully in the future.

This portfolio is not a hypothetical example. It is a pension fund with about 6,000 participants and a value of approximately $114 million. The time is May 1977. The yield is 5.5%.

The portfolio was diversified among fixed income securities (43%) and equities (57%). The average Taft-Hartley fund would not have been tilted toward equity that much, but this fund anticipated good, positive cash flow, was concerned with accelerating inflation and, therefore, was trying to get into a position to take advantage of having some assets offering growth in value.

What types of assets were used? Roughly, half of the fixed income was in marketable bonds, rated A or better. About 24¢ of every dollar was invested in the guaranteed investment contracts (GICs) of insurance companies. Because of concern about rising interest rates, 17% of the fund was invested in money market instruments.

Also, at that time, we were beginning to participate on a commingled basis in a private placement fund. This can be done through banks, insurance companies, and other media. No matter what the medium, it is a way to participate in lower credit securities. The insurance company loans the money, for example, to companies rated Baa or Bbb that you may not feel comfortable investing in directly. That way, you can go through the keyhole of a commingled fund to achieve a higher yield.

You have less liquidity, but you have the diversification offered by that insurance company since you share with other investors in a portfolio of hundreds of loans. You are passively invested, but reaching for higher yield than you can achieve with marketable bonds.

What about the equity side? It was decided—because of the experience of the fund with several money managers who had done relatively well, but, unfortunately, several managers in the common stock area who had done relatively poorly—that a portion of the common stock should be passively invested in an index fund. An index fund is merely a way of replicating the return of a market, for example Standard and Poor's 500. By participating in all 500 issues, you can achieve the market's return.

No superior knowledge is involved. Active managers have to give evidence of possessing superior knowledge to provide you with value in excess of the market's return, so this fund embraces a combination of passive (index fund) and active (two investment counsel firms) management.

Part of the 57% in equity is allocated to equity real estate: warehouses, office parks, shopping centers and office buildings. Why? Because if inflation were going to get worse (and it did), then real estate could be a way of diversifying out of dollar-denominated assets into a commodity. We are going to see more of this tactic. You are going to see pension funds participating as limited partners, in some way, in bricks and mortar, commodities, oil, gas, timber, etc.

Assumptions and Expectations

What were the expectations at the time (Table III)? After seeking professional counsel, we concluded that it was reasonable to assume over the next five to eight years an average inflation rate of 5%. Were we wrong? Yes! For decades, inflation had been 2% or 2½%, but all of a sudden it shot up to 6% and 7%.

The money market at that time was 5%. There was no reason to expect with inflation at 5% that money markets would pay any more than 5%.

Table III

EXPECTED RETURN FROM PORTFOLIO PROJECTED IN MAY 1977
(Assuming 5% rate of inflation)

	Expected Return
Fixed income	8.0%
Bonds	8.4%
GICs	9.0%
Money market	5.0%
Private placement fund	9.0%
Equity	12.6%
Common stock	13.5%
Real estate	9.9%
Combined portfolio	10.7%

That's what savings accounts paid. For the private placement fund—because it reaches for lower credits, more illiquid investments—it was reasonable to expect 9%. Adding it all together and weighting accordingly, we expected a net of 8% from fixed income investments.

As for the equity expectations, remember that we had a combination of common stock actively managed, an index fund and real estate. At that time many banks and people doing this type of work thought it was reasonable to expect an annualized rate of return of 13.5% from common stock. When I said that in the summer of 1977, I heard from the audience, "Good luck." That was the attitude—people were very skeptical about whether you could get a 13.5% return. Today, what are the experts telling us? People who are doing market research say you should be able to achieve 18% from common stock.

The projection for real estate was 9.9% based on the properties in the portfolios and the economy at that time, never expecting inflation to be higher than 5% on a net basis. These assumptions were reasonable at that time.

Putting it together, based on the mix in the portfolio and assuming a rate of inflation of 5%, we could expect a combined return from the portfolio of 10.7%.

Results

What happened (Table IV)? We were assuming inflation of 5% and a combined portfolio return rate of about 10.7%. We were looking, then, for a real return of the difference between the inflation rate and the combined portfolio return rate—about 6%.

Was it reasonable to expect a real rate of 6%? Let's look at what occurred the first year. Inflation started going up. From May 1977 to May 1978 it was 7.2%, higher than expected. What happened to the various classes of assets?

As inflation was going up, interest rates were following it; that's what happens. Consequently, our fixed income didn't do as well as we expected. The marketable bonds really got hit. In fact, during that period there was perhaps, on a total return basis, zero return from the marketable bond portfolio. We got 8% or 9% in clipping coupons, but the principal dropped in value because interest rates were going up.

Table IV

**EXPECTED RETURN VS. REALIZED RETURN
1977–1982**

	Expected Return (May 1977)	Realized Return 5/77-5/78	Realized Return 5/78-5/79	Realized Return 5/79-5/80	Realized Return 5/80-5/81	Realized Return 5/81-5/82
Fixed income	8.0%	5.4%	6.0%	4.0%	−0.01%	13.5%
Equity	12.6%	12.8%	11.6%	18.4%	26.4 %	1.2%
Common stock						
Actively managed	13.5%	16.8%	6.5%	12.7%	31.0 %	−6.8%
Index fund	13.4%	6.4%	7.3%	18.5%	25.5 %	−9.8%
Real estate	9.9%	8.4%	26.0%	33.2%	18.4 %	23.0%
Combined portfolio return	10.7%	9.3%	9.2%	12.3%	14.3 %	5.6%
Inflation rate	5.0%	7.2%	10.9%	14.4%	9.8 %	6.7%

The only reason we were able to get 5.4% was because part of the fund was passively invested in GICs and in private placements. GICs are not marked to market. Some people say they should be, but we know that we have a certain income stream out of the contract. Our fixed income return was hurt by an inflationary environment; our expectations were not on target.

In the equity column, we didn't do too badly. We said that we expected about 12.6%. Let's see how we realized it. Wow! Our active managers made some good strategic moves out of yield stocks into growth companies.

If you look at the New York Stock Exchange as a total over the last five years, and if you could have purchased a share in the total exchange, you could have had very high rates of return on a five year basis from 1974. Many smaller capitalized growth companies have done very well. Inflation can be very disruptive, but in that particular environment our active managers did well.

The index fund was a drag on our return, at least for that year.

In real estate, we didn't reach the 9.9% goal. What happened? We started accumulating the properties in the early 1970s, and there was a real estate recession in 1974 and 1975. We were still suffering some leasing problems, since the properties were not fully leased. Consequently, we did not reach the objective of 9.9%.

On a total basis, then—with inflation higher—although we had expected to get a combined rate of return of 10.7%, we got 9.3%. It was above the inflation rate of 7.2%, but not nearly as much as we expected.

The important thing in this review is not whether each class reached its objective on an annual basis, but that we may see the value of diversification. In that particular year, the active managers did very well for us. The index fund did not. Bonds were lagging because of inflation. Real estate lumbered along and gave us a good rate of return, although slightly under the objective. The result was a net return of 9.3%.

Effects of Inflation

Still looking at Table IV, let's move to the next year—May 1978 to May 1979. Remember that when we projected these rates of return we said that they were reasonable to expect over the next five to eight years. Therefore, they should still have been valid. See what happened. From May 1978 to May 1979, point to point, the annualized inflation rate was 10.9%, *twice* as high as we expected. What did it do to the assets?

Look at the real estate return—26%! This rate was not unusual during that period; many of the commingled funds—the larger funds—had this type of return. They got it by rolling over leases at higher per square foot rates and by increased investor interest in real estate. Investors were willing to pay a higher price. Investors from Argentina, Italy, the United Kingdom and Canada were buying up our real estate. They were willing to buy it, believe it or not, at negative cash flows, counting on inflation to increase the value over time. These investors are seeking the stable political environment of the U.S. and they are seeking hard assets.

Therefore, we realized 9% from net lease rentals for the period and added 17% from capital appreciation increases. That result shouldn't surprise you. Many of you live in neighborhoods where such increases took place. What has impacted real estate? Inflation. Everybody is losing purchasing power in dollar-denominated assets; the purchase of real estate is a flight away from dollars into a commodity—in this case, bricks and mortar.

What happened in the other accounts? The index fund returned 7.3%. It was very tough to make money from common stock during that 12 month period. Active managers didn't do as well as the index fund. At that point, you could say, "Well, maybe the index fund is the best investment," but we don't make these decisions year by year. A ten, 12 or 15 year period will go by before we make any real changes. From equity (not necessarily with thanks to our common stock, but certainly to our real estate portion) we came up to 11%. Our targeted rate of return was 12.6%.

In the bonds, there were still problems. Why? Look what rising inflation does to fixed income contracts. Eighty-eight percent of return from a long term bond investment depends on the reinvestment rate. In the past, deflation has always followed inflation. What happens when we roll these bonds over into 5%, 6% or 7% paper? I'm not saying that will happen, but that's the risk that you run with bond portfolios. At any rate, we didn't reach our 8% because the value of our portfolio was marked down as interest rates went up.

However, because of our diversified portfolio, and thanks to real estate in particular, we achieved a 9.2% rate of return for the year in total.

What about May 1979 to May 1980? Inflation was at 14.4%!

Thank goodness we had some bricks and mortar, a nonfinancial asset: Real estate was up 33% (because of leverage)! Conversely, for fixed income contracts, we couldn't even hold onto all of our coupons—they were up only 4%. The index fund, up 18.5%, outperformed the counseled accounts (12.7%) because of oil company stocks and small capitalization companies in Standard and Poor's 500.

From May 1980 to May 1981, inflation was a little better—"only" 9.8%. Fixed income securities were a disaster, while equity was a bonanza. All in all, the portfolio produced a 4.5% real rate of return. Now for the most recent year, the year ended May 31, 1982. Disinflation was in progress; year-to-year price increases were only 6.7%. As you would suspect, bonds did very well at +13.5%. Stocks did poorly, with poor profits resulting from a squeeze on margins. All in all, not a good year for the portfolio; the unstable environment resulted in a +5.6% rate of return.

Expectations vs. Realities

Let's put the five years together (Table V) and compare expectations to reality. We expected inflation to be 5%; it was 9.7%. You would expect real estate ownership to be profitable; it was at 22%, far more profitable than expected. Common stock kept pace with inflation; bonds, as expected, did not.

Thanks to diversification and realizing the "unexpected," the portfolio's return for the five years worked out just about as was expected five years ago. We expected 10.7% per year and achieved 10.2%. The ideal, however, would have been to have produced the originally expected *real* rate of return +5.7%. Producing a positive real rate of return should be the goal for your pensions funds.

Have we learned something from the exercise? Yes. We had certain expectations, now we have realities. Somehow or another as we oversee these funds, we have to modify hope with reality. We have to learn from our experience.

The Future

Unfortunately, we don't have the luxury of sticking with any 12 month period. We have to move ahead. In fact, just to remind you, we are encouraged to be mindful of changing circumstances, and we did have changing circumstances during these recent years. We have to continue to choose a course of action.

What about the next five years? How are the movements in inflation going to affect our bonds, stocks, real estate investments or any of the other classes of assets we may embrace?

Bonds

Until the recent upturn, I don't have to remind you that investment in bonds resulted in disaster. Unfortunately, since World War II, we have basically been in a bear market in bonds, primarily because inflation has only gone one direction during that period of time—up! For example, during a 66 month period, if you had purchased an 8¼% 30 year U.S. Treasury bond on January 1, 1977 for slightly over $1,000, the value of that bond in five and a half years would have decreased to $650, a 41% loss in principal. This is hardly the way to finance escalating benefit payments. That's the bad news. The good news is that for the first time in decades, we have an opportunity to reinvest our bond coupons and any cash flow in a bond market that is giving us the potential for significant *real* rates of return. Instead of the approximately 2% real rate of return that has been achieved in the past, we may be on the threshold of real rates of return anywhere from 4-8% in the future. Of

Table V

EXPECTED RETURN VS. ANNUALIZED REALIZED RETURN

	Expected Return (May 1977)	Realized Return (Annualized) 5/77–5/82
Fixed income	8.0%	5.3%
Equity	12.6%	13.9%
Common stock		
Actively managed	13.5%	11.3%
Index fund	13.4%	8.9%
Real estate	9.9%	22.0%
Combined portfolio return	10.7%	10.2%
Inflation rate	5.0%	9.7%

course, it all depends on the level of inflation in the ensuing years.

The recent dramatic drop in interest rates has enabled our portfolios on a total return basis to perform extremely well. When Treasury bonds were recently at the 14½% level, in retrospect they represented significant opportunities. With rates dropping to the 12% level, total rates of return of 35% or 36% could have been achieved in just a one year period. To do equally well in the stock market, the Dow Jones Industrial Average would have to rise to the 1120 level. Thus, although bonds have been a disaster in the past, many think that they could represent significant opportunities at this level. Remember, bonds are financial assets; during stable inflation, disinflation or deflation, they can do very well on a total return basis.

Common Stock

What may we expect from common stock over the next five years? Before speculating on the future, we should remind ourselves of why we buy stock anyway. Increased earnings by companies should lead to the declaration of increased dividends, which should in turn impact the prices of common stock shares. If we sell those shares at prices above what we purchased them, we achieve a gain on sales, which in turn enables us to pay benefit payments in the real dollars that the future will require. The good news from common stock ownership is that historically it produces a higher rate of return for the commensurate higher risk taking. Unfortunately, we are painfully aware that there are short term periods where we experience a significant drop in value of the stock in our portfolios.

More recently, when comparing the cash yield on bonds versus stocks, bonds have had the edge with their high cash return. This occurrence is particularly valuable to tax exempt investors such as our plans. However, when comparing relative stock prices to asset values of the companies issuing the stock viewed historically, stock is selling very cheaply. In fact, even though companies have adjusted to inflation and have increased their earnings growth, the value of their shares has not increased proportionately. One of the reasons is that investors have asked, "Why should we take a chance with stock when we've been able to get such a high return from either bonds or money market instruments?" Remember, stocks have proven in the past to do very well when inflation is stable. Double-digit real rates of return have been achieved. During the period from 1949 to 1968, stocks did very well because of the stable inflationary environment. The Reagan Administration claims that we are about to enter a relatively stable inflationary period; thus, the stocks in our portfolio, if properly supervised, may do very well over the next few years.

Real Estate

In many ways, real estate is comparable to common stock. It has the financial characteristics of a going business while having certain tangible asset characteristics. This combination permits it to have somewhat more stability in maintenance of value than even common stock does. Additionally, at this time, the real estate industry needs the pension industry's money very badly and therefore is willing to offer attractive deals. We are warned, though, that it takes good real estate management to produce good returns. Because commercial income-producing properties have done very well these last five years, there might be a period of moderate returns particularly impacted by the recessionary environment. It is my opinion that, despite where the level of commercial real estate prices may be, any pension plan with good cash flow expectations should have at least 10% of its portfolio invested in equity real estate. Also, with the flexibility and adaptability of the mortgage industry, employee benefit plans are well-advised to examine mortgage investing opportunities.

Bonds may represent value at this time, stocks may be poised for a continued growth in value and real estate will continue to maintain its value. Let's return to our case study and see how this representative portfolio is positioned. Learning from the past, how do we face the future in this actual portfolio?

The Portfolio—May 1982

Look now at the portfolio as it was positioned in May 1982, and what could reasonably be expected in rates of return over the next five years. The portfolio (Table VI) was 62% in equity and 38% in fixed income. Included in equity are the actively managed and index fund common stock and real estate holdings. Included in fixed income are the bonds, guaranteed investment contracts, money market instruments and continued involvement in the private placement fund.

Our equity position is considerably higher than the average Taft-Hartley fund. However, because of the nature and characteristics of this particular plan, and because of our outlook for continued inflation, we are tilting the portfolio toward growth from equity participation. Our equity real estate

Table VI

THE PORTFOLIO–MAY 1982
Yield (at cost)–8.9%

Fixed income–38%
    Bonds 62%
    GICs 21%
    Money market 12%
    Private placement fund 5%

Equity
    Common stock
        Actively managed 48%
        Index fund 14%
    Real estate 38%

Table VII

EXPECTED RETURN FROM PORTFOLIO PROJECTED MAY 1982
(Assuming 9% rate of inflation)

Fixed income   <u>11.5%</u>
    Bonds 12.8%
    GICs 9.0%
    Money market 9.0%
    Private placement fund 12.0%

Equity   <u>18.2%</u>
    Common stock 20.0%
    Real estate 14.7%

Combined portfolio .... <u>15.6%</u>

---

now represents better than one-third of our equity dollars, which is really a maverick position; as you know, most pension funds are struggling to get even 2% or 3% in equity real estate.

We are counting on our two common stock managers to do better than the index fund. You can see that most of our equity money is with the two active managers—one a growth stock manager and the other a manager who rotates from sector to sector, wherever the values are, in his opinion. We use the index fund as the "core" portfolio of the stock portion of the fund.

Roughly one-half of the bonds are relatively longer term. As bonds rally, this particular part of the portfolio should do very well. As you have noticed before, it has been the laggard sector in the portfolio over these last five years. Twelve percent of the fixed income is in money market instruments.

Now, what do we expect over the next five or so years (Table VII)? Remember, this expectation was determined in May 1982. If you recall, we had assumed a 5% rate of inflation in May 1977; we are now assuming 9%. We hope we are wrong and that is too high, but only the future can tell. We let the *market* tell us the inflation rate that investors are anticipating. We use the spread that exists between the AAA-rated bond yield (approximately 14%) and the dividend yield of Standard and Poor's 500 (approximately 5%). This technique assumes that the dividend yield of Standard and Poor's 500 at any given time represents the expected real rate of return. The difference in the spread in May was 9%.

From fixed income, the rate of return in the aggregate should be 11.5%; from the equity, 18.2%; for the combined portfolio, 15.6%. Stocks should do much better than real estate.

In money markets, we are just assuming that we will earn the inflation rate because this rate has been the longer term history of any short term monies. You merely get the inflation rate. More recently, it's been tough to get even that.

We are locked into 9% GICs. You, of course, could do a lot better in the current market, but we are dealing with a real portfolio that locked up monies at lower rates.

The bonds are at 12.8%. We have an income stream at this point that is approximately 11%, and we are estimating conservatively that in the next five years or so we will pick up an additional 2% from reinvesting that income at slightly higher rates. We look at the bonds as an income stream rather than attempting to increase value from making astute portfolio moves with the principal. We did start a $10 million contingent bond immunization program last year, and the year's experience was favorable.

Conclusion

Finally (Table VIII), let's compare the overall expectations versus realized returns. Remember, we are dealing with the period of May 1977 to May 1982. We will look at what was expected in May 1977, what we realized and what we expected as of May 1982.

Inflation: We expected 5%. We experienced 9.7%; almost double what we anticipated. We presently are expecting 9%.

Fixed Income: In 1977, the income stream indicated that we would get 8%. Unfortunately, since we measure our portfolio on a total return basis,

Table VIII

EXPECTATIONS VS. REALIZED RETURN
May 1977–May 1982

	Expected May 1977	Realized	Expected May 1982
Inflation	5%	9.7%	9%
Fixed income	8%	5.3%	11.5%
Equity	12.6%	13.9%	18.2%
Common stock			
Actively managed	13.5%	11.3%	20.7%
Index fund	13.5%	8.9%	18.3%
Real estate	9.9%	22.0%	14.7%
Combined portfolio	10.7%	10.2%	15.6%
Real return	5.7%	0.5%	6.6%

part of that income stream was diluted by a drop in principal value, so we only achieved 5.3%. Presently, we are anticipating 11.5%, which would be 2.5% above inflation. People talk about real rates of return from bonds of 3%. In recent years, bonds have produced *less* than that, on a real basis.

Equity: In 1977, we expected 12.6%. We picked up a real rate of return of better than 4%, since we achieved 13.9%.

Common Stock: We expected 13.5%. Neither the active managers or the index fund produced that return. Our two active managers did outperform the index fund slightly with their 11.3% versus 8.9%. We expect almost 20% from common stock at this level of the market.

Real Estate: We expected 9.9% and we achieved 22%. This rate was a significant change resulting from grossly accelerating inflation and the fact that half of our portfolio was leveraged during the time (mortgaged at 9%). We actually *doubled* the inflation rate for the period. At this point, we expect less than 15%. Real estate did very well in inflation. It should perform more modestly in disinflation.

In the aggregate, then, in the combined portfolio in May 1977, we expected 10.7% and realized 10.2%. At this point, we are expecting 15.6%. But on a real rate of return basis, it's not all that much different because we were expecting 5.7% in May 1977 and now are expecting 6.6%.

As you can see, the good news is that we realized just about what we expected. That is good for planning purposes. The bad news is that we only kept slightly ahead of inflation, and that goal is what we strive for.

I need not remind you that supervising these portfolios is a very humbling experience. We have managed to muddle through a very difficult environment. We feel that if some things in our economy can go right for a change our portfolio is positioned to participate in the growth of this country.

The record shows that having a fully diversified portfolio has narrowed the range of probabilities in outcomes from year to year, while producing over the longer period a return that has significantly exceeded return assumptions used by the actuary and a modest real rate of return. It is a continuing challenge for professionals and trustees alike to keep our portfolios competitive with changes in inflation and its impact on the value of plan assets.

The present study points out the importance of keeping our eyes on the road ahead and attempting always to recognize changing circumstances. We must always be mindful of the risks that we are taking. Also, we should recognize the disruption of the financial markets that we're investing in by changes in inflation and the importance of diversifying the portfolios to narrow the range of probability. Last, but not least, we must maintain reasonable expectations in our topsy-turvy world.

The Evolving Role of Labor in Pension Fund Investment

BY JACK SHEINKMAN

WITHIN THE LAST five years, union leaders have become concerned over the administration of union pension funds by pension managers designated by employers.[1] What triggered our concern was the increasing evidence that a substantial portion of the assets of pension funds controlled by employers and managed by banks and professional pension managers is invested in a manner that conflicts with, and may indeed undermine and frustrate, the immediate and long term objectives of the union members for whom the funds were established.

Initially, labor leaders felt a sense of frustration and outrage at this realization. As far back as 1978, I testified before the Senate Judiciary Subcommittee on Citizens and Shareholders Rights and Remedies. I said:

> The American labor movement can no longer sit idly by. It is obligated to prevent its pension funds from being used in such a manner as will be inimical to the welfare of working men and women. We can no longer tolerate such abuse of assets held in trust for our workers.

Research

We then began the search for the hard facts that would justify the intervention of labor union leaders into pension fund investing. We knew that without the hard facts, we would be unable to shake the firm hold of traditional pension management on the investment of pension fund assets. A committee of the Industrial Union Department of the AFL-CIO (the "IUD committee")[2] retained Corporate Data Exchange of New York to undertake in-depth studies of pension plans administered by employers or their hired managers to

Mr. Sheinkman has served as international secretary-treasurer of the Amalgamated Clothing and Textile Workers Union since 1972. Prior to that, he served as vice president. He is vice president of the Industrial Union Department of the AFL-CIO and chairman of its Pension Committee. He also serves as chairman of the board of directors of the Amalgamated Bank of New York. Mr. Sheinkman served two terms as a member of the Board of Directors of the International Foundation and has been active on several committees, including chairmanship of the Trustees Committee.

provide reliable data on the performance of those pension fund monies.

There were two major findings of the Corporate Data Exchange studies. The first and most significant finding was that the rate of return on company-controlled pension investments over the last decade has not only lagged behind the inflation rate and average stock market yields, but has amounted to less than the interest rate on savings accounts. This finding is consistent with those of the well-known A. G. Becker Securities Evaluation Service, which in 1980 found that the total return on pension funds was only 4.3% during 1970-1980.

Recommendations

These findings led the IUD committee to conclude that the immediate and long range interest of pension fund beneficiaries would be better served if unions representing employees covered by pension funds became active in the manage-

---

1. Some major firms in the business of pension fund management are Morgan Guaranty Trust Company of New York, Equitable Life Assurance Society of the United States, Bankers Trust Company, The Prudential Insurance Company of America, Citibank and Chemical Bank.
2. The AFL-CIO Industrial Union Department Executive Council's Committee on Benefit Funds.

ment of such funds. To achieve this objective, the IUD committee recommended that where the employer alone controlled the investment of pension fund assets, the union use its leverage in collective bargaining with the employer to obtain a voice in the management of the funds covering its union members.

The IUD committee further recommended that the union require fund investment managers to follow investment guidelines that optimize return on sound and secure investments and that serve the present and long range needs of the labor union members who are the beneficiaries of the fund. Some examples of sound investments suggested by the IUD committee are: residential mortgages and other investments that promote the development of communities in which fund beneficiaries work and live, firms with large domestic workforces and firms that have good labor relations records and support their employees' organizational rights under the Fair Labor Laws.

Reactions

As soon as organized labor began to point out that traditional pension management had not performed well financially and to object to pension fund investments that were in conflict with the objectives of the labor union members who were the fund's beneficiaries, representatives of the traditional pension management and employers began to vigorously oppose labor's demand for a role in pension fund investment. They contended that the obligation of pension fund management was to act prudently and that the revisions in investment approach sought by labor almost certainly would jeopardize the safety of the pension funds involved. They argued that the use of the expertise of traditional pension management was essential for the safe and most productive investment of pension funds and, in any event, union participation in pension fund management was unworkable.

Our answer was that, of course, those who control the pension funds, whether labor or management, had to be concerned primarily with prudent investments to secure expected benefits for the workers covered by the funds. We pointed out that prudence did not, however, require that pension funds be invested against the economic interest of the workers. For instance, prudence does not require a pension fund to invest in a multinational corporation when such investment is likely to contribute to the outflow of capital investment and to unemployment in the United States. Other investments that would not produce such results are generally available. Similarly, there are many prudent investment opportunities available that do not involve antiunion firms.

Our answer to the argument that labor's influence on pensions and decisionmaking could produce financial disaster for the pension funds is to point out that the few funds that take socially responsible criteria into account in determining investments have sustained a better record of performance than traditionally managed funds. The Teachers' Insurance and Annuity Association, composed of 650,000 members, has an $8.6 billion fund that has had an average annual return of 11.1% over the last five years, using an investment approach that takes consumerism, environmentalism, product safety, hiring practices and investments in South Africa into account. Another example is the Dreyfus Fund, a $200 million fund, which increased the value of its net assets by 31.6% in 1981 by using an investment approach that took into account environmental protection, occupational health and safety, consumer protection and product safety. A third example is the Hospital and Health Employees $360 million pension fund, which, as a result of union demands, sold off $6 million of stock in 19 auto, oil, drug and financial companies with an active presence in South Africa in 1978. The alternative investments selected produced a 30% return on the equities in the fund.

Union Objectives

Union leaders have the same fiduciary obligation as does traditional pension management to make certain that pension funds are managed to optimize the plan benefits for union members. However, the union leader is also accountable to his members for poor fund performance or poor investments. Intervention by union leaders in the investment of pension plan assets is therefore essential if union leaders are to satisfy their legal obligations to their members.

Organized labor is searching only for lawful ways of influencing the use of pension funds. We do not advocate the elimination of the ERISA requirements that pension fund assets be invested prudently and be used for the exclusive benefit of the plan beneficiaries. Nor does organized labor have any quarrel with the recent Supreme Court holding in *NLRB v. Amax*, 453 U.S. 322 (1981), that the duty of loyalty of the trustee to a plan must overcome any loyalty to the party that appointed him.

Our objective is to have union pension funds avoid investments that conflict with the interests of plan beneficiaries. It is against the interests of labor union members covered by a pension plan to invest their pension fund's assets in antiunion firms or multinational firms, whose operations are overseas. It is against the interests of labor union members to invest in companies with strong connections in South Africa, when so many labor union members are morally outraged by the notion of dealing with a country in which the rank discriminatory doctrine of apartheid is state policy.

Legal Implications

The elimination of investments in corporations engaging in morally repugnant activities will violate no legal rule, if alternative suitable investments are available, as they always are. There is no legal obligation on the part of fund managers to search out investments in entities that are so tainted morally that they may yield an extraordinarily high return. The applicable rule is set forth in Scott's *Law of Trusts*:

> Trustees, in deciding whether to invest in, or to retain, the securities of a corporation, may properly consider the social performance of the corporation. They may decline to invest in, or to retain, the securities of corporations whose activities or some of them are contrary to fundamental or generally acceptable ethical principles. They may consider such matters as pollution, race discrimination, fair employment and consumer responsibility.[3]

As I said before the Senate Judiciary Subcommittee on November 22, 1978:

> No one is advocating imprudent investment of pension funds... But, within the area of equally acceptable investment risks, there are often alternative choices. It is in this area that broader social and economic criteria can be used to take advantage, without sacrificing the dollar return or the invested funds.

This approach has been approved by the United States Department of Labor. In 1979, Ian Lanoff, who was until recently the administrator of Pension and Welfare Benefit Programs at the Department of Labor, testified before a Senate subcommittee in February 1979:

> If, after evaluating other factors, two investments appear to be equally desirable (in economic terms) then social judgments are permissible in determining which to select.

In my view, union leaders have a fiduciary obligation to influence the investment of union pension funds in a manner that promotes the interest of the members of the union covered by such fund. I can see no justification whatsoever for barring participation of union leaders in the investment of assets of union pension funds. These pension funds have been built up solely by contributions obtained as a result of the efforts of unions through collective bargaining. They were created by the efforts of unions; their assets are held exclusively for the benefit of union members, and their assets increase whenever unions, through collective bargaining, obtain an increase in contributions.

Traditional pension management has attempted to discredit union influence in pension fund investing by contending that the leaders of unions are ignorant of the intricacies of investment practice and are ill-equipped to make sound judgments in the selection of investments. This claim is totally unwarranted. Almost every major union has millions of dollars of its own funds to invest and does so, generally with its own expert personnel cooperating with investment counselors or financial institutions such as the Amalgamated Bank. Indeed, unions such as Amalgamated Clothing and Textile Workers Union, United Federation of Teachers and the International Ladies Garment Workers Union have obtained much higher returns on their investments than the returns secured on the pension fund investments managed by traditional pension management.

Union leadership does not wish to substitute the standard of "socially responsible" investment for prudent, financially responsible investment. Where an investment deemed injurious to union members is eliminated, there is no desire by responsible union leadership to substitute any investment, whether or not it serves some social objective, with an investment that is not financially sound. Similarly, investments that improve the economy, job opportunities and public services available for union members in urban centers need not, and should not, be made with pension funds unless they are financially sound. The recent experience of public pension funds investing in New York City with special safeguards at a time when New York City was in financial distress indicates that innovative investment in such areas may be prudently made.

Economic Impact

The potential impact of union attempts to have pension funds with socially responsible and

---

3. Scott, Austin W., *Law of Trusts,* 6 vols.; 3rd ed. Boston: Little, Brown & Co., 1980.

union-oriented investments should not be minimized. The total amount of nonfederal pension plan assets has been estimated as of 1980 to be in excess of $650 billion, of which union pension funds constitute several hundreds of billions of dollars.

What Does "Socially Responsible" Investing Mean?

Since the late 1970s, the leaders of organized labor have asserted the right to use union influence to assure that union pension funds shall not be used for purposes conflicting with the interests of the union's members. This proposition is one that, although first advanced only a few years ago, is beginning to gain acceptance even in the world of traditional pension management. Indeed, some of the leading investment firms—Drexel Burnham Lambert, Inc., The Prudential Insurance Company of America, National Bank of Washington, Aetna Life Insurance Company—have established funds that will invest primarily in union-built construction. What is far less accepted, and would indeed require federal legislation, is the next logical step—the use of union pension funds to assist their own ailing industries to renovate and replace equipment, thereby helping to eliminate unemployment in industries covered by union pension plans.

Labor leaders have announced programs to provide mortgages for middle income residential housing and investments in nursing homes, nursery schools and similar nonprofit entities. Some labor union leaders have been able to get their pension funds to agree to invest in union-built construction. The Marine Engineer's Beneficial Association plans to use some of its $400 million in pension funds to construct union-built ships and a pension-owned shipping company.

Although these programs move in the right direction, we need even more affirmative action and swift implementation. Thus far, pension funds have been used to create jobs for union workers primarily in the construction industry. Most union leaders outside the building trades have done little more than use their influence to prevent pension funds from being invested in a manner that clearly conflicts with the objectives or welfare of the union members covered by such funds. Although such efforts are significant and will ultimately operate to the benefit of union members, so far they have had little impact on eliminating unemployment among union workers.

We are all sadly aware that the current recession is deep and particularly painful for the over ten million workers, including millions of union members, who are unemployed in this country. Many industries are unable to compete in the marketplace because of their failure to replace worn-out or outdated equipment. One of the major reasons imports have made significant inroads in several product areas, such as steel, is that the domestic manufacturers of such products are producing with outmoded equipment. An industry that has largely obsolete equipment may have unemployment even where general demand for the industry's product exists.

What Legislation Is Necessary?

Organized labor believes that this country must use all available tools to eliminate unemployment. Certainly, it is in the interest of labor leaders and union members to stimulate employment in the very industry that employs or has employed them. At various times in its history, this country has determined that the health of one or more of its industries or the production of certain products or services justified the use of federal guarantees or insurance. The housing industry still benefits from Federal Housing Administration insurance of mortgage loans. A significant amount of American industry has for many years received direct or indirect assistance from federal and state governments designed to assure its survival and ability to compete. The use of guaranteed pension loans to industry, which are essential for the program I suggest, is certainly not without precedent.

It is true that if a pension fund lends money to a manufacturer in the industry covered by such fund to enable him to retool and compete more effectively, such loans may violate the party-in-interest standards of ERISA. However, if legislation is adopted by Congress providing for a guarantee of such loans by either the U.S. government or an appropriate agency of the government, such loans would then be prudent under the standards of ERISA, and the welfare of the pension fund's beneficiaries could not be jeopardized. Loans by pension plans to an employer secured by certain real estate or the marketable securities of an employer in a principal amount exceeding 10% of the fair market value of the pension fund's assets, and all other loans by a pension plan to an employer not secured by marketable securities or certain real estate of the employer, would constitute prohibited transactions under ERISA. However, an exemption for such prohibited loans can be granted by the U.S. Department of Labor. Such an exemption has, in fact, been granted recently for a pension fund loan to the employer of an amount equal to 21% of fair market value of the assets of the pension fund.

The legislation providing for establishing such guarantees should establish a federal administrative agency like the Federal Housing Administration to determine which employers merit this type of guaranteed financing. The enabling legislation should also amend ERISA to authorize the Department of Labor to establish regulations that simplify the process of obtaining Department of Labor exemptions for loans to employers that qualify for the federal agency guarantee.

Under the program, the agency would have the obligation to determine that other commercial financing was not available and that, with the guaranteed financing furnished by the pension fund, the company would be able to survive in the marketplace. Strict enforcement by the agency of these conditions is essential to limit the exposure of the federal government under the guarantees used in the program and to assure the achievement of the objective of the program: to make employers more competitive and capable of surviving in the marketplace.

The use of such guaranteed pension fund loans would complement other efforts of the AFL-CIO to establish an independent institution, similar to the New Deal's Reconstruction Finance Corporation, to facilitate the reindustrialization of America. It hopefully would allow a substantial portion of this country's industry to regain the competitive position it has lost in the United States market and world markets over the last several decades. Such a gain in competitive position should help eliminate much of the unemployment plaguing our domestic industry and make available many of the jobs lost as a result of deterioration of plant equipment.

Some Possible Results

One of a union leader's most important objectives is the full employment of the members of his union. Indeed, union pension funds have actuarial difficulties if too many covered members are unemployed. Every union leader who is a trustee of a pension fund, or is able to influence pension fund investment decisions, should encourage affirmative investments that are prudent and likely to reduce unemployment in his members' industry.

The proposal I have advanced arises out of the growing conviction in the circles of labor, industry and economics that traditional approaches to the complex economic problems that have affected the health of American industry are not likely to yield a solution. If we fail to solve our economic problems, the working men and women of this country will suffer greater and greater hardship.

Organized labor must lead the way toward regeneration of the nation's economic health. Financing plays the critical role in the reactivation of any economy. Pension funds, with their abundant assets amounting to hundreds of billions of dollars, are available in every sector of industry throughout the country. Trustees are generally knowledgeable about the industry covered by their own pension fund and are well-equipped to make the initial financial judgments required for pension fund loans to employers in the industry. These trustees, subject to supervision by the federal agency established to administer the proposed guaranteed loan program, can serve as part of the administrative structure of the agency, thereby minimizing the amount of governmental personnel required and the time needed to initiate the program.

Admittedly, this approach to pension fund investment is new. However, the technique suggested is substantively the same as was used in the New York City fiscal crisis several years ago. The trustees of the New York City municipal employees' pension plans, after obtaining certain legislative safeguards, committed a substantial portion of the assets of their pension plans to buy all the New York City bonds that no one else wanted. This investment saved New York City from default, gave the pension funds an excellent return on interest on their bonds and secured the jobs of the thousands of municipal workers who were covered by the pension funds that assisted the city in its crisis. As the experience of New York City's municipal pension funds indicates, pension fund investments in the very industry that employs the beneficiaries of the pension fund may at times be necessary to secure the jobs of those beneficiaries.

Conclusion

In this country whole industries have failed to modernize their equipment, and the result has been a steady attrition of the industry's workforce. Substantial portions of numerous other industries suffer from obsolete and worn-out equipment that employers do not have the funds to replace. I do not believe we can wait much longer before direct measures are taken to eliminate this type of unemployment. Such unemployment will be permanent unless we remedy the loss of a competitive posture.

The proposal is basically simple. I believe that affirmative action, making use of the pension funds created by union members, can play an important role in reducing the high rate of unemployment now crippling the nation. This process will not only help the economy—it will help strengthen the pension fund system participating in the new program. By reducing unemployment, it will increase the contributions into pension funds.

Organized labor now has an opportunity to provide a meaningful counterthrust to the decline of American industrial strength, by using its political and economic power to press for a major retooling of American industry. Such an endeavor is one in which labor and management combine for their common good to restore the employers' prosperity and ability to employ a full complement of union workers. I submit that labor leaders, employers and others sharing their concerns throughout the country should lend their support to this initiative, an initiative born out of watching the sadness and despair of those workers who already have lost their means of earning a living in a country known for so long as a land of opportunity.

Tying Defined Contribution Plans to Investment Earnings

BY JON S. BRIGHTMAN, CPCU, CFA

THIS ARTICLE WILL address but one segment within the whole issue of retirement planning. When focusing on defined contribution plans and tying investment earnings to these types of plans, however, it is instructive to review these plans within the broad arena of retirement benefits. When planning for any human endeavor, choices are involved. Whenever alternatives are evaluated, one must attempt to understand the benefits and costs associated with choosing one method over another. The whole field of pensions and retirement is fraught with choices, each with a unique benefit and cost.

First and foremost, pensions are a form of deferred compensation. Consequently, the first choice you are faced with is whether you should take compensation that you earn today in your paycheck or reduce your present paycheck and defer your compensation to a later date—for instance, at retirement. Once a decision has been made to reduce your current income and defer part of it, there are a host of other decisions required so that this deferred income will be managed properly and will achieve the objectives you had in mind when you deferred your income.

The decisions that must be made to manage a pension plan are the responsibility of either the participants of the plan or the trustees of a pension plan acting on behalf of the participants. Perhaps many of the decisions are made during the bargaining process. To understand these decisions, it is worthwhile to review the evolution of pension plans, describe the factors that influence that evolution, review why defined contribution plans are in vogue today and indicate the types of choices that one may be faced with as an individual participant in a defined contribution plan.

Defined Benefit Plans

Pension plans have, of course, been with us for many years. Most familiar to us is a defined benefit plan. In its simplest form, it states that an individual will receive so many dollars a month per year of service with an employer. For example, a defined benefit plan might state that for every year of employment, an individual would receive $10 per

Mr. Brightman is vice president of Harris Trust and Savings Bank in Chicago, where he is manager of the Master Trust Division. He previously was corporate vice president and manager of the Milwaukee office of Meidinger, Inc. and, prior to that, was manager of the Retirement and Insurance Department of the Air Line Pilots Association, representing 36 airlines, with fiduciary responsibility for pilot pension plans. Earlier, he held several positions with Travelers Insurance Co., including manager of pension services and portfolio manager of the Investment Department. Mr. Brightman received his A.B. degree from Bowdoin College and holds the professional designations of chartered property casualty underwriter (CPCU) and chartered financial analyst (CFA). He is a member of the Institute of Chartered Financial Analysts and the Milwaukee Society of Investment Analysts. Mr. Brightman is chairman of the International Foundation's Consultants Committee and a member of the Educational Program Committee. Mr. Brightman has spoken at several International Foundation educational programs.

month at age 65 retirement. With 30 years of service, the individual would receive $300 per month. This type of program is easy to understand and is excellent for planning. It is a basic foundation for one of the four legs of retirement that are being discussed so much today. The other three legs are Social Security, personal savings and supplemental part-time work after retirement.

Defined Contribution Plans

Another basic form of retirement planning focuses on the contributions that are made to the plan rather than describing the benefit that will be earned in the future. These types of programs are called defined contribution plans. For example, they might state that so many dollars per hour are going to be placed in a fund and that fund will grow through investment earnings and receive additional contributions throughout the years. At some future point there will be a lump sum of money available for the participant to receive. Historically, these types of plans have been used for plans with rather short term horizons. We are all familiar with Christmas funds that require one to set aside so many dollars a week to provide a nest egg for the holidays. Many organizations have "banked" hours to be used for vacation funds or sick days. This framework also applies to defined contribution retirement planning.

Combination Plans

Through negotiations, in response to industry trends and demands and perhaps even to make the bargaining process easier, there evolved a blending of these two concepts into one plan, which has been called a combination plan. These combination plans provided a defined contribution, perhaps $1 per hour, that is translated into a defined benefit program. During the bargaining process, both the benefit and the contribution level are specified. This approach makes the bargaining process much easier and on the surface it is intuitively appealing—a defined contribution equals a defined benefit.

Unfortunately, contribution plans are highly dependent on many assumptions. Consequently, the administration of a combination plan is extremely difficult for actuaries, consultants, investment managers, trustees, etc. For a combination plan to work, all the assumptions concerning investment return, mortality, turnover and work history must be precise. Otherwise, the benefits will not live up to the promises made to the participants. Since nobody is able to forecast the future with any real precision, many of the assumptions used for combination plans have not worked out over time. In my opinion, this eventuality is one major reason for the Multiemployer Pension Plan Amendments Act of 1980 (MPPAA). There was not enough money going into the combination plans to provide the benefits that were promised to the participants, so Congress did something about it.

Multiemployer Pension Plan Amendments Act

MPPAA is a fact of life today. We do not completely understand it; the law has not been completely litigated, nor have all the regulations been finalized so that it can be administered, but one thing seems undeniable: Today, employers who participate in multiemployer plans have a higher liability than they had prior to enactment of this law. Plan liabilities are defined as unfunded vested benefits. Employers who participate in such a plan ultimately are obligated to fund their portion of this liability, and their liability could cost them 100% of the net worth of their business! The unfunded vested benefit liability is computed as the difference between the assets of the pension plan less the present value of all the future benefits that the participants have earned and are vested in, as of a specified date.

Because of the unlimited obligation of employers, there may be a reluctance in the future for employers to increase their liabilities to a pension plan. Future increases to defined benefit plans and combination plans may be extraordinarily difficult to achieve at the bargaining table. Since there are no vested liabilities associated with defined contribution plans, it is my judgment that defined contribution plans and the management of defined contribution plans will become an ever-increasing factor in the pension industry field.

Advantages

What are the advantages and disadvantages of defined contribution plans, the cost and benefits? The first benefit is that there is no increase in employer liability by increasing contributions to a defined contribution plan. Essentially, what goes into the plan is owned by the employees and the employer's obligation ends at the time that a contribution is made. Secondly, with defined contribution plans, the amount of the benefit is tied directly to the work level. Either the harder or the longer an individual works, the more the contribution—and the ultimate benefit—will increase. A participant who works 1,000 hours in a year will receive only half as much benefit as a participant who works 2,000 hours in a given year, all else being equal. Third, it provides for investment flexibility. In defined benefit programs, investment decisions are made for the pension plan as a whole; under a defined contribution plan the investment vehicles can be designed to take into consideration the individual participant's tolerance for taking investment risk. Consequently, investment decisions and how the assets of the pension fund are invested in a defined contribution plan can be tailored to the unique requirements of a participant, rather than looking at the broad perspective of the pension fund as a whole.

Another advantage of defined contribution plans is that they are encouraged by the government. In recent years, we have seen enabling legislation to allow all working employees to establish individual retirement accounts (IRAs) up to the amount of $2,000 per year. In addition, the government has encouraged salary reduction plans called "401(k)" plans, which are also a form of defined contribution plans. Recent legislation has strengthened employee stock ownership plans in the form of pay-related plans. Self-employed individuals have had more favorable legislation allowing them to defer more income than in the past. This pattern of defined contribution legislation, which allows avoidance of present income tax on one's contribution and the avoidance of income tax on the investment return earned on their contributions, leads one to think that there is perhaps a trend in Washington to encourage defined contribution plans, which we as employees should take advantage of.

Finally, another advantage of a defined contribution plan is that participants can actually watch their benefits grow. Money is set aside on behalf of an individual; it is real money, not promises that a future benefit will be provided should an individual reach retirement and should all the assumptions work out. Today, there is an often articulated concern among employees not only about the health of their own defined benefit program, but about all defined benefit programs, whether they are government-sponsored (Social Security), a single employer plan or a multiemployer plan. Defined contribution plans eliminate the concern that promises will not be kept.

Disadvantages

However, there are also many disadvantages with defined contribution plans. The first and foremost is that the future benefits are uncertain. Although dollars are set aside today, nobody knows for certain how much those dollars are going to be worth in the future, nor what amount of goods and services that those dollars will be able to buy. Future benefits are uncertain, although the contributions that are being made today are certain.

Another disadvantage of defined contribution plans is that they only reward a person for future service. It is very rare that a defined contribution plan takes into consideration past service with an employer. Future benefits are a function of future service and not past service.

Another disadvantage of defined contribution plans is that the future pay-out of the plan is uncertain. Even though one can determine what the lump sum asset value of an individual's account balance is, translating that asset value at age 65 into periodic payments and annuities is difficult and highly dependent on interest rates and the availability of insurance vehicles at the time one retires.

Finally, and I feel most importantly, all the risk of investment return is placed on a participant. If investments in a defined benefit plan are poorly made, it is up to the employer(s) to make good on those investments and increase contributions to the plan. In a defined contribution plan, if the investment return is poor, the only person to suffer is the individual participant. Therefore, anyone who is in a defined contribution plan should understand the capital markets in order to choose how to invest his defined contribution account balances to best meet his own investment needs.

Capital Markets

After examining the evolution of pension plans and the factors that have influenced the evolution of defined contribution plans, it is now worthwhile to focus on the capital markets and the choices that are available. As alluded to previously, in my judgment the single most dramatic difference between defined contribution and defined benefit plans is the transfer of investment risk from the plan to the participant. The participant must make choices about how he wishes to place his assets within the investment vehicles offered by the defined contribution plan, if choices are available.

To do so, one must make a sequential decision. First, an individual has to determine what amount of risk he wishes to take over what investment horizon. This choice is highly individualistic and one that needs thorough financial planning, taking into consideration income needs, age, available resources, etc. After making the determination of risk level, he must then translate that choice into selecting the appropriate investment vehicle most apt to provide him with the returns associated with the risk level he has chosen over his remaining working career—not an easy task!

To shed some light on how to choose these investment vehicles, it may be appropriate to look backward for 55 years and to try to understand what the capital markets have produced over that period. Fifty-five years is an appropriate time frame to look at when analyzing a pension plan. An individual who enters a pension plan at age 25 can expect to work for approximately 40 years. At age 65, one's life expectancy is in the neighborhood of 15 years. Therefore, a 55 year period is

Figure 1

INFLATION

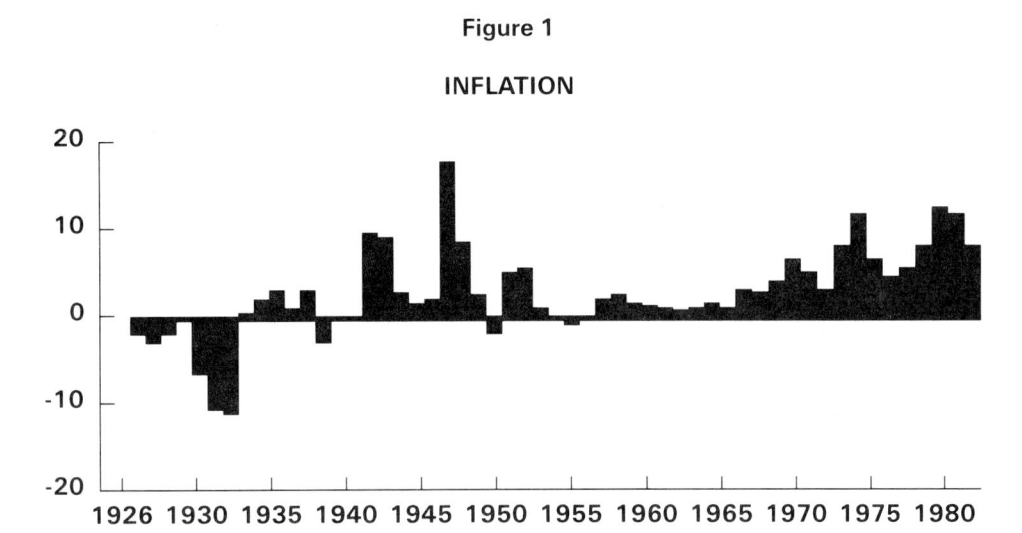

Figure 2

UNITED STATES TREASURY BILLS

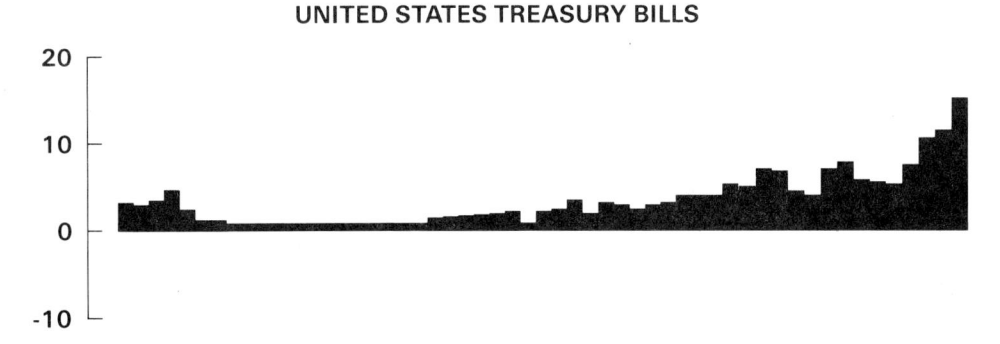

Figure 3

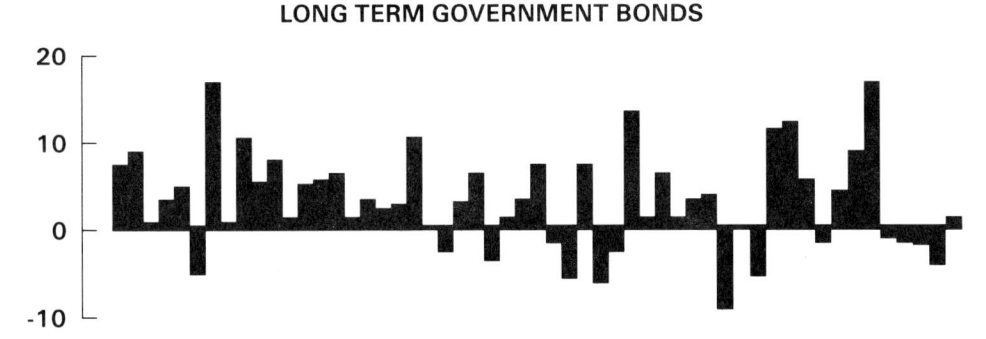

LONG TERM GOVERNMENT BONDS

representative of a hypothetical participation in a defined contribution plan.

Figures 1-4, which show year by year total returns on inflation, Treasury bills, bonds and common stock, are attempts to display the risk and returns that one would have experienced if he were to invest money during the past 55 years.

Figure 1 is labeled "Inflation." One can see that inflation has been highly variable over the 55 year period. In fact, in ten of the 55 years there has actually been deflation, where the value of a dollar has been more in the following year than it had been in the preceding year. Inflation has been high, reaching 18% in 1946 and 13.3% in 1980. Inflation

Figure 4

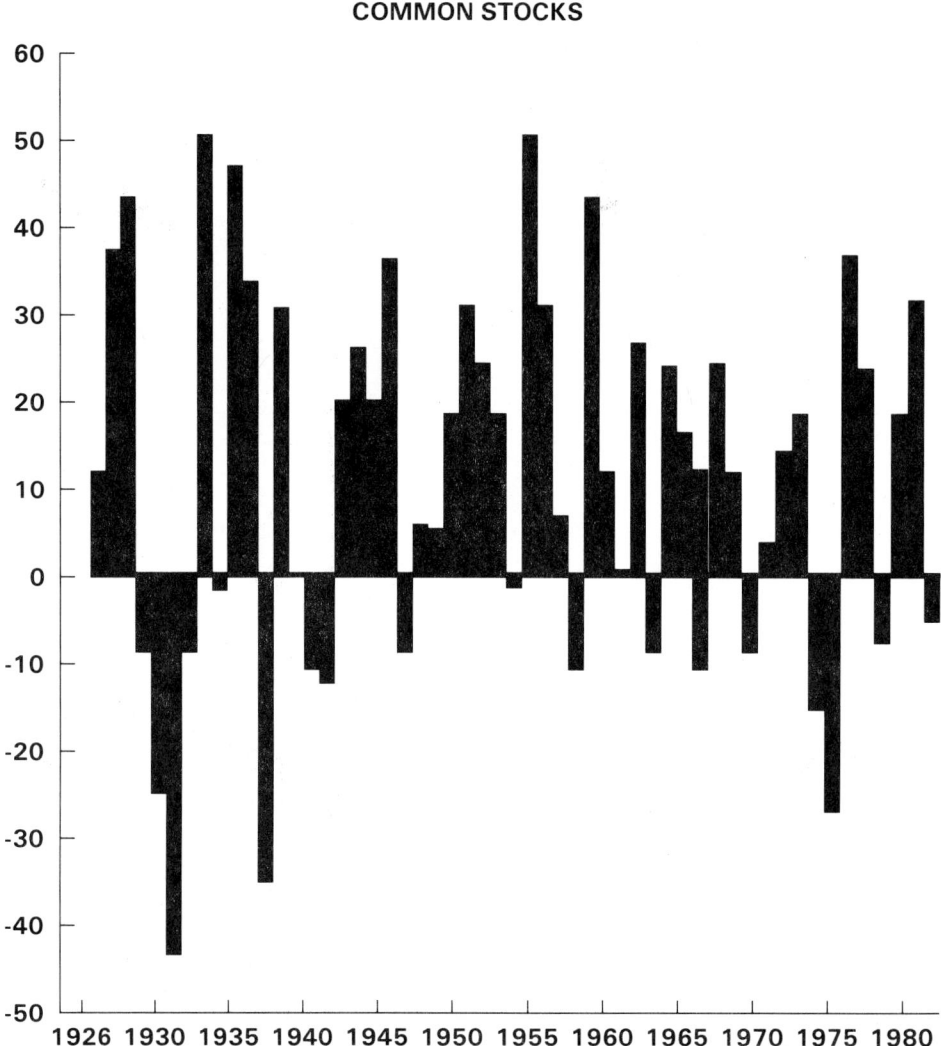

COMMON STOCKS

in 1981 was 8.9%. Throughout the whole 55 year period, inflation has been equal to a 3% annual rate. If one were to physically hold dollars in a safety deposit box, not investing any dollars at all, the purchasing power of that dollar would have been reduced by 3% for each of the 55 years.

Figure 2 is entitled "United States Treasury Bills." Perhaps the most dramatic aspect of this chart is that there was never a negative return for U.S. Treasury bills over the 55 year period. Further, Treasury bills have been extraordinarily stable. Returns have sometimes been relatively low, ranging in the 1% range between the early 1930s and the late 1940s. However, throughout the whole 55 year period, Treasury bills maintained a 3% annual rate of return, the same as inflation. Consequently, if one were to choose to invest in Treasury bills, he would have maintained the value of the dollar throughout this period.

Figure 3 is called "Long Term Government Bonds." One can observe readily that, when compared to United States Treasury bills, long term government bonds are quite variable. In fact, in 14 out of the 55 years, long term government bonds have declined. The highest return from government bonds was in 1932, when they earned 11%. However, over the total 55 year period, bonds earned 3%, about the same as inflation or Treasury bills.

Figure 5

**WEALTH INDEXES OF INVESTMENTS
IN THE U.S. CAPITAL MARKETS
1926–1981**

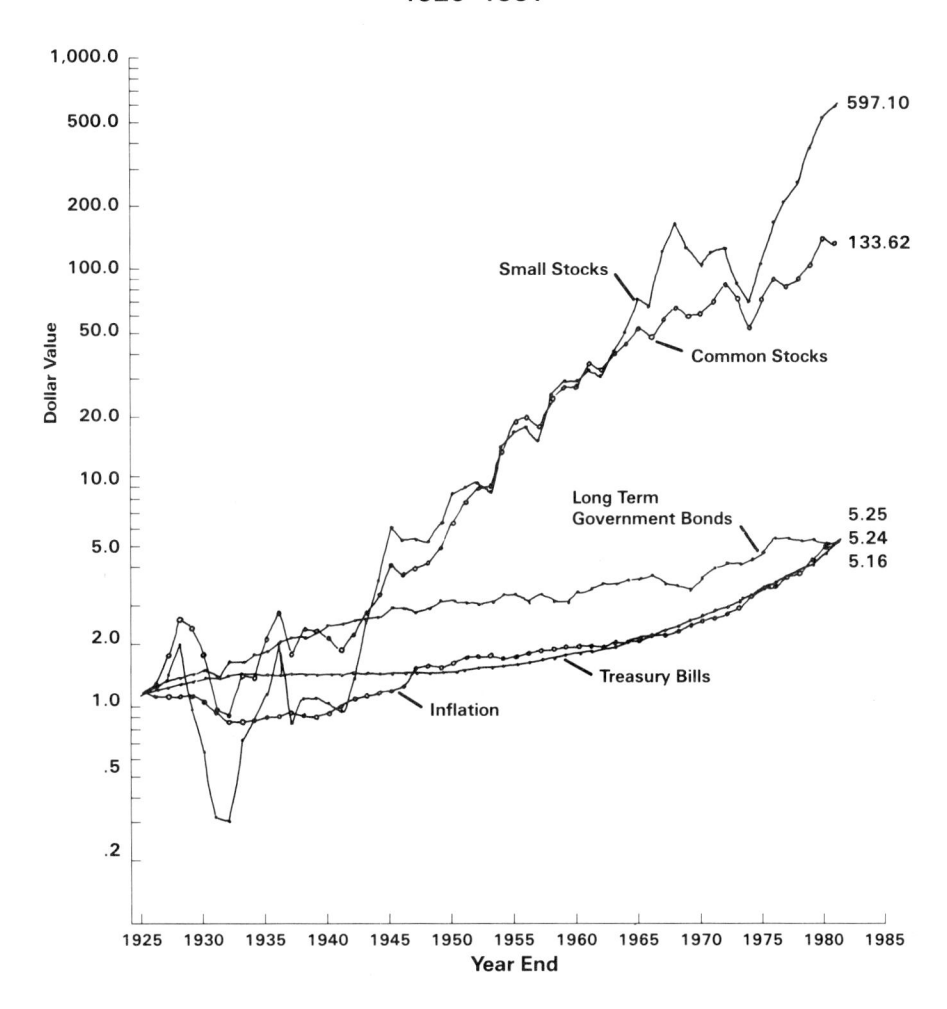

Turning to common stocks (Figure 4), it is readily apparent that there has been a great deal more uncertainty or volatility associated with common stocks over this 55 year period. In 19 of the 55 years, stocks went down. The highest return from stocks was in 1933, when they returned 54%. In 1980 they returned 32%, but in 1981 they declined 4.9%. It is clear that anyone over this period who put money in common stocks should have been ready to accept the huge upside and downside returns that are so graphically portrayed in common stock annual returns.

Wealth Accumulation

What does this type of volatility within the capital markets relate to in terms of wealth accumulation? Figure 5, "Wealth Indexes of Investments in the U.S. Capital Markets," indicates wealth accumulation available in the capital markets over the past 55 years. This figure dramatically displays the rewards that were received for exposing oneself to high risk and uncertainty over the past 55 years. Treasury bills, long term government bonds and inflation all have increased the nominal value of a dollar that was invested in 1926, and kept in those indexes until 1981 to roughly $5.20, not much difference. On the other hand, a dollar invested in common stocks and kept in the common stock market through the wide variations in returns would be worth $133 over the same 55 year period. Certainly, over the past 55 years, investors have been rewarded for taking the high risk associated with common stocks. High risk has meant high return over a long period.

This discussion does not imply that the next 55 years will in any way reflect the past 55 years; it just indicates what would have happened had an individual allocated his assets to different investment vehicles in a defined contribution plan over this period. Exercising different investment choices and tying those choices to a defined contribution plan can have a great impact on the ultimate value of such a retirement plan.

Solving Investment Problems for Small Funds

Definition of a Small Fund

Since no trustee wishes to believe that he is spending his time and efforts in overseeing an insignificant sum of money, I have found that it is very difficult to define what a small fund really is in the employee benefits area. However, there are some measures that we can use to help us.

Asset base would be a reasonable place to start. Interestingly enough, however, large banks or insurance companies who might combine or commingle any account under $5 million have a distinctly different view than does the independent investment counselor who might take on the management of an account of the $100,000 or $250,000 size. Estimates of a small fund range from under $5 million to $50 million.

"Small" then becomes a matter of perspective to the vendor of investment services, depending on his ability to service the more modest sized accounts. Regardless of size, I think that it is critical that the trustees of a fund make sure that they do have the vendor's attention. If they do not, the fund is not therefore of sufficient size to the provider of the investment services and its investment results may well suffer.

Second on our possible list of frames of reference would be a discussion of contribution size. Although a fund might be considered to be small in asset base, the sheer size of its annual contributions could well make it a large fund. A good example would be a new health and welfare fund that has several thousand covered employees. Certainly, it is a small fund today, but will be a sizable fund to be administered and managed later. Today's estimate of a small contribution base would range from $500,000 to $5 million.

A third way to view the issue of size is to look at the number of participants. A health and welfare plan for a large number of participants in a mature industry with a declining asset base and contribution levels might now qualify as a large fund, but might be a small fund tomorrow. Estimates of a small fund range from 100 to 1,000 participants.

As you can see, the actual definition of a small fund tends to be illusive because size is really in the

BY F. GILBERT BICKEL, III, CEBS

Mr. Bickel is director of consulting services for E. F. Hutton and Company, Inc. in St. Louis, responsible for consulting employee benefit plans regarding investment goals, asset allocation and implementation. Mr. Bickel was formerly president of Donelan-Phelps Investment Advisors, Inc. He received his B.S. degree in business administration from Washington University, his M.S. in commerce from St. Louis University and has attended the graduate school's Investment Management Course at Stanford University. He has taught finance at Lindenwood College, St. Louis University and Washington University. Mr. Bickel is a member of the St. Louis Society of Financial Analysts and of the charter class of Certified Employee Benefit Specialists (CEBS). He served three years on St. Louis County's Board of Equalization and currently serves as a member of the Missouri Governor's Commission on Crime.

eyes of the beholder, who has a number of personal biases.

Considerations in Structuring an Investment Program for a Small Fund

Trustee Interest

I have always found that the level and sophistication of trustee interest is paramount in the decision of what type of investment alternatives will be used in a given fund. If the trustees do not take their job seriously or conscientiously, they will take the easy way out or maybe make no decision at all. Cash equivalents have been an easy alternative in 1982.

Typically, I find that one or two trustees will be very interested in seeing that the fund strives to obtain a superior rate of return and will therefore work very hard to make sure that the remaining trustees participate to some extent. On the other side, those active trustees tend also to scrutinize the various investment alternatives carefully to prevent a potential undiversified disaster.

Ease of Administration

Another important consideration for trustees is the question of an administration of the fund. Many trustees do not want the supervisory job that goes with holding a diversified portfolio with several different investment managers. For the extremely small fund, size constraints probably would not allow that flexibility anyway. But for anything other than a very small fund, the trustees must make a commitment to providing the needed guidance and supervision.

Conceptual Simplicity

I have seen cases in which trustees actually have been bowled over by the hard realities of owning a diversified investment portfolio. To be effective, an investment program must be easily understood by each trustee. The concepts must be understandable and workable for the most inexperienced trustee or there are going to be problems down the road. I believe that it is the investment manager's job to ensure proper communication with the trustees.

Cost

A smaller fund cannot bypass the very important element of cost, since it represents a bigger percentage of the assets of a smaller fund than of those of a larger fund. However, the axiom, "You get what you pay for," is one of the great truths that trustees learn through the years. The trustees must weigh the relative potential return with the relative expense when deciding on the cost of purchasing various investment services.

Investment Goals

Regardless of the relative fund size, it is imperative that the fund's investment goals be set out in clearly defined terms. Without a roadmap, the trustees will never know whether they have arrived at their destination. Topics that should be covered include:

1. General attitudes toward the fund's management
2. Short term/long term economic outlook
3. Potential alternative investments
4. Potential asset sector outlook
5. Investment attitudes toward different classes of assets
6. Quality standards
7. Purchasing power risks
8. Definition of risk
9. Investment parameters:
   - Liquidity needs
   - Current income needs
   - Comfort level
   - Actuarial needs
   - Retention of principal values
10. Type, method and form of investment reports
11. Investment advisor relationships and communications
12. Custodian relationship.

Future Contribution Estimates

For the smaller fund, I believe that it makes a lot of sense to budget for estimated cash flow as well as possible. This tactic should not only help the trustees forecast cash flow, but also will give them a fairly good picture of how much money they will have available for investment at any one time.

Performance Needs

In structuring the investment program, the trustees should consider the issue of potential investment performance and how that issue might impact their attitudes and contributions and the fund's management. The potential rewards of any investment alternative should be weighed carefully against the expected return.

Need for Flexibility

Whatever decisions current trustees make for the investment of the fund's assets, they must provide a back door, an escape hatch—better known as investment flexibility. What may seem to be the ultimate investment answer today may prove to be tomorrow's mistake. The smaller the fund, the greater the need for investment flexibility.

Providers of Alternative Investments

Regardless of whether your portfolio might contain cash equivalents; fixed income alternatives such as corporate bonds, insured contracts, real estate mortgages and U.S. government bonds; the equity alternative of common stocks, preferred stocks and real estate; or alternatives in the miscellaneous classification, which covers commodities, metals, covered options, timber, coal, oil and gas, some provider or vendor will be there to help guide you through the investment maze.

Some of these alternative providers and their approximate costs are:
- Bank trust operations ($3/10$ of 1% to 1%)
- Brokerage firms ($1/2$ of 1% + commissions or 3% wraparound fee)
- Independent investment advisors ($1/8$ of 1% to $1 1/2$%)
- Insurance companies ($1/10$ of 1% to $9/10$ of 1%)
- Syndicators ($1/2$ of 1% to $2 1/2$%).

Operationally, you may have a separate or individual account relationship or you may have a pooled or commingled account. The fund's size, the type of investment and the type of provider's vehicle will greatly determine whether your fund is commingled or a separate account. The actual form of investment vehicles will depend on the specific provider and its need or desire to invest the trusts' funds individually.

The Trustees vs. the Providers

In my opinion, the decision of whether the fund operates in the commingled fashion versus the separate account form should depend on the trustees' perceived needs for:
- Asset diversification
- Reporting
- Service
- Flexibility
- Risk versus return balance.

Summary—Keys to a Successful Program

Although success is in the eye of the beholder and may only be relevant to other alternatives, I think that trustees have to do their best to:
- Accomplish the fund's stated investment goals.
- Satisfy the fund's actuarial requirement.
- Maintain diversification.
- Retain flexibility.
- Make administration as easy as possible.
- Balance costs with potential and actual return.

Fixed Income Alternatives

BY GEORGE J. COLLINS

IN THIS PRESENTATION I will try to give you a look at a couple of different alternatives to fixed income management in the context of what has been a highly volatile fixed income market—one that recently has been very good to us, but which over the last couple of years has been very volatile and has eroded the values of most of your fixed income portfolios substantially. It is interesting to note that at this time last year, we were talking about substantial negative rates of return. For the 12 months ending October 1981, bonds produced total rates of return of between –10% and –12%, and that return includes the coupon income. Today, for the 12 months ending September 1982, those same fixed income securities, using the Salomon Brothers Index as a measure, have produced rates of return of almost +45%. If you include the month of October, the total return for the last 13 months has increased to almost +55%. During this period, stocks have not done nearly as well as bonds.

Although the news today is better, the fact is that bonds are a lot different today than they used to be. Bonds cannot be relied on to produce the nice, stable rates of return for which they have been known in the past. Undoubtedly, you have spent a lot of time wondering what to do about your fixed income portfolio.

I will also try to give you some perspective on a couple of relatively new alternatives in the areas of immunization and dedication. A lot of attention currently is being paid to these concepts and, most importantly, a lot of money is being moved into immunization-related products. Just a short while ago, a statement was made by a representative of Salomon Brothers that almost $15 billion of fixed income assets have been either immunized or put into dedicated portfolios. The majority of this money, in my opinion, has come from the corporate sector. I have not seen that much coming from the multiemployer area, but certainly it has been a major trend in the corporate sector of the market.

A major consideration in the scope of fixed income portfolio management is the choice between active and passive management. The distinguishing feature between an active portfolio manager and a passive portfolio manager should be obvious to all of us: The passive manager sits

Mr. Collins is director of the Fixed Income Division of T. Rowe Price Associates, Inc. He is responsible for $6.5 billion in assets and directs a staff of 40. Mr. Collins additionally serves on the firm's board of directors and investment policy committee and is president of T. Rowe Price's new income fund, tax free income fund and tax exempt money fund, as well as vice president and director of the firm's prime reserve fund and U.S. Treasury money fund. Active in the employee benefit field for over 11 years, both in multiemployer and corporate areas, he previously served as bond portfolio manager and senior security analyst for the U.S. Fidelity and Guaranty Company, and as financial analyst for Diversified Services, Inc. Mr. Collins earned his B.A. degree in history and economics at Virginia Military Institute, Lexington, Virginia, his M.B.A. degree with distinction in finance at the American University School of Business, Washington, D.C. and his certificate of completion from Stanford University Executive Program. He is chartered investment counselor for the Investment Counsel Association and is a member of the Bond Portfolio Managers Association and the Municipal Bond Club of Baltimore.

on his assets while the active manager manages his assets. I will try to address the following questions: What is the bond environment? What are the styles of an active manager? How should you measure an active bond manager? How should these managers be organized? What do these managers look at? How important is the interest rate forecast? What should be your fixed income strategy?

Bond Environment

Figure 1 shows a decline in the value of bonds corresponding to increases in interest rates. What

Figure 1

CORPORATE BOND YIELDS BY RATINGS
Long Term Monthly Averages

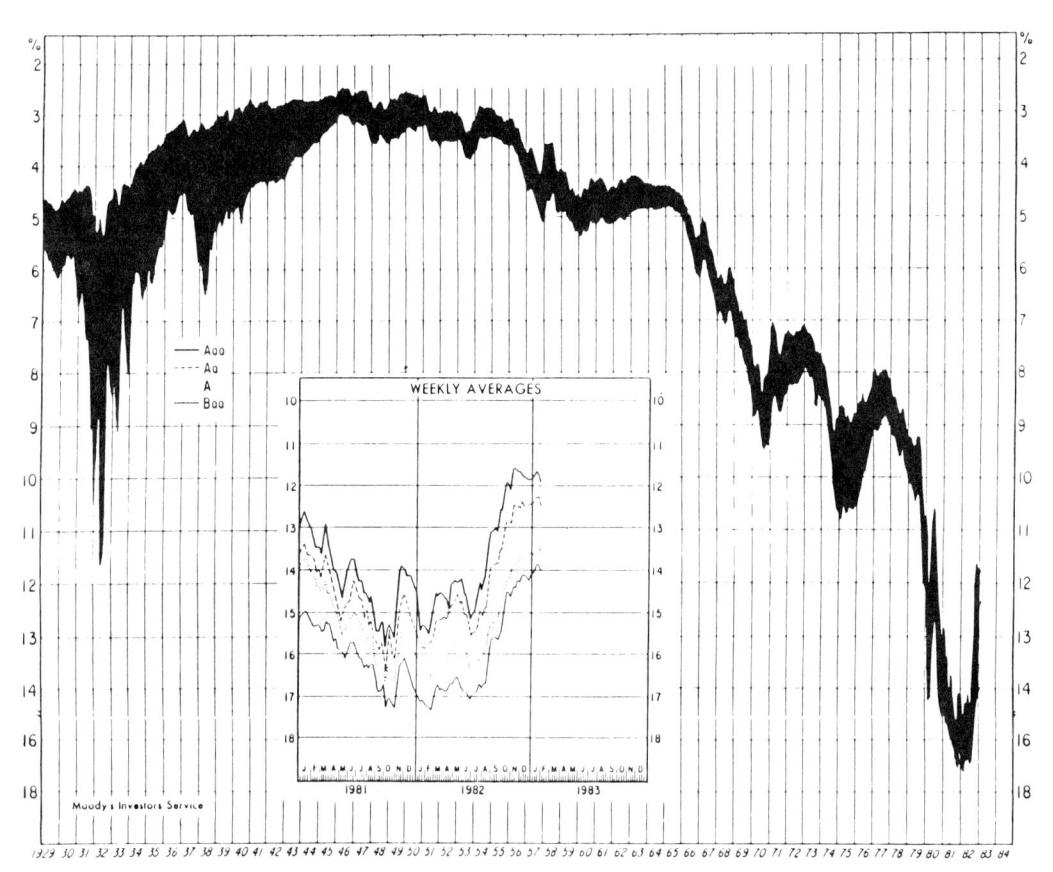

Source: Moody's Investors Service

is portrayed is a very bad market environment: the great bear market. The only bull markets during this period were the small rallies around the recessions of 1970, 1975, 1976 and, more recently, in 1980 and 1982. This environment has not been particularly good for the active bond manager to work in. As a result, we have seen a tremendous growth in defensive products, such as the immunization techniques I mentioned previously.

Figure 2 depicts the fixed income environment for the past year and, more importantly, the past quarter: a period that was quite explosive. The highest yields a year ago were in the short term area. A three month domestic certificate of deposit (CD) a year ago yielded 16.30%; today's rate is around 9%. During this period, the long term market also gave up a lot of yield, with corporate bond coupons declining from 18.55% to 12.30%. It is even more dramatic when you look at the long market and the short market together during the past quarter. During these three months, short rates declined over 5½ points, while long rates declined over four points. Again, this quarter obviously was very explosive. In this short period of time, the market has turned from illiquid to very liquid, and bond prices have risen very sharply.

Figure 3 portrays bond volatility by comparing the average annual standard deviation of the total returns of stocks and bonds. It shows that in more recent periods, particularly since the Federal Reserve changed its basic approach to monetary policy in October 1979, bonds have been more volatile than stocks. I am tempted to say that this pattern probably will continue in the future, but

Figure 2
YIELD CURVES

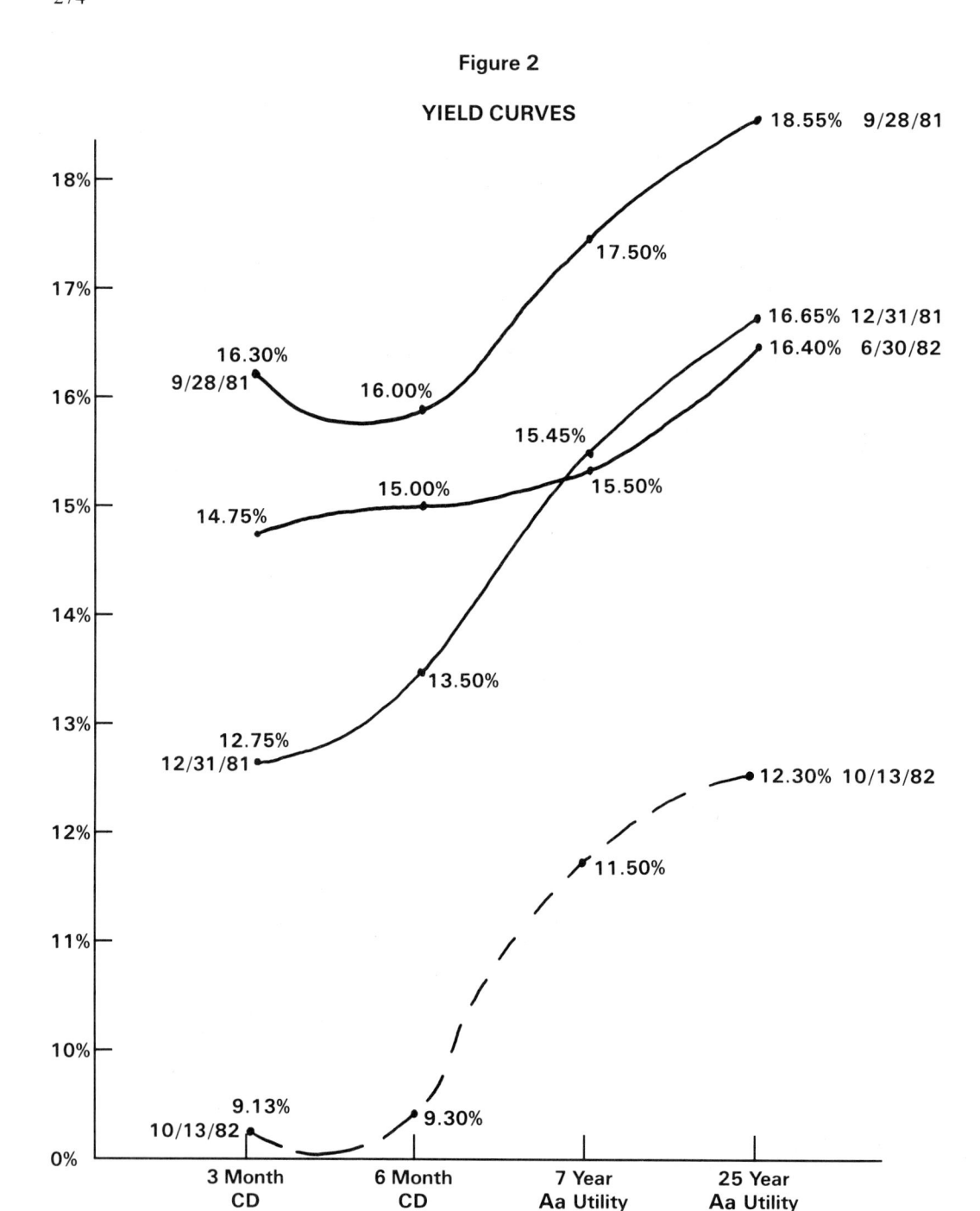

- 18.55% 9/28/81
- 17.50%
- 16.65% 12/31/81
- 16.40% 6/30/82
- 16.30% 9/28/81
- 16.00%
- 15.45%
- 15.50%
- 15.00%
- 14.75%
- 13.50%
- 12.75% 12/31/81
- 12.30% 10/13/82
- 11.50%
- 9.13% 10/13/82
- 9.30%

X-axis: 3 Month CD, 6 Month CD, 7 Year Aa Utility, 25 Year Aa Utility

the point is that in the past three years bonds have been very volatile and, in fact, have been more volatile than stocks.

The best fixed income returns over the bear market environment of the past 30 or 40 years have been from Treasury bills. The simple rolling over of 90 day Treasury bills would have produced higher returns than any other single, repetitive strategy, particularly in more recent times, since Treasury bill yields normally move hand in hand with the rate of inflation, as shown in Figure 4. Since there is no credit risk and no market liquid-

Figure 3

COMPARATIVE STOCK AND BOND VOLATILITY

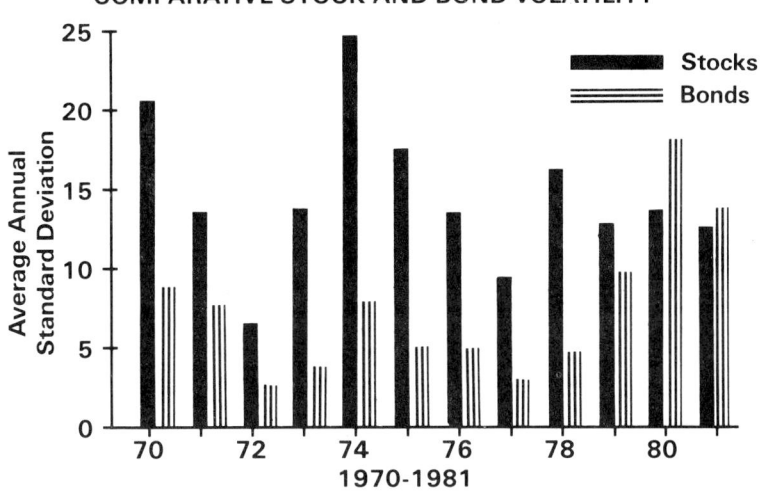

1970-1981

ity risk with T-bills, only the reinvestment risk is of concern, that is, the risk that the rate might fall significantly by the time your Treasury bill matures and needs to be reinvested. Reinvestment risk has been the only major risk, until the last quarter, of keeping your portfolio very short.

Table I compares performance for the various fixed income markets. I have taken the past 35 calendar quarters, from January 1974 to September 1982, for 90 day Treasury bills, the Lehman Brothers Kuhn Loeb (LBKL) Intermediate Bond Index, the LBKL Long Bond Index, our own "Best of Best" index and the Lipper Bond Funds Averages, which is a composite of the 40 bond funds that Lipper monitors. What this table shows are the total returns and the average annual returns for each of these indexes.

Table I

PERFORMANCE MEASUREMENT

	Total Return	Average Annual Return
Treasury bills	+108.4	8.8
LKL intermediate	101.7	8.4
LKL long	63.5	5.8
Best of Best index	379.9	19.6
Lipper bond funds	96.6	8.0

Period: 1/1/74–9/30/82
35 Quarters

The Active Bond Manager

Based on this information, how do you measure an active bond manager? Certainly one of the most obvious comparisons should be against Treasury bills. If an active bond manager is worth anything, he or she should add value to the portfolio. In adding value, a comparison should be made to 90 day Treasury bills. The T-bill is a simple, risk free security that anybody can invest in safely. If you can't outperform 90 day Treasury bills over a full market cycle, you are *not* a good active manager. Recently, this performance goal has been a very tough target because of the negative returns in the marketplace. However, the intermediate and long term indexes are also important.

Depending on the objective of the portfolio, the "Best of Best" index also could be considered, and it is the goal that the active manager should be aiming for. In constructing the "Best of Best" index, we have taken, over the last 35 quarters, that sector, whether short, intermediate or long, that has yielded the highest total return for each particular quarter. As shown in Table II, in 17 of the last 35 quarters, short term instruments have given the best return. The intermediate sector performed the best only three times, whereas the long sector was the best in 15 quarters. As you would expect, there are no negative returns in the short term sector, but there were ten quarters of negative total returns in the intermediate sector and 15 quarters of negative total returns in the long sector.

Figure 4

TREASURY BILL RATES VS. INFLATION

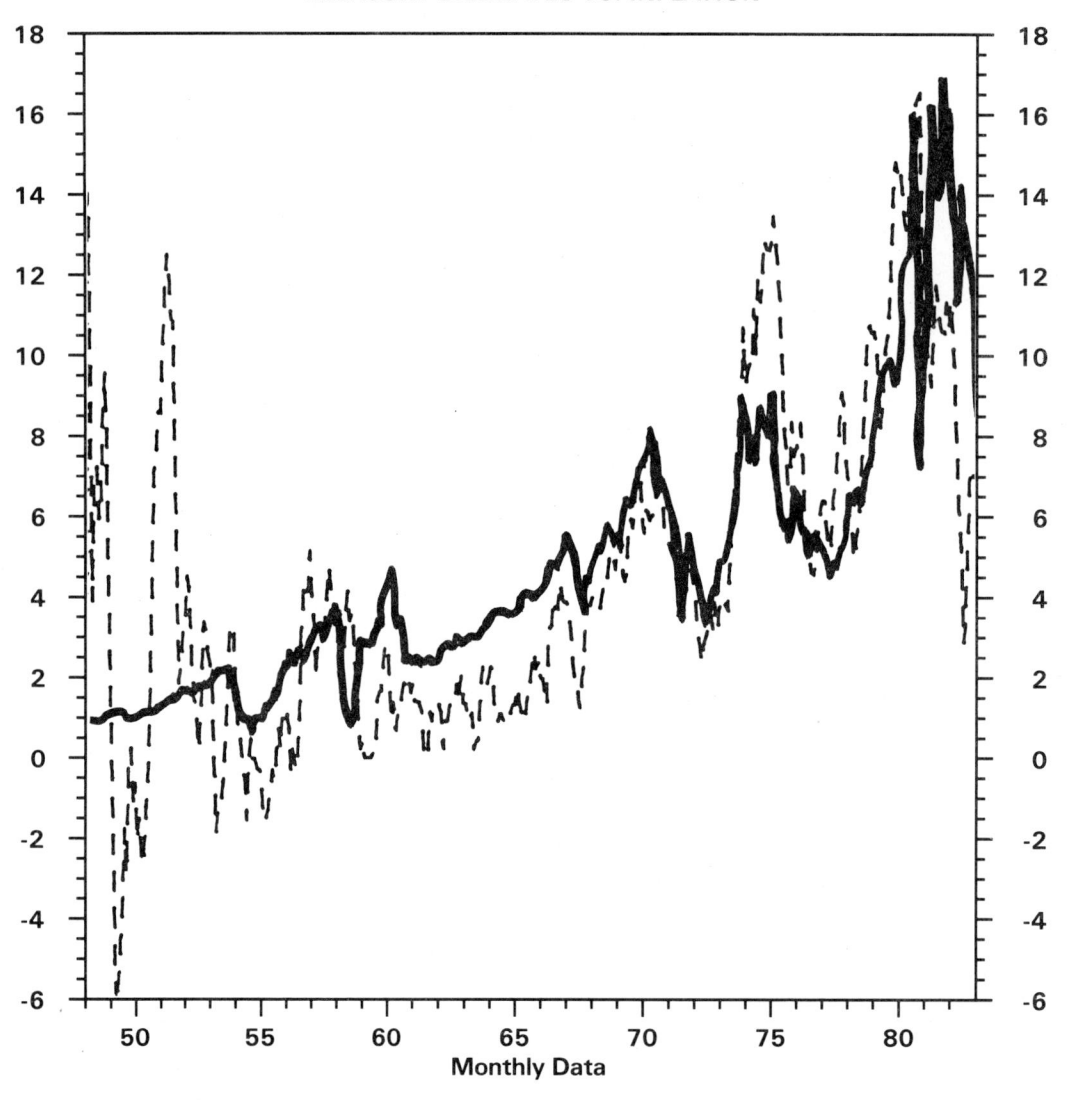

Sources: U.S. Treasury, Bureau of Labor Statistics

— Interest Rate on 3 Month Treasury Bills
--- Inflation Over 6 Month Spans, CPI

Obviously, longer term bonds were not a very stable investment environment. The "Best of Best" index works out to a 20% average annual return, and almost 400 percentage points for the full 35 quarters. Table III is a performance summary, on a quarterly basis, where the "S" signifies the 17 times that the short sector came out ahead, "I" where the intermediate sector is the winner and "L" where the long sector won.

Areas of Concern

With regard to what areas the active manager should be concerned with, put most of his or her time, effort and research into, very clearly the ma-

Table II

BEST OF BEST INDEX

(Last 35 Quarters)

Sector	No. Periods
Short term	17
Intermediate	3
Long term	15

Negative Quarters	
Intermediate	10
Long term	15

Table III

BEST OF BEST INDEX

Quarters

1974	S	S	I	L
1975	L	L	S	L
1976	L	I	L	L
1977	S	L	L	S
1978	S	S	L	S
1979	I	L	S	S
1980	S	L	S	S
1981	S	S	S	L
1982	L	S	L	

turity selection of the portfolios is the most important. The greatest risk to the portfolio is price, or market, risk. For this reason, most of your time and research money should go into that maturity selection process, as depicted in Figure 5. I am not saying, as in the "Best of Best" index, that the active bond manager can be, or should be expected to be, perfect all the time, but he should be correct in the majority of the markets and with the bulk of his assets. This consistency is crucial in order to avoid negative returns and to perform ahead of Treasury bills. Additionally, credit research, which I will discuss in greater detail, is very important because this area is where we find the raw material to invest in. Industry sector selection is also crucial: One need only look to the housing industry, the forest products industry and even the telephone industry, areas that were once very sacred in the marketplace and were considered very high quality, to see the importance of sector analysis.

There are several active management styles or techniques that can add value to a fixed income portfolio:

- Sector plays
  1. Industry/coupon/credit
  2. Junk
  3. GNMA/mortgages
  4. Sinking funds
  5. Private placements
- Arbitrage
- Interest rate plays.

Sector swaps, industry selection, coupon and credit are all very important. Upgrading or downgrading of credits at the right time, and using low or high coupons at the right stage in the interest rate cycle, can both add value. The area of coupon selection has grown tremendously in recent years and has produced many new opportunities now that we have deep discount bonds and zero coupon bonds, as well as the higher and current coupon issues. Ginnie Maes and mortgage-related securities are also very important, as are sinking funds, private placements, arbitrage and the interest rate plays.

The active, fixed income markets are:
- Governments
- Mortgage-backed securities
- Corporates
- Agencies
- Money market
- Coupon range
- Rule 415.

Among the markets that active bond managers use most often, the government bond market is, by far, the most important because of its size. It is an extremely liquid market and it is one that is virtually risk free. Another market, the mortgage-backed securities, has grown tremendously in recent years and I would now rank it second behind the government market but ahead of the corporate market in terms of size. Here again we are talking about, for the most part, a market with excellent quality, good liquidity and with no significant size limitations. Finally, though not least in importance, is the money market. To maintain a positive return in negative bond markets, it is often necessary to shorten the portfolio substantially and to go in the money market, buying Bankers' Acceptances, CDs, commercial paper, repos, etc. For this reason, the money market will always be an important resource to the active bond manager.

The Importance of Interest Rates

All active portfolio managers have an interest rate forecast, whether explicit or implied. In fact, most economists now come up with as many as three separate forecasts, assign a probability to each and defend each scenario individually.

Figure 5

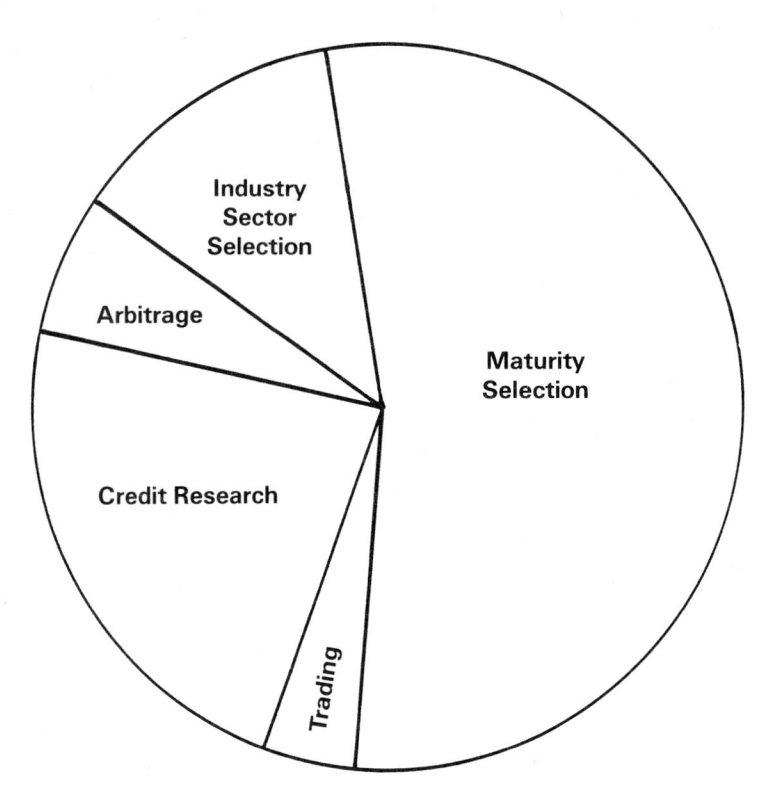

STRATEGY EMPHASIS

[Pie chart showing segments: Industry Sector Selection, Arbitrage, Credit Research, Trading, Maturity Selection]

What are the important elements in such a forecast?
- Federal Reserve policy
- Fiscal policy
- Economy activity
- Inflation
- International markets
- Politics
- Internal rates of return
- Shape of yield curve.

First and foremost is Federal Reserve policy. All we have to do is look at the last three years, the changes in Federal Reserve policy and their impact on the markets, to see how important that policy has been. Fiscal policy is also growing in importance because of the amount of debt the U.S. government has issued and the effect that this large volume of Treasury securities is having on the markets. The importance of economic activity to the forecast is obvious. If economic activity increases, we have greater demands for credit; if we have greater demands for credit, we are going to have rising interest rates. Inflation is also very important, particularly over the long run, as are the influences of the international markets. Domestic and international politics have become very important in recent years and have exerted their own influence on the shape of the yield curve. Therefore, we develop an interest rate forecast based on, and in consideration of, each of these factors.

Table IV is an example of an interest rate forecast and how, as a result, an active bond manager might structure his portfolio over the next couple of years. Remember that this forecast is predicated on those factors that we just looked at: the trend and level of real economic growth, the money supply, the basic Federal Reserve statistics and the inflation rate. What this forecast shows is a continuation of the decline in both short term rates (Treasury bills) and long term rates (Aa utilities). This decline being the pattern, one would be moderately bullish and extend portfolio maturities, on market weakness, where one could find value. This strategy should increase the return from the portfolio.

Table IV

**INTEREST RATE FORECAST
AND LONG TERM BOND STRATEGIES**

	1982	1983	1984
Real growth	−1.4%	3.3%	3.2%
Money	5.8	5.9	6.0
Inflation	6.2	5.6	5.9
T-bills	10.3	8.1	8.5
Aa utilities	14.8	13.0	12.5

Strategy: Moderately bullish—extend portfolio maturities on weakness.

How that strategy might look in more detail is shown in Table V. This table reflects a short term and long term strategy, the positives and negatives affecting those strategies and the inevitable uncertainties. What is extremely difficult to build into this process are those market occurrences that the portfolio manager hasn't anticipated or can't anticipate in the interest rate forecast: irresponsible fiscal policy, uncertainty surrounding the Federal Reserve's monetary targeting policy, the transitional phase of the economy, the cyclical or perhaps secular change in inflation, etc.

Credit Research

To the active bond manager, it is very important to have the necessary raw material so that he or she can move confidently in the marketplace. There are always opportunities to add value from good credit research. Certainly, a good bond manager should have a credit staff which is active in contacting the financial managements of organizations in which the fund invests. The work that the credit analyst does should include:
- Establishing direct contact with the financial management of organizations
- Establishing a system that studies cash flow analyses, developing ratios for liquidity, capitalization and profitability assessments
- Monitoring external credit ratings
- Determining internal credit rating system
- Working from approved list.

Table VI shows how the use of credit analysis can add value in the money market area. Here you see the mid-1974 "flight to quality" in the marketplace, when the yield spreads between Treasury bills and bank CDs were as high as 500-600 basis points following the Franklin National Bank failure. In the next column, you see the more normal spread of 14-30 basis points and, in the last column, the recent spread of 200-300 basis points.

Doing adequate and thorough credit research can give a portfolio manager the confidence in a select group of banks or investments, which at times can add tremendous value to the portfolio—in this case, 200-300 basis points.

In value analysis—also important to an active bond manager—one must:
- Identify opportunities for active repositioning along the yield curve.
- Monitor yield differentials among various sectors and securities.
- Employ credit analysis to identify securities that are over or undervalued.
- Capitalize on trading opportunities.

What is cheap? What is rich? Where should one position along the yield curve? Monitoring the yield differentials among sectors and among different credits and capitalizing on trading opportunities in the marketplace are important aspects of active bond management. A good example, shown in Table VII, is the historical yield spreads in the corporate market looking at industrials and utilities from a credit standpoint. What this table shows is that weaker credits can add value. Right now, the Baa and A credits—if you do the proper research—can represent exceptional values.

An Example Portfolio

How should an actively managed bond portfolio look over time? An illustration is shown in Figure 6 where all this business of credit research, interest rate forecasting and sector evaluation is reflected. What I have done in this figure is to compare an active manager's portfolio to the Lehman Kuhn Loeb Index, a well-known example of a passive portfolio. The chart at the top shows the weighted average maturity. Note that, for the active manager, the maturity has ranged from 14-18 years, down to around four years, back up to 14, down to six and more recently up to around the 14 year area. As shown in the middle chart, the weighted average coupon has trended upward along with the rise in interest rates, although, if one shifts a portfolio from long to short at the right time (that is, if one catches the downturn in prices properly), one will be giving up coupon yield initially. Hopefully, that will be made up in total return, as was done in this example with the shortening of the portfolio in 1977, 1978 and again in early 1979. Finally, the last chart shows the variation in quality ranging from as low as Baa+ to as high as Aaa−.

Management Constraints

Should there be constraints on the active portfolio manager? We believe that there should. The

Table V

STRATEGY

Short Term

Reserves (0-1 year)

Recommended Action: Reserves should average 180 days.

Reasons:
- Positive yield curve
- Stress liquidity and quality
- Sector spreads remain wide
- Short term rates could spike higher.

Alternative: Lengthen reserves less aggressively. Money growth targeting could reappear in 1-6 months.

Short-Intermediate (1+ - 5 years)

Recommended Action: BUY

Long-Intermediate (5+ - 10 years)

Recommended Action: BUY
- Buy aggressively
- Stress investment grade
- Watch call provisions.

Long Term Bonds (10+ years)

Recommended Action: BUY

Reasons:
- Positive yield curve
- Yield spreads should close.

Alternative:
- Build moderate long position.

Long Range

Reserves (0-1 year)

Recommended Action: Capitalize on positive curve.

Short-Intermediate (1+ - 5 years)

Recommended Action: Short-intermediate issues should perform well.

Long-Intermediate (5+ - 10 years)

Recommended Action: Long-intermediates should give high positive returns. Marketable issues should be favored.

Long Term (10+ years)

Recommended Action: Long term bonds should perform well.

Critical Factors Impacting Strategy

Near Term

Positives	Negatives	?
• Easier Federal Reserve	• Staggering world-wide debt burden	• Responsible fiscal policy
• Positively sloped yield curve	• Bank problems	• Fed monetary targeting policy and inconsistencies
• Positive dealer carry	• Bankruptcies expected	• Middle East
• Recession/slow growth	• Large structural gov. deficits and borrowing needs	• Transition in economy
• Stable inflation rates	• High private credit demands	• Inflation cyclical/ secular change
• Easing of wage pressures	• Money growth above target.	• Midelection cycle outlook.
• Bond market liquidity.		

Future Concerns
- Market volatility
- Government borrowing "crowding out"
- Europeanization of bond market
- 1980s decade of geopolitical confrontations.

Table VI

CREDIT ANALYSIS

	Mid-1974 "Flight to Quality"		4/22/77 ("Normal")		8/20/82 ("Recent")	
	Yield	Spread	Yield	Spread	Yield	Spread
90 day Treasury bills:	7.41%		4.56%		7.13%	
90 day domestic CDs:	12.65%	+524 B.P.	4.70%	+14 B.P.	9.50%	+237 B.P.
90 day Eurodollar CDs:	13.69%	+628 B.P.	4.88%	+32 B.P.	10.00%	+287 B.P.

Having confidence in a select group of banks can enhance yield substantially.

Table VII

HISTORICAL YIELD SPREAD RELATIONSHIPS (BASIS POINTS)

Sector	1971-1981			
Industrial	Range	Mean	Standard Deviation	10/1/82
Aa vs. Aaa	12-51	27.7	12.0	25
A vs. Aaa	35-117	58.7	21.2	75
Baa vs. Aaa	72-225	134.5	47.6	160
A vs. Aa	23-66	34.8	13.5	50
Baa vs. Aa	50-175	107.2	37.0	135
Baa vs. A	24-109	72.3	27.0	85
Public Utility				
Aa vs. Aaa	12-39	26.2	10.2	25
A vs. Aaa	24-106	61.0	27.3	100
Baa vs. Aaa	57-193	120.3	45.8	215
A vs. Aa	12-85	36.5	21.7	75
Baa vs. Aa	45-152	94.2	36.5	190
Baa vs. A	33-88	59.3	20.6	115

questions you should ask of your manager are very important. For example, should industry sector limitations apply to telephones or public utilities? Certainly there shouldn't be any sector limitations on Treasuries. Do utilities hold any special risk, such as that from a nuclear accident? What about preferred stocks? Should they be included in the portfolio when they are priced cheaply and perhaps sell at higher yields than bonds? How do you determine the credit worthiness of short term investment funds (STIF accounts) when you don't know what's in the pool? Single issuer limitations are also important. What about Yankee, Eurodollar, Canadian or other foreign issues? Should there be limitations on these as well?

These types of questions should be addressed by establishing portfolio diversification guidelines, such as:
- Industry sector limitations
- Utilities
- Nuclear risk
- Preferred stocks
- STAP/undetermined credits
- Credit ratings
- Single issuer limitations
- Issue limitations
- Private placements
- Eurodollar, Canadian, foreign.

Immunization and Dedication

At this point I would like to say a few words about fixed income investing for pension plans and some of the latest techniques in immunization and dedication. In this regard, I don't want you to think that my remarks are sour grapes. Active portfolio managers have the capability to immunize and dedicate for their clients, and many of our clients view this service as just another of our products.

However, I consider myself an investment counselor and I take the active management function very seriously. If you immunize or dedicate, you should be doing it for the right reasons and you should recognize your decision for what it is. It should be viewed as an active decision in a continuing active context, and you should be aware of what the consequences are likely to be.

Many plan sponsors and trustees seem to think that immunization and dedication are passive approaches. But, as I will illustrate, there is still a large dose of active management and, hence, risk in them. For instance, a typical reason given for setting up a classic "duration matching" or "bullet immunized" portfolio is to lock in today's interest rates because they are particularly appealing. What is implicit in such a decision is the assumption that rates are expected to decline and that bond prices are expected to go up. If that active conviction is really present, then why not put your money into long bonds where you will get a bigger play? Why do I say that? Because immunization caps the upside potential as well as the downside risk.

Another reason often cited for immunization is the desire to escape the volatility in bonds. This

Figure 6

ACTIVE MANAGEMENT

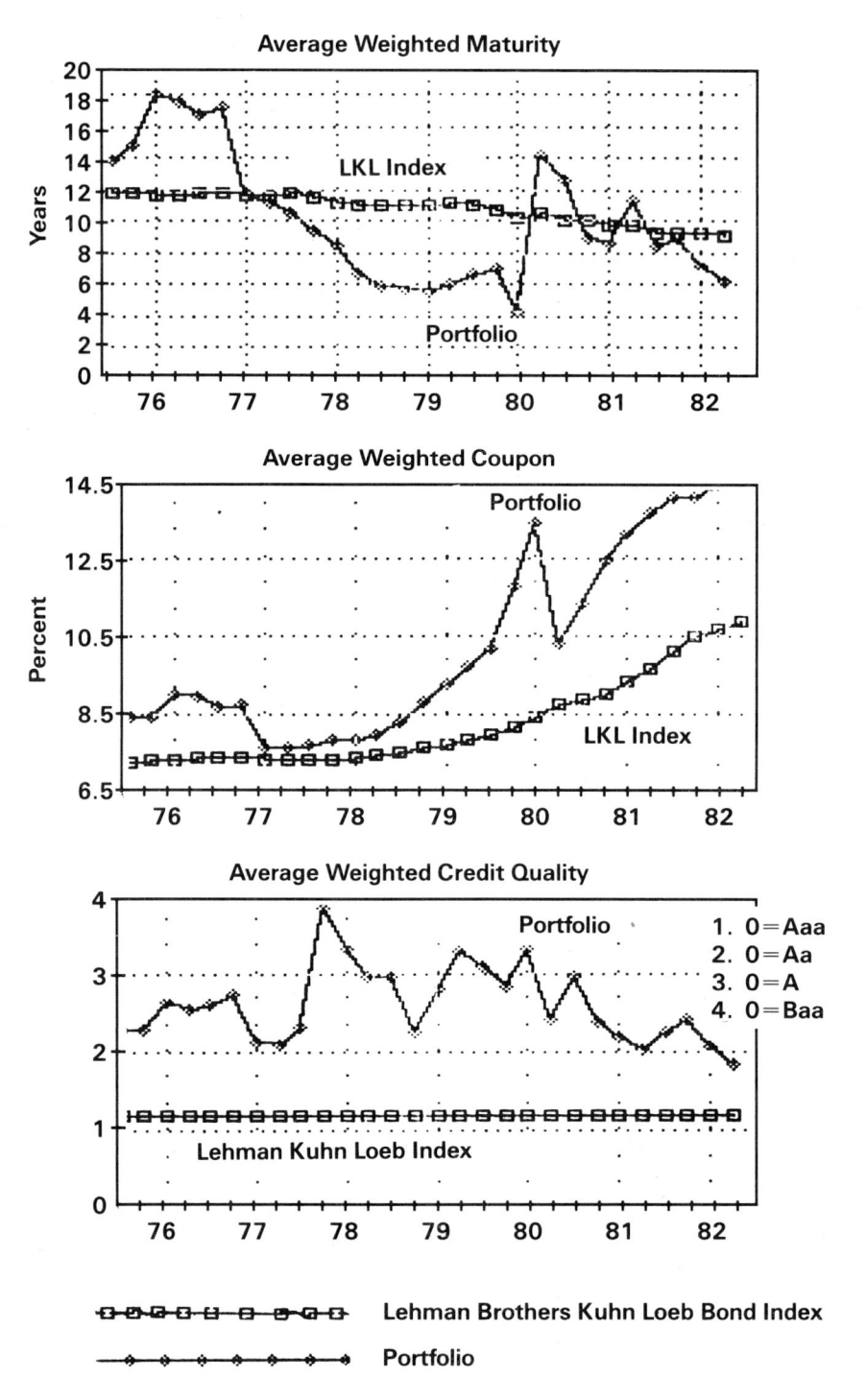

Average Weighted Maturity

Average Weighted Coupon

Average Weighted Credit Quality

1. 0=Aaa
2. 0=Aa
3. 0=A
4. 0=Baa

Lehman Brothers Kuhn Loeb Bond Index
Portfolio

reason is often another way of saying, "I have seen nothing but the bad aspects of volatility," which could mean that this time is the worst to eliminate volatility from the portfolio, since volatility on the upside is good. True, an immunized bond portfolio is less volatile than an active one, but the expected return is also lower. Immunizing bonds without altering the risk of other assets in the plan, for example by taking more risk in stocks or in bonds, decreases the expected return of the total portfolio.

I am also concerned about the tracking record of immunized portfolios and what it may eventually turn out to be. A few years ago, we heard original estimates of plus or minus five basis points; I am now hearing 50 basis points. I wonder if it eventually might approach 100 basis points or more.

Dedication, liability immunization or whatever you might call this approach to cash flow matching has been practiced for many years. Typically, a bond portfolio is dedicated against a series of liabilities because bond prices look attractive at the time. Again, the decision is an active one, but this approach has some hidden time bombs, too. What happens if retirees don't die nicely—that is, according to actuarial calculations? Second, although pension contributions are reduced in earlier years using dedication, contributions can turn out to be larger in later years than they would have been if no dedication had been used—but how much larger? That depends on the characteristics of the plan, but it is an issue that can't be ignored.

That observation brings me to the larger, asset mix question of how much to immunize and/or dedicate. For a dedicated portfolio, the question seems easy to answer at first: Dedicate against liabilities for retirees and terminated vested employees. But what happens when next year's group of retirees enters the retired population? Do you re-dedicate? Will rates be as good? Should you dedicate now for those who are going to retire next year? What about those who are going to retire in three, four or five years? These questions require some tough active management decisions.

For an immunized bullet portfolio, finding an answer is even tougher. The typical approach is to use a computer-based, asset allocation model. However, I don't think these models are really adequate to answer the question. Besides, the technical problems of simply describing the immunized portfolio in quantitative terms, and the choices available regarding the particular time horizon, really influence the answer. With a time horizon equal to the life of an immunized portfolio, typically five years, immunization looks terrific.

However, what is sacred about a five year horizon, or any other fixed period? Try a simulation with an immunized portfolio lasting five or seven years and then tack on another five years of investment after the immunized portfolio expires. You will find that the models don't like immunization quite as much. The problem is that you have a static model applied to a dynamic situation.

Finally, I will mention that maturity selection, which I have ranked as the number one decision for the active bond manager, is preempted by the mathematics of duration and immunization. How about credit analysis? Setting up an immunized or dedicated portfolio is the start of the process, not the end. In immunization and dedication, portfolio techniques are not special properties of the financial instrument used. Unless one employs Treasuries exclusively, which can get very expensive in terms of yield giveup, the contents of the immunized/dedicated portfolios are the same as the contents of other active fixed income portfolios—namely bonds—and they require constant watching. I wonder how many Johns Manville bonds are out there now in existing immunized/dedicated portfolios? My point is that these techniques require serious thought, both in advance of establishing the portfolio and on an ongoing basis after implementation. Immunization is not the pot of gold at the end of the rainbow. In some cases it may be a pot, but it might not be filled with gold.

Options for Employee Benefit Funds

BY HERBERT B. SOROCA

OPTIONS ARE an investment tool. They can be used to tailor the risk profile of the portfolio, to generate additional income, to protect profits or to speculate. The purpose of this discussion is to describe the various strategies and their strengths and weaknesses so that an informed judgment regarding their use can be made.

The first step is to provide the basic language and terms of options:
- *Call Option*—A contract giving the buyer the right to purchase 100 shares of stock at a specified price for a certain period of time
- *Put Option*—A contract giving the buyer the right to sell 100 shares of stock at a specified price for a certain period of time
- *Strike Price*—The price at which the 100 shares of stock are bought or sold
- *Maturity*—The date on which the option expires
- *Exercise*—The purchase or sale of 100 shares of stock according to the terms of the option contract.

Mr. Soroca serves as manager of options and related investment matters for L. F. Rothschild Asset Management, a subsidiary of L. F. Rothschild, Unterberg, Towbin of New York, New York. Mr. Soroca received his A.B. degree from Columbia College and his LL.B. degree from Columbia University School of Law. He has spoken before the New York Savings Bank Association.

Strategies

There are four major strategies that could be used by employee benefit funds. The first is "covered call writing" with its substrategy, the "overwrite or shadow" program. The second is "buy stock–buy put." The third is "sell put." The fourth is "buy T-bill–buy call/put."

Covered Call Writing

This strategy is the most popular and the easiest to explain. An example:
Buy 1,000 shares of XYZ Corp. at $40 = $40,000
Sell ten calls of XYZ Corp. for six months = $4,000

If XYZ is at or above the $40 strike price at expiration, the option will be exercised and the stock called away (sold) at $40. This sale would result in no gain on the stock, but a gain of $4,000 (the proceeds of the option) at *any* price in excess of $40. If the stock were to decline below $40 at expiration, the option would not be exercised. The fund keeps the premium, which offsets the loss incurred on the stock. For example, if the XYZ were to decline to $36, resulting in a loss of $4 per share or $4,000, this would be offset by the option premium of $4,000—resulting in a breakeven situation, rather than $4,000 loss.

In a covered writing transaction, the stock is purchased and the option is sold simultaneously; the stock is delivered to the custodian bank, which issues a depository receipt indicating that the account owns the security on which the option has been sold. The proceeds of the option sale are sent to the bank when the depository receipt reaches the executing broker. If and when the option is exercised, the bank delivers the stock held by the account to satisfy that exercise.

The two primary benefits of a covered writing program are additional income and reduced risk. In a market that is relatively unchanged, the writing of calls will provide income from the otherwise static assets. In a down market, the option premiums will offset the decline in the stock portfolio.

The primary drawback of this program is that the upside is limited to the amount of the premium. If the stock written against has a vigorous move up, participation will be cut off and the benefits of a major price move lost. In addition, protection is limited to the amount of the premium written and a decline of significant magnitude will exceed the premium rather quickly.

Overwrite or Shadow

The overwrite or shadow program is a variation of covered call writing. The major distinguishing factors are the separation of the stock and option decisions and the prohibition against delivering stock from the existing portfolio to satisfy an exercise. The mechanics are essentially the same as covered writing, except that the bank is not permitted to deliver the stock from the account to satisfy an exercise. The option manager either must close the option position before exercise or purchase stock in the open market to satisfy the exercise.

There are three general styles of overwriting. The first is market timing, by which the manager tries to catch the major market swings; the options are heavily written at the top of the swing and lightly written at the bottom of the swing. The second is the computer-directed approach, where a computer program dictates when and which option should be sold. The third is the continuous writing approach, where options are sold constantly without regard to market cycle or other considerations.

There are many advantages to the overwrite program. There is additional income generated and the overall risk of the portfolio is reduced. There is no limit on the upside for stocks because they cannot be called away. The managers of the equity portfolio have complete freedom and are not affected by the option manager. The program uses existing assets and therefore requires no cash funding to start.

The only drawback of the program is the losses generated in the option account. In a vigorous market it will be difficult for the option manager not to lose money. However, in a situation in which the overwrite account was losing money, the underlying portfolio should be doing well enough to offset these losses by a wide margin.

Buy Stock—Buy Put

An illustration of this strategy is:
Buy 1,000 shares of XYZ at $40 = $40,000
Buy ten puts XYZ for six months at $4 = $4,000

If the stock is at $50 at expiration, there is a $10,000 profit in the stock, which would be reduced by the $4,000 cost of buying the put. If the stock is at $40 at the time of expiration, there will be no gain on the stock but there will be a loss of $4,000, the cost of the put. However, if the stock would drop to $30, the $10,000 loss in the stock would be offset by $6,000 profit in the put, resulting in a loss of only $4,000. The mechanics of buy stock–buy put involve the normal purchase and delivery of the stock and the purchase of the put, which would then remain at the executing broker.

The technique of buy stock–buy put provides several benefits. The risk of owning the stock is significantly reduced by owning the put. In fact, the position is insured against decline for a specific period of time, i.e., the life of the put. In addition, the full profit potential of the position can be realized, since there is no limit on the upside. It should also be pointed out that a put can be purchased to protect profits. The only drawback is the cost of the put. If the insurance can be obtained at a low enough cost, then this is not a severe negative.

Sell Put

The third strategy is the sale of the put, which can be done to acquire stock. An illustration is:
XYZ Corp. at $40
Sell ten puts XYZ for six months at $4 = $4,000

Here, the fund has sold a put for $4,000. The fund does not own XYZ but is obligated to purchase the stock at $40 per share for the life of the option. If the option is exercised, the true cost will be the $40 strike price less the $4 premium or $36 at expiration. If the stock is above $40, the put will not be exercised and there is a gain of $4,000 from the sale of the put. The mechanics of put selling require segregation of collateral. Proceeds of the sale are sent to the customer. The exercise of the put results in a purchase of the stocks in the normal manner.

Put selling permits the fund to acquire stock at a price below the current market. If the put is not exercised, then the gain is the proceeds of the sale of the put. As long as the fund is willing to acquire the stock at the adjusted price, there is no negative associated with selling puts. Puts can also be sold as part of a shadow writing program. In fact, it is the mirror of call writing and should be used with call writing to provide a stronger writing program.

Buy T-Bill—Buy Call/Put

The structure of such a program is to couple a riskless investment—i.e., T-bills—with a highly speculative tool—i.e., calls and puts—to create a defined risk instrument with significant potential for gain. The usual form of this strategy is to speculate in options with the income generated by the T-bill. Even if the option portfolio were to lose everything, the loss would not exceed the income for the period. In any case, the principal would remain intact.

The benefits of this program are leveraged speculations with limited risk and the ability to take bull or bear positions to suit the perceptions of market direction. The drawbacks are that as interest rates decline, fewer dollars are available for option purchases and that it requires precise timing to trade options successfully.

Summary

This presentation is a broad overview of the option market. Each of the approaches discussed can be used by employee benefit plans; the specific strategies depend on the size and objectives of the individual fund.

Investing in Real Estate

BY VINCENT F. MARTIN, JR.

OUR BUSINESS has been getting some negative press coverage recently. However, I think that the marketplace today represents some unparalleled investment opportunities and, certainly, opportunities that we haven't seen for the last ten years in the real estate business. I will spend some time, before getting into the meat of the discussion—the conditions of the marketplace today, where I see investment opportunities and how plans can participate in the market—going over a few of the basic elements that characterize the real estate investment industry, to accommodate the wide divergence of experience among my readers.

History of Real Estate Investing

The first question that many funds have is, "Why should we even be in real estate?" Back in 1970, when my firm started its first fund operation with Coldwell Banker, our representatives talked to various employee benefit plans around the country. People would ask us, "What is real estate?" At that time, it was an investment medium that really, for all practical purposes, had no place in their employee benefit plan portfolios. Today, 12 or 13 years later, we've crossed a major barrier. Real estate has become an accepted part of most employee benefit plan portfolios; there has been a big movement of capital into the real estate markets. The biggest feature that I think everyone must understand about the real estate area—as opposed to the stock and bond area, which most of us are familiar with—is the nature of the asset.

What is the big attraction of the real estate industry right now? The biggest attraction is that real estate represents a tangible asset. Some people call it a nonmonetary asset; other people call it a hard asset. Basically, the value of ownership of a tangible asset lies in its utility. The bricks that you put in the building have a certain utility value to someone who can use them. If, during inflation, the purchasing power of the dollar goes down and the utility value of that brick stays the same, then the price of the brick goes up. It's as simple as that. When you deal with tangible assets you're dealing with the ownership of hard assets that theoretically will reflect any changes in the inflation rate.

For years, economists have been saying that in periods of high inflation a large segment of portfolios should be invested in tangible assets—inflation-sensitive investments. Because we've been very fortunate in our country for a long period not to have long term inflation, most pension plan people, as well as investment managers, have concentrated on the financial asset side—stocks, bonds and so forth. People thought that if we ever did have inflation, the stock market would certainly reflect it and protect their capital. However, when the '70s began and we really got into a serious inflation problem we began to learn what our European counterparts learned a long time ago—that the stock market is not going to protect your money from inflation and the bond market is an investment position that you take when you expect a recession or a depression. Therefore, people be-

Mr. Martin is managing partner of Westmark Real Estate Investment Services. Prior to his present position, he was senior vice president and general manager of Coldwell Banker Capital Management Services in Los Angeles and chairman of the Investment and Administrative Committees of Coldwell Banker Commercial Group, Inc. Mr. Martin's responsibilities include consulting and counseling clients on the desirability of real estate investments, as well as the structuring and presenting of investment packages. He was involved in the conception, development and operation of commingled real estate funds for pension fund investors. Mr. Martin received his B.S. from Boston College and his M.B.A., with distinction, from Harvard University Graduate School of Business Administration. He is a member of the International Foundation's Corporate Investment Policy Guidebook Ad Hoc Committee and has spoken at previous Foundation educational programs.

gan to look around; all of a sudden they found the oldest investment market in the world—the real estate market—and began to study it.

About four or five years ago, the results of that interest became apparent, as major flows of capital came from the pension fund community into the real estate markets. Within that period, real estate has become a permanent part of employee benefit plan portfolios.

Along with that development came a little problem, in that there were no experienced investment managers, plan sponsors or trustees who were familiar with the real estate investment medium. People viewed real estate as if it were a homogeneous market—if they bought a house, a piece of land, a warehouse or whatever, they were in the real estate market. However, the real estate market is as diverse and complex as any other investment market. It is not homogeneous; there are many positions that you can take in it. In fact, one study identified 880 real estate investment positions. Therefore, when you begin to look at this market, it's very important to break it down into its components and understand the different risk and reward aspects in each segment. This subject is quite involved and I'll only touch on it briefly during this presentation. The important factor to understand is that there are many aspects in this marketplace.

Real Estate Performance

A few statistics give some new historical data concerning the performance of real estate investments. For years, getting such numbers has been difficult because real estate was always a very private industry. However, I think that these data indicate what real estate can do for the investment performance of many employee benefit plans.

Over the last ten years, the Consumer Price Index (CPI) increased at an annual compounded rate of 8.4%; if a dollar had been invested ten years ago, that dollar would have lost buying power at the rate of 8.4% a year on a compounded basis for ten years. The S&P 500 increased at a rate of only 6.4% a year compounded. Therefore, the S&P 500 lost about two points in the inflation index during that period. Salomon Brothers Bond Index showed a 3% annual compounded rate of return growth for those ten years. Therefore, if you invested your dollar in a bond ten years ago and held it, you would have lost 5 1/2%. U.S. Treasury bills came closest to matching inflation; they showed a compounded growth rate of 7.9%. On the other hand, the index for all of the commingled open ended real estate funds (I will explain what these funds are all about a little later) showed an annual compounded growth rate of 11.3%. The real estate funds, in fact, did beat the inflation rate by about three points per year; that number is called "real rate of return."

The closed end variety of real estate funds showed a 16.3% average annual compounded growth rate—that is, these funds just about doubled the inflation rate for that time. Such statistics will prove to people that real estate is an investment to be considered for their portfolios. The big questions that remain now are: What types of real estate investments should be made? How much money should be invested? When? Before I answer those questions, though, I think that it's important to differentiate how real estate creates value from how it realizes value. If you understand this difference, you can begin to put all the alternatives that I'll be discussing into some sort of context.

The value of real estate is based on its utility. The only value that any real estate asset has is based on what someone will pay to use it. All office buildings are based on what rent someone will pay to use the space. Residential land value is identical to what a builder will pay to buy the land, which is related to what a homeowner will pay to own a house on that piece of land. The trick in real estate investing is to be able to forecast, to anticipate, changes in demand. By and large, that's 90% of the ability to be successful in this business.

Investment Categories

Market Segments

Market segments can be broken down very simplistically into two areas—residential and commercial. In the residential area, the primary purpose is to provide shelter for people to live in. The commercial side's primary purpose, on the other hand, is to create income. Therefore, when we talk about the institutional investment market in real estate, we're basically talking about the commercial side of the business.

The commercial side is broken down into six categories: office, industrial, retail, multifamily housing, transient residential (hotels, motels and convalescent hospitals fall into that category) and other special uses (such as bowling alleys, restaurants, etc.). The first three segments are the largest part of the commercial market—the office, industrial and retail areas, "retail" mainly meaning shopping centers.

Investment Positions

The other differentiation to fix in your mind at the beginning of your study of the real estate market is that the investment position that you take in the market can fall into one of two categories: equity (which is the ownership of real estate assets) or debt, i.e., mortgages (which is simply using real estate as collateral for your loan). The inflation sensitivity of real estate relates to the attributes of ownership, not to those of real estate, because it's only the ownership of the income stream that those buildings can generate that really provides inflation protection.

Today, a third category is emerging, which is really a mixture of equity and debt. Participating mortgages are an example; they share not only in the collateral value of the property but also in the income stream. This hybrid fits in a certain investment situation, which I will discuss later.

Unique Characteristics of the Real Estate Market

There are a few caveats about the real estate market that are very important to understand. The real estate market is very inefficient. There isn't any central stock exchange that people can go to and get a fix on the value of an asset. It's a "caveat emptor" market, one of negotiation—a throwback to the old days of the securities markets. (To transact the purchase or sale of a piece of property, two people would sit underneath a tree and bargain back and forth until they came up with a value that both of them agreed to.) Therefore, when you deal in the real estate market, it's really very difficult to get good price or value information. The process is very subjective and plays a big part in determining the types of structures that really can be used in our business and used in evaluating performance measurements, because most performance measurements are based on appraisals.

I think that most people are familiar with the subjectivity of the appraisal process. It's very difficult to get good data. We don't have large central data banks. When you look at a piece of property, you really have to create your own information about supply and demand in the area, operating factors and so forth.

There are not many experienced real estate investment managers in this business because the field has only been in existence for about the last four or five years. Care must be taken when selecting the method and organization to use to manage your money, since ERISA has introduced some very tricky aspects to investing in real estate with pension plan money.

The biggest factor in managing real estate investments is that they operate in a local marketplace. These local markets do relate to overall economic conditions. However, local supply and demand are extremely critical in making your investment decisions, particularly in this day and age of social investing as a major topic for many employee benefit plans. Real estate values are based on utility; you have to have somebody who wants to use your properties—a very simple process. If you have no demand in an area, it doesn't matter how great the building is—you're not going to make any money from it. It is very important to understand that concept.

Current Market Conditions

In most parts of the country, our real estate markets are overbuilt. We have high vacancy rates in office space, industrial space, shopping centers and condominiums. In this situation, you might question why you should invest in real estate at all. However, another very interesting situation should affect your thinking.

We have an almost total lack of long term mortgage money in our business right now. Historically, the real estate market has been very leverage conscious; perhaps 60% of the assets in the real estate industry were leveraged at one point, representing mortgages on property. When you take away 60% of the capital from the marketplace, the people who do have money in the market are going to realize a premium yield.

Absorption rates, the rates at which available space is leased or sold, is at an all-time low. Therefore, rental rates are decreasing very rapidly because developers and owners of property are competing for tenants. There is a serious decline in the capitalization rates and in the yields that owners of property can realize by selling their assets. Put all of these factors together; if we have money, if we understand the nature of local market conditions in terms of supply and demand and if we can project what we think growth rates will be in various cities, we can take advantage of this situation. We can take advantage of the absence of capital; we can take advantage of low rental rates. In fact, in our investment position we hope that rental rates continue to decline. Develop your strategies around three broad areas: identifying the growth factors in different cities, developing product strategy and, very importantly, setting your investment position in the marketplace.

History

Why did we get into this mess? Two years ago, whatever mortgage money was in the market became relatively expensive; it was costing 12-13% for a 30-32 year mortgage. Lenders were asking for participations. They wanted to share in the income stream—share in the value of these properties. The developers looked at this situation and said, "That's so expensive we can't afford to build buildings." Therefore, they went to their bankers, who were hurting for commercial loans at the time. (Construction loans had probably been one of the most profitable parts of their portfolios.) The developers convinced many big bankers that two or three years hence—after their buildings were built and on the market—there would be a permanent mortgage market. The developers looked to those projected permanent mortgages from the insurance companies to pay off the bank mortgage loans.

The bankers accepted this reasoning. A great deal of construction (some estimates say 70-80% in the commercial sectors) was started using short term construction loans without a permanent mortgage to pay off the construction lender. Unfortunately, two years have passed and there still is no long term mortgage market. The developers and the banks are faced with a situation in which even leased buildings won't produce enough cash flow to cover the short term debt at the present rates—a situation of, in essence, slow death.

The bankers are putting pressure on the developers now to find some alternative, when really the only alternative is to deal with people who have money and are willing to buy these buildings. Therefore, the situation is similar to that of the mid-'70s with the real estate investment trusts, in which banks got greedy and developers got a lesson.

Don't believe that interest rates are going to be so volatile or that the market structure can ever change. Throughout the country there is a large inventory of construction that has been financed principally with short term money. This situation has put the banks in a very tenuous position.

How Can Funds Take Advantage of Current Market Conditions?

The way to take advantage of the situation is to use fund money in an ownership position. Say to the developer who has a building under construction, "We will make an agreement with you now to purchase your building when you finish construction and lease the building." In making such an agreement now, you will fix the multiplier or the capitalization rate that you will price that income on later.

You will be saying, "We will buy your building; the price will be based on the income you have in place when it's leased at a 10% capitalization rate (or 11% or 12%)." In a year, when the building is leased, if the income in place is a million dollars, the fund pays the developer $10 million. If the income is $800,000, the fund pays $8 million; likewise, if it's $2 million, the fund pays $20 million. What you're really doing is taking advantage of the softness in the capitalization rates by fixing that number today. You're also betting that for the next six months to a year rental rates are going to continue to decline, which means that the net income of that building will decline. When that building is leased, you'll be able to buy it at a cheaper price than you would have paid today or would have paid a year from now if the rate weren't already fixed.

The thing you don't want to do is take a risk concerning leasing. The leasing risk is the risk that the developer took when he decided to build the building; it was the risk that the banks took when they decided to finance it. Therefore, funds must take advantage of those poor investment decisions made two or three years ago and position themselves so that they can purchase buildings at a very low price. Two things can happen when a building is bought in this manner.

In the investment business, people talk about what would happen if we have deflation—if inflation disappears and prices actually decline. If that happens, the funds are putting themselves into a position in which they would have a 10-12% current yield with no inflation; the 10-12% would be a real rate of return, competitive with anything you can make in the marketplace today. If, in fact, the market recovers again, if the inventory burns itself off—gets absorbed through an economic recovery to a point where new construction will start again—and if construction costs increase (and they will), then the newer buildings that get built two or three years from now will have substantially higher rental rates than are available today. If that's the case, the buildings that the funds bought at low rental rates are going to have an opportunity to increase rental rates dramatically when the leases expire and the space comes back to market.

The other thing that could happen is that the yields that investors will take will decrease from the 10-12% rate to the 7-9% rate. Therefore, the fund positions itself for a very substantial capital appreciation if, in fact, the economy recovers. If the economy doesn't recover, the fund positions will have a very competitive, attractive real rate of return.

Tax Exempt Status

Pension funds should be aware of another investment vehicle, i.e., the fact that they're all tax exempt investors. They don't need depreciation or tax shelter; it's a waste of good economic benefits not to use that aspect of a real estate deal. Therefore, an investment vehicle called a convertible mortgage has been designed. In essence, the convertible mortgage splits the tax benefits from the economic benefits of a piece of property. In exchange, the fund obtains a lower price for the property than it would have gotten if it had bought it for cash or 100% ownership. The convertible mortgage is an equity ownership position. The fund does, in fact, own the building; it does, in fact, operate the building as if it owned it. Using a variety of convertible mortgages and forward purchase commitments appears to be another way to attack the market today.

Geographic Strategy

The other important factor in real estate investments, as I mentioned before, is developing a geographic strategy. It's one of the most important topics to explore because many funds related to the construction industry are getting involved in the social investing aspect of using money to create jobs. If you take part in such a program, you've got to understand the economics of your marketplace first. If you're going to invest in a building to create jobs, you've got to be sure that there is a reason for that building to be built. If there isn't a reason, then you're putting yourself in a position to lose money—and that doesn't benefit anyone.

In a geographic strategy, you observe employment trends across the country, because people wanting to use your real estate product create its value—demand again. Employment trends help you get a handle on who wants to use these properties in the '80s, how much they will spend and what type of property they want. For example, when you look at the employment growth of the '60s, you see that the manufacturing segment of the economy was responsible for about 15.5% of all new jobs created. The service sector at that time created about 26%. In the '70s, we saw a dramatic shift: Manufacturing dropped 15%, to 4% of all new jobs created; services, on the other hand, jumped from 26% up to about 42%.

Most economists today are projecting that, in the '80s, the service sector will be responsible for 55% or more of all new jobs created, and that manufacturing may even turn negative in this respect. What does this projection say about where we want to place our money? It says that we want to identify those cities that have very high service employment sectors, because those cities will be in the best position to grow in the future—simply because of their economic profiles. In developing your investment strategies the key becomes "city, city, city," not "location, location, location."

What cities are going to experience future growth? The way to determine that is, as I said previously, to break the employment sectors down into service categories and to identify the cities that have experienced a positive job growth during the last three years, but did not have a negative employment number during the last three years. That's a difficult test for many cities to pass, given economic conditions. Contrary to what much of the general press has been reporting, my firm found that there were 44 major cities that experienced positive job growth on average during 1979-1981.[1] Therefore, these cities became our "universe," our targets for investment or capital allocations.

Taking Inventory

Your next question should be, "What's the supply situation?" That is, how much office space is available? These data become very interesting. Adding together all the office space in the 44 cities mentioned—I'm talking about Class A office space—you get a total of roughly 1.1 billion square feet. Office space currently vacant in those marketing areas, plus office space becoming available this year and next year through current construction equals about 333 million square feet.

Such data begin to put the oversupply situation into focus. About 34% more office space will be added in these cities in two years. The average absorption rate—how many square feet of office space the real estate markets have absorbed on average during the last five years—was about 56½ million square feet; the highest absorption in one year was 80 million square feet. Therefore, there will be about 3.8 years' worth of office space on the market to absorb in two years.

Of course, not all of these office buildings are competitive—some shouldn't have been built in the first place. However, in general, I don't expect to see very much in the way of new construction starts (for office space in particular) for about another year to a year and a half—just because that inventory must get down to the level of a two year supply. When that level is reached, I think that there will be another rise in construction. A two

---

1. A partial list includes Anaheim, Boston, Camden, Dallas, Hartford, Houston, Los Angeles, Nassau, Phoenix, Reno, San Francisco, Suffolk, Tulsa and Washington, D.C.

year absorption period is one that most developers can live with. Even though the bad news is that commercial construction is going to be slow for a while, I think that the investment side is going to be quite positive.

Determining Which Type of Property Is Right for Your Fund

The other aspect that you have to concern yourself with is what product you should be investing in—office buildings, industrial buildings, shopping centers or apartments.

Office Buildings

The employment growth previously mentioned also indicates what sectors you should be investigating. The service sector, the fastest growing part of the economy, creates a demand for office buildings. Therefore, the office side of the market should be the strongest.

Industrial Buildings

Conversely, look at the decrease in the manufacturing side of the economy. Many companies have had terrible experience with carrying their inventories, given economic fluctuations and interest rates. There is a long term trend for companies to try to decrease inventory levels permanently and to use alternatives, such as overnight transportation or making consumers wait a week for delivery of goods, because these businesses are not willing to take the risks inherent in short term financing anymore. Therefore, I think that a very soft industrial market, particularly in the warehouse sector, is likely for the next three or four years. Now is the time to begin to move away from industrial buildings if you're in that sector; stay away from the industrial sector if you are not now involved.

Shopping Centers

Shopping centers really have not been economical for about the last three years. The major tenants—the large department stores and supermarkets—have insisted on lease terms that are uneconomical from an investment standpoint. They've kept themselves in that position during the recession simply because they're not in an expansion mood right now.

The side shops (the satellite shops—mall shops, as you may call them) are where the real profit comes for the owner. However, rental rates have gotten so high that it's almost impossible now for the small retailer to make a profit. If he can make a profit, it's almost impossible for him to pay any percentage rent, which is where inflation protection comes from. These spaces are beginning to be leased more along the lines of office leases—a lease rate with CPI increases annually; however, most of these retailers can't afford that arrangement either. Therefore, some basic changes must be made in that whole retailing area before much fund money is moved into that segment of the marketplace.

Apartment Buildings

The multifamily area is one that is mentioned frequently. There are very low vacancy rates throughout the country in the apartment area, for a good reason: Apartments have gotten so expensive to build that the rents charged to make them profitable are beyond most people's reaches, just like mortgage payments on houses are. Many areas of the country have set up laws instituting rent controls that restrict the economics of your investment. A lot of people don't want to own an apartment building where the government is going to come in and tell them how much they can make from it. There also are problems with condominium conversions. The quality apartments already have been converted to condominiums, or if you try to buy one you're going to buy at a condominium conversion price.

There are several negative factors to consider in the multifamily housing area, including management aspects—it's very difficult to manage these investments. However, one of the main reasons that many funds have stayed away from apartments is the social issue. We all know that housing costs so much money that people can't afford shelter anymore. Such an investment is attractive because it is sensitive to inflation. "Sensitive" means that if inflation goes up next year by 10%, the owner will have to raise the rents by 10%. The fact that many people just can't pay this kind of money any longer makes it very difficult for employee benefit plans to invest in apartments. Unfortunately, housing as a social issue is going to have to involve some sort of government intervention to solve the problem nationwide.

If you elect to go into the multifamily area, just be certain that you're going into it in locations that do not have rent control programs in effect or in the planning stages. Also, be sure that this type of investment really does fit into your portfolio.

Market Implications

Because there is low demand, funds can buy office buildings at much lower prices than were possible previously. They should welcome falling rents, but shouldn't buy existing buildings that were leased two years ago, because those buildings were leased at rental rates that reflected a supply-constrained market. Such buildings are in a position to expect lower rents when leases roll over. They were purchased at capitalization rates that were in the 7-9% range; if they were to be liquidated today they'd be liquidated in the 10-12% range—which means that those buildings, in essence, have suffered a capital loss.

As the market conditions change, investment strategies have to change, too. The position outlined here is based on current conditions, but, as the conditions change, funds may opt to move into the development side, or into the market side. Recognize that your investment strategy should not use a single dimension as these cycles occur. Always look for the opportunity today to get the most premium for your dollar with the lowest risk. The dynamics of the marketplace will define your investment criteria.

The whole issue comes back to understanding demand. If people want to use a particular type of real estate, then you supply it to them. If they don't, you just don't go out and build something on speculation and hope that someone is going to come along and use it. We've got to get back to a much more rational development process. Southern California has probably been the biggest instigator of this whole problem. In the Los Angeles area, when the economy was booming people just built buildings; they didn't worry about where the tenants were coming from. They knew that sooner or later someone would come along and lease a building. Now, however, heavy preleasing and confirmed major tenants are necessary before the construction process is actually started.

Participating in the Real Estate Marketplace

Participation in this marketplace creates problems for some funds because real estate is a "big ticket" item. If someone says to you, "I have a million dollars—invest it for me," you almost can't do anything with it. It's incredible to have a million dollars available and not be able to make a sound commercial real estate investment with it! The problem is that prices have gotten so high that you can't leverage your investment by combining equity with debt. You really have to work at figuring out exactly how you can participate.

There are a number of ways to do so. On the equity side, you have a basic choice between developing your own investment program or using a separate account. If your fund is large enough, you allocate a certain percentage of your portfolio to the real estate area. Then, either you develop an internal staff to search and evaluate investments or you hire an outside investment manager to do it for you. However, this opportunity is really only available to the large funds; I think that you need to be in the vicinity of $700-$800 million or above to work in that area successfully.

Another aspect is the commingled fund area. Commingled funds are simply set up by large insurance companies, some with the private real estate companies, to put you together with eight or nine or 50 other pension funds. You each contribute money to a fund; the manager then invests it. I think that this route is the most viable, for most of the smaller funds particularly, to invest in the real estate area. You can get into many of these funds with a minimum $100,000 investment. Some have a minimum of $1 million. Commingled funds offer a very attractive way for most funds to invest, with good management for a very cheap price. Usually, the management fees run about 1-1½% per year.

To get into real estate investments, a fund can involve itself in private syndications. A private syndication is simply a partnership arrangement in which someone invites you to invest in a particular deal with eight or nine other investors, with a minimum investment of perhaps half a million dollars. The problem with such an arrangement is that it doesn't give you a lot of diversification. You're really investing a large part of your funds in a very small number of properties. Diversification is very important; commingled funds can offer you more diversification because they invest nationally.

Public syndications usually are offered as a tax shelter. Today many such syndications work so that the money from pension funds, which don't need the tax benefits, can be used by taxable investors as leverage. By and large, you're going to find that those arrangements aren't economical because the public area takes about 20-25% off the top in fees. That situation just doesn't make a whole lot of sense to many investors.

Many other areas for real estate investment are beginning to crop up. Some bank trust departments are offering opportunities in which you can buy a certificate of deposit (CD) and they'll pledge that money to specific investments for you—in essence, underwriting that type of arrangement. Another idea, one of the most interesting, is the foundation. A foundation is a combination of commingled funds and separate accounts. A small fund, which perhaps has only $50,000 to invest, can participate with other people in a $5 million or

$30 million deal. However, each participant reserves the decisionmaking right for itself. It has the right to decide on each particular deal whether it will contribute. That idea is unique, I think; many investors are reluctant to give up control to a money manager.

The mortgage area, which I haven't really touched on, offers several attractions. Keep in mind that a mortgage is an alternative to a fixed income investment, a bond. The difference between it and a bond is that the mortgage uses real estate; the hard asset itself is security for the loan. On the other hand, bonds depend on the overall business management acumen of particular companies for the repayment of the loan. In periods of high inflation, the underlying value, the asset value, of real estate increases dramatically. Where you might have started out making a loan that was 75% of the value of the property, five years later you might find that the loan represents only 30% of value. Therefore, you have the unique characteristic of an increase in security for your loan. Conversely, most bonds (most company earnings) went way down and their collateralization went down with them. Therefore, mortgages as an alternative to bonds are extremely attractive.

The problem is that the markets have not been very efficient in the past. Many people, including mortgage holders, don't understand the mortgage side of the market. However, the mortgage market is really beginning to come of age. For those of you with an orientation toward current income, the mortgage market is definitely something you should investigate.

The participating mortgage area is also very interesting. As I mentioned before, it's rather a hybrid between the equity position and the mortgage position. Let's assume that the average mortgage is at 16% interest. With the participating mortgage, the lender would accept perhaps 13% interest, but in exchange would take a 30% share in the gross revenue of the building. With this arrangement, the lender is trying to realize a higher current yield than he would through buying a building, trying to obtain some degree of inflation protection by participating in the rents. Such an arrangement won't have a perfect correlation with inflation; nevertheless, when you're in an uncertain situation and you need cash flow, these types of mortgages can offer substantially higher rates of return than bonds or straight mortgages can, because of that participation in future revenue.

I'm of the opinion that participating mortgages will be the major forum for mortgage lending in the future. Lenders have finally gotten wise; they've said to themselves, "We're not going to take the risk of inflation anymore; we'll make the borrower take that risk." Taking the inflation risk was how lenders got themselves into trouble in the first place. If you are making mortgages directly, or are interested in doing so, I think that you should look very hard at participating mortgages, because this structure makes the most sense for you.

The Real Estate Life Cycle

The other aspect of looking at your alternatives is to decide what position in the life cycle of real estate you want to invest in. Do you want to invest in raw land? Do you want to make development and improvement loans? Do you want to invest in a development project itself—actually be involved in developing the building? Do you want to invest in buildings only after they're built and leased? Each of these phases has very different characteristics to it, as well as very different rewards.

In the development phase, the biggest risk you are taking is on the demand side. You are betting that you guessed right, that someone will come along and lease your building. If no one leases, you've lost a lot of money; if someone does, you've made a lot of money. On the other hand, when buying leased buildings you know that the tenant is there and you know that you have income in place. Therefore, it's important to ascertain the different risk positions you're willing to take.

Conclusion

Pension funds have finally put themselves back into the position of controlling their own destiny. In years past, pension funds were very passive; they were content to give money to the insurance companies and let those companies do what they wanted. Now that the funds have the money back, it is incumbent upon them to develop expertise in all investment areas.

CHAPTER 6

Cost Containment: Issues and Strategies

Larry M. Fisher

President
A. S. Hansen, Inc.
Lake Bluff, Illinois

Glen Slaughter

Chairman of the Board
Glen Slaughter & Associates
Oakland, California

Edgar G. Davis

Vice President of Corporate Affairs
Eli Lilly and Company
Indianapolis, Indiana

Charles J. Mazza, CEBS

Vice President and Manager
Meidinger, Inc.
Milwaukee, Wisconsin

Frederick Klein

President
National Pharmacies, Inc.
Elmwood Park, New Jersey

Medical Care in the '80s

BY LARRY M. FISHER

TWO MAJOR POINTS should dominate your thinking as welfare fund trustees for the next ten years.
- The single most important challenge you face during the 1980s is your ability to maintain the level and scope of medical benefits that you have provided in the past.
- Your successful response to that challenge will involve you in influencing fundamental changes in the medical care delivery system in this country and in the lifestyles of your participants.

Planning for the effective use of your available medical benefit dollars is the most complex part of your job because of the multiplicity of outside factors over which *in the past* trustees have been able to exercise little or no control, such things as:
- An inflation rate approximately three times greater than that of the economy as a whole
- A medical delivery system that varies dramatically by location with respect to quality, efficiency and availability of services
- Constant exposure to unnecessary costs ranging from lack of sophistication in purchasing medical services to deliberate abuse by the participant or the provider
- A bewildering array of state and federally subsidized programs that at times overlap and duplicate benefits available through private plans and create enormous pressures for the time and energies of medical personnel, plants and equipment
- The two way squeeze caused by this country's commitment to medical care for the indigent and the aging. Philosophical issues aside, these two groups drive the price of medical care up because of the increasing demand for services, and since they don't pay their own way, the deficit is passed along to your participants.

We will deal in greater detail with each of these factors later, and it's not a very pretty picture—but before we start, let's reaffirm the positive aspects of what you are trying to do. In my opinion, the most devastating financial hazard facing most *working people*—not the poor and not the rich—is the exposure to major medical expense. The *most effective* protection against this hazard is to be a participant in an industrywide welfare plan, with

Mr. Fisher is president of A. S. Hansen, Inc., a consulting and actuarial firm for employee benefit plans, both single and multiemployer, throughout the United States and abroad. He has over 26 years of experience in consulting with welfare and pension funds, as well as major corporate clients. Prior to joining his present firm, Mr. Fisher was associated with Blue Cross-Blue Shield and Hewitt Associates. He has lectured on industrial relations at Roosevelt University and the University of Chicago, on insurance at Indiana University and has published in major employee benefit publications. Instrumental in establishment of the International Foundation's Trustees Institutes in 1967, Mr. Fisher has served on the Board of Directors and CEBS Committee and as chairman of the Trustees and Consultants Committees. He has spoken at numerous Foundation educational programs and presently serves on the Educational Program and Compensation Committees and is chairman of the Corporate Program Committee.

reciprocal rights to coverage if you make a temporary or permanent change in job location. Therefore, in spite of the problems we'll be talking about, your role in providing this kind of protection to your members and the employees of the companies you represent should be viewed as an important reward for the time and effort you spend on the job as trustee.

There are three main issues I want to cover in some depth:

First, we'll talk about some of the statistical measures of the cost of health care nationally, an overview of the medical environment of the '80s.

Second, I want to tell you about what I believe to be the most exciting development that has taken

Figure 1

NATIONAL HEALTH SERVICES COSTS
($ billions)

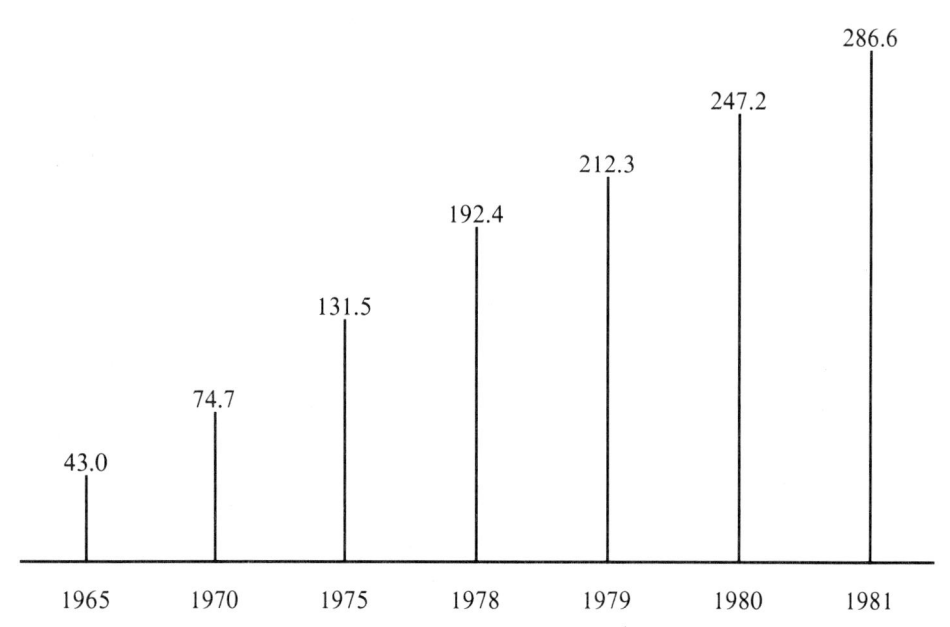

1965	1970	1975	1978	1979	1980	1981
43.0	74.7	131.5	192.4	212.3	247.2	286.6

place in years for tackling the health care cost problem: the joint efforts of labor, employers and health care providers at the local community level to provide medical services to your participants on an effective and lower cost basis than has been done in the past, without reducing the quality of care. I believe that I can show you that your fund, combined with all of the other sponsors of prepaid medical care, is probably financing as much as 70% of the total cost of medical care in your community. When this purchasing power is used effectively, it can lead to a new definition of the buyer/seller relationship in the marketplace for health care services. Some of you may already be included in *community health care coalitions.*

Third, I want to describe some of the specific programs being implemented through these community coalition efforts, as well as by individual health and welfare funds, that are beginning to show real progress and success in containing costs. I will emphasize things you could be doing right now in your own health program.

Measures of Health Care Costs

In looking at the nature of the problem, I believe that it is critical to sort out various segments to identify those elements that we as the buyers of health care services can start to have some effect on. To put these elements into context, let's also look at some of the overall trends of health care cost growth over the last ten years.

Here are a few of the latest statistics on medical care, nationally (Figure 1). In calendar year 1981, the nation spent an estimated $287 billion for health care. This figure is up from $74 billion just 11 years ago, and from only $43 billion just 16 years ago. This $287 billion in 1981 represents almost 10% of the nation's Gross National Product (Figure 2), up from about 6% in 1965. On a per capita basis, total spending for health care amounted to nearly $1,225 per person in 1981 (Figure 3). This figure is up from only $359 per person in 1970, an increase of 340% in just 11 years.

Let's take a look at where this money came from and, of particular importance, where it has gone (Figure 4). Nearly 43% of this $287 billion came directly from government, principally through the Medicare and Medicaid programs and some of the specialized public health programs; 57% came from the private sector. Government's share of total funding is growing more rapidly than the private sector. Without changes in the types of coverages under government programs, more than half of total spending for health care will be paid for by government by the end of the 1980s.

Figure 2

TOTAL HEALTH CARE SPENDING'S SHARE OF GNP
(in percentages)

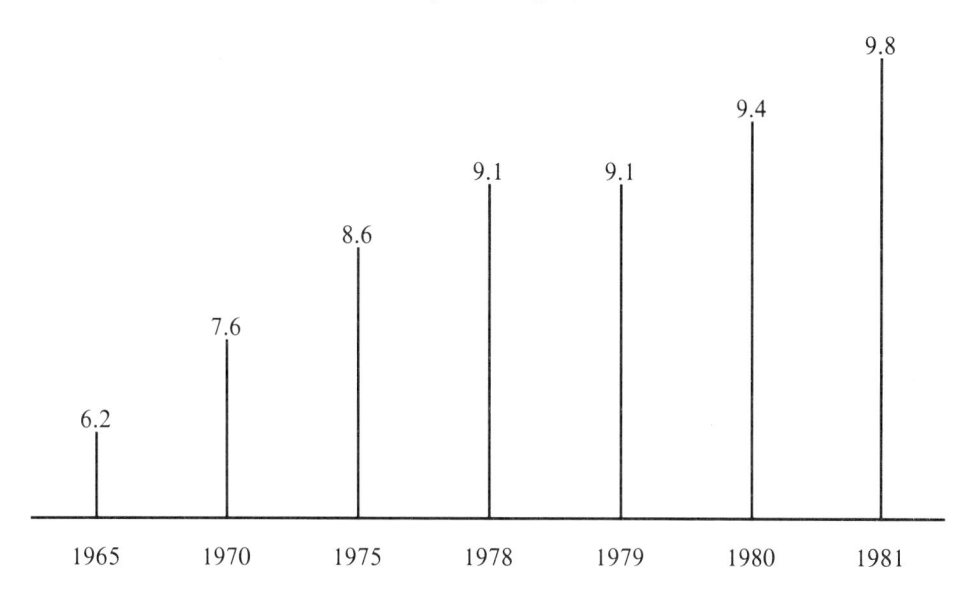

1965	1970	1975	1978	1979	1980	1981
6.2	7.6	8.6	9.1	9.1	9.4	9.8

Figure 3

PER CAPITA SPENDING FOR HEALTH CARE

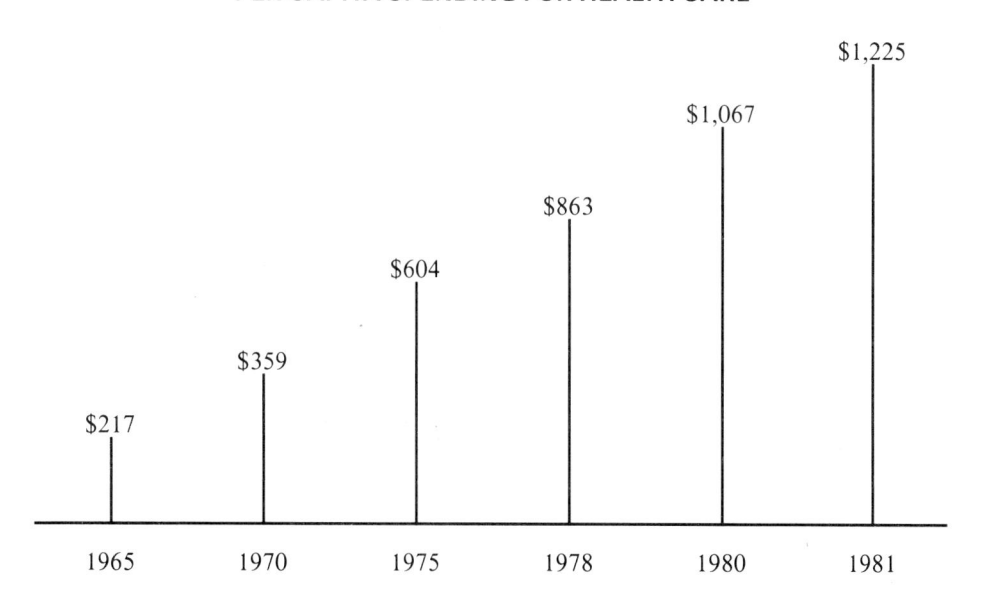

1965	1970	1975	1978	1980	1981
$217	$359	$604	$863	$1,067	$1,225

Figure 4

SOURCES OF FUNDING FOR ALL HEALTH CARE SERVICES AND SUPPLIES (1981)
($ in billions)

13.5%	29.2%	57.3%	
___ 42.7% ___			
$38.6 State and Local Govt.	$83.9 Federal Government	$164.1 Private Sector	$286.6 Total

Figure 5

SOURCES OF PAYMENT FOR PERSONAL HEALTH SERVICES 1981

Direct Payment by Individuals — 32.1

Third Parties — 67.9

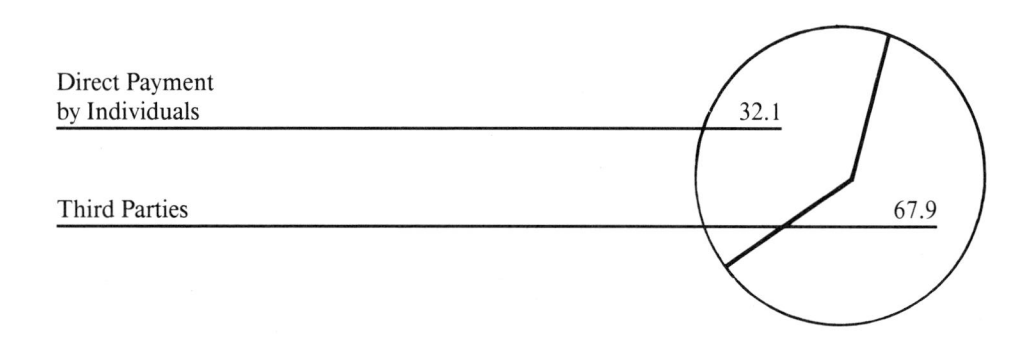

Figure 6

AVERAGE HEALTH CARE COSTS FOR PRIVATE PLANS ROSE 19% IN 1980 DUE TO:

• Price Increases	11.1%
• Increased Intensity/Technology	3.2%
• Demand	1.7%
• Cost Transfer from Government Programs	3.0%
TOTAL	19.0%

Let's focus a little further on current spending within the private sector, that is, the $164.1 billion we spent in 1981 (Figure 5). Sixty-eight percent of this $164.1 billion was paid for by private parties—insurance companies and self-insured health and welfare funds. Individuals paid 32%. Again, if you looked at a similar chart for the 1970s, you would see that the third-party's share of private sector spending has grown rapidly while direct payments by individuals have declined. What is significant about this trend is that the average individual covered under a private health insurance program has a declining incentive to be a wise consumer of cost-effective health care services.

Also of great importance is where private individuals have spent their health insurance money. Nearly 60% of all private sector health care dollars is now going to hospitals. About 30% goes to physicians. The remaining 10% is spent for drugs and other incidental medical services.

Third parties pay 89% of all hospital expenses, including government and private sector insurance programs. Third parties pay 62% of all physician charges and 41% of all other services. What is important here is that the more costly services were paid by the buyers of health care—health and welfare funds and employer-sponsored plans—and that this portion is growing as third parties pick up an ever-larger share of the total bill.

Let's look now at some of the items contributing to increased costs so that we can begin to sort out those areas where we can have some impact (Figure 6). Average health care costs for private plans rose about 19% in 1980. Inflation or price increases for services and supplies purchased by doctors and hospitals to run their businesses contributed 11 percentage points; increased intensity of services and increased use of technology on behalf of the average patient added a little over 3%. Increased demand for services, meaning that people went to the doctor or hospital with greater frequency, added another 1.7%. The final contributor and one that will haunt all of us in the private sector increasingly is the 3% resulting from hospitals and physicians transferring unreimbursed government-sponsored patient costs to private payers to maintain an acceptable profit margin. This is the two way squeeze I referred to earlier; in addition to the direct taxes your participants are paying, they are also subsidizing the inadequate funding of government programs.

One Fund's Experience

So much for national trends. Let's talk now about a real world situation, a projection of what

Table I

HEALTH AND WELFARE CONTRIBUTIONS AS A PERCENT OF PAY

Year	Monthly Contribution	Percent of Pay
1980	$ 95	8%
1982	140	10
1984	212	13
1986	320	17
1988	485	22
1990	733	29

might be considered a reasonable expectation of the cost through the 1980s of providing the *same* benefits—no new benefits or benefit improvements—for a food industry fund in a metropolitan area (Table I). In 1980 the monthly contribution was $95 or about 8% of the average monthly compensation for the group. In 1982 this number had increased to $140 a month or about 10% of pay, still a pretty manageable number. But these costs take off—in 1986, 17%; 1988, 22% and by 1990, a totally unworkable 30% of a participant's wages for health and welfare, all resulting from the four factors I described earlier:

- Inflationary price increases
- Increased intensity of medical treatment
- Increased demand for medical care
- Inadequate governmental funding of public programs.

This projection illustrates all too dramatically the gap between the rate at which wages are expected to increase during the 1980s and the projected cost to the participants for medical benefits. The bottom line, it seems to me, is that even in the unlikely event that labor and management could agree to pay these costs, the vast majority of fund participants would not accept diverting 25-30% of their total compensation for medical benefits alone.

Solutions

Your plan participants as a group cannot absorb the financial impact of the gap that will exist if we continue to attempt to provide today's *current level of protection* within our *current medical delivery system*. I believe that the solution lies in two fundamental areas, both of which will require significant education to promote change on the part of plan participants and major new areas of involvement by labor and management trustees:

- The first solution is to reduce the total cost of medical care in this country through a coordinated area by area attack on the waste inherent in our piecemeal approach to medical care. For the first time in our history, we have agreement between such divergent forces as the AMA and the AFL-CIO that 10-20% of our total medical expenditures can be eliminated without reducing the quality of care. I will describe such efforts that are already being pursued today by groups that three years ago would have been viewed as strange bedfellows indeed.
- The second solution is to change the notion built up over 30 years that participation in a welfare fund relieves the individual of any responsibility for exercising the same judgment in spending the fund's money that he would over his own. You can help by providing financial incentives to accept new, more efficient methods of treatment, but in the long run it is the fund participant who will have to be educated to accept the tradeoffs involved in the form of equitable cost sharing of some of the benefits that have historically been paid by the fund.

Let's explore each of the four cost-increasing factors to further identify issues that you as buyers *can* have an impact on in reducing fund costs in the 1980s.

Inflationary Price Increases

All four of these areas—inflationary price increases, increased intensity of treatment, growing demand for services by patients and government cost shifting—are closely linked. The first, inflation caused by higher labor costs, energy costs and the cost of supplies incurred by hospitals and physicians in running their facilities, has to be passed on to the buyers of their services. To a considerable extent these costs are more a function of the general rate of inflation and a reflection of the economy as a whole.

There are important areas where these costs, however, can be constrained. These constraints come under the heading of "improved efficiencies" or higher productivity in the use of both capital and labor. Although there have been significant advances in recent years in the health care field, by both doctors and hospitals, in making better use of their facilities and in increased outputs from the average health care worker, much more can be done. Let me describe several examples for you, particularly with regard to how these link to the other three areas.

Labor costs account for about 60% of total hospital costs and have been going up rapidly, not because average wages are going up any faster than in other industries, but because hospitals are employing many more highly skilled and professional people than in the past. One important way to improve labor productivity is to broaden cross training; another is to share highly skilled personnel among hospitals in a community; still another is to avoid duplication of services and programs among hospitals so that some of these high cost personnel are not needed. All three of these programs are now being implemented in some communities, especially where multihospital systems are being established, i.e., where individual hospitals come together to participate in joint purchasing programs and the sharing of high cost equipment. (Ethnic elitism—i.e., Methodist Hospital is best, or Alexian Brothers if you are Catholic, or Mount Sinai if you are Jewish—is a hindrance in dealing with such a community problem.)

The single most important ingredient for advancing the development of such interhospital cooperation is strong community leadership by the employers and labor leaders who pay the health care bill. All of the areas we're concerned with are closely linked to the inflation problem. For example, increased technology use by doctors is one of the reasons why every hospital wants to have every new piece of diagnostic equipment, which adds to that hospital's total costs because a new high cost professional must be hired to operate that equipment. Closer cooperation between hospitals and doctors is the key. We have to provide them with the incentives to be more cooperative.

Moving on to the areas of technology and intensity, increased demand by patients and government cost shifting—again, I want to emphasize examples of what you as buyers of health care services can do to restrain costs for your members. In each of these cases there are now numerous experiments to which we can point where cost containment successes are being achieved.

Increased Service Demand

Some of our health care plans are simply too generous, particularly in regard to coverage for the more costly services; there is little patient incentive to restrain demand for care. Many physicians now say that they are unable to discuss fees or costs with their patients because the patients are not interested. The comment repeated is, "Don't worry about the cost because my health care plan will pay for everything, especially if you put me in the hospital." Perhaps the strongest research evidence

Figure 7
**BREAKOUT OF INPATIENT HOSPITAL EXPENSES
MAJOR HEALTH AND WELFARE FUND**

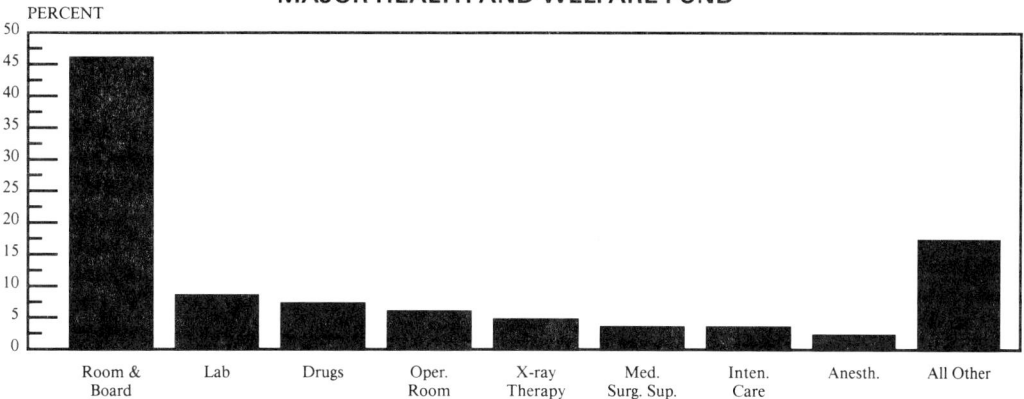

[Bar chart showing percentages by category: Room & Board ~46%, Lab ~8%, Drugs ~7%, Oper. Room ~6%, X-ray Therapy ~4%, Med. Surg. Sup. ~3%, Inten. Care ~3%, Anesth. ~2%, All Other ~17%]

concerning the importance of cost sharing is given by the recent seven year nationwide study by the Rand Corporation, which showed that families with annual cost sharing responsibilities of between $500 and $1,000 for medical services used hospitals up to 40% less than families with little or no cost sharing. Another interesting point many physicians now make is that patients demand office or hospital emergency room treatment for matters that do not require physician attention. Doctors estimate that at least one out of three visits to their offices or hospitals is unnecessary. Again, the Rand study is highly instructive—individuals or families with significant cost sharing visited the doctor's office up to 40% less. Even HMOs, where the physician has no incentive to overutilize services because all care is paid for on a predetermined annual payment, are finding meaningful cost sharing necessary to provide financial incentives to limit unnecessary office visits or emergency room usage.

This important nationwide study and its findings suggest that if we are to use available benefit dollars wisely, we need to look at appropriate types of participant cost sharing to encourage the most efficient use of health care services.

Reimbursement Biases

Many of our plans continue to encourage inpatient care over outpatient care, which in turn provides an incentive both to the patient and the doctor to use the most costly critical care hospital facility for noncritical health care services. This practice leads to excessive and inefficient use of hospitals and inadequate use of the following five less expensive services. If greater use were made of outpatient surgery, pre-admission testing, outpatient diagnostic testing, home health care and skilled nursing care, your fund's costs for hospital care would be significantly reduced. Putting the issue another way, we can eliminate the incentives to use high cost inpatient care by providing comparable or higher coverage levels in our plans for these five less costly services. A number of statistics identify the opportunities for cost savings.

Outpatient Surgery and Pre-Admission Testing

As stated earlier, about 60% of all plan costs go to pay hospital charges, the item that is affected most by inflation. Nearly 50¢ out of every dollar paid to hospitals goes for room and board, compared to all other hospital services (Figure 7). That 50¢ could be significantly reduced in the following ways:

Currently, about 55% of all hospital admissions, nationwide, are for surgery. Technological advances now make it possible for up to 40% of all surgical procedures to be done on an *outpatient* basis. Theoretically, over 20% of all hospital admissions could be avoided, thereby saving 50¢ out of every dollar spent on room and board for the in-hospital surgical patient. Putting it another way, between one and two dollars out of every ten in our health care plans could be saved if surgery were shifted to an outpatient basis whenever possible. It clearly makes sense to pay at least as much for outpatient surgery as for inpatient surgery. Some plans are even paying higher levels of coverage for outpatient surgical procedures today to provide strong positive incentives to use surgi-centers or other noncritical care facilities. One of our clients saved $600,000 for 7,000 covered employees last year on increased use of outpatient surgery alone.

Pre-admission testing is another important

area where reimbursement biases play a role. Many tests can be done prior to hospital admission for surgical procedures or even medical procedures. When done in the hospital, these tests frequently take one to two days' time prior to the day of surgery or other medical treatment. Since the average length of stay for all under age 65 patients is about six days nationally, the significant savings potential is obvious.

Outpatient Diagnostic Testing, Home Health Care and Skilled Nursing Facilities

These three types of care provide particularly important alternatives to inpatient care for the very high cost, severely ill individual. It is these people, as we will see a little later, who account for the largest share of all dollars spent by health care plans. Providing positive incentives to use these three approaches to health care could reduce in-hospital patient days for severely ill individuals by as much as 20-30%.

Yet another hospital cost containment alternative is being developed for the very ill. One of the most startling statistics I ever came across is that of the total Medicare hospital expenditures of $36 billion paid out by the federal government in 1980, some 60% or $22 billion went to cover expenses of people with 30 days or less to live.

Whether we like to talk about it or not, this pattern of inpatient use of our most expensive critical care facilities by the terminally ill must be examined and consideration given to providing alternative arrangements, such as hospice programs, for providing terminal care for participants. A hospice is not a facility. It is an interdisciplinary program designed to minimize the trauma associated with a terminal illness. Care can be provided on an inpatient basis or by providing for supportive services at the home such as 24 hour nursing care and visits by medical social workers, physical and speech therapists and nutritional counselors. The significant consideration is that cure is not the objective, and nothing is gained by confinement in a critical care facility except astronomical costs. Hospice programs are useful not only for the Medicare elderly but also for working age adults and children suffering from terminal illnesses.

Are the Alternatives Effective?

Can these five alternatives to in-hospital patient care work together to reduce your fund's hospital costs? Here is dramatic evidence to answer that question. Health maintenance organizations, because of the financial incentives to physicians to limit the use of the hospital as much as possible, make broad use of all five of these alternatives. In 1979 nationwide, the ten million people belonging to the HMOs were in the hospital only 440 days for each thousand HMO members. All other under 65 individuals experienced at least 700 hospital days per thousand population that year. Obviously it pays to provide proper incentives, both to the physician and the patient, to use the most cost-effective setting for care.

Physician and Hospital Incentives

We have covered demand and technology issues that are causing health care cost increases, and have looked at several specific examples of savings related to cost sharing and reimbursement biases. These savings generally relate to patient incentives regarding economical use of health care services. Now let's look at savings relating principally to incentives to physicians and hospitals to economize. Again, I will focus particularly on issues which you as a buyer of health care services can do something about.

In the past, much of our attention has been in the area of excessive or unnecessary use of health care services and inefficiencies in the day-to-day delivery of those services. These issues continue to be increasingly relevant, primarily because of the tremendous growth in the number of physicians in the United States. The number of physicians is growing so rapidly that between 1970 and 1990, the ratio of physicians to the population will drop from about one for every 1,000 people, to one for every 250. Obviously, if all of these doctors are to maintain their high incomes, both the volume and price of services will have to continue to grow very rapidly—at a tremendous cost to welfare funds. Certainly the volume of services and the price of services will continue to grow if the buyers of those services do not become more informed and judicious and if they do not work to identify less costly and more efficient health care providers.

Unnecessary health care services already are and will continue to be a major source of the growing cost problem. Four principal causes of unnecessary services have been identified:
- Variations in medical practices among physicians increase costs with little or no effect on the overall quality of care.
- Retrospective reimbursement by third-party payers—payments by insurance plans based on whatever cost the patient, the physician and the hospital incur—provides incentives for at least some patients and providers to use unnecessary services.
- Lack of price competition between physi-

cians and hospitals, again related to retrospective cost-based reimbursement of billed charges, which eliminates economic incentives to providers to economize
- Defensive medical practices by physicians that add significantly to the cost of medical testing.

Variations in Medical Practices Among Physicians

The first of these four causes of unnecessary services is a very interesting one. Perhaps the best discussion of this issue currently available can be found in an April 1982 article in *Scientific American* entitled, "Variations in Medical Care Among Small Areas," by John Wennberg and Alan Gittelson. I recommend this article to you for immediate reading. It is in layman's language and easily understood.

The findings from this study indicate that physicians' practice patterns differ widely from community to community, even when population characteristics affecting health, age and sex are similar. The authors found in a six year study in New England that "... the amount and cost of hospital treatment in a community has more to do with the *number of physicians,* the *medical specialties represented* and the *procedures they prefer to use* than with the health of the residents."

For example, there is a city in Maine where surgery for the removal of the uterus was done so frequently in the past decade that, if the rate persists, 70% of the women there will have had the operation by the time they reach the age of 75. In a city less than 20 miles away, the rate of this procedure is so much lower that, if it persists, only 25% of the women will have lost their uteri by age 75.

What could account for this disparity? It seems unlikely that there would be any large difference in the general health of the populations of the two neighboring cities, and after looking into the matter, the researchers found none. The populations are similar in economic status. The difference in the number of physicians, the supply of hospital beds and coverage by medical insurance plans cannot explain the difference in the rate of surgery. Instead, the most important factor in determining the rate of hysterectomy seems to be the style of medical practice of the physicians in the two cities. In one city, surgeons appear to be enthusiastic about hysterectomy; in the other they appear to be skeptical of its value. I cite just one example of medical procedures from the many discussed in the article. The article goes on to discuss the effect of the supply of physicians, the availability of complex technology and hospital beds, the nature of medical training and the reliance on medical specialists as factors contributing to variations in medical practices. A variety of means are now being used to address these issues.

Open heart surgery is clearly one of our most costly types of hospitalization. Coronary bypasses and heart valve replacements are among the most common open heart surgery procedures. Their use varies tremendously among populations with apparently similar levels of healthy hearts. A number of dramatic changes in physician use of these procedures have been reported in the medical scientific literature in communities where effective peer review programs among physicians have been implemented to evaluate use of these procedures. For example, in a major teaching hospital in New York City the frequency of heart valve replacement dropped by 50% in one year after cardiac surgeons began reviewing one another's cases. This took place without any changes in physician or hospital reimbursement practices. Comparable or even greater reduction in surgical cases has been reported where peer review was initiated involving the use of coronary bypasses.

Retrospective Reimbursement

Let me cite another dramatic example with large potential for savings. One of the most common causes of hospitalization for most plans is childbirth. In fact, I know of many funds where admissions for childbirth account for as much as 40-50% of all incurred claims for hospital-based care. Because the plans generally pay on a retrospective basis for all billed charges, the patient and physician can choose whatever hospital they please without consideration of cost. Likewise, the full cost reimbursement provides little incentive to minimize expenditures through prudent and judicious use of the latest technology. For example, a health care coalition in Philadelphia found that total costs for a routine childbirth varied as much as four to five times among hospitals. Still more interesting is the fact that many of the obstetricians and gynecologists supervising childbirths in the most costly hospitals are also on the staffs of some of the least costly hospitals, where they also oversee childbirths. If the health and welfare plans in Philadelphia reimbursed routine childbirths for a standard fee based on the less costly hospitals, both the physicians and the patients would quickly increase their use of the less costly hospitals for childbirth. The major teaching hospitals and other high cost hospitals would then use their complex technology primarily for childbirths involving complications, where that technology is really needed.

Lack of Price Competition

In my discussion on the effects of cost-based retrospective reimbursement, I have also hinted at the effects of the lack of price competition among health care providers as a source of unnecessary services. Retrospective reimbursement and lack of price competition are essentially different names for the same phenomenon, which grows out of the way our plans reimburse for medical care.

For example, if all private insurance plans in Philadelphia started reimbursing routine childbirths based on the costs of the least costly hospitals in Philadelphia, other hospitals would quickly swing their costs into line. As another example, many hospitals around the country have adjusted their charges downward for surgical procedures done on an outpatient basis as soon as a freestanding surgical center operated by physicians has been opened up in the hospital area. Where a fund has incorporated significant cost sharing incentives, the participants quickly recognize the economic advantage of having surgical procedures performed in these less costly surgical centers. Hospitals are very quick to change their pricing to remain competitive.

The best possible example of price competition, however, is now occurring in communities with well-established HMOs or other prepaid care programs. The HMO provides the opportunity to compare costs at the time coverage is selected. Many employers and funds are now offering HMO choices to their employees or members. In many cases, the HMO provides a more comprehensive set of services at a cost lower than the costs for participants in the traditional health and welfare plan.

Health and welfare plans can begin to take advantage of price competition as a means for restraining unnecessary services and unnecessary costs by, for example, providing plan members choices involving use of hospitals in just the area of childbirths, based on standardized fees, or by offering members choices between fee-for-service plans and prepaid plans or between preferred providers with whom lower payment rates have been negotiated.

"Defensive" Medicine

Another major cause of unnecessary services is defensive medicine. Unnecessary services are performed in the name of defensive medicine because of the rapid deployment of medical technology and excessive medical malpractice awards granted by some juries. Both issues again are being dealt with in some areas through effective cooperative action among employers, health and welfare funds and health care providers.

Defensive medicine is costly; it involves physicians performing every possible test with the latest available technology to avoid even the remotest possibility of a malpractice claim. Their concern is driven by the fact that a growing portion of malpractice claims involve awards in the millions of dollars. This issue is one of the causes of the rapid growth of Caesarean sections—the doctors prefer to avoid some of the risks of natural childbirth. It is important to put these malpractice costs in perspective in terms of total operating costs for the physician or the hospital. Annual malpractice insurance premiums for the more complicated medical specialties, including most surgeons, anesthesiologists, radiologists and pathologists, are in the area of $40,000-$50,000. Premiums are equal to as much as half of their total annual net income, and run even higher once the physician has lost a case in court. Malpractice insurance costs for hospitals run as high as 4-5% of the hospital's total annual operating budget.

For example, the malpractice insurance premium for a medium sized hospital in the northwest suburbs of Chicago was $25,000 in 1976. In 1981 it was $1 million and the hospital has had no malpractice claims filed against it. Media exposure has made more people aware of the possibility of suing, which may have caused the increase. It doesn't take much imagination to see why hospitals and physicians will take every defensive measure possible to avoid claims being filed against them. There are several states where the medical liability amount is now being controlled through arbitration systems and liability limits adopted through legislation. A concerted combination of efforts by employers, health and welfare plans and hospitals and physicians was necessary to get this legislation passed.

High Cost Claimants

Another factor contributing to the cost problem is the effect of high cost users of health care services. We have all heard about the importance of preventive medical care, but many of us tend to react with a certain degree of cynicism about the "health nuts" and about whether health care problems can be avoided. Let's look at some statistics that can help put our cynicism into perspective. Again I want to refer to recent medical economic research, a year long study in six major hospitals in the Boston area reported in the *New England Journal of Medicine* in 1980. The study produced the following important conclusions regarding the relationship of high health care costs to poor individual health practices.

Thirteen percent of all patients admitted to the six hospitals studied over the course of a year accounted for 85% of all costs incurred by those hospitals that year. Nearly all of those patients had chronic health problems, e.g., heart disease, cancer, arthritis and lung, liver and digestive tract problems. The health problems of over half of this 13% were related to the presence of three or more poor health habits—alcoholism, heavy smoking, serious obesity, poor nutrition, little or no exercise and inadequate rest. Remember, half of these patients practiced at least three of these bad health habits simultaneously. The conclusions seem obvious. Bad health habits early in life contribute to the development of chronic health problems, which account for an increasingly larger share of total health care costs from about age 40 on. Only a very small portion of plan participants will incur these high costs because only a few—about one out of ten—have practiced several of these bad health habits in tandem, but as we operate now, *all* participants are paying for them. Clearly, there are incentives and long term educational efforts that we can undertake to help control these costs and, even more importantly, to improve the lives of the few individuals who will incur these problems.

Government Cost Transfer and Prospective Reimbursement

You may recall from Figure 6 that this area accounted for approximately three percentage points out of the 19% increase in private sector health plan costs in 1980. Government cost transfer is the effect of cost shifting by hospitals and other health care providers in the face of tightening limits by government to control outlays for medical services for the elderly and the poor. This cost shifting takes place because the majority of health care services are paid for on a retrospective cost basis. If we move increasingly toward *prospectively* reimbursed health services this problem will be resolved.

The State of Maryland is a good example of how fairly simple solutions can work when the proper pressure is applied. Uniform reimbursement levels have been established for each patient in advance and applied equally to Medicare, Medicaid, Blue Cross, commercial insurers and self-insured welfare funds. This predetermined price provides a guaranteed amount of revenue so that the hospital can budget its costs and services over all patients, and it must live within that budget. It may also retain any profit recognized from increased efficiency of operation.

In Baltimore alone this approach has turned, for 18 hospitals serving large segments of the Medicare and Medicaid population, an aggregate loss of $275,000 in 1975 to an aggregate net profit of $9 million in 1980. More importantly, fund participants are no longer subsidizing losses from public programs. Important innovations are now being considered by the federal government and some states to move their public health problems toward a prospective reimbursement approach. These innovative government policies deserve support and implementation. This is another area with potential for active involvement by the groups I consider to be the most important part of my presentation—*community-based coalitions.*

Community Coalitions for Health Care

This movement is the one that I believe to be the most effective step yet taken to begin to build a more efficient medical delivery system—the joint efforts of labor, employers and health care providers to control costs. Earlier, I used the term *buyers* of health care services several times. I used that term advisedly to describe a new role for the trustees of jointly managed health and welfare funds in working with the suppliers of health care services in a buyer role on behalf of their participants. The key concept that has developed over the last several years is the existence of a buyer/supplier relationship between the managers of health care plans and the physicians and hospitals providing services to plan members and employees. We have come a very long way from the idea of considering health benefits solely as an arm's length insurance transaction.

This new approach to managing health care services received monumental support early in 1982 with the announcement of an agreement among six major national organizations representing labor, employers, hospitals, physicians and insurers. The policy agreement was signed by officials representing the AFL-CIO, the Business Roundtable, American Medical Association, American Hospital Association, Blue Cross-Blue Shield Associations and the Health Insurance Association of America. The central thrust of the policy agreement is being backed by the federal government as well as several states.

The agreement recommends creation of coalitions of employers, labor and insurers at the community level, where the *buyers* of health care can work with physicians and hospitals as *suppliers* of health care. The agreement further calls for these parties to work as buyers and suppliers in cooperative efforts to set cost containment priorities based on the analysis of the leading problems in the local community contributing to excessive health care costs and to implement cost containment programs by working together on a communitywide basis.

This agreement at the national level suggested a number of priorities for early consideration by community-based health care coalitions. They are:
- Improve the efficiency of existing health care services.
- Reform reimbursement practices to provide positive incentives to physicians, hospitals and patients to promote more efficient use and delivery of health care services.
- Effect local community decisions on additions to health care services and facilities to avoid unnecessary duplication.
- Assure that adequate services are available for the poor and aged.
- Promote the expansion of improved health status through preventive care programs and employee education.

Interestingly, each of these priorities relates to the specific problems I identified earlier as contributing to the health care cost problem. This national agreement represents an unprecedented accord among all the sectors of the health care equation concerning potential solutions for rising health care costs. I think you'll agree that it is a powerful and unique group—the strange bedfellows I mentioned before.

This important national level policy commitment provides the essential impetus to the rapidly growing development of community-based coalitions for health care. At present there are some 130 community groups in existence, about 80 of which could be considered active. About 25 to 30 are actually implementing specific projects across the country. In general, most of the coalitions today are made up principally of employer representatives. In most cases, formal working relationships have been developed with local medical societies, hospitals, selected insurers and other health care organizations such as medical foundations and professional standard review organizations. Less than 20 have any labor involvements at this point, but a concerted effort is planned to change this situation. These existing coalitions and the national policy statement I have referred to represent a major opportunity for Taft-Hartley health and welfare plan involvement at the local community level. The coalition initiative is new, and the vast majority of the groups have developed within the past two years.

Why is the pattern of community-based health care cost containment and local coalitions that is now arising the best alternative for solving the long range health care problem? I would like to explore that question with you and lead you through some of the specifics of how these community-based coalitions are working and how they have to be structured to be fully effective. My discussion here is drawn from the growing experience our consultants are gaining from working with existing community coalitions and from our ongoing study of and discussions with many of these groups around the United States.

These new approaches are developing because third-party payers and fund managers are becoming increasingly frustrated in their attempts to contain health care costs through the usual methods of the last 15 or 20 years. For example, usual and customary reimbursement restrictions have had little effect. In communities where the supply of physicians is increasing rapidly, the usual and customary reimbursement method in fact facilitates accelerated physician fees rather than restricts them. Stricter claims control is also limited because the controls are still after the fact, and frequently serve only to alienate participants by forcing them to pay for excessive charges. Finally, efforts by individual parties to negotiate charges have failed due to lack of sufficient volume to provide a benefit to the provider for cooperating. Again, lack of leverage is the problem.

New Concepts, New Responsibilities

Clearly, concepts must change. Trustees of health and welfare funds must become active in their true role as buyers. The complexity of the health care system requires a more active role on behalf of the individual participant. Physicians, hospitals and other medical providers also have to become more responsible as suppliers of health care services. Interestingly, many physicians and most hospitals welcome this new approach to the health care equation, recognizing the need to establish a more responsible accountable basis for providing health care services. Finally, participants also need to recognize that they have new roles to play in terms of making more informed choices among health care providers, based on costs as well as quality. These changes require new communitywide efforts to inform employees and to help them recognize that the cost containment solution requires that they make more effective use of health care services. They need to understand why specific incentives are designed to promote efficient use of the fund's resources.

The buyer/supplier relationship I am describing works when we consider the local nature of health care. Part of the problem in the past has occurred because we have attempted to apply uniform policies across widely different communities and populations. As a result, national policies frequently conflict with local needs or capabilities for delivering care. Perhaps the strongest proof of the need to develop health plans with the flexibility to meet local needs can be drawn from the fact that nearly all of us receive most of our health care services within three to four miles of our homes.

This new concept requires new roles for all three of the major parties in the health care equation: from trustees of funds as buyers; from physicians, hospitals and other health care providers as suppliers; and from participants.

Trustees

In the past, trustees were principally concerned with providing adequate health care for their participants. Their involvement went no further. The new approach requires a significantly expanded set of responsibilities if they are to be effective in addressing solutions to the cost problem. Trustees must become concerned with provider capabilities in their own communities. They must become aware of the specific service facilities that exist, of the opportunities to promote the use of more cost-effective existing alternatives or of the development of new alternatives. They must also become aware of community cost factors such as the need for health services for the aged and the poor.

As buyers of services, trustees must become involved directly with physicians, hospitals and other health care providers to identify opportunities for working together in ways that will control costs. Most physicians will tell you that they have never been able to talk to trustees of funds about their concern and preferred approaches for controlling costs. This new approach also means considerably expanding thoughts about the design of health plans. The principal new emphasis here is in providing participants with choices and alternatives that contain economic efficiencies as well as quality of care. It involves broadening our fund administrative role to do more than just pay claims by collecting data and analyzing usage patterns to work with providers for improved efficiencies. Finally, trustees must actively involve plan participants in the development and implementation of cost control measures.

Health Care Providers

In this new approach, health care providers also have new responsibilities as suppliers of cost-effective health care. They need to be frank in identifying current mistakes and misuse and take leadership on behalf of their peers to address these problems. Many local medical societies and hospital groups are now actively taking up this cause. They are coming forward themselves with new approaches and suggestions for plan design that promote less costly services, such as the development of prenegotiated payment programs—the highly innovative project now in its third year in Rochester, New York, where all hospitals are paid on the basis of a prenegotiated budget and specific hospital charges along the lines of the Baltimore example given earlier.

Participants

Fund participants also have important responsibilities. They must understand the importance of using appropriate low cost services. In most cases, individuals are willing to cooperate once they believe they have choices that are real and will be to their advantage. Finally, individuals must recognize the importance of taking care of themselves and in turn be willing to pay a financial price if they practice poor health habits. For example, we long ago accepted the concept in both automobile and life insurance that higher premiums are charged for individuals who have avoidable problems such as excessive drinking or heavy smoking. Why not do the same for the majority of participants who try to maintain good health by rewarding them with lower cost sharing without denying treatment to those with several addictions?

Cooperative Measures

The new approach of necessity requires joint action by employers and health and welfare funds in the community to provide common direction to providers. It also involves elements of common plan design and administrative approaches within the community to effectively direct the providers. It is critical that buyers share data to identify problems such as excessive hospital use or unnecessary services, described earlier. A benefit to joint action is that participation cost can be reduced through economies of scale. Perhaps the most important reason for joint action is to promote change where resistance may occur on the providers' side through the combined purchasing power of the buyers (leverage, if you will).

Figure 8

TYPICAL ORGANIZATION

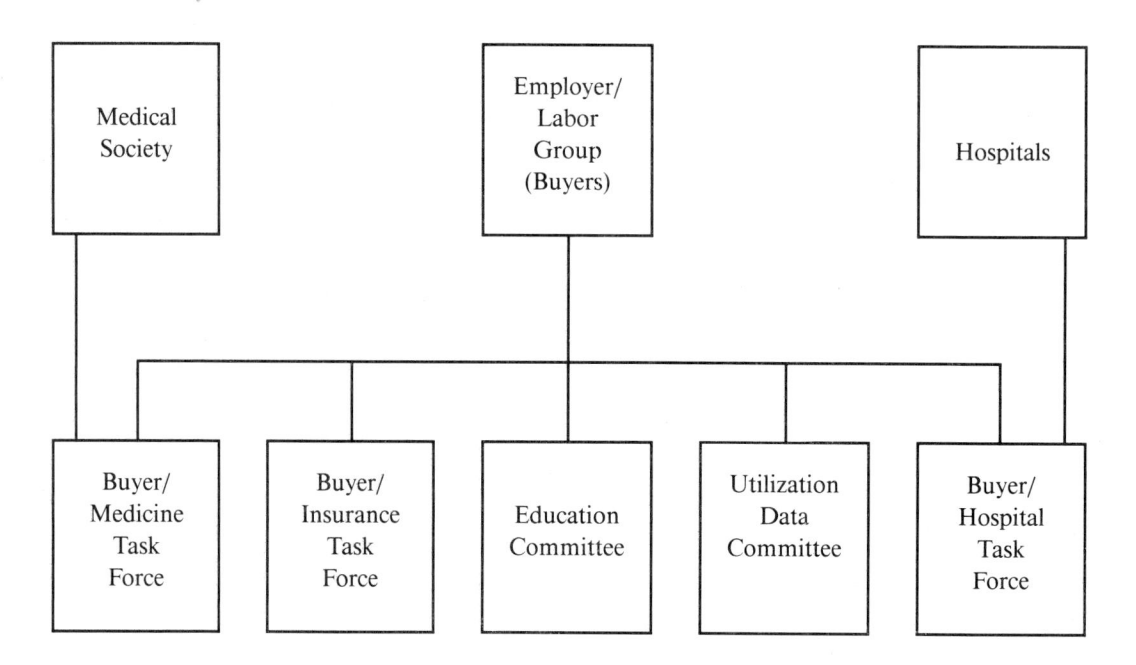

```
                      ┌──────────┐
  ┌──────────┐        │ Employer/│        ┌──────────┐
  │ Medical  │        │  Labor   │        │          │
  │ Society  │        │  Group   │        │ Hospitals│
  │          │        │ (Buyers) │        │          │
  └────┬─────┘        └────┬─────┘        └────┬─────┘
       │                   │                   │
       └───────┬───────┬───┴───┬───────┬───────┘
               │       │       │       │       │
          ┌────┴──┐ ┌──┴───┐ ┌─┴────┐ ┌┴─────┐ ┌┴─────┐
          │Buyer/ │ │Buyer/│ │      │ │Utili-│ │Buyer/│
          │Medicine│ │Insur-│ │Educa-│ │zation│ │Hospi-│
          │ Task  │ │ ance │ │ tion │ │ Data │ │ tal  │
          │ Force │ │ Task │ │Commit│ │Commit│ │ Task │
          │       │ │Force │ │ tee  │ │ tee  │ │Force │
          └───────┘ └──────┘ └──────┘ └──────┘ └──────┘
```

Typical Organization

The organization of community-based programs differs by location. Here is an example of one structure that has been created in a community where we have been working for several years (Figure 8). After a review of the buyer's objectives, I will discuss the various committee structures and task forces that have been created to identify priorities, develop programs and implement specific projects in support of those programs. I will then move into a general description of the kinds of cost containment projects being implemented and the progress being achieved. First, let's reemphasize the buyer's objectives.

Buyer Objectives

The first step in creating an effective community cost containment program is the creation of a coalition of employers and labor representatives. In general, without the initiative coming from employers and labor as buyers, there will be no effective cost containment program. The principal objectives of the buyer group in the community are:

- Employer/employee education, the first step in becoming an effective initiator. In most cases this effort is taken with indirect input from providers and insurers until the parties feel they have sufficient knowledge to interact effectively with the more technically knowledgeable physicians and hospitals. This interaction quickly leads to preliminary identification of cost containment opportunities.
- Building relationships with doctors and hospitals to gain support and participation from them in identifiable cost containment programs
- Changes suggested by the employer/labor group for plan design and administration to be implemented by other employer plans and welfare funds within the community
- Examination of how the group's efforts will impact on the community and consideration of the needs of other segments of the general public who also receive their health care services from local providers.

Buyer/Physician Task Force

The next step is creating a task force of the buyer group and the physicians. We recommend that the task force include representation from the buyer group, the medical society and the elected presidents or chiefs of the hospital medical staffs from all community hospitals. The basic purpose of this task force is to assure cooperative efforts with physicians and hospital medical staff. The goal is to create change within the existing medical practice structure.

In almost every case, the buyer/medicine task force finds itself working through the following set of objectives. First, there is a period of mutual education regarding one another's problems in the health care equation. The second objective growing out of these discussions becomes one of exploring ways of improving physician and hospital practices to contain costs, e.g., better use of outpatient surgery, controlling the use of hospital emergency rooms and all the other factors touched on previously. Discussions quickly move to ways of improving benefit plan design to provide the proper positive, as well as negative, incentives to both patients and physicians to use and provide services efficiently. Additional objectives frequently involve consideration of legislation to achieve specific purposes, e.g., how to control medical liability claims in order to limit defensive medicine. Another important role is communicating policies agreed to by the task force to all other physicians, patients and participants, to hospital medical staff and to others in the community. The final objective is creation of a database to monitor physician and hospital performance as well as the outcome of specific plan design incentives. A common database, which all parties will accept as technically valid and accurate, is essential for progress.

Buyer/Hospital Task Force

A comparable task force is created between the buyer group and hospitals. The development of this task force follows a process similar to the discussions with physicians. Again, one of the first efforts is to educate one another regarding each other's problems, and particularly to identify excessive use of inpatient services. Generally, discussions then move directly to ways of modifying hospital operations to improve the availability of outpatient services and preventive care.

Another objective is to determine which physician demands and uses of the hospital are not cost-effective. For example, a frequent problem causing high hospital costs has to do with the ways in which physicians schedule admissions of patients to the hospital. Making better use of costly hospital facilities such as surgical suites and diagnostic equipment by broadening their use into afternoons, evenings and weekends is another important objective.

Plan design changes are also critical. For example, one of the greatest problems hospitals have is in controlling inappropriate use of emergency rooms. Plan design changes to provide patient incentives to use emergency rooms only when needed for true emergencies is a critical step.

Gaining access to hospital medical record data to evaluate physician practices and employee health problems is another major objective. These data are important in assuring effective utilization review for individual patient admissions.

Buyer/Insurer Task Force

Another task force is frequently created with the insurers. Their involvement is necessary because in most communities many smaller employers do not have the capacity to become involved with the employer/labor coalition; rather, they must depend on the initiative and policies that are set by the coalition. Participation of insurers is frequently the most important step in permitting participation by the smaller employer. Initially, these discussions include sharing information on plan design problems based on local experiences and obtaining the insurer's ideas for specific cost containment approaches in that community.

Another important step is to gain commitments from insurers to implement plan design changes locally once new approaches built around those plan design changes have been negotiated between the employer/labor coalition and the physicians and hospitals. A principal reason for this development is the need to avoid conflicting goals and approaches between insurers and health care providers and between the employer/labor coalition and providers. Insurers also must assist the smaller employers and their covered beneficiaries in the education effort so the individual consumer is aware of cost containment options.

Finally, broadening hospital utilization review programs to include as many patients as possible within the review process is important to complete success. Since some decisions regarding hospital operations of physician performance can only be objectively made after reviewing service use data for large numbers of individuals, it is necessary to include as many covered employees as possible.

Education Committees

Education committees are another important part of the coalition structure. These committees oversee the important shift in attitude that is necessary to promote effective changes. Principal objectives for this committee are to provide common information for all buyers in the community on new approaches and on existing analyses of cost problems. A second objective is to develop employee education programs on how to use the health care services in the community more efficiently—how to select less costly providers, which frequently includes publishing information on costs and sources of less costly care. Providing information to employees on how bad decisions on their part regarding the use of services contributes to costs is another important role for the education committee.

Finally, many coalition programs provide employees with information on preventive care programs and the need for improved health as a way of containing health care costs. If you are over 50, you'll remember the pamphlets on good health habits that the Metropolitan Life Insurance Company used to distribute when the agent came to the door to collect 27¢ from your mother—nothing new here. Education committees also frequently find it necessary to undertake general public information programs to acquaint the community at large with the overall nature of the community cost containment effort, in order to assure cooperation by other needed groups in the community.

Utilization/Data Committee

A utilization and/or data committee is also necessary. The objectives of such a committee generally start with developing agreements between the employer/labor coalition and the physician and hospital sector for implementation of concurrent utilization review programs for hospitalized participants. The data committee also oversees the development of data collection systems frequently based on patient and physician information contained in hospital medical records. Approaches for maintaining patient confidentiality are a critical part of this discussion.

The third key role is to analyze data on physician and hospital performance to identify instances of inappropriate utilization. In some cases, this analysis must move down to the individual physician and/or hospital level. Technical support from physicians and other medical specialists in the community familiar with analysis of medical utilization data is critical.

The problems identified through these data then move to the appropriate task forces with physicians and hospitals for agreement on corrections. For example, a particular physician may always perform a specific type of surgery on an inpatient basis that his colleagues routinely perform on an outpatient basis. These types of negotiations are best left to the members of a particular hospital medical staff to work with their fellow physician on ways to modify his practices. This process is the type described earlier that took place in the New York City hospital with regard to open heart surgery. The key to success, however, lies in the fact that physicians know that the employer/labor coalition has data identifying general physician community practices as well as individual physician practices. Again, leverage on your part, as the buyer, helps to solve cost problems.

Overall Objectives

All common buyer efforts and activities are directed toward reducing costs for individual illnesses, encouraging the appropriate level of care through plan design incentives and communications. Other important roles include assuring cost-effective high quality care and providing leadership for change in the entire community. To be effective, cooperative relationships must be developed among the buyers, hospitals and physicians. Community programs to improve the health of the employees to reduce future demand for health services is another major goal. Finally, efforts must be directed toward modifying government influences on the local health care system where those influences may be driving up costs or blocking changes that could help eliminate or constrain costs.

From my description of the development of a coalition, I hope that you can see major opportunities for yourselves in working with other funds and employers to begin to have a strong buyer impact on the health care system in your communities. We can no longer look to third parties such as government or insurers to solve *our* problems.

Maintaining Your Medical Benefits in the '80s

In conclusion, let me leave you with a five point strategy for your own fund that, effectively implemented and coordinated with the community efforts I have described, can help you provide your participants with an acceptable level of protection against the hazards of major medical expenses for the balance of this decade.

1. Plan Design Changes
   Build financial incentives into the plan to encourage both the participant and the provider to make cost-efficient choices regarding the location and use of services.
2. Education and Communication
   Begin the process of educating your participants toward acceptance of change in how their medical care will be provided in the future, their own responsibility to cooperate with better ways of providing medical care

and the various sources of care and their associated costs/prices.

3. Utilization Review
On your own, or in conjunction with your community coalition, use a monitoring mechanism that will permit you to identify and be responsive to the need for change as your own experience dictates.

4. Preventive Care
Encourage attention to the maintenance of good health by incorporating some or all of these preventive measures in your plan:
- Early detection screening
- Nutrition education
- Immunization programs
- Physical fitness
- Weight loss
- Stress management.

5. Multiple Choice of Plans and Providers
Provide participants with real choices concerning the desired coverage in the form of flexible levels and types of benefits, and encourage the use of alternative providers of care based on cost-effectiveness.

You have your work cut out for you. I hope that at least some of these ideas will be useful to you as you attempt to maintain your own fund's commitments during the balance of the 1980s.

Cost Containment Through Plan Design

BY GLEN SLAUGHTER

BACK IN 1967 when I was the immediate Past Chairman of the Foundation, I gave a speech to the American Society of Internal Medicine entitled "Is God Dead?" Its theme was cost containment. Preparing for this presentation, I reread that speech. It was like opening a time capsule. I was astounded to realize nothing has changed but the prices quoted. In that speech, I said " . . . a complete plan of family protection now costs close to $30 per month . . . individuals and employers will balk at $40 to $50 monthly premiums."

If it didn't hurt so much, you would have to laugh at those words. Fifteen years later we are far beyond that balk point. What are you paying now? Even HMOs must charge $100 a month for all the benefits mandated by Congress. The average indemnity plan well exceeds that figure. A typical dental plan costs $25 per month. After you add vision, drug, disability and a retiree program, many labor-management principals find themselves sitting at the bargaining table looking at $200 or more per month diverted from the paycheck for health plan coverage. For what? Certainly not better coverage. We all have been part of the great American process of ever-higher provider fees and overexpanding hospitals and health-related facilities—all of which must be financed through benefit payments.

Some of us get tired of taking all the blame and being castigated because we as trustees, administrators or insurance company claims managers can't stem this upward spiral. We do our best through pre-authorization, negotiated discounts, utilization review procedures, etc. You can frustrate the obvious bandits by such measures, but they are ineffective in stemming the general tide of rising medical costs.

What Did We Do Wrong?

The principal culprit in the cost spiral is faulty plan design. Thus, the principal solution will come from a drastic revision in plan design, which requires a drastic revision in the understanding and attitude of trustees, labor-management principals, government officials, legislators and, finally, of all of us as covered beneficiaries.

Mr. Slaughter is chairman of the board of Glen Slaughter & Associates of Oakland, California. His firm has specialized in serving as consultants and administrators to labor-management trusts for over 27 years. He holds a B.A. degree from the University of California at Berkeley and an M.A. degree from American University. An active participant in civic and national affairs, Mr. Slaughter was one of the initial members of the Advisory Council on Employee Welfare and Pension Benefit Plans, U.S. Department of Labor. Mr. Slaughter served as one of the outside consultants working with the PBGC Special Project Team that prepared the multiemployer plan study presented to Congress on July 1, 1978. Actively involved in the International Foundation since its early days, he has served on the Board of Directors and was Chairman of the Board in 1965. He is a former chairman of the Past Chairmen's Council, 25th Anniversary and Employer Liability Study Committees and a former member of the Research, Public Relations, Cash Reserves Ad Hoc, Employer Liability and Educational Program Committees. He is presently a member of the Foundation's Government/Industry Relations Committee. Mr. Slaughter has appeared as a speaker and moderator for numerous educational programs and has written articles for the Foundation's monthly Digest. *He is currently the president of the Society of Professional Benefit Administrators.*

History of What We Did Wrong

The Blues

Blue Cross and Blue Shield were born in the '30s. They were sponsored and controlled by the hospital associations and the medical societies, respectively. Therefore, naturally, the benefits were designed for the economic interest of hospitals and doctors, namely, to get their bills paid by their patients.

Consequently, early Blue Cross plans paid 100% of the ward rate and hospital extras. However, as you may remember, most were limited to 31 day coverage. Why? Because few hospital stays exceed 31 days and well over 90% of a hospital's total billings will be paid with 31 day 100% coverage.

Some of you will remember, in pre-Medicare days, that under Blue Shield plans, doctors accepted Blue Shield plan benefit schedules as payment "in full" if your income did not exceed a specific dollar limit.

Thus started the first step on the primrose path. The basic plan design features lauded by both providers and claimants were *first dollar coverage with payment in full.*

The Insurance Companies

Not to be outdone, along came the insurance companies with the Siamese twin plan design concepts of *major medical* based on *usual and customary charges.* These concepts answered two needs: First, for the claimant, major medical coverage meant true insurance protection extended for months and even years beyond a 31 day limit, and that idea made sense. We all know that extended benefits are relatively inexpensive in terms of overall experience.

Second, for the insurance companies, usual and customary provided a marketing answer to the scheduled rates arranged by the Blues and their member hospitals and doctors. There was one serious flaw—the allowable charges set as usual and customary by most insurance companies were set so high that they could only be described as overcharges rather than reasonable. This situation appealed both to the doctors and to the claimants who always got their bills paid.

Taft-Hartley Trusts

Let's face it. The pressure on the union business agent is to cover everything, 100%, on a first dollar and forever basis. Under the Landrum-Griffin Act, it is difficult enough for union representatives to get reelected, so what you want is a plan that pays the bills, whatever they are, like clockwork, with no screams from the members. Besides, what could one poor union member do to object to a course of treatment or the charge while he is lying on his back? Just pay the bill!

The Government

I appreciate that governments must properly reflect the desires and needs of the citizens, but when it comes to Medicare and Medicaid, Congress went overboard. The government managed to incorporate all of the bad design principles of the Blues, the insurance companies and of plan trustees, while adding two more design concepts guaranteed to boost charges. Those two new concepts were that the aged and the indigent were entitled to mainstream medical care. That concept meant not being sent to county hospitals and not receiving care from doctors under tightly controlled fee schedules. It meant that they could go to hospitals and doctors of their choice. That concept also meant that those hospitals and doctors were to be paid the same as for services provided to their private patients.

The law actually said that it would pay "reasonable" charges, but that provision was interpreted by regulation to mean "usual and customary." Since providers were to be paid the same for private patients and Medicare patients, there was a whole new quantum leap in the "usual and customary" definition. All providers did not charge the same; therefore, uniform usual and customary charges could not be established according to "community profiles," as the insurance companies theoretically did. It meant allowing each provider to establish an *individual profile* of usual and customary charges, for which he would be entitled to reimbursement.

Therefore, you have the new concepts of mainstream medicine and individual "usual and customary" profiles pushed upward by the full force of your tax dollars. Against that kind of force, all the utilization reviews in the world are like coughing into the face of a hurricane.

We now spend more than $280 billion on medical care each year. That figure is more than we spent annually for all goods and services in the U.S. 35 years ago, the year the Taft-Hartley Act gave birth to jointly administered trust funds.

How to Change Course?

The mood of the nation is prepared for a new course. A new course means a change in government policies and programs, and a change in our attitudes and design practices as private purchasers of medical benefits.

First, let's all recognize that no one in the government or Congress any longer advocates socialized medicine with the $280 billion price tag as a part of the national budget. Bills considered by both parties call for mandated benefits, which employers and/or negotiated plans would be required to provide employees.

Until recently, the trend of thinking within the bureaucracy and on Capitol Hill followed the same historical primrose path described previously. Suddenly, however, there is a new mood—and in all fairness to the Democrats, the present regime in Washington didn't invent it. Nature is just catching up with our past improprieties. In fairness to the Reagan Administration, it is stirring the pot and calling for cost containment measures, concepts not voiced previously, in my memory, in Washington.

Let's not get upset because we know that "competition" is not created by requiring every employer of 100 employees to have all his employees covered by three carriers. Let's grab at the chance to work cooperatively with the government so that constructive changes in both government and private plan design and cost containment will occur. If cost containment can be made part of that design, so much the better. We have a wealth of practical experience to share with government policymakers.

In addition, there have been many private and government-sponsored studies conducted to identify how different types of plan design affect cost and the level of health care. Within the government itself, on the leading edge of the effort to alter government policy and to provide the research tools necessary for intelligent government and private policy decisions is the Competition Work Group in the Department of Health and Human Services. In the private sector, the Rand Corporation designed and conducted the massive Health Insurance Study under a Health and Human Services grant.

Why Is a Change in Labor-Management Attitude Critical?

The government is going to move in the area of plan design, hopefully with the benefit of the studies available. We not only should influence those changes but take direct action in our private plan design decisions. If we don't, projected costs will destroy our ability to protect our members from either medical or financial catastrophe.

A Business Perspective on the Management of Health Care Costs

BY EDGAR G. DAVIS

AT THE NATIONAL level, I think it is safe to say that the business community generally feels that our present health care system, in spite of its problems and faults, is the best in the world and far better than any kind of system the federal government could ever devise. Thus, I believe that the general business community will continue to support the country's basic, private, pluralistic health system vigorously and will resist any major political encroachment of a negative nature at the national level. Further, we all recognize that a major part of the high cost of health care can be attributed directly to the regulations already in place. We need to undo regulations rather than pile more on top of what we already have. The business community is working to make that happen.

The business community has listened to the debate over rising health care costs with interest and concern. Cost increases have become, in fact, a topic of major importance to the majority of the large corporations of this country. The reasons are obvious. First, employee health plans pay for approximately 25% of the entire personal health bill of this country, which is something of the magnitude of $50 billion to $60 billion. Further, the costs of these benefit plans have escalated alarmingly, to a point where they are a significant portion of the total payroll dollar—up to 10% in some instances. While business profits have been declining, health benefit costs have continued to rise.

Problems in Health Care

In recent years, the business community has become more knowledgeable about the workings of the country's health care system. Consequently, the business community now tends to be concerned and apprehensive about the consequences of many of the proposals offered in the political arena to "correct the problems." We, therefore, are helping you and others to find alternatives. Community health coalitions are one of the alternatives being tested.

Mr. Davis is vice president, corporate affairs for Eli Lilly and Company. He is a member of The Conference Board, Public Affairs Research Council; vice president and member, board of directors, Washington Business Group on Health; director, Public Affairs Council; member of the Business Roundtable Task Force on Health; and director, Legislative Advisory Committee of the Business Roundtable Task Force on Regulation. Mr. Davis received his A.B. degree from Kenyon College, his M.B.A. degree from Harvard University School of Business and attended the "Washington Semester" of Honors Study in Political Science at American University.

The typical businessman *does* worry that there may be inefficiencies in the health system that tend to inflate the cost of the services provided. He also worries that providers of care may not be exerting enough self-discipline on their activities or giving enough attention to the cost/benefit ratios of services. These are serious concerns.

More to the point, businessmen are looking in the mirror and are wondering if their companies have gone too far in providing benefit programs that are too open ended and too broad in scope—thus unleashing a tremendous demand for services from a system that is perceived by employees as being "free." This dilemma may be the biggest one of all.

Indeed, many businessmen feel that they and the federal government have almost signed blank checks for health care delivery. Many businessmen, like many politicians, have sought (and some continue to seek) culprits who are responsible for perceived problems.

However, in my opinion, businessmen are beginning to realize that, largely, the general economic environment and the institutional arrangements for payment for care have helped to cause cost escalation. For example, I believe it is becoming increasingly clear—though far from universally accepted—that the general inflation of the past decade or so has been, by far, the largest single cause of price and cost escalation in health care. Health care is inherently very labor-intensive and so far has not experienced strong labor productivity growth. Health care providers, thus, have been hard hit by wage inflation.

Since general inflation cannot be controlled to any significant degree by health policy actions alone, business and the public will look more and more to the areas of utilization and intensity of care for the causes of unwarranted cost escalation problems that are specific to health care. With utilization review they will seek short run solutions—perhaps within the framework of local health care coalitions.

Possible Solutions

I believe that businessmen are finding, or expecting to find, that in many areas there *has* been overgrowth in some kinds of hospital capacity. Physicians and their patients have not had sufficient incentive to economize on the use of a community's total facilities. The need for newer facilities can always be rationalized, but then it becomes painfully clear that they must be at least partially paid for through cost-based reimbursement systems. The growth of so-called alternative delivery systems has helped reveal this sequence of problems, as has the experience gained from close examination of individual businesses' health program costs. Business thus realizes that its benefit plan design may be contributing to the problem.

The Business Roundtable, therefore, encourages business to design benefit plans that lead to more prudent use of all types of health care services. This design may include such things as copayments, deductibles, etc., to provide economic incentives for individuals to control health costs. The Task Force on Health especially urges that companies avoid benefit plan provisions that give a higher rate of reimbursement for a more expensive type of care when a less expensive one would do just as well. Other possibilities include provider selection, utilization review and alternative delivery systems, such as HMOs, as well as reimbursement for pre-admission laboratory testing, ambulatory surgery and health care at home, as opposed to that in a hospital setting.

Reviewing a Benefit Plan

Although each company has its own set of experiences and competencies with which to develop an internal assessment of health care benefit programs, it is possible to describe the more obvious checkpoints for such a review. Working with their own corporate staffs, benefit plans consultants and others, a company should be able to develop a series of checkpoints grouped under at least four major subject areas.

In the same sense that a multiphasic physical examination may provide a "snapshot" of an individual's current health, a similar examination of health benefit program design could, at least, raise questions that should be thoroughly reviewed and thoughtfully answered by corporations in considering the best possible way to address the issues of health care cost management without compromise of quality or of access to proper care. Again, a key issue will be management's communication of the employees' interests, so that these costs are being addressed for *their* personal benefit, both financially and for *quality* of care in the long view. These four subject areas are:

Management of Claims Control

- Claims data accuracy
- Coordination of benefits
- Management by exception
- Industrial medicine/medical community liaison.

Management of Data Analysis

- Cost comparisons
- Provider comparisons.

Programs to Improve Health Status of the Individual and Dependents

- Health education and screening
  1. Early detection screening programs
  2. Accident prevention and safety training programs
  3. Immunization
  4. CPR programs
  5. General hygiene and wellness
- Health promotion programs
  1. Smoking cessation programs
  2. Stress management
  3. Employee counseling programs
  4. Self-care programs.

Working With the Medical and Hospital Community and Other Interested Parties

- Cooperative analysis and health planning efforts
  1. Working with the medical and hospital community
  2. Coalition activities.

Business Roundtable Health Initiatives' Survey

To develop our own understanding at the Roundtable of the current situation concerning aspects of employee benefit design and other corporate health programs, in March 1982 the Roundtable's Health Initiatives' staff conducted a survey of more than 160 Roundtable companies. One hundred and thirty-five companies responded. Although the final results of this survey are not yet available, it is possible to share some general results with you now.

The survey consisted of two major parts. The first part concerned some specifics of firms' benefit plans and other cost management programs. The second part sought more in-depth data on community activities and the activities in which members would like to see involvement by Health Initiatives. Some of the more salient results from the survey are:

- Most firms have begun to implement cost management programs.
- Greater than 25% of the companies indicate that they have recently increased employee cost sharing.
- Greater than 68% of responding companies indicated their willingness to participate in Health Initiatives' activities.
- Data standardization for utilization comparisons was identified as an area of great interest.
- Approximately 120 companies are active in more than 80 local, state and regional coalitions of different compositions.

The Local Approach to Cost Management

The Roundtable Task Force on Health has long urged executives to participate meaningfully on hospital boards and work actively on management problems. It also urges companies to examine corporate giving programs to make them consistent with appropriate community efforts. I personally know of one sizable community in which *every* hospital has a capital fund drive under way. In recessionary times, as a businessman I would say that something is seriously wrong in that situation—which leads me to my next point.

The need for changes in the delivery of medical care varies from community to community, as does the demand for, and the supply of, health care resources and the financial needs of health care institutions. That's why the local approach to health care cost management makes sense. Obviously, this feeling is widespread, for the number of local health coalitions has been growing rapidly. The real challenge is to make each local coalition a truly effective instrument for health care oversight.

Effectiveness at health care oversight inevitably involves finding a way for interested parties to "face up" together to some very basic questions. One way or another, these questions will touch on such basic issues as:

- Do we really understand what is going on in the delivery of health care in our community? In other words, do we really understand how a system is or is not working effectively? What information do we need, and how can we obtain it, in order to make knowledgeable and informed judgments?
- How do we feel about the adequacy of the system in our community for providing access to quality, cost-effective care?
- How willing are we to listen and learn from each other's concerns about these questions? How willing are we to build a plan of action for community self-discipline and to use our leadership roles to develop the necessary public consensus to accept those actions that may represent significant change from the status quo?
- Can the coalition develop to the point that the members can and do address these and other fundamental health policy questions? If so, that will signal an important achievement, which demonstrates that health policy can rise above the parochial concerns of any component group. If members of coalitions, as professionals, can accomplish constructive change of public attitude about health care delivery through leadership, they will have acted as true stewards of the public interest.

The Role of Business

In our opinion, the senior corporate executive brings a special talent to the local coalition. He or she is used to being part of a team and planning for the long run. He or she has experience and competence in managing the inevitable conflict that emerges in a coalition of various interests. Managing this conflict, by keeping attention focused on the issue and on substantive alternatives rather than on personalities or constituencies, and helping to move from points of difference to areas of agreement are important skills of most senior corporate executives.

Business should—and I hope will—come to these local coalitions with a broader objective than simply reducing the cost of their own benefit plans, important as that is to their individual corporate "bottom line." In the process of effective coalition development, employers (like any other single constituency group) may *initially* work together and learn about the health system to better understand how to exert positive influences on the structure and costs of health care delivery. Beyond that, however, business can best serve its own interests and further its corporate social responsibility to all segments of the public by concentrating on the broader goal of better allocation of health care resources for the entire community.

One danger that must be avoided is perpetuating or furthering "cost shifting" from one segment of the public to another. Coalitions with too narrow a base of community participation can inadvertently have this result. The cooperation and participation of business, hospital management, physicians, insurers, labor and other community interests are needed.

Problems in Developing Coalitions

I do not believe that an ideal coalition will ever be defined for all communities and all times. The problems of each community are different—and, quite frankly, it is likely that in some communities part of the problem will be that some of the groups whose management should be a part of any such coalition will concentrate on their own short term self-interest.

Trying to achieve greater cost-effectiveness for health care while improving—or at least not harming—the quality of care and necessary access to it cannot be easy in any community. The crosscurrents of public programs, private interests, subsidized capital for hospitals and consumers seeking better health care without personal cost pose enormous difficulties and promise conflicts. Just the agreement on a particular local problem with a workable solution is a challenge equal to any we face in managing either businesses or hospitals.

Business alone will not be able to solve very many local problems; I hope that businessmen will not try. They will need the support and help of hospital managements and other parties concerned about health care. In my view, health care coalitions must be as broadly based as possible, with all parties as equally motivated as possible, to represent total community interest. I am sure most business participants in health care coalitions recognize this need.

As I see it, perhaps the two most unfortunate sorts of local coalition that could result are first, the one that is dominated by self-interested providers seeking to preserve the status quo from even being critically examined and second, the one that is directed by a small set of narrow business interests seeking only to enhance the bottom line of member companies. It will take the cooperation of business, hospital management, physicians, insurers, labor—all interested parties—to guard against such developments and to modify them if they occur. I hope that the International Foundation and its members will continue its work with businesses toward the formation, development and success of many more successful programs of improved health care cost management.

Conclusion

I know that you share the thought that the U.S. does have the world's greatest health care system. It is the result of the efforts of literally thousands of people who have worked together over many, many years in a free, pluralistic society. In spite of its shortcomings, it is a vast, varied and dynamic system that has done a remarkable job of fulfilling society's needs. However, just as American industry is not as efficient as it should be, I am sure that you will agree that neither are hospitals as cost-effective as they should be.

I can assure you that the objective of the business community is to enhance the inherent benefits of our system by making it work still better. The job ahead of us is clearer than the possible solutions, but if those of us in the private sector continue to pull together in addressing the issues, we can achieve a great degree of success.

Cost Containment Through Health Education and Welfare Programs

BY CHARLES J. MAZZA, CEBS

HEALTH CARE is a major concern for all employers and employees, as well as trustees and participants of a Taft-Hartley trust. Articles abound in newspapers and periodicals; the media highlight the mounting costs of room rates and complex operations; Congress is constantly debating what to do about Medicare, or the lack of competition in the health care industry, or changing the beneficial tax implications regarding deductibility of medical expenses for a firm and its employees, etc. In short, health care is a critical issue; one of the reasons it will remain so is that there is no single answer to getting our arms around this problem and reducing it to a manageable size.

Since it is an issue of major proportions, we must segment it, break it down into significant parts and deal with those issues in a manageable way.

I intend to discuss ways in which this problem can be addressed in the workplace, that is, in the relationship between employer and employee. There are other ways to deal with this problem, such as legislation. However, legislation in particular is a reactionary solution—in effect, a knee jerk reaction trying to solve the problem because other alternatives haven't worked. Historically, when other alternatives haven't worked, government has stepped in and provided us with solutions, whether desired or not.

However, the employer-employee relationship is one in which there is a mutual self-interest in trying to resolve the problem. If the resolution is effective, the employer receives lower costs, more productivity, less turnover and a more effective use of its salary and wage dollar. Employees receive much greater rewards—a healthier, more productive, longer and more enjoyable life.

The premise of this discussion is that neither employers nor employees will take any action unless they perceive it to be in their own self-interest. Likewise, I don't expect you to make a commitment to carry this message back to your own companies or trusts unless I convince you that the

As manager of Meidinger's Milwaukee office, Mr. Mazza has overall responsibility for the preparation, delivery and quality of compensation and employee benefit consulting services throughout Wisconsin and Minnesota. He is also an instructor in the Certified Employee Benefit Specialist (CEBS) program at Marquette University in Milwaukee. His previous position was as director, compensation and benefits for the Jos. Schlitz Brewing Company, Milwaukee and his responsibilities there included all compensation programs for salaried employees and executives, as well as the design and administration of approximately 25 welfare and 12 retirement plans for salaried and union employees. He has also served as trustee for the Milwaukee Brewery Workers Pension Plan. He earned a B.S. degree in civil engineering and a master's degree in business administration at Marquette University.

subject is worth your consideration. Therefore, I first will summarize all the data you may have seen to indicate that health care costs are really running out of control. Then I'll briefly identify four ways in which costs can be contained and dismiss the first two—not because they are unimportant, but because they are beyond the scope of this presentation. I will then deal with the two remaining alternatives that have real potential for cost savings.

Why Cost Containment Is Needed

Two common ways to measure the increase in health care costs have been by comparison to the

Consumer Price Index (CPI) or as a percentage of the Gross National Product (GNP).

CPI

The medical cost portion of the CPI rose 12.5% in 1981, compared with an overall increase in the CPI of 8.9%—medical costs increased almost 50% more than the overall CPI. This disparity is not unique to 1981; it has been occurring for the past several years. For example, since 1972, the overall CPI rose 133% and the medical CPI rose 149%— but the cost of a hospital room rose 221%! This higher rate will not change soon. Although the CPI currently is around 5-7%, the increase in the medical component of the CPI from July 1981 to July 1982 was 11.6%.

The unfortunate point to note is that the medical CPI understates the real increases in medical care. One reason is that it includes routine dental care, routine eye care and nonprescription medicines, all of which are rising moderately. The second reason is that 34% of the medical CPI is based on employee contribution rates for fixed benefit individual policies, which tend to increase very little. Thus, since these items are included in the index, but rise very slowly, the remaining items rise disproportionately faster.

A better barometer of medical care costs would be the increases in group insurance premiums, which increased by over 20% in 1982; for small firms, increases of 50-60% were not uncommon. Some insurers are even scrapping 12 month premiums and are going to six month renewals.

GNP

In 1960, the GNP was $507 billion; health care was 5.3% of that amount. In 1981, the GNP rose to $2,859 billion, but the portion attributable to health care was 9.6%. In other words, while our GNP grew to five times its 1960 rate, the health costs portion grew to over ten times its 1960 level.

Why are costs increasing so rapidly? As is true of most major problems, there are several causes. Some of the *major* ones are:

- Inflation. Just as inflation affects us personally, it impacts medical costs through higher labor costs, higher material costs and interest rates.
- Government's cutback on Medicare reimbursement formulas. Since hospitals can't get reimbursed fully for Medicare patients, they collect disproportionately from private sector patients.
- Aging of the population. There is no argument about the fact that older people need more medical care, and the fastest growing part of our population is the people over 65. The second fastest growing segment is age 55-65. This situation has tended to foster the increased utilization rates that have occurred.
- There are many more doctors today. In 1950, there were approximately 14 physicians/ 100,000 persons; in 1980 the number had increased 40%, to approximately 20 physicians/100,000 individuals. In 1990, the ratio is expected to be at 24 physicians/100,000. In that context, in 1965 there were 7,700 surgical operations for every 100,000 citizens; in 1980 it nearly doubled to 14,000. A recent Cornell study suggests that the rate of surgery is increasing $3\frac{1}{2}$ times faster than the population growth rate.
- Another significant factor is that, because of the liberal medical benefits programs most of us are fortunate to have, insurance firms insulate us from the real costs of medical care.
- The overriding reason is lack of competition in the health care industry. The provider determines the type of care, amount of care and extent of care. His or her preoccupation is to get us well and not to worry about cost. Since our preoccupation is also to get well, and since we have insurance, we don't worry about costs either; since the hospitals get paid for services provided—after the fact—they also don't have to worry about costs.

What will be the outcome of this scenario if it doesn't change? Failure to stem these costs is leading to:

- A disproportionate amount of employer funds going to pay medical bills instead of into our pockets as increased wages and salaries
- Some citizens are not able to afford medical care. This situation is particularly apparent in our current recession, when hospitals are seeing reductions in their patient days because laid-off employees can't afford to pay insurance premiums and so simply go without needed medical care.
- Government intervention. Congress is seriously considering several pieces of health legislation. By its already approved actions on limiting Medicare reimbursements, it is affecting our pocketbooks. As an example, with the passage of the new tax act, employers are now responsible for providing medical benefits for employees between the ages 65-69. Before the passage of the act, employers

needed only to pay that portion of medical expenses not covered by the government's Medicare program.

How Costs Can Be Contained

There are four major ways in which costs can be contained. The first is through the redesign of our benefit programs. I don't necessarily mean cutbacks such as increasing the employee's portion of the premium, or raising the coinsurance or deductible portions. There are cost-effective designs that can be added on, such as second opinion surgery, pre-admission testing, outpatient reimbursement equal to or greater than inpatient care, etc.

A second way is to review the administrative and funding costs of operating our plans. Consider, for example, minimum premium plans, administrative services only (ASO) plans, experience-rated premiums, etc. This area, too, is beyond the scope of this presentation, but it should be noted that even though savings in this area are attractive, they are limited to impacting the administrative portions of total health care expenses, or about 5-15% of the total bill.

The third and fourth options available in reducing costs are involvement of the employer/trustee and involvement of the employee/participant. The reason for the distinction here is that there are several actions that the employer/trustee can take unilaterally, without employee/participant involvement. Employee/participant involvement occurs in the implementation of wellness programs, which I will cover shortly. However I will talk about employer-instituted programs first.

Employer/Trustee Involvement

Education

Consistent with my premise that no one will take action unless he perceives it to be in his own self-interest, let's take a look at what we have to do to convince employers that they must get involved. There are four key reasons for employer involvement (I should mention at this point that I will use the term "employer" for shorthand only, since many of these considerations do apply to trustees of Taft-Hartley welfare plans as well):
- Cost of health benefits. Employers pay nearly half of all health costs in America today.
- Increased absenteeism. As the result of poor health, substance abuse, etc.
- Decreased employee productivity
- Premature loss and replacement of valued key employees. For example, Xerox recently indicated that it costs $600,000 to replace a high level executive who suffers a coronary disease.

In 1975 the cost of these four items was $50 billion. Considering inflation, today's cost would be about $100 billion or $1,000/year/employee. Clearly, the employer has a stake in cost containment.

But where do employers start? First of all, by educating themselves. They should evaluate and analyze data on incurred claims. It is critical to establish a baseline so that employers can measure the cost-effectiveness of any programs they implement.

I was talking to the executive director of a professional standards review organization (PSRO) recently and asked how effective his programs were in the community. He indicated that the average length of hospital stay had declined by a full day in the last couple of years since his plan was implemented communitywide. However, because employers previously did not have any good data with respect to incurred claims, he couldn't say for certain that the reduction of one day per hospital stay was because of the PSRO and, therefore, was reluctant to use it as a marketing tool.

The data we need to educate ourselves have always been available. For example, hospital invoices carry the diagnosis code and all pertinent financial data. But it isn't enough just to have proper data; you must know how to interpret them. Only when you can understand these data can you begin to manage them.

For example, these slides show the type of data analysis currently available from some insurers and independent consulting firms. (These slides are somewhat difficult to read because they are copies of computer reports. But it is not important that you see any figures. What is important is that you understand that this type of data is available from your own carrier.)

You can now diagnose claims by:
- Type of service provided (rather elementary) (Appendix A)
- Length of stay, by diagnosis, comparing actual stay to expected length of stay. A caution to note here is that you have to be aware of any reason that might prolong the stay, i.e., perhaps the patient put off one illness and decided to get that treated while being hospitalized for another (Appendix B).
- Hospital confinements analyzed by hospital and by diagnosis (Appendix C)
- Analysis of admissions by hospital and by day of week (Appendix D). Ask yourself why are there Friday or Saturday admissions.

- Analysis of discharge by day of week (Appendix E). This report is not quite as useful as the last one, but it may pose some additional questions.
- Length of stay by hospital (Appendix F)
- Second surgical opinions. Savings (net) by not having surgery performed (Appendix G)
- Second surgical opinions. Analysis of how savings were computed (Appendix H).

These services are the ones your insurance carrier or third-party administrator (TPA) should be providing so that you can evaluate your health expenses intelligently and determine where abuse is occurring.

Once you have these data, you must then know how to evaluate them—i.e., you must not only know how to ask for the data, but how to determine what the baseline is.

Action

Once the educational process is under way, the employer can begin to take positive action to contain these costs. Some effective action plans are:

Join a PSRO

As I mentioned before, because of the lack of baseline data, sometimes it is hard to say just how effective the PSROs are. However, all Medicare and Medicaid patients are subject to PSRO review, and thousands of companies have signed up as well. PSROs check admissions, not only for length of stay, but also for necessity of admission, as well as quality of care received while in the hospital. Typically, the patient's folder is noted, on admission, that admission is subject to PSRO review.

If the hospital stay exceeds the allowable limit, benefits usually are not cut off, although with some plans they are. However, for extended stays the physician must confer with a review board of his peers. The "sentinel" effect of this technique is obvious, even if not all PSRO admissions are checked; often only a statistical sampling is performed. The end result of PSRO participation has been a reduction in the average length of stay in hospitals.

To check whether there is a PSRO in your area, contact the American Association of PSROs, 11325 Seven Locks Road, Potomac, Maryland 20854.

Join Local Coalitions

Though this option will not have an immediate effect on an employer's health dollars, it may well have the greatest effect in the long run. Primary aims of business coalitions include involvement in hospital planning, particularly capital expenditures; coordination of health services between providers—often by assisting the local health systems/planning agency and encouraging hospital utilization review; reducing hospital beds; promoting alternate delivery forms, health maintenance organizations (HMOs); increasing outpatient or ambulatory care; coordinating a database, etc.

The contact for information is: *Directory of Health Action Programs,* published by U.S. Chamber of Commerce, 1615 H Street N.W., Washington, D.C. 20062.

Evaluate Coordination of Benefits (COB)

Though this procedure is included in most plans, its effectiveness varies considerably. Cost savings run from 3-20%, with most firms on the low end of that range. Though it is affected by employee makeup (the higher the female count, the higher the COB savings), high benefit levels and noncontributing plans, it is also affected by the insurer's or administrator's commitment to making it work, and such a program should be reviewed with them periodically.

Hospital Audit Reviews

There have been "horror" stories of some overcharges by hospitals. This is not to say that hospitals deliberately overcharge. Rather, with the myriad of charges that are involved in a typical hospital stay, there are bound to be errors involved. Currently, there are several services available that perform such reviews, either before or after the claim is paid. The usual savings are $3-$4 for every $1 spent on the audit.

These four items can all be implemented by *unilateral* action on the part of the employer or trust, with a minimum of time and effort, especially when considering the savings involved. Again, as a reminder, another significant area involving only employer initiative, but which will not be covered in this presentation, is the administration of health plan operations, particularly the funding arrangements.

Just as there are two areas of cost containment involving the employer only, there are two areas that require employee involvement. The first—that of negotiating changes in benefit plan design—is not within the scope of this paper. The other is that of employee involvement in wellness programs. (When I refer to "employees," please construe it to mean participants in a Taft-Hartley welfare trust as well.)

Employee/Participant Involvement

Education

Again, the first step in any such program is education, which is necessary to get the commitment to follow through with the program. In this instance, the educational process is addressed to both the employer and the employee.

The employee's attitude may well be: "Heart attacks will hit the other guy. I take reasonably good care of myself." The employer's attitude may well be: "Where do I start? I don't want to put in a series of programs that may not address the issues and have a minimal pay-out—and then only after several years."

Thus, the place to start the educational process is to look at the causes of death and determine which risk factors tended to be present in people who died from those causes. Heart disease accounts for nearly half of the deaths each year in the United States and cancer accounts for over 20%. Accidents are the third leading cause.

Which risk factors are present in these deaths? It is important to note that despite all the testing, it cannot be said with certainty that these factors are causal factors. What can be said is that people who have died from these diseases tended to have these factors in common. The common risk factors for the three leading causes of death in America are:

- Smoking
- High blood pressure
- Eating habits.

High risk individuals, or about 10% of a company's personnel, can account for 40-60% of annual medical care spending. Thus, by paying attention to programs that address these high risk areas, and by calling attention to those employees who exhibit those risks, cost-effective programs can be implemented that have a reasonable chance of succeeding. Here are some specific examples.

Smoking

> The combination of cigarette smoking and physical inactivity probably accounts for nearly one-half of all premature deaths in the U.S.
> (R. O. Keelor, Ph.D., 1976, President's Council on Physical Fitness)
> and
> One pack a day smokers have a 50% greater absenteeism rate and a 50% greater hospitalization rate than non-smokers. Two pack a day smokers have a 100% greater absenteeism rate than non-smokers.
> and
> Smoking contributes to 350,000 deaths annually (due to lung and other cancers, cardiovascular disease, emphysema and chronic bronchitis). (1979 Surgeon General's Report)

In addition to those statements regarding the health dangers to the smoker, consider that studies have put the cost of medical treatment for smoking at about $300/year for each employee who smokes, with an additional $300/year for absenteeism, loss of productivity and other related costs. Hopefully, this type of data will induce both employers and employees to at least consider causing lifestyle changes to reduce this terrible waste.

High Blood Pressure

The problem with this disease is that it has no symptoms and thus many times is left untreated. Ten percent of our citizens have high blood pressure and, of that number, 20% have it high enough to run a 3:1 chance of serious cardiovascular complications within three years.

Eating Habits

We live a good life, and unfortunately one of the byproducts of our eating habits is high blood fats (cholesterol). High blood fats produce high serum cholesterol counts, which lead to arteriosclerosis (narrowing of arteries because of fat deposits).

> Too much fat, too much sugar or salt can be and are linked to heart disease, cancer, obesity, stroke. In all, 6 of 10 leading causes of death in the U.S. have been linked to our diet. (1977 U.S. Senate Select Committee on Nutrition and Human Needs)

> High blood fats, high blood pressure, and cigarettes are strongly associated with about 80% of disability or fatal arteriosclerosis in our society. ("Prudent Eating after 40," *Geriatrics*, May 1974)

The relationship between our lifestyle and our chances of living long and productive lives is clear and unequivocal. The decisions we make today on how we want to live, work, eat and play affect our chances of living tomorrow. Other statistics could be cited, but it would be overkill. The conclusions are clear. Employers have at risk significant costs for health benefits, absenteeism, productivity and replacement of valued personnel. Employees risk their opportunities for continued living and for the quality of their very lives.

Action

What types of action can be taken to encourage good lifestyles? Have they been proven to be cost-effective? Unlike COB and hospital audit reviews, these data are not as "hard," primarily because of the lack of good recordkeeping and the relatively recent emphasis on wellness. However, there are many activities that can be implemented:

- Smoking cessation
- Diet and nutrition classes
- High blood pressure testing
- Weight control
- Stress management
- Exercise and fitness
- Employee assistance programs
- Cancer risk reduction exams
- CPR training
- Heimlich maneuver training
- Glaucoma screening
- Testing for sickle-cell anemia.

Some successful examples are:

- New York Telephone—alcoholic rehabilitation—85% success rate
- New York Telephone—nine programs—$2.7 million net savings annually
- Campbell Soup—smoking cessation programs—25% success rate
- Dow Chemical (Texas)—smoking cessation program—25% success rate
- General Motors—employee assistance plans have a 3:1 return.
- Cannon Mills—screening exams—discovered 1,600 hypertensives, 80 diabetics and 21 employees with cancer in 18 month period.
- Equitable Life—employee assistance plans have a 5.5:1 return.
- Kennecott Copper—employee assistance plans have a 6:1 return.
- Burroughs Wellcome—routine physical exams—discovered 8% of employees had potential health problems; reduced absenteeism from 6% to 3.5%.
- Generally acceptable rules of thumb for savings generated by screening programs—hypertension, $2-$6 saved for every $1 spent. Cancer, $3-$5 saved for every $1 spent.

Other Considerations

The last two points for consideration are in the form of "caveats."

With respect to planning, health care/wellness programs must be developed on a long range basis. Some of these activities do not show immediate results, and an employer must not be tempted to cut them during annual budget-cutting exercises. Indeed, with some creativity and hard work, many of these programs can be established with local governmental units, community hospitals or service organizations at little or no cost. In one instance, we staffed an entire 26 week series of seminars with qualified individuals from sources as I just mentioned, at no cost whatsoever. Those agencies are anxious to provide assistance because it is their job and because it preserves the justification to continue those jobs.

Communication of these programs must exhibit that same careful planning. Communications must be regular, relevant and upbeat. Notices tacked onto a crowded bulletin board will not generate the necessary participation, nor will a column or two in a hastily prepared company newsletter. There must be a set of objectives, a logical flow of information, a common theme and easy accessibility to the information and the events for programs to be successful.

There is no substitute for careful planning and communication to obtain commitment. There is nothing so worthy of commitment as the quality of our own lives.

Summary

There is significant economic justification for employers/trustees to consider implementing programs designed to monitor the expense of health care. There are equally strong data to encourage employees/participants to review their lifestyles with an eye to improving the quality of their own lives. As one physician noted, 90% of the illnesses/diseases we treat today are *not* caused by the outside environment, but rather by how we choose to live our lives.

Appendix A

MEDICAL UTILIZATION SUMMARY
EMPLOYEES AND DEPENDENTS COMBINED
2/1/82–4/30/82
(prepared 8/10/82)

All Locations Combined

| | Current Quarter |||| Year to Date ||||
Type of Service	Covered Expenses	Annualized Per 1000 Employees Number of Services	Number Admits	Average No. of Services	Covered Expenses	Annualized Per 1000 Employees Number of Services	Number Admits	Average No. of Services
Room + board	491,833.52	3,100/day	373	8.3 days/admit	491,833.52	3,100/day	373	8.3 days/admit
Anc fees								
Inpatient	630,003.48				630,003.48			
Outpatient	151,865.24				151,865.24			
Surgery	233,851.94	1,444/proc			233,851.94	1,444/proc		
Physicians								
In hospital	80,160.04	2,337/visit		8.1 visits/clmt	80,160.04	2,337/visit		8.1 visits/clmt
Office	103,046.80			visits/clmt	103,046.80			visits/clmt
Other	13,649.14			visits/clmt	13,649.14			visits/clmt
Diag XR+lab	149,178.07				149,178.07			
Drugs	61,568.90				61,568.90			
All other	132,119.34				132,119.34			
Total	2,047,276.47				2,047,276.47			

1982 Annual Conference   327

Appendix B

DAY OF ADMISSION/DAY OF SURGERY SUMMARY
(BY HOSPITAL)

This report identifies hospital admission patterns and compares the actual length of stay, by diagnosis, to an expected length of stay. It also identifies the time between admission and the day surgery is performed. The report is available by hospital provided there have been at least ten assigned claims involving surgery during the period.

Payment Date Range   1/15/82–3/31/82
Service Date Range   1/01/81–3/31/82

Control # 12345   Branch # 095   Date of Run   4/15/82
                                                        Page   1

Hospital Name and Address   Baptist Memorial Hospital
                                         100 Madison Avenue
                                         Anytown   TN 38146

Day of Admission		Mon	Tues	Wed	Thurs	Fri	Sat	Sun	Summary
Total claims		18	16	7	5	2	2	4	54
Duration/claim		6.8	6.3	6.5	7.8	9.0	8.7	9.6	7.1
Expected duration		6.4*	6.7	6.3	6.9	7.6*	7.5	7.4	7.0
Day of surgery	Mon	4	1		2	1		1	9
	Tues	6	4				1	2	13
	Wed	5	6	3			1		15
	Thurs	3	1	2	1				7
	Fri		4	1	2	1			8
	Sat			1					1
	Sun							1	1
	Over 1 week								

*Note: Diagnosis not available on one or more claims.

Appendix C

DIAGNOSIS BY HOSPITAL

This report identifies length of stay and charge patterns. The actual duration, by diagnosis, is compared to an expected length of stay. The report is available provided there have been at least ten assigned admissions for a specific diagnosis in any one hospital during the period.

Payment Date Range 1/15/82–3/31/82
Service Date Range 1/01/81–3/31/82

Control # 12345   Branch # 095   Date of Run 4/15/82
                                                                    Page   1

Diagnosis Hospital Expected Duration of Stay*	Number of Claims	Total Days	Avg. Dur. of Conf.	Avg. Pre-Op Stay	Total Charges	Total Elig. Charges	% Ancl. Chrg.	Male by Age 0 to 19	20 to 34	35 to 49	50 to 64	65 & up	Female by Age 0 to 19	20 to 34	35 to 49	50 to 64	65 & Up
Appendectomy																	
Baptist Memorial Hospital 4.7	10	30	3.0	1.0	12528	12350	54.6	30	10	10			40		10		
All other hospitals (2) 4.7	2	6	3.0	1.0	2505	2475	54.6	50					50				
Total (3) 4.7	12	36	3.0	1.0	15034	14826	54.6	33	8	8			42		8		
Normal Delivery																	
Baptist Memorial Hospital 3.3	18	87	4.8		26561	26126	53.3						11	78	11		
Methodist Hospital 3.8	11	40	3.6		11948	11748	49.7						9	82	9		
All other hospitals (2) 3.3	10	20	2.0		6908	6700	60.0						60	40			
Total (4) 3.4	39	147	3.8		45419	44575	51.8						23	69	8		

*This figure is determined by experience in a geographical region. For the "all other hospitals" and "total" categories, expected durations were combined to produce an average.

Appendix D

HOSPITAL ADMISSIONS/DISCHARGES BY DAY OF WEEK
EMPLOYEES AND DEPENDENTS COMBINED, NONMATERNITY
2/1/82–4/30/82
(prepared 8/10/82)

All Locations

				Admissions (%)				
Hospital ID	Mon	Tue	Wed	Thu	Fri	Sat	Sun	Total
0	60.0	20.0	.0	20.0	.0	.0	.0	5
390,286,215	.0	.0	.0	33.3	.0	33.3	33.3	3
390,794,174	21.4	14.3	.0	21.4	14.3	7.1	21.4	14
390,806,155	21.4	25.0	3.6	17.9	7.1	10.7	14.3	28
390,806,181	13.8	20.7	17.2	17.2	3.4	3.4	24.1	29
390,806,204	22.2	22.2	.0	11.1	27.8	5.6	11.1	18
390,806,237	10.4	19.4	17.9	14.9	7.5	17.9	11.9	67
390,806,296	16.7	16.7	16.7	33.3	.0	16.7	.0	6
390,806,302	.0	33.3	33.3	.0	33.3	.0	.0	3
390,806,315	15.4	15.4	23.1	23.1	7.7	7.7	7.7	13
390,806,347	100.0	.0	.0	.0	.0	.0	.0	1
390,806,393	.0	100.0	.0	.0	.0	.0	.0	1
390,806,429	.0	.0	.0	100.0	.0	.0	.0	1
390,806,438	24.0	8.0	8.0	20.0	8.0	4.0	28.0	25
390,807,063	.0	20.0	20.0	60.0	.0	.0	.0	5
390,808,443	.0	.0	.0	100.0	.0	.0	.0	1
390,808,480	.0	.0	.0	33.3	33.3	33.3	.0	3
390,808,503	100.0	.0	.0	.0	.0	.0	.0	1
390,808,509	100.0	.0	.0	.0	.0	.0	.0	1
390,810,534	.0	.0	.0	.0	100.0	.0	.0	2

Appendix E

HOSPITAL ADMISSIONS/DISCHARGES BY DAY OF WEEK
EMPLOYEES AND DEPENDENTS COMBINED, NONMATERNITY
2/1/82–4/30/82
(prepared 8/10/82)

All Locations

	Discharges (%)							
Hospital ID	Mon	Tue	Wed	Thu	Fri	Sat	Sun	Total
0	20.0	.0	20.0	20.0	40.0	.0	.0	5
390,286,215	.0	.0	50.0	.0	50.0	.0	.0	2
390,794,174	14.3	.0	21.4	.0	21.4	28.6	14.3	14
390,806,155	3.6	21.4	14.3	10.7	10.7	21.4	17.9	28
390,806,181	15.4	26.9	15.4	11.5	7.7	15.4	7.7	26
390,806,204	16.7	22.2	.0	11.1	11.1	16.7	22.2	18
390,806,237	12.3	12.3	12.3	12.3	20.0	20.0	10.8	65
390,806,296	.0	20.0	20.0	20.0	20.0	20.0	.0	5
390,806,302	66.7	.0	.0	.0	33.3	.0	.0	3
390,806,315	15.4	23.1	.0	.0	7.7	38.5	15.4	13
390,806,347	100.0	.0	.0	.0	.0	.0	.0	1
390,806,393	.0	.0	.0	.0	.0	100.0	.0	1
390,806,429	.0	.0	.0	.0	.0	100.0	.0	1
390,806,438	4.0	24.0	28.0	.0	8.0	24.0	12.0	25
390,807,063	.0	20.0	.0	.0	20.0	60.0	.0	5
390,808,443	.0	.0	.0	.0	.0	.0	100.0	1
390,808,480	66.7	.0	.0	.0	33.3	.0	.0	3
390,808,503	.0	.0	.0	.0	.0	.0	100.0	1
390,808,509	.0	.0	.0	.0	.0	100.0	.0	1
390,810,534	.0	.0	.0	.0	50.0	50.0	.0	2

Appendix F

**DISTRIBUTION OF HOSPITAL CONFINEMENTS BY DURATION
COMPLETED CONFINEMENTS
EMPLOYEES AND DEPENDENTS COMBINED
2/1/82–4/30/82
(prepared 8/10/82)**

All Locations

% of Confinements by Duration

Hospital ID	Number of Admissions	1-3	4-7	8-12	13-25	26-40	41+	Average Duration
390,816,857	85	29.4	48.2	10.6	4.7	5.9	1.2	7.3
390,806,237	70	27.1	28.6	22.9	14.3	4.3	2.9	9.4
391,022,464	50	44.0	44.0	8.0	4.0			4.7
390,987,025	43	30.2	65.1	2.3	2.3			4.7
396,080,562	39	38.5	35.9	20.5	5.1			5.9
390,806,155	31	35.5	22.6	25.8	12.9		3.2	8.0
390,907,740	31	54.8	38.7	3.2	3.2			4.0
390,806,181	29	48.3	34.5	6.9	10.3			4.9
390,826,292	28	42.9	32.1	17.9	7.1			5.3
391,077,992	28	46.4	28.6	21.4	3.6			5.1
390,806,438	27	44.4	25.9	18.5	11.1			6.1
390,853,528	27	37.0	40.7	7.4	11.1	3.7		6.7
390,910,727	23	39.1	30.4	21.7	4.3	4.3		6.7
396,005,720	22	50.0	31.8	4.5	9.1		4.5	6.8
390,806,204	21	52.4	33.3	4.8	9.5			4.2
390,812,532	21	57.1	23.8	9.5		9.5		5.8
390,794,174	17	29.4	58.8	11.8				4.2
390,829,030	17	41.2	29.4	17.6	5.9	5.9		6.8
390,806,315	15	46.7	40.0	6.7	6.7			5.0
580,833,515	14	35.7	57.1	7.1				4.3
390,836,072	11	18.2	27.3	36.4	18.2			9.0
390,861,620	11	54.5	36.4		9.1			4.2
390,872,192	11		9.1	27.3	36.4	18.2	9.1	19.5
396,105,970	11	36.4	27.3	36.4				5.4
390,806,296	6		66.7	16.7	16.7			7.0
0	5	40.0	40.0		20.0			6.4
390,807,063	5	60.0	40.0					3.0
391,150,165	5	40.0		40.0	20.0			10.2
581,034,851	5	40.0	60.0					3.4
410,944,601	4				100.0			14.5
581,091,080	4	25.0	75.0					4.0
390,286,215	3	33.3		33.3	33.3			11.3
390,806,302	3	66.7	33.3					3.7
390,808,480	3	33.3	33.3		33.3			9.0
390,879,446	3				100.0			19.0
390,975,167	3					100.0		28.0
396,006,492	3	100.0						3.0
390,810,534	2	50.0	50.0					4.0
390,819,992	2			100.0				10.0
390,830,664	2		50.0	50.0				6.5
390,868,982	2	100.0						1.0

Appendix G

SECOND SURGICAL OPINION PROGRAM
NET SAVINGS REPORT

The second surgical opinion program net savings report provides a summary of the cost effect of Prudential's second surgical opinion programs. For a voluntary program, "Total Gross Savings" represents the estimated savings of charges that could have been incurred in the absence of an unconfirming opinion (total savings illustrated in the savings report of nonperformed surgery). For an incentive program, the total gross savings also include the savings that result when a lesser benefit is paid as a result of the absence of a confirming second/third opinion. The total expenses shown reflect the dollars spent on consultations and testing. Additional reports providing a breakdown of total expenses and total savings are available.

#12345-06   Date Range 01/01/81–7/22/81

	$ Total Gross Savings	$ Total Expenses	$ Estimated Net Savings
Employee (M)	18,029	3,986	14,043
Employee (F)	56,774	5,138	51,636
Spouse (M)	2,906	680	2,226
Spouse (F)	22,976	4,173	18,803
Child	11,847	4,175	7,672
Other	0	0	0
Total	112,532	18,152	94,380

An "I" (incentive) or a "V" (voluntary) appears in the upper righthand corner of the report to identify the type of second surgical opinion program.

Appendix H

SAVINGS REPORT OF NONPERFORMED SURGERY, UNCONFIRMING SECOND/THIRD OPINIONS

The savings report of nonperformed surgery, unconfirming second/third opinions is an analysis of estimated savings of charges that could have been incurred in the absence of an unconfirming opinion. Estimated savings for surgery, assistant surgery and anesthesia are calculated using the current usual and prevailing amount for the nonperformed surgical procedure. Hospital savings are calculated by the system using the number of avoided hospital days (from a hospital duration guide) times the current average semiprivate room rate plus a percentage (based on the number of days) for ancillary charges. All savings estimates (except days) are based on the geographical area indicated by the claimant's zip code.

#12345-06   Date Range 01/01/81–7/22/81

	# of Proc.	$ Surgery	$ Asst. Surg.	$ Anesthesia	$ Hospital	Total Days	$ Total Savings
Employee (M)	4	5,310	1,065	970	6,952	19	14,297
Employee (F)	14	20,670	3,830	4,945	21,748	65	51,193
Spouse (M)	1	620	125	240	1,145	4	2,130
Spouse (F)	5	6,570	1,315	1,675	7,289	23	16,849
Child	5	2,305	190	1,025	4,670	12	8,190
Other	0	0	0	0	0	0	0
Total	29	35,475	6,525	8,855	41,805	123	92,659

An "I" (incentive) or a "V" (voluntary) appears in the upper righthand corner of the report to identify the type of second surgical opinion program.

A Major Innovation in Controlling Prescription Costs

BY FREDERICK KLEIN

PROVIDING A PRESCRIPTION benefit and encouraging employees to use appropriate medication not only relieves the employee of a financial burden, but can have a value far beyond its immediate visible cost to the sponsor—that is, to reduce absenteeism and/or hospitalization. The major types of prescription services being offered are:
- Major medical (using any local pharmacy)
- Sponsor-designated pharmacies
- The third-party "plastic card" companies
- The mail prescription service
- The mail prescription service in conjunction with a plastic card program.

The term "sponsor" refers to the company or welfare fund. When the term "patient" is used, it means the eligible employee or recipient of the medication. In discussing the various routes available, the important advantages and disadvantages will be highlighted. Each will be examined in turn from the standpoint of the sponsor, the patient and sometimes the pharmacy.

Mr. Klein is president of National Pharmacies, Inc., one of the country's largest mail prescription delivery systems. He is vice president and director of the National Association of Pharmaceutical Manufacturers and the National Association of Mail Service Pharmacies. Some of the techniques and procedures in the use of the mail as a prescription delivery system are a direct result of his involvement in this uniquely efficient means of providing prescription service. He is a graduate of Long Island University, College of Pharmacy.

Major Medical Program

Under this plan, patients are permitted to go to any pharmacy they choose (Figure 1). The prescription is filled and the patient requests a receipt form from the pharmacist or, where required, gives the pharmacist a claim form to complete. The patient then pays for the medication and submits the claim to the sponsor or the sponsor's administrator for reimbursement, less the deductible if there is one.

On the surface, this plan appears to be relatively simple but there are advantages and disadvantages to both the sponsor and patient that may not be so obvious. First, let's review the program from the patient's viewpoint. What are the disadvantages?
- The patients must pay for the medication—they have to lay out the money.
- A claim form must be filled out and filed.
- They have to wait a month or more for reimbursement.

However, the main advantage to patients is that they have their choice of pharmacy. They can take advantage of convenience and familiarity.

From the local pharmacy's point of view, this plan is the most desirable because it allows the pharmacy to maintain its individual pricing structure.

The effect on the sponsor is:
- The sponsor is paying full price for the drugs, less the copayment. There is very little incentive for the patient to question price. Moreover, the sponsor may be charged an inflated price and will probably never know it.
- The sponsor, administrator or whoever processes the claims for reimbursement is burdened with a great deal of clerical expense above and beyond the cost to produce and mail the reimbursement check, *all* of which the sponsor is obliged to pay. In addition, there may be a significant error factor because nonprofessionals review the claims. For example, an analysis of such a plan found that 6% of the claims reimbursed were for noncovered drugs, mostly over-the-counter preparations.

Figure 1

MAJOR MEDICAL

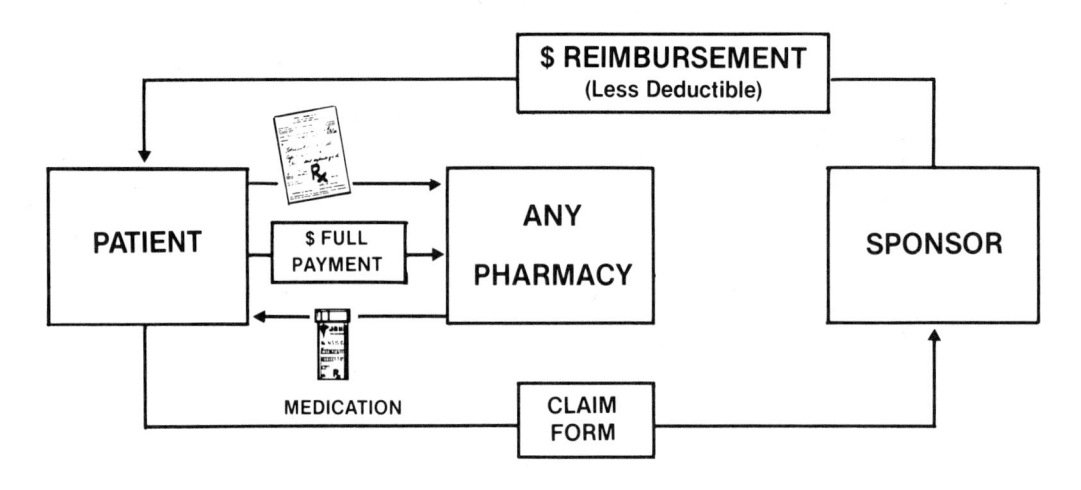

Figure 2

SPONSOR-DESIGNATED PHARMACIES

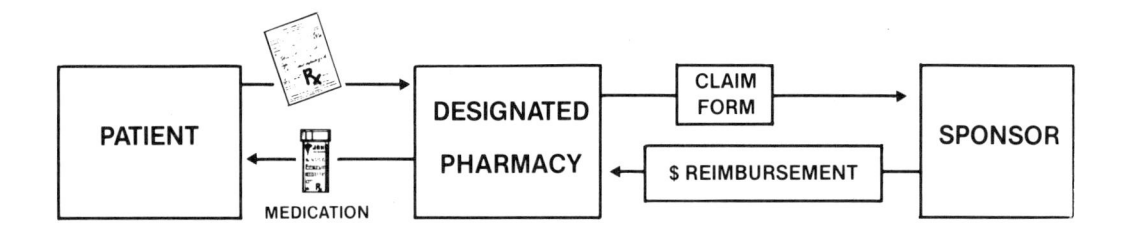

- With older workers, there is a rapid increase in the number of medications required. The plan's overall deductible, usually $100, is easily satisfied by the doctor's charges and the sponsor really pays on the first dollar for drugs. This situation could have negative effects on the sponsor's premiums by further inflating them.

Sponsor-Designated Pharmacy

This second type of program is not too popular. Here the patient must use certain, specified pharmacies. This plan has an important disadvantage in that many patients may have to go far out of their way to find one of these designated pharmacies. Even more important is the fact that the patient may be treated like a second class customer because the pharmacist is giving preferential treatment to the regular or full-paying customers. Under this plan, the pharmacist has agreed to accept a lower fee arrangement and smaller profit for plan customers (Figure 2).

There is a variation of the preceding plan that is only in the experimental phase at present. Here, some pharmacists provide prescriptions under a so-called capitation plan. Each pharmacy is paid a fixed monthly fee for each patient assigned. The patient then receives the medication from that particular pharmacy at no charge. There is no documentation to support the advantages and disadvantages claimed for this program. It is feared by some that profit might be placed before services, thus encouraging some pharmacies to provide less-than-satisfactory service. In Iowa, a recent experimental capitation program was terminated three months early because administrative costs

Figure 3

PLASTIC CARD COMPANY

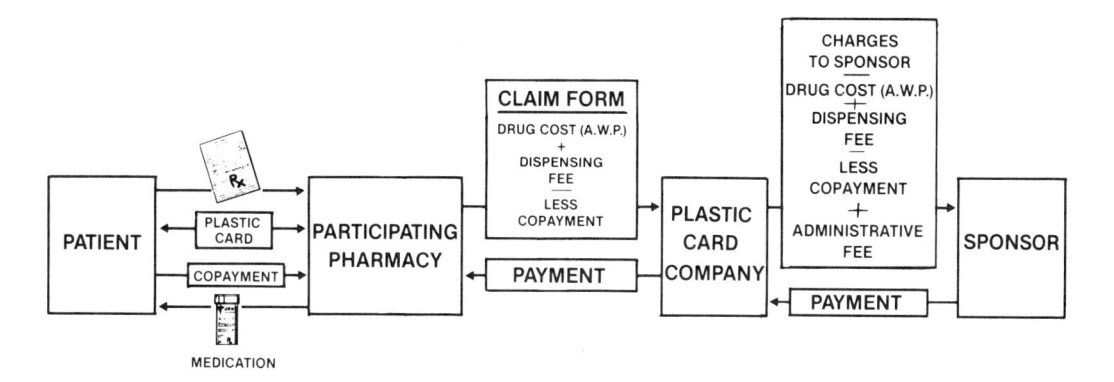

[Flow diagram: Patient → Participating Pharmacy (via Plastic Card and Copayment; receives Medication) → Plastic Card Company (via Claim Form: Drug Cost (A.W.P.) + Dispensing Fee − Copayment; Payment returned to pharmacy) → Sponsor (Charges to Sponsor: Drug Cost (A.W.P.) + Dispensing Fee − Copayment + Administrative Fee; Payment returned to Plastic Card Company)]

had grown too great. The Iowa Pharmacist Association suggested that others hold off until the data could be evaluated.

Third-Party Plastic Card Program

Under this plan, a network of pharmacies is offered to the sponsor's employees (Figure 3). The patient is served better than under the sponsor-designated pharmacy plan, because there are many more participating pharmacies, thus making it easier for the patient to find one that is convenient. The patient presents an embossed plastic card to the pharmacist, who uses it to imprint a special claim form. In most cases, the patient is required to pay the pharmacist a copayment of between 50¢ and $3. This copayment is deducted from the invoice submitted by the pharmacist.

The sponsor is usually charged the wholesale cost of the drug plus the negotiated dispensing fee. Some states prohibit the negotiated fee arrangement. Instead, they require what is called "usual and customary charges." Because these "usual and customary" charges are nearly always higher, many pharmacists, through their state associations, are lobbying to obtain legislation mandating "usual and customary" charges. As more and more states pass such legislation, the cost to the sponsor increases. In the passing on of these costs to the sponsor, the plastic card company also adds an administrative charge for each medication.

Some of the abuses previously discussed are less likely to occur under the plastic card system because of the card companies' field audits and the more sophisticated programming of their data processing centers.

Mail Prescription Service

This fourth method for delivery of prescription benefits is most unique and is fundamentally different from the other three systems (Figure 4). For most sponsors, it is inherently more efficient and significantly less costly. In this method, cost containment is highly visible and remarkably easy to achieve. Of course, it is essential that the mail prescription service has the sophisticated tools to handle large volume, is well-staffed, uses the latest automated equipment and has developed the software to maintain patient profile data. It should also be large enough to realize the maximum in purchasing power to reduce cost. Using these criteria, the increase in cost efficiency above the previously mentioned systems should be great enough so that *the sponsor can effect a savings even after offering the employees the prescriptions at no cost.*

The patient benefits in two important ways: in savings and in convenience. The savings can be in the form of a reduced copayment, or in elimination of it altogether. The convenience is in having the medication delivered to his front door. There is no waiting; in some cases, driving long distances to obtain the needed medication also is avoided.

What are the advantages to the sponsor? First, the fee structure is considerably lower because the pharmacist's time and skill are used more effectively. He is not required to perform the many nonprofessional tasks associated with retail drugstores. Second, the sponsor or the sponsor's administrator is not burdened with processing thousands of claims. Third, the abuses associated with retail-oriented programs as previously discussed

Figure 4

MAIL PRESCRIPTION SERVICE

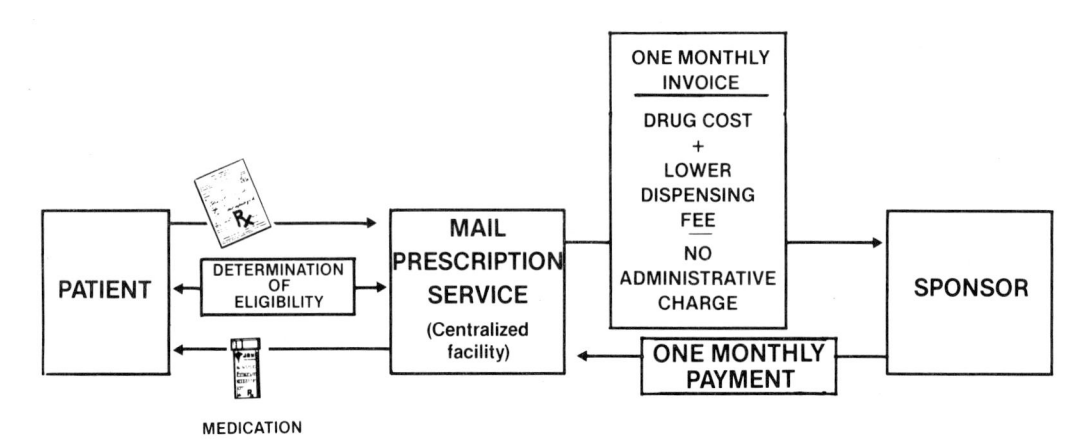

are eliminated. Another important feature in this type of program is the maintenance of a patient profile, which lists all prescriptions filled. This profile allows the pharmacist to compare current medication to previously dispensed drugs. Should a problem develop the doctor is contacted.

How is it that the mail prescription service can deliver so much more in service and still cost less? The answer lies in the fact that mail permits the use of a single centralized operation with all its attendant economies and controls. Since about 80% of the dollars spent on medications are for maintenance drugs, the type that can be obtained by mail easily, the impact on the total cost structure is immense.

Plan Mechanics

What are the mechanics of the mail prescription service? To begin with, the service should supply the sponsor with the following items:
- A descriptive brochure explaining the program to the employee
- Preaddressed reply envelopes. The employee is required to fill in a few simple items on the flap of the envelope such as name, address, Social Security number and whether the medication is for himself, spouse, dependents, etc.
- A patient profile questionnaire card. This card should be very simple, asking if the employee, spouse and covered dependents have any drug allergies or chronic medical conditions.

The sponsor distributes the provided material. All the employee does is complete the information on the flap of the envelope, and enclose a doctor's prescription, with a copayment if required.

When the prescription is received by the mail prescription service company, it is immediately checked for eligibility. There are several ways information on eligibility may be made available. One way is on computer tape, in which case the service company must have a data processing capability. Eligibility can also be determined by the use of lists or ID cards. If ID cards are used, then the employee includes the card with the prescription and it is returned with the medication.

As soon as the patient is determined to be eligible, the prescription can be processed. In processing, some steps are:
- Determine if the drug is covered under the plan.
- Review the patient profile.
  1. To verify that there is no conflict between previous medication dispensed and the current prescription and
  2. To check for potential abuses such as reordering too frequently, duplication of medication from different doctors, excessive dosage, etc.

After determining that these basic requirements have been met, the prescription will be filled and the medication mailed. In each step of the filling process, there must be careful controls to ensure that the prescribed medication is correct. With the medication there is also included perti-

Figure 5

**COMBINATION PLASTIC CARD COMPANY
AND MAIL PRESCRIPTION SERVICE**

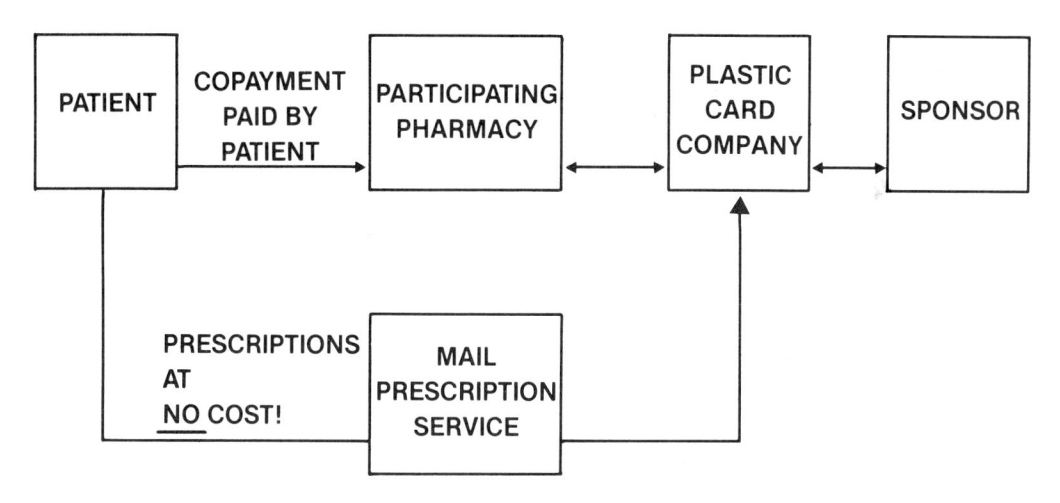

nent information such as authorization for refills, etc., and a new preaddressed reply envelope.

The turnaround time is about seven to ten days, which presents no obstacle when medications are taken over periods of months and years. The patient is instructed to reorder in time to avoid running out.

The mail service company prepares a single monthly computerized billing; only one check is required. Auditing is very easy. The sponsor or sponsor's administrator is relieved of an enormous clerical burden and, of course, cost.

Emergencies

"What about emergency medication?" The answer is simple: The patient obtains such medications locally. You have the choice of offering one of the following arrangements:
- Allow the patient to purchase medication under the existing major medical or plastic card plan.
- If you have no such plan, you can provide a comprehensive mail-order program with a provision for the supply of emergency medication.

The Combination Program

The fifth type of program combines the mail prescription service with the third-party plastic card program (Figure 5). In a typical plastic card program, the three main cost elements are:
- A predetermined price for the drug itself (usually the average wholesale price, referred to as AWP)
- A predetermined professional fee for each prescription medication
- A predetermined administrative fee.

For example, in such a card program the cost of one month's supply of a drug might be its AWP of $10 plus the average professional fee of $2.75 and the average administrative fee of 75¢, for a total cost of $13.50 for a 30 day supply of medication (Figure 6). Of course, these figures can vary slightly.

The mail prescription service, however, is able to increase the limit for each prescription from a 30 day to a 90 day supply–a much more realistic quantity for maintenance medication. This increase results in a cost for the AWP of $30 for a 90 day supply of drugs plus *one* professional fee of $2 including postage and an administrative fee of 75¢, for a total of $32.75, a savings of $7.75 per medication to the sponsor. As mentioned previously, these figures can vary slightly. Thus, the sponsor has avoided two professional fees and two administrative fees, making it possible for him to eliminate the copayment paid by the employee and still save on each maintenance medication. There is no question that this plan is an opportunity to improve your current program, if you have one, and reduce costs at the same time.

To ease this combination of plans, the mail prescription service would have to provide the plastic card company with a computerized billing

Figure 6

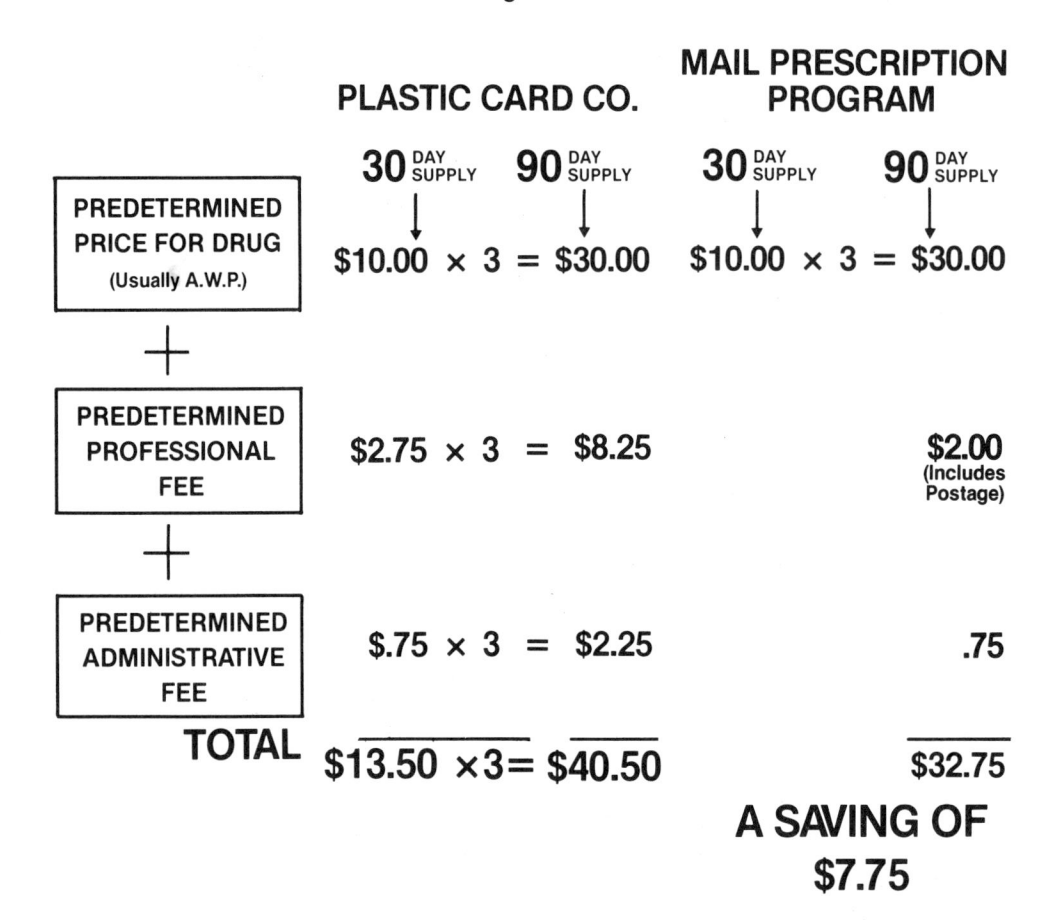

	PLASTIC CARD CO.		**MAIL PRESCRIPTION PROGRAM**	
	30 DAY SUPPLY	90 DAY SUPPLY	30 DAY SUPPLY	90 DAY SUPPLY
PREDETERMINED PRICE FOR DRUG (Usually A.W.P.)	$10.00 × 3	= $30.00	$10.00 × 3	= $30.00
+				
PREDETERMINED PROFESSIONAL FEE	$2.75 × 3	= $8.25		$2.00 (Includes Postage)
+				
PREDETERMINED ADMINISTRATIVE FEE	$.75 × 3	= $2.25		.75
TOTAL	$13.50 ×3	= $40.50		$32.75

A SAVING OF $7.75

in the universal format. The plastic card company, in turn, would then be able to provide the sponsor with a fully consolidated report.

There is still another advantage to this combination of plastic card company and mail prescription service. Customarily, the sponsor is charged for the medication when he neglects to retrieve the plastic card from a terminated employee who uses the card in a participating pharmacy. However, under the mail prescription service, eligibility is verified *prior* to dispensing; thus, the terminated employee's prescription is not filled in the first place.

This combination of plastic card company and mail prescription service reduces the sponsor's cost, while offering the employee three very important advantages:

1. The copayment is reduced or eliminated, saving the employee money.
2. It reduces the number of visits to the pharmacy and eliminates any hassles and waiting.
3. Where travel was required previously, there is also a savings on transportation.

Supplementing the plastic card company's service with a mail prescription service is not merely an idea whose time has come–it's a reality. Right now, it is saving sponsors and covered patients substantial sums.

CHAPTER 7

U.S./Canadian Relations

John Crispo, Ph.D.

Professor
Faculty of Management Studies
Department of Political Economy
University of Toronto
Toronto, Ontario, Canada

William A. Rivers

President
Martin E. Segal Company, Ltd.
Toronto, Ontario, Canada

Canadian-American Relations: A Canadian Perspective, or a Latent Continentalist Comes Out of the Closet

BY JOHN CRISPO, Ph.D

LET ME START OUT by sharing some of my biases on the subject of Canadian-American relations. It is important that I begin this way since this subject is so controversial and sensitive from a Canadian point of view.

First of all, I want to make it clear that I am a Canadian through and through without, at the same time, feeling any need to be anti-American, as are so many Canadian nationalists. Given that it is our fate to share this continent with a monster, I like to remind my fellow Canadians that we are lucky to be sharing it with you. When one looks at the alternatives, you don't look too bad at all. That, by the way, is meant to be a compliment, even if you don't recognize it as such.

I also want to state that I am optimistic about our respective long term futures. You are going to do well because you are viewed as just about the last safe haven for capital and because your labor costs are becoming much more competitive. We should do well if only because of our bountiful natural resources.

Finally, I wish to declare my belief that we will both be better off if we work together. Unfortunately, from our point of view, you will only be marginally better off since you are the elephant in our mutual relationship and don't really need us very much. We, being the flea, depend more on you and, therefore, have much more to gain or lose from the state of the relationship.

Having stated some of my biases, let me now turn to some facets of our common heritage and history. After that, I will offer a partial thesis about the irritants and issues that inevitably arise between us. I will then examine some of Canada's alternatives and options and some of its concerns and fears in relation to the United States. This discussion will set the stage for a few words on the challenge that lies ahead.

Our Common Heritage and History

There are many intriguing things to be said about our common heritage and history. Some of them are almost mythical in character. Take that

Dr. Crispo is a professor in the Faculty of Management Studies and in the Department of Political Economy at the University of Toronto. In 1981, Dr. Crispo took a leave of absence from this position to assume the responsibility of Chevron Visiting Professor of Management at Simon Fraser University. He is also an associate of the Centre for Industrial Relations and the Centre for Policy Analysis. Since graduating in 1960 from Massachusetts Institute of Technology with a Ph.D. in industrial economics, he has combined research and teaching with other professional activities. He was founding director of the Centre for Industrial Relations and first dean of the Faculty of Management Studies at the University of Toronto. His publications include several books, the latest of which is entitled A Mandate for Canada. *Dr. Crispo has been a member of the Prime Minister's Task Force on Labour Relations; director of research, Royal Commission on Labour-Management Relations in the Construction Industry; director of research, Select Committee on Manpower Training; research consultant for the Economic Council of Canada; chairman, Ontario Union-Management Council; and research consultant for the Prices and Incomes Commission. He has given his energies to conciliation and mediation in numerous instances, and is often interviewed by the media.*

longest undefended border about which we both like to boast. The fact of the matter is that we could not defend it, even if we wanted to. Moreover, given the state of your armed services—if I may say something somewhat tongue in cheek—we're not even sure you could invade us if you wanted to.

We do have a common language, except in Quebec and now in various parts of your South. We just wish that if you are going to go bilingual you would adopt French rather than Spanish as your second language. If you were just to beam one TV network across our border in French, we English Canadians would probably learn French and thereby solve our language problems.

We are both federal countries, but with some marked differences. Whereas your Constitution calls for a highly decentralized federation, you have gone the other way in practice. In contrast, we have twisted our Constitution in just the opposite manner.

Of special importance is the fact that we are our own best customers. Here again, however, there is a big difference that makes Canada much more vulnerable to any disruption in our trading ties. We send roughly 70% of our exports to you, whereas we only take back from you about 10% of your exports.

Most disturbing is the fact that we are both showing serious signs of becoming more protectionist in our trade relations. You are doing so in the name of fair trade, reciprocity or reindustrialization. We are doing so under the guise of some new national policy as yet unnamed.

A Thesis About Our Mutual Irritants

Even though we have much in common we are bound to have our differences. In part, those differences come down to variations in the personalities of our leaders. Right now, for example, you are led by a refugee from acting while we are led—misled might be a better term—by a refugee from academia. Any two such refugees are almost certain to clash on something or other.

Then there is the differing political complexion of our two countries. At the one extreme, you have your potentially authoritarian moral majority right. At the other extreme—if you choose to term it that—we have our supposedly socialistic New Democratic Party.

As well, there are differences in our political systems that complicate relations between us from time to time. Under your system of checks and balances, your Administration cannot deal with certainty with us because it cannot be sure of Senate ratification of its position. Under our parliamentary system we can deal with certainty, even though there may be great internal opposition from the provinces and other quarters.

A particularly telling factor is the state of our economies. When we are both booming, it is much easier to resolve our differences. When prosperity gives way to recession and worse, however, our differences become more intractable. Right now, therefore, it is not surprising that we have many issues to resolve.

Nor should anyone be surprised that Canada tends to have a longer list of grievances than the United States. That is the prerogative of the flea, though we can only make you itch or twitch at worst. Your list of grievances is shorter but no less significant. In fact, it is more significant if only because you as the elephant can give us more than an itch or twitch if you become aggravated enough.

My purpose is not to review our mutual grievances but rather to offer you a partial thesis about them. In general, it is my conviction that whenever one of our countries acts contrary to the interests of the other, it ends up operating contrary to its own interests as well. Let me illustrate this conviction, partial thesis or whatever it is by drawing on some current irritants from both sides of the grievance ledger.

I will begin with two of your grievances, one concerning FIRA, our Foreign Investment Review Agency, and the other concerning NEP, our National Energy Program. Regardless of how much damage these policies may be doing to you, my point is that they are also hurting us. Under FIRA, for example, we have been discriminating blatantly against foreign firms. As a result, we have been scaring away a lot of capital, one of the key ingredients for economic growth.

We have done even more harm to ourselves with NEP. In the name of Canadianization we did immense harm to the many Western-based small and medium sized companies that were in practice gradually Canadianizing the oil and gas industry. In the name of self-sufficiency we killed the two big tar sands projects, thereby setting back that goal.

Along the way we created Petrocan to serve as a window on the industry. We needed such a window because it is a very peculiar industry, dominated as it has been by a few multinational firms and OPEC. However, we've provided Petrocan with so many advantages that it no longer provides a legitimate benchmark against which to assess the performance of other firms in the industry.

I now turn to two of our concerns: acid rain and the auto pact. Too many Americans seem as unaware of the killing effect that acid rain is having on lakes in Michigan and New England as they are of what it is doing to Canadian lake country. As for the auto pact, you can obviously survive more readily without it than we can. On balance, however, it has worked to your advantage so far, thus suggesting that it would be ill-advised for you to risk it as part of your overall protectionist drive.

Canada's Alternatives

With so many issues up in the air both between our two countries and among Western countries in general, Canada has to think carefully about its options. We could go the "fortress-Canada" route, but that solution is not even being advocated by the most narrow minded of the Canadian nationalists. Our population of under 25 million is simply not large enough to support the scale of industry required of an advanced technological society.

Another possibility is our Prime Minister's so-called third option. This solution would have us build up our trade with Europe and the Pacific Rim in order to reduce our trading dependence on the U.S. The problem with this approach is twofold; the Atlantic and the Pacific both represent major obstacles to trade. For this and other reasons, the proportion of Canadian trade with the U.S. has risen from 60% to 70% since Trudeau promulgated his vaunted third option.

Still another possibility lies with the multilateral approach. As a major trading nation, Canada has consistently backed GATT (the General Agreement on Trade and Tariff) and other measures designed to free up international trade. Canada should continue this backing but recognize the risks involved. If world protectionism beats a world recovery, Canada is going to find itself terribly exposed on its own.

As for the U.S. option, whether we like it or not, you represent our natural trading partner. Throughout our history we have tried to ignore this economic fact of life by forcing trade within Canada on an east-west basis, when it has always wanted to flow between our countries on a north-south basis.

Despite valiant efforts to the contrary, we have been backing into closer and closer economic ties with you. My position is that we should stop backing into this kind of relationship and face up to it. It's time that Canada thought about a new economic deal with the U.S.

Now is not the time to talk to you about it, however, since you are being savaged by a combination of imports and a recession. Actually, at this time, we are in no position to talk to you anyway since we haven't begun to think through our own priorities.

If we choose to go for a new deal with you, maybe we should only strive for a series of pacts similar to the auto pact. Certainly, anything beyond this scope—such as a free trade area or a common market—would raise difficult issues concerning the viability of several of our major industries. We would probably require some sort of production-sharing arrangements no matter how much further we went with you.

Assuming you were willing to offer such guarantees (a big assumption), we might eventually be willing to talk about some form of sovereignty association along the lines of that called for by the Premier of Quebec in relation to the rest of Canada. Thus, we would have our own political sovereignty within an economic association with you.

Canadian Concerns and Fears

The question is, why Canada has been so reluctant to pursue closer economic ties with the U.S. The answer lies in two parts: the vested interests that are opposed to any such move and the legitimate concerns and fears that they are able to exploit.

As for the vested interests, they are pervasive and strong. They range from academics and advertisers to manufacturers and publishers, all of whom have found it profitable to seek protectionist measures of one kind or another by wrapping themselves in the Canadian flag. These private vested interests are aided and abetted in their self-serving causes by public vested interests, in the form of government bureaucrats and politicians. The latter gain immense manipulative scope with the discretionary powers they grant themselves under the various protectionist measures they introduce.

Unfortunately, it is all too easy for these private and public vested interests to exploit the legitimate concerns and fears that many Canadians have about any kind of closer ties with the U.S. Some fear any kind of economic interdependence with the U.S. in and of itself because they see the sun setting on the American empire. For reasons cited earlier, I totally disagree with this interpretation of your economic prospects.

Others fear the loss of our cultural sovereignty, if not in Quebec then at least in the rest of the country. I again take exception to this view since I do not perceive a much greater threat to our cultural independence because of closer economic ties to the U.S. If anything, within the U.S. itself, there are encouraging signs of the reemergence of some cultural diversity.

Still others fear the loss of our political sovereignty, a concern which cannot be dismissed lightly. The point is that closer economic ties with the U.S. could further reduce our political sovereignty below that which we have already lost in such spheres as defense and foreign policy. If I thought any significant further diminution of our political sovereignty was inevitable because of a closer economic association, I would not advocate that association as strongly as I do.

Ultimately, of course, there is underlying fear for our very existence as a separate country or national entity. In this regard, I think that Canadians have less to fear from any lingering manifest destiny in the U.S. than from our own apathy and indifference. I don't perceive any American interest in taking over Canada. It would be terrible for your international image. Moreover, those persons most prone to think in such terms in your country are your political right-wingers and they would hardly want to take in what they perceive to be a lot of left-wingers.

The real threat to Canada's existence as an independent entity comes from within, because we don't have enough confidence and pride in our country. Ironically, it could be the narrow-minded nationalists who do us in. They could have this perverse effect by standing in the way of closer economic ties with the U.S. and thereby jeopardizing our prospects for maintaining our present standard of living in relation to yours.

If any single consideration could tempt Canadians to give up their citizenship, it would probably be a decline in our standard of living in comparison with yours. It is in this sense that the nationalists' policies of protectionism could prove so self-defeating in the long run.

The Challenge

The Canadian challenge is to get our act together. To do so, we must get over our unwarranted inferiority complex and recognize the economic facts of life. Maybe then we can stop backing into closer relations with America, decide what kind of a deal we'd really like, determine what we're prepared to trade off for it and prepare to sit down with you when the circumstances become appropriate.

Our mutual challenge is to work out our common destiny. Whether we like it or not we are inextricably and irretrievably bound together. Our mutual independence is inescapable and even desirable. For all these reasons and more it will be a tragedy if we don't find a satisfactory accommodation.

With this objective in mind I will conclude with these thoughts. I hope you share my view that our two countries have much more in common than anything that could ever divide us. I trust you share my concern about the present mismanagement of what has been a deteriorating relationship between us.

I further trust that you recognize that there are many Canadians like me who wish to improve our relations by pursuing that which is to our mutual advantage. Of like-minded Americans, I would ask that you assist in this process if only by demonstrating as much sensitivity as possible to the legitimate nationalistic aspirations of me and my fellow Canadians.

Author's note: This paper was prepared using the rough notes for my informal address.

U.S./Canadian Reciprocity

BY WILLIAM A. RIVERS

Mr. Rivers is president of Martin E. Segal Company, Ltd., responsible for the company's Canadian operations. He has worked in the multiemployer trust fund field for the past 14 years, the last eight as a consultant to trust funds throughout Canada. He received a B.A. from Albion College in 1966. Mr. Rivers has been a speaker at previous International Foundation educational programs and is a member of its Consultants Committee.

YOU AND I have a real challenge. I don't know you; you don't know me. Yet, we have to communicate on the subject of U.S./Canadian reciprocity, which on any day lacks "pizzazz." In addition, my detailed remarks on tax implications are highly technical in nature. I will try my best to develop the subject gradually, clearly and thoroughly.

We are going to look at reciprocal agreements from a new and different perspective. I believe I am correct when I say that this is the first time that the International Foundation has presented a reciprocal agreement forum from the point of view of its international scope. This presentation is timely, as there are several such agreements in existence, at least within the construction industry. Also, many of the "megaprojects," such as oil refineries, require members from each country. Operating Engineers, Ironworkers, Bricklayers and the Pipe Trades are but a few trades that have U.S./Canadian reciprocity.

Perhaps you are not familiar with Canada's benefit systems. Health and welfare trust funds provide benefits identical to a U.S. fund, except that the basic physicians, surgical and medical benefits are provided through the Federal/Provincial Medicare system—which for all intents and purposes is a national program. For private pension plans in Canada, it may surprise you to know that Canada does not have the advantages of one uniform pension act like ERISA. Rather, we must comply in some areas with the Department of National Revenue, which is federal. In other areas, such as vesting and funding, we must register provincially. In the last few years, vesting minimums have become dissimilar in the various provinces, creating burdensome problems in all aspects of plan operations.

Obviously, as trustees you will have to study Canada's provincial pension legislation carefully whenever reciprocal agreements are being designed. I have chosen not to pursue all of the various and sundry peculiarities of this legislation. However, I wanted each of you to be cognizant of our system differences, especially at this time when most provinces are reviewing their legislation and will likely be drastically liberalizing their vesting provisions.

Definitions

My experience suggests that almost any discussion or review of reciprocity will sooner or later lead to a reference to the terms "portability" and "vesting." There is evidence of this tendency in the pre- and post-ERISA dialogue in the United States, where considerable reference to pension portability, the impact of earlier vesting and the effectiveness of reciprocal agreements can be found.

In Canada, the provincial government of Ontario has conducted an exhaustive study on the status of pensions in Ontario, tabled in the legislature earlier this year. To give you a brief insight into their recommendations on the overall issues of portability, reciprocity and vesting, I will quote excerpts from the *Final Report 1982 of the Select Committee on Pensions:* First, "the Act should be amended to require for multi-employer plans full and immediate vesting and that members' benefits be fully and immediately locked in." Second, "the Select Committee endorses the principle of pensions being *deferred wages . . .*" This very succinct statement has far-reaching implications. Third, "the Select Committee endorses the principle of 'the-money-follows-the-worker' and reciprocal transfer agreements are the means by which portability among members of multi-employer plans may be achieved. . . ."

Although these recommendations are not yet law, it is clearly a signal of the tendencies of one government in Canada to make pensions more portable. The growing importance of the principles underlying portability in its various forms, I believe, is well-documented by these examples of government leanings in our two countries.

The terms "reciprocity," "portability" and "vesting" all have different meanings, but invariably all three appear whenever the rights of an employee in a pension plan are discussed. All three terms are common to multiemployer Taft-Hartley funds, with reciprocity being quite commonplace.

Portability

I would suggest that this term has a broader, more global meaning in that it is defined as the "capability of being carried." The Canadian Life Insurance Association introduced in 1981 what to them was a revolutionary idea of "pension portability." It meant that the employees of participating companies were able to carry their accumulated pension benefits or their pensionable service from job to job. To most of us in this industry, the idea is far from revolutionary, especially in the 1980s. Other illustrations of portability are government retirement systems, such as Social Security in the United States, or Canada Pension Plan in Canada. They are among the largest systems wherein a person's retirement benefits are completely portable.

Reciprocity

Reciprocity is a form of portability. It means a "mutual exchange of privileges or rights." Reciprocal agreements are a means of preserving ultimate pension rights through the mutual cooperation of two or more pension plans. They were originally introduced in our industry funds in the 1950s.

Vesting

The term "vesting" is most commonly used in the unilateral context of one plan to mean "the conveying of an inalienable right of a benefit to an employee."

Types of Reciprocity

Our objective is to focus on portability through reciprocal agreements. To achieve further insight into portability through reciprocity requires analysis of the different formats or means of designing reciprocal agreements.

For most reciprocity discussions, and certainly this one, there are two basic types of reciprocal agreements—one is called "money-follows-the-worker" and the other is called "pro-rata." While "money-follows-the-worker" is used both in health and welfare and in pension plans, "pro-rata" is used almost exclusively in pension plans. It is recognized that there are other types of agreements, such as "point-of-claim-origin." However, money-follows-the-worker and pro-rata cover the great majority of reciprocity arrangements.

Space does not permit us to pursue the intricacies of these two types of agreements, but I believe that we have to review the distinguishing features of each briefly. This review will assure that we are all familiar with the underlying concepts, and will enable us to better understand the problems and tax implications to be presented later.

Money-Follows-the-Worker

This type of reciprocity involves the transfer of contributions from one fund to another. If a member works outside his own local union in the jurisdiction of another local union, both of whom participate in a "money-follows-the-worker" reciprocal agreement, then the contributions made on the member's behalf to the other local union's fund are transferred to his own local union fund. In this way, the member is able to maintain his eligibility and earn additional benefit credits in his own fund. If both the sending and receiving funds are in the same country, there are no tax implications. However, as we will find, if one fund is in the United States and one in Canada, there are implications worth considering.

Pro-Rata

The other basic type of reciprocity is "pro-rata." Under this arrangement, there are no actual contribution transfers. The member who, during his career, works in the jurisdiction of different funds that participate in the "pro-rata" agreement, earns credits that are maintained and then aggregated on retirement to recognize his employment in the industry and determine his total pension. In most instances, the member receives a pension check from each fund.

Legislative Implications

In analyzing the problems of U.S./Canadian reciprocity, one must study the applicable legislation, especially tax matters. It should come as no surprise when I tell you that the tax implications of reciprocation across the 49th parallel are full of uncertainties and complexities. However, I am sure that readers who have spent the past eight years maneuvering through the minefields of ERISA are well-prepared for uncertainties, complexities and even more.

Examination of the various tax considerations of U.S.-Canadian reciprocal agreements requires an orderly distinction of the many different possibilities that could arise.

Health and Welfare or Insurance Funds

As "money-follows-the-worker" agreements are most common to these types of funds, I have limited my remarks to this form of reciprocity. We will assess the tax consequences of such an agreement for a person from the United States working in Canada and for the Canadian employed in the United States.

The U.S. member works in Canada under a collective bargaining agreement requiring contributions to a Canadian-based health and welfare trust fund. The Canadian fund must, under the terms of the reciprocal agreement, transfer the contributions to the fund in the area of his home local in the United States. The same principle would apply if the member were from Canada working in the United States.

After considerable research and discussions with the requisite authorities, I came to a very simplistic conclusion. It would appear that there is no tax to be withheld by the Canadian fund if it is the exporting fund, or by the U.S. fund if it must transfer the contributions to Canada. The contributions are being transferred between trust funds, thereby creating no taxable circumstances for the trust funds or the individual involved. Whether by design or oversight, existing laws are silent on this type of transaction.

I'll let you be the judge of whether my findings on the tax implications for pension reciprocity were fortunate or unfortunate. My initial thoughts, after my simplistic conclusion concerning health and welfare funds, were that this subject and my speech would quickly become a "scratch" on the IF Conference charts. However, to my good fortune, pension and tax legislation in both countries do have direct application to U.S./Canadian reciprocal agreements.

Pension Funds

Money-Follows-the-Worker

The "money-follows-the-worker" reciprocal agreement for a pension fund operates under the identical principles of such an agreement for a health and welfare fund.

In the situation of a person from the United States working in Canada, a Canadian trust fund is obliged to transfer pension contributions to a pension fund in the United States. As expected, it is the Canadian tax law that is applicable. The Canadian law relating to the transfer of contributions from one pension plan to another pension plan is written to apply to a domestic transfer—that is, all within Canada. The existing law apparently did not contemplate the transfer of contributions between pension plans on an international basis. Accordingly, interpretations have been offered by the nonresident tax department at Revenue Canada. I want to clearly underscore that the following items are opinions based on discussion and are not formal rulings.

Canada—Section 212 of the Income Tax Act

Under Section 212 of the Income Tax Act in Canada, every nonresident person receiving "amounts" for services rendered in Canada must pay a special tax in accordance with Part XIII, Section 212 of the act. A payment of a superannuation or pension benefit is deemed to be one such "amount." I might add at this juncture that this part of the act does not in any way refer to health and welfare or insurance plans, which is the reason why there is no withholding on such plans.

Information Circular 76-12R

What is the formula for this special tax? On June 18, 1979 the Department of National Revenue issued Information Circular 76-12R, which sets forth the rate of tax on "amounts" paid or credited to persons in treaty. To digress briefly, there is a point that deserves some explanation before we identify the exact amount of the tax. First, in my reference to the Information Circular 76-12R, I stated, "the rate of tax on 'amounts' paid or credited." The Department deems the contributions transferred from the Canadian pension plan are to the individual, even though they are in fact made to the U.S. pension plan. The Department's position is that they do not know if and when the individual will ever receive the contributions or the *"amount"* credited as a result of the contributions. Therefore, to assure that it is taxed at some point, they deem withholding the tax before the credited amount leaves Canada.

The amount of withholding tax on a United States resident by the Canadian pension fund is 15%. For those who may be interested in the reference, this information is contained in Appendix A to Information Circular 76-12R.

Canadian authorities admitted the potential double taxation that could occur in these instances. They advised that the U.S. resident can, within 60 days after the calendar year in which the contributions were transferred, file a Canadian individual tax return, Form T1. The individual could report the amount of contributions transferred, claim the standard deductions and possibly receive a refund of the tax withheld. You could assume, in most instances, that the full amount of tax would be refundable as the basic personal exemption in Canada is approximately $3,200.

Currency Values

To do our subject justice, I do not believe that we can overlook one other very significant and real issue—currency values. Simply put, one U.S. dollar is worth about $1.20 in Canadian currency. Conversely, a Canadian dollar is worth only 80¢ in U.S. value. Therefore, consider the U.S. resident who works 500 hours in Canada, for which $1 per hour is contributed to the Canadian pension plan. The $500 is first slapped with a 15% withholding tax and the balance is converted to U.S. dollars for deposit in the U.S. pension plan, leaving a net amount of approximately $340.

Canadian Working in the U.S.

To conclude our review of the tax implications on the transfer of contributions between pension plans domiciled in our two countries, we must consider the Canadian person working in the United States. It is my understanding that the Internal Revenue Service would view such a transfer as being from pension trust fund to pension trust fund. Accordingly, no withholding tax would be required.

ERISA Concerns

So much for the tax implications of "money-follows-the-worker" reciprocity between the United States and Canada. Are there other implications in particular for trustees of a U.S. pension trust fund? I must first readily admit to a personal lack of expertise on the intricacies of ERISA, but I feel compelled to raise just a few possible nontax ERISA concerns. It is my understanding from some of my consultant associates practicing in the United States that the transfer of contributions between funds is not without its share of onerous responsibilities under ERISA.

Delinquency in Fund A involving contributions due to Fund B is but one example of these fiduciary obligations. I submit that if Fund A happens to be in Canada, the legal proceedings to collect the delinquent contributions could be very entangled. Another inherent problem with an international money-follows-the-worker agreement under ERISA is the funding of service with insufficient contributions. Recall, if you will, my earlier comments about the $500 of Canadian contributions for 500 hours worked that dwindled to $340 by the time the money reached the U.S. fund. Will the U.S. plan recognize the 500 hours for vesting and/or benefit accrual credit? If so, how will the funding be made up if only $340 is received?

What if the U.S. fund has a $1 contribution rate, and the Canadian fund has only a 60¢ rate? The reciprocal agreement permits the U.S. fund to transfer only 60¢ to the Canadian fund. Under ERISA, are the trustees of the U.S. fund obligated to provide pension credits to the Canadian member based on the 40¢ per hour that remains in the U.S. plan?

Pro-Rata

From my introductory remarks, you will recall the "pro-rata" reciprocal agreement that is frequently in use with pension plans. Briefly, there is no transfer of contributions. Rather, all credits are maintained in the respective plans and aggregated on the individual's retirement.

A U.S. resident could be eligible under such an agreement for a pension from a Canadian pension plan on retirement. The Canadian plan would pay a pension in Canadian currency and under the *current Canadian law* would not have to withhold any tax. Rather, the U.S. employee, whom we have assumed resides in the United States at retirement, would simply add the income from the Canadian plan to his total income and file it in his U.S. tax return.

1942 U.S./Canada Tax Treaty

I emphasized *current law.* A word of explanation or caution is needed. In 1942, the United States and Canada signed a treaty called the 1942 Canada-U.S. Tax Convention. Article VIA of the treaty dealt specifically with the taxation of pensions and annuities. It provides that pensions and life annuities derived from, for example, Canada, by a resident of, for example, the United States, shall be exempt from taxation in Canada. This convention is still the operative law today and, therefore, a Canadian pension fund is not required to withhold tax on a pension or annuity payment to a U.S. resident.

Canada-U.S. Income Tax Convention

However, during President Carter's Administration, a new Canada-United States Income Tax Convention (1980) was signed. This convention was intended to replace the 1942 convention. Article XVIII of the 1980 convention suggests that pensions and annuities may be subject to a maximum 15% withholding tax. This new agreement would require a Canadian pension fund to withhold tax on any pension or annuity payment to a U.S. resident.

I want to emphasize that this new convention has not been ratified by either country as of this date, and there is good reason to believe that it may never be ratified in light of U.S. Administration changes since 1980. I thought as trustees, however, you should be aware of this new convention and of the changes it would introduce in case it is ratified.

Tax Equity and Fiscal Responsibility Act

What are the conditions under a pro-rata reciprocal agreement for a U.S. pension fund paying a pension to a Canadian? *At the present time,* it is my understanding that there is no withholding tax by the U.S. pension fund when a pension or annuity payment is made, unless the pensioner requests that tax be withheld. This procedure applies to payments made to a U.S. or to a Canadian resident.

With the new Tax Equity and Fiscal Responsibility Act, however, this procedure will soon be changed. The Tax Equity and Fiscal Responsibility Act passed in the United States in August of 1982 and recently signed will require the trustees of a pension plan to write to a pension applicant advising of his choice to either waive withholding tax or to have withholding tax on his pension payments. If the applicant does not reply, it is deemed that he did not waive the provision and tax will be withheld.

Conclusions

In my opinion, this review of the tax implications of reciprocity identifies the methods and problems that are unique to plan participants who work in both Canada and the United States. There are, of course, other matters to be considered in the establishment and maintenance of a U.S./Canadian reciprocal agreement. I do believe, however, that they are similar to the concerns you would have to address in establishing and maintaining a reciprocal agreement of a domestic nature—that is, between plans in the U.S. only or exclusively in Canada. We therefore will leave any review of those concerns for another day.

On reflection about my findings, I asked myself, "What does this information imply, if anything, and does it in any way suggest some new beginnings for pension plan portability?" It seems to me that, although there are some important tax considerations to be examined, there is nothing to preclude the establishment of a "money-follows-the-worker" or "pro-rata" reciprocal agreement between U.S. and Canadian funds.

There may be some deterrents, however, that will pressure trustees to find other means of handling U.S./Canada benefit portability. Some of these deterrents are administrative in nature, affecting both the trust funds and the individual plan participants. Another deterrent is the legislation within the two countries. It not only differs in each country. In Canada, it appears to have some inequities mainly as a result, I think, of the legislation not being drafted with such reciprocity even contemplated. In the United States, there are fiduciary responsibility questions that must be answered.

Perhaps of even greater significance for the future is the apparent trend in both the United States and Canada toward earlier vesting. I think you would agree that, if further liberalizations of minimum vesting standards are mandated, such as Ontario's "full and immediate," reciprocal agreements most certainly will be in jeopardy.

I hope that my remarks have been informative and have nurtured some thought processes in each of you, so that as trustees you can develop sound and practical solutions to portability for the future, especially between the United States and Canada.

CHAPTER 8

Benefit Plan Design Options

William R. Breher

Executive Director
Michigan Educational Special
Services Association
East Lansing, Michigan

Denis Stallings, PE

Construction Consultant
Howard, Needles, Tammen & Bergendoff
Evansville, Indiana

Robert J. Leaf, D.M.D.

President
American Dental Examiners, Inc.
New York, New York

William M. Kirschner

Attorney-at-Law
Burger, Kramer, Feldman & Kirschner, P.C.
Hauppauge, New York

Alec M. Schwartz

Executive Director
American Prepaid Legal Services Institute
Chicago, Illinois

Cheryl Denney White

Associate
Dickstein, Shapiro & Morin
Washington, D.C.

Flexible Benefits for Multiemployer Plans

BY WILLIAM R. BREHER

THAT THERE IS little, if any, meaningful discussion centering around flexible benefits for multiemployer plans seems unarguable. The literature is sparse, perhaps nonexistent. Why is that?

Is it because flexible benefits for single employer plans, despite fast growing activity, are still only on the threshold of credibility for corporate decisionmakers? Are the rewards for employers and employees not worth the effort? Is it perhaps that the very real difficulty of achieving desired results has discouraged benefits planners?

My assignment in this presentation, as set forth by the International Foundation, is to commence the dialogue on this subject. I am to broaden the discussion that is now taking place freely on the subject of single employer flexible benefits and initiate communication and seek an exchange of information among multiple employer plans.

Whether this discussion and ensuing ones eventually lead to the proliferation of multiemployer flexible benefit plans is problematical, but I hope that we become convinced that the research and investigation undertaken, whatever the outcome, will at the minimum sharpen views on fundamental compensation theory. We should commend the Foundation for leading the way.

How MESSA Is Organized

Before I set forth my organization's experience on this subject, you will need to know what kind of organization it is so that you can relate its experience to your own situation.

I understand that perhaps a great majority of attendees at the Montreal Conference where this paper was first presented were labor-management trustees and/or staff, and that the balance was single employer representatives, third-party administrators, insurers, consultants, attorneys and other professional and technical personnel. The organization I represent, Michigan Education Special Services Association (MESSA), engages in activities as though it were almost all of these organizations.

MESSA, a nonprofit corporation, was formed in 1960 under the sponsorship of the Michigan Education Association (MEA) because the MEA felt a need for group insurance programs designed for educators. It is tax exempt under Section 501(c)(9) of the Internal Revenue Code as a voluntary employee beneficiary association (VEBA). It is first and foremost an employee membership organization and we provide life, health, accident and similar benefits to 90,000 insured members and their families.

Mr. Breher is chief executive officer of the Michigan Education Special Services Association (MESSA), a nonprofit corporation that is tax exempt under 501(c)(9) as a voluntary employee beneficiary association. He is responsible for the development, marketing and administering of a variety of insurance plans for 90,000 public school employees and their families. Prior to joining MESSA, he held various analyst and management positions including service on the Ford Motor Company central benefits and compensation staff; before that, he was benefits analyst for the U.S. Department of Labor. Mr. Breher is a member of the American Public Health, Michigan Education, National Education and National Economic Services Associations, and has spoken before several of these organizations and Michigan State University Economics Symposium. He earned his B.A. degree in economics at Michigan State University, East Lansing and his M.S. degree in labor economics at the University of Wisconsin, Madison.

In the name of and for the benefit of its members, MESSA acts as policyholder for more than $150 million 501(c)(9) type benefits. Most of these benefits are under minimum premium arrangements that gain for our membership the benefits of self-funding, while preserving for them, when needed, the benefits of fully insured plans.

MESSA designs the plans, tailoring them to the needs of its membership, and then negotiates with

Table

NET IMPACT ON EMPLOYERS AND EMPLOYEES
$100 PAID IN SALARY VS. $100 PAID IN BENEFITS

Employer Costs			Employee Taxes	Single*	Married*
Retirement plan contributions	5%		Fed income tax	22%	33%
FICA	6.7%		FICA	6.7%	6.7%
Salary related (e.g., paid time off)	15%		State and local income tax rates	5%	5%
Total	26.7%		Total	33.7%	44.7%

* * * * * * *

				Single	Married
Salary increase	$100.00		Salary increase	$100.00	$100.00
Additional costs	26.70		Taxes	33.70	44.70
Total	$126.70		After tax pay	$ 66.30	$ 55.30
			Before tax salary increase needed to equal $100 after tax	$150.83	$180.83

*Assumes 1982 annual taxable income is $15,000 for single employee, $30,000 for married filing joint return.

---

carriers to provide required coverages at appropriate premiums. With MEA's assistance, MESSA then markets the benefits against the strong competition of Blue Cross-Blue Shield of Michigan, other commercial carriers, plans sponsored by the state school board association and self-funded plans.

MESSA has benefit plans in countless variations of benefit levels and coverages for its members, who are employees of approximately 550 local school districts. It bills and collects contributions from these 550 employer accounts, reviews member applications submitted during annual enrollment periods and administers and pays claims.

To accomplish this task, MESSA employs a staff of over 200 persons, most of them performing functions similar to those of a life and health insurance company.

If that information doesn't confuse you, the next comment might. One thing MESSA is *not* is an organization that falls under ERISA. Its members are employees of local public school districts and are therefore exempt. Nevertheless, 501(c)(9) rules and regulations demand strict accountability to the membership through the requirements of prudence and conservation of membership funds.

On the face of it, it should be obvious that our organization is very unlike the typical Taft-Hartley multiemployer plan. Public school employees have far different work and compensation patterns and the basis for rating benefit plans in the education industry varies widely from that in Taft-Hartley type industries. Nevertheless, some fundamental similarities exist. These include dealing with large numbers of employees and dealing with a good measure of confusion, sometimes bordering on anarchy, to achieve a modicum of sound personnel pay practices. Most of us seem to have this problem in common.

In this presentation I will set forth three main points: first, a brief review of the advantages of flexible benefits over other forms of compensation; second, an explanation of what might be called the "multiemployer complication"; third, some of the approaches MESSA uses to develop and make available a shelfful of benefit plan choices to its membership.

Why Flexible Benefits?

The position in favor of single employer flexible benefits plans has been well-documented and can be summarized briefly if one can accept a few oversimplified assumptions.

The Table shows that nontaxed benefit plans provide great values to both employers and employees. For example, an employer's wage-related costs are about 25% greater if he provides an increase in straight wages rather than in nontaxed benefits. For employees, tax law provides startling advantages in the choice of benefits over straight wages. Some double income families may have a taxable income of $30,000 or more. When FICA, state and local taxes are added to federal income taxes, a double income family may pay taxes at an equivalent 45% tax rate. If so, that family would need more than $180 in wages to equal $100 paid in nontaxed benefits.[1]

It is appropriate at times to remind ourselves of the value of economies of scale. Group purchase discounts for life, health and disability benefits are often taken for granted. When there are multi-employer group purchases, the discounts can be very large indeed.

At MESSA, we are constantly reminded of this point by those of our members who must leave employment in the education industry, and find that they now have available only individually purchased benefits or benefits purchased by their new small employer at relatively high prices. It is perhaps almost axiomatic among actuaries that large group size = high credibility factor = low risk charge in the pricing of benefit plans.

Economic theory also tells us that free choice by individuals produces greatest results, that the invisible hand of the free market results in optimal allocation of scarce resources—in this case, of benefits. In our experience, this theory seems validated. Flexible benefits made available through a wide array of choices avoid duplication and waste and minimize unwanted, partially used benefits.

In addition to the economic basis, there is also a strong philosophical basis for flexible benefits that may be summarized in the following questions: Shouldn't we be searching for ways to preserve free choice and independence? Can't our employees be treated as individuals, able to make judgments about their own economic futures? Do we have to mandate, to substitute our judgment for theirs, to insulate them from any risk taking?

Along this line of thought, Professor Yair Aharoni wrote recently that ". . . the more government protects the individual against risks, the more it feels entitled to restrict individual choice." That's a pretty heavy thought, isn't it? Could the same point be made by merely substituting employer for government? In Japanese industry the workers apparently accept a very disciplined approach to their jobs and compensation. But one can speculate that what fits in the Japanese heritage could, justifiably, fail miserably in our U.S. society, where workers generally strive for workplace independence.

We have all witnessed, and participated in, the great changes that have occurred over the last few decades in the traditional family, in personal values and in lifestyles. Who in the 1930s and 1940s could have dreamed of the vast social revolution that would take place in the next 50 years? Yet science tells us that "we ain't seen nothin' yet." Microtechnology, robotics and genetic engineering portend even more rapid and sweeping changes. Personal commitment to the care of one's body and mind produces individuals that are healthier and more independent at age 85 than would have seemed possible only a few decades ago. In this scenario, age-based programs are truly becoming irrelevant.

The question should then be whether we can be at all prepared unless we adopt flexibility as a fundamental process that can carry us through these changes.

Why So Few Flexible Benefits Plans?

Thus far, relatively few single employer plans around the country have flexible benefits, but activity seems to be picking up very recently. Although there may be some multiemployer plans that provide small and varying degrees of options, presumably such options were not developed as a matter of system or policy. However, if one accepts the premise that there is sound justification for flexible benefits in economic and philosophical terms, as noted previously, what are the reasons for inaction?

Perhaps just plain inertia is one principal reason. We often are comfortable doing things in the same way. Also, experts inform us of the potential costs and risks involved. There seems to be a good deal of fear and intimidation, much of it self-imposed, concerning the problems encountered if one permits employees to exercise choices over their own economic futures.

Finally, the apparent magnitude of the job of installing flexible benefit programs seems to inhibit both single employer and multiemployer plans from initiating them. Employers think that surveying employee attitudes, designing plans, estimating costs, educating employees and developing administrative tools and follow-through procedures make the process too big of an undertaking. But it doesn't have to be that way.

---

1. The "tax effect" formula is quite simple: wage increase equivalent equals the benefit increase divided by the difference between 100% and the assumed tax rate (e.g., wage increase = $100/(100%–45%) = $182; or wage increase = $100/(100%–30%) = $143.)

There is a germ of truth behind all these reasons for inaction. In my view, however, the risk/reward ratio may be so biased in favor of benefits over wages, of choice over nonchoice, that it becomes imperative to explore flexible benefit plans.

The First Step—An Action Step

To confirm these conclusions, I would propose that the decisionmakers in an organization should do a quick study, the purpose of which is to prove (or disprove) the theory that action should be taken. Once convinced, they should proceed without delay.

In MESSA's view, the health care plan option represents the "base plan" decision, around which other option decisions could be made. For example, some employees may be willing to pay large deductibles and have minimal prescription drug coverage in order to use the differential premium savings/cost for some short term disability coverage. Others may not need health care coverage because the family is covered under another plan provided by the spouse's employer—the entire premium savings/cost might be used for several lower priced coverages such as life, disability or dental. The point to be made here is that employers are not paying for unneeded health care benefits for double income families; employees may exercise voluntary, individualized options about their economic lives.

"Adverse Selection"—Problems Overemphasized

At this point, a vague uneasiness begins to take hold. A definitional term is applied that builds on the uneasiness. "Selection" is a positive word; but "adverse" means hostile, inimical, opposed to one's interests, counter. The combination, "adverse selection," becomes a term that turns people off before they can understand the positives of employee options.

Why is it that whenever options are discussed in this context everyone states that an "adverse selection" problem arises because the benefit plan selected is "more likely to be used"? But of course! "It also will affect the rates." Again, we agree. However, unless we are ready to admit that we cannot develop reasonable eligibility standards through plan design and underwriting rules, or that we cannot control fraud and abuse through sound benefits administration, the benefit plans are merely performing their substantive function.

Benefit checks, after all, reimburse the employee for expenses incurred; the charges would have been paid, out of pocket, from aftertax dollars. Is this not the purpose of large group, spread the risk, low retention insurance purchasing? Does this not meet the purpose of longstanding public policy: to encourage installation of employee benefit plans by offering substantial employer and employee tax benefits?

Offering individual options does not imply that one has "bought" all known risks. Rather, it implies that the rating must move from absolute neutrality caused by a mandated 100% mix to a rating that is somewhat biased because some of the better risks have opted out for other plans. In MESSA's experience, this bias is small. But even if it were as much as 10% or 20%, the advantages of group purchasing and tax benefits far outweigh the additional premium charge.

The Multiemployer Complication

If these basic views are understandable, if the risk/reward ratio seems positive, then single employer plans, anyway, might well consider flexible benefits worthy of further investigation. But what if you must deal with 550 employers, each one of whom negotiates contracts, including benefit plans, with at least one local union? What if each employer also wants to provide different packages of benefits for the clerical staff, the custodial staff and the administrative staff? What if some negotiations settle on single year contracts while others use multiple year contracts; what if some have effective dates for benefit coverages on July 1, while others have September 1 or October 1? What if all 550 want annual reenrollment dates, where individual employees may opt annually for changes in levels of benefits and coverages?

These "what ifs" set forth what we term the "multiemployer complication." They are compounded by the fact that multiemployer plan administrators may need to meet strong, continuing competition from several outside sources ranging from small specialized carriers to multibillion dollar annual sales hospital/medical service corporations.

Service! Service! Service!

If there is a single characteristic that is required of multiemployer plans promoting flexible benefits, it is the ability to provide service to its various constituencies. If it is a VEBA membership plan, it often must find ways to handle widely diverse (e.g., small rural school and sophisticated city school) problems. It must develop complete and accurate master files of data on its individual members. It must develop census data on school employees in various combinations and apply those data to preprogrammed benefit factors and actuarial charges so that it can make bids on negotiated life, vision, dental and long term disability business put out for bid by each school. It must develop good working relationships with providers and their office staffs; with local union leaders, negotiators and union headquarters staffs; and with school business managers.

For a multiemployer plan, the name of the game is service to its constituents. The plan must find ways to simplify the life of its members, employers and providers. It must develop tools to make it easy for local union leaders to negotiate the multiemployer plan benefits, not some competitor's benefits.

Especially if the plan is a large one, dealing with number-crunching problems, it is axiomatic that almost any time, effort and initial expense to improve systems will be rewarding many times over. Improved data processing, microfilm/microfiche and work flow simplification are all improvements that can minimize complaints, followups and inefficiencies.

Following is a list of some administrative tools, aids and systems that may be used to accomplish the basic flexible benefits objectives of the multiemployer plan—a wide selection of cost and tax efficient benefit plans, made available to large numbers of employers, with individual employee options available on annual reenrollment dates:

- Direct phone contact with members, employers and providers, including WATS lines
- Standardized letters with variable information inserts—a system that interfaces data processing with word processing
- Specialized literature for negotiators and field representatives summarizing the many plans that are available, with emphasis on coverage explanations, underwriting requirements and costs (the Appendix—excerpts from *Bargaining Briefs, 1982-1983*)
- Preprocessed, computer-printed multiple benefit plan application, color coded to minimize errors and simplify the annual reenrollment process
- Computer-printed "schedule of benefits" pocket card, listing benefits that had just been applied for in the annual reenrollment
- Plastic identification card, useful for verifying eligibility to providers and also for processing of drug prescriptions with participating pharmacies
- Certificate booklets with simplified language
- Greatly simplified claims forms useful in most claims situations
- Handy reference manual for employers' business offices
- Periodic bulletins and newsletters to notify business offices of changed procedures, new governmental regulations, etc.
- Computer-processed billing system that minimizes the reporting requirements of employers
- Regional summer workshops for employer business office personnel to exchange information, clarify procedures and promote good will.

Conclusion

My assignment was to commence the dialogue on flexible benefits for multiemployer plans. I hope that I have met that assignment, at least partially. It seems clear perhaps that no multiemployer organization could adopt MESSA approaches, unmodified, in any substantive way. Most multiemployer plans have far different, and perhaps in some ways far more perplexing, problems facing them.

I would hope, however, that some plans become encouraged, or motivated, to consider a process that will move them along the flexible benefits path. In my view, the risks are small in relation to the rewards, and both employers and employees will greatly appreciate any leadership efforts that result in meaningful flexible benefit plans.

Appendix

MESSA OPTIONS[1]

General Information

MESSA recognizes that not all employees of a school district need identical insurance protection, as many school employees are covered by health or dental care programs through another source. In such cases we believe that the best approach is to provide alternative programs which will eliminate unnecessary duplication. This represents a savings to the employer while at the same time providing more meaningful coverage to the employee. If employees are permitted to elect among various benefit programs (MESSA programs or otherwise), and if any such programs offer taxable benefits, then it is imperative that the Board of the school district adopt a written tax qualified cafeteria plan. Taxable benefits would include such benefits as auto insurance, homeowner's insurance, dependents' life insurance and group term life insurance coverage in excess of $50,000. (For information concerning most of these taxable benefit plans, consult your MEA and MEFSA descriptive materials.)

Eligibility

To be eligible for MESSA Options the employee group must be a MESPA or MEA unit, or otherwise "grandpersoned" by action of the MESSA Board of Trustees, effective March 1, 1982. In addition, the employee group must also have MESSA health insurance available.

The Option Concept

A. *The Variable Option Plan*—allows an employee to choose the benefit or combination of benefits for which his/her school subsidy may be used. No percentage of employees is required to participate in order to make these programs available.

It is important to note that many combinations are possible under the variable concept. The inclusion of MESSA Options, or other employee benefit programs, often will reduce the overall cost of an insurance package since employees not presented with an alternative will often "double insure" rather than give up their fringe subsidy.

B. *The Fixed Option Plan*—substitutes a specified benefit for all employees who choose not to utilize a Super Med program.

Important Note

The options available through MESSA are continually being updated and improved. Therefore, when you are negotiating for the MESSA Variable Options as a part of your fringe benefit package, *do not list the options.* By referring only to the Variable Options Package available through MESSA, any new benefits will become automatically available.

Here are some examples of contract wording for MESSA Options:

Example 1

Fixed Option Approach—Employees not electing MESSA health insurance will receive Delta Dental Care Plan _____ for themselves and their eligible dependents, as provided through the MESSA/Delta Dental Program.

Example 2

Combination Fixed and Variable Options—(On a fixed dollar basis) Employees not electing MESSA health insurance will receive Delta Dental Care Plan _____ for themselves and their eligible dependents as provided through the MESSA/Delta Dental Program. The balance of the subsidy will be applied to the MESSA Variable Option Package.

---

1. THIS BRIEF OUTLINE IS FOR BARGAINING PURPOSES ONLY. For additional information, please contact the MESSA office or your MESSA representative.

Example 3

Variable Option Approach—In the absence of guidelines from the Department of Labor, we believe the following variable option approach to Health will minimize the potential for discrimination by marital status.

The Board shall provide without cost to the employee for a full twelve month period a choice of either:
- a) MESSA SM2 for self and eligible dependents plus $XX per month to be applied toward optional benefits; or
- b) An amount equal to single subscriber coverage to be applied toward optional benefits.

The agreement in this section shall be subject to the following guidelines:
1. Eligible dependents and underwriting guidelines are as defined by MESSA and its underwriters.
2. Where applicable Limited Medicare Supplement contributions and Medicare premiums will be paid in lieu of SM2 contributions.
3. Any amounts exceeding the Board subsidy shall be payroll deducted.
4. An open enrollment period shall be provided whenever contribution subsidy amounts change for the above groups.
5. The variable option program shall consist of:
   - a) MESSA Short Term/Long Term Disability
   - b) MESSA Term Life Insurance
   - c) MESSA Survivor Income Insurance
   - d) MESSA Dependent Life Insurance
   - e) MESSA Hospital Confinement Indemnity
6. The amount stipulated in Example 3 a) and b) shall be apportioned as determined by the Association and/or split between the fixed and variable options.

MESSA FIXED AND VARIABLE OPTIONS SUMMARY

Type of Plan	Programs Available	Coverage	Fixed[1] or Variable	Health? or Pre-X	Underwriting Requirements (all have at work Req.)	Cost Consideration
DENTAL	Dental Option for all employees not taking health	Variety of programs available See DENTAL Section	F	No	Premium must be fully Board paid. 100% participation of definable group	Contact MESSA Rep for quote
VISION	Vision Plan I	Pays a scheduled benefit based on type of service See VISION Section	F	No	Requires 100% participation of definable group	Rates based on composition of group. See Vision Section for census information.[2]
	Intermediate Vision	Pays 80% of R&C charges See VISION Section	F	No	Requires 100% participation of definable group	Rates based on composition of group. See Vision Section for census information.[2]
	Vision Plan 2	Pays 100% of R&C charges See VISION Section	F	No	Requires 100% participation of definable group	Rates based on composition of group. See Vision Section for census information.[2]
INDEMNITY	Group Hospital Confinement Indemnity Insurance	Choose amount from $10 to $100 reimbursement for each day hospitalized as inpatient	V	Pre-X applies	No	See RATE chart.[2]
LIFE	Basic Term Life[3]	$5,000 Life $5,000 AD&D	V	No	Those not electing MESSA Health Insurance	$2.36/Month
	Dependent Life[3]	Program pays $2,500 for death of dependent spouse— $1,250 for each dependent child	V	No	Must be enrolled in Basic Term Life or a SMIAD, Super Med 1, or Super Med 2 program	$1.48/Month (includes all dependents)
	Supplemental Life[3]	Selection of life & matching AD&D: $5,000, $10,000 $15,000, $20,000	V	Health question applies	Must be enrolled in Basic Term Life or a SMIAD, Super Med 1, or Super Med 2 program	See RATE chart.[2]
	Negotiated Life	Min. available: $2,000 Max.: 2½ x salary up to $100,000	F	No	See NEG. LIFE Section.[2]	Need census, i.e., sex, birthdate, and amount
	Negotiated Optional Life	Up to ½ face value of Neg. Life	V	Health question applies if less than 75% participate	Must be in addition to a MESSA negotiated life package	Based on census of those who enroll
	Negotiated Dependent Life	Spouse—up to ½ face value of Neg. Life to $25,000 Dependent children—up to 25% of face value to $12,500	F or V	No	Must be in addition to a MESSA negotiated life package. 75% minimum participation requirement. See NEG. LIFE Section.[2]	Based on census of those who enroll

Type of Plan	Programs Available	Coverage	Fixed[1] or Variable	Health? or Pre-X	Underwriting Requirements (all have at work Req.)	Cost Consideration
LIFE (continued)	Survivor Income Insurance[3]	Upon death of insured member, spouse receives $200/month and child(ren) receives $100/month	V	Health question applies	Must be enrolled in Basic Term Life or a SMIAD, Super Med 1, or Super Med 2 program	See RATE chart.[2]
	Group Term Life	Coverage available in units of $10,000. Minimum $10,000 Maximum $100,000	V	No health question on family basic unit during open enrollment	No	See RATE chart.[2]
INCOME PROTECTION PLANS	Negotiated Long Term Disability	Benefits provide either 50, 60 or 66⅔% of contractual salary with various monthly maximums	F	No health question. If 50 or more emp., no Pre-X	See NEG. LTD Section.[2]	Need census, i.e., sex, birthdate, salary, accumulated sick leave and type of plan.[2]
	Short Term Disability[3]	Weekly benefit from $20 to $300 payable up to 52 weeks. Waiting period is either seven or 28 days for illness, 1st day for injury.	V	Pre-X applies	Must be enrolled in Basic Term Life or a SMIAD, Super Med 1, or Super Med 2 program	See RATE chart.[2]
	Optional Long Term Disability[3]	Monthly benefit from $100 to $1,000, payable after one year waiting period. Plan pays up to five years or age 70. A rider may be added to extend benefit period to age 70 without five year limitation at extra cost	V	Pre-X applies	Must be enrolled in Basic Term Life or a SMIAD, Super Med 1, or Super Med 2 program	See RATE chart.[2]

1. See pages 360-361 for definition of fixed and variable.
2. Available from MESSA.
3. For further information, please refer to the MESSA Options Brochure.

PLEASE NOTE: THESE SHOULD NOT BE USED AS BIDDING SPECIFICATIONS. THIS LIST IS PRIMARILY TO IDENTIFY THE DIFFERENCES BETWEEN THE OPTIONS PROGRAMS AND THEREFORE DOES NOT INCLUDE THEIR MANY OUTSTANDING BENEFITS. REFER TO THE EQUITABLE CERTIFICATE BOOKLET FOR ALL THE BENEFITS COMMON TO OPTIONS PROGRAMS, OR EXCLUSIONS AND LIMITATIONS.

Employee Assistance Programs for Alcohol and Drug Abuse

BY DENIS STALLINGS, PE

TO START WITH, I thought I would add a couple additional items as part of my biography. First, my interest and work in employee benefit programs are not as a result of my association with Howard, Needles, Tammen & Bergendoff. That is an endeavor I have followed part time since my retirement. For 30 years I worked in the heavy construction field, all with one employer, and much of that time was spent as a management trustee of Operating Engineers Local 181, Health and Welfare Fund, headquartered in Henderson, Kentucky.

Second, I am an alcoholic, which probably accounts for my interest in the field of employee assistance programs. If I hold out another three weeks, it will have been five years since my last drink. I feel if you know this, perhaps you will better understand the sincerity with which I approach this subject.

Mr. Stallings currently serves as a management trustee in the health and welfare area, a position that he has held for over 14 years. As construction consultant with Howard, Needles, Tammen & Bergendoff, he represents the firm of architects, engineers and planners on a part-time and consulting basis in Indiana, Kentucky, Tennessee and Mississippi. In addition to his professional responsibilities, Mr. Stallings serves as volunteer coordinator of the Southwestern Indiana Council of Alcohol Problems.

Statistics

There are many statistics available these days concerning alcoholism and drug abuse. Many persons and organizations connected with this problem use a figure of 10% to represent that part of the population with these and other personal problems. Probably something less than 10% of the population are alcoholics, but when you consider that nearly every alcoholic or drug abuser seriously affects one or more other persons, mostly family members, then you realize that regardless of what percentage you use, the problem is monumental and becoming increasingly worse.

What Is an EAP?

The phrase "employee assistance program" (EAP) is intentionally broad for two reasons. First, the program is intended to assist employees who either have job performance problems or are likely to have them as a result of personal problems. This criterion applies regardless of what the problem may be. Consequently, identifying the program with a single disorder would be inappropriate. Secondly, one of the major concerns of the employee assistance program is to help alcoholic people, and experience is showing that people with alcohol problems do not respond to a program and staff labeled with the terms "alcoholism" or "alcoholic." When such labels are applied, those employees most needing the program tend to avoid it.

Where alcoholic or other chemically dependent people are concerned, the object of the EAP is to confidentially assist the large majority of sufferers who are not readily recognized as alcoholic because of stereotypical bias. This large segment has been estimated to be as much as 95% of those employees who are chemically dependent in one way or another. It should be the aim, therefore, of any EAP not only to help the 5% who are obvious but also to assist that other 95% who often have serious financial, medical, social and legal problems. Obviously, therefore, the identification technique used in the employment setting is of major importance. A good EAP must deal with a wide range of problems; one major aim of such a program is to take that 95% who may have serious personal problems and prevent them from becoming part of the 5% who are in obviously serious trouble.

One of the principal goals of any EAP should be education—help for those with a problem, but also help for those loved ones who are also seriously affected. Knowledge concerning the problem and what to do about it may go far toward a solution.

Also high on the list of reasons for an EAP is the fact that early help for an alcoholic person or one otherwise chemically dependent does much toward reducing unnecessary or preventable claims. Aside from the tragic human waste, a substantial percentage of medical costs borne by union health and welfare funds are the direct result of neglected and untreated alcoholism.

Different Types of Programs

Single Employer-Predominately Single Union

Two programs I know of in Southern Indiana in this category are at Alcoa and Whirlpool. Each of the concerns employs approximately 5,000 persons and both have an established employee assistance program.

Single Employer-Multiunion

In this category would be a large construction firm with its own individual program. This type employer traditionally deals with a number of unions.

Single Union-Multiemployer

The best example in this category with which I am familiar is that of Local No. 3, International Union of Operating Engineers, with jurisdiction in Northern California and surrounding states. This program covers some 38,000 employees in four states and the Mid-Pacific Islands. Gary Atkinson, director of Local 3's program, tells me that one of the biggest problems he has is lack of employer participation in a multiemployer plan. He estimates that he gets cooperation from only 20% of his employers, perhaps less.

Multiemployer-Multiunion—Multiple Industry

Included in this category is the program for the Westchester and Mid-Hudson region of New York State. This program services employees and employers in the building, construction and realty industries and is headquartered in White Plains, New York.

Plan Development

In-House vs. Outside Programs

Probably one of the first, if not the first, question to be decided once the decision has been made to start an EAP is whether it is to be an in-house or an outside-administered program. A program may be instituted and administered wholly within the company, union or industry itself without outside assistance or it may be initiated and operated by an outside consultant in that business.

Personnel, Medical or Employee Relations

Traditionally, a company-operated program is part of the personnel, medical or employee relations departments. A study completed by Paul M. Roman, Ph.D. of Tulane University, arrived at this breakdown by departments:

Personnel/industrial relations	28.9%
Medical employee health service	23.2%
Combined personnel and medical	46.5%
Independent department	1.4%

Mr. James L. Francek, corporate coordinator of the Ford Motor Company Employee Assistance Program, further suggests that programs affecting 2,500 or more employees should be in-house programs without outside consultants. Obviously, those programs for a lesser number of employees might be developed with or without an outside consultant.

How to Start a Program

With all of the information currently available on this subject, which I will discuss later, there are any number of ways to start an EAP. I recall an incident many years ago in which a concession I made in a bargaining session with the Ironworkers was severely criticized by one of the partners in my company. In discussing this criticism with the other partner, he made this observation: "It is almost impossible for one person to handle labor matters to the satisfaction of anyone else."

Therefore, what I say and the example I use are my personal opinion and certainly are not ironclad rules for how to start.

As a framework from which to begin, I use the following items in setting up a program:

- *Management Guide on Alcoholism.* This particular publication is put out and available from the Kemper Insurance Companies, Long Grove, Illinois.
- *What to Do About the Employee With a Drinking Problem.* This presentation is also a Kemper publication.
- *A small booklet for all employees.* This booklet might be published expressly for the employees of the company or group of firms starting the program or for the members of the particular union or group for which the program is intended.

As the program progresses, obviously other material can and should be used, but these three items should provide an adequate place to begin.

Cost of Some Programs

An outside consultant that I know will start and operate a program for a cost varying from $20-$40 per covered employee per year. This program includes such services as management training, employee counseling, program promotion and a variety of other related services.

Local No. 3, Operating Engineers at San Francisco covers some 38,000 members. It currently operates with an annual budget of $200,000, a full-time director and 13 recovery program coordinators who are also business representatives of the local.

The program in White Plains, New York earlier referred to covers some 30,000 union workers and 2,000 member firms and has a current annual budget of $105,000. This budget is projected to increase by 10% annually for the next two years.

The United Labor Assistance Program in St. Louis, Missouri is a statewide program of organized labor representing the AFL-CIO, Teamsters, United Auto Workers and United Mine Workers—some 250,000 members. The cost to the employer is negotiable, generally in the range of $10-$15 per employee per year, depending on the program components and sophistication.

McDonnell Douglas Corp. of St. Louis states that, based on the 12 years that its program has been in effect, its records show a net savings, after all program costs are taken out, of $4,171,000.

Source of Funds

Company or Employer

For a single company or employer, this program most likely would be funded as part of the cost of the personnel, medical or other department operating the program with or without a separate budget.

Health and Welfare Funds

A program operated solely as a part of the health and welfare program would normally be financed the same as any other fund activity, such as administration, claims paying, etc. Ideally, the administrator of the EAP would be a full-time employee whose duties were limited to that particular activity. The costs of such a program could thus be more easily defined and the program could operate either with or without a separate budget.

Per Man-Hour Directly to the EAP

Some programs for union employees are financed by a separate contribution per man-hour worked. This method is similar to financing vacation programs, training programs and others. These contributions would go directly to the EAP.

Annual Grants From the Health and Welfare Fund (IUOE Local No. 3)

The $200,000 annual budget previously referred to for the Operating Engineers Local No. 3 is, as I understand it, a separate grant from the health and welfare fund and is used solely for the EAP.

Per Man-Hour From Health and Welfare Funds

Such a method of financing not only provides the funds with which to operate but also serves as a budgetary limit and control on expenditures. Periods of high employment naturally provide more money to operate this program, as well as other activities of the health and welfare program such as medical and hospital benefits, etc.

Industry Advancement Funds

Some EAPs are financed as one of the activities covered by industry advancement funds and, thus, are largely separate from the health and welfare or trust program. EAP programs thus financed appear to be few.

Federal Funding—Grants

People active in employee assistance programs tell me that this method of financing is rapidly drying up and initiation of any new program should not consider the federal government as a likely source of funds.

Sources of Information

You may be surprised at the number of companies, organizations, foundations, etc., that make such information available (see Appendix).

Some Final Facts

Jellnik Curve—IUOE Local No. 3 Version

As an educational tool in the field of alcoholism, this curve in one form or the other, is widely used. I like Local No. 3's version (see Figure) because it is simplified, hard hitting and to the point. This curve is used to demonstrate one of the basic facts of alcoholism—that it normally develops over a long period, worsening as time goes on. This progress is identified on the curve at various stages of a person's drinking. Continued drinking leads to the bottom of the curve. Late stages list such items as being unable to work, obsession with drinking and complete abandonment. At the bottom of the curve are such items as calls for help and medical help; up the other side of the curve, there is continuing improvement and, at the top, recovery.

I like the bottom of this curve and the line sloping on off to the right. Continued drinking and deterioration lead to death or insanity—or both. That item is about as simple as you can make it.

Another generally accepted fact associated with this curve is that a person on the way down may, of course, at any point—by outside help or otherwise—quit drinking; one's descent on the curve would naturally stop at this point. It is also a generally accepted fact, however, that after a period of sobriety, even for many years, a person who resumes drinking does not again start at the top and gradually continue downward as before, but will in a very short time be at the point at which the drinking stopped; downward progress will continue from that point.

Some people with extended periods of sobriety feel that they can resume drinking on a social or limited basis. Without exception, these attempts fail; one merely resumes the downward journey on the curve from where it was stopped.

Fatality in IUOE Local No. 181

A claim processed by our health and welfare fund involved a fatality apparently caused by the mixture of alcohol and a strong painkilling drug. This statistic is a hard one, involving a young operator whom I have every reason to believe is not alive today because of a lack of knowledge that such a mixture can be and is fatal. What a real service a little education might have provided for this man and his young family.

What One Union Is Doing

In addition to the EAP operated by Operating Engineers Local No. 3, its international union is providing information to its members on a nationwide basis. Its monthly *National Magazine,* for example, has included the following articles:

December 1981:   "Alcoholism—A Treatable Disease'"
January 1982:   "Part II—Excerpts from Local No. 3 (San Francisco EAP Program)"; "Drug Abuse, The Scourge of the Nation"
February 1982:   "Part III"—on the same subjects
March 1982:   IUOE Special Report, "Drug Abuse."

Heredity

I thought it would be interesting for you to learn a bit on the part heredity seems to play in alcoholism. Studies in Scandinavia and in the U.S. now show conclusively that children whose parents were alcoholics have four or five times the risk of becoming alcoholic—even though they were raised separately from their parents from the time of their birth—than do children of nonalcoholic parents who were placed in adoption.

Dr. T. K. Lee, of Indiana University, maintains that the son of an alcoholic father is nine times more susceptible to the disease. He has discovered that the congenital linkage runs from father to son and from mother to daughter.

Brain Damage

I had originally intended to present three slides at this point, showing progressive brain damage. However, X-rays and CAT scan pictures do not reproduce very well.

It is enough to say, however, that one group of these films showing moderate brain damage was, unfortunately, pictures taken in 1975 of me. The doctor showed me that my damage only differed from that of a person suffering irreversible and irreparable damage in degree. This experience, I assure you, was shaking and one I want never to encounter again.

This fact effectively demonstrates the old cliche´ that every person may have at least one more binge but may not have one more recovery.

Educational Aim of EAPs

It should be the aim of every EAP to work toward the early identification of the problem drinker and to educate that person in ways to combat the problem. Experience has shown that the recovery of the substance-abusing worker is possible and can be achieved with greater success if the problem is identified and dealt with in its early stages. Such programs will assist in the reduction of unnecessary or preventable claims to your health and welfare programs, while assisting employees with the personal responsibility of maintaining better health standards.

Appendix

SOURCES OF INFORMATION
ON EMPLOYEE ASSISTANCE PROGRAMS

1. Employee Assistance Program for the Building, Construction & Realty Industries
   600 North Broadway
   White Plains, New York 10603

2. Hazelden Educational Services
   Box 176
   Center City, Minnesota 55012
      Ask for: Catalogs on Educational Services.

3. International Telephone & Telegraph Corporation
   320 Park Avenue
   New York, New York 10022
      Ask for: Information on the Employee Assistance Program as advertised.

4. The Christopher D. Smithers Foundation
   41 East 57th Street
   New York, New York 10022
      Ask for: List of Foundation publications.

5. Public Relations
   Kemper Insurance Companies
   Long Grove, Illinois 60049
      Ask for: *Management Guide on Alcoholism; What to Do About the Employee With a Drinking Problem; Guide for the Family of the Alcoholic; The Way to Go.*
   Up to 25 copies free.

6. McDonnell Douglas Corporation
   P.O. Box 516
   St. Louis, Missouri 63166
      Ask for: *Historical Background of Employee Assistance Programs; Employee Assistance Programs in the St. Louis Marketing Area.*

Figure
DISEASE OF ALCOHOLISM

PROGRESSION

EARLY STAGES
- INCREASE IN ALCOHOL TOLERANCE
- DESIRE TO CONTINUE WHEN OTHERS STOP
- RELIEF DRINKING COMMENCES
- PREOCCUPATION WITH ALCOHOL (THINKING ABOUT NEXT DRINK)
- DRINKING TO CALM NERVES
- DRINKING BEFORE A DRINKING FUNCTION
- UNCOMFORTABLE IN SITUATION WHERE THERE IS NO ALCOHOL
- OCCASIONAL MEMORY LAPSES AFTER HEAVY DRINKING
- SECRET IRRITATION WHEN YOUR DRINKING IS DISCUSSED

HEAVY SOCIAL DRINKING — 3 OR MORE PER OCCASION · 3 OR MORE TIMES PER WEEK

LOSS OF CONTROL PHASE—RATIONALIZATION BEGINS
- INCREASING FREQUENCY OF RELIEF DRINKING
- SNEAKING DRINKS
- DRINKING BOLSTERED WITH EXCUSES
- INCREASED MEMORY BLACKOUTS
- TREMORS AND EARLY MORNING DRINKS
- COMPLETE DISHONESTY
- LOSS OF OTHER INTERESTS
- EFFORTS TO CONTROL FAIL REPEATEDLY
- FAMILY AND FRIENDS AVOIDED
- LYING ABOUT DRINKING
- HIDING LIQUOR
- URGENCY OF FIRST DRINK
- INCREASING DEPENDENCE ON ALCOHOL
- FEELING OF GUILT ABOUT DRINKING
- UNABLE TO DISCUSS PROBLEMS
- PROMISES AND RESOLUTIONS FAIL REPEATEDLY
- GRANDIOSE AND AGGRESSIVE BEHAVIOR
- FAMILY, WORK AND MONEY PROBLEMS
- NEGLECT OF FOOD
- DRINKING ALONE - SECRETLY

HELP NEEDED

MIDDLE STAGES

LOSS OF JOB
- RADICAL DETERIORATION OF FAMILY RELATIONSHIPS
- PHYSICAL DETERIORATION
- MORAL DETERIORATION
- URGENT NEED FOR MORNING DRINK
- SANITARIUM OR HOSPITAL
- PERSISTENT REMORSE
- LOSS OF FAMILY
- DECREASE IN ALCOHOLIC TOLERANCE
- HOSPITAL/SANITARIUM
- UNABLE TO INITIATE ACTION
- OBSESSION WITH DRINKING
- COMPLETE ABANDONMENT
- "SQUIRREL CAGE" DRINKING AWAY HANGOVERS IN VICIOUS CIRCLES
- NOW THINKS: "RESPONSIBILITIES INTERFERE WITH MY DRINKING"
- UNREASONABLE RESENTMENTS
- "WATER WAGON" ATTEMPTS FAIL
- LOSS OF WILL POWER
- ONSET OF LENGTHY DRUNKS
- GEOGRAPHICAL ESCAPE ATTEMPTED
- IMPAIRED THINKING
- DRINKING WITH INFERIORS
- SUCCESSIVE LENGTHY DRUNKS
- UNABLE TO WORK
- INDEFINABLE FEARS
- ALL ALIBIS EXHAUSTED
- DESIRE FOR ALCOHOL PERSISTS
- EXPRESSES DESIRE FOR HELP
- DRYING OUT/MEDICAL HELP

ALCOHOLIC RECOVERY
OPERATING ENGINEERS
LOCAL UNION NO. 3
474 Valencia Street
San Francisco, CA 94103
415/431-1568

LATE STAGES

CALLS FOR HELP

CONTINUED DETERIORATION — INSANITY OR DEATH OR BOTH

RECOVERY
- LIFE GETS BETTER AND BETTER
- SOBRIETY CONTINUES
- FULL APPRECIATION OF SPIRITUAL VALUES
- BEGIN CONTENTMENT IN SOBRIETY
- INCREASED INTEREST ACTIVITY IN GROUP THERAPY
- APPRECIATION OF REAL VALUES
- REBIRTH OF IDEALS
- NEW INTERESTS DEVELOP
- NEW FUTURE FACED WITH DETERMINATION AND COURAGE
- DESIRE TO ESCAPE PASSES
- SOME SELF ESTEEM RETURNS
- FAMILY AND FRIENDS APPRECIATE EFFORTS
- BEGINNING OF REALISTIC THINKING
- REGULAR NOURISHMENT TAKEN
- DESIRE FOR GROUP THERAPY GROWS
- SPIRITUAL NEEDS EXAMINED
- CARE OF PERSONAL APPEARANCE/HYGIENE BEGINS
- STARTS TO REACT TO GROUP THERAPY
- ATTEMPTS TO STOP DRINKING
- LEARNS ALCOHOLISM IS A DISEASE
- MEETS RECOVERED, NORMAL, HAPPY ALCOHOLICS
- IMPROVED PEACE OF MIND
- CONFIDENCE OF EMPLOYER BEGINS
- RATIONALIZATIONS RECOGNIZED
- FIRST STEPS TOWARD ECONOMIC STABILITY
- INCREASE OF EMOTIONAL CONTROL
- ADJUSTMENT TO FAMILY NEEDS
- NEW CIRCLE OF STABLE FRIENDS
- NEW SET OF MORAL VALUES START UNFOLDING
- NATURAL REST AND SLEEP
- DIMINISHING FEARS AND ANXIETIES
- APPLICATION OF SPIRITUAL VALUES BEGINS
- BELIEF THAT A NEW LIFE IS POSSIBLE
- DAWN OF NEW HOPE
- ATTEMPTS AT HONEST THINKING
- TOLD ALCOHOLISM CAN BE ARRESTED

Dental Insurance: Goals, Plan Design, Choosing an Administrator and the Role of Dental Consultants

BY ROBERT J. LEAF, D.M.D.

Dr. Leaf is founder and president of American Dental Examiners, Inc. (ADE) of New York City, the largest dental consulting firm in the United States. ADE's four regional offices serve over 40 major insurance companies and corporations. Dr. Leaf graduated in 1965 from Cornell University, New York, with a major in economics, and received his D.M.D. in 1969 from Harvard University School of Dental Medicine. He is a member of the American Dental Association, First District Dental Society, New York State Dental Society and the Northeast Gnathological Society and has spoken at numerous educational conferences including the Midwest Claims Conference, Eastern Claims Conference, Detroit Claims Conference and Health Insurance Conference.

DENTAL INSURANCE today is a $4-$5 billion a year industry, which is growing at an extremely rapid rate. As president of American Dental Examiners (ADE), the largest dental insurance consulting firm in the United States, I have been intimately familiar with the development and growth of this industry.

In this article, I will attempt to provide an indepth insight into those features that are important to the purchasers of dental insurance, but before discussing the ideal features of a dental plan, it is important to agree on goals or objectives. Based on ADE's extensive experience, we have developed four basic objectives that we believe are desirable.

Goals

Maximize Benefits to All Employees

Unlike most insurance plans, which are designed to provide a large amount of dollars to very few people, dental insurance provides a relatively small amount of money to many people. In fact, it is not insurance at all in the true sense of the word. The administrator of the plan has a limited amount of dollars. He can use this money to provide very expensive and comprehensive dental care to a few people, or he can use this same money to provide basic dental care to all insured.

We believe that making benefit dollars available to all members to encourage them to obtain sound basic dental care is the method of choice. The plan design and administration should have a primary purpose of maximizing the usefulness of the benefits for all covered individuals. To provide an analogy, if one had 1,000 employees who were all covered for dental care, it would be preferable to pay $100 per employee for preventive and basic care rather than pay $10,000 for ten employees to have extensive crowns, bridges and periodontal treatment.

Encourage Prevention

The ideal dental plan encourages the patient to visit the dentist. Only 30-40% of the population of the United States visits a dentist regularly. The average person in the United States who doesn't have dental insurance has 0.4 cleanings a year. The average person insured under a dental care program that does not emphasize prevention has 0.8 cleanings a year. The average person insured under a preventive dental plan has 1.0 cleanings a year. If the insured can be encouraged to visit the dental office frequently, little problems can be fixed inexpensively, before they become big problems. This method provides more inexpensive care for more people.

Discourage Overtreatment

One of the problems of a dental insurance program is that it can encourage overtreatment. It is, therefore, extremely important that the plan be designed to reduce overtreatment. Expensive dentistry such as crowns, bridges and orthodontic care should never be paid for at more than 50% coinsurance. Some statistics may be interesting. If the cost of insuring crowns and bridges under a standard dental plan with 50% coinsurance equals *one*, the cost under an 80% coinsurance plan is *2.3*; the

Figure 1

PREVENTION	BASIC	MAJOR	ORTHODONTIA
Oral Exams X-rays Teeth Cleaning Fluoride Treatments Space Maintainers Lab Tests Emergency Treatment	Fillings Extractions Gum Treatments Repairs of Bridges Repairs of Dentures Root Canal Therapy Drugs Oral Surgery	Gold Inlays Crowns Bridges Dentures Gum Surgery Porcelain Crowns	Teeth Straightening

cost under a capitation plan is *0.3*. It is obvious that who pays for this type of dentistry determines how much will actually be done. Under a capitation plan, where the dentist is paying for them entirely, crowns and bridges are performed infrequently. Under an insured plan where the insurance company pays 80% of the cost, these same services become quite popular. Other types of overutilization are the frequent repetition of such items as scaling and root planing, and occlusal adjustments which cannot be proved to have been performed. Policy frequency limits protect against this type of overutilization.

Discourage Claim Abuse

The vast majority of people in the dental profession are extremely honest. However, when insurance companies have $100 bills in large baskets with nobody watching the basket, it becomes very tempting to reach in. A small percentage of dentists do reach into this insurance basket. If the basket were watched carefully, this percentage would be markedly reduced. The watchers are claims processors and, more importantly, dental consultants. The proper use of the dental consultant is critical to the overall success of a dental plan.

Goals Summary

In summary, these four basic objectives are essential to keep in mind when designing a dental plan, when choosing an administrator and when evaluating the program chosen:
- *Maximize benefits to all employees.* The plan should benefit the majority of employees, not a select few.
- *Encourage prevention.* Routine office visits are encouraged to promote dental health and to correct minor problems before they become major.
- *Discourage overtreatment.* Policy design and administration can deter the overtreatment of the insured.
- *Discourage claim abuse.* Proper administration will protect the insured from fraud and unnecessary treatment.

Dental Insurance Plan Design

The purchaser of a dental insurance program should be aware of the various features of plan design. This process is very complex, requiring decisionmaking for hundreds of variables. An understanding of each of these variables is important to the ability to design a plan properly. An overview of a basic dental plan follows. Special design features and some of the more important variables are then discussed. This analysis is followed by a brief discussion of the merits of a scheduled plan vs. a comprehensive plan.

Standard Plan Design

The standard plan design divides dental treatment into four categories. These categories are outlined in Figure 1. Most plans pay:
- 80-100% of the cost of preventive care
- 70-85% of the cost of basic care
- 50-80% of the cost of major care
- 50-60% of the cost of orthodontia.

The most popular plans pay 100% of preventive care, 80% of basic care, 50% of major care and 50% of orthodontia. Usually there is an annual deductible of $25 or $50 per covered individual. Those plans that stress prevention pay 100% of the prevention costs with no deductible applied to prevention benefits.

Many plans have a lifetime maximum of $500-

$1,000 applied to orthodontia care. In addition, most plans have an annual maximum of $1,000-$2,000. The maximum is the least effective cost saving device, and can be increased easily without a great effect on premium. Most plans pay for the least expensive professionally adequate treatment. In addition, many plans will not pay to replace a tooth extracted prior to the beginning of the insurance plan. Although this last feature is not consistent with good dental practice, it is a major cost saving feature, saving as much as 10-12% of the premium.

Special Design Features

The more sophisticated plans have a number of special design features that reduce overtreatment and claim abuse. These features include exclusions to eliminate certain types of very expensive dental treatment, frequency limits on many types of treatment and other limitations such as patient age, combinations of treatment and replacement of prostheses rules. In evaluating or designing a dental plan, these special design features must be analyzed and understood thoroughly. They are critical to the success of the plan.

Other Details

It is very important that as many details as possible be clearly spelled out in the contract. A list of some of the more essential items follows.

- Definition of date insured—to make sure participant is eligible for benefits for crowns, bridges, partial dentures, full dentures, root canal therapy, orthodontia
- Takeover provisions and their applicability to deductible, annual maximum, orthodontic maximum, continuity of coverage, work not completed while insured by previous carrier
- Extension of benefits
- Late enrollment penalty
- Coordination of benefits between medical and dental plans
- Internal limits
- List of covered expenses
- Predetermination of benefits
- Proof of claim
- Exclusions and limitations.

In evaluating a dental insurance plan, it is important to have a dental consultant involved who will explain how each of these features affects the insured. The dental consultant, if sufficiently knowledgeable, should be able to describe the effect of each plan design feature in simple terms. The critical elements here are that each of these topics is addressed, that each topic is clearly understood and that each topic then is addressed in the actual contract.

UCR vs. Scheduled

The great majority of dental plans written in the last three years have been usual and customary (UCR) plans. This phrase means that benefits are based on a dentist's usual fee for a service or on the fee customarily charged in a geographic area, whichever is less. Another type of plan is the scheduled plan. In a scheduled plan there is a listed allowance that will be paid for a particular procedure. The insured has a booklet that lists what is covered and how much will be paid. Theoretically, the dentist should not charge more than his usual fee even if the scheduled benefit is more. Practically speaking, the dentist will charge at least the scheduled amount listed regardless of his usual fee. Therefore, a rich schedule (one that approaches a UCR plan) is more expensive than a UCR plan. Since UCR plans are more popular with both employers and employees, and the benefits more closely reflect fees actually charged, they are preferable when the premium costs are comparable. Scheduled plans have a place only when they provide less than 60% of the benefits provided by a UCR plan.

How to Choose the Best Insurance Company Administrators for Your Plan

In selecting an administrator for your dental insurance plan, there are several factors that should be analyzed. These factors include the obvious ones such as experience, financial strength, size (ability to handle your group) and preexisting relationships. A discussion of factors that are not so obvious follows.

Philosophy

It is important to be sure that the philosophy of your company is the same as that of the insurance company. Some companies are extremely benevolent and paternalistic toward their employees. All they want is for benefits to be paid quickly, with a minimum of administrative expense and with no questions asked. The benefit expenses of such a plan will be fully absorbed by the rich, benevolent corporation. It is obvious that an insurance company with thorough and extensive cost containment programs would not be appreciated.

On the other hand, some companies are extremely concerned with cost containment and the total cost of their employee benefit programs. As the economy falters and as the cost of health care skyrockets, more and more corporations are be-

Figure 2

PERCENTAGE OF CLAIMS REVIEWED BY DENTISTS

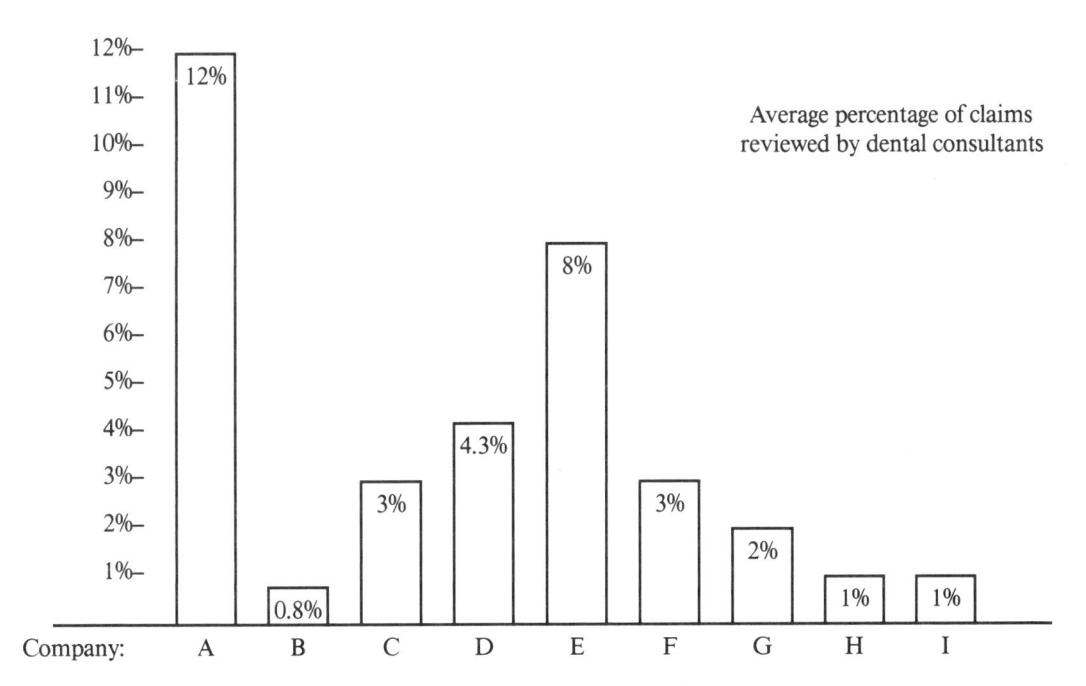

Average percentage of claims reviewed by dental consultants

Company:	A	B	C	D	E	F	G	H	I
%	12%	0.8%	3%	4.3%	8%	3%	2%	1%	1%

coming concerned with cost containment. It is equally obvious that these corporations are not going to appreciate an insurance company that makes little or no effort to contain costs.

The important factor is that the philosophies of the insurance company and the employer company coincide. We did a survey of several insurance companies to compare the percentage of dental claims being reviewed by dental consultants. The following companies were surveyed: Aetna, Connecticut General, Equitable, John Hancock, Massachusetts Mutual, Metropolitan, Pacific Mutual, Prudential and The Travelers. The results indicated huge disparities among these companies. Without indicating the companies specifically, the results are shown in Figure 2. We believe that the percentage of claims reviewed by dentists is one indicator of the concern that the insurance company has for a cost containment program.

Location of Branches

It is important that the insurance company has branch offices that are reasonably close to where your employees work. A regional office within 300-400 miles of your employees would meet this criterion. If all of your employees are in one location, then one claim office near that location would suffice. If your company is spread throughout the United States, then at least seven regional offices would be preferred.

Special Dental Claims Processors

Insurance companies handle dental claims in one of two ways. Some insurance companies have special dental claims processors. These processors have been trained to handle only dental claims. Many of them will have had previous training and experience working in dental offices as assistants or hygienists. Other insurance companies will use general purpose claims processors who handle both medical and dental claims. These general purpose processors tend to have a much better understanding of medical claims than of dental claims. It is our opinion that those corporations that are concerned about how their benefit dollars are being spent would be better off with well-trained dental-only processors handling their dental claims.

Please note that the use of dentists or dental consultants to review a high level of claims (7-10%) will offset the lack of expertise when using general claims processors. However, using a lay dental claims specialist will not be sufficient to offset the lack of dental consultant review.

Figure 3

PERCENT OF CLAIMS REVIEWED BY DENTAL CONSULTANTS BY INSURANCE COMPANY REGIONAL BRANCH

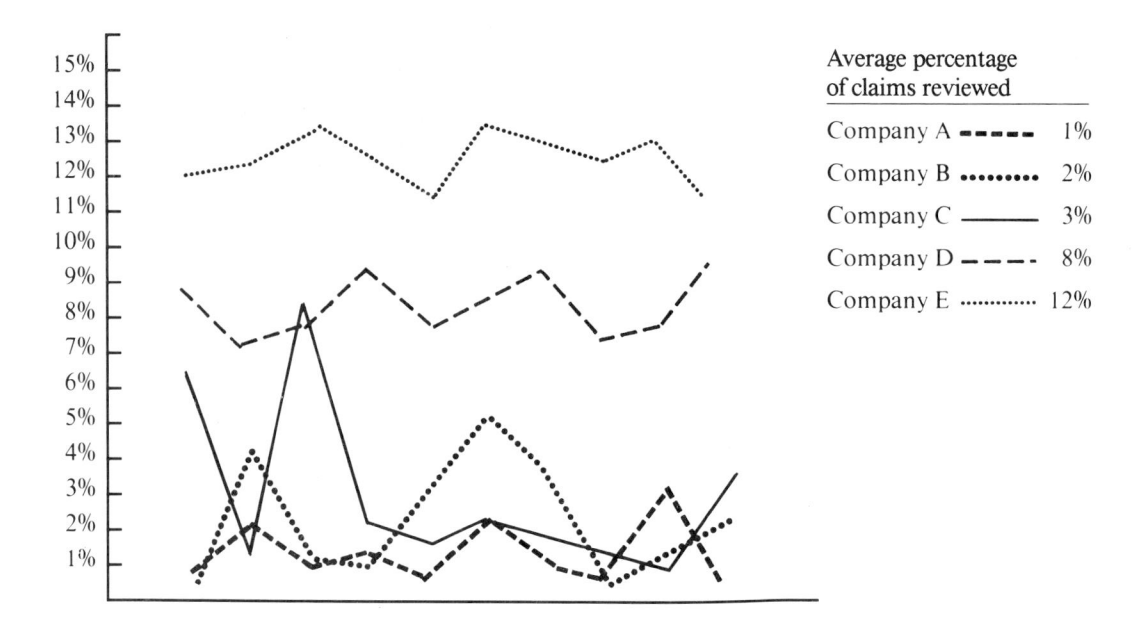

Average percentage of claims reviewed	
Company A ▬▬▬▬	1%
Company B ●●●●●●●●	2%
Company C ————	3%
Company D ─ ─ ─ ─	8%
Company E ············	12%

Consistency

If your corporation is nationwide, it is very important that the regional claim offices handle your account in a consistent manner. Some insurance companies make great efforts at quality control and consistency, whereas others seem not at all concerned. We have seen some insurance companies in which every claim office makes its own decisions on administrative practices and some insurance companies whose branches are carefully monitored by the home office. One measure of consistency is the use of dental consultants. Using statistics for ten branches each of five major insurance companies, Figure 3 shows that there are a huge disparity in use of dental consultants for some companies and a consistency for others.

Obviously, if your claims are paid by more than one branch of the insurance company, consistency is important. One solution is to have all of your claims paid by one branch. This practice will improve the consistency significantly for those companies experiencing problems in this area, but will have the negative impact of losing close geographical proximity of claim offices to all of your employees.

Computer System

The ideal handling of dental claims should be through the use of a computer system. Most large insurance companies are computerized. The more sophisticated systems will subject the claims to a series of automatic edits. The very sophisticated system will have many hundreds of these edits for dental claims. We have designed a system used by some insurance companies that has 3,400 edits and is very advanced. These edits permit a precise selection of claims for dental consultant review as well as an automatic rejection of most claim abuses.

Turnaround Time

How long does it take from the day the insurance company receives a claim until some action is taken? (We define "action" as a request for more information, approval or denial of a claim.) How long does it take once all information is received for the claim to be approved or denied? You should receive reports providing this type of information on a regular basis. You have the right to expect five days or less average turnaround time for the standard claims, and no more than two to three weeks for nonstandard claims, once all the information is received.

UCR Definitions

If your plan is a UCR plan, be sure to determine how the UCR is calculated. Some companies use the 50th percentile, others use the 90th (which is most common). This definition makes an enormous difference in the cost of the program and the amount of benefits paid. A recent study done in Washington indicated a difference of 800% between the lowest UCR and the highest UCR for the same procedure in the same geographic area. Be sure that the insurance company's definition corresponds to your company's policy.

Training Program

It is important that claims processors be well-trained. Determine whether the insurance company has a well-thought-out and thorough training program for the claims processors that will teach them dental terminology, what is included in paying for each procedure and how to protect against claim abuses. This training is particularly important for those companies with general claims processors and not dental-only processors.

Courtesy

There are several types of services that indicate that the insurance company really cares. We call them courtesies; however, they are important to the smooth administration of a dental insurance plan. Included in this category is the tone of all correspondence. If the correspondence is cold and bureaucratic, it conveys one image. If, on the other hand, the insurance company's approach is polite and not unnecessarily authoritative, it creates a completely different atmosphere. Among the items to look for are:

Delay Letters

Whenever a claim will be delayed, either because additional information is required or because the claim will be professionally reviewed, it is polite to write a brief note to the policyholder. This note can explain that the claim will be delayed as a result of _____, but everything possible is being done to expedite the claim. As soon as the missing information is received, the claim will be processed. This type of note lets the policyholder know that the insurance company normally gets claims out very quickly and is concerned about them.

UCR Letters

Whenever a benefit determination is made that will reduce the amount paid because the dentist's charges exceed UCR, a very carefully written letter should be issued to the dentist *and* the insured. Many insurance companies write to the patient stating that benefits are reduced because the dentist's treatment is not usual or customary; others go even further, implying that the dentist is overcharging his patients. This type of correspondence disrupts the dentist-patient relationship and creates real antagonism on the part of the dentist toward the insurance company. The same information can be provided in a much more tactful letter, which smoothes rather than ruffles feathers. For example, "We have compared your fees with our customary fee data and find that some of the fees on this claim are in excess of the customary fees for your area." Again, this approach is indicative of the concern that the insurance company has for its policyholders.

Special Telephone Personnel

Some insurance companies have special personnel just to answer policyholders' questions. These well-trained processors will skillfully and patiently answer any questions concerning a claim. These processors are trained in public relations as well as dental claims processing.

Dentist-to-Dentist Discussions

Some insurance companies encourage their dental consultants to discuss the claim review directly with the providing dentist. The providing dentist will thus have an opportunity to discuss his treatment with a dentist, a peer, not with a lay claims processor. This tactic also markedly improves rapport between dentist and insurance company.

Open Reconsiderations

The best of the dental consultants will have a significant error rate (1½-4%) in reviewing claims. The reason for this error rate is inadequate information. Frequent seeking of additional information will markedly reduce this error rate, but not eliminate it. The insurance company should, therefore, encourage honest reconsiderations of the claims when provided additional information.

Visit

Careful attention to all of the previously mentioned features does not substitute for an actual visit to a claim office. Select the office yourself. Be sure that this office will be handling some of your claims. Spend some time speaking to actual processors. Do they seem intelligent and knowledgeable? Is the office well-organized? Is there a large backlog of claims? It is amazing what can be learned in a one hour visit to a claim office.

Comparison

Finally, you should add up all of the advantages of each company and compare them with your corporate philosophy. No company will be perfect. The one that meets most of your objectives is the one you should choose.

How Do Dental Consultants Affect Your Dental Insurance Program?

A dental consultant is a licensed dentist who reviews dental claims from a professional viewpoint and recommends to the insurance company which claims should be paid and which ones are not covered. A preselected sample of claims is sent to the consultant for review. These claims are monitored to determine the appropriateness of care, the quality of care, the possibility of fraud and contractual liability. Professional claim review should not be primarily concerned with cost containment; however, its direct result can be a substantial savings (10-20% of premium) to the insurance company and, therefore, to the purchasers of dental insurance programs. The primary goal of the dental consultant should be to improve the quality of care and reduce overtreatment of patients.

Choices in Dental Consultants

Insurance companies have four basic choices in selecting a dental consultant.

- *Full-Time In-House Consultants:* Dentists who have given up their dental practices to work for the insurance company on a full-time basis as employees. They review the claims at the insurance company's claim office and, hopefully, will be able to provide on-site training of the claims processors.
- *Part-Time In-House Consultants:* Basically the same as the full-time consultants, except that they continue to practice dentistry. We believe that this distinction is important. By remaining in dental practice, the consultant is continually reminded of all of the problems of the dental practitioner.
- *Part-Time Independent Consultants:* Dentists who review claims on a part-time basis in their own dental offices. They typically do not provide on-site training for the claims processors. Since they are called on to review a very small percentage of claims, they frequently have insufficient claim review training and experience to be excellent dental consultants.
- *Outside Professional Review Boards:* Two nationwide independent professional review boards review dental claims for insurance companies. Each of these boards has regional panels of dental consultants. Among the advantages of these panels are: The dental consultants receive extensive training; they are practicing dentists and, therefore, in touch with the dental community; and they are monitored for consistency of review decisions. Furthermore, these panels provide a nationwide network that complements the regional claim office structure of most insurance companies.

Selecting Claims for Professional Review

The usefulness of dental consultants is directly affected by the selection of claims for review. The better the selection process, the greater the potential for the dental consultant to have a positive influence. Claims can be selected by very broad screening criteria, such as all claims over $1,000, or by a long list of very specific criteria. An example of an item on such a list would be "all claims that have a new crown on a front tooth that doesn't require root canal or post and core." It is our experience that using a dollar amount as a screening criterion is not very effective, since many claims get by without review that should be reviewed. The very detailed list is excellent if the computer is used to select claims. However, even the best of dental claims processors will lose effectiveness with a complicated list.

In the absence of a sophisticated computer system, we suggest a simple list of eight to ten "screens" or reasons for selecting a claim for review. It is essential that the claims processors do not have discretion in employing these screens. When given the discretion, the claims processor, who is judged primarily on productivity, will not select a claim for review.

Once the screens are chosen, there must be a method for determining their economic effectiveness. One should not want to pay more for professional review than the cost savings produced. After the screens are used for several months, they can be adjusted to obtain a desired ratio. (For example, let's say that the desired ratio is a savings of six times the cost of reviewing claims for crowns. The initial screen may be "all claims with two or more crowns." If, on the other hand, the savings is two times cost, we may decrease the screen to "all claims with three or more crowns.") The important feature is the monitoring of the effectiveness of each screen, with adjustments made as indicated.

Getting Complete Information

Before a consultant can review a claim properly, he must have a great deal of information. He must have a working knowledge of the dental contract being interpreted as well as an understanding of the insurance company's administrative practices. Ideally, large purchasers of dental insurance will be consulted in setting up these administrative guidelines.

In addition, he must have a copy of the claim and the proper x-rays. Frequently, insufficient x-rays are sent, or x-rays are sent that were taken after the work was started. It is essential for the consultant to have preaccident or pre-operative x-rays. In the absence of x-rays, a complete, detailed written report and models will sometimes suffice.

Other information that the consultant may need is pathological reports, cephalometric x-rays and study models. Frequently, additional information must be requested prior to determining benefits. Examples of this additional information are:
- The dates when teeth were extracted
- The ages of previous crowns, dentures and fixed bridges
- The reason for replacement of crowns or bridges
- Name and address of prior dentist who extracted teeth
- Reason denture or bridge cannot be repaired
- Clarification of dates of service
- Exact date work was started
- Exact date work was completed.

In writing for this type of information, the tone of the letter is very important. It should be polite and nonthreatening, and should clearly state that such information is not requested routinely.

All of the necessary information must be obtained prior to making a benefit determination. Frequently, one piece of information will be overlooked that would completely change the benefit determination. The system should be such that a claim cannot be paid until all of the necessary information is received.

Qualifications of Dental Consultants

A dental consultant should have a minimum of ten years in practice. Also, he should not be in his retirement years. He should be active in his dental practice and keep up with all of the newest technological improvements in dentistry. Ideally, he should have had some teaching experience at a major dental school. Most important, he should be well-respected by his peers and known for his honesty and integrity. The ability to handle difficult situations with great tact is also helpful.

Once a dental consultant with all of these qualifications is chosen, he must go through a formal training program. This program must be designed to teach the consultant the fair and correct method of claim review. It is rare to find a consultant who is capable of handling claims properly without either years of consulting experience or a formal training program.

Using the Consultant

For a consultant to be effective, he must review 3-10% of total dental claims. The richer the plan, the higher the percentage of claims requiring review; the more carefully designed the plan, the higher the percentage of claims requiring review. The analysis of nine large insurance companies in Figure 2 indicates a wide variation in the overall use of dental consultants. It is obvious that a consultant who reviews only 1% of the claims will have less ability to affect benefit determination than a consultant who reviews 10% of the claims.

Consistency of Consultant Review

The consultant review program must be monitored continually for consistency. It is imperative that well-qualified senior dental consultants monitor the dental consultants to assure that all are maintaining a consistent standard. It is equally important that a comprehensive dental consultant manual be distributed to all consultants reviewing claims for the same company. An attempt must be made to avoid approval of a claim by one consultant and denial of an identical claim by a second consultant. Extremely liberal and conservative consultants should not be retained by the same company without changing their prior methods. It is also important that consultants meet on a regular basis to exchange ideas. The most difficult idea to inculcate in a dental consultant is never to impose one's personal views on the dental profession. All claims should be judged within the context of the contract and whether the treatment has a reasonable chance of success, not "I wouldn't do it that way."

Reports

Each claim that is professionally reviewed should be evaluated as to the effect of the professional review. A true cost containment program is only as effective as can be demonstrated clearly.

The evaluation should include a determination of the savings resulting from the review. "Savings" is defined as the amount of benefit that would be payable without a dental consultant minus the amount payable after the dental consultant's review. Regular reports should be available to the chief dental consultant to determine consistency of reviews. These reports should also be provided to the insurance company and to the purchasers of dental insurance programs to clearly demonstrate an effective cost containment program. These reports should not be used to stimulate dental consultants to recommend reduction of dental benefits where reductions are not warranted.

Ideal Professional Review Mechanism

Following is a list with brief descriptions of the ideal qualifications of a dental consultant program that would best serve the insurance company, dental community, insureds and purchasing company in a fair and objective way.

- *Independence:* The dental consultant should be as independent as possible. Therefore, hopefully, he will be as free as possible from outside influence and be in a position to make as objective a decision as possible.
- *Direct Communication:* The dental consultant must be encouraged to communicate directly with provider dentists. This free and open communication will provide the consultant with more information and permit a more accurate review determination. In addition, the provider dentist has a peer with whom he can communicate. This dentist-to-dentist relationship is helpful in fostering good will between the consulting dentist and the provider dentist.
- *Availability to Processors:* The dental consultant must be continuously available to the claims processors to answer their questions. The availability of the dental consultant will markedly improve the ability of the dental claims processors to correctly handle the claims that are not normally sent to a consultant.
- *All Specialties:* All claims submitted by specialists should be reviewed by specialists in the same discipline. It is important to have periodontists reviewing periodontal claims and orthodontists reviewing orthodontic claims. In this way, a fairer and more accurate benefit determination is accomplished.
- *Reconsideration by Other Consultants:* All consultants should have a backup consultant who can reconsider disputed claims. This feature permits a fair reconsideration by another impartial consultant. In addition, the backup procedure permits a group discussion of the more difficult claims.
- *Consultant Guide Manual:* All consultants must have a comprehensive guide manual. This manual will encourage consistency of reviews across the country. It will also permit the consultant to have his reviews more accurately reflect the administration of the insurance company and the philosophy of the employer.
- *Reasonable Consulting Fees:* The consultant must not be too expensive. If too expensive, the consultant's services will not be used sufficiently.
- *Well-Respected:* The consultant must be well-respected by his peers and by organized dentistry. He is in a position of tremendous responsibility and his past experience and background must be commensurate with this responsibility.
- *Practicing Dentist:* The consultant must be a practicing dentist so that he is continually reminded of the problems of the practicing dentist. It is very easy for a consultant to become jaded. This situation must be avoided.

Summary

When you are choosing a dental plan, each of the four areas discussed in this paper must be carefully considered, for they are integrally related. Through a careful analysis of these issues, a proper dental plan can be selected by the employer.

Prepaid Legal Plans: Structure and Implementation

BY WILLIAM M. KIRSCHNER

THE PURPOSE OF this article is to present a pragmatic approach to the structuring and implementation of a legal service plan—advising you, the trustee, on how to comply with the underlying intent of ERISA that a benefit promised be a benefit delivered. The benefit being promised is quality legal services at a reasonable cost. Although the trustees are ultimately responsible for taking all actions necessary, appropriate and prudent to guarantee that quality legal services are delivered at a reasonable cost, and for protecting the financial integrity of the fund, practicality dictates that the day-to-day responsibility rests with the administrator and the providers.

To meet these responsibilities, to structure a plan that will satisfy the obligations mandated by ERISA and to comply with the provisions of the Internal Revenue Code, the initial step to be taken by the prudent fiduciary will be to review alternative methods of administration and delivery of services. First, however, some background in reference to the benefit itself will be helpful.

Benefit Classification

All legal plans provide benefits classified as either preventive law benefits or as major legal benefits.

Preventive Law Benefits

These benefits are designed to prevent more complex legal problems and potential litigation by advising a client of rights and obligations before he or she has a problem. They include advice and consultation (either in person or by telephone), document review, document preparation and the preparation of wills and trusts.

Preventive law benefits are the essence of every legal plan. It is most unlikely that employees have attorneys to whom they may turn to review a simple document, such as a lease or a bank loan statement, or to whom they may turn for consultation on an everyday problem regarding a consumer or other matter that may be of great concern to them. A Bar Association study revealed that 83% of Americans don't use lawyers because they don't know one who is available to handle their needs. By making an attorney available for advice and consultation, a more serious legal problem may be prevented from developing, which might cause greater concern to the client at a later date and potentially reduce his or her effectiveness on the job. As we will also see later, consultation at an early stage may well save the fund extensive legal costs later; thus, the preventive law benefits may well be the most effective element of cost control.

Mr. Kirschner is a senior member of the New York lawfirm of Burger, Kramer, Feldman & Kirschner, P.C., which serves as general counsel to Nationwide Legal Services, Inc. He is directly responsible for the administration and provision of legal services presently being provided to members of groups including the New York State United Teachers, Public Employees Federation, depositors of Citibank, the Grumman Corporation and others. He is also director of legal services for the State of New York for the Retail Clerks Union Local 1262. Mr. Kirschner earned a B.A. at University College, New York University and a J.D. degree at Brooklyn Law School. Prior to entering private practice, he served with the Manhattan District of the Internal Revenue Service. He is admitted to the practice of law before the Supreme Court of the State of New York, the United States District Court for the Southern District of New York, District of Columbia Court of Appeals and the Supreme Court of the United States of America. Mr. Kirschner serves as a frequent lecturer and has authored an audiocassette, reproduced and disseminated by the New York State Bar Association, entitled "Settlement and Distribution—Estate Probate and Administration for Estates Up to $500,000."

Major Legal Benefits

The major legal benefits to which I refer consist of those benefits for which it is more likely that employees will realize they should seek legal advice. These benefits, for example, include representation in the purchase and sale of a principal residence or representation in some type of family dispute, be it separation, divorce, custody, etc. They are more expensive to provide than the preventive law benefits, but are of equal importance in implementing a comprehensive legal plan. Other major legal benefits are landlord/tenant problems, adoptions, debtor counseling, bankruptcy counseling, traffic offenses, litigation matters and probate matters, as well as criminal matters.

Although a comprehensive legal plan ideally will include both preventive law benefits and major legal benefits, the actual decision concerning which benefits should be included in a plan usually will be determined by the extent of funding available.

Delivery of Legal Services

In addition to determining the level of benefits, the trustees are charged with the responsibility of prudently determining the method of delivery of those services. A large area of concern for the prudent fiduciary should be the determination of how that promised benefit—quality legal services at reasonable cost—shall be delivered and by whom it shall be delivered. One of the most sensitive areas of fiduciary responsibility, and potential criticism, is the choice of the provider of the service. A fiduciary is obliged to avoid even the slightest appearance of impropriety and, as Marvin P. Lazarus, resident counsel for Martin E. Segal Company, stated:

> Perhaps the person the Trustees have in mind is the employer's attorney, a Fund counsel, or counsel to the Union. What is more natural, more human, than to have the legal services under the plan delivered by lawyers whom you trust, with whom you are familiar? But a Trustee whose personal liability is now involved must take into consideration that plans are established for the exclusive benefits of participants, not for the benefit of insurance agents, relatives, or friends.

and the trustee "... should remain cognizant of the fact that good faith, friendship and trust are not defenses under the fiduciary section of ERISA."

Delivery Methods

In determining the method of delivery of legal services, there are various alternatives available. The fund could implement a staff plan, whereby attorneys are hired by the fund and operate one or more offices, which in effect constitute a fund lawfirm. These staff attorneys would provide the preventive and major legal benefits and would be paid salaries by the fund. In the event that services were required to be provided in geographical areas that were not advantageous for the staff attorneys to handle, or in highly specialized fields of law not within the expertise of the staff, they could be provided by outside attorneys who would be paid by the fund. It is believed, at this point, that the comprehensive prepaid legal service plan being structured—and soon to be implemented—pursuant to the United Auto Workers contract, will follow this format and will service approximately 500,000 members through staff and outside attorneys.

Most plans implemented around the country have fallen into categories familiarly classified as open panel, closed panel or modified open panel.

Many people have various definitions that they attribute to each of these classifications, and the title doesn't always fit the description of the type of panel. Be that as it may, a true open panel will generally allow all attorneys who choose to participate in a plan to do so, whereas a closed panel generally consists of a limited number of attorneys chosen by the fund. The insurance company-sponsored plans generally favor the true open panel (with several state laws requiring same), whereas most of the union self-insured plans have favored the closed panel.

In one Retail Clerks' closed panel plan, the trustees designated a lead lawfirm. That lawfirm subcontracted with other lawfirms in key geographical areas of that state to provide the services, but the ultimate responsibility for delivery of services remained with the lead lawfirm.

In what I refer to as a modified open panel, the attorneys participating are generally selected either by the administrator or director of delivery of services of the plan or by the fund's trustees. The attorneys must agree to abide by the fee schedule set up by the plan and, of course, to meet the requirements such as malpractice insurance coverage, etc., designated by the fund. In most modified open panel situations, the supervision of the plan is handled by the lead lawfirm. Referrals are made to the panel participants on the basis of geographical considerations as well as relevant expertise; some panels consist of literally hundreds of attorneys with expertise in all areas of law. There are, of course, various combinations of the staff and panel programs that can be implemented, and it would not be surprising to see unique combinations of all of these methods tried by various groups within the next several years.

Plan Administration

Of great importance in structuring and implementing a legal service plan is a determination of the administration method to be used. There are various methods of administration available, including direct responsibility remaining with the trustees themselves. However, it is most likely that the trustees will delegate this responsibility and retain a professional administrator. The administrator could be a staff administrator hired and paid by the fund, such as an administrator who presently is administering other benefits (e.g., medical, dental and optical) as was done in the Retail Clerks' plan. Other plans have chosen to retain supervising attorneys or professional organizations that specialize in administering legal service plans.

To assist you in determining the method of administration most appropriate for your plan, you should review the specific responsibilities involved in administration. The administrator will be charged with the overall responsibility of making sure that the plan operates in a prudent fashion, delivering those promised benefits to the beneficiaries at reasonable cost. The specific responsibilities of administration include the collection of assets, the verification of eligibility, compliance with filing requirements, paying the expenses of administration, disseminating information about the plan to the membership, payment of the attorneys, compiling and maintaining statistical data and encouraging proper utilization. These general responsibilities of administration are self-explanatory, but the more technical and professionalized responsibilities relating to cost and quality control require detailed amplification—beginning with the selection of the administrator.

Selection of Administrator

A prudent trustee will screen potential administrative candidates carefully to ascertain their methods of ensuring quality and protecting the financial integrity of the fund.

The administrative commitment to quality must commence with the initial structuring of the legal service plan. The administrative person or organization must possess the expertise to analyze the demographics, sociographics and psychographics of a particular group to determine which benefits are most needed by the members of that group and how many attorneys located in which geographical areas and with which areas of expertise should be retained to render the services.

For example, if most of the members are young and single, there is less need for estate planning services than there would be in a group whose members are older. Likewise, a group whose members are predominantly in their mid-30s probably requires more family-related services (matrimonials, adoptions, custody and representation in real estate matters). A careful analysis is therefore needed before starting the plan. Even after the plan has been started, analysis will help in using the data that should be collected during the early operation of the plan—to make sure that you are meeting the needs of the members and to determine whether benefits should be modified.

Selection and Supervision of Attorneys

The choice and training of the attorneys who will be providing the services are major quality control responsibilities of both the administrator and the trustees.

It is imperative to recognize that providing services to large groups of people is a specialty in itself and requires a very different set of qualifications than do other specialized areas of law. For example, an attorney employed in a large Wall Street lawfirm, who has spent the first eight years of his career devoting 95% of his time to working on one particular antitrust case, is no more qualified to render advice about recent changes in the divorce laws than is the matrimonial specialist qualified to advise Wall Street clientele in reference to antitrust law. It is thus important to select attorneys who have the proper expertise and ability to render quality services in what may be referred to as the people-oriented areas of the law. They must also have the ability to function with a high volume practice.

The attorney must be extremely sensitive to the emotional and psychological needs of a client with even the slightest of problems—with a utility bill for example—as oftentimes these are major concerns that can detract from a member's productivity. If a member is unable to perform at maximum efficiency, it is obviously to the detriment of his or her employer. It is that employer who would like to see this plan, for which he is footing the bill, benefit him in terms of increased productivity. The trustees should screen potential providers carefully to ensure that they have the proper backgrounds, levels of experience, conscientiousness and devotion to this specialized area of practice. It should not be merely a sideline that helps to meet overhead.

It is critical that, when dealing with a volume of this nature and with situations that may be extremely impersonal by virtue of extensive telephone communications, attorneys be provided with and trained in using management-oriented systems. These procedures should guarantee that no piece of paper gets lost, no record gets lost, no client fails to have a telephone call returned and no situation arises in which something that is supposed to be done by a certain time is not done by that time. Every client must be notified and kept apprised of the progress of his case. The trustees should satisfy themselves that "foolproof" procedures have been implemented to ensure delivery of that promised benefit—quality legal services at reasonable cost.

Statistical Data

Foolproof procedures also must be implemented to collect appropriate data.

Under ERISA, the fund is required to maintain records in a businesslike manner. Trustees are required to report on their plan's activities, using an annual report Form 5500, for example—a plan description plus description of major changes in benefits and termination reports. Records must be maintained on such items as participant enrollment, benefits, contributions and claims. Records must also be kept concerning the approval or denial of claims under the terms of the plan.

Plans should also be making decisions about future benefits, coverage, size of staff and evaluations of the adequacy of the services. To accomplish these things, the identification of patterns and trends in numbers and types of clients and problems is essential.

There are many ways of presenting what's commonly referred to as utilization rates. These rates are, of course, related not only to quality control but also directly to cost control.

The gross utilization rate would be the number of clients divided by the number of members. For example, if 300 clients called and the membership were 1,000, then the utilization rate would be 30%.

The adjusted utilization rate would be the number of matters divided by the number of members, which would reflect the fact that one particular client might call with several matters. Thus, the adjusted utilization rate would be higher than the gross utilization rate.

Perhaps the most reflective statistic is the time utilization rate, that is, the number of hours of services expended divided by the number of members. This statistic is the one that will always provide you with an accurate picture of the amount of time spent delivering legal services to the membership. It seems to me that it's just as important to know how many hours have been expended to service those 1,000 members as it is to know how many members call. For example, if 300 members use the plan, in terms of computing a cost for the plan it is crucial to know that 250 members called merely for advice on the telephone, with an average call duration of eight minutes, and the other 50 called for matrimonial services, which required an average of 20 hours per member.

My point here is that a major area of both cost and quality control is keeping accurate statistics on the utilization by the members and breaking down that utilization into the exact areas of law and geographic areas in which the services were provided.

Grievance Procedure

Every legal service plan is required to have a grievance procedure, which should address itself to problems of coverage (that is, whether a particular problem is one for which the plan provides a benefit) as well as to complaints or disputes over the quality of the service provided. Fee disputes can arise in group and prepaid plans where the fee is, for example, for excess coverage provided for a matrimonial benefit. This subject should be of concern to the administrator, regardless of whether the fees are subject to reimbursement by the plan. ERISA establishes certain standards for determining whether claims are to be paid and for reviewing the appeals of denied claims, but a detailed discussion of these standards is beyond the scope of this paper.

Cost Control

Cost control is a direct responsibility of both the trustees and the administrator of the plan. It is an essential ingredient of quality and at the same time is essential to ensure the financial integrity of the fund.

Payment of Attorneys

One of the most sensitive areas of fiduciary responsibility relates to the amount and method of payment for legal services provided by the plan. Basically, two methods of payment for legal services have developed: first, the annual retainer where the contributions are transferred from the fund directly to the providers; second, what is commonly known as fee-for-service, where an attorney will be paid a specified sum after providing the service.

As you can readily understand, the attorneys may be undertaking some degree of risk in gearing themselves up to provide the benefits. For example, if the plan has a closed panel and a lawfirm is to provide services to 10,000 members, then this firm will obviously have startup costs for readying itself to render the service. This problem, however, does not exist in the modified or open panels, in which each firm will be responsible for providing services to a smaller number of members.

In any event, if an annual retainer is paid, a problem arises for the fiduciary. The fiduciaries have, in fact, delivered a sum of money to attorneys who have yet to provide a service. The fiduciaries do not know with any degree of certainty the extent of the services that will be provided in that particular year and have no way of knowing whether the attorneys will make $50 per hour, $100 per hour or perhaps substantially more than that. Even if the fiduciaries knew with some degree of certainty the extent of services that will be rendered, there is a significant problem in that the fiduciary has sanctioned a system whereby the less service the provider renders, the more profit he makes.

Under fee-for-service remuneration, no such problem exists. A provider only gets paid for services actually rendered.

There are various types of fee-for-service schedules. The attorneys could be paid a set fee for a particular service, for example, $750 for a matrimonial, $600 for representation in a real estate matter or $100 for preparation of a will. Whatever the number might be, it would be a set fee. Some plans have provided for a percentage discount from the "usual and customary rate" (whatever that means), whereas others have provided for payment to be made to the attorneys on an hourly rate. Under still other plans, the attorneys are paid a minimum fee for specific services, but, in the event that the providing of those services should require more than a designated number of hours, they are paid on an hourly basis in addition to the minimum fee.

In the plans I prefer, attorneys are paid for services actually rendered at prescribed hourly rates, through a maximum fee schedule. By placing a maximum fee in the plan, you are, of course, helping to ensure the financial integrity of the plan. You are also providing a degree of protection for those who claim (with some justification) that attorneys, despite all of their intellectual prowess, occasionally encounter difficulty with the simple mathematics involved in counting hours.

There may well be situations where it is entirely justified for the attorneys to receive a combination of a retainer to help them meet their startup costs plus fee-for-service remuneration. I caution you, however, to be careful that the fiduciaries are protected from liability in these situations.

Reducing Financial Risk

There are various other measures that may be taken to ensure the financial integrity of the fund. You could merely purchase an insured plan. There are several major carriers who are now either involved in or are preparing to be involved in the group legal field, each having varying degrees of commitment to responsibility for quality.

The self-insured plans have various methods available to them to protect their financial integrity. The initial step will be to determine the level of eligibility. For example, will the plan cover just full-time employees, or will it also cover part-time employees, retirees and dependents of plan members? In one plan, we initially covered only full-time employees, and expanded to cover part timers, dependents and retirees after an appropriate reserve had been created.

Another method available to the trustees to control costs is to limit the utilization per member in each year of the plan. For example, you could limit a member to one or two cases per year, or perhaps only a specified number of hours per year or per matter could be expended on behalf of that member. In one plan we initially limited matrimonials to ten hours of legal services. After the ten hours, arrangements had to be made for the member to pay for future services. After about one year of the plan's operation, the reserve had grown and we were able to expand this limit to 20 hours. We have maintained this 20 hour limit in the plan, despite the fact that the reserve is now adequate to expand it. One reason we have done so is that if a fund is responsible for the entire legal fee, it is entirely possible that the parties will choose to litigate beyond that reasonable time when a settlement should be reached.

In structuring legal plans, it is not uncommon for the attorneys to share in the financial risk. By this I mean that various plans have developed unique formulas whereby if utilization is high and the fund is unable to afford it, the risk of providing the services will be borne by the attorneys. For example, one of the insurance carriers has a somewhat complex formula whereby a portion of the fund is set aside and is shared by all attorneys in proportion to the amount of services that each has rendered over the year. In the event that this portion of the fund is not sufficient to compensate the attorneys adequately for the services rendered, then they, in effect, share the loss in percentage to the amount of services they've rendered.

A rather unique method of sharing the risk with the attorneys was implemented by the Retail Clerks Union, where the attorneys are paid on an hourly basis. However, this hourly rate has a cap on it, which is a percentage of the fund. In effect, the plan makes 90% of the annual contributions to the fund available for the payment of attorneys fees. In the event that the billing to the fund at the hourly rate exceeds 90% of the fund, then the attorneys will receive a lower hourly rate so that the fund will not be depleted. In the four years of experience with the plan, this structure has not yet been a problem from the provider's standpoint. In a plan with adequate funding and good structuring of benefits and eligibility, there is probably minimal risk to the attorneys and maximum protection to the fund.

Telephone Advice and Consultation

The final cost control item to review is the use of the telephone. Many plans, both insured and uninsured, provide for preventive law benefits to be delivered by unlimited telephone advice and consultation. National surveys have shown that the first benefit every consumer group wants is advice and the knowledge that competent legal representation is merely a phone call away. The National Resource Center for Consumers of Legal Services has reported that clients always regard advice as the primary benefit, with representation in specific matters secondary.

The center further reports that the fastest growing type of legal service plan is the telephone advice and consultation plan, which permits a member to call a central number and speak with an attorney immediately. To properly use this benefit, members should be encouraged to call whenever they have a problem. Carefully trained attorneys should be assigned to handle these telephone calls, as early use of this telephone system may solve a problem or prevent one from developing. If an attorney can resolve the problem by merely rendering advice or sending a third party a letter, he will do so.

National statistics indicate that 70-80% of all calls result in the problem being resolved without the member having to visit the attorneys office. The member's time is saved in that he doesn't have to visit an attorneys office and possibly lose time from work, and the fund saves dollars in that telephone advice and consultation are obviously less expensive than are office visits. If the matter is more complex, it will be assigned to an attorney for appropriate disposition, including personal consultation with the client.

Types of Plans

With the distinction between preventive legal benefits and major legal benefits and emphasis on the fiduciary's responsibilities for cost and quality control in mind, I will outline some of the alternative prepaid legal service plans presently available. Legal service plans are similar to medical plans in that money is paid, by or on behalf of a subscriber, into a fund of money in advance of the providing of the service, on the assumption that the service will be needed in the future. There are many types of prepaid legal plans developing; all of them can be classified as either comprehensive prepaid plans or access plans.

Comprehensive Prepaid Plans

These plans provide a wide variety of preventive law and major legal benefits, with the fund being responsible for the payment of all legal and administrative fees. Under this type of plan, the member will only be responsible for some payment if a matter has been specifically excluded or if coverage has been specifically limited. For example, many plans exclude personal injury matters and place a limit on the number of hours of representation allowed for contested matrimonial actions. However, even if a matter is excluded from the plan, it is within the prerogative of the trustees to provide a mechanism whereby members may receive a discount in the amount of the fee for which they will be responsible.

Access Plans

If adequate funding for a comprehensive prepaid plan is not available, you may wish to structure what is commonly called an access plan. In an access plan (100%), the fund will pay an enrollment fee for each member. This fee will be used to pay for the cost of administrative services and the cost of providing preventive law benefits. The major legal benefits generally will be provided at a discounted fee, with the member being responsible for the payment of all or part of these fees.

The 100% access plan is an excellent vehicle for commencing a prepaid plan where limited funding is available. All members receive the preventive law benefits at no personal cost and major legal benefits at discounted fees. If funding is available, a portion of the discounted fee can be absorbed by the fund. As additional funding becomes available, either through increased contributions or by the accumulation of reserves, the portion of the discounted fee paid by the fund can be increased. Eventually, what started as an access plan will become a comprehensive prepaid plan.

Conclusion

Although the basic purpose of this presentation has been to alert the prudent fiduciary to alternative methods of structuring legal service plans and delivering the promised benefit—quality legal services—I must caution you not to become overwhelmed by the various alternatives, thereby losing sight of the primary goal. In the forefront of your thinking should always be the objective of using the combined purchasing power of your members to provide them with quality legal services at reasonable cost, something heretofore not available but greatly needed by a large segment of our population.

Prepaid Legal Services as an Employee Benefit

BY ALEC M. SCHWARTZ

THE IDEA OF an employer furnishing services or payment for services related to the personal well-being of employees has been recognized as an integral part of compensation packages for many years. The 1940s marked the development of plans designed to pay for the cost of basic medical and hospital services. In the 1960s and '70s we saw tremendous growth in plans that pay for dental services.

Extending the concept of employee welfare to areas other than physical health, labor unions over the last ten years have taken the lead in advocating benefit plans designed to provide legal services, and there is evidence that the number and variety of these plans will grow markedly during the coming decade. Already, the number of people affected by these plans has grown from a few hundred thousand in the early 1970s to an estimated six million by mid-1983. This number includes the recently negotiated plan for UAW employees of General Motors, which will provide legal service benefits for over 350,000 hourly workers and retirees.

Prepaid legal service plans have been recognized by both consumer groups and the legal profession as being an economically and socially desirable way of giving middle income Americans access to the American legal system. The rise of consumerism has spawned the concept that an individual can successfully mount a battle against a major corporation and win that battle—so long as the needed legal help is available.

Recognizing the need for personal legal services for workers has not been difficult for the labor union movement. In the early 1970s, the AFL-CIO, the UAW and other major unions acknowledged the desirability of developing plans and programs that would provide needed legal services to members. Opposition from the organized legal profession has turned to active support, following a number of Supreme Court decisions in the late '60s that affirmed the rights of consumer groups to make legal representation available to their members in a manner appropriate to the needs and desires of the group.

Changes in the law, especially federal law relating to employee benefits and taxation, have further paved the way for the expansion of legal service plans. Prepaid legal services are now established under Section 302(C)(8) of the Taft-Hartley Act as mandatory items of bargaining and are defined as employee welfare benefit plans under ERISA. With the enactment of Section 120 of the Internal Revenue Code, which permits employer payments to and value of benefits received under a legal service plan to be excludable from employee taxable income, the barriers that remain to widespread implementation of these plans have been greatly reduced.

Mr. Schwartz is executive director of the American Prepaid Legal Services Institute in Chicago, Illinois. Active in legal services delivery for over nine years, he has been involved in prepaid legal services since 1973. Before joining the Institute in March 1979, he served as technical advisor to the National Council of Senior Citizens, Washington, D.C. for developing group and prepaid legal service plans for senior citizens. Prior to that, Mr. Schwartz was vice president of Group Fifty Corporation, assigned as senior consultant to the State Bar of Michigan to coordinate their statewide prepaid legal services effort. He is a frequent speaker at Bar Association functions, conferences and workshops on group and prepaid legal services and is the author of several articles and publications on the subject. Mr. Schwartz holds an undergraduate degree in economics from Williams College, Williamstown, Massachusetts and has done graduate work in business administration at the University of Colorado and Michigan State University.

In addition, most of the technical problems associated with designing and administering plans have been solved over the last ten years. Actuarial information of the type to which employee benefit plan designers are accustomed has not yet been gathered in quantity. However, there is sufficient knowledge about the utilization of benefits by plan participants, the costs of providing those benefits and the costs involved in plan administration to make it possible to design and implement a program for a specific group.

Need for Legal Services

Much has been written about the need for legal services. The American Bar Association has estimated that two-thirds of the population that encounters problems with legal implications may do without needed legal services because of fear of high cost, ignorance of when a personal problem has legal implications, inability to find a lawyer and the desire to solve personal problems without help.

However, it is clear from observing the operation of group and prepaid legal plans that their potential contribution to an employee's well-being and productivity should not be underestimated. The impact of health problems on an employee's ability to work effectively is universally recognized, but the similar effect of legal problems is sometimes not so apparent. However, a legal problem may draw the employee's attention away from work duties and even result in absenteeism. The following case history illustrates this phenomenon and points out the way in which a relatively minor event that has legal implications can lead to major problems.

Case History

Robert Martin (fictitious name) had worked as a quality control inspector in an electronics plant for six years. During that period, his performance evaluations had been excellent and his attendance record perfect. Mr. Martin was well-liked by his fellow employees and was credited with making a number of suggestions that improved quality control procedures markedly. He was active in his local union and was being considered by management for promotion to supervisor of his section.

In the seventh year of his employment, the quality of components coming off the assembly line where Mr. Martin was stationed dropped off sharply. In addition, his attendance record began to deteriorate and he was absent from a number of important union meetings. Supervisors and co-workers tried unsuccessfully to ascertain the reason for this change in Mr. Martin's behavior. He became somewhat short-tempered, explaining that he had a few minor problems he would take care of shortly. At one point, Mr. Martin's job performance declined so that both his co-workers and management feared that he might not only lose the chance for a promotion but might even lose his job.

Mr. Martin's job performance suffered because of a problem which affects many American workers today: He was distracted by serious legal difficulties. Following is a chronological sequence of events which transformed Mr. Martin from a conscientious and effective employee to a state of inefficiency.

At the conclusion of Mr. Martin's sixth year of employment, he moved his family to an older apartment building in a northwest suburb of the city. He entered into a two year lease agreement but did not consult an attorney as to the terms of the agreement. A month after he moved in, a small fire broke out on the first floor and Mr. Martin, who lived on the third floor, became somewhat concerned over the need for fire protection. The landlord refused to provide alarms and extinguishers, and Mr. Martin, not the smartest of businessmen, decided to purchase, on an installment note, $2,400 in fire protection equipment.

Had Mr. Martin talked to a lawyer before purchasing the equipment, he would have discovered that the landlord was obligated by both state law and municipal ordinance to provide fire protection equipment. He would also have realized that the lease agreement that he entered into specifically stated that the landlord would provide such equipment on request and that rent could be withheld if such a request was not honored.

Three months after purchase of the equipment, Mr. Martin discovered that he could not meet the installment payments. The finance company refused to listen to any excuses and promptly sued Mr. Martin for $2,400 in the municipal court. Mr. Martin, unaware of the ramifications of the suit and without the funds to retain a lawyer, failed to answer the complaint and a default judgment was entered. The fire equipment was repossessed, sold at sheriff's sale for $400, with a deficiency balance of $2,000 showing as an unsatisfied judgment on the records of the municipal court. Mr. Martin was called into court on a judgment-debtor hearing and his wages were immediately garnisheed.

Over the next six months, as Mr. Martin attempted to pay off the judgment against him, his other monthly obligations fell into arrears. Mr. Martin lost his gasoline credit card, his bank credit card, the rent was always paid late and his creditors began harassing him for prompt payment of his obligations. Several small lawsuits were filed, all resulting in default judgments. Mr. Martin attempted to secure a loan to relieve the financial burden, but loan companies refused to consider his application because of the court judgment. Mr. Martin became short-tempered with his wife and children and somewhat impossible to live with.

Because of the change in him and the pressure of continual harassment from creditors, Mrs. Martin informed her husband that she had had enough and filed for divorce. Mr. Martin was served the complaint at work, much to his embarrassment, along with motions for expense money, temporary alimony and support and custody of the children. Ironically, on the same day, due to the fact that the rent was once again late, the landlord filed an action to evict. During the next six months, numerous hearings on the pending divorce were held and Mr. Martin had little time for anything but the legal battles that surrounded him.

Need for Attorney

Could an attorney have prevented many of Mr. Martin's problems? Probably. Certainly an attorney's review of the original lease agreement might have prevented the credit purchase of the fire prevention equipment which seems to have led to Mr. Martin's other difficulties. Even assuming the purchase had been made subsequent to an attorney's advice, many of the judgment-debtor problems would have been immediately relieved through trusteeship, or an attorney's active participation with creditors. The divorce might well have been avoided if the credit problems had been alleviated initially. Even if the divorce were unavoidable, the availability of an attorney prior to the initiation of the suit by Mrs. Martin could have prevented a lengthy contested proceeding.

Is this case untypical? We don't think so. The way in which Mr. Martin's problem developed points out the benefit of receiving legal services on a preventive basis. Numerous operating prepaid plans that feature consultations with a lawyer either in person or by telephone have statistically demonstrated that preventive use of lawyer services can be quite valuable. These plans report that somewhere between 60% and 80% of the problems presented to lawyers by plan participants can be resolved simply through advice by the attorney combined with self-help efforts by the plan participant. In addition, many of these plans offer free document review services. If Mr. Martin had been a member of such a plan, even if he could not have taken time off from work to go to a lawyer's office, he might have been able to consult the plan lawyer by telephone during his lunch hour, mailing the original lease agreement to the lawyer for quick review before he signed it. Thus, he would have avoided, certainly, the initial purchase of the $2,400 worth of fire prevention equipment.

Basic Considerations

We assume that the reader has been exposed previously to a discussion of the basic elements of prepaid legal service plans. In its simplest form, a legal service plan pays for the services of lawyers the same way that a medical plan pays for the services of doctors or a dental plan pays for the services of dentists.

Prepaid plans can vary widely in cost, benefits and the way in which legal services are furnished. However, in recent years, there have emerged two basic formats for these plans, which I choose to designate as Type 1 and Type 2.

Type 1: The Prepaid "Access" Plan

The term "access" is used to describe the primary purpose of the Type 1 plan—to provide easy access to a lawyer for legal advice and other noncomplex preventive services. The prepaid "access" plan provides an enrolled plan member with limited basic legal services for which money is paid in advance, plus additional noncovered services at a "discount."

The basic service—which is completely paid for by the prepaid fee—normally includes consultation with lawyers by telephone, brief office consultations, one simple legal document per year, and also may include letters written or phone calls made on behalf of the plan member. If the plan member wants or needs services beyond the limited items prepaid by the subscription fee, he/she and the lawyer arrive at a mutually satisfactory fee which the participant pays to the lawyer directly, based on the plan's fee schedule per hourly rate. In some plans, lawyers who provide the basic services do not provide further services; rather, the plan participant is referred to a participating lawyer who has agreed to furnish the additional services according to the plan's fee schedule.

Type 2: The Comprehensive Prepaid Plan

The comprehensive prepaid plan goes considerably beyond the "access" plan in providing truly "prepaid" services. In fact, the common usage of the term "prepaid legal service plan" generally applies to this comprehensive benefit form.

Figure

IN A NUTSHELL...

A prepaid plan involves:

The prepaid fee or premium

---

which is paid by

An employer on behalf of all covered employees as an employee benefit negotiated under collective bargaining or provided voluntarily by employer
or
An individual member of group through payroll deduction allowed by an employer or by individual remittance
or
An individual not affiliated with group

---

to

A trust fund for legal services
or
An insurance company
or
A private entrepreneurial plan

---

which pays

Staff lawyers who work entirely for the plan
or
One or more law firms who handle plan services
or
A broad group of lawyers who participate in plan
or
Any licensed lawyer anywhere

---

for service to

The individual beneficiary or member of group (who also may pay additional fees to lawyer for services not covered under the plan)

Used with permission of the American Prepaid Legal Services Institute.

Under this form, all plan benefits are available to the plan member at no additional cost, once the prepaid subscription fee or contribution has been paid. Typical benefits may include unlimited legal advice on any subject, negotiation with adverse parties, drafting legal documents such as contracts, wills and deeds, and representation in court or before administrative agencies. Although even the most extensive plans limit or exclude coverage on certain items, most comprehensive plans are designed to meet 80-90% of the legal service needs of the average middle income family.

Other elements of plan organization and operation are similar to those of any welfare plan. The plan may be administered on a self-funded trusteed basis, or coverage may be purchased either directly by an employer or by trustees from an insurance carrier. So far, the access to this latter option has been limited because major insurance carriers have not yet developed insurance products on a widespread basis. In fact, most employee welfare benefit plans, both those funded by employers and those financed by employee organizations, are of the self-funded trusteed type.

Provision of Services

Arranging for provision of services also follows models developed for other benefits. Services can be provided by any attorney of the plan participant's choice, by attorneys who are members of a participating or cooperating panel selected by the plan sponsor or administrator, by a small group of lawfirms designated by the plan sponsor or by a staff of lawyers hired by the trust fund for the exclusive purpose of providing benefits to participants. Whereas there has been and still continues to be some controversy over the best method of organizing providers, it is fair to say that all of these provider arrangement options can work effectively, depending on the particular needs and desires of the group of participants and the plan sponsor.

As with other benefit plans, the cost per participant can vary widely. The most important determinants of that cost are the scope of the benefit offered and the enrollment basis under which the plan will operate. Voluntary enrollment plans have proven to be significantly more expensive because of the phenomenon of adverse selection. Most employer-funded benefit plans do not face this problem since they involve 100% of the participating employee group automatically.

Plans that provide a simple schedule of benefits, such as those afforded under the access plans, can be operated quite economically. Such plans can cost as little as $20 per year and range up to $75 a year when the entire group is not enrolled automatically. Plans which offer comprehensive benefits have ranged from $40 a year to $300 a year, with the average ranging in the area of $100.

Plan Design Issues

Although there remain a number of technical issues that warrant further examination, we would like to address briefly those that we think have direct bearing on the use of legal service benefit plans by participants. The first of these involves the impact of a benefit schedule design.

We have categorized plans as falling into two types, the access plan and the comprehensive plan. In reality, plan benefits range from very basic to very extensive. Assuming there is sufficient money to fund a very comprehensive benefit schedule, which provides any and all legal services possibly needed by an employee, there is evidence to indicate that the degree to which participants internalize the need for a particular benefit will have a direct relationship to the extent to which they value the prepaid legal plan as a whole.

For example, when asked why she decided not to enroll in the plan offered through her credit union, the credit union member explained that the plan provided liberal benefits in the area of divorce, bankruptcy, eviction matters and criminal defense. She not only had none of those problems, she said, but she certainly hoped she would not ever face them. The only benefit that seemed attractive to her was the four hours per year of consultation with a lawyer. She reasoned, however, that she could obtain consultation services outside the plan at a cost lower than the subscription charge. In this situation, although the plan offered a wide range of benefits whose value exceeded several thousand dollars, it is our contention that the benefit schedule was not presented in a way which would allow prospective participants to perceive a personal need for the benefits.

The opposite may be true for a plan whose benefits are stated in more general terms and which emphasizes access to lawyer services. A plan which emphasizes that its main benefit is consultation with a lawyer at any time on any legal matter, especially where the telephone can be used, may serve to illustrate this point. Obviously, Mr. Martin in our case study did not feel that the signing of what he assumed was a routine form lease agreement would lead to the legal battles which he eventually faced. If Mr. Martin's prepaid legal service plan, assuming he was fortunate enough to be a member of one, emphasized the availability of lawyer's advice on any problem, whether or not he really believed the problem had legal implications, he might very well have been encouraged to call a plan lawyer before signing the original lease agreement.

Plans which state benefits in terms of the amount of services available for solving problems are not always inappropriate. A plan for a group which had a high incidence of home ownership among participants might be very well-advised to specifically cover legal services related to real estate problems. A plan for retirees could emphasize wills and estate planning and assistance with Social Security and other benefits.

However, we submit that unless the specific legal needs of the employee group are well-documented, it may be more appropriate, even in a comprehensive plan, to concentrate on a benefit scheme that makes initial contact with a lawyer as simple as possible for the participant prior to his or her taking any action which might have legal ramifications.

Open vs. Closed Panels

Another issue involves the effect of the arrangement of service provider panels on plan utilization. As the reader may be aware, the debate over whether a prepaid legal service plan should provide services through an open or closed panel of attorneys continues. The open panel system allows the plan participant to choose his or her own attorney whom the plan then pays for services rendered according to the plan benefit schedule. The closed panel system involves the selection by either the plan sponsor or administrator of plan lawyers to whom participants must go to receive services covered under the plan. Generally speaking, the "closed panel" consists of a fewer number of lawyers than does an "open panel" system or may even involve a staff of attorneys hired by plan trustees to provide services exclusively to plan participants. Each of these mechanisms has its own advocates. We would like to confine our discussion to some potential effects on the propensity of plan members to use the service.

To some extent, experience gained from the federally funded legal services program to the poor and from commercial legal clinics indicates that physical access to plan lawyers may have a significant impact on the extent to which the services are utilized. The federally funded legal services program for the poor has emphasized the concept of neighborhood law offices located near where the potential client population lives. Similarly, legal clinics that have opened up small branch offices throughout a city have experienced greater demand for their services than those who consolidate operations in a central office. As we have pointed out before, access to plan attorneys may not only be a function of physical proximity to the employee's workplace or home. Plans which provide access by telephone generally have higher utilization rates than plans that do not provide this service.

A number of the more highly developed plans have set up the multilevel service provider network in recognition of this problem. Basic services such as legal advice and simple document drafting are made available to participants via a single lawfirm or a legal staff. If they require more complex attention, participants are given the option of being referred to a plan lawyer, or, in some cases, using an attorney of their own choosing to perform the additional services covered by the plan.

The important thing in our view is to tailor the provider network to the particular needs of the membership. In this regard, attention must be given to plans covering employee groups whose members reside in more than one state. In the New York City area, many plans arrange for services to be provided by lawyers licensed in New Jersey and Connecticut as well as in New York State. The United Auto Workers–Chrysler Plan, which covers active and retired employees of Chrysler Corporation located in 44 states, has adopted a combination of staff offices, attorneys under contract and independent cooperating attorneys to be able to make plan benefits accessible to all participants regardless of where they may live or work.

Prepaid Legal Plans and ERISA

In most respects, the development and administration of a prepaid legal plan as an employee welfare benefit are no different than any other plan falling within the definition contained in Section 3a of ERISA. However, the requirements of Section 404 relating to fiduciary responsibility have special application to a legal service plan, which may not be obvious. As the reader is probably aware, trustees as fiduciaries must act solely in the interest of the participants and beneficiaries and must discharge their duties for the exclusive purpose of providing benefits to participants and their beneficiaries. In developing legal plans, this standard must be applied to all aspects of plan design and operation. But, particular attention should be paid to the impact of these standards on the way legal service providers are chosen and the method by which those providers are to be paid for covered services.

The history of the development of legal service plans established pursuant to the collective bargaining process has shown that trustees, unions and employers have tended to turn either to counsel for an existing welfare trust fund, the union counsel or counsel for the employer when it comes to setting up the service provider mechanism. Of course, it is natural to assume that if a particular group is satisfied with the services of lawyers with whom it has dealt for a number of years, it will tend to rely on those lawyers either to provide services or for advice as to who should provide services. We submit, however, that the fiduciary standards under ERISA require trustees to go a number of steps further in assuring that selection of service providers is made solely with the interest of plan participants in mind.

In the previous section we have noted that certain service provider arrangements may influence the ability of a participant to utilize services under the plan. The selection of a lawfirm which has traditionally provided services either to the union, the trust or the employer because of the quality of the firm's work, the fee arrangement or more subjective judgments may be wholly justified. However, recent developments in Department of Labor enforcement proceedings indicate that trustees must make every effort to objectively evaluate the alternatives open to them and make their choices based on arm's length dealings with prospective lawyers or lawfirms. In this regard, it should be noted that any participant may challenge the actions of trustees in selecting plan attorneys should the participant feel that he or she is effectively precluded from utilizing plan benefits because the attorney selected by the plan is inaccessible or because it would be inappropriate for that attorney to be handling a particular type of legal matter.

In some instances, trustees may choose not to select attorneys for participants but rather allow participants to use any attorney they wish as long as that attorney agrees to the terms and conditions of the plan. In yet other instances, plan counsel may finally be selected to provide or coordinate the provision of services to participants (see ERISA Section 408(B)(2) with regard to exemptions from prohibited transactions); however, the final selection, we suggest, should be based on some objective procedure, hopefully documented, which has allowed trustees to consider all possible alternatives and then arrive at a conclusion based on their estimate of what would be in the best interest of plan participants.

Fee Arrangements

Similarly, the question of the amount and basis on which plan attorneys are to be paid for their services is an important decision, which must be made by trustees consistent with the requirements of Section 404.

Some plans collect monies from an employer, place them into a trust fund and pay lawyers only for each unit of work they perform for plan participants. Other plans have seen fit simply to pay plan attorneys a portion of the employer contribution on a per capita basis, leaving it to the lawyer to provide all the covered services as needed for that fixed fee. Under this latter system, if the aggregate amount of the contributions paid to the lawfirm has a reasonable relationship to the amount of work that lawyers perform for plan participants during a given year, there may be nothing wrong with this mechanism of payment.

For example, a plan that pays the attorney $100 per year per participant with 1,000 participants in the plan should assume that the value of services rendered to members of the participating group will approach $100,000. If it turns out that either very few participants use the benefits or that the type of services rendered are not very extensive, the value of legal services rendered by the lawfirm may be significantly less than the $100,000 fee paid. If this is the case, trustees must ensure that their actions are consistent with the fiduciary responsibilities by either reassessing the fee paid to the attorney or increasing plan benefits.

Of course, the per capita payment system may work to the advantage of a plan if the value of benefits provided to participants exceeds the prepaid fee paid to the attorney. Usually, the contract between the trust and the attorney stipulates that the attorney must absorb losses in this regard. However, expecting a lawfirm to continue absorbing such losses is unrealistic, and it certainly will behoove trustees either to decrease benefits available under the plan or to increase compensation to plan attorneys. In the latter instance, however, such increased payments may require renegotiation of the contribution rate paid by the employer.

In an attempt to avoid problems associated with renegotiation, many plans have erred on the side of providing too high a fee to the attorney rather than too low. Again, such an approach may be justified during initial years of the plan when precise figures on utilization of plan benefits are unknown. However, it is assumed that trustees acting prudently will only agree to a contract that provides for renegotiated fees in accordance with plan utilization, as evidenced by records kept by plan attorneys on the use and value of services provided to plan members.

Financing the Benefit

Until recently, most plans operated in the employee benefit context have been financed directly through employer and/or employee contributions. Generally such funds are either directly paid to an insurance company or legal services provider, or are deposited in the account of a special legal services trust fund established in accordance with the requirements of Section 501(c)(20) of the Internal Revenue Code.

With regard to this latter arrangement, the Tax Reform Act of 1976 includes an amendment to the Internal Revenue Code of 1954 establishing, under Section 120, a mechanism for qualifying legal service plans such that the value of contributions made by the employer on behalf of an employee and the value of services rendered to the employee by the plan are not considered as part of the employee's taxable income.

Qualifying a prepaid legal service plan under Section 120 is an important step for a plan funded in whole or in part by the employer. Although it is beyond the scope of this article to discuss in detail the features a plan must exhibit in order to qualify, it is sufficient at this point to indicate that the plan must be a written plan of an employer, must be funded in whole or in part by the employer and must be limited to furnishing personal legal services to employees and their dependents as defined in the statute and regulations. Proposed regulations relating to Sections 120 and 501(c)(20) were issued by the Internal Revenue Service on June 29, 1980 and it is anticipated that final regulations will be issued by the summer of 1983.

The establishment of a 501(c)(20) trust fund assumes the existence of plans qualified under Section 120 to which that trust fund can relate. Such a trust fund operates similarly to an employee welfare plan established under Code Section 501(c)(9), except that its exclusive function is restricted to forming part of a plan qualifying under Section 120. Proposed regulations issued by the Internal Revenue Service governing the operation of 501(c)(9) trust funds state that the term "other benefits," as used in Section 501(c)(9) include prepaid legal services and that funds from a 501(c)(9) welfare fund can be transferred to a 501(c)(20) legal services trust in order to finance a qualified prepaid legal service plan.

Another option to be considered by employers, employee organizations and trustees is the purchase of an insurance policy that pays for certain legal service benefits. As with other types of benefits involving insurance, a special trust fund may be unnecessary, with the employer simply paying a premium on a group basis to an insurance company to cover all employees. Although such an arrangement removes the underwriting and much of the administrative burden, the decision concerning the use of an insurance policy to provide benefits must be made in light of comparison between premium rates charged by the insurance company and an estimate of the costs of administering and providing services on a self-funded basis. Since insurance company offerings in the legal expense field are not yet plentiful and are not even available in all states, plan sponsors must use caution in ascertaining the availability of such coverage, especially where multistate employers or multiemployer plans are involved.

Future of Legal Plans

In summary, we have concentrated on illustrating some of the reasons why legal services are an important benefit and what, from the employee benefit designer's perspective, are some problem areas to consider in implementing a prepaid legal service benefit plan. We do not mean to leave the impression that problems abound or are insurmountable, or that a prepaid legal service plan as an employee benefit is particularly difficult to establish. To the contrary, the last several years have seen a significant and successful effort to remove the institutional and regulatory barriers to plan development. In fact, it is our experience that, once a decision is made to start a legal service plan and funding for the plan has been successfully established through collective bargaining or otherwise, groups (along with their attorneys) have found it relatively simple to begin a program and to successfully administer it.

The active interest of some major insurance carriers in entering the market, as well as evidence that self-funded trusteed plans continue to be formed even in light of the economic downturn, indicates that this benefit is considered a valuable addition to wage and salary packages. In many instances, legal service plans will be the next major undertaking at the negotiating table, as far as fringe benefits are concerned, during the 1980s.

Legal Service Plans: Legal Basis, Legal Developments

BY CHERYL DENNEY WHITE

THE LEGAL BASIS for prepaid legal service plans, and the rules governing their operation, is contained in three separate statutes: the Taft-Hartley Act, the Employee Retirement Income Security Act (ERISA) and the Internal Revenue Code.

The Taft-Hartley Act

In 1973, Section 302(c) of the Taft-Hartley Act[1] was amended to give unions the right to bargain with employers for contributions to plans to provide for legal services to members. The Taft-Hartley Act sets several requirements that still apply to collectively bargained legal service plans. First, funds must be held in jointly administered trusts, with union and employer trustees. Second, an annual independent accounting for trust funds is required. Third, the Taft-Hartley Act limits the use of funds in a collectively bargained legal service plan by prohibiting payment for suits against the union, against participating employers or for legal services that the union could not pay for directly because of the Landrum-Griffin Act. It is important to note that the Taft-Hartley Act does not set any standards for what a plan may provide in legal services.

ERISA

The second important statute governing prepaid legal service plans was enacted in the following year. The Employee Retirement Income Security Act of 1974 sets comprehensive requirements for all kinds of employee plans, including employee welfare benefit plans as well as retirement plans. ERISA defines "employee welfare benefit plan" to include prepaid legal service plans that are set up by an employer or a union to cover employees.

The Department of Labor has ruled on several limited exceptions to ERISA coverage for prepaid legal plans. In some cases, the legal service plan is not covered by ERISA because it does not fit the

Ms. White is an attorney with the Washington, D.C. lawfirm of Dickstein, Shapiro & Morin, specializing in employee benefits issues. She provides legal counsel to multiemployer, multiple employer and single employer retirement plans, welfare plans and a prepaid legal service plan. Her responsibilities include monitoring changes in tax and labor law in the employee benefits area, requesting rulings or Advisory Opinions from government agencies, advising plan fiduciaries on questions of administration and statutory compliance and assisting in an increasing volume of litigation over employee benefits claims and delinquent contributions. Ms. White previously served as trial attorney with the Tax Litigation Division, Office of Chief Counsel, Internal Revenue Service and, before that, as consulting assistant specializing in pension administration with a Kansas City, Missouri consulting firm. She received her B.A. from the University of Missouri, Columbia, her J.D. from the University of Missouri, Kansas City Law School and her master of laws in taxation from Georgetown University Law Center, Washington, D.C.

definition of an employee plan, either because it was not established by an employer or a union or because it covers not only employees but is also open to the public. In another case, the plan is not subject to ERISA because it is sponsored by a state government and is therefore exempt from ERISA generally as a governmental plan.

There are two major areas in which ERISA applies to a legal service plan: the reporting and disclosure requirements and ERISA's fiduciary standards.

---

1. 29 U.S.C. §185(c).

Reporting and Disclosure

ERISA's reporting requirements for prepaid legal service plans are the same as for any other welfare plan. The annual report to the federal government is a fact of life for all employee plans. More important for prepaid legal service plans, however, is ERISA's requirement of disclosure to plan participants through the summary plan description, the summary of material modification, and the summary annual report. These publications and notices are valuable opportunities to communicate with plan participants, to remind them of the benefits available through the plan (benefits that may be underutilized) or to inform them of benefit improvements. Good communication with participants is also the key to ERISA's requirements that any denial of benefits must be in writing and that participants must be given the right to appeal any denial of benefits.

Fiduciary Standards

The most important ERISA requirements are the standards for fiduciary conduct. Although these standards apply to all types of employee plans, certain of the standards raise special problems for prepaid legal service plans.

ERISA sets four duties for plan trustees. The first duty of the trustees is the duty of loyalty to plan participants, a duty to administer the plan for the exclusive benefit of participants. This principle underlies all the other requirements of ERISA. A plan is permitted to pay administrative costs and benefits, but the plan should not use its funds to benefit anyone other than its participants.

This exclusive benefit rule is the reason behind ERISA's list of specifically prohibited transactions, which include situations where the plan in some way profits an employer, union, trustee or service provider instead of benefiting plan participants. When plan funds are used for other purposes, directly or indirectly, they are not available to pay benefits when claims come in from plan participants. ERISA provides a few specific exemptions from the prohibited transaction rule, including an exemption for reasonable arrangements between a party in interest and the plan for office space, or legal or other services necessary to establish or operate the plan, provided that compensation for these services is reasonable.

This exemption can be applied to permit a prepaid legal plan to make arrangements for legal services with a person who is an employee of the union or a participating employer, for example, without violation of the prohibited transaction rule. However, such arrangements must meet the tests of the exemption (reasonable cost, necessary to plan operation) and must not violate any of the other standards ERISA sets for plan administration.

ERISA's second fiduciary requirement is that the trustees must act prudently in administering the plan. The hallmark of prudence is a full investigation and consideration of the available alternatives before making a choice among them. Prudence is usually thought of in the context of selecting plan investments, but prudence is required in every step in plan administration. Trustees must act prudently not only in selecting and managing plan assets, but also in collecting contributions to the plan, in making benefit payments under the plan and, most importantly, in the prepaid legal service plan context, the trustees must act prudently in the selection, retention and compensation of plan service providers.

The Department of Labor certainly ascribes to this requirement. In 1979, the Labor Department brought suit against the trustees of a union-negotiated prepaid legal service plan, charging that they had acted imprudently in choosing the son of one of the trustees to provide the plan's legal services without using prudent selection procedures and in overpaying the attorney for his services. In this case, *Donovan v. Sackman*,[2] the trustees agreed to entry of a consent decree under which they are obligated to accept a neutral trustee, neither union nor employer-appointed, who will choose the legal service provider under detailed rules set by the court. These requirements apparently include that the neutral trustee obtain a number of competitive proposals from law firms and that evaluation of the proposals be made with the assistance of consulting attorneys who are not candidates for the service provider position.

ERISA's third specific duty is a duty to diversify plan assets to minimize risk of loss. This requirement is another aspect of general prudence in plan investment.

Finally, ERISA requires that the plan be administered in accordance with the terms of the written plan documents. Very often, what this requirement means to plan trustees is that they must say no. Plans are set up to pay benefits, but to pay benefits when the plan prohibits it may mean that the necessary funds will not be available to pay plan participants with legitimate claims for benefits.

---

2. S.D.N.Y., No. 79-Civ.-838 (ADS), consent order entered June 4, 1981.

Preemption of State Laws

One other provision of ERISA that is important to prepaid legal service plans is ERISA's preemption of state laws regulating employee plans. ERISA specifically does not preempt state insurance law, nor does it preempt state laws that regulate professions or conduct of business. That means that states may still set requirements for service providers, such as the insurance companies who now provide prepaid legal services, through state insurance laws and that state laws on licensing of corporate offices to do business and laws on attorneys code of professional responsibility are intact. These state laws will apply to attorneys who provide legal services to prepaid legal service plans.

Internal Revenue Code

Neither ERISA nor the Taft-Hartley Act sets any restrictions on what the prepaid legal service plan must contain. The third major statute in this area does. When Congress enacted the Tax Reform Act of 1976, it added Section 120 to the Internal Revenue Code. Section 120 of the Code sets five requirements that prepaid legal service plans must meet.

First, a prepaid legal service plan must be in writing and must be for the exclusive benefit of employees. These requirements echo basic requirements under ERISA and the Taft-Hartley Act.

The second requirement under Section 120 of the Code is that the plan must not limit participation to members of the prohibited group of officers, shareholders, business owners, or highly paid employees and their families. There are special limitations on the amount of benefits or contributions a prepaid legal service plan may provide on behalf of these prohibited group employees and their families.

The third requirement under Section 120 is that a plan may be funded in only one of four ways: (1) by insurance; (2) by a trust limited to providing funds for prepaid legal service plans and qualified under Section 501(c)(20) of the Code; (3) by another trust, such as a welfare plan trust, under Section 501(c) of the Code, that channels funds to a Section 501(c)(20) trust or organization; or (4) by prepayment directly to the service provider—the attorney providing services under the plan. The IRS will also permit the use of some combination of these four methods.

The fourth, and most important, requirement of Section 120 is that the plan must provide "personal legal services" to participating employees and their families. Exactly what "personal legal services" is is not defined by the statute.

The Internal Revenue Service has issued a proposed regulation, Section 1.120-2,[3] that defines personal legal services very strictly. Under the proposed regulation as it now stands, personal legal services do not include legal services connected with a trade or business, legal services related to management of property held as an investment or for the production of income or legal services in the collection or production of income. IRS makes exceptions for legal services to obtain, increase or collect payments of alimony and child support, or in connection with an inheritance or for damages other than personal injuries; these exceptions are permitted on the theory that these expenses are inherently personal in nature.

IRS originally took such a hard-line position in refusing to allow a plan to cover any business-related expenses that at first the IRS did not even allow a plan to provide initial consultation on business matters. The IRS now takes the position, stated in Private Letter Ruling 8038029, that a prepaid legal service plan may provide an initial consultation with a plan attorney to figure out whether the matter is business-related or is one that can be covered by the legal service plan.

The proposed regulations on prepaid legal service plans were originally issued in April 1980. A final version of the regulations has been drafted and circulated within the IRS, but is presently stalled in review, perhaps because the revisions are viewed as noncontroversial and because there have been so many recent statutory changes in the employee benefits area. The revisions are thought to be significant, very probably taking into account the extensive criticism of the strict definition of "personal legal services" that the IRS has applied in the past.

The final requirement for a prepaid legal service plan under Section 120 of the Internal Revenue Code is the filing of a notice with the IRS. Of the three regulations IRS has proposed for prepaid legal service plans, the only regulation that has been issued in final form is the regulation on how to file a notice with the IRS.[4] The legal service plan must file IRS Form 1024 and the form's Schedule L with the IRS Key District Director in the region where the plan is administered to be qualified under Section 120 of the Code.

---

3. Prop. Treas. Reg. §1.120-2, proposed April 29, 1980, 45 *Fed. Reg.* 28360.
4. Treas. Reg. §1.120-3.

Why bother to get the plan qualified under Section 120 of the Code? It makes a big difference in the tax treatment of the trust and of the participating employees. If the plan qualifies under Section 120, then its related trust is exempt from tax on its investment income under Section 501(c)(20) of the Code. Tax exempt status normally results in significantly faster compounding of the funds available to pay promised benefits. When the plan is qualified under Section 120, then the participating employees do not have to include in their taxable income any of the employer's contributions, any of the amounts that the plan pays for legal services or the value of any legal services the employee and members of his family receive under the plan. The personal legal services that these plans can provide are generally legal expenses that the employee could not deduct on his tax return if he paid them himself, so when the benefit is paid to him tax free, the employee is in a much better position than if he had to pay for the services himself.

Sunset for Prepaid Legal Service Plans?

Ironically, in proposed regulation Section 1.120-2(b)(1), the IRS requires a prepaid legal service plan to be permanent, not just temporary, in order to qualify as a plan under Section 120 of the Internal Revenue Code. That requirement is ironic because the statute itself has a sunset provision, an automatic termination date. Originally, Section 120 was supposed to terminate on December 31, 1981, but as part of the Economic Recovery Tax Act of 1981 the deadline was extended to December 31, 1984.

What would happen if the deadline were not extended again? The best estimate of what would happen can be made by looking at prepaid legal plans before Section 120 was enacted in 1976. Employers deducted contributions to prepaid legal service plans under Section 162 of the Code before 1976. Plans often were administered by the union staff or were set up with a welfare plan as a conduit for legal service plan contributions, which meant that funds contributed to provide legal services accumulated tax free anyway. Treasury representatives, testifying at hearings on the proposed Section 120, admitted that they did not know how or when employees should be taxed on prepaid legal plan benefits.

Fortunately, the question of how to treat prepaid legal service plans if Section 120 is not extended is unlikely to arise. Prospects for extension of the deadline, if not the outright elimination of the sunset provision altogether, are very good. Section 120 is considered a part of the fringe benefit area. Congress has put a freeze on regulatory development of fringe benefit taxation until it has made a comprehensive review of fringe benefits, but there is no indication of when Congress will undertake that task.

If extension of Section 120 is reviewed on a piecemeal basis by Congress, as seems most likely, there is no reason to anticipate any opposition to an extension. The last extension was noncontroversial and was approved without any serious debate. No abuses have arisen to generate the notoriety that could jeopardize the future of prepaid legal service plans. On the whole, it is probably easier for Congress to extend the provision than to resolve unanswered questions about how to handle the shutdown of formerly qualified prepaid legal service plans and trusts. Extension of Section 120 of the Code seems assured.

CHAPTER 9

Alternatives in Health Care

James F. Doherty

Executive Director
Group Health Association of America, Inc.
Washington, D.C.

Karen Ignagni

Assistant Director
AFL-CIO Department of Social Security
Washington, D.C.

Richard L. Epstein

Senior Vice President
American Hospital Association
Chicago, Illinois

James S. Todd, M.D.

Member, Board of Trustees
American Medical Association
Ridgewood, New Jersey

Alternative Health Care Delivery Systems

BY JAMES F. DOHERTY

THE MOST INTERESTING facet of the subject of alternative health care is its relative novelty. Ten years ago, a discussion of alternatives in health care was confined to a half dozen proposals for national health insurance, which were not taken very seriously by the national legislature, and to the debate surrounding the enactment of a little known and unheralded bill called the Health Maintenance Organization Act of 1973. True, there was concern ten years ago about health care cost inflation, but then the basic approach was to contain rising costs through several legislative efforts, notably the passage of certificate-of-need laws and the 1974 National Health Planning Act, as well as outright wage and price controls. An irony during that period was the almost simultaneous enactment of health workforce legislation, one of the effects of which was a fueling of an already uncontrolled inflation by adding a new factor—physician inflation.

Today, the inflation numbers continue to rocket upward, forcing all concerned to cast about for new ideas predicated on new ways of addressing the problem of health care cost inflation. Hence my presentation will explore some of these options. The newest options have their roots in meetings in a private sector environment to discuss private sector initiatives, a sad reflection of the government's inability to offer any meaningful reform thus far.

Rate of Cost Increases

Everyone, I assume, has heard the unhappy dollar numbers on health care costs, so they don't need to be reviewed here in detail. We all know that the health care inflation rate has been little retarded by the Reagan Administration's budget cuts and deficit reduction efforts and we all should be more than a little fearful of the ominous nature of the rate of growth. When Medicare was enacted, its initial projected cost was expected to be $4.5 billion per year, with an inflationary rise to $9 billion in 1990.

Today's projections have the cost at $50 billion in 1983; a doubling of that number is expected by 1987. Senator Edward Kennedy, at a press con-

Mr. Doherty is executive director of the Group Health Association of America, Inc. (GHAA), the largest national trade association for group model health maintenance organizations. Before joining GHAA as legislative counsel in 1970, Mr. Doherty served as counsel to the Committee on Banking and Currency of the U.S. House of Representatives. Prior to the Capitol Hill appointment, he worked as a legislative representative under the AFL-CIO's legislative director, Andrew Biemiller. Mr. Doherty founded, and served as president from 1972 to 1978, the National Health Lawyers Association, a 1,500 member organization of health attorneys. He also chaired a committee responsible for drafting the HMO solvency requirements adopted by the National Association of Insurance Commissioners. Mr. Doherty is a graduate of the Georgetown University Law Center and has been on the faculty of the George Washington University Law School. He has also been a lecturer at the University of Pennsylvania's Wharton School, the University of Pittsburgh and Cornell University. He is a member of the International Foundation's Health Care Services Committee and has participated in previous Foundation educational programs.

ference heralding the development of his Health Security Act in 1972, decried with understandable alarm the explosion of the nation's total health care bill to $88 billion; today the number is $300 billion. Conservatively, one can posit that a continuation of this phenomenon will result in a collapse of the health care system as we know it and, the greatest tragedy of all, in a magnificent health care system that only a privileged few can afford to use.

Initial Federal Response

The federal government's response to this sad situation so far is less than reassuring. Already the Congress has authorized borrowing from an about-to-go-broke Medicare trust fund to replenish a depleted Social Security fund. One member of the National Commission on Social Security Reform has observed that a continuation of this practice will render the Medicare trust fund insolvent by the end of 1984. The government also has resorted to cost shifting through new restrictions on federal health programs, which force hospitals and other providers to make up their losses through price increases to private patients—resulting in increased premiums for health insurance. The Health Insurance Association of America (HIAA) has estimated this initial cost shift to be in the neighborhood of $6 billion. There's more bad news to come with the soon-to-be-implemented requirement that Medicare be secondary coverage for the working aged.

Some Positive Developments

Against this dismal backdrop, there are some encouraging developments. Most significant are the meaningful steps taken by major purchasers and those persons and organizations who influence the purchase of health care toward containing health care costs. Even more encouraging is the growing support that these efforts are gaining from providers and third-party payers. No longer is the determination of need for a health care service and the payment for that service an automatic process. Increasingly, reviews of utilization, appropriateness and price are becoming the business of employers, unions, community groups and others who are now beginning to look at health care and health care resources and practices with a critical eye toward cost-effectiveness.

Another significant activity is the willingness of purchasers and others to develop or offer alternative delivery and financing systems with proven effective records. The alternative system not only has the advantage of efficiency and economy, but also can have a profound effect on the management of health care in the community. Studies have verified that alternative systems can serve as a measure by which existing health care practices are improved. It's the old competitive rule of a market response to a better product.

HMOs

Health maintenance organizations (HMOs) are the forerunner of all alternative delivery systems. In the few areas where they have been tried, significant reduction in resource utilization has been accomplished. Unfortunately, before the HMO Act was passed, HMOs were viewed with hostility by organized providers and were restricted by law in over 30 states. A few dozen HMOs served less than five million people. The HMO Act removed state restrictions, provided modest seed money for development and, most importantly, required employers to offer HMOs as an alternative health plan. Today HMOs number over 250, serve 12 million people and continue to grow at a 10-15% rate.

The driving force behind this extraordinary growth has been the growing general concern over health care costs. Double-digit indemnity rate increases and cuts in benefits also have made HMOs increasingly attractive. Member satisfaction is rated at 85-90%. Benefits are comprehensive with only nominal copayments; care is prepaid and delivered through an organized and effective use of professional personnel. Also, HMOs' rates are based on carefully constructed budgets sufficient to meet the needs of the populations that they serve.

Although all HMOs meet these general principles, the form and shape of specific HMOs differ. Some are operated through consumer-elected boards, some are for profit, some are employer- or labor-sponsored and some are sponsored by major insurance companies—Prudential, Hancock, INA, Blue Cross-Blue Shield. There are 44 hospital-sponsored HMOs. All HMOs have one thing in common—they are expansionist in outlook and are growing.

Those of you who still consider HMOs to be the baby of the political left and just another federal program should realize that HMOs have received the active support of the last four Administrations, including the present one. You should also be aware that 85% of the funds for expansion have come from the private sector.

Problems

HMOs still suffer from many problems. Unfortunately, knowledge about the system is not widespread. HMOs boast of high member satisfaction but have been short of the mark in explaining themselves to those persons who should be interested in becoming members. The Group Health Association of America (GHAA) has assigned a high priority to meaningful dialogues with employers, unions and providers. Our less-than-satisfactory progress in this effort means that either there are none so deaf as will not hear or that the fault is with us, or that both problems exist. That is why we are so enthusiastic about opportunities to meet with audiences and so chagrined at the failure of some business, labor and community coalitions even to consider a role for us.

Another problem arises from distorted and widespread publicity received over the dozen or so HMO failures attributed to insolvency, poor management or bad luck. I read about an HMO failure in Fort Collins, Colorado in a Fort Lauderdale, Florida newspaper, but a hospital failure in Fort Collins likely would not make even the Denver papers.

Controls

HMOs are a highly complex business, expensive to start and manage. Experienced managers are in woefully short supply. Nonetheless, we in the HMO industry took the initiative and secured the imposition of state and federal solvency requirements to assure the parties with whom we contract that we are financially responsible.

We also urge and welcome scrutiny from payers and consumers. We freely invite inquiry and inspection. As a precondition of participation, sophisticated employer inquiry, inspection and analysis are sound and constructive processes. Advance examination of physician/patient ratios and physician and management qualifications, and review of utilization patterns and financial practices minimize later misunderstandings.

Reasons for Starting HMOs

As I mentioned previously, one of the major causes of increased willingness to offer or join HMOs is the rather dramatic rate increases by Blue Cross and indemnity plans. Last year, the Federal Employees' Program issued rate approvals ranging from 20-30% in the indemnity plans, whereas HMO rate increases averaged from 10-14%. The increased indemnity rates were accompanied by mandated benefit cuts in the 14-16% range; HMOs were required to cut their benefits by 6%. Although early data show significant growth of federal employee membership in HMOs, there were equally significant shifts to higher and lower option indemnity plans.

Data are far from conclusive, but GHAA is watching developments in this program with a little anxiety. At least one study shows a high degree of adverse selection for the higher benefit programs, including HMOs. If this phenomenon holds true, then we will have to do some heavy thinking about higher copays and deductibles and their impact on our ability to compete. This situation becomes particularly important if some of the pro-competition schemes, which include tax limitations on employer health insurance deductions, are adopted.

PPOs

HMOs are not the only alternatives that have become fashionable of late. The health care literature is now giving some attention to a hitherto unheralded concept—the preferred provider organization (PPO). Little is known about the effectiveness or acceptability of these programs, but we do know something about the general principles under which they operate. PPOs, like HMOs, are prepaid contracting entities that seek to encourage consumers to use providers who have agreed to restrict their behavior concerning price, at least, if not mode of practice. PPOs offer purchasers and users a more comprehensive set of health care benefits if the consumer uses contracting providers. If the consumer does not elect the provider panel, then he or she can be covered under normal insurance with increased out-of-pocket payments.

Like HMOs, PPOs take on several forms. They contract with physicians, specialists and hospitals for preset, usually discounted, fee schedules. Aetna instituted a program in the Chicago area—Choice Care—that allows a free choice of primary care physicians, with specialty referrals and inpatient care handled by contracting providers.

I do feel some faint skepticism, admittedly stemming from my HMO bias, when I read that PPOs solicit provider participation on the basis of maximizing patient loads and bed utilization. However, the true test of any scheme is experience; those PPOs that demonstrate cost-effectiveness and a high quality of care may well be a desirable alternative for consumers.

Preliminary Results From Alternative Systems

As I mentioned, the thrust of alternative systems is to subject health care to a free market choice with the hoped-for result of cost containment for all. HMOs and PPOs now service such a small percentage of the total population that we cannot be absolutely certain of their results, but the studies and experience we have, coupled with the crisis level of inflation, leave all of us little choice but to try out these alternatives.

No matter what system we try, we should always bear in mind that the key relationship we are talking about is that of physician and patient. That relationship should always remain a sacrosanct and independent part of any health care delivery system. One, particularly a nonphysician, would be presumptuous and foolish to permit quality and privacy of care to be sacrificed for economy.

Some Important Governmental Policies

Finally, note the ongoing development of some governmental policies that may impact on the growth of alternative delivery systems. Recently, the State of California enacted a dramatic new process in an effort to control spiraling Medicaid (medical) costs. State agencies now are empowered to contract fees for Medicaid services directly with providers. A particularly significant provision added to that legislation was an amendment that empowered insurance companies to contract with providers generally.

Arizona has adopted legislation under which competitive bidding on a fixed price basis is the basic Medicaid funding mechanism. Successful bidders contract for the provision of care; eligibles may choose the organization in which they enroll.

New York, Illinois and several other states are adopting variations on this theme of mandated, competitive alternatives. Although no one, including the drafters, knows the shape of the Reagan Administration's vaunted competition proposals, we can conclude that inflationary health costs drive legislatures to require alternatives in the interest of cost containment. We should all, in the words of the Irish patriot, "Beware of the thing that is coming."

Prospective hospital reimbursement is another subject of concern. In October, Congress instructed the Secretary of Health and Human Services to develop and submit a proposal for prospective reimbursement of hospitals under Medicare. Again, the Congress is taking some of its cues from states that already have enacted prospective reimbursement proposals—New Jersey and Massachusetts, for example. Current information indicates that the scheme decided on by the Reagan Administration is based on reimbursement by diagnostically related groupings. Organized providers may prefer a cost per discharge or some other base. Collaterally, some insurers want any system adopted to apply the new mechanism to all payers as well as to Medicare.

Although it's too early to predict any certain outcome of all this activity, you can be fairly sure that prospective fixed payments to hospitals will result in increased hospital competition. You may see imaginative financing and service arrangements that are a little bit different from what you've seen before.

Conclusion

If the last decade has any clear message, it is that things are going to be different in the health field and that people in the employee benefits field are going to participate in and shape those changes. Health care crises and tragedies aside, we are all in for exciting times.

Labor's Involvement in Health Care Coalitions

BY KAREN IGNAGNI

Ms. Ignagni joined the staff of the American Federation of Labor in March 1982 as the assistant director of the Department of Social Security and is responsible for all health care issues. Prior to joining the AFL-CIO, Ms. Ignagni spent three years as a staff member on the U.S. Senate's Labor and Human Resources Committee. She was legislative assistant for Senator Pell from Rhode Island and handled health, labor, employment and other domestic policy issues. From 1977-1979, Ms. Ignagni served as research director and then assistant director for the Committee for National Health Insurance. From 1975-1977 she was a health care research analyst for the Department of Health, Education and Welfare.

AS TRUSTEES OF employee benefit plans, you have a unique role in our health care system. If the economy continues to decline and health care expenditures continue to rise, you may be forced to make extremely difficult decisions concerning the future financing and benefit structure of your plans.

As a representative from organized labor, I will focus my remarks around three central issues concerning community health care coalitions: how the AFL-CIO became involved in the coalition movement, our experience to date and how local coalitions fit into our overall health care strategy.

AFL-CIO Involvement

Participation in community health care coalitions is a new experience for many union members. Organized labor did not join the voluntary effort (VE) from which many local coalitions developed. Instead, we chose to pursue a national strategy in support of federal hospital cost containment legislation. Considering the inability of the VE to make a dent in soaring hospital cost inflation, I would say that we made the right choice. It was unfortunate, however, that a majority of the members of Congress did not support our position.

A year ago John Dunlop, of Harvard University, suggested to AFL-CIO President Kirkland that the AFL-CIO participate in discussions on cost, access and quality of health services with the American Hospital Association, the American Medical Association, Blue Cross, the Business Roundtable and the Health Insurance Association of America. Last February, our executive council voted to endorse a statement, along with the other five organizations, pledging a determined effort to promote the development of local coalitions. However, the decision to participate in the Dunlop group has in no way diminished our efforts at the national level to improve the delivery of health care services and to restrain soaring health care inflation.

Many of you have been requested to join local health care coalitions. I thought it would be useful to discuss some of the issues that you, as potential members, will have to deal with in your own communities and, in the process, shed light on organized labor's views on and expectations for local health care coalitions.

Problems With the Present Health Care System

Three major problems exist in our health care system: excessive annual cost increases, insufficient access to services and uneven quality of care. These problems are not new. For some time, annual increases in health care expenditures have risen at more than twice the rate of increase in expenditures for all other goods and services in the general economy. At present, health care costs are rising at three times the rate of increase in the Consumer Price Index (CPI).

Poor Access

Twenty-five million people in our country have no health insurance whatsoever. Unemployment has added another 20 million to that number, bringing the total number of people without health care protection up to 45 million. An additional 15 million people have inadequate coverage. Needless to say, this entire group has little, if any, access to health care services. In addition, there has been a dramatic increase in the number of physicians who refuse to accept Medicare or Medicaid payments, a development that has made it more difficult for the elderly and the poor to obtain health care services.

Uneven Quality

Another problem in the system is the difference in the quality of health care dispensed to individuals covered by private insurance and to people covered by public programs. We have in the past referred to a two tiered health care system. I would suggest that we have a multitiered system, where the services you get depend very much on what you can pay.

Causes

The roots of these problems can be found in the dramatic changes that have occurred in the past quarter century in the practice of medicine and in the structure of our health insurance system. The explosion of information and rapid technological development during the 1950s and 1960s encouraged physician specialization, which led to a decline in primary care physicians, a dramatic increase in ancillary services and, therefore, to higher health care costs. The expansion and modernization of health care facilities rival that of big business. In many cases, hospitals have been forced to acquire new, expensive (and not necessarily cost-effective) technology to recruit and retain physicians.

The Reimbursement System

As a nation we are spending almost $300 billion on health care; however, there is not a great deal of evidence to suggest that we are healthier because of it. The cost of health insurance premiums has skyrocketed, but there are still tremendous gaps in coverage. For instance, in spite of our national concern about wellness, individuals rarely are covered for preventive health care or outpatient diagnostic services. Most insurance packages emphasize hospital care—the most expensive service in our system—and leave out cost-effective primary care that keeps people healthy.

The fact that the health care reimbursement system is open ended, with little incentive for providers to control costs and strong incentive to overutilize services, has been stated many times. This statement deserves to be made again because there has been, up to this point, no significant leadership in Congress to change this situation. Finally, despite the great expectations of policymakers who supported the passage of Medicare and Medicaid, we still have serious access problems in our system.

Solutions

Why are problems in our health care system so difficult to solve? There are many reasons, including the unwillingness of certain participants in the system to discuss comprehensive solutions to one of our nation's most serious problems. As a society we believe that medical care is in a class by itself. We don't purchase health care the way we purchase used cars. Patients are not the real buyers in the system; physicians are their purchasing agents. All of us want the best for our family and friends.

The solution to our problem lies in our ability to reduce the rate of increase in health expenditures without reducing quality or further inhibiting access to services. Organized labor has a plan to control increases in all health care costs. National standards would be set for states to develop prospective budgeting systems for all payers. The program would include hospital and physician services. However, it is not my aim to discuss that proposal in this presentation.

As you join coalitions, many of you may hear that so-called pro-competition plans are the answer to our problems. Proponents of this view would place limits on the amount that employers could contribute to health insurance for their employees and give consumers strong financial incentives to choose less insurance. This idea creates a perverse economic incentive for families that are trying to make ends meet to gamble with their health care and choose less expensive plans. If they are wrong and anyone in their family experiences an unforeseen illness, they will be financially obligated to pay uncovered expenses despite great financial strain. If workers are unable to pay for uncovered services, the cost of health care could increase for individuals who are covered by more comprehensive plans, not to mention the already overburdened state and local governments.

Given the problems in our system, we are advising our members to do six things: work for cost containment legislation, national and statewide; encourage primary care; negotiate reimbursement in advance with providers; monitor utilization; incorporate mandatory second surgical opinions into collective bargaining agreements and encourage alternative forms of health care delivery.

Conclusion

We have encouraged our affiliates and local unions to participate actively in local health care coalitions. In Chicago and Kansas City, organized labor has formed its own coalition. In other parts of the country, organized labor is working closely with business, providers and insurers to solve local problems. We believe that it makes sense to encourage individuals to solve as many problems as possible at the local level.

However, the recent increase in the number of

local health care coalitions may reflect desperation rather than real progress in the field. Those coalitions that survive will have to make hard decisions that may please no one.

The AFL-CIO is involved in the coalition movement because we want to do our part to help reduce health care costs, which affect all of us. Unless every group is willing to do its part, we can look forward to higher inflation, less access and more uneven quality in the delivery of health care.

Encouraging Hospital Involvement in Health Care Coalitions

BY RICHARD L. EPSTEIN

As senior vice president of the American Hospital Association, Mr. Epstein has responsibility for the AHA's legal affairs, directing all litigation and legal activity in which the Association is involved and supervising the AHA office of general counsel. After graduating with a B.A. degree, cum laude, from Amherst College, he received his law degree from Yale Law School. He has specialized in labor and health law and was a trial attorney with the Rochester, New York firm of Harris, Beach, Wilcox, Rubens and Levey. From 1970 to 1978 he served, by appointment of the President, as a member of the Federal Impasse Services Panel, which mediates labor cases involving unionized federal government employees and the agencies employing them. He was also a member of the U.S. State Department's Foreign Services Disputes Panel. Mr. Epstein is currently serving as cochairman of a task force on antitrust and health planning of the Section of Antitrust Law of the American Bar Association and as chairman of the Lawyer's Task Force on Legal Implications of Competition in the Health Field of the American Enterprise Institute. He serves as a member of the editorial board of Employee Relations Law Journal *and is listed in* Who's Who in American Law *and* Who's Who in America.

AS A REPRESENTATIVE of the American Hospital Association (AHA), I want to tell you what we are telling our members about the health care coalition movement, and why we are putting emphasis on it. Recently, we opened an office devoted entirely to health care coalitions and to the needs of our members in dealing and working effectively with such coalitions. The reason we opened this office is that there are several remarkable threads that characterize health care coalitions.

First, although they have many configurations, every one of them is a nontraditional alliance of some sort—nontraditional in the sense that representatives of business, labor, medicine, commercial insurers, hospitals, Blue Cross-Blue Shield and sometimes state government are all sitting together around the table.

Second, health care coalitions are entirely an activity of the private sector. They are not ordained by any federal government regulation or requirement. They are not even put in place as the result of any kind of governmental incentive. They are entirely and solidly a private sector activity.

Third, as we get acquainted with these emerging coalitions, we notice an interesting crochet, if you will, of overlapping but as yet disparate interests. There are any number of things that all of the participants agree on, including the observation that this health system is a good one. They acknowledge that we all need to address the rate-of-cost increases for care. However, there are also things that they do not necessarily agree on, particularly not on how the problem should be approached.

AHA Recommendations

We urge our hospitals to join and participate in the health care coalition movement. For those persons who think perhaps that joining would be an obvious kind of inclination on the part of institutional providers—it is not. In some places there are pockets of ambivalence, but it is an understandable kind of ambivalence. It is based on, among other factors, the human reaction to the unknown. There is also a concern about how much willingness there will be on the part of others who make up the health delivery system to shoulder and share the activities that are necessary to address the problems. Therefore, it is helpful for us to start out with realistic expectations about hospital ambivalence.

There are seven reasons why we think that hospitals ought to join, ought to encourage, ought even to initiate coalitions.

First, coalitions represent an opportunity for hospitals to assert leadership in their local communities. In talking about leadership, I speak of it in the sense of the hospitals' knowledge of available health care resources, their knowledge of needed care (and how to access it) and their knowledge and appreciation of the importance of the quality of care. Leadership means appreciating the role of the other community segments in addressing those very factors. Also, in so many communities, it includes such things as the problem of the disinsured (unemployed workers no longer covered by insurance) and how those people will be taken care of when they need health care.

Second, we encourage our hospitals to realize that joining a coalition is an opportunity either to make or to enhance alliances with other components of the health delivery system. The coalition table encourages the exchange of views and interests. Such an exchange is not necessarily a natural, and it certainly is not a historic, coalescing of interests. However, the coalition table is a marvelous opportunity for hospitals to enhance their relationships at the community level with each of their counterparts.

The third reason is that the involvement of hospitals in the coalition can serve as a catalyst within the hospitals to bring together trustees, management and medical staffs to address the issues of cost containment. That means looking specifically and constructively at patterns of practice and patterns of management behavior—elements that contribute to the cost problem.

The fourth reason is the opportunity for hospitals to educate their own community (staffs, etc.) about the people who are its patients and the problems that go with serving them. I am referring here to that portion of the population that is aged, indigent, uninsured or unemployed. I also mean the problems of medical care, the problems of institutions with respect to research and education and the special problems of small or rural hospitals, as well as access and quality issues.

The fifth reason is that hospitals are a unique source for data. Not only can they provide the data concerning such issues as utilization, but they also can intelligently and usefully evaluate that data for their partners at the coalition table.

Sixth, we point out that hospitals can insist that the other components of the health delivery system become actively engaged in the pursuit of the demand side of this equation—another of the causes of health care cost increases. The equation of cost increases has two sides. One side is certainly the supply-side. I made previous reference to the response of the health delivery system to the incentives, in place now for decades, that have encouraged expansion. If that problem is to be addressed and solved, so too should the demand side be examined. The coalition table is a marvelous setting for hospitals to bring this concept to the attention of their partners.

The seventh reason is that hospitals can help and encourage a private sector mechanism to work effectively. Why? Because the health care coalition provides a place where problems peculiar to a community can be addressed by that community. As an example, I refer to the disinsured. Coalition communities can address that problem at a local level, where unemployment may be particularly high. One community's situation will be different from the situations in other communities around the United States.

Conclusion

In closing, I want to make an appeal that coalition activity and involvement be approached realistically. A health care coalition is not a neighborhood Welcome Wagon. The stakes in this business are substantial for each participating entity and for the patients who are served. This approach requires that we address these issues with thorough candor. Such candor may cause some discomfort and perhaps some tensions in some places, but we cannot really solve a problem without a realistic assessment of it.

If the effort is to be effective, it must be joint, direct and open. Coalition activity is and should be marked by self-interest without self-consciousness. Participants should be able to discover and pursue areas of mutuality while discovering areas of difference and seeking to make appropriate accommodations.

People involved in employee benefits can be singularly helpful in that process because of their unique relationship to the health care cost problem and to the phenomenon of coalitions. With respect to cost issues, they represent buyers; with respect to people issues, they represent accountability. With respect to the institutions that provide health care, it seems to me that they are uniquely situated to provide logical and easy access to all of the components that can help address and work to solve our jointly felt concerns about health care costs.

Health Care Coalitions: A Perspective From the Medical Profession

BY JAMES S. TODD, M.D.

IT IS A REAL privilege for a physician to address those who can and should have a significant influence over the health care system in this country. I am aware of the huge resources you as employee benefit trustees have, and of your responsibility to use them prudently and in the best interest of those you represent.

If anything is certain in this world, it is that we live with ever-increasing change. Nowhere is this change more evident than in health care. There has been a phenomenal technological explosion, to the point that perhaps one-third of the items now routine in medical practice were not available five years ago. More people are receiving more care and demanding more care. The system has done just what it has been rewarded to do; to date, all the incentives have been toward expansion. Now it appears that resources are no longer available for the sort of open ended care to which we have become accustomed, and increasingly the focus has been on cost as a limiting factor, not infrequently to the exclusion of considerations of quality and need.

It almost seems that, without looking at its own contribution to the problem, society expects the health care system to correct itself. The question of health care costs is a complex problem without simple solutions or quick fixes. All segments of society, the medical community included, have contributed to the problem and all must participate in its solution. That solution must be reached cooperatively, avoiding the imposition of unreasoning regulation or legislative constraints. Before the solution can be discussed, however, we must be clearly aware of the contributing causes.

Factors Contributing to Health Care Costs

Probably the largest contribution to increasing health care costs comes from inflation itself, representing some 60% of increased cost. Only 10% comes from population growth and perhaps 30% from increased demand by patients. Inappropriate utilization of health care services, both by patients and physicians, adds its share to health care costs. It has been estimated that 50-80% of emergency room visits, for example, are really not necessary.

Dr. Todd serves on the board of trustees for the American Medical Association, Ridgewood, New Jersey and has served in various capacities for the AMA since 1972. His professional activities include chief of vascular service and associate director of surgery at Bergen Pines Hospital, Paramus, New Jersey; chairman of the intensive care unit and private practice of vascular and neoplastic surgery at Valley Hospital, Ridgewood, New Jersey; visiting attendant in surgery at Francis Delafield Hospital, New York City; and instructor in surgery at Columbia College of Physicians and Surgeons and Columbia Presbyterian Medical Center, New York City. Dr. Todd received his A.B., cum laude, from Harvard College and his M.D., cum laude, from Harvard Medical School. He has served as member/trustee/chairman of numerous professional medical associations and societies and has written a variety of articles for medical publications.

First dollar insurance coverage without doubt contributes to increased health care costs, when it becomes easier to go to the emergency room than it is to keep Band-Aids in the medicine cabinet. There are no incentives to cost or utilization restraint when there is no economic impact on the patient directly. Those patients with first dollar coverage use the health care system twice as much as those without it.

Technology has found more disease, more ways to treat it and obviously has increased the demand for health care. The cost of supporting all who now can be helped by the improvements in medical care has also increased.

We must be aware of the effect of the steady aging of the population as a contribution to our problem. People over age 65 use a decidedly disproportionate share of health care resources, usually of the more expensive kind.

Finally, we must look at what unhealthy lifestyles do to the cost of health care. It has been estimated that if the diseases associated with tobacco were eliminated, health care costs would fall by 11%; if diseases associated with alcohol were eliminated, the decrease would be 10%. Indeed, if the effects of poor lifestyles and accidents were subtracted, it is estimated that health care in this country would cost one-half of what it does now, to say nothing of the reduction of productivity losses.

The Medical Community's Reaction

Let me assure you that the medical profession is just as concerned as you are over these issues. In 1977, the American Medical Association convened the national commission on the cost of health care, which provided some 48 recommendations on how to reduce health care costs. In 1978, the American Medical Association began its corporate visitation program, meeting with the Fortune 500 companies to convince them that the physical well-being of their employees was as important to them as their fiscal well-being. Then, in 1980, came the development of health care coalitions with the American Hospital Association, the Health Insurance Association of America, the National Blue Cross-Blue Shield program, the Business Roundtable, AFL-CIO and the American Medical Association joining in activities calculated to strengthen cost consciousness and to encourage addressing these problems voluntarily.

Local Coalitions

It soon became clear that only so much could be done globally—that local problems and needs required local solutions. Each one of us can and should participate in the solution of these more local concerns. To the medical profession, it seems the local health care coalition program offers great promise. Now better than 100 are in operation throughout the country and, while they vary in composition, the best results have been obtained when all the concerned factions are involved. For any cost containment system to work it must be acceptable to all involved, especially patients; reduce demand for services; and increase and reward cost-effectiveness on the part of all concerned.

Local coalitions have many potential areas of action, none of which really should be ignored. Among these areas are utilization review, development of employee health policies, redesign of benefit packages, health facilities planning, plans to use less expensive modalities, health education programs for employees, alteration of incentives through reimbursement programs, data collection to identify continuing or emerging problems and last (and not to be underestimated) political pressure to accomplish those items deemed worthwhile by the coalition.

Conclusion

Such an operation sounds complex, and it is. We should not anticipate any quick earthshaking results. There are too many attitudes to be changed; there is no clear indication that patients are ready for such restraints. Obviously, we cannot in one action reverse a generation of procedures and attitudes. Indeed, I'm not at all sure that the rush to high technology, high cost care can be slowed.

However, I am absolutely sure that as acknowledged leaders we must try to look cooperatively at what we are individually and collectively about. We need to open lines of communication, develop a better understanding of each other's problems and needs and attack local problems one at a time, thereby perhaps producing a partnership among all the diverse elements involved. Everyone is going to have to give a little, but none should be or need to be compromised in the process.

The American Medical Association stands ready to participate at all levels and makes information, resources and expertise available wherever necessary and desired. Indeed, a whole department has been created within the American Medical Association organization to focus on the problem.

Clearly, more than economics is involved. The goal is to provide quality, cost-effective medical care to all who need it, at a cost we can all afford. We in the medical profession see the coalition movement as a way to accomplish this goal. Organized medicine is committed to finding a cooperative solution to the problem of health care costs, and you must be also.

CHAPTER 10

Retirement

Todd Aldrich

Branch Manager
American Benefit Plan Administrators, Inc.
St. Paul, Minnesota

R. George Martorana

Senior Vice President
Retirement Advisors, Inc.
New York, New York

Steven A. Harrold, FSA

Consulting Actuary
Tillinghast, Nelson & Warren, Inc.
Overland Park, Kansas

Matthew M. Lind, Ph.D.

Vice President, Corporate Planning and
Research Department
Travelers Insurance Companies
Hartford, Connecticut

Marilyn S. Albert, Ph.D.

Assistant Professor of Neurology and Psychiatry
Massachusetts General Hospital
Department of Psychiatry
Boston, Massachusetts

Donald H. Rowcliffe, Jr., CPA

Administrative Manager
Carpenters Welfare & Pension Funds of Illinois
Geneva, Illinois

Pre-Retirement Preparation Assistance

BY TODD ALDRICH

THERE IS GROWING interest from both corporations and union pension funds in retirement preparation assistance. Although corporations and union funds that do provide retirement preparation programs are still in the minority, it is widely believed that in the next five to ten years it will be a rare major corporation that does not provide some assistance to older workers. The major impetus for these programs has been inflation, as well as the necessity of sound financial planning. Many employers and unions also share a sense of social responsibility toward the older worker. This concern may be prompted by ERISA's communication requirements, a desire to encourage early retirement or, in many cases, a response to the growing importance of human resources planning and employee benefits. Finally, as a result of advances in medicine and changing, more healthful lifestyles, people's retirement years have been significantly lengthened. It is estimated that one American in ten is 65 or older today, with one in five expected to be in that category by the year 2030, according to the Bureau of the Census.

A New Definition of Old Age Security

Social scientists, not minimizing the effect of inflation on the retirement experience, have taken a longer view. Since the enactment of Social Security legislation, and a period of increasing industrialization, the nature of physical and emotional security in old age has changed. Today, the role of family in providing security for the aged has been replaced by government, employers and individual initiative. We have created a situation in which individuals must plan for financial security with uncertainties over Social Security payments, changing tax laws and employment opportunities.

In a study of issues and trends in pre-retirement education, U. Vincent Manion (1974) felt that primitive and agrarian societies treated their elderly more humanely than we do. The elderly had an enhanced role in their families, a role supported by systems of property rights transferred through inheritance. Now that these same dependencies and supports have been stripped away in modern society, "retirement poses a major threat to the individual. Pre-retirement education is needed, not just to prepare individuals for a non-work role in

Mr. Aldrich is manager of the St. Paul branch of American Benefit Plan Administrators, Inc. and serves as administrative manager for multiemployer benefit fund pension and welfare programs for a variety of construction and service trades, ranging in size from 50 to approximately 20,000 participants. He previously served as vice president of Midland Administrators, Inc., and prior to that as account executive for American Benefit Plan Administrators, Inc. Mr. Aldrich received his B.A. degree with distinctive scholastic achievement from the University of Wisconsin, Madison and is a candidate for the Certified Employee Benefit Specialist designation.

society, but to add dignity and meaning to one-fourth to one-third of the life cycle."

A Need for Planning

For most, the retirement transition is spun with common thread: uncertainty over when one will die, what future financial resources will be, what basic retirement needs will be, what lifestyle one will ultimately choose, when one will retire, what future rates of inflation will occur that will depreciate the value of retirement assets and reduce the buying power of income from those assets and what the future economic growth will be to the extent that it affects one's economic position relative to the working population. More important, perhaps, is the immediate adjustment to retirement—loss of income and peers and a developing sense of aimlessness—particularly so for male retirees, who have come to depend on work for so much of their sense of identity.

These latter concerns are rarely addressed in pre-retirement programs, however, since many have been designed to provide last minute presentations to members of the pension plan concerning plan provisions and perhaps how they should go about obtaining Social Security benefits. The more ambitious programs treat retirement planning from the perspective of the whole person and provide planning that emphasizes economic as well as family and psychological considerations. Some programs use group discussion techniques or a combination of lecture and group discussion. Although there is naturally room for modification, the following list of requirements has been most often cited for a pre-retirement program to be comprehensive (Monk 1979).

1. Program delivery should be through counseling or group activities or both.
2. The program's starting point should be at least five years prior to retirement.
3. The program is mostly conducted on employers' time.
4. Employees are exposed to more than ten hours of counseling.
5. The employer will foster consultation and provide for counseling services.
6. The counseling program will cover all or most of the following issues:
   a. Pension and Social Security matters
   b. Personal financial planning and consumer problems
   c. Health and personal care
   d. Housing and living arrangements
   e. Leisure and post-retirement employment
   f. Legal aspects.

Statistics show that comprehensive programs, as described, probably do not reach more than 10% of our working population. Most deal with employees between 60 and 65 years of age, although it is preferable to address retirement concerns much earlier.

Why Have Programs Failed?

Studies by the National Council on Aging (NCOA) and the William M. Mercer Company were done on the attitudes of employers who did not start pre-retirement preparation programs in their companies. The NCOA study covered chief executive officers (CEOs) and personnel directors of the Fortune 1000 companies, their attitudes toward older workers and retirement and their companies' employee retirement preparation practices.

Unfortunately, despite awareness of the inflationary effect on retirement security, the issue has "low priority" among companies without programs. A significant minority, about two in five CEOs without programs, doubt that they have the in-house expertise to develop one. Finally, even where programs exist, there remains a problem in getting all qualified employees to participate—"fear of facing retirement" is a difficulty still to be overcome.

In both the NCOA and Mercer studies, reasons for not implementing programs were:
- Not enough people to implement programs
- Other work priorities
- Shortage of time at the moment
- Employees spread over too large a geographic area
- A lack of interest among top people
- Budget restrictions
- Program is intrusive or invades privacy.

Many employers use group counseling or workshops that fail because they put people together on the basis of age, and such a group is likely to be comprised of people with quite varied interests and backgrounds. Information can be too elementary for some or too complex for others, which can create confusion and frustration. Giving generalized information may be practical, but it may not always be useful because participants have difficulty applying it to their own circumstances.

Finally—and this is a key point of failure in programs—participants already in their sixties may find that information they receive may be too late since they've already made many decisions, financial and otherwise, during a career that may have already greatly determined what their lifestyle will be. People who started an investment plan in their fifties and find out in their early sixties at a pre-retirement planning session that they should have done it just the opposite way are going to be confused and feel that the whole effort was not worth it.

The point is, major financial and lifestyle habits are developed over many years, and retirement preparation programs will have a very difficult time trying to change behaviors during the latter stages of the individual's life. This is not to say that the effort should not be made, only that programs must establish realistic expectations of change.

Designing a Program

Along with realistic expectations of change, employers or trust funds must consider other basic issues in designing a program, such as:
- Who is responsible for providing pre-retirement education?
- What does the company or plan hope to accomplish?

- Are these aims consistent with sound business objectives and the objectives of the plan?
- What subjects or topics of interest should be included?
- What age and service breaks should the plan target for participation?
- Should spouses be included?
- What are the best methods to use with the group: oral and/or written communication, audiovisual aids, etc.?
- How can the effectiveness of the program be assessed?

One of the obvious first steps is to get agreement from the company or benefit plan that retirement preparation assistance is a worthwhile goal. The issue of who is responsible for pre-retirement education has been debated for several decades, with little agreement except that most feel that government should not get involved. Many people favor community education, because of the natural advantages of facilities and trained teaching personnel. All agree, and this finding was overwhelming in the NCOA study—that responsibility should be shared between employer and employee.

As another initial step, you may wish to poll a representative group of retirees to determine, for example, what aspects of retirement they most or least enjoy and in what areas were they least prepared for the changes associated with retirement. These questions and others put to retirees can help establish priorities for the type of information and assistance to be made available.

Then, determine what local sources of information and referral are available at little or no cost. Depending on the extent and availability of community services—such as pre-retirement education courses at community colleges, the United Way, area offices on aging, printed materials devoted to concerns of the elderly published by local banks and insurance companies, legal aid services, housing agency publications, etc.—you may wish to tailor a program using an information and referral approach strictly based on "outside" sources. An "inside" or in-house program could address specific topics not adequately provided for by the community at large.

In gathering the information, a good place to start is your state office on aging, which in Minnesota is responsible for administering over 450 programs with a budget of over $15 million from federal and state grants. It's also responsible for administering the Older Americans Act programs in the areas of transportation, homemaker care and legal aid. The State Board on Aging usually publishes a newsletter for seniors—in Minnesota it's the *Senior Spotlight,* which could be made available by funds. Such a newsletter can be a good source of reference for pre-retirees as well as retirees. A recent issue of *Senior Spotlight* contained articles on new developments in health (the "wellness" movement, education), experimental learning programs developed by Control Data Corp. in which computers do the teaching and an editorial that describes the success of and need for further volunteer programs in the state.

In the private sector, there is the United Way in your community. In Minneapolis/St. Paul there are over 200 United Way agencies geared to community action and service programs for the elderly, in the areas of medical and rehabilitative care, housing and home services and job opportunities. A directory (updated annually) of these services can be purchased currently for $7.50. Among the many other free reference and referral guides available are publications from local banks and their trust departments on estate and financial planning; legal aid society publications on the rights of seniors that cover issues such as Social Security, Medicare, consumer fraud, practical advice on setting up a will and on establishing power of attorney or guardianship. The Civil Liberties Union publishes in paperback *Rights of Older Persons.* This publication is an excellent reference work on legal rights and delineates the basic framework of public agencies and services available.

Conclusion

Planning a pre-retirement education program should be viewed as any other worthwhile long term business venture. Serious thought should be given to the characteristics of a particular employee group. It may not be necessary to commit large amounts of resources and effort to the project until it is definitely found to be useful to employees and supported wholeheartedly by corporate management or the fund trustees.

What is called for is some strategic planning—i.e., what can be done this year and how it can be improved and expanded the year after, and the year after that, etc. For example, you may wish to limit your initial effort to a "no frills" approach. Your personnel or fund office staff could be asked to gather the type of materials on local services and facilities previously described. A phone "hotline" list tailored to your geographic area—similar to that shown in the Appendix—could be distributed (at a minimum) to members of the plan who are nearing retirement and to those already retired. Periodic announcements of the existence of the library of materials could be made in company or union meetings. Those employees applying for benefits could be encouraged to pursue their individual concerns with the appropriate sources.

However you decide to start the program, the important thing is that you recognize that retirement preparation assistance should be an integral part of your employee benefits package. It's time to do more than just agree that retirement planning is a good idea—it is time for action.

Bibliography

Manion, U. Vincent. "Issues and Trends in Pre-Retirement Education." *Industrial Gerontology* 1, No. 4 (1974): 28-36.

Monk, Abraham, and Rebecca Donovan. "Review of the Recent Literature: Pre-Retirement Preparation Programs." *Aged Care and Services Review* 1, No. 5/6 (1978-1979): 1-6.

Appendix

PHONE HOTLINES
MINNEAPOLIS/ST. PAUL AREA SERVICES FOR THE AGED

Information
Minnesota Board on Aging's INFO-LINE   1-800-652-9747
Federal Information Center   612-349-5333
County Welfare & Social Service Department's contact,   612-298-5351   (Ramsey)
  "County Coordinator on Aging"   612-348-8585   (Hennepin)
Metropolitan Senior Federation   612-645-3795
  —Insurance   612-645-1398

Financial
Social Security and SSI   612-378-1151
Veterans Administration   612-726-1454
Tax Help; Minnesota Department of Revenue   612-296-3781
Tax Help; Internal Revenue Service (ask for booklet,
  Tax Benefits for Older Americans)   612-291-1422
Food Stamps Hotline   1-800-652-9747
Insurance Information Center   612-339-9273
State of Minnesota Insurance Division   612-296-2488

Jobs or Job Help
Minnesota Department of Economic Security
  (local Job Service office)
"Green Thumb" Program   218-631-3483
Foster Grandparents and Senior Companion Programs   612-827-5641
"Green View" Program   612-646-2292
Senior Aide Program (sponsored by National Council
  of Senior Citizens)   612-224-3727
Seniors in Community Service   612-874-7080   (Minneapolis)
  (National Urban League program)   612-224-5771   (St. Paul)
U.S. Forest Service Senior Employment Program 218-335-2226
RSVP of Greater St. Paul (volunteer services) 612-221-2820
RSVP of Greater Minneapolis (volunteer services)   612-827-8158

Housing
Housing and Urban Development (for federally
  subsidized housing in Minnesota)   612-349-3195
Minnesota Housing Finance Agency
  (low interest housing loans)   612-296-7615
Share-a-Home Program for Minneapolis/St. Paul 612-871-0221

Education
Elderhostel—Summer programs at 23 participating
  state colleges   612-376-2704
Minnesota Private College Council   612-228-9061

Health & Nutrition
Medicare   612-378-1151
Health Maintenance Organizations (HMOs)   612-474-1176
Public Health Nursing Service—St. Paul   612-298-4548

Legal Aid
Minnesota Bar Association   1-612-333-0921
Legal Aid Services   612-332-1441   (Minneapolis)
                                                     612-224-7301   (St. Paul)

Miscellaneous
Consumer Complaints
  Minnesota Attorney General's Office   612-296-3353
  Office of Consumer Service (Minnesota Department
    of Consumer Service)   612-296-2331

Retirement Counseling—Necessity or Frill?

BY R. GEORGE MARTORANA

RETIREMENT PREPARATION PROGRAMS are a concept whose time has come. No longer experiments, they have demonstrated a number of encouraging results throughout the country.

Now in our 25th year of operation, we at Retirement Advisors, Inc. (RAI) have seen a dramatic upsurge not only in interest in this topic, but in the action taken to do something to provide assistance to the employee approaching retirement. Throughout labor and industry, instead of a low priority item that merited little more than "lip service," retirement planning programs are receiving increasing attention. Pension funds that have had programs in existence are taking steps to review and improve them. Moreover, organizations that have stayed on the sidelines while making lengthy studies on whether they should adopt a program in this area are now swinging into action.

I'm often asked whether retirement preparation programs are a necessity or a frill. Can retirement counseling be considered a frill? I wouldn't be honest if I said that retirement preparation programs are never a frill. Several organizations have spent money for programs that have missed the mark because they were not properly planned or were poorly executed. A poor retirement planning program is the most expensive kind.

As senior vice president of Retirement Advisors, Inc. in New York, Mr. Martorana serves as a consultant to management in the areas of sales and marketing and administration, and as director of marketing to multi-employer pension funds. Active in the multiemployer benefits field for over 32 years, he specializes in pre-retirement planning and retiree relations, and has spoken before organizations including the American Management Association, American Society of Personnel Administration, American Society of Insurance Management, Profit-Sharing Council of America and the Pre-Retirement Planning Seminar at the University of Houston, Texas. Mr. Martorana earned his B.B.A. degree at St. John's University, New York.

Background

I might ask the question, "Why get involved with a retirement planning program?" The old attitude was, "Why bother with good old Joe, why help him plan when he will not be working much longer?" This feeling has given way to a more constructive approach involving pre-retirement and post-retirement counseling. Numerous organizations have met their objectives in such programs and have seen benefits accrue to both their senior employees and retirees as well as to the sponsoring organizations themselves.

An effective program should benefit both participants and the organization for it to be judged a worthwhile expenditure of time and money. Also, as with any program, it is important that top management give full support to the program to guarantee its success. If an organization believes that it should make a commitment to older workers and retirees beyond the pension check for either humanitarian or economic reasons, it's important to pay more than lip service to this obligation.

Retirement preparation programs are no longer novel or rare. There has been considerable experience with the benefits of these programs to the participants as well as to their pension funds and the trustees.

The last few years have witnessed a dramatic change of thinking on behalf of the labor-management community. For want of a better term, I'll label this movement "social responsibility awareness." Although much of this concern is being channeled toward other directions, some of it is being focused on the older worker and the retiree. There was a time when retirement counseling was not even thought of and, what's more, was quite unimportant. Several factors have changed this situation. Both labor and management have felt a growing responsibility toward older workers. Of course, the emphasis on communication in ER-

ISA also contributed to the increase in interest, as did the Age Discrimination in Employment Act (ADEA).

Retirement is that stage in life for which the institutions of our society provide the least built-in preparation. The reasons all seem to derive from the fact that retirement in its present scope is only a recent phenomenon. That is, a significant number of people no longer work at a job until they die or become enfeebled, but retire with a prospect of 15 or more years of life remaining. Yet, the changes that come with retirement are more radical and abrupt than between other stages in life and they occur when most people are least able to adapt to change.

Benefits to the Participant

A number of research studies by academic institutions and business research organizations, as well as our long experience in the field, demonstrate that some of the benefits to the participant of an effective pre-retirement program are:

- *Provides a personal formula for a satisfying retirement life.* Pre-retirement planning is no panacea, but it provides sound guidance and direction before retirement, on which a person can plan retirement living that can be meaningful, productive and personally satisfying. Moreover, it will help a person maximize his or her financial resources through careful management.
- *Develops realistic expectations regarding retirement.* An effective program deals honestly with the realities of retirement living. It will enable the employee to look ahead thoughtfully, so that retirement will bring few "surprises." Retirement planning helps people cope with the new experiences that lie ahead.
- *Reduces anxiety related to vague expectations.* From the employee's point of view, the prospect of retirement after a structured life of many years can be terrifying. What will I do with all that time? Can I live on a reduced income? What if I become seriously ill? Can my spouse and I cope with being together every day? Retirement planning can give employees a head start on making adjustments to a new lifestyle.
- *Generates a preventive rather than remedial philosophy.* Such programs help the employee take pre-retirement action regarding expected problems, plan for appropriate action to be taken at the time of retirement and adopt alternative plans for implementation after retirement.
- *Increases understanding and appreciation of retirement benefits.* Benefit communication is an integral part of a pre-retirement planning program. This type of program gives participants the motivation to seek additional information which leads to a greater appreciation of the scope and value of retirement benefits.

For most people, the great change in their pattern of living from being actively at work to being retired is a momentous and, in many cases, a traumatic experience. Although that experience remains in the distant future, it is often an inviting prospect. Many employees have the attitude that retirement will be a ball. No more commuting to work—no more taking orders. But as the time of its actual occurrence draws nearer, it looms up in a different light for many people. Doubts and uncertainties, anxieties and apprehensions become the prevailing mood.

By the time an employee has reached age 60, the passage of the months and weeks can remind him ever more insistently that he is growing older. As he looks ahead, he may see those fearful things that man has always dreaded: idleness, disability and death. "It's a strange thing," commented one union official, "but the older you get the more you like work."

Programs

Sustained and systematized advisory services are now available in a wide range of industries to men and women who have attained the status of seniors in their work. In the last few years, these programs have been offered to every occupational level.

Objectives

Through trial, error and testing, certain basic programs have emerged that effectively meet the desired objectives. These objectives are largely the common aim of all retirement counseling, though their priority may vary from one organization to another. Let's review what most experts consider are the major pre-retirement planning objectives:

- To motivate participants to prepare for retirement
- To help participants develop a favorable attitude toward retirement
- To help participants and retirees achieve realistic expectations
- To show that the sponsoring organization cares
- To influence the retirees' attitudes toward the employer and the union.

Types

The variety of retirement planning programs runs the gamut from individual counseling to group sessions to printed matter. The established formulas for successful counseling programs recognize two basic factors: first, that an effective program should cover a defined subject area and, second, that printed material is essential in communicating a major part of the information to be conveyed.

Individual counseling relies on a specially trained person to impart his expertise to an employee approaching retirement. It's more than having a person explain the benefits that an employee is entitled to. In some organizations, trained psychologists, financial planners, lawyers and other professionals offer this service. Although individual counseling can be tremendously effective, it is quite an expensive technique.

Group counseling sessions have been given on and off company time. Here there are a variety of choices, such as with or without the spouses in attendance or conducted entirely by company personnel or with the help of outsiders. Even though the advantages of effective group counseling far outweigh the disadvantages, a number of pitfalls should be noted. Experience has shown that attendance may be lower than expected regardless of the caliber of the speakers. What's more, those who need retirement counseling most may be the very people who stay away from the sessions, because they do not realize that there is a problem.

Certain other observations regarding group sessions have surfaced. For example:
- Group participants do not usually take copious notes during the session.
- The amount of detailed information that a participant absorbs during the session is limited.
- Retention of the information covered at a group session is also limited.

Although there are negative aspects of a group program, there are also many positive results that can be achieved. Here are a few:
- The support given each other by the participants is reassuring.
- Personal contact can influence the participants' feelings and, therefore, greatly affect their attitudes.
- The skill of the group leader can make a valuable contribution to the end result.

Subjects

The program will be comprehensive even though not all of the subjects it covers are of equal importance to each individual for which it is provided. Experts in the field of retirement preparation are quick to point out that if a pension fund is, in fact, providing retirement counseling, the programs will cover all or a majority of the following subjects:
- Pension and Social Security benefits
- Personal financial planning
- Attitude adjustment
- Health after retirement
- Housing and relocation options
- Activities—leisure and employment possibilities (both part-time and full-time)
- Family relations
- Legal considerations—wills, starting a business, buying or selling a home, etc.

Example

An important concept that can be communicated effectively in a retirement counseling program is a concept from the general field of financial planning—gross income vs. usable income.

Throughout our working years we have always thought of our compensation in terms of gross dollars: $20,000 a year, $30,000 a year, etc.—whatever amount we were being paid. For one thing, it sounded better that way. Those gross dollars give us a greater feeling of success and security than did take-home pay. On the other hand, most of us have complained at one time or another, maybe constantly, about the taxes that reduce our take-home earnings, whether they were Social Security taxes, withholding for federal income taxes or, sometimes, state and city taxes. These deductions are money we don't have available at our fingertips for day-to-day living expenses. They are what we call nondiscretionary funds—money we never see.

However, as you begin your financial planning for retirement, it's important to take a truly objective look at the way well-adjusted retirees view the subject of income AFTER they retire from their active careers. Simply said, a retired person stops emphasizing gross income and concentrates on usable income—the discretionary dollars.

The retirement incomes of most Americans are considerably less than their final salaries or wages before retirement. That is to say, they find themselves with a lower gross income. But if you examine what happens to one's buying power before and after retirement, you can see why retired people should concentrate on the difference in their spendable income—their discretionary dollars—rather than on gross earnings. The happy fact is that these spendable dollars are not reduced anywhere near as much as one might expect after regular salaries or wages are stopped.

Suppose we consider that the retiree's gross income is going to be cut in half after retirement, which is about par for the course. The first reaction is, "How will I be able to get along on half my income?" But if we look at this situation in terms of spendable dollars, the actual difference is not nearly as staggering as it seems at first.

To illustrate this point, let's take a couple, both 64 years old, whose gross income just prior to retirement is $24,000 and who plan to retire at 65. Using our half salary yardstick, they can expect a retirement income of $12,000 from pension checks and Social Security benefits. That's quite a reduction! Now let's look at these figures in terms of spendable income.

This couple, claiming only themselves as exemptions and taking the standard deductions, pay a federal income tax on $24,000 of almost $3,800. In addition, there may be state and local taxes. Approximately $1,600 is withheld for Social Security tax. Some experts agree that 5% of gross income is spent on work-related expenses such as commuting, lunches, some clothing, etc.—which amounts to another $1,200 that may not be needed when one retires. If they contributed 2% of their income to charity, that's another $480. Savings for retirement can also be substantial and considered mandatory—therefore, not spendable. Suppose they put $2,000 a year into retirement savings.

Add up all that nonspendable money that was deducted from their gross income before retirement:

$1,608	Social Security tax
3,800	Federal income tax
1,200	Work-related expenses
500	Charity (approximate figure)
2,000	Retirement savings
$9,108	Total

A total of $9,108 out of their $24,000 was never available to begin with, leaving less than $14,000 of spendable dollars (usable income).

Take a look at their retirement income to see how much is available for spending. Remember, retirement income came to a total of $12,000. There is no longer any Social Security tax deduction and the Social Security benefits that they will collect are not taxable. Federal income tax on the pension income may well drop to zero. Many people feel that once they have retired, they no longer need to add to their retirement savings; after all, they've been saving for retirement. There are no longer any work-related expenses, because the work has stopped. If they continue giving 2% of their income to charity, the dollar amount drops to about $250. Therefore, they can expect to have $11,750 of spendable income. What looked like a huge drop of $12,000 in income is actually the realistic difference between $15,000 and $11,750 of spendable income—a reduction of only $3,142, not $12,000.

When a working person thinks along these lines he or she finds out that the financial adjustment as a retiree will be much less traumatic than originally anticipated. Furthermore, the approach is realistic.

Publications

Previously, I mentioned the need for publications, but will they be read? I think I know what many of you are thinking: "Our people will never read any of that material—they don't read anything we send them." I wouldn't blame you for feeling that way; 25 years ago I would have said the same thing. However, because of some surveys of our clients, I know that good publications are read, understood and appreciated. I'm not saying that the construction worker or truck driver is waiting for the mailman and grabs the retirement publication before *Playboy* or *Sports Illustrated,* but the results of surveys conducted by our clients demonstrate clearly that the publications are read. The Appendix gives some examples.

Post-Retirement Contact

In addition to retirement planning, another development that has gained popularity and impetus is a program involving contacts with retired participants. You can expect an acceleration of these efforts. Programs in this field run the gamut from providing specialized informational services that help a person as he or she faces life in retirement to retiree clubs and group activities. Many experts in the field of aging, as well as most persons experienced in retirement counseling, share the opinion that an effective retirement counseling program should not terminate at retirement. In fact, many feel that meaningful post-retirement contact is, in some ways, more important than a pre-retirement program.

This opinion is substantiated by a survey conducted by the University of Michigan/Wayne State University: "Post-retirement seminars and counseling can often be more crucial than pre-retirement preparation. Assistance is often required because for the first time the reality of retirement is being experienced." No matter how effective a pre-retirement program is, the retiree very often has the feeling that "They have forgotten me." Increasing importance will be attached to eliminating this concern. If your pension fund has done nothing in this area, it is a worthwhile concept to investigate.

The Louis Harris & Associates *1979 Study of American Attitudes Towards Pensions and Retirement* emphasizes another point. Of the four major findings in the survey, the first was on "Inflation and the Quality of Retired Life." The following information was taken from the overview and summary of this major finding:
- Inflation is clearly the number one problem facing retirees and the providers of retirement income today.
- Spurred by inflation, retirement income expectations are rising, and the providers of retirement income are likely to feel increasing pressure for larger benefits in years ahead.

However, besides increasing pension benefits to existing retirees, what can trustees of a pension fund do to help retirees cope with inflation? There are no easy answers to this question, but what can be provided is a practical demonstration of the trustees' continuing concern. They can provide information about how to make the most of retirement income and about services and benefits that are available under federal, state and local community programs.

This kind of bread and butter information can be helpful to all retirees. If you can then supplement the general material with individual assistance to retirees who find themselves in dire financial need, you have a well-rounded retiree service. The personal help can be coordinated by someone who has the experience and expertise to do so.

Using an Outside Service

Many pension funds are availing themselves of comprehensive retiree services offered by professional organizations specializing in such programs. However, as with other consulting services, trustees must be careful in locating the appropriate professional organization.

Here are some guidelines that may be helpful to you in choosing an outside retirement counseling service.
- Does the service include a program of integrated publications?
- Is the program flexible enough to suit your needs?
- Does the service include individual assistance for participants?
- Can the program be identified as your program?
- Does the program contain material that is written in a style that will be clearly understood by your participants?
- Do the publications contain advertising or editorials that could have a backlash effect on your organization or trustees?
- Can the program be personalized with material written by you?
- Does the organization providing the service have a professional reputation and a track record with multiemployer pension funds?

Conclusion

Let's face it, not only the humane incentives for pre-retirement counseling and retiree relations have led many more organizations to provide these programs. For what is an inconsequential amount of money—both in absolute terms and in comparison with what is being spent for pension coverage—many of these pension programs have become a better, more effective vehicle to give advantages to the employer, the union and the pension fund. This value has been achieved by attaching to the program a service that personalizes its benefits for retirement while the participant is still at work. Such a program convinces the participant that when he retires he is more than just a name and address in the pension records.

Appendix

SURVEY CONDUCTED BY A BUILDING TRADES PENSION FUND TO DETERMINE WHETHER PRE-RETIREMENT PLANNING PUBLICATIONS DISTRIBUTED TO PARTICIPANTS APPROACHING RETIREMENT ARE READ AND APPRECIATED

Results of the Survey

Total questionnaires mailed	350 (100%)
Total questionnaires returned	102 (29.1%)
Favorable responses	98 (96.1%)
Negative responses	2 (1.9%)
Undecided	2 (1.9%)

Of the 102 persons who returned the questionnaire, 66% took the time to write a comment.

Comments

"I am very quickly approaching retirement and consider myself of more than average intelligence—yet—these booklets have exposed me to thoughts and ideas I would never have dreamed of."

"They are very helpful to us since we are nearing the retirement age. My husband has no idea whatsoever about retirement and refuses to think about it or discuss it. Your booklets are very helpful, especially the one on Fraud."

"Excellent coverage on potential pitfalls—the average person is vulnerable at one time or another—concise advisement—thank you—We are pleased with the information."

* * *

SURVEY CONDUCTED BY A NATIONAL PENSION FUND IN THE BUILDING TRADES TO DETERMINE WHETHER THE NEWSLETTER DISTRIBUTED TO RETIREES IS READ AND APPRECIATED

Results of the Survey

Total questionnaires mailed	1,000 (100%)
Total questionnaires returned	619 (62%)
Favorable responses	613 (99%)
Negative responses	5 (0.8%)
Undecided	1 (0.2%)

Of the 619 retirees who returned the questionnaire, 143 took the time to write a comment.

Comments

"I appreciate the pension check, but the Newsletter brings such helpful information and a caring attitude. Thanks."

"They tell one thing in particular. At least we have not been written off and completely forgotten."

"I have gotten some real help thru them by contacting the right people."

"Dear Sir: I find this newsletter most interesting and educational and even profitable. Thanking you."

Funding Retirees' Health and Welfare Benefits

BY STEVEN A. HARROLD, FSA

COLLECTIVELY BARGAINED PLANS have enjoyed a long and successful period of providing pension and health and welfare benefits to their union members:
- Pension benefits to provide (along with Social Security benefits) adequate income during periods of disability and after retirement
- Health and welfare benefits to provide protection from the ravages of medical care expenses during the working years
- Health and welfare benefits to supplement Medicare in helping retirees cope with the same medical care expenses experienced by active plan members.

The funding of these benefits almost always is done through negotiated contributions by the employers, usually on a cents per hour basis. In the area of employee benefits, funding means to me the systematic accumulation of money to provide for the benefits promised under the fund. By "systematic," I mean that the monies are accumulated regularly (each day period, each month, each year or some other regular period) and that these payments are made according to an organized plan.

There are several "game plans" under which funds can be accumulated to pay for benefits:
- Pay-as-you-go funding: Under this game plan, a retiree welfare fund would simply wait for the retirees to present their medical bills to the fund and use contributions to pay only these bills.
- One year term funding: Under this game plan, contributions to the fund for the year are intended to provide for those claims that are *started* during the year, even though they may not be *paid* until a later year. You will notice that some planning is required under this method; someone must figure out what portion of the claims that started during the year will be paid at some later time. This amount is called a "reserve"—which will be discussed later.
- Advance funding: Under this game plan, contributions would be accumulated and set aside during the member's active service. Therefore, when he retires, enough money would be

Mr. Harrold is a vice president and principal of Tillinghast, Nelson & Warren, Inc. and manages the employee benefits practice of the firm's Kansas City office. He serves as consultant and actuary to pension and health and welfare plans in the multiemployer field and consults corporate management on matters dealing with employee benefits. Mr. Harrold is a graduate of Carleton College and has been in the benefits field for more than 16 years. He is a fellow of the Society of Actuaries, a fellow of the Conference of Actuaries in Public Practice, an enrolled actuary under ERISA and a member of the American Academy of Actuaries. Currently, he is president of the Kansas City Actuaries Club and vice president of the Heart of America Employee Benefits Conference.

available to pay for all of his medical care benefits thereafter.

For a typical retiree welfare plan, these three game plans—or funding methods—have very different requirements for fund accumulations (as shown in Figure 1):
- Under pay-as-you-go funding, typically very little money is needed when the fund first offers retiree medical care benefits (unless, of course, there are many retirees at the start). As time goes on, however, and the retiree group grows, more and more money is needed to pay the benefits.
- Under one year term funding, there is basically the same cost pattern—very little money needed at first, but much more needed later. Because of the reserve requirements, however, the money needed under one year term fund-

Figure 1

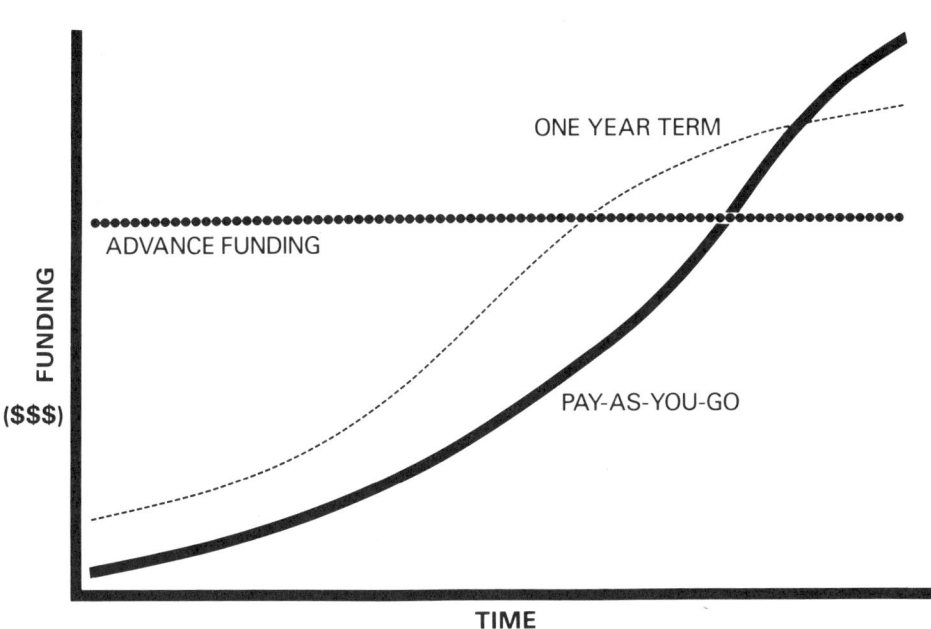

[Graph showing FUNDING ($$$) vs TIME with three curves: ADVANCE FUNDING (horizontal dotted line at top), ONE YEAR TERM (dashed S-curve), and PAY-AS-YOU-GO (solid S-curve starting lower and rising above the others)]

ing is larger at the start than under pay-as-you-go. Because more money is coming in at first, less money will be needed in later years.
- Under advance funding, much more money will be put in at first, to pay not only for current retirees' benefits but also to start to build a fund for future retirees—today's actives. In this situation, future years' funding requirements will be less than in the other two plans, because of the asset buildup in early years.

For those of you who are involved with pension funds, you know that the law requires funds to be accumulated by an advance funding method. Now, although there are many types of advance funding, the situation for pension funds is basically quite simple: The level cents per hour contributions must be enough to accumulate at retirement to the amount needed to pay for the retirees' pensions.

The situation for welfare funds—both for actives and retirees—is not nearly so clear-cut. In the first place, there are no legal funding requirements as there are for pensions. As you might expect, the practices in this area are more diverse.

For many years, welfare benefits for actives (and for retirees) were well-served by setting a level cents per hour contribution equal to the average expected claims over the period of the collective bargaining contract. (Sometimes this contribution was figured on a pay-as-you-go basis, but usually on the one year term basis.) There were two reasons that this procedure worked well:
1. Medical care claims were reasonably level and predictable from year to year, because inflation was relatively stable.
2. The economy was healthy and more members were enrolling in these funds. Remember—under a plan whose membership is growing, fewer cents per hour are needed than under a plan whose membership is declining.

Then three things happened:
1. Medical care claims costs began to escalate dramatically, at a rate that was often more than 50% greater than the rate of increase in the Consumer Price Index, which itself was going up at unheard-of levels. This development means that more cents per hour are now needed to provide benefits for the same number of fund members.
2. Because of the recent downturn in the economy, employment levels fell off and the hours-worked base also declined, sometimes very dramatically—up to 50% or more. Although this development makes the situation bad for the active group, it is even worse for retiree welfare benefits—because as the active membership base declines, more cents

Table I

LOCAL UNION NO. 1 WELFARE FUND
Ten Year Projection of Plan Costs
(millions)

Year	Incurred Medical and Dental (Excluding Med. Supp.) Amount	Cost per Hour	Medicare Supplement Amount	Cost per Hour	Other Amount	Cost per Hour	Net Costs Amount	Cost per Hour
1978	$ 4,732	$ .68	$ 380	$.05	$ 711	$.10	$ 5,823	$ .83
1979	5,182	.74	500	.07	738	.11	6,420	.92
1980	5,703	.81	579	.08	775	.11	7,057	1.01
1981	6,277	.90	671	.10	815	.12	7,763	1.11
1982	6,905	.99	777	.11	861	.12	8,543	1.22
1983	7,599	1.09	900	.13	910	.13	9,409	1.34
1984	8,359	1.19	1,028	.15	964	.14	10,351	1.48
1985	9,198	1.31	1,174	.17	1,034	.15	11,406	1.63
1986	10,113	1.44	1,341	.19	1,101	.16	12,555	1.79
1987	11,131	1.59	1,532	.22	1,175	.17	13,838	1.98
1988	12,245	1.75	1,750	.25	1,257	.18	15,252	2.18

per hour are needed to pay for the retirees' benefits.
3. Finally, Medicare cut back the benefits it will pay. This cut affects only the retiree group, the subject of this paper. When Medicare pays less, other plans—your funds—must pay more.

The Problem

Now, if you will let me put on my actuary's hat for just a minute, I would like to show you some examples that will illustrate some of the ideas discussed previously. The point of these examples is the need to *measure accurately* the current and future costs of welfare benefits for retirees.

Table I shows a ten year financial projection made for a client that I'll call Local Union No. 1. This plan provides for its members:
• Medical care and dental benefits for actives
• A Medicare supplement for retirees
• Weekly disability income and life insurance benefits for actives.

Shown in the table are the estimated costs of the program, the related cents per hour contributions for those three classifications of benefits and the total. (The "other" category also includes estimated projections of expenses less self-payments and investment income.)

To perform the projection, we assumed that medical care costs for both actives and retirees would increase at the rate of 10% per year (in retrospect, this rate was less than the actual increase in medical care costs to date). We also assumed that the hours-worked base would be seven million hours each year. To complete the background, the average contribution rate during 1978 was 77½¢ per hour; at the end of the year, the rate was scheduled to increase to 85¢ per hour.

Several conclusions can be drawn from analyzing these results:

• First, looking at the far righthand columns, the overall plan costs in 1988 are expected to be *2.6 times* that in 1978 (going from 83¢ per hour to $2.18 per hour).
• Second, looking at the far lefthand columns, the medical and dental claims costs for actives in 1988 are also forecast to be *2.6 times* the 1978 claims (going from 68¢ per hour to $1.75 per hour).
• Finally, looking at the second set of columns, the Medicare supplement benefits in 1988 are predicted to cost *five times* the 1978 benefits (going from 5¢ per hour to 25¢ per hour).

Note that the heading for medical and dental benefits for actives is *incurred* claims, but there is no such heading for the Medicare supplement for retirees. The funding for this plan was a combination of pay-as-you-go for retirees' welfare benefits and one year term for the actives' benefits.

To emphasize the need to measure the experience under these plans accurately, let's take a minute to look at these things I have called reserves. As you'll see, this part is vitally important to the measurement process, and not everyone looks at reserves in the same way.

When I use the term "reserve," I mean the dollar amount of an obligation to pay a benefit in the future, as a result of some accident or illness (or other situation) that has already occurred. For example, at the end of the fund's plan year, the following obligations can be identified:

- The amount that the fund's auditors have to be paid for the annual audit, which won't be completed until after the year is over, would be set up as an *"accrued expense" reserve.*
- For claims that have been processed, but for which the check has not yet been delivered to the fund member, an amount would be set up for a *"claims reported but not paid" reserve.*
- For claims that have been started—or incurred—but for which the member hasn't yet submitted his claims form to the fund's administrator, an *"incurred but not reported" (IBNR) claims reserve* would be set up.
- For members who have accumulated hours in the fund's hour bank, so that they can continue their eligibility even though their future hours worked may fall way off, an *"hour bank" liability* would be set up.

In measuring the fund's experience for the year, it's important that all of these reserves be evaluated accurately. The first two types of reserves are really very simple to calculate—you could use the accountant's estimate of his expense for the year or you could add up the "processed but not paid" claims. Sometimes, for example, the books of the fund are held open after the end of the year so that these claims can be paid; then, these reserves can be reduced. They are very often small amounts.

The other two reserves mentioned, the IBNR and hour bank reserves, involve actuarial calculations, based on analyses of historical claims and employment patterns under the fund. The three key elements in an actuarial reserve are:

- The probability that some future event will take place
- The amount of money needed to be paid at that future date
- An interest rate used to figure how much money is needed now to accumulate to the necessary amount in the future.

Following are three examples of reserve calculations, showing some problems that can arise.

The first example is the same one used for the financial projection. It illustrates the need to review the financial results shown in the annual report of the fund carefully. When we began our work with this fund, we first reviewed the audited financial statements for 1976 and 1977 (see Table II).

Note the following items:

- First, the assets have grown from $3,390,000 to $3,873,000.
- Second, although the assets have increased, the liability for accrued claims has actually decreased, from $815,000 to $677,000.
- Next, notice that the assets are exactly equal to the plan liabilities, with a balancing item called "unassigned funds."

I said that the assets were up, but the claims reserve was down. Further investigation showed that the paid claims for the current year were almost 25% higher than last year, yet the reserve decreased—all without disclosure of a change in the method of calculating the reserve amount (see Table III).

Table II

LOCAL UNION NO. 1—WELFARE FUND STATEMENT OF ASSETS AND LIABILITIES
(millions)

	Year-End 1976	1977
Assets		
Total	$3,390	$3,873
Liabilities		
Accrued claims	$ 815	$ 677
Accounts payable and accrued expenses	28	89
Unassigned funds, reserved for future benefits and administration	2,547	3,107
Total	$3,390	$3,873
(Surplus/(Deficit)	–0–	–0–

Table III

LOCAL UNION NO. 1— WELFARE FUND RESERVE ITEMS
(millions)

1. Hour bank liability—No number
2. Change in claim reserve

	1976	1977
Claims paid (incl. exp.)	$3,114	$3,855
Claims reserve	815	677
Ratio: Reserve/paid	26%	18%

Table IV

**LOCAL UNION NO. 1—WELFARE FUND
ASSETS AND LIABILITIES**
(millions)

Assets	$3,873	$2,750
Liabilities	Year 1977 (Auditors)	Year 1978 (Actuary)
Accrued claims	$ 677	$1,630
Accounts payable and accrued expenses	89	50
Hour bank liability	—	1,730
Unassigned funds reserved for future benefits and administration	3,107	—
Total liabilities	$3,873	$3,410
(Surplus/Deficit)	–0–	$ (660)

Table V

**LOCAL UNION NO. 1—WELFARE FUND
ASSETS AND LIABILITIES**
(millions)

	1978
Assets	$ 2,750
Liabilities	(Actuary)
Accrued claims	$ 1,630
Accounts payable and accrued expenses	50
Hour bank liability	1,730
Unassigned funds reserved for future benefits and administration	—
Subtotal	$ 3,410
Present value of future medical claims on current retirees	$ 6,650
Total liabilities	$10,060
Surplus/(Deficit)	($ 7,310)

Now, look at Table IV, which compares the balance sheet status of the fund for the years 1977 and 1978.

- First, note that the assets on hand actually were reduced by 30%, from $3,873,000 to $2,750,000—as a result, as you might expect, of excesses of claims plus expenses over contribution income.
- Next, note that a new liability item has been introduced: the hour bank liability. Under this plan, hours worked but not needed to preserve current eligibility go into an hour bank. The member who works an insufficient number of hours to maintain his current eligibility may draw on his hour bank to preserve his eligibility for a limited period of time.
- Finally, note that the accrued claim liability (or the IBNR reserve) in year 1978 is exactly double the amount that it was *two years previously*—$1,630,000 compared with $815,000.

Therefore, instead of inserting a balancing item to maintain the balance sheet equation, a determination of each individual liability was made, using standard actuarial techniques. The result, as Table IV clearly indicates, is that the fund is in a deficit position: Liabilities exceed assets by $660,000, a figure that represents almost 20% of the liability amount.

One other item: Remember that the Medicare supplement benefit for retirees was funded on a pay-as-you-go basis from current employer contributions. If we include on the balance sheet (see Table V), the present value today of all future medical benefits for only today's retirees, here's what happens:

- Total liabilities now exceed total assets by $7,310,000.
- Assets are only 27% of total plan liabilities.

A footnote to these results: In the following year, the auditor's request carried the following statements:

> ... before we can complete our audit report for The Fund, we need the amount of the liability with respect to the value of future medical benefits on current retirees. ...
>
> Please indicate if the liability was determined in accordance with the actuarial assumptions utilized the prior year or, if there were changes, the nature of the changes and the net effect on the amount. ...

Two other examples of the importance of reserves will be useful:

Local Union No. 2

The first example concerns a situation in which the welfare benefits were being funded through an insurance company. At the end of 1979, the insurance company requested a 30% rate increase, which would have caused medical care expenses to increase from $5.6 million to $7.3 million. At that

Table VI

LOCAL UNION NO. 2
SELECTED FINANCIAL INFORMATION
(millions)

	For Year Ending December 31	
	1979	1980
Medical expenses	$5.6*	$5.5
Net gain for the year	(0.5)	0.8

*Insurance carrier request for 30% rate increase to $7.3 million, which was actual experience.

Table VIII

LOCAL UNION NO. 2
CONCERNS

1. Earnings Distortion
   A. Year of change—major
   B. Subsequent years—minor, unless substantial growth

2. Unreported Liability
   A. Continual, unless corrected by changes of policy
   B. Potential implications—merger or acquisition (if a regular employer)

Table VII

LOCAL UNION NO. 2
SELECTED FINANCIAL INFORMATION
(millions)

	For Year Ending December 31		
	1979	1980	
		As Reported	Correct
Medical expenses	$5.6	$5.5	$7.3
Net gain for the year	(0.5)	0.8	(1.0)

Table IX

LOCAL UNION NO. 3—
HEALTH AND WELFARE FUND

BALANCE SHEET—SEPTEMBER 30, 1981
PER AUDITORS

Liabilities and Fund Balance
(dollars)

Liabilities	
Accounts payable	$ 5,071
Claims payable	537
Claims incurred but not reported	78,774
Hour bank liability	217,961
Total liabilities	$302,343
Fund balance	$200,892
Total liabilities and fund balance	$503,235

time, the fund decided to terminate its insured arrangement and go "self-funded." In doing so, the treatment of the IBNR claim reserve was changed; Table VI shows the medical expenses reported during the next year, along with the fund's net gain for the year.

Note that I used the term "self-funded," not "self-insured." I did that for a very important reason: The minute that an insurance company no longer covers the reserves, there is no longer any "insurance" involved. Members can look only to the fund for their benefits. So the term "self-insured" really isn't correct, is it? Under "self-insurance," there is really no insurance—so let's think in terms of "self-funded."

Getting back to the example, what actually happened after all the claims were in proved that the insurance company was right! Table VII shows what the real medical expenses and gain for the year were at the end of the next year (1980).

Table VIII highlights these issues and the possible impact of an incorrect treatment of reserves during a year of transition from being insured to being self-funded.

Local Union No. 3

As a final example, we were asked to make an actuarial review of the following health and welfare plan (Local Union No. 3). As Table IX shows, the plan apparently has a surplus (labeled "Fund Balance") of $200,892, 66% of total liabilities.

Table X

LOCAL UNION NO. 3—
HEALTH AND WELFARE FUND
BALANCE SHEET—SEPTEMBER 30, 1981

Liabilities and Fund Balance

Liabilities	Per Auditors	Per Actuary
Accounts payable	$ 5,071	$ 5,071
Claims payable	537	537
Claims incurred but not paid	78,774	99,463
Hour bank liability	217,961	557,621
Total liabilities	$302,343	$662,692
Fund balance	$200,892	$(159,457)
Total liabilities and fund balance	$503,235	$503,235

Table X shows the results of applying standard actuarial techniques to the fund. Note the difference in the IBNR reserve ($99,463 versus $78,774), but note especially the difference in the hour bank liability: $557,621 versus $217,961. As a result of these actuarial calculations, the fund balance changed from a $200,892 surplus to a $159,457 deficit (24% of plan liabilities).

Retiree Welfare Costs

We've spent some time looking at projections of welfare costs under high inflation and at the importance of reserves in measuring plan experience. Both of these factors are important in determining the level of retiree funding, even though we haven't limited our examples to retiree plans. For the balance of this presentation, we will focus on some of the things that are applicable solely to retirees' welfare costs.

As stated previously, inflation, declining employment and Medicare changes were the key elements that made funding welfare benefits different from funding pension benefits for retirees. Now take a look at the impact of 1982 changes in Medicare on the potential costs of providing Medicare supplements to retirees. Shown in Table XI are two sets of results, drawn from the Local Union No. 1 example:

- The first set of results at the top of the table are the Medicare supplement numbers from the first table.
- The set on the right demonstrates the impact of the changes made in Medicare for 1982.
- At the bottom is an individual claim analysis.

Effective in 1982, Medicare reduced its level of payments to covered beneficiaries. Based on a review of a typical plan of benefits, Medicare would have paid 85% of the retirees' claim in 1981, but only 80% of the claim in 1982. If the claim were $200, then the Medicare supplement plan would have paid $30 in 1981 (15% of $200 is $30) and $40 in 1982 (20% of $200 is $40). This increase from $30 to $40 represents *a 33% increase* for the Medicare supplement plan.

As shown in Table XI, a 33% benefit increase adds 4¢ per hour to the retirees' costs in 1982, and 8¢ per hour in 1988. These results do *not* reflect changes in Medicare scheduled to take effect during 1983.

Review of the Questions

Consider the following questions:
1. Are retirees' medical care costs significant? Look again at Table I:
- During 1978, it's clear that the answer to this question is *no*. Total plan costs are 83¢ per hour; the retirees' costs are only 5¢ per hour (or about 6% of the total), which is probably an affordable level.
- However, as the retiree group gets to be a bigger percentage of the total group and as inflation increases, even pay-as-you-go funding costs increase by five times, from 5¢ per hour to 25¢ per hour (or 11% of the total).
- Further, when the Medicare changes are taken into consideration, the pay-as-you-go cost for retirees is almost *seven times* what it was, projected at 33¢ per hour (or 15% of the total).

We would conclude that retirees' welfare benefits are expected to be a significant portion of the total plan costs. Also, if I were a betting man, I'd bet that the younger worker, who is being asked to give up 28¢ per hour more to fund retirees' benefits, will agree with me!

We must consider two other things to answer question 1:
- At the time our analysis was made, we estimated that the amount of money needed to fund (in one shot at that time) all future welfare benefits for only the current retirees was $6.65 million. This amount is what would have been accumulated had this plan always been using advance funding, and it's exactly like the unfunded past service costs you've heard about under a pension plan. At seven

Table XI

LOCAL UNION NO. 1—WELFARE FUND

Ten Year Projection of Retirees' Medical Care Costs

Year	Before 1982 Medicare Cutback Amount	Cents per Hour	After 1982 Medicare Cutback Amount	Cents per Hour
1978	$ 380	5	$ 380	5
1979	500	7	500	7
1980	579	8	579	8
1981	671	10	671	10
1982	777	11	1,036	15
1983	900	13	1,200	17
1984	1,028	15	1,371	20
1985	1,174	17	1,565	22
1986	1,341	19	1,788	26
1987	1,532	22	2,043	29
1988	1,750	25	2,333	33

Average Claim: $200

In 1981:	Medicare pays	$170	(85%)
	Plan pays	30	(15%)
		$200	

In 1982:	Medicare pays	$160	(80%)
	Plan pays	40	(20%)
		$200	

Table XII

RETIREE WELFARE COSTS

Summary—Local Union No. 1

1978—5¢ per hour
1988—25¢ per hour (retiree growth plus inflation)
1988—33¢ per hour (Medicare)
1988—39.5¢ per hour (past service liability)
1988—Declining hours worked?

million hours a year, funded over 30 years like a pension plan, it would take another 6½¢ per hour to pay off that liability at 6% interest (see Table XII).

- Even under pay-as-you-go, there will come a time when the relationship of retirees to total plan participants will level off; retiree costs won't be eating up a larger and larger percentage of the fund's assets. However, if the "hours-worked" base declines, you would still need more cents per hour, just because retirees' benefits are there.

2. Should this type of projection be performed for your fund?

You, as a trustee, can make your decisions about retirees' benefits in a proper fashion only if you have all the facts in front of you. I urge you strongly to work with your advisors and actuaries to have this work done.

You may review the results of all this work and choose to proceed just as you have in the past, and that's all right, too. My only point is that you should have all the facts in front of you, so that you can make intelligent decisions about plan benefits and how they are to be financed.

3. What types of funding arrangements are currently in existence, and what are some of the other issues?

Funding

Different funds have approached the funding of retiree welfare benefits in different ways. Some examples are:
1. Eliminate the benefit.
2. Establish a separate trust for retirees' welfare benefits.
3. Use the current trust already set up for active members, but keep track of the retirees' experience separately.
4. Use the pension plan vehicle.

Take a look at these four alternatives:
1. Eliminate the benefit.

Don't laugh! This solution may prove to be the only workable one, once the size of the emerging obligations is identified and translated to a cents per hour basis. But we must look at the situation this decision puts our retiree group in. What are their choices?
- They can go without insurance, which is a pretty risky situation, even for those fortunate enough to have accumulated a tidy little nest egg at retirement. It doesn't take much of an illness to wipe out a life's savings.
- They can purchase insurance coverage from a commercial insurance carrier. The problem with this solution is that for individual policies most commercial carriers require that, at most, only 60¢ out of every premium dollar goes for paying claims, leaving 40¢ of every dollar for expenses and profit. Based on the experience of the funds that we've seen, that's not a very good buy.

Is there another option? Yes! That is to permit retirees to buy their medical care benefits from the fund! Under this alternative solution, the retirees as a group fund the entire cost of their benefits.

Remember our Local Union No. 1 example? This is the solution it chose, and after three years of experience it seems to be working pretty well. However, during the transition period, there were some significant problems. The main one was that only those retirees who thought they needed medical care signed up for the coverage, and there was no premium that could have been charged that would have provided sufficient money to pay for the benefits.

Therefore, the fund agreed to use some of its current assets and income to make it through the transition period. As time went on and more and more new retirees elected the coverage, the average age of the retirees became much lower and the overall cost per retiree dropped to a manageable level. Today, the retirees as a group support their own claim expenses.

There was one other problem when the transition was made from using cents per hour contributions to using self-pay, and that was: What sort of promises had been made to current retirees and what sort of legal problems might arise if, for example, a retiree sued the fund? Let's hold that issue for a while, and come back to it after we look at the other three funding vehicles.

2. Set up a separate retiree trust fund.

This course might seem to make the most sense from a theoretical point of view:
- A separate trust is set up to receive contributions (either cents per hour or self-pay) and pay benefits.
- The retirees can look only to their own pool of money to provide benefits.
- The actual costs of the retiree benefits program will be clearly identified.

However, there are some disadvantages. We don't feel that this solution really is necessary. Not only will there be extra administrative work in handling another trust, but there's no reason why the separate experience of the retirees can't be kept track of in the active members' fund. Plus, as in the Local Union No. 1 situation, the larger fund for active members can be used as a buffer against temporary bad experience for the retiree group.

3. Use one fund for actives and retirees.

This solution seems to be the practical way to handle the situation, although you must be careful to keep track of retiree claims and contributions for retirees. It accommodates nicely either the pay-as-you-go method, the one year term method or the advance funding method. Both cents per hour and self-pay contributions can be funneled into the same trust and used together for investment purposes.

4. Use the pension plan as the funding vehicle.

There are some pension funds, which have been in existence for several years, that pay medical care benefits to retirees right out of the funds' assets. The pension plan vehicle might look like a natural place to use the advance funding technique because, as we've seen earlier, monthly pensions are required by law to be advance funded.

There are, however, potential dangers if this approach is taken:
- In some funds, to figure the annual cost requirements, the actuary uses advance funding techniques for the retirement pension benefit and one year term for the disability, death, termination *and* retiree welfare benefits. As seen earlier, as the retiree group grows to be a larger percentage of the total group, and as inflation continues, the costs of their medical

Table XIII

ADVANCE FUNDING—SAMPLE COSTS

Benefit	Cost (Cents per Hour)
• $360 per month *pension*	90¢
• $36 per month *medical care* (no inflation)	9¢
• Add a spouse	18¢
• Add inflation at 5% per year	27¢
• All this in addition to actives' costs	

care benefits will increase on a cents per hour basis if the one year term costing is used for their benefits.
• How do the Pension Benefit Guaranty Corporation's obligations relate to welfare benefits? The PBGC at least knows the problems associated with monthly pension benefits, but what about welfare benefits? Are they covered? Would participants *think* they're covered? We would guess that the PBGC would not cover these benefits, but the question is what the plan's members might be led to believe.

The pension plan could be broadened to include an additional monthly benefit, one intended to cover the anticipated premium requirements for retirees' welfare benefits. This idea might at least be one answer to the PBGC question, as the welfare benefit is now expressed as a dollars per month benefit. You could even plan to have the benefit increase as inflation increases, like any other cost-of-living pension adjustment.

Costs

We don't feel that the pension plan is necessarily the best vehicle to use for funding retirees' welfare benefits. Even if you decide that you want to apply advance funding concepts, that can be done just as easily through the welfare plan trust.

Look at what such a plan might cost; use the pension plan example in Table XIII to get started. Assume that pension benefits for new retirees average about $360 a month—(that's $12 a month for a worker with 30 years of service) and that the pension plan costs 90¢ per hour. Also assume that the right monthly cost for the retirees' welfare benefit today is $36 a month, or one-tenth of the pension benefit. Then, using the same advance funding methods as the pension plan, the retiree welfare plan ought to cost 9¢ per hour—one-tenth of the 90¢ per hour rate needed for pension—and that's what ought to be going into the welfare fund to provide for current and future retirees' benefits.

Now, what happens if all our members are married and all spouses are covered by the welfare plan? The cents per hour cost for the welfare plan would be 18¢ per hour—exactly double the cost for "members only" coverage.

Finally, what happens if we assume that future inflation will go up at, for example, 5% per year? Then the advance funding cents per hour costs would increase by about 50%, to 27¢ per hour for the retiree and spouse.

Other Issues

Let me just touch on four other issues related to retirees' welfare benefits:
• Legal problems and members' expectations when benefits are reduced or eliminated
• The treatment of "early retirees" compared with "normal retirees"
• The problem of younger members' reactions to the cost of retirees' benefits
• Communications.

Take, for example, the fund that has been providing retiree welfare benefits for some years, which decides it wants to eliminate them. Further assume that the collective bargaining agreement defines only the cents per hour amount that employers must contribute and that the trust document states that retirees' benefits are to be the same as those for actives, except that Medicare pays first. Finally, assume that the summary plan description given to members reflects all of this information accurately.

Legal Problems and Member Expectations

What do you do for the retiree who, at the time these benefits are eliminated, is in the middle of recovering from a heart attack, with huge medical expenses still ahead? Do you (can you) say: "No more benefits for you!"? What about retirees who have had their retiree medical costs covered in the past? Can you say that they're no longer covered? What if they're uninsurable? What about those workers eligible to retire? They've given up their cents per hour in the past in anticipation of future benefits. If you continue benefits only for current retirees, do you penalize these members just because they elected to continue to work and not to retire? Finally, what about other active members? They, too, have given up current wages in anticipation of future benefits. What do you tell them? At least the issue is clear for *future* new members of the fund: Since they haven't yet been covered, they should have no future expectations.

Let's assume that one of the current retirees on claim decides that he's been wronged and brings suit against the fund. Who is liable—the fund, from future contributions? Or the trustees?

We believe that, in the words of one attorney, careful drafting of the plan instruments is vitally important. For example, language should be in the document that says specifically that the continued provision of benefits under this fund will be made only to the extent that monies are available. Also, the plan document should permit the trustees to be able to reduce benefits if they find that current and expected future contributions will not be sufficient to provide for the current level of benefits. Finally, it's most important that these provisions of the plan be communicated clearly and effectively to all plan participants.

Early Retirees

As you know, medical costs for members who elect early retirement before age 65 are much larger than the costs for retirees over age 65, because once you reach age 65, Medicare benefits help fund a large portion of the medical bills. Do (or should) funds treat these early retirees any differently than those over age 65? I suspect that, as a result of cost considerations, most funds require substantially higher self-payments from early retirees than from retirees over age 65.

Younger Members

One of the crucial issues you will have to deal with is how to convince the younger members of the fund to give up current income to provide welfare benefits for retirees, assuming that retirees aren't being asked to fund the entire cost. Perhaps the one major advantage of the advance funding system is that younger members can honestly be told that the current income they're giving up will ultimately be returned to them in the form of their own medical care benefits, just as they are giving up current income in anticipation of future pension benefits. This approach seems to me to be a much easier sale than convincing them to give up ever-increasing amounts for the benefit of current retirees.

Communications

Communications was touched on briefly during the discussion of legal issues and member expectations, but it deserves special mention. Just as it's important to draft the plan documents carefully, it's even more important that members be told exactly what promises are being made to them by the fund.

Absolutely the worst situation I can imagine is to have a member give up current income during his working years in anticipation of future welfare benefits, only to find out the money's not there when he gets ready to retire.

Therefore, we should keep our members aware not only of the benefits available under the plan, but also of the financial status of the fund. ERISA requires that we provide summaries of the plan's financial status once a year. Use your summary annual reports as a communications tool! Don't just fill in the blanks on some form prepared by a bureaucrat—a form that no one can read; dress it up!
- Use charts.
- Show the fund's history.
- Sell its financial strength to the members—or, if the financial position is getting worse, tell them about it. They appreciate the benefits and will be more supportive of additional cost requirements if things are explained properly.

Summary

Here is a brief summary of the discussion about the funding of retirees' welfare benefits:
1. The major problems are runaway inflation, declining contribution bases, Medicare cutbacks and measuring future costs accurately through financial projections.
2. There are three major ways to fund the cost of these benefits: pay-as-you-go, one year term or advance funding.
3. These benefits can be funded through either a separate welfare trust for retirees, the same welfare trust used for actives or perhaps even the pension plan.
4. Some special problems might arise in the areas of:
    - Employee expectations not met
    - Lawsuits from unhappy members
    - Larger benefits for retirees under age 65
    - Resistance from younger plan members
    - Communications.

Course of Action

In conclusion, here is a three step plan that seems to me to be the only way to resolve these questions.
1. *Plan* for the benefits.
2. *Provide money* to fund the benefits.
3. *Communicate* the benefits and the fund's status effectively.

You must first identify what level of benefits you want to provide. You then must measure your obligations accurately, working with your fund's actuary to develop cost projections. Then you must decide how to pay for the benefits—cents per hour or self-pay. Finally, and most important of all, you must tell your members about the benefits, about the cost requirements and about the plan's financial status.

Work: The Fourth Leg of Retirement

BY MATTHEW M. LIND, Ph.D.

I WILL BEGIN by providing you with some perspective on our economic security structure and its components.

The role of each leg in the "retirement income stool" has undergone significant change during the last several decades. The most striking change has been the increasing dependence of elderly households on Social Security for income. Even in the relatively short span from 1967-1977, the proportion of income from Social Security for households consisting of persons ages 65-71 grew from 28% of income to 38%. For households over age 75, of course, this shift is even more dramatic, with Social Security accounting for 48% of income.

During the same years, wages and salaries from employment fell a whopping 40% for households of ages 65-71, to only 21% of retirement income. Only income from occupational pensions remained relatively stable during that period. Asset income, including personal saving, increased slightly.

The decline in the share of income derived from wages and salaries reflects the increased ability of the elderly to afford leisure, a triumph resulting from Social Security advancements and our national economic prosperity. It is also a reflection, however, of national policies that favor retirement over work.

The hard questions before us are: Do these policies make sense in today's economic and social climate? Do most older people wish to cease working? Are they able to work?

Some Considerations

Increased Older Population

First, the combination of longer life expectancy and a drastically lower birth rate will result in a much higher proportion of older people in the population—people over age 65. This high proportion of potential retirees to active workers suggests that great stress may be placed on our Social Security system, precipitating not only intergenerational conflict but also a heavy cost burden on our industries in an increasingly competitive international marketplace.

Mr. Lind, as vice president of corporate planning and research for The Travelers Insurance Companies, is responsible for planning and performance monitoring of the company's diverse businesses and for major corporate development activities. Prior to joining Travelers in July 1979, Mr. Lind was executive director of the Pension Benefit Guaranty Corporation. He has also served as a management associate at the Office of Management and Budget, where he was actively involved in the development of national health insurance legislation and the policy analysis and implementation of pension reform legislation. During 1980, he served as staff director for the Technical Committee on the Economy for the 1981 White House Conference on Aging and most recently was appointed by Governor William A. O'Neill to the Connecticut Teachers Retirement Board. In addition, Mr. Lind heads The Travelers National Leadership Program, which is focused on applying the company's full corporate resources to meeting the needs of older Americans. He received S.B. and S.M. degrees in electrical engineering from Massachusetts Institute of Technology and M.A. and Ph.D. degrees from Harvard in applied mathematics. A frequent lecturer, Mr. Lind has spoken at numerous Foundation and other educational meetings and is currently chairman of the Foundation's Government/Industry Relations Committee and a member of the Educational Program Committee.

Increased Desire for Post-Retirement Work

Next, as people live longer and enjoy more healthy, vigorous years after age 65, being sidelined full time makes less and less sense to them. In 1981 pollster Lou Harris found that 73% of people age 65 and older would like some type of part-time paid work after retiring. They see work as a way to remain active, alert and useful and as a way to earn badly needed extra income in a time when inflation is draining fixed income.

This desire to remain active and productive in later years is also reflected among workers in their 50s, who are looking ahead to retirement. In a 1980 study conducted in my own company, The Travelers, fully 85% of employees over age 55 responding to the survey indicated a preference for some form of paid work following traditional retirement.

A recent National Council on Aging study showed that 43% of the labor force age 55 and above wishes some kind of employment after retirement. Among those persons who would like post-retirement employment, there is a strong preference for part-time work and for the same kind of work as performed during the respondent's career.

Above all, the rapid rise in the numbers of older Americans expected over the coming decades is creating the need for a new definition of the word "old." This need leads to my third point: There is growing medical evidence to support the fact that many people are intellectually and behaviorally as alive at age 75 and 80 as they were in their 40s and 50s.

Abilities of the Older Worker

We have an outmoded view that "old" is "sick." In fact, sick old people are sick because they are sick, not because they are old. Over 95% of the old people in this country don't live in nursing homes. The proportion of individuals who have not seen a doctor in two years is 13% between ages 25 and 50, 11% between ages 50 and 65 and 13% between ages 65 and 74. The elderly are vulnerable, of course, to a greater loss of health with the onset of any disease that comes on the heels of normal aging changes.

Further, we know that a major loss of mental function is not an inevitable change that we see with age. What happens to us after age 60? As Marilyn Albert points out in "Myths and Realities of the Older Worker" (this volume, pp. 445-452), there are indeed some real declines in some selected abilities—principally in recalling names and places and in divided attention tasks. However, these declines are selective; they occur in some abilities, but not in all—and in only some people, not all. The key message, however, is that older people are not only willing, but also able to work ... and to work productively.

Advantages to Business

If providing work opportunities can help people psychologically and economically, the benefits to business and to our national economy are equally impressive. Population forecasters tell us that, over the next 20 years, the nation's pool of new workers ages 18-24 will shrink by 16%. Meanwhile, our over 65 population will grow by 28%.

These facts make it simple common sense for employers to seek employees where the potential supply is great and growing, i.e., among older people. Some companies have already begun experimenting with expanded employment of older people. Some banks, for example, report that older workers make better, more accurate check processors than do their younger counterparts.

Advantages to the National Economy

Finally, expanded job opportunities for older people promise to be good for the nation's economy. A major economic study completed in the past few years has estimated that if the numbers of older people in the workforce increased to the higher rates prevailing in 1970, when 26% of men over age 65 worked compared to 20% today, the results over the next 25 years would be impressive:

- Real GNP would be improved by almost 4%. This increase would come from increased consumption and savings generated by higher numbers of employed persons and from the stimulation of business investment that typically follows consumer demand.
- Expanded economic growth could mean about $40 billion more in federal, state and local revenues by the year 2005.
- Finally, because of the projected decline in young entrants into the labor force, a tight labor market will offer increased opportunities for older people without closing off job opportunities for younger workers.

Problems and Possibilities

These findings underscore the growing importance of work for older people as a source of retirement income. With this thought in mind, my presentation and that of Marilyn Albert have been designed to shed further light on the aging process and on the disincentives to employment of older people. Finally I will suggest some of the public and private initiatives that might make sense to expand employment opportunities for older workers and also make them more productive.

Disincentives to Work for Older People

You have learned thus far that older people want to work more, are able to work and that expanded employment of older people would be good both for business and our national economy in the long run. Why, therefore, have we in fact experienced a declining rate of employment among older people? There are many reasons, but one of the biggest barriers is on the public side.

The Social Security Earnings Test

This test adds a 50% tax on benefits with respect to earnings above $6,000, in addition to payroll and income taxes. Simply, the test works this way: One dollar in benefits is withheld for each two dollars of annual earnings above the exempt amount. Earnings above this amount reduce benefits and any benefits for a spouse or child who is entitled to them because of the earnings record. The test applies to people younger than 70. The earnings or "retirement" test has been present in the Social Security system since the beginning, but it has never enjoyed unanimous endorsement from the public or from the Congress.

The debate over the earnings test focuses on issues of equity and the costs of elimination. However, few argue that the test is not a barrier to employment of older people or that it does not figure substantially into retirement plans as well as into current participation in the labor force by older people.

What would happen if we eliminated this test? Recent research indicates that if just 13% of nonworking persons ages 65-69 returned to work full time, the combined incremental taxes—personal income and payroll taxes—would equal $2.1 billion, exactly the amount of increased Social Security benefits. The government could then justify an increase in Social Security tax rates sufficient to meet the increased benefits by reducing income tax rates by a corresponding amount.

Even more important, the increased labor supply would raise total income and GNP. It is estimated, for example, that if just 10% of nonworking people ages 65-69 returned to work as a result of the elimination of the earnings test, wages of the elderly would increase by at least $5.1 billion and GNP would rise by about $9 billion.

Private Disincentives

On the private side, there are numerous barriers to work for older Americans in private pension provisions and in personnel policies, compensation and benefit structures. Mandatory retirement is, of course, the most obvious barrier. Despite recent legislative changes raising the age of retirement and strengthened age discrimination laws, many businesses retain policies that favor compulsory retirement.

Many pension programs also have structural characteristics that encourage retirement. In most cases, workers must terminate employment to start benefits. Further, for those workers seeking part-time work options following traditional retirement, there is typically a ceiling on the number of hours of work allowed within sponsoring companies. Beyond that ceiling, pension benefits are lost.

Example

Let me illustrate how these disincentives work and how they combine to levy an almost confiscatory "tax" on the work of older people through the interaction of Social Security, federal income taxes and pension benefits. Consider the case of an employee of "retirement" age who is single with a pre-retirement income of $20,000 and 20 years' service. For the purposes of this simple case, we'll use the provisions of my own company's former pension program and ignore the impact of asset income on income tax rates. We'll look at the average "effective" tax rate on earned income for the individual.

Now let's ask: "As this person works for earned income, how much actual additional income does he get to keep? How much income is taken away by income taxes, Social Security taxes, lost Social Security benefits and lost pension benefits?"

Because of pension income, our hypothetical employee faces a stiff tax bite from the first dollar of earned income. Working just one-eighth time, with an earned income of about $2,500, 17% of earned income would be drawn off by the combined effect of federal income taxes and Social Security taxes. At just $6,000 of earned income, the effective average tax jumps sharply—with little more than a one-fourth time work effort. The jump in effective average tax, of course, comes from a loss of Social Security benefits—a dollar lost for every two dollars of earnings above $6,000. In fact, the marginal tax rate on each extra dollar above $6,000 would be about 70% from federal income taxes, Social Security taxes and lost Social Security benefits.

This 70% marginal tax rate on earned income above $6,000 is most certainly a powerful barrier to employment. However, the problem is compounded by the interaction of private pensions.

Most private pensions also have an earnings test, at least for earnings with the sponsoring company, which may be even more stringent than the Social Security earnings test.

An employee who worked more than one-fourth time in any month at The Travelers lost all pension benefits for that month under the former pension plan. In our example, that represents an average effective tax rate of over 70% for any work effort above one-fourth time.

Given these disincentives, logically—and quite sadly—many people conclude that even part-time work just isn't worth the effort. If we are truly serious about helping older people in America, we would do well to review such public and private policies. Do such barriers create more problems than they solve? If so, we should begin toppling them—sooner, not later.

Possible Remedies

I personally believe that our first step should be to make public policies neutral. That is, I favor the elimination of the Social Security earnings test. In the private sector, however, I believe that although we should encourage a lifting of barriers to employment, businesses should retain the flexibility of their own earnings tests and other disincentives. This policy recognizes the diversity of industries, jobs and local labor market conditions.

I might add that, even without a Social Security earnings test, companies will be able to provide substantial work disincentives for older workers if that is their decision. Ultimately, however, through the free play of market forces and requirements, I think that many businesses will discover that their own best interests will be served by opening employment options to older people.

Creating New Employment Opportunities

Beyond these policy changes, we must begin to resolve the biggest barrier of all to expanded employment opportunities for older people: simple lack of choice. All too often in our nation, the only choices open to older people are two extremes—full-time work or full-time retirement.

We need, in short, to begin the experiment with a whole range of work options for older people: part-time employment for retirees or job sharing with younger workers; job redesigns to make use of special qualifications of older people, such as their vast experience; work-education combinations to help older workers take on new responsibilities; reassignments to lesser responsibilities for those employees who want to work, but need to taper off; phased retirement programs, with fewer hours of work; at-home work programs for retirees with computer links to business sites.

Example

At The Travelers, we've opened up employment options for Travelers retirees. We started by eliminating all mandatory retirement ages in Connecticut where required by law, and we continued to do so across the nation in all of our field offices.

Next, we looked at our temporary employment needs at the home office. We use about 63 temporary workers each day to fill in for our employees on vacation and sick leave, as well as for workload peaks. We asked: Why not use our retirees for these temporary spots? Therefore, we've started a temporary employment program for retirees. Now we make it possible for retirees to earn more through us than by working for an outside employment agency.

We've also surveyed our home office and found that at least 300 positions could be turned into part-time work opportunities for our retirees, who would work on a shared job basis. Our decision was to open up these jobs to retirees as they become available.

In keeping with our commitment to use the skills of the rapidly expanding retiree population, we are now assessing the feasibility of establishing a computer programming subsidiary operation, in which retirees can be trained in computer programming skills and employed as independent contractors. This operation would allow retirees to meet their income needs and their interests while responding to the severe nationwide shortage of computer programmers. Not only would such an operation help Travelers, but it could also help other corporations throughout the country to fulfill their programming requirements.

To put teeth into all of these programs, we changed our pension policy—a policy that specified that any retiree who worked more than 40 hours a month would lose pension income. Now, any retiree will be able to work up to 960 hours a year—nearly half time—without loss of Travelers pension income. The average effective tax rate faced by our hypothetical Travelers employee now is far less onerous for half-time work or less. If part-time jobs are made available, we could expect more retirees to return to work.

Although these actions may not be appropriate for every employer, they have proved successful for us. Today, 60% of all of our daily home office temporary positions are filled by retirees. Our experience has convinced us that these efforts work. Many other companies are instituting similar programs, which serve not only the well-being of older workers but also the interests of their own businesses.

Conclusion

We need to signal the nation's older people, and those workers who are moving toward retirement, that enforced idleness will not be their inevitable fate in the future. Building this "fourth pillar" to support retirement income will not be easy. We will need to change habits, entrenched policies and established stereotypes. The effort will require answers to dozens of questions about the capacities of older people and the kinds of work schedules that are appropriate for them. However, by expanding choices for older people we can benefit from their experience and their wisdom—assets we can least afford to waste in America.

Myths and Realities of the Older Worker

BY MARILYN S. ALBERT, Ph.D.

ASIDE FROM THE numbers involved of younger vs. older workers, why were rules established in the first place to restrict the employment of the elderly? Why did the perception develop that older workers were not desirable in the workplace, that they were over the hill, that they were more trouble than they were worth?

Some of these perceptions were based on facts that used to be true about the elderly but are no longer and some of these perceptions were based on myths that many years of research are finally beginning to dispel. In trying to explain what current research shows to be the *myths* and *realities* of the older worker I will discuss three areas related to aging: physiological aging, intellectual aging and personality changes with age.

Physiological Aging

It is often thought that "old" means "sick." Although this perception used to be true of the elderly, it is no longer so. Therefore, let me first explain why "old" and "sick" used to be synonymous and why that situation has changed.

Physiologically, most people reach a peak in early adult life and then decline gradually thereafter. There is no pleasant plateau of the middle years when you stay in your prime to age 50 or 55 and then suddenly start to decline. You can see from Figure 1 that there is a fair amount of linearity in these changes. That is, old people aren't aging any faster than young people—they've just done more of it. They've lost function; they have less reserve.

Now, what is the impact of these age-related physiological changes? Let us take the case of the function that changes the most with age: breathing capacity. By age 80, breathing capacity is about 50% of what it was at age 30. But we all know that one can remove a lung in a young man without adverse effects. So the 80 year old man with 50% of his original lung function is *fine for everyday life*. He's simply at greater risk, if he gets sick with pneumonia or a lung infection, than a 30 year old because *he has less reserve*. The elderly are thus vulnerable to a greater loss of health, given any disease that is superimposed on their normal aging changes. When medicine was less able to treat common illnesses, such as pneumonia, the result was

As assistant professor of neurology and psychiatry at Massachusetts General Hospital, Dr. Albert researches aging and dementia, and directs clinical evaluation of patients with memory disorders. She has served as research associate at Boston University Medical School and as a lecturer at Clark University. Dr. Albert earned her B.A. degree at the University of Rochester, Rochester, New York and her M.A. and Ph.D. degrees at McGill University, Montreal, Quebec, Canada.

that the people who had less physiological reserve—the elderly—were sick.

Many illnesses that used to stress the reserve of the elderly aren't that common anymore. Thus the elderly are, on the *average*, quite healthy. Of course, this fact is the major reason that the elderly population is increasing so rapidly. More and more people are living out their normal life span. Their medical history is more and more rapidly approaching the ideal where serious illness is postponed till later and later in life.

Intellectual Changes

What about the thinking ability of these relatively *healthy* older people? Has that ability been declining steadily since age 30, leaving people with smaller and smaller reserves? The answer is no!

It used to be thought, as Figure 2 shows, that cognitive and intellectual changes paralleled physical changes. Individuals were thought to be at their peak when they were in their 30s and that afterward mental function began to deteriorate. Research during the past two decades has clearly indicated that this belief isn't the case.

Figure 1

PHYSIOLOGICAL CHANGES WITH AGE

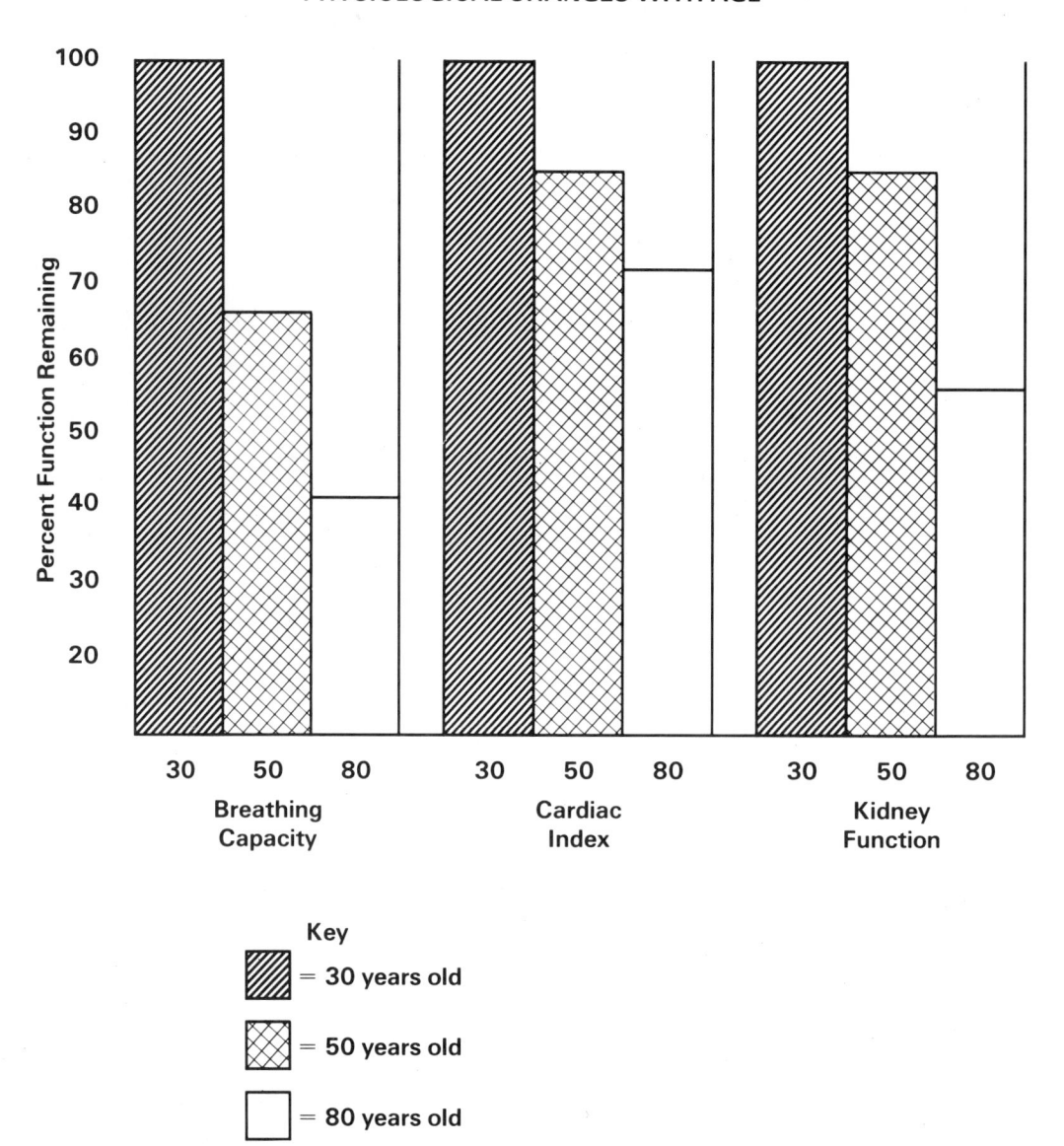

[Bar chart showing Percent Function Remaining for ages 30, 50, and 80 across three measures:
- Breathing Capacity: 30 yrs ≈ 100%, 50 yrs ≈ 66%, 80 yrs ≈ 40%
- Cardiac Index: 30 yrs ≈ 100%, 50 yrs ≈ 85%, 80 yrs ≈ 72%
- Kidney Function: 30 yrs ≈ 100%, 50 yrs ≈ 85%, 80 yrs ≈ 56%]

Key
- ▨ = 30 years old
- ▩ = 50 years old
- ☐ = 80 years old

It turns out that generational differences were confused with aging differences. First, elderly people 30 years ago had very different life experiences than the younger people they were being compared with. They had different *education*, different *health care*, different *sociological* pressures, different *nutrition* and, of course, as I just said different *health status*. Again we come back to the importance of health status—not only in preventing older people from being sick but in improving their mental status as well.

It's becoming increasingly clear that, as people get older, a wide variety of medical disorders—disorders that don't seem to affect the intellectual functioning of younger people—do affect the intellectual function of older people. The Table shows the things that cause mental changes in older workers that are treatable and reversible: drugs taken in quantities that are too large or in the wrong combinations; medical illnesses such as diabetes, thyroid disease, kidney disease or disease causing metabolic imbalance; poor nutrition; heart disease;

Figure 2

INTELLIGENCE TESTING
(uncontrolled for generational changes)

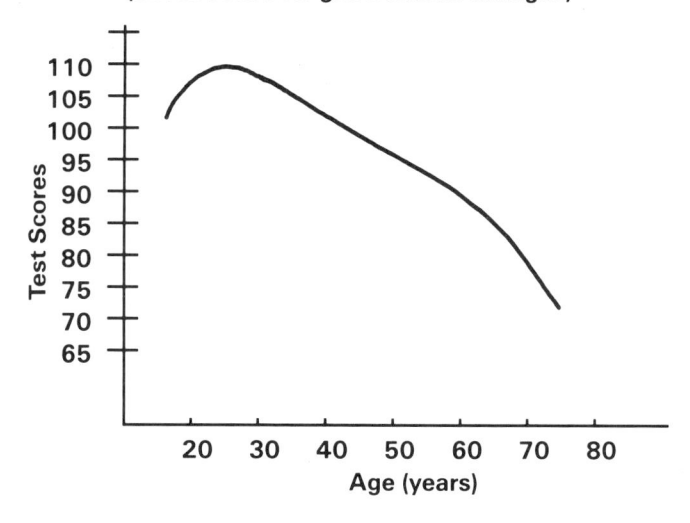

[Graph: Test Scores (y-axis, 65-110) vs Age in years (x-axis, 20-80). Curve rises from ~102 at age 20 to peak ~110 around age 25, then declines gradually to ~85 at age 60, dropping more steeply to ~72 at age 75.]

Table

REVERSIBLE CAUSES OF COGNITIVE CHANGE

Drug intoxication
Metabolic and nutritional imbalance
   systemic disturbance (e.g., pulmonary, renal, hepatic)
   endocrine disturbance (e.g., hypothyroidism, diabetes)
   electrolyte disturbance (e.g., sodium, calcium)
   nutrition (e.g., thiamine, folate, B12)
Infection or fever
Cardiovascular disorders
   congestive heart failure
   arrhythmia
Neurological disorders
   subdural hematoma
   subarachnoid hemorrhage
   meningitis
   brain abscess
Disorders related to hospitalization
   anesthesia
   sensory deprivation

even pneumonia. All of these factors can affect an older person's intellectual ability in ways different from a younger person. It's easy to understand that when diseases were harder to treat and occurred earlier in life, their effect on mental function served to further advance the idea that people were beginning to decline after age 30.

However, it is now clear that the myth of mental decline after age 30 was based primarily on generational differences in health and education. Current results of standard intelligence tests in the elderly illustrate this fact most dramatically (Figure 3).

On the verbal scale of the Wechsler Adult Intelligence Test (the most widely used intelligence test

Figure 3

INTELLIGENCE TESTING
(controlled for generational change
by repeated testing
of the same generation)

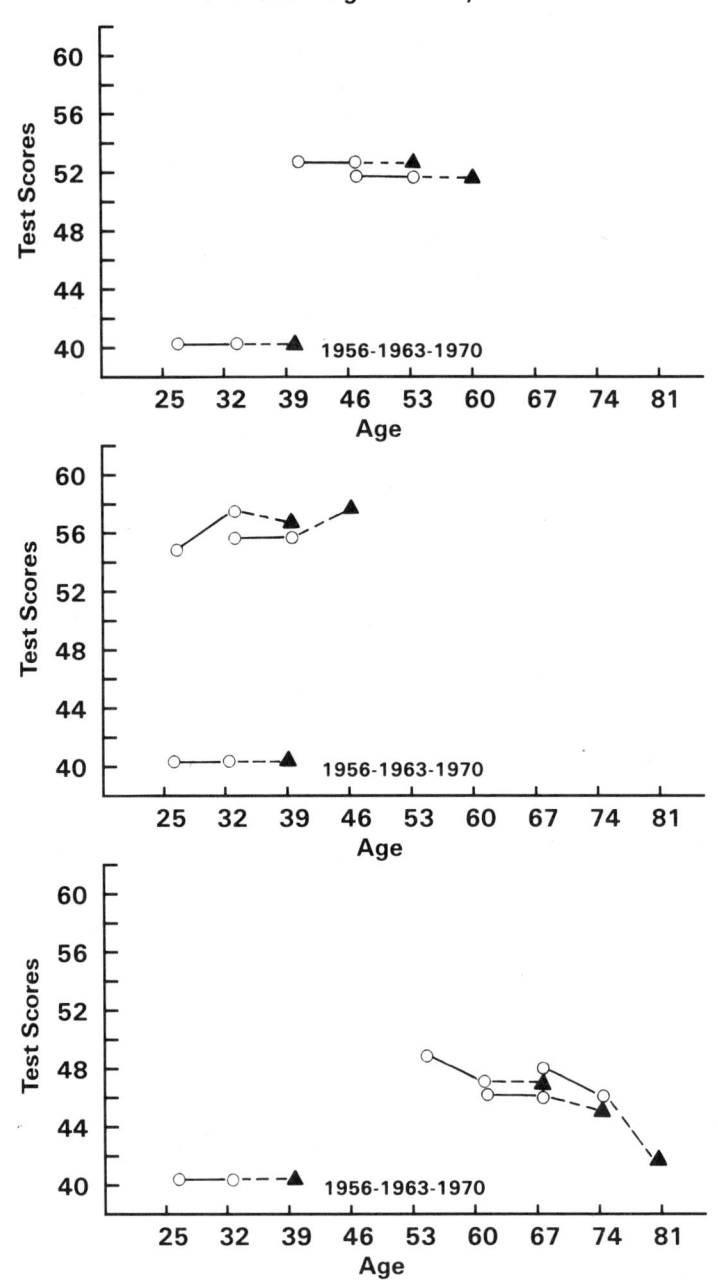

Figure 4

VERBAL INTELLIGENCE TESTING

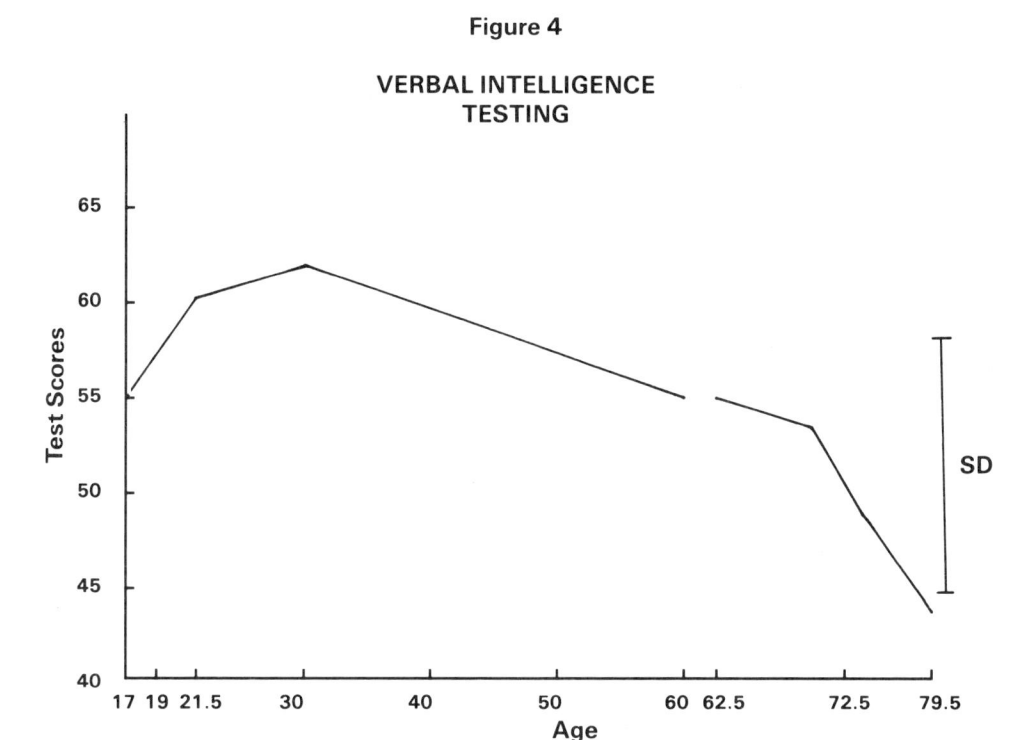

in the United States and perhaps in the world), there is barely a change of even one standard deviation from the age of 17 until the age of 80. There are very few changes in intellectual function with age, not in general information about the world, comprehension, ability to make judgments about the outcomes of various circumstances, arithmetic or vocabulary. If you look at Figure 4, you will see that scores remain remarkably stable over time.

Other Intellectual Changes

However, some abilities, *not* tested by IQ tests, do change. What are they?

The most common complaint that you hear among older people is, "My memory isn't as good as it used to be." Experimental investigation supports this conclusion, with some interesting and very important exceptions. In laboratory tests—such as word lists, where you give somebody a list of dissociated words to learn—older people as a group remember considerably less than do younger people. But on material organized in a paragraph format, where there is a logical coherence to the information—a situation that's much more like real life—there are no differences between young and old people (Figure 5)!

Therefore, there is a seeming contradiction: If memory differences in old and young people become less and less evident as the task gets closer and closer to real life, then why do we hear old people say that their memory ability is getting worse? I think that there are basically two age-related changes in intellectual performance that explain this:

First, people in their 60s and 70s show changes in their ability to produce the names of objects or people. In fact, it's not uncommon to hear people say, "My memory is getting worse. I just can't remember people's names anymore." If we test naming ability in the laboratory with pictures of objects or with faces of people that are thoroughly familiar to all of us, older people know the use of objects, or pertinent facts about the people. But they have much more trouble than younger people producing the appropriate names. Let me emphasize, however, that this problem isn't really a memory problem—it's a naming problem, a language problem (Figure 6).

The second age-related change in performance—change in attention—probably contributes even more to the older person's self-perception of a memory change with age. One of the clearest results from the psychological aging research done over the past 20 or 30 years is that as people get older they have more and more difficulty in dividing their attention. Suppose we ask someone to scan

Figure 5

MEMORY FOR STORY

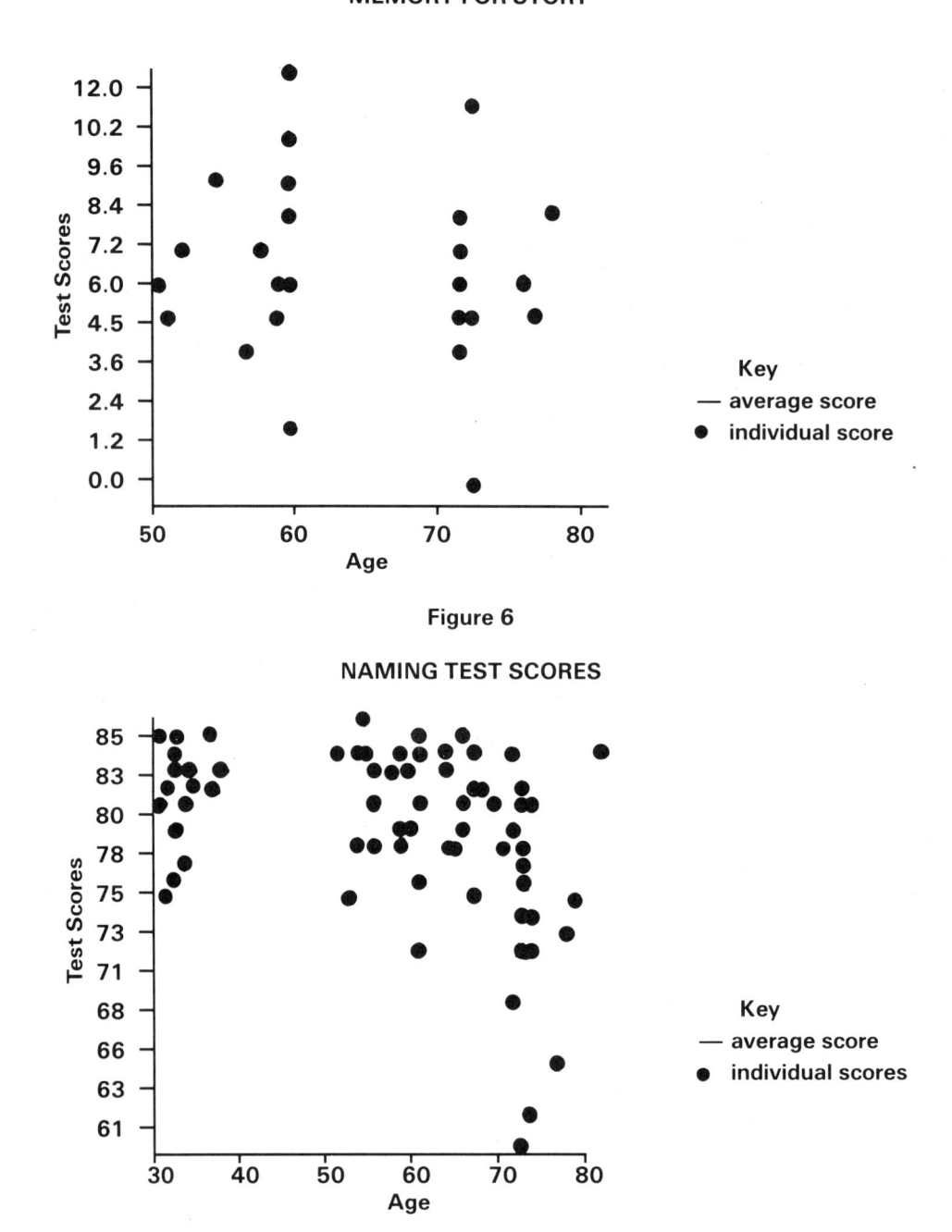

(scatter plot: Test Scores vs Age)

Key
— average score
● individual score

Figure 6

NAMING TEST SCORES

(scatter plot: Test Scores vs Age)

Key
— average score
● individual scores

an array of letters, cross out all the letter "As" and, at the same time, listen to a tape and identify a repeating letter. Now, young people cope moderately well with such simultaneous tasks. But older people tend to concentrate on one task while performance deteriorates on the other. Figure 7 shows the performance of young, middle aged and older people on a task of divided attention. As you can see, until the end of their 50s, people are able to do such divided attention tasks fairly well. Then, there's a drop-off in performance.

If you consider the structure of the typical work

Figure 7

DIVIDED ATTENTION TASK

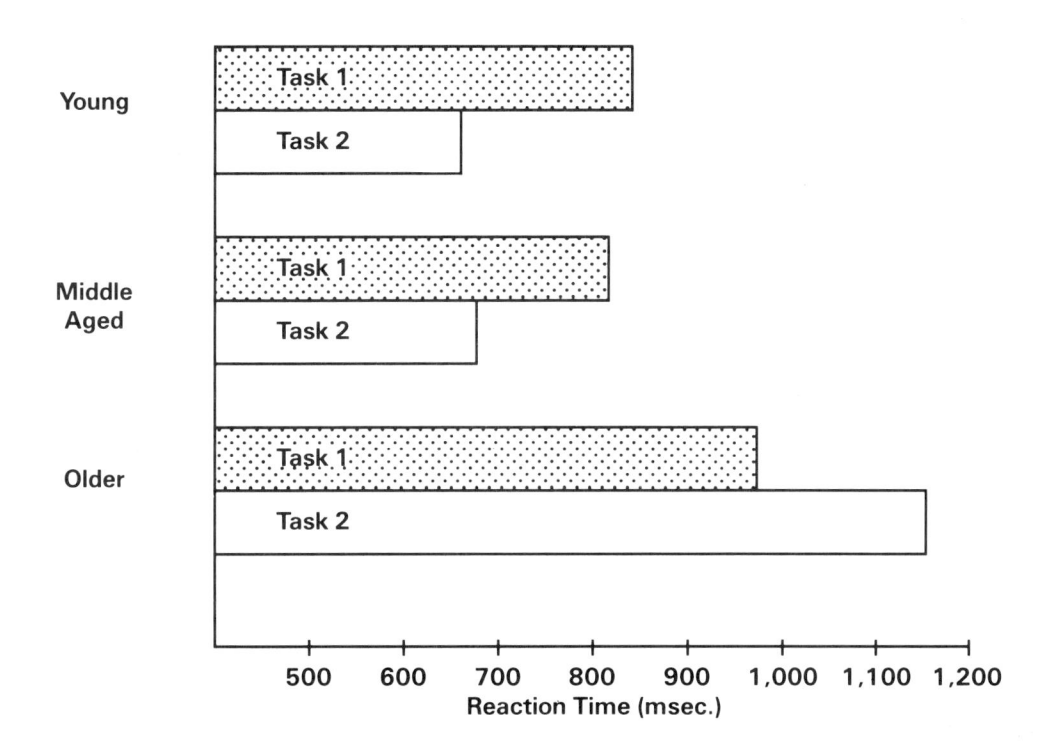

environment—at least if your work environment is anything like mine, where there are 20 different things going on simultaneously—it becomes apparent that decrements in intellectual capacity could produce reductions in performance. This situation occurs not because the ability to process information has actually decreased, but because the concurrent attentional demands make it more difficult for the individual to perform at his best.

Therefore, age-related changes in attention can produce changes in performance. One can imagine that the older worker, experiencing difficulty with the old ways of performing a task, would seem the perfect candidate for what is often referred to as job burnout. Not realizing that he has to change the way in which a job is normally performed to accommodate to such changes, the older worker might set unrealistic goals for himself. He might find, time and again, that these goals cannot be met. Then he might get frustrated, apathetic and ultimately become unable to cope. In my opinion, any program for rehiring the older worker, or redesigning jobs for older workers, must also make older workers aware of these mental changes and must take these intellectual changes into account.

However, if one wants to restructure jobs for older workers there is one additional consideration. How adaptable is the older worker? How willing is he or she to make changes in his or her work style or to accept changed responsibilities? Is it true, as is often thought, that as people get older they become more rigid and less willing to make changes?

Personality Changes

Literally hundreds of studies have been done in the past two decades to evaluate personality change with age. The general outcome of all of them has been that individual differences in aging appear to far outweigh any uniform direction of change. There is continuity and consistency of personality with age. Older people, like younger ones, have different capacities for coming to terms with changing life situations. Some do it well; some do it poorly. Knowing an individual's age does not enable us to predict how well that person is going to adapt to change. Since we now have some ways of measuring adaptability in workers, it is theoretically possible to determine who would adapt easily to changes in job situations and who would need special guidance and training to become more adaptable.

Although some people might need extra help in adapting to redefined or restructured jobs, it is my opinion, however, that all older workers need at least some education, if not specific training, concerning the cognitive changes associated with aging. It's important for employees to recognize and understand the possibility of selective changes in intellectual function with age. Programs of career planning and development, or programs of health care in the workplace, might serve well as devices for conveying this important information. Such programs could also prepare older workers for the possibility of changing their jobs or their work habits to compensate for such changes.

Once such selected changes are recognized and accepted, however, what then can be done about them?

With regard to "naming" deficits, what can or should be done? The implications of changes in naming for work depends entirely, of course, on how important it is for a person to remember names in his job. Remember: People don't forget an object—only its name. They don't forget who a person is or the important things about that person. They just have difficulty producing the name. So many jobs can be done perfectly well, even if naming ability is altered.

For the salesman or manager, however, ability to produce a name may affect his social encounters and, therefore, his success on the job. There are a variety of memory training tricks that can be used to improve naming. There are various books that describe these techniques. They could be developed into short courses, available at the workplace, on how to improve memory for names.

Now, what about memory? Given that memory problems among older people are most evident where information is abstract and disconnected, improving memory in the older worker would seem primarily a matter of organizing material so that it has *logical and contextual coherence*. Rather than an abstract list of changes or directives, reasons for changes and the background of the thinking related to why certain decisions have been made, etc., should be given. Wherever possible, new information should be related to information already in memory, and vocabulary should be used with which older workers are already familiar. The business world, not to mention the scientific community, adds new jargon all the time. Imagine the plight of the older worker trying to learn something new but having to absorb the new phraseology at the same time.

However, in my opinion, the most important change to which older workers must be sensitive is the change in divided attention. For individuals in managerial positions, this change might be expected to take the biggest toll.

Simple awareness of the problem may be enough to enable many individuals to analyze the job they have and try to figure out better ways of coping. One person, for example, might find it helpful to take careful notes of meetings and phone calls and then review them later before making a decision. Another might find it necessary to have phone calls screened more often so that there are fewer interruptions.

Some workers, however, may need actual training in how better to focus their attention. It may be necessary to show people how to set tasks for themselves, one at a time; to perform them to a certain degree of completion before they begin other competing tasks. This area is really one where research in the workplace seems to me to be most necessary. We know very little about the capacities that people draw on to accomplish a particular job, and different jobs necessarily make different intellectual demands. I would think that jobs with high attentional demands should be targeted first for some sort of in-depth examination and be evaluated systematically concerning how best to alter the flow of events and the attentional demands, so that if older workers encounter difficulties, they will know how to adapt to them.

Summary

Older workers are, by and large, healthy and as adaptable as when they were young, but there are unquestionably changes in mental performance for most individuals as they grow older. However, these changes are selective and by no means universal. There are, after the early 60s, changes in some capacities, but not in others—and in some people, but not in all. Although it is certainly clear that it is incorrect to assume that all abilities change extensively, I think it would be just as unwise to pretend that no abilities change—because it is only when we recognize and understand real changes that we can find ways of adapting to or circumventing them. In addition to encouraging the older worker to adapt to the physiological and psychological changes that occur with age, changes in rules and regulations, hiring and training programs that affect the older worker must take place.

Communication With Retirees

BY DONALD H. ROWCLIFFE, JR., CPA

THE ACT OF COMMUNICATING has been defined as the exchanging of ideas or the conveying of information. As such, it seems to me that the better we know the person with whom we are communicating, the better our chances of success in any communication endeavor.

Most of the communication in my organization is with persons that we do not know—at least not intimately. We often do, however, know something about the person or persons with whom we are communicating, and every little bit helps. For example, if we were communicating with children, we certainly would want to keep that in mind. We would use shorter, less complex words, shorter sentences and the subject matter itself would, hopefully, be of interest to the children addressed.

The Concerns of the Retiree

When we communicate with retirees we more than likely do not know the retirees personally, but we certainly know something about them as a group. First, we know their work background because of the requirements necessary for receiving a retirement benefit from our fund. I believe that we also can presume some other information that we should keep in mind in developing our communications with our retirees.

There is little doubt that each retiree gave consideration to his financial status in retirement. He spent some time determining the sources and amounts of income that he could expect after he was in retirement status, i.e., his Social Security award, his retirement benefit with our fund, other pension benefits to which he may be entitled, his personal savings or other forms of investments he may have, etc. He may have even planned some part-time work to further augment his retirement income. He then spent some time in determining and budgeting the various costs and expenses that he might expect to incur while in retirement. Hopefully, his anticipated income more than offset his anticipated expenses, so that he could retire in dignity.

I believe that we can also expect that the retiree thought about what he planned to do with the great amount of time that would be available to him after retirement. I'm sure that his wife was most interested in this aspect of his retirement because many, if not most, wives hope that their husbands will not be continually underfoot during their retirement years. After all, doesn't absence make the heart grow fonder?

Physical and mental well-being may have played a most important part in pre-retirement planning. Health may have been the sole reason for the retirement, even to the point that the worker is receiving a disability retirement benefit. No one looks forward to the prospect of death, even though we all know that it is inevitable. Some people may have postponed retirement, fearing that inactivity might hasten death's occurrence.

There is no question that some retirees have given these pre-retirement considerations much

Mr. Rowcliffe is administrative manager of the Carpenters Welfare & Pension Funds of Illinois in Geneva, Illinois. His office also provides administrative services to 18 other construction industry welfare, pension, apprentice and vacation funds. His experience encompasses 15 years in the multiemployer benefits field as an auditor, contract administrator and salaried administrator, serving welfare, pension, apprenticeship and vacation funds. He is a past president of the Fox Valley Chapter of the Illinois Society of Certified Public Accountants and a member of the American Institute of Certified Public Accountants. Mr. Rowcliffe has written articles for the International Foundation's Digest *and* Employee Benefits Journal, *has spoken at various Foundation educational meetings and has been heard several times on the Foundation Forum cassette program. He serves on the Foundation's Board of Directors and is a member of the Accountants Committee.*

more thought and planning than others. However, "the best laid plans of mice and men" often go awry. After retirement, there are many forms of indirect communication reaching the retiree that can have devastating effects. How many times have the media raised the question of the impending doom of the Social Security system? How many times has the retiree heard of reductions or eliminations of Social Security or other welfare benefits? Remember, Social Security is one of the items of income, and perhaps even the major one, that the retiree was counting on. Thus, such reports of impending disaster are not welcome to the retiree.

How many times in the last year alone has the retiree heard of other pension plans that have terminated, jeopardizing the pension benefits of their members? Certainly, the retirees and employees of Chrysler, International Harvester, Braniff and others have much concern for their current and future pension benefits. How can this news help but raise the question of the safety of every retiree's own pension plan?

The financial market also leaves a lot to be desired. When the retiree receives an annual summary report of his own plan, which may indicate a sizable drop in the market value of its assets, he does not feel reassured that his own monthly pension benefit check will continue.

Add to all of this tension the inflationary spiral that for some time has had a horrendous effect on the purchasing power of fixed retirement income! Is it any wonder that when the retiree receives a piece of correspondence from our office he opens it with trembling fingers? I'm almost hesitant to send a Christmas card!

This is the person with whom we are trying to communicate. This is the person who was either overly optimistic or overly pessimistic or had no choice in planning for his retirement some time ago. In today's faltering economy, I believe it would be difficult to find a retiree who is doing better financially than he had planned. Let's keep this fact in mind when we develop pieces of communication for him.

When and What to Communicate

To communicate or not to communicate? That is the question—and, I believe, a most important one. If the communication is not necessary, don't send it! With all that must be on the retiree's mind regarding his ability to keep his head above water and live a little, rather than just exist, he doesn't need a shot of adrenaline from you. He gets that every day when he picks up a newspaper or turns on the television or radio.

If you must communicate with the retiree, keep it short and direct. Remember, the best piece of mail he receives from you is his monthly benefit check. Every piece he receives after that he opens with apprehension—if he opens it at all. Therefore, including the necessary communication with his pension check not only saves postage but catches him at a time when he is in a better frame of mind.

If you have both good news and bad news to impart, tell him the good news first. Lay it out up front in the opening sentence. Make every effort to use simple and direct terms that cannot be misunderstood. You can embellish on this news in later paragraphs, but I know of no better way to get the reader's attention than to relate that good news in the opening sentence. Give him a reason to read further.

If you also have some bad news that you must tell him, cover this next—also in simple and direct terms that cannot be misunderstood. Notice that I said "must tell him." If you don't have to tell him the bad news, don't! If you must tell him, don't drain all of your energy in discussing the good news before you get to the bad news. By the time he gets through the good news discussion, you may lose his attention and fail to get the bad news through to him. Get both the good and bad news spelled out immediately. You can elaborate on both later.

However, when you do elaborate, don't get all wrapped up in your own writing ability. Say what you have to say in the most understandable terms you can. Once you've made your point, stop. Don't oversell! Remember, if the reader doesn't understand it, you've wasted your time and the cost of distribution. A friend of mine runs his communications by his eighth grade daughter. If she doesn't understand it, "it's back to the drawing board."

I've talked about communicating both good and bad news, but there are times that the bad news really doesn't have to be communicated to the retiree. For example, let us assume that the trustees have approved a 10% increase in retirement benefits to all new retirees and a 5% increase to all current retirees. Now, that is good news to the active participant, who not only can expect a greater benefit when he retires but is made aware of a board of trustees with compassion for current retirees, which will, hopefully, be of the same frame of mind after he retires.

As for the current retiree, it's good news that his benefit will increase but bad news that he is not getting the same percentage increase that a new retiree will enjoy. Therefore, why not tell him only the good news that really applies to him? Tell him with exuberance that his pension benefits are being increased 5%! Why tell him that others will be getting a 10% increase? Of course, a few retirees will hear about the 10% increase in new retiree benefits, but they will not have heard it from you.

Another example: Assume that the trustees approved an increase in the welfare plan of benefits, but that none of these increases apply to retirees or beneficiaries. You will, of course, transmit this information to all participants—all participants except retirees and beneficiaries. You won't make many friends or influence many people if you tell the retiree about some fine benefit improvements that apply to everyone but him! Skip the unaffected parties with this piece of communication.

Recordkeeping

I wish to bring up another point—recordkeeping and its importance in communications. I've really been discussing the "rifle approach," as opposed to the "shotgun approach," to communications. However, it doesn't help much to develop specific communications for a specific group if your recordkeeping does not enable you to segregate the specific group to whom you wish to direct a piece of material.

Be specific in your communications and have the capability of directing each piece only to the person or persons you want to receive it. Even all retirees aren't in the same group. Don't you have early retirees, disability retirees or vested retirees, as well as normal retirees? Many times your information may have a different effect on these various classes of retirees. If so, why not address each group specifically? Of course, it's a little extra work but the extra effort may well be worth it.

Do you routinely verify the existence of retirees and beneficiaries and verify the continuing disability of disabled retirees? If not, perhaps a true story may point out the error of your ways. Several years ago, I was involved with a fund that instituted a new annual program to verify the existence of retirees as well as the continued disability of disabled retirees. One response from a widow advised that her husband had died some five years ago! There were no survivor benefits available to this participant, so the trustees were faced with the unpleasant task of collecting 60 months of overpayments from the widow.

I don't doubt the possibility that this widow had assumed that she was entitled to this benefit for the rest of her life. The fact that the benefit checks continued to be issued in her husband's name didn't bother her since she had been endorsing them for him for some time anyway. If this was the case, didn't the fund fall down on its communication with this participant and his spouse?

I expect that most people involved in pension funds have had problems in transmitting information to retirees about the new suspension of benefit regulations. Depending on your own plan rules, if any, covering suspension of benefits prior to the new regulations and your trustees' decisions following the new regulations, I suspect that you had either good news, bad news or good and bad news to impart. How well did you handle it? Have you analyzed the responses received from retirees following this mailing to determine what kind of job you did in getting the message across? You should. It is a good barometer of any communication and may give you some clues to handling future communication responsibilities better.

Special Retiree Summary Plan Descriptions

We are all aware of the requirements for summary plan descriptions (SPDs) as set forth in ERISA. Are you also aware of the somewhat lesser requirements for SPDs prepared especially for retirees and beneficiaries? If you're not, an SPD for retirees and beneficiaries may omit information that is not applicable to them. Again, why provide a retiree with an SPD with only a small amount of the information applicable to him? I'll admit that the retiree may have more free time to read an SPD, but I've yet to see any SPD reach the bestseller list.

Such an SPD cannot help but be smaller than the SPD prepared for other participants. The smaller size not only means smaller mailing costs but also can easily provide for smaller production costs. These savings may not be in evidence in the original printing, but I would expect that changes in the plan that would affect retirees and beneficiaries would occur far less frequently than for your active group. This SPD would require far less modification and, therefore, less frequent updating than your main SPD.

Oral Communication

To this point, I've directed my remarks toward written communications. However, I can't recall any previous comment that does not also apply to oral communications, except that oral communications are primarily engendered by questions from the retiree and generally occur over the telephone. Of course, we all get involved at one time or another in addressing groups of retirees, but my remarks on written communications are applicable to such speeches.

One-on-one communication is better than written communication, but only because it is more specific. It involves a specific person, his question or questions and the application of the plan or plans to him. Such communication is, however, far more demanding and requires greater exactness. In this instance, we must know the person we are addressing specifically! I don't mean that we must know him personally, but we must know exactly who he is and in what plan or plans he participates. He usually is not interested in general information; he is interested in information as it affects him personally. His questions may require that we review his record in the plan or plans so that the information provided to him is based on his record and not someone else's.

Points to Remember

The communicator must be capable of handling communication with care and accuracy. The communicator must also be pleasant and take sufficient time for the discussion. Keep in mind that the retiree may not only have more time on his hands, but he may also be lonely and just want someone to talk to. Remember that many, if not most, pension plans were created by the vote of today's retirees. Younger employees do not give pension plans a very high priority; they forget that some day they will be old, too. Give that retiree some of your time. Above all, know exactly to whom you are talking. Understand his questions thoroughly, so that you can respond with accuracy.

Conclusion

Most of the remarks I've made in this presentation apply to communications with any group of people. However, let's give some extra effort to communicating with retirees with one goal in mind: making our communications to them understood, not misunderstood. Who knows? Some of this care may rub off and our communications with other groups will also improve.

CHAPTER 11

Communications Programs

Joseph A. Brislin

Director of Special Services
Timber Operators Council Inc.
Tigard, Oregon

Edward M. Finkelstein

President
Union Communications Corporation
St. Louis, Missouri

Developing Communication Material

BY JOSEPH A. BRISLIN

THIS PRESENTATION WILL explore the process of developing communication material from the trustees' point of view. Regardless of the trust's size or the industry that it serves, there are several basic techniques that will assist trustees in developing effective methods of communication. This article will review a basic rule and a model for good communication. By implementing the principles contained in the basic rule and the model, trustees can solve some of the special problems they may have in controlling communications.

Some of the special problems that will be discussed are: (1) Communication that is dictated by governmental regulations may conflict with the trustees' desire to send a simple message. (2) Communication barriers may prevent a participant from understanding or receiving the trustees' message (e.g., a 19 year old's lack of interest in reading the pension plan booklet). (3) Feedback from the participants oftentimes goes to persons other than the trustees so that the trustees do not have a way to measure the effectiveness of their communications. (4) Sometimes there is a tendency to design the message to fit a traditional type of media (e.g., the plan booklet) rather than selecting the media forms that will disseminate the trustees' message most effectively.

Good communication takes thought and planning. The suggestions outlined in this article will assist trustees in the planning process.

The Basic Rule of Good Communication

For communication to be effective, both the sender and the receiver must have the same interpretation of the message. The basic rule of good communication is to remember that the person who is receiving the message (the receiver) *always* controls the communication. The sender cannot and should not assume that the message is automatically received and understood just because the sender has the authority.

A good example to illustrate this basic rule is the plan booklet that the trustees prepare for the participants. The plan booklet contains the policies and procedures that the trustees desire the participants to know and understand. Normally the plan booklet is extensive, well-thought-out and

Mr. Brislin, as staff attorney and director of special services for Timber Operators Council, Inc. (TOC) of Tigard, Oregon, advises association members on all aspects of labor law and serves as advisor and trustee to six health and welfare and five pension funds in the forest products industry. TOC is a forest products manufacturing employer association that represents approximately 580 companies in Oregon, Washington, Alaska, California, Montana, Idaho and Nevada. Prior to joining TOC, Mr. Brislin served as attorney with the lawfirm Dezendorf, Spears, Lubursky & Campbell. He is a graduate of Paul Smith's College of Paul Smiths, New York, earned his B.S.F. and master's degrees at the University of Washington and received his J.D. degree from the University of Oregon School of Law. Mr. Brislin is a member of the Oregon State Bar and Western Pension Conference.

provides excellent directions for the participant to follow. The booklet is distributed, but some of the participants do not read it. The participant who does not read the plan booklet controls the communication because this participant has not received the message. There is no communication because the participant does not have the same understanding of the plan's policies and procedures as the trustees.

As previously stated, the goal of communication is for the sender and the receiver to have the same understanding of the message after it has been sent and received. The model in Figure 1 shows the cycle for good communication.

The cycle contains three elements: message, feedback and followup. Feedback gives the receiver the opportunity to enhance his understanding of the message by asking questions or by

Figure 1

THE CYCLE FOR GOOD COMMUNICATION

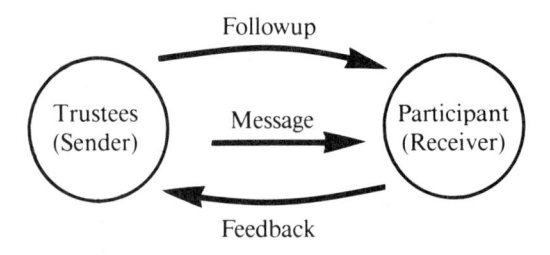

Trustees (Sender) — Message → Participant (Receiver)
Followup
Feedback

providing input. Followup allows the sender to assure that the receiver's questions are answered and allows the sender to respond to the receiver's input. This cycle is continuous until both the sender and receiver have the same understanding of the message.

An illustration of how this cycle may be used by trustees is a continuation of the previous example of the participant who does not read the plan booklet. The trustees sent their message through the plan booklet, but because the participant did not read the booklet, the message was not understood. The trustees will receive "feedback" that the booklet was not read when the participant asks a question that is covered clearly in the booklet or seeks benefits without following established procedures. Undoubtedly, the trustees have a "followup" procedure through the insurance carrier, administrator or some other person to assure that the participant's questions and/or problems are resolved. Following the model, the trustees not only have to send an accurate message, but they must also provide a system for obtaining feedback and providing followup. If any of the three elements—message, feedback or followup—in the communications cycle is missing, the communication will not be effective.

Special Problems Trustees Have in Controlling Communication

In preparing communication material, the trustees of a Taft-Hartley trust face some problems that may not be present in their position as a union or management representative. Several of these problems and suggestions for solutions are discussed below.

Simplicity vs. Mandate

Trustees will sometimes encounter a conflict between their desire to send a simple message that the participants can understand and the requirements placed on the message by governmental regulations, legal counsel, the insurance carrier, the administrator and other professional advisors. Whenever possible, trustees should stand firm for the principle of keeping the message simple. Advisors tend to use technical language, so trustees must be prepared to force the advisors to translate the technical terms into simpler language. If the advisor insists that the technical language is mandated, the trustees should follow up the mandated language with examples or other simplified clarifications.

An example of simplicity versus mandated language that can cause confusion is found in the following two eligibility rules. The first phrasing is what the trustees wanted to use and the second phrasing is what the insurance carrier required:

What the Trustees Wanted to Say:

There is a six month waiting period before you are eligible for dental and vision benefits.

What the Insurance Carrier Wanted to Say:

A new employee and his dependents will be covered for dental and vision care benefits of the plan commencing on the first day of the month following four months of eligibility under the fund. This would require a minimum of six consecutive months of employment, with 80 or more hours worked in each of those six months.

In setting forth a plan's eligibility requirements, examples for clarification should be used whenever possible. The insurance carrier's language above was technically correct, but very difficult to understand. The use of an example can simplify eligibility rules and make the rules more understandable (e.g., Joe Doe works 80 hours during each of the months of June, July, August, September, October and November. Joe's coverage starts on the first of December).

Communication Barriers

A communication barrier is any external factor that prevents the participant from receiving the trustees' message. Some of the barriers that trustees may encounter are:

- *Lack of interest.* The participant doesn't bother to take the time necessary to receive the message (e.g., a 19 year old's lack of interest in reading the pension plan booklet).
- *The message is too complicated to under-*

stand. The participant tries, but doesn't comprehend.
- *An easier (but often very unreliable) source to go to.* After the claim is denied, how many times have you heard a participant state that "so and so" told him that he was eligible for coverage? In this case, "so and so" was the easier source to go to.
- *Message competition.* Competition from too many messages sent at the same time or sent at the wrong time (e.g., Christmas holidays).

Trustees can avoid or penetrate communication barriers by applying the basic rule and the model. Since the participant always controls the communication, the trustees have to design a message that will be compatible with the participant's interest and attitude. Also, the communication system must include the three elements in the cycle: message, feedback and followup. Consider the following suggestions for overcoming these barriers:

- *Keep the message simple.* Sometimes the sender thinks that the message is so important that it needs to be profound. This point is illustrated by a bit of second grade humor. The second grader asked his father, "What did George Washington say to his troops before they got into the boat to cross the Delaware River?" Expecting to hear a profound inspirational and historical reply, the father said he did not know. The second grader replied, "Get into the boat, men." What trustees need to tell participants most of the time is simply to get into the boat—not a dialog or legal treatise on the dynamics of boating.
- *Send the message in the form that is the easiest to receive.* Message or media forms can be plan booklets, letters, notices, posters, videotapes or any other form that transmits the information to the participant. Trustees should take the time to consider not only which media forms will reach the participant, but which will also be easiest for the participant to understand. For example, if participants are not reading and following the plan booklet, would a poster in appropriate areas at the workplace or a notice and article in the union and/or company periodical be helpful? The poster and notice would warn participants that problems with medical claims payments or pension applications could be avoided if participants follow the procedures outlined in the booklet. In this example, the poster is a constant reminder and the notice in the union and/or company periodical may get the spouse involved.

When technical language has to be used, examples should be used for clarification. Participants may not even try to comprehend a technical term but normally they will read and apply an example to their own situation.

Do not send your message at a time when the participant's attention may be focused elsewhere or when there is competition from outside sources such as the Christmas holidays, the first week of hunting season or Superbowl weekend. The timing of the message can be a very important factor in obtaining maximum reception.

- *Control feedback from participants.* This suggestion will be discussed in more detail later.
- *Follow up the feedback.* If feedback from participants indicates that they are not reading the plan booklet, a followup message may be desirable. If the feedback indicates that participants are obtaining their information from an unreliable source, the trustees may want to follow up and counter the other source. In a plan with which the author is associated, the trustees constantly warn participants that eligibility determinations are made only by the plan administrator. Reliance on any other source regarding eligibility is at the participants' peril.
- *Do not be afraid to change.* If one method of communication is not working, trustees should try another method. Avoid the "we have always done it this way" trap.

Developing Feedback

The communication model previously shown in Figure 1 may not always be realistic. One of the problems trustees face is that they send the message to the participant but they may not receive the feedback. The feedback from the participant may look like the diagram in Figure 2 because it often bypasses the trustees and goes to the insurance carrier, administrator, co-workers, company personnel officer, union representative or other person.

When the trustees do not receive feedback they become isolated and cannot gauge whether their communication is effective. Without access to feedback, the trustees may feel that the message was properly communicated and well-received but, in reality, confusion and dissatisfaction may reign. The trustees must develop procedures for keeping informed of any participant feedback that goes to other persons. Some suggestions are:

- *Encourage input from field representatives.* The best source of feedback is from the people who have the most contact with the employee

Figure 2

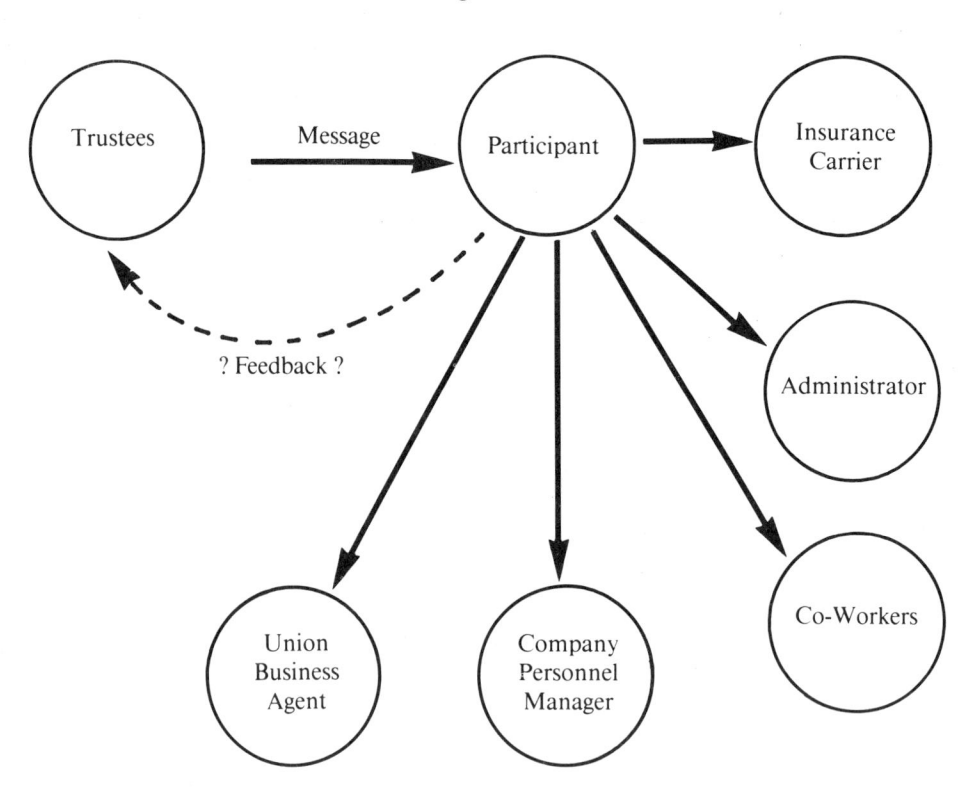

Diagram: Trustees → Message → Participant, with Participant sending arrows to Insurance Carrier, Administrator, Co-Workers, Company Personnel Manager, and Union Business Agent. A dashed arrow labeled "? Feedback ?" returns from Participant to Trustees.

participants and their families. These people normally are the local union representative and the company personnel manager. These individuals should be encouraged to alert the trustees (or a representative of the trustees) regarding problems or questions that participants bring to their attention.

- *Form a subcommittee to work with the advisors.* The trustees should form a subcommittee that meets regularly with the professional advisors to discuss what is occurring within their areas of responsibility and any problem that they may have. Whenever possible, the subcommittee should have the authority to resolve any matter that is within the policy guidelines established by the board of trustees. It is suggested that the subcommittee form proposals and recommendations for the full board of trustees on matters that will require the establishment of a new policy or an amendment to existing policy.

For example, a trust with which the author is associated has a subcommittee of one union representative and one management representative that meets at least monthly. The meeting normally includes a review of pension applications, claim appeals for both pension and health and welfare, and a general discussion with the administrator, attorney and actuary. The advisors discuss items that are of concern to them and the subcommittee reports problems that have been brought to its attention by local union representatives and company personnel managers. In most cases, all matters are resolved at this meeting. If a policy must be adopted or amended, the subcommittee and the advisors make a proposal and recommendation to the board for action at the next quarterly meeting.

- *Maintain a telephone log.* The insurance carrier and/or administrator should keep a telephone log of inquiries and complaints made by the participants. The telephone log produces two worthwhile benefits. First, it makes the carrier or administrator aware of what its employees are doing and gives the carrier or administrator the opportunity to make internal adjustments. Second, a quick review of the log provides the trustees (or the subcommittee) with an excellent overview of what feedback the participants are providing. The subcommittee previously mentioned recently

observed a high number of inquiries about layoff coverage. This observation prompted the board of trustees to issue a special notice to participants outlining eligibility rules for layoff coverage.
- *Review correspondence.* The trustees (or the subcommittee) should periodically review the administrator's and/or carrier's correspondence to participants. ERISA (Employee Retirement Income Security Act of 1974) requires the trust to provide the participant with a written explanation whenever there is a denial of a benefit. The trust has a problem if there is either too much or too little correspondence. If there is too much, something has not been properly communicated to the participants or there is a problem with a trust policy or procedure. If there is too little, either the trust has very liberal benefit provisions or it is not meeting the ERISA notice requirements.
- *Do not be afraid to change.* Again, avoid the "we have always done it this way" trap. If one method of communication is not working, try another.

General Considerations Before Selecting a Media Form

The trustees have access to many types or forms of media. These forms include booklets, letters, notices, posters, magazines, newsletters, videotapes and many others. Before the trustees decide on what type of media they want to use to send their message, they should evaluate the factors that may influence that decision. This evaluation will avoid designing the communication to fit the media form. Rather, it will permit using the form of media that will disseminate the message most effectively. Several of the factors to consider are listed below:
- *What message do the trustees want to send?* For example, if the trustees are amending the plan to provide a new level of benefits, is reprinting the plan booklet the best way to convey the message? Sometimes the trustees cannot overcome the "we have always done it this way" trap or the "then the participants will have all of the current benefits from one reference" argument. If these traditional arguments cannot be avoided, at least consider using followup communication such as posters announcing the change, announcements in the union and/or company periodical(s) or other complementary media forms.

Trustees should use the media form that will best disseminate the message. Trustees should not design the message to fit the traditional form of media.
- *What are the time limitations?* How soon does the message have to reach the participant? How long will the message remain accurate? One large bank with many multistate branches produced an excellent videotape presentation that explained health and welfare benefits to its employees. The videotape was in living color, stereo sound and had the right mixture of humor and serious discussion to convey the message. The presentation even won a gold medal in a film exhibition. The only problem was that after six months the bank discontinued using the videotape because the health and welfare plan had been amended and there were no provisions made for the film to be modified or updated. This example of an expensive and elaborate presentation that could only be used for six months illustrates a lack of planning.

When there is a short period between trust action and the effective date, posters at the workplace and in the union halls with a followup notice in the union periodical are effective ways to communicate a message. A trust with up-to-date addresses of participants can use letters very effectively. A small trust that has a good working relationship with participating employers can use stuffers in pay envelopes.
- *How many people need to receive the message?* If the message is only for a select group of participants, an individual letter may suffice. However, an individual letter may be impractical if the message is to go to every participant in a very large trust (especially if the trust does not maintain an accurate participant address file). If the select group of participants are relatively easy to contact, such as retirees, a simple notice or letter included in with the retiree's monthly check works well. On the other hand, if the select group of participants are those workers on layoff and the trust covers four states, the communication may need to take several forms to be effective.
- *What is the cost/benefit ratio?* In the example of the bank's elaborate videotape presentation that was only used for six months, there is questionable cost/benefit ratio. Reprinting the plan booklet after every benefit change can also have a questionable cost/benefit ratio when the administrator, local unions and par-

ticipating employers discard thousands of unused copies.

In a plan with which the author is associated, we had a consultant develop a pre-retirement program. The program was presented to participants who were 55 and older and their spouses. The program was made available to every local union throughout the four state jurisdiction of the pension trust. The cost of each session was approximately $1,000 and during the first year it was well-received and well-attended. During the second year, however, attendance averaged five employee participants per presentation. The $200 cost per participant produced an unfavorable cost/benefit ratio. With this experience in mind, the sponsoring union now presents a pre-retirement program as part of its annual convention. This annual program is followed up by a set of pre-retirement booklets for participants who request them. The positive results of the annual program have a very favorable cost/benefit ratio for the plan. Again, trustees must not be afraid to change.

- *What is the expected success of the different forms of media?* What has past acceptance and effectiveness been? What do the advisors and consultants recommend? What is the feedback from the participants, union representatives and company personnel officers? All of this input should be considered along with the simple rules that the participant (receiver) controls the communication and that the three elements of the communication cycle are accurate messages, feedback and followup.

Should Consultants Be Used?

There are many situations in which the use of a consultant and/or advisor is mandatory, or at least highly advisable. For example, it should be mandatory that before any communication from the trustees is sent to the participants legal counsel review the content of the message. Trustees may only be telling the participants to "get into the boat," but legal counsel will probably change how they get into the boat or what life jacket they should wear to comply with some regulation or to prevent a potential liability to the trust. In addition, the content should also be reviewed by the administrator. How many times have trustees been told by the administrator that the message that has already been approved by legal counsel will not work because it cannot be programmed into the computer?

The Process of Preparing Communication Material

Reviewing Policy Questions

The trustees should review some basic policy questions as part of the process of preparing their communications. A thorough review and consideration of all potential problems in the preparation process will save considerable time and potential liability in the future. Some of these considerations are:

- *The trustees should know exactly what policy they want to communicate.* Or, put another way, *poor communications should not set trust policy.* An example: Participants who make self-payments for health and welfare coverage during layoff must make the payment by the tenth of the month to be eligible for the next month's coverage (e.g., a payment on June 10 provides July coverage). In January, the trustees change the amount of self-payment a participant must make to maintain health and welfare coverage. The effective date is July 1. The administrator sends out timely notices to all participants. *Question:* What is the trustees' policy? Should participants who make self-payments remit the new amount in June or July? In this real life example, the trustees intended for the increased payment to commence in June for July coverage. The trustees did not adequately communicate when payments were to commence, so the poor communication changed the trustees' effective date from July 1 to August 1.
- *The trustees should know what the limitations are.* These limitations would include those dictated by legal counsel, the administrator or other advisor. Time limitations or other requirements that may influence the content of the message should also be considered.

Methods Trustees Can Use

There are many methods trustees can use to prepare communication material. All of the methods have their strong and weak points and trustees must select what is right for them. Following are some of the most common methods to get the job done:

- *Turn the project over to a consultant or an advisor.* Since most trustees have other responsibilities and do not have all of the time that they would desire to dedicate to developing the communication, this method is often

the most practical. A caution, however, is to be sure that the consultant and/or advisor implements the trustees' policy and does not dictate it. To avoid this problem, a system of checks and balances should be used to monitor the consultant or advisor.
- *Have someone prepare the communication and then have a subcommittee and/or all of the advisors and trustees review the draft and submit comments.* This system offers effective checks and balances to control the preparer. One big drawback is that commenters tend to procrastinate. Reviewing a draft, especially a long, complicated one such as a revised plan booklet, tends to get low priority. To keep the review process moving, the board should set a specific deadline for submitting comments. Setting a deadline is helpful, but Murphy's Law normally prevails. Applying Murphy's Law, the person who should have reviewed the draft and submitted comments misses the deadline. The communication is finalized and is sent to the participants. Then the person reviews the communication and finds several items that are incorrect. In this example, the deadline was met but an accurate message was not sent. Another drawback of the "prepare and review" method is that individuals commenting separately can "what if," "what about" and "suppose that" a policy to death. In many instances, all of the "what ifs," "what abouts" and "suppose thats" have to be recommented on in second, third and fourth drafts. Thus, this method can be time-consuming and has the potential of neglecting the rule of simplicity.
- *Have a subcommittee of knowledgeable union and employer trustees sit down in a room with the necessary consultants and advisors and hammer it out until it's done.* This procedure has been found to be a very successful method to get the job accomplished efficiently. All interested parties can add their input to the project at the same time and all of the "what ifs," "what abouts" and "suppose thats" are considered in one joint session.
- *Any combination of the previous three methods that will provide the best results for the trustees.*

Summary

Each trust has its individual characteristics concerning size, geographical jurisdiction, type of industry, benefits and purpose. A trust covering one local of 500 participants in a single city has a different objective and purpose than a large trust covering thousands of participants located throughout several states. A trust covering participants in a seasonal industry has different objectives and purposes than a trust covering employees in a stable industry. Trustees should strive to develop communication techniques that will best serve their particular goals and objectives.

Regardless of trust size, industry or purpose, several basic rules will help trustees develop communication systems that will be effective. First, good communication must have all three of the elements in the model: accurate message, feedback and followup. Second, trustees must remember that the plan participant (receiver) controls the communication. Identify the barriers that would hinder participants from receiving the message and design methods that will penetrate or eliminate those barriers. Third, trustees send the message but often do not receive the feedback from participants. The trustees must develop a system to monitor feedback so that they have an accurate measure from which to determine if the message has been received and understood. When it comes to feedback, no news is *not* good news. Fourth, the trustees must evaluate all items that can influence their message before they select the media form. What policy do the trustees want to maintain? Who is to receive the message? Are there any legal or administrative limitations? What will the cost/benefit ratio be? What feedback are the trustees receiving from the field? Fifth, trustees must be adaptable to change. Sixth, trustees should not allow bad communication to set trust policy. Good communication takes thought and planning. The proper consideration of all of these elements will permit trustees to send a message that will meet their goals and objectives.

Understanding Production

BY EDWARD M. FINKELSTEIN

FOR CLARIFICATION OF this subject, based on your needs as administrators as I understand them, what I am referring to when I say "production" is really printing. It is the art of getting out a good quality, readable piece of printed material so that your fund's beneficiaries can better understand what the employer is providing and the union negotiated for them.

To many, printing is simply like "magic." You give a bunch of papers to a guy called a printer and lo and behold he comes back with a beautifully printed piece—a newsletter or benefit booklet or whatever. Simply magic? Not quite. What happens between the time you hand your printer that pile of papers and the time he brings back your finished product is a specific, sometimes overly complicated, process. Understanding that process can save your fund a great deal of money—and save you a great many headaches and heartbreaks later.

Frankly, I don't have all the answers. But some 18 years of experience in the communications and public relations business has given me an appreciation for the problems and concerns on both sides: you as the client and buyer, and your printer as the supplier. I'll try to cover as many aspects of the nitty-gritty as possible so that you can better understand the roles of the various players in the production process.

Although I'm going to cover production as a process, I'm going to spend more time on the upfront requirements, the *business side* of production that, if managed properly, can save your fund a great deal of money—and save you a lot of problems. This aspect should be far more profitable to you than a review of the physical, backshop aspects of production that will be of little practical value to you. I'll cover the business of production, the creative aspects of production, some of the actual production itself so that you have a feel for the processes and for critiquing your printed pieces and, finally, a few buying hints designed to help you be a sharp production purchaser.

The Business of Production

If you can master this aspect of the production process, you'll find that the rest will come much easier and at far less cost.

Mr. Finkelstein is president of Union Communications Corporation (UniCom), a full-service communications agency in St. Louis, Missouri that writes and produces health and welfare and pension newsletters for several multiemployer AFL-CIO and Teamster union trust funds. Mr. Finkelstein works closely with the trade union movement and is publisher of the St. Louis Labor Tribune, *one of the largest circulation local labor newspapers in the United States. He is a member of the Governor's Economic Development Advisory Council (Labor and Employment Committee), counselor to the United Labor Committee of Missouri, Missouri State Labor Council—AFL-CIO, Greater St. Louis Labor Council—AFL-CIO and the St. Louis Building and Construction Trades Council—AFL-CIO. He currently is involved in helping organize a new St. Louis labor and management group dedicated to finding ways to curtail the skyrocketing cost of local health care. He received his bachelor of journalism degree from the University of Missouri. He is also a member of the Public Relations Society of America (and a member of the Society's Counselors Section), Sigma Delta Chi (the professional journalism organization) and the Advertising Federation of Greater St. Louis. He has participated in previous International Foundation educational programs.*

Determining Your Own Role

Just how far do you want to go? What are your choices? You can take the role of the executive, the general overseer of the project. You can take the role of the producer, actually pulling together all the different pieces of the production process to make sure they get to the right place at the right time—a time-consuming responsibility. You can play the role of the art director, but that takes a very special talent that few managers really have if they are honest with themselves. You can play the role of the photographer, actually taking or at least setting up the photographs you'll need for your printed piece. Finally, you can play the role of the copywriter and write everything you want to print.

The most important point is that you must evaluate your own limitations honestly, admit to them and understand that they are human; you can't be all things—you can't be Clark Kent and Superman. Knowing your own limitations is a critical first step in the production process. Why? Because once you know your own limitations, you can get some professional help. Now I can appreciate that this may seem a bit self-serving as I'm a communications professional who does consulting work on proper communications. But the realities of life are what they are: If you want to produce a professional communications piece, you should consider professional help at some level. Again, the role you want to play will determine what kind of professional assistance you seek out.

A suggestion: In a single week, literally dozens of newsletters and other printed materials come across your desk. Why not start an "ideas file"? When you see an item that's particularly good, file it away. When it comes time to deal with a professional—whether he or she is a communicator, artist or photographer—pull out your ideas file to show them samples of what you like and don't like. Use the same technique with your printer.

Points of Decision

In determining your role in the production process, there are some decisions that you simply cannot defer, decisions that you must make in coordination with the other policymakers in your organization.

First, there's the strategy of the communications piece. What is its goal? It's important to let your suppliers and/or professionals know, at least in general terms, the kind of money you have for this project. They may tell you right away that you can't get what you want for that money; then you'll need to reevaluate the project. Second, what is the timetable or schedule for the piece? Be realistic. Early planning and giving yourself time to get the job done right the first time will save you a lot of money! Finally, you cannot defer the overall responsibility for the printed piece. If it is good, you'll get the compliments; conversely, if it is bad or too expensive or incomplete, your head is on the chopping block. Therefore, it is imperative that you maintain overall responsibility for the project. You see, the simple truth of the matter is that the buck does stop at your desk.

Quality

The next concern you must take into consideration when planning the "business" of production is the quality level you expect to receive. Your choices fall into three categories, what I call the three "Ps"—*pretty, practical* or *plentiful.*

A *pretty* piece is designed to impress someone or persuade the reader to a point of view. It is usually an advertising or promotional piece and is usually the most expensive to produce.

A *practical* piece is something that's both attractive and affordable. It won't be as handsome as an advertising item, but it can be attractive. Practical items are usually mass communications items such as newsletters, brochures or magazines. Although they are fairly expensive, they don't cost what a *pretty* advertising item would cost.

Finally, there are the items that I call *plentiful.* Items in this category are a necessity and, because they are for mass distribution, must be as economical as possible. In this category are mass circulation newspapers, sales and instruction manuals, and sales directories or catalogs like Sears' or J. C. Penney's.

A definition of what it is you are looking for is important for you and your professional help. This definition will go a long way toward helping determine your overall cost.

Scheduling

Next in the "business" of production is scheduling, that is, the time you have to get the job done. Herein lies a major cost consideration. I would like to introduce you to scheduling through the letters "GFC." They stand for "Good/Fast/Cheap." No matter how inventive or creative you are, chances are you can only accomplish any two qualities in combination for your projects. It is impossible to accomplish all three in the same project.

You can get a good project fast, you can get a good product cheap, or you can get a product fast and cheap. But you just can't get a good product done in short order and have it cost you nothing! What you can expect is a good product at a fair price if you give yourself a reasonable schedule in which to accomplish the task.

Time is a major cost factor. If you have a tight deadline and want a quality product, you're going to pay an arm and a leg for it! You'll have overtime, the need to put other jobs aside, etc.; before you know it, the job's costs are out of sight.

However, you can affect the time elements in your job. As an administrator, here's where your role can be critical. Think in terms of a circle. This circle represents the TOTALITY of your project, from start to finish. Within this circle you have various elements of your project. First, one slice of the "pie" is the organization of your task—that is, you're making the various decisions outlined previously. The second slice is the schedule you've established and the time you will need to get it done. The third slice is the actual time it will take to do the job—writing, designing, typesetting and getting it ready to be printed. Finally, the fourth slice will be the time needed to make any needed changes once you have gone all the way through the process and just before it is ready to go to the printer. Big or little, at this stage, changes are costly.

Now the secret: You can't shrink this circle. What you *can* do is alter the size of the slices. If you don't give yourself adequate time to organize the project and don't leave adequate time to get it done, you pay for it in the actual time the job will take. An example: The writing was not well thought out and not cleanly typed when it went to the typesetter. Your artist was rushed so he or she gave a very rough layout to the typesetter. Therefore, the copy doesn't fit the specifications. On top of that, there are many, many errors because the typesetter couldn't read someone's handwriting or scribbled corrections. Not only are you increasing the production time, but when someone reads it and discovers the errors just before it is ready to go to the printer, you have to make massive alterations. What have you done? You haven't changed or shrunk the circle; you've only made various segments within that circle larger and increased your costs substantially.

If you as the administrator take the time *at the beginning* to get your project organized, make sure that it is well-written and cleanly typed, and that your professional help will be given ample time to produce it, then you can alter the size of the time pie slices when it comes to production and corrections. You come out with a better job within budget.

A good friend of mine is a typesetter. He has a key saying that I've come to learn is the truth. In his honor, I've titled this truism "The Hempen Imperative." It goes like this: "There's never enough time to do the job right . . . but there is always time to do it over."

All of these processes, then, make up the business of production. If this is the point where you want to end your personal involvement, that's fine. Remember, you have to make an honest evaluation of your own skills and ability. To stop at this point is no shame. After all, you are an administrator; you are the overseer. If that's where your real skills lie, then use them to the fullest and from this point on in the production process, get some professional help.

Creative Aspects of Production

The graphics designer can help you translate your message into a well-thought-out, attractive brochure, newsletter, etc. The functions of the design of your item are to help you establish individual identification, to provide information of course, and to help persuade the receiving audience. A lot of information poorly displayed will accomplish nothing. That's the reason for good design—to help you communicate your message in a visually pleasing format that enhances the desire to read the message.

However, designers have to understand what you are trying to accomplish. The designer must know your objectives and what you expect from the printed piece before the design process can begin. I would urge that when you are dealing with graphics designers, you encourage them to read your copy. After all, if they don't understand it, how can they help to display the material so that it will be understood by others? And listen to their advice. Because he or she comes into the challenge fresh, often your designer can make positive suggestions that will help you produce a better item.

Keep in mind that, although you probably have a concept in your head, there is always more than one solution to a problem. Asking for alternative solutions, if you have planned your time properly, may be a little more costly, but will help you get the very best results.

While we are talking about costs, which is obviously a very important item, I would like to make a suggestion about the alternative of using a college student learning the trade instead of a professional graphics designer. Quite often there are good college students around and they often work very, very cheaply. But . . . keep in mind that they are students, and you only get what you pay for. An experienced graphics designer can save you a great deal of money in the long run through experience with paper sizes, printing techniques, quality control and much more. I am all for giving students an opportunity to learn, but you have to gauge whether it is worth doing on your job! If you're on a limited budget and have time constraints, as is usually the case, then you had better stick to a professional designer.

Layouts

A key element in dealing with a designer is to ask for a layout of your piece as the designer sees it after reading your copy and working up an approach to accomplish your objectives. A layout is like a blueprint; it helps everyone understand what is going to happen to the printed piece.

There are three basic kinds of layouts: a rough layout—basically a very loose sketch to give you a general feel of what the finished piece might look like; a "semicomp" layout—much more specific, with copy blocks sketched in, headline areas noted and generally everything in the approximate place you could expect it to be in the final product; and a "tight comp"—an exact blueprint of your printed piece, with all copy sized and located on each page so you can have a good idea of what your newspaper or brochure will look like when it's done.

Which kind should you ask for? That depends on the confidence you have in your creative person and what you need or feel your supervisor needs to be able to approve the project. In many instances, if you know your staff graphics people well, you can agree on concepts from a rough layout. This procedure saves time and some costs, but if you don't know your graphics designer, I would suggest that you ask for a "tight comp." In fact, a tight comp will aid you in getting some very specific printing cost quotations. With a tight comp, a printer knows what he can expect and from that can give you a bid.

Production

To this point, you've gotten your copy written and approved, your graphics designer has taken that copy and prepared a tight comp layout for your consideration and you've approved it; and the type has been set and pasted to production boards so that you have camera ready copy boards for your printer. What now?

Bids

First and foremost, with bids from a printer, you know if you can afford the item and if it fits your budget. If it doesn't, bring your graphics people back and tell them the problem. They can help reduce costs with some positive suggestions for change.

When you're dealing with a printer, there are a few essential points you must be aware of. I mentioned printer quotations. At this point, let me offer a word of caution: There are printer "estimates" and printer "quotations"; there is a difference between them. Estimates are not, I repeat, *not*, firm figures on which you can rely. If you don't have a tight comp and your graphics people have not specified paper, ink colors, etc., then the printer is really flying blind. Therefore, you'll get an estimate, but the final price could be substantially different.

On the other hand, if you give your printer all the information needed, you can get a firm quotation. It may be slightly higher than you might expect, but the printer is looking out for the one or two surprises that always crop up once the graphics people are finished. But at least with a quotation, you have reliable figures you can count on when budgeting.

Customs of the Trade

In the printing business, there are sets of rules called the "customs of the trade." It is important that you know these rules because there are several essential elements. Notable among them is the "plus or minus 10% rule." That means your printer has a right to overprint by 10% and charge you for it, or underprint your jobs by 10% and not be penalized by you. Why? Because today's high-speed presses are costly to run and there is a certain amount of spoilage as the printer gets ready, especially in preparing the inks. Thus, in an effort to keep costs down, the printer may shut off his presses a moment too soon and you come up 10% short on your run. If you need an exact number of printed pieces, let the printer know so he can be sure to get them all printed. In this case, you can expect an overrun, but you are sure of getting the exact number to meet your needs.

When dealing with a printer, I strongly urge that you put everything in writing, and then go over those written instructions with your printer. A friend recently ordered 5,000 brochures over the phone but 50,000 were delivered! He didn't have a written backup, and it was impossible to place specific responsibility for the goof. Guess who ate the cost of 45,000 brochures? *Put your request in writing!*

Scheduling

An important element to your printer is time. If you are in a rush because you scheduled this job poorly, and your printer already has a job on the presses, for him to meet your deadline he will have to pull that work off and put your work on . . . or bump someone out of rotation for presswork that's already been scheduled. By giving your printer ample time, he can fit your work into his schedule and save you costs. You need it yesterday? You pay a premium for it!

Don't be afraid to call your printer to ask for his advice. Quite often he can help you save money. Every printer has different equipment. Each usually has a stock of paper that he may give you a deal on.

That fact alone can help you and your graphics designer. So let your printer give advice. It's often a real money saver.

The Critique

Finally, after your piece is printed, you need to critique it with your staff and others who receive it. Did the piece do the job it was intended to do? You can learn a great deal for the next project if you discover how well the planning and execution of the present job went.

Practical Buying Hints

- Know your printer. It's critical. Ask for samples of work he has done. You've got to know his capabilities and his limitations. Some printers are great with two colors of ink, but four or more colors are a different story. Most printers will never say "no." If they can't print it themselves, they'll job it out to a larger printer, tack on their fee and you'll never know the difference. Small printers can do small jobs inexpensively. Large printers usually do small jobs expensively. It is best to have two or three printers with whom you can deal, printers of equal capabilities so you can get bids and compare them properly.
- Good service comes because of one good habit—paying your bill promptly! That means within 30 days. That printer had to buy the paper stock, the ink, pay his pressmen, etc. If you make him wait 60 or 90 days, you are costing him money. Do that regularly and you will find that your service deteriorates.
- Most of you probably have regular printers that you deal with. You are comfortable with them. Fine. But periodically, get comparative bids, especially on larger jobs. You see, it is not beyond a printer to give you work perhaps at cost or with minimal markup for a time, just to get you comfortable. Then, over a period of time, the costs rise ever so slowly. You fall into the comfort rut; you don't like to change... no one does. But once in a while, put your jobs out for bid—just to make sure "Old Charlie" is still giving you the best price.
- Think quantity on standard items you use all the time. Remember, the larger the printing run, the cheaper the unit cost. I ran into one instance where one organization had eight different sized envelopes, ordered by various departments from different printers!
- Don't be afraid to consolidate your buying needs and let one person do all the ordering. That way, that person can constantly be on the lookout for other economies. Also, don't be afraid to modify forms to fit standard sized envelopes.
- Demand quality. Don't be intimidated. You are paying the price; expect the work. When a printer sends you a job that's not right, if you have the time, send the job back and demand that it be reprinted. I can guarantee that the next time your job will get special attention from that printer. He can't afford to do otherwise. Once the printer knows you expect it to be right, you'll get it right. Also, don't let them give you a "price reduction" if you will take the botched job. If you have the time, send the job back.
- Finally, a word about bids. I use a rule of thumb when reviewing bids—eliminate the highest and the lowest and look at the midranges. The very highest bidder really doesn't need the work. He is usually very busy and if he gets your job, it's all gravy. On the other hand, the very lowest, especially if it's far below the others, means that the printer is looking to cut corners some place that you won't know about until you see the final product. The printers in the midranges will usually be pretty close to each other, if you have given them all the same set of written specifications from which to bid.

Now there are exceptions to that rule of thumb: If you know the low bidder, and he has given you quality before, chances are that his workload is down and he wants the job badly enough to give you an extremely good price. In that case, go with it. Also, if the low bids are close, and you have a printer with whom you deal but he was not quite as low, let him know how much he is off. Usually, he will agree to meet the low price if it is within his ability to do so.

Summary

There's no magic to understanding production. It is not so important for you to understand the technical aspects of how your job is produced in the plant. But, as a manager, you should understand the essentials of the job that affect the final product and its price. With this information, you should be able to go back to your fund with the assurance that it is getting the best value for the dollars spent.

Index

Author Index

Albert, Marilyn S.
Myths and realities of the older worker, (82) 445-52
Aldrich, Todd
Pre-retirement preparation assistance, (82) 415-21
Baum, Bernard M.
The board of trustees and its counsel: a question of professional responsibility, (82) 223-26
Bickel, F. Gilbert, III
Solving investment problems for small funds, (82) 269-71
Breher, William R.
Flexible benefits for multiemployer plans, (82) 355-63
Brightman, Jon S.
Tying defined contribution plans to investment earnings, (82) 262-68
Brinson, Gary P.
You and your investment manager, (82) 227-29
Brislin, Joseph A.
Developing communication material, (82) 459-65
Burroughs, Eugene B.
Spectrum of investments: 1977-1982, (82) 244-55
Carroll, Michael J.
Trustees' responsibilities for collection of employer contributions, (82) 168-74
Chadwick, William J.
Fiduciary responsibility and prohibited transactions: 1982 update, (82) 141-50
Cohen, Bonnie R.
Evaluating your investment manager, (82) 230-35
Collins, George J.
Fixed income alternatives, (82) 272-83
Courtney, Joseph M.
CEBS: a view from the center of the action, (82) 207
Crispo, John
Canadian–American relations: a Canadian perspective, or a latent continentalist comes out of the closet, (82) 343-46
Davis, Edgar G.
A business perspective on the management of health care costs, (82) 317-20

Davis, Richard J., Jr.
Trustees' personal liability under ERISA and the importance of proper "defensive" documentation—the fabled "paper trail," (82) 151-53
DeCori, Robert A.
Collecting withdrawal liability, (82) 163-67
Doherty, James F.
Alternative health care delivery systems, (82) 401-04
Elberts, Lee
Legal odds and ends, (82) 46-48
Epstein, Richard L.
Encouraging hospital involvement in health care coalitions, (82) 408-09
Finkelstein, Edward M.
Understanding production, (82) 466-70
Fisher, Larry M.
Medical care in the '80s, (82) 297-313
Friedman, Margery Sinder
Confidentiality of information and plan records, (82) 23-40
Gentile, Carolyn D.
Considerations of post-MPPAA benefit improvements, (82) 41-45
Gertner, Marc
Attitudes and approaches of trustees toward MPPAA, (82) 175-80
Gibson, Virginia L.
Marital property interests in retirement benefits: treatment on divorce, (82) 56-71
Golumbic, E. Calvin
The role of a trustee in a collectively bargained pension trust, (82) 115-16
Greenfield, Michael C.
Legal odds and ends, (82) 46-48
Handel, Bernard
Administrative considerations in establishing voluntary and deductible employee contributions to multiemployer defined contribution plans, (82) 135-40
Harrold, Steven A.
Funding retirees' health and welfare benefits, (82) 428-39
Hass, Lawrence J.
Fiduciary responsibility and prohibited transactions: 1982 update, (82) 141-50
Hesse, Katherine A.
Suspension of pension benefits, (82) 17-22

Horn, Stephen, II
Fiduciary liability insurance—its place in the insurance program of a multiemployer fund and how to buy the cover, (82) 158-62

Ignagni, Karen
Labor's involvement in health care coalitions, (82) 405-07

Jones, Edwin M.
Current PBGC legislative and regulatory developments, (82) 3-12

Joseph, Earl C.
Computers with human characteristics—threshold to the future, (82) 100-11

Kirschner, William M.
Prepaid legal plans: structure and implementation, (82) 379-85

Klein, Frederick
A major innovation in controlling prescription costs, (82) 335-40

Leaf, Robert J.
Dental insurance: goals, plan design, choosing an administrator and the role of dental consultants, (82) 370-78

Lewis, Sheldon P.
We had a barbecue and nobody came except the fire department, (82) 202-06

Lind, Matthew M.
Work: the fourth leg of retirement, (82) 440-44

Majich, Leo A.
Policy manuals, (82) 197-201

Martin, Vincent F., Jr.
Investing in real estate, (82) 287-94

Martorana, R. George
Retirement counseling—necessity or frill? (82) 422-27

Mazza, Charles J.
Cost containment through health education and welfare programs, (82) 321-34

Melchiori, Maria F.
The legal right to die, (82) 72-81

O'Reilly, Timothy P.
Collecting withdrawal liability, (82) 49-55

Perreca, John S.
New trends in forecasting the future of pension plans, (82) 85-89

Reeves, Gilbert K.
An auditor looks at monitoring cash flow, (82) 117-29

Rider, David L.
The legal right to die, (82) 72-81

Ridley, Robert W.
Trustee education and expenses for educational programs, (82) 192-96

Rivers, William A.
U.S./Canadian reciprocity, (82) 347-51

Rowcliffe, Donald H., Jr.
Communication with retirees, (82) 453-56

Salisbury, Dallas L.
Employee benefits: a transformation, (82) 90-94

Saltzman, Warren H.
Fiduciary liability insurance—what the policies cover and what they don't, (82) 154-57

Sass, Martin D.
An investment strategy for the 1980s, (82) 239-43

Schwartz, Alec M.
Prepaid legal services as an employee benefit, (82) 386-93

Sheinkman, Jack
The evolving role of labor in pension fund investment, (82) 256-61

Silverman, David W.
The trustee examines special problems, (82) 185-91

Slaughter, Glen
Cost containment through plan design, (82) 314-16

Smart, Donald A.
The role of the plan professional, (82) 211-13

Soroca, Herbert B.
Options for employee benefit funds, (82) 284-86

Sprinkel, Beryl W.
U.S. monetary policy: looking forward, (82) 95-99

Stallings, Denis
Employee assistance programs for alcohol and drug abuse, (82) 364-69

Storke, Charles A.
Marital property interests in retirement benefits: treatment on divorce, (82) 56-71

Thurau, Russell W.
The actuarial effects of MPPAA on benefit improvements, (82) 181-84

Todd, James S.
Health care coalitions: a perspective from the medical profession, (82) 410-11

Weinstein, Stephen A.
Prohibited transaction exemptions—1982, (82) 13-16

White, Cheryl Denney
Legal service plans: legal basis, legal developments, (82) 394-97

White, Geoffrey V.
The trustees' duty to monitor and evaluate professional advisors, (82) 214-22

Zimmerman, Edward F., Jr.
Techniques for monitoring cash flow, (82) 130-34

Subject Index

Notes on arrangement:

Alphabetization is letter by letter.

Acronyms are treated as single words. For example, "OSHA" appears after "Organizations." However, all acronyms are cross-referenced to their descriptive phrases.

Legal decisions are alphabetized according to the first significant word in their titles; introductory Latin phrases, initials, etc., are ignored. Such legal decisions are not separate entries. Rather, they appear under appropriate subject headings.

A

Accountant *see* Professional services, accountant
Actuarial assumptions, (82) 47
   MPPAA effect on, (82) 182
Actuarial science
   employer liability data, (82) 50
   MPPAA effects on benefit improvements, (82) 181-184
   withdrawal allocation method, (82) 163-164
Administrator *see* Professional services, administrator
Aged and aging
   adaptation abilities, (82) 451-452
   intellectual changes, (82) 445-451
   life expectancy increase, (82) 86, 90
   personality changes, (82) 451-452
   physiological aging, (82) 445
AHA *see* Organizations, American Hospital Association
Alcoholism
   Jellnik curve, (82) 366-367, 369
   see also Employee assistance program
Attorney *see* Professional services, attorney
Auditor *see* Professional services, auditor

B

Benefit plans
   administration
      policies, (82) 197-201
      security, (82) 202-206
   Canada, (82) 347
   corporate, suspension of pension benefits, (82) 19
   defined benefit, (82) 262
   defined contribution, (82) 135-140
      investment earnings, (82) 262-268
   documentation, (82) 151-153
   EDP impact on, (82) 100-111
   improvements
      MPPAA effect on, (82) 41-45
   investment advantages, (82) 290-291
   multiemployer
      cafeteria approach, (82) 355-363
      defined contribution, (82) 135-140
      employer liability, (82) 163-167
         collection of, (82) 49-55
      fiduciary liability insurance, (82) 154-157, 158-162
      suspension of pension benefits, (82) 19-20
      unfunded liabilities calculation before MPPAA, (82) 178
   right-to-die provisions, (82) 72-81
      based on privacy right, (82) 73-74
      Berman v. Allan, (82) 74
      definition of death, (82) 74
      In re Dinnerstein, (82) 77
      Eichner v. Dillon, (82) 77-79
      impact on plans, (82) 73
      law, (82) 75-80
      litigation procedure, (82) 80
      living will, (82) 75, 80-81
      payment of guardian *ad litem* fees, (82) 79-80
      procedure for court review, (82) 78
      In re Quinlan, (82) 74, 76
      Satz v. Perlmutter, (82) 75-76
      specific plan provisions for, (82) 74, 80-81
      In re Storar, (82) 73, 78-79
      Superintendent of Blechertown v. Saikewicz, (82) 74, 77
      Wilmington Medical Center v. Severns, (82) 79-80

role of federal government, (82) 48
small, (82) 269
  investment program for, (82) 269-271
Benefits
  disability
    divorce rights, (82) 59-61, 64
    short term, deducting Social Security from, (82) 46, 145-146
  flexible *see* Cafeteria approach
  improvement
    actuarial effects of MPPAA, (82) 181-184
    arbitrations, (82) 182
    post-MPPAA practices, (82) 183-184
    procedure for determining, (82) 42-44
  medical, maintenance of, (82) 312-313
  pension *see* Pension plans
  post-retirement, (82) 428-439
    communications, (82) 438
    funding, (82) 428-439
      approaches, (82) 436-437
      background, (82) 428-430
      costs, (82) 434-435
      examples, (82) 431-434
      problems, (82) 430-431
    institution of, (82) 438-439
    legal problems, (82) 437-438
    retiree expectations, (82) 437-438
    retirement, early, (82) 438
    working participant attitudes, (82) 438
    see also Employment, retirees
  suspension *see* Employment, retirees
  unfunded vested, (82) 181-184
Breaks in service, (82) 165-166

C

Cafeteria approach
  administration, (82) 358-359
  advantages, (82) 356-357
  adverse selection, (82) 358
  benefit plans, multiemployer, (82) 355-363
    sample plan, (82) 360-363
  disadvantages, (82) 357-358
Canada
  benefit plans, (82) 347
  economic conditions, (82) 343-346
  foreign relations, U.S., (82) 343-346, 347-351
  legislation, (82) 343-346, 347-351
  politics and government, (82) 343-346
Cash flow
  cash held by investing agency, (82) 118
  financial statement review, (82) 118
  investment agent monitoring, (82) 118
  lockbox for employer contributions, (82) 117

manager evaluation, (82) 134
monitoring, (82) 117-129, 130-134
performance measuring service, (82) 119, 123-124
portfolio characteristics
  credit quality, (82) 133
  maturity risk, (82) 133-134
  scope, (82) 131-133
reporting, (82) 130-131
zero balance checking accounts, (82) 117
CEBS *see* Certified Employee Benefit Specialist
Certified Employee Benefit Specialist *(CEBS),* (82) 207
Coalitions *see* Health care, coalitions
Collective bargaining
  agreements, employer contributions, (82) 170-171
  Bonanno Linen Service v. NLRB, (82) 188
  Labbé v. Heroman, (82) 188
  MPPAA, (82) 179-180
  NLRB v. Erie Resistor Corp., (82) 187
  NLRB v. Great Dane Trailers, Inc., (82) 187
  Producer's Dairy Co. v. Western Teamsters, (82) 187
  trustee responsibility, (82) 115-116, 186-188
  UAW v. Cadillac Malleable Iron Co., (82) 188
  Vesuvius Crucible Co. v. NLRB, (82) 188
  Wiegand v. NLRB, (82) 187
Communication of benefits
  developing material, (82) 459-465
  suspension of benefit provisions, (82) 22
Communications
  administrator's role, (82) 466-467
  barriers, (82) 460-461
  consultants, (82) 464
  controlling, (82) 460-461
  creative aspects, (82) 468-469
  employee contributions, (82) 137
  employer liability, (82) 53-54
  media selection, (82) 463-464
  participant divorce rights, (82) 69-70
  participant feedback, (82) 461-463
  policies, (82) 464
  policy manuals, (82) 197-201
  preparation of material, (82) 464-465
  pre-retirement, (82) 425, 427
  production, (82) 466-470
    bids, (82) 469
    buying hints, (82) 470
    "customs of the trade," (82) 469
    schedules, (82) 469-470
  professional services, (82) 211
  quality, (82) 467
  regulations, (82) 460

Index 477

retiree, (82) 425-426, 427, 438, 453-456
    oral, (82) 455-456
    recordkeeping, (82) 455
    retiree concerns, (82) 453-454
    SPD, (82) 455
    subjects, (82) 454-455
    timing, (82) 454-455
rules, (82) 459-460
schedules, (82) 467-468
strategy, (82) 467
subjects, (82) 464
Computers *see* Electronic data processing
Confidentiality *see under* Records management
Consultant *see* Professional services, consultant
Consumer Price Index *(CPI)*, (82) 322
Contributions
    employee
        administrative problems, (82) 137-139
        advantages, (82) 135-136
        benefit plans, multiemployer, defined contribution, (82) 135-140
        collection, (82) 137
        communications, (82) 137
        costs to plan, (82) 135-140
        disadvantages, (82) 136
        divorce rights, (82) 58, 62
        forms and procedures, (82) 137
        investments, (82) 139
        method, (82) 136-137
    employer
        Audit Services, Inc. v. Stewart & Janes, (82) 190
        Audit Services v. Rolfson, (82) 190
        collection, (82) 147-148, 168-174
            administrative office action, (82) 172-173
            delinquency, (82) 171-172, 173
            disclosure, (82) 147-148
            procedures, (82) 168-170
        collective bargaining agreement, (82) 170-171
        economic conditions affecting, (82) 173-174
        Ethridge v. Masonry Contractors, Inc., (82) 146
        Griffith Company v. NLRB, (82) 191
        Metropolitan Detroit Bricklayers v. Hoetger, (82) 191
        NLRB v. Burns International, (82) 190
        NLRB v. Haberman Construction, (82) 191
        NLRB v. Scott Printing Corp., (82) 191
        Pacific N.W. Chapter AGC v. NLRB, (82) 191
        return of mistaken contributions, (82) 146-147
        Schriver v. NLRB, (82) 191

        Soule Glass & Glazing Co. v. NLRB, (82) 190
Corporate plans *see* Benefit plans, corporate
Cost containment *see* Health care, costs
Counseling, pre-retirement, (82) 415-421, 422-427
    background, (82) 422-423
    benefits, (82) 423
    communications, (82) 425, 427
    justification, (82) 415-416
    objectives, (82) 423
    problems, (82) 416
    professional services
        consultants, (82) 426
    program design, (82) 416-417
    publications, (82) 425
    social issues, (82) 415
    statistics, (82) 427
    subjects, (82) 424-425
    types, (82) 424
CPI *see* Consumer Price Index

D

Data processing *see* Electronic data processing
Defined benefit plan *see* Benefit plans, defined benefit; Pension plans, defined benefit
Defined contribution plan *see* Benefit plans, defined contribution; Pension plans, defined contribution
Demographics, (82) 90-91
    impact on pension plans, (82) 86
Dental care, prepaid *see* Insurance, dental
Dental insurance *see* Insurance, dental
Department of Labor *(DOL)*
    prohibited transaction exemptions, (82) 16
    regulations
        diversification, (82) 244-255
        trustee compensation, (82) 193-194
Discrimination, age, (82) 445-452
    see also Aged and aging; Employment, retirees
Divorce *see* Pension plans, divorce
DOL *see* Department of Labor
Drug abuse *see* Employee assistance program

E

EAP *see* Employee assistance program
Economic conditions, (82) 241-242
    effect on employer contributions, (82) 173-174
    impact on pension plans, (82) 91
    North America, (82) 343-346

retirement income, (82) 440-441
underground economy, (82) 88
Economics
    domestic policy, U.S., (82) 95-98
    international policy, U.S., (82) 98-99
    monetary policy, U.S., (82) 95-99
EDP *see* Electronic data processing
Education
    trustee compensation for, (82) 192-196
Electronic data processing *(EDP)*
    artificial intelligence, (82) 104-108
    computers with human characteristics, (82) 100-111
    distributed data processing, (82) 109-111
    impact on benefit plans, (82) 100-111
    office automation, (82) 109
    personal computer trends, (82) 101-104, 109-111
    robots, (82) 108-109
    security, (82) 202-206
    simulators, (82) 108-109
Employee assistance program *(EAP)*, (82) 364-369
    costs, (82) 366
    definition, (82) 364-365
    education, (82) 367
    funding, (82) 366
    information sources, (82) 368
    starting, (82) 365-366
    types, (82) 365
Employee Retirement Income Security Act of 1974 *(ERISA)*
    employee census data, (82) 165-166
    fiduciary responsibility, (82) 141-150
        delegation, (82) 214-222
        liability, (82) 151-153
            insurance *see under* Insurance, liability
        professional services, (82) 223-226
    insurance, legal *see* Insurance, legal
    legislation to include public employees, (82) 92
    liability, employer
        statute of limitations, (82) 52
    MPPAA effects on benefit improvement, (82) 181-184
    no preemption of state marital property laws, (82) 66-68
    participant rights, (82) 188-190
    PBGC, (82) 3, 6
    prohibited transactions, (82) 141-150
    reciprocity, (82) 350
    reporting and disclosure, (82) 459-465
        retirees, (82) 455
        see also Summary plan description
    Section 203, (82) 17-18
    service, definition, (82) 18-19
    trustee compensation, (82) 192-193

    trustee responsibility, (82) 185-191
        collective bargaining, (82) 115
        personal liability *see* fiduciary responsibility
Employer liability, (82) 178-179
    actuarial data, (82) 50
    benefit plan, multiemployer, unfunded liability, (82) 178-180
    calculation of, (82) 49-51, 52-53
    collection of, (82) 49-55, 163-167
    collective bargaining, (82) 179-180
    communication with employer, (82) 53-54
    consultants' role, (82) 51, 52, 53, 54, 55
    contractual obligations, (82) 50
    Ells v. Construction Laborer's Pension Trust, (82) 179
    employee census data, (82) 165-166
    employer histories, (82) 49-50
    enforcement, (82) 54-55
    identification of withdrawing employers, (82) 51-52
        abatement provisions, (82) 165
        communication, (82) 165
        withdrawal tests, (82) 165
    interest assumption, (82) 47
    Nachman Corp. v. PBGC, (82) 179
    payment schedules, (82) 53
    Peick v. PBGC, (82) 179
    recordkeeping, (82) 49-52, 164
    statute of limitations, (82) 52
    withdrawal allocation method, (82) 163-164
Employer records *see* Records management
Employment, retirees, (82) 89, 445-452
    abilities of older workers, (82) 441
    adapting job to circumstances, (82) 452
    business advantages, (82) 441
    creating new opportunities, (82) 443-444
    discrimination, age, (82) 441
    disincentives, (82) 442-443
    economic advantages, (82) 441
    sample program, (82) 443-444
    social considerations, (82) 440-441
    suspension of benefits, (82) 17-22, 48
        benefit plans
            corporate, (82) 19
            multiemployer, (82) 19-20
        ERISA, Section 203, (82) 17-18
        notification, (82) 20-21, 22
        plan provisions for, (82) 22
        resumption of payments, (82) 22
        retirement, delayed, (82) 20, 21-22
        review of status, (82) 22
        service, definition, (82) 18-19
        suspendible amount, (82) 18
    see also Aged and aging; Discrimination, age
ERISA *see* Employee Retirement Income Security Act of 1974

F

Federal Insurance Contributions Act *(FICA) see* Social Security
FICA *see* Federal Insurance Contributions Act
Fiduciary responsibility, (82) 141-150, 185-191
  Bay Area Painters Pension Trust Fund, (82) 176
  Blankenship v. Boyle, (82) 177
  Borden, Inc. v. United Dairy Workers Pension Program, (82) 176
  Bueneman v. Central States, Southeast and Southwest Areas Pension Fund, (82) 175
  collection and disclosure of contributions, (82) 147-148
  conflicts of interest, (82) 149-150
    Donovan v. Cunningham, (82) 149
  decisionmaking procedures, (82) 214
  delegation of, (82) 152, 214-215
    Donovan v. Mazzola, (82) 215-216
    Fentron Industries, Inc. v. National Shopmen's Pension Fund, (82) 215
    litigation, (82) 215-216
    Marshall v. Glaziers Pension Plan, (82) 216
  deposit of plan assets, (82) 150
  documentation, (82) 151-153
  Donovan v. Bierwith, (82) 177
  Donovan v. Cunningham, (82) 186
  Donovan v. Mazzola, (82) 186
  Donovan v. Sackman, (82) 395
  Hopkins v. FMC Corporation, (82) 148
  insurance, legal *see* Insurance, legal
  liability, (82) 151-153
    co-fiduciary, (82) 153
    employer, collective bargaining, (82) 179
    individual, (82) 152
    insurance *see* Insurance, liability
    joint, (82) 152
  Marshall v. Glass/Metal Assoc. & Glaziers, (82) 186
  MPPAA impact, (82) 176-178
  Nichols v. Board of Trustees of the Asbestos Workers Local 24 Pension Plan, (82) 147
  North Texas Carpenters Pension Plan, (82) 177
  participant-directed transfers of assets, (82) 145
  Pierce v. NECA-IBEW Welfare Trust Fund, (82) 176
  plan asset regulations, (82) 142-144
  plan counsel, (82) 148
    Washington-Baltimore Newspaper Guild v. The Washington Star Company, (82) 148
  pre-MPPAA guidelines, (82) 175-176
  professional services, (82) 223-226
    monitoring, (82) 211-213, 214-222, 230-235
  return of mistaken employer contributions, (82) 146-147
  transfer of surplus assets, (82) 144-145
  United Mine Workers v. Robinson, (82) 177-178
  Winpisinger v. Aurora Corp. of Ill., (82) 175
  withholding from short term disability benefits, (82) 145-146
Flexible benefits *see* Benefits, flexible

G

GNP *see* Gross National Product
Government
  effect on health care costs, (82) 307, 315
  impact on pension plans, (82) 86
Gross National Product *(GNP)*, (82) 322-323

H

Health care
  alternatives, (82) 401-404
    government policies, (82) 403-404
    preliminary results, (82) 402
    see also Health maintenance organizations, Preferred provider organizations
  coalitions, (82) 307-312, 319-320, 405-407
    American Hospital Association recommendations, (82) 408-409
    health care personnel involvement, (82) 410-411
    hospital involvement in, (82) 408-409
  costs, (82) 297-313, 410-411
    Blue Cross-Blue Shield, (82) 314-315
    Business Roundtable Health Initiatives Survey, (82) 319
    changing attitudes, (82) 315-316
    coalitions *see* Health care, coalitions
    communication, (82) 326
    cost shifting, (82) 307, 401-402
    CPI, (82) 322
    defensive medicine, (82) 306
    education, (82) 321-334
    employee/participant involvement, (82) 325-326
    employer/trustee involvement, (82) 323-324
    GNP, (82) 322-323
    government, (82) 307, 315
    health care personnel reaction to containment efforts, (82) 411
    high cost claimants, (82) 306-307

incentives for physicians and hospitals, (82) 304-307
inflation, (82) 302, 401
insurance companies, (82) 315
justification, (82) 321-323
lack of price competition, (82) 306
local approach to containment, (82) 319
management, (82) 317-320
methods, (82) 323
plan design, (82) 314-316, 321-334
prescription drug plans, (82) 335-340
problems and solutions, (82) 317-318
reimbursement
   biases, (82) 303-304
   prospective, (82) 307
   retrospective, (82) 305
reviewing a benefit plan, (82) 318
role of business, (82) 319-320
statistics, (82) 298-302, 327-334
utilization increases, (82) 302-303
variations in medical practices, (82) 305
welfare plans, (82) 314-316
home, (82) 304
personnel
   involvement in health care coalitions, (82) 410-411
system, (82) 405-406

Health maintenance organization *(HMO)*, (82) 402-403
controls, (82) 402
justification, (82) 402
problems, (82) 401

HMO *see* Health maintenance organization

Hospitals
health care coalition involvement, (82) 408-409

I

Inflation, (82) 251-252, 302, 401
impact on pension plans, (82) 85-86

Insurance
companies, effects on health care costs, (82) 315
dental, (82) 370-378
   administrator choice, (82) 372-376
   consultants, (82) 376-378
   goals, (82) 370-371
   plan design, (82) 371-372
legal, (82) 379-385, 386-393, 394-397
   administration of plan, (82) 381-382
   benefits, (82) 379-380
   case history, (82) 387-388
   cost control, (82) 382-384
   delivery of services, (82) 380-381, 389
   ERISA and, (82) 390, 394-396
   fee arrangements, (82) 390-392
   fiduciary standards, (82) 395
   financial risk, (82) 383-384
   financing, (82) 392-393
   future of, (82) 393
   history, (82) 386-387
   IRC and, (82) 396-397
   justification, (82) 387-388
   open vs. closed panels, (82) 390-391
   plan design, (82) 390
   plan statistics, (82) 382
   reporting and disclosure, (82) 395
   selection of attorneys, (82) 381-382
   sunset provisions in IRC, (82) 397
   Taft-Hartley Act and, (82) 394
   telephone advice and consultation, (82) 384
   types of plans, (82) 384-385, 388-389
liability
   automobile, (82) 159-160
   fiduciary, (82) 154-157, 158-162
      application for, (82) 161-162
      intent, (82) 158
      purchase, (82) 160-161
      summary of policies, (82) 155
   general, (82) 159-160
   workers' compensation, (82) 159
prescription drug, (82) 335-340
   mail prescription service, (82) 337-340
   major medical, (82) 335-336
   sponsor-designated pharmacy, (82) 336-337
   third-party plastic card program, (82) 337
property
   EDP losses, (82) 204-206
   records *see* Records management

Insurance Information and Privacy Protection Model Act, (82) 26-27

Internal Revenue Code *(IRC)*
amendments to, (82) 46-47
insurance, legal, (82) 396-397

Internal Revenue Service *(IRS)*
withholding from short term disability benefits, (82) 145-146

Investment manager *see* Professional services, investment manager

Investments
alternatives, (82) 270-271
benefit plans, small, (82) 269-271
bonds, (82) 240-241, 252-253
capital markets, (82) 264-268
cash held by investing agency, (82) 118
characteristics, (82) 247
classes, (82) 247-248
common stock, (82) 253

contributions, employee, (82) 139
daily activities of investing agent, (82) 118
defined contribution plans, (82) 262-268
economic conditions, (82) 241-242
equity market, (82) 239-240
fixed income
  alternatives, (82) 272-283
  bond environment, (82) 272-275
  credit research, (82) 279
  dedication, (82) 281-283
  immunization, (82) 281-283
  interest rates, (82) 277-279
  management constraints, (82) 279-281
future of, (82) 252-255
inflation, (82) 251-252
labor union involvement, (82) 256-261
manager evaluation, (82) 134
MPPAA influence on, (82) 182-183
options, (82) 284-286
overview, 1977-1982, (82) 244-255
performance evaluation, (82) 235
policy, (82) 227-228, 231-232, 239-243, 244-246
portfolio characteristics, (82) 131-134
real estate, (82) 253, 287-294
  categories, (82) 288-289
  history, (82) 287-288
  life cycle of, (82) 294
  market
    characteristics, (82) 289
    conditions, (82) 289-291
    implications, (82) 292-293
    inventory, (82) 291-292
    participation, (82) 293-294
  performance, (82) 288
  prohibited transaction exemptions, (82) 148-149
  property types, (82) 292
risks of ownership, (82) 246-247
sample portfolio, (82) 248-252
security selections, (82) 242
social, (82) 256-261
IRC *see* Internal Revenue Code
IRS *see* Internal Revenue Service

J

Jellnik curve, (82) 366-367, 369

L

Labor unions
health care coalition involvement, (82) 405-407
investments, (82) 256-261
  economic impact, (82) 258-259
  fiduciary responsibilities of union leaders, (82) 257
  legal implications, (82) 258
  objectives, (82) 257-258
  reactions of employers and administrators, (82) 257
  research and recommendations, (82) 256-257
  social investing, (82) 259-260
Legal insurance *see* Insurance, legal
Legal service plans *see* Insurance, legal
Legislation
medical records, confidentiality, (82) 37
PBGC, (82) 3-12

M

Medical personnel *see* Health care, personnel
Medical records *see* Records management
MESSA *see* Organizations, Michigan Education Special Services Association
Monetary policy, U.S. *see* Economics
MPPAA *see* Multiemployer Pension Plan Amendments Act of 1980
Multiemployer Pension Plan Amendments Act of 1980 *(MPPAA)*
actuarial effects on benefit improvements, (82) 181-184
arbitrations, (82) 47-48
Borden, Inc. v. United Dairy Workers Pension Program, (82) 43
collective bargaining, (82) 45, 179-180
constitutionality of, (82) 55, 179
defined contribution plans, (82) 263
effect on benefit improvements, (82) 41-45
employer liability, (82) 6, 41, 178-179
fiduciary responsibilities, (82) 175-180
genesis of, (82) 6-7
implementation procedure, (82) 180
intentions limited, (82) 43
issues, (82) 41-42
In re Labor Trustees and Management Trustees of the Bay Area Painters Pension Trust Fund, (82) 42
litigation, (82) 6
NLRB v. Amax Coal Co., (82) 42
PBGC, (82) 6-8
Penn Textile Corporation v. Textile Workers Pension Fund, (82) 47
problems and solutions, (82) 7-8
remedial thrust of, (82) 44
trustees, (82) 175-180

In re Union Trustees of the Northern Texas Carpenters Pension Plan and Management Trustees of the Northern Texas Carpenters Pension Plan, (82) 43
Multiemployer plans *see* Benefit plans, multiemployer

N

National Labor Relations Board *(NLRB)*
confidentiality rulings, (82) 37
NLRB *see* National Labor Relations Board
Nursing facilities, (82) 304

O

Occupational Safety and Health Act of 1970 *(OSHA)*
medical record release rules, (82) 36
Office automation *see* Electronic data processing
Option purchase *see* Investments, options
Organizations
American Hospital Association *(AHA)*
health care coalition recommendations, (82) 408-409
Business Roundtable
Health Initiatives Survey, (82) 319
Michigan Education Special Services Association *(MESSA)*, (82) 355-363
OSHA *see* Occupational Safety and Health Act of 1970

P

Party in interest, (82) 13
PBGC *see* Pension Benefit Guaranty Corporation
Peer review organization *see* Professional standards review organization
Pension Benefit Guaranty Corporation *(PBGC)*
assets, (82) 3
bankruptcies, effect of, (82) 4
benefits paid, (82) 3
Congressional requirements, (82) 4
corporate insurance program, (82) 4-6
legislation status, (82) 5-6
creditor status, changes in, (82) 5
"safe harbor" tests, (82) 6
secondary liability, changes in, (82) 5-6
"trigger" event for coverage, changes in, (82) 5
premium increase, (82) 4
deficit, (82) 4-5

ERISA, (82) 3, 6
termination liability, (82) 6
legislation, (82) 3-12
lives covered, (82) 3
multiemployer insurance program, (82) 6-8
MPPAA, (82) 6-8
genesis of, (82) 6-7
problems and solutions, (82) 7-8
regulations, (82) 3-12
administrative relief category, (82) 9-10
clarification category, (82) 9, 10-11
withdrawal rules, special, (82) 8-9
responsibilities, (82) 4
single employer insurance program *see* corporate insurance program
Pension plans
administration
policies, (82) 197-201
benefits, improvement
MPPAA effect on, (82) 183
combination defined benefit and defined contribution, (82) 263
defined benefit
popularity declining, (82) 88
defined contribution, (82) 262-263
advantages, (82) 263-264
disadvantages, (82) 264
MPPAA, (82) 263
popularity increasing, (82) 89
delayed retirement, (82) 86-87
demographics, (82) 86
divorce
American Tel. & Tel. Co. v. Merry, (82) 67
Ball v. Revised Retirement Plan, Etc., (82) 69
In re Marriage of Brown, (82) 59
Busby v. Busby, (82) 60
In re Marriage of Campa, (82) 67
Carpenters Pension Trust, Etc. v. Kronschnabel, (82) 67
Carpenters Pension Trust Fund v. Reyes, (82) 67
Cearley v. Cearley, (82) 57, 58, 59
Central States, Southeast and Southwest Areas Pension Fund v. Parr, (82) 67
Cody v. Riecker, (82) 67
common-law states with equitable division statutes, (82) 61-64
deferred vested retirement benefits, (82) 62-63
disability retirement benefits, (82) 64
employee contributions and benefits in pay status, (82) 62
nonvested retirement benefits, (82) 63-64

community property states, (82) 57-61
   benefits, disability retirement, (82) 59-61
   benefits regarded as separate property, (82) 61
   employee contributions and benefits in pay status, (82) 58
   nonvested retirement benefits, (82) 59
   court orders against plans, (82) 66-69
   division methods, (82) 64-66
   "terminable interest" rule, (82) 66
   Ellett v. Ellett, (82) 58, 59
   Farver v. Department of Retirement Systems, (82) 58
   Flowers v. Flowers, (82) 61
   General Motors Corp. v. Townsend, (82) 67
   Guy v. Guy, (82) 60
   Hisquierdo v. Hisquierdo, (82) 67
   Matter of Marriage of Huteson, (82) 60
   T. L. James & Co., Inc. v. Montgomery, (82) 59
   Johnson v. Johnson, (82) 59
   In re Marriage of Kittleson, (82) 60
   LeClert v. LeClert, (82) 59
   Leighton v. Leighton, (82) 64
   In re Marriage of Lionberger, (82) 69
   Luna v. Luna, (82) 61
   McCarty v. McCarty, (82) 68
   military retirement, (82) 68
   Monsanto Co. v. Ford, (82) 68
   Operating Engineers, Etc. v. Zamborsky, (82) 67
   plan administration, (82) 69-71
   Senco of Florida, Inc. v. Clark, (82) 67
   Shill v. Shill, (82) 59
   Sims v. Sims, (82) 58, 59
   In re Marriage of Stenquist, (82) 60
   Stone v. Stone, (82) 67
   Varsic v. U.S. District Court, (82) 68
   Waite v. Waite, (82) 66
   Wilder v. Wilder, (82) 59
economic conditions and, (82) 91
future of, (82) 85-89
government and, (82) 86, 91-93
increasing life expectancy, (82) 86
inflation, (82) 85-86
legislation, (82) 92-93
mandatory coverage foreseen, (82) 94
personal savings, (82) 87-88
portability *see* Reciprocity
retirees, employment *see* Employment, retirees
retirement, delayed, (82) 89
Social Security, (82) 87, 92, 93-94
suspension of benefits *see under* Employment, retirees
trends impacting, (82) 85-89, 90-94
underground economy and, (82) 88
vesting, (82) 347-351
   unfunded vested benefits, (82) 181-184
Personal computers *see* Electronic data processing
Personal liability *see* Fiduciary responsibility, liability
Physicians *see* Health care, personnel
Plan counsel *see* Professional services, attorney
Plan records *see* Records management
Portability *see* Reciprocity
Post-retirement benefits *see* Benefits, post-retirement
Post-retirement communication *see* Communications, retiree
PPO *see* Preferred provider organization
Preferred provider organization *(PPO)*, (82) 402
Pre-retirement counseling *see* Counseling, pre-retirement
Prescription drug plans *see* Insurance, prescription drug
Privacy, right of
   basis of right-to-die controversy, (82) 73-74
   see also Records management, confidentiality
Professional services, (82) 185-186
   accountants
      sample engagement letter, (82) 221
   administrator, (82) 211-212, 372-376, 381-382
      CEBS, (82) 207
      collection of employer contributions, (82) 172-173
      communication, (82) 466-470
      employee contributions, (82) 135-140
      fiduciary responsibility, (82) 141-150
      flexibility, (82) 94
      monitoring cash flow, (82) 117-129, 130-134
      participant divorce effects, (82) 69-71
      policies, (82) 197-201
      prohibited transactions, (82) 141-150
      security, (82) 202-206
   attorney
      conflicts of interest, (82) 224-225
      duties, (82) 223-226
      fiduciary responsibilities, (82) 148
      model rules of conduct, (82) 224-225
   auditor, (82) 117-129
   consultant
      communication, (82) 212, 464
      counseling, pre-retirement, (82) 426
      dental, (82) 376-378
      role in establishing employer liability, (82) 51, 52, 53, 54, 55
   evaluation of, (82) 211-213
   fiduciary responsibility, (82) 214-215

investments manager, (82) 118, 227-229, 230-235
   active, (82) 275-283
   sample financial summary, (82) 222
jealousies among professionals, (82) 212-213
monitoring of, (82) 211-213, 214-222

Professional standards review organization (PSRO)
dental care, (82) 376-378

Prohibited transactions, (82) 141-150
definition, (82) 13
deposit of plan assets, (82) 150
exemptions
   1982, (82) 13-16
   advantages, (82) 16
   class, (82) 14-16, 148-149
   definition, (82) 13-14
   DOL attitude toward, (82) 16
O'Toole v. Arlington Trust Company, (82) 150
party in interest, (82) 13
plans paying employer portion of Social Security tax, (82) 46-47

Prudent man rule, (82) 185-191
trustee compensation, (82) 192-193

PSRO *see* Professional standards review organization

Publishers and publishing *see* Communications, production

R

Reciprocity
definitions, (82) 347-348
ERISA, (82) 350
tax implications, (82) 347-351
TEFRA, (82) 351
types, (82) 348
U.S./Canada, (82) 347-351

Recordkeeping
communication, retirees, (82) 455
employer liability, (82) 49-52, 164

Records management
confidentiality, (82) 23-40
   Detroit Edison Co. v. NLRB, (82) 37
   employer
      employee access to records, (82) 24-25, 32-33
      employer use and disclosure of records, (82) 25-26
      state laws affecting, (82) 23, 24-26, 32-34
   General Motors Corp. v. Director of NIOSH, (82) 29, 36
   Horne v. Patton, (82) 28
   insurance
      state laws affecting industry, (82) 23-24, 26-27
   Insurance Information and Privacy Protection Model Act, (82) 26-27
   medical
      legislation, (82) 37
      NLRB rulings on, (82) 37
      OSHA rule revisions, (82) 36
      release of information, (82) 36-37
   plan
      laws affecting, (82) 24, 27-30
      Privacy Protection Study Commission, (82) 31, 38-40
      types of information available to participants, (82) 30-31
   United States v. Westinghouse Electric Corporation, (82) 29, 36
   United Steel Workers of America v. Marshall, (82) 29-30, 36
   Whalen v. Roe, (82) 29, 36

Regulations
administrative relief category, (82) 9-10
clarification category, (82) 9, 10-11
communication, (82) 460
DOL
   diversification, (82) 244-255
PBGC, (82) 3-12
withdrawal rules, special, (82) 8-9

Retirees
benefits *see* Benefits, post-retirement
communication *see* Communications, retirees
concerns, (82) 453-454
employment *see* Employment, retirees

Retirement
delayed, (82) 20, 21-22, 86-87, 89
employment after *see* Employment, retirees

Retirement counseling *see* Counseling, pre-retirement

Retirement income
economic conditions, (82) 440-441
personal savings, (82) 87-88
underground economy, (82) 88
see also Employment, retirees

Retirement planning *see* Counseling, pre-retirement

Retirement plans *see* Pension plans

Right to die *see* Benefit plans, right-to-die provisions

S

Sickpay *see* Benefits, disability, short term
Single employer plans *see* Benefit plans, corporate

Social investing *see* Investments, social
Social Security
  benefits, disability, short term, (82) 145-146
  earned income offset, (82) 87
  employment, retiree, (82) 442-443
  pension plans and, (82) 87, 92, 93-94
  short term disability benefits, (82) 46-47
  see also Counseling, pre-retirement
Social Security Act
  amendments, (82) 46-47
SPD *see* Summary plan description
Statistics *see* specific subject
Summary plan description *(SPD)*
  retirees, (82) 455
Surgery
  outpatient, (82) 303-304
Suspension of benefits *see under* Employment, retirees

T

Taft-Hartley Act, (82) 186-191
  insurance, legal, (82) 394
  role of trustee in collectively bargained pension plan, (82) 115, 116
Tax Equity and Fiscal Responsibility Act of 1982 *(TEFRA)*
  reciprocity, (82) 351
TEFRA *see* Tax Equity and Fiscal Responsibility Act of 1982
Testing
  outpatient, (82) 304
  pre-admission, (82) 303-304
Trustees
  compensation, (82) 192-196
    DOL regulations, (82) 193-194
    problems, (82) 194-196
    propriety of, (82) 192-193, 194
  education, (82) 192-196
  MPPAA effect on, (82) 175-180
  responsibility, (82) 185-191
    cash flow monitoring, (82) 117-129, 130-134
    Caudle v. UMW, (82) 189
    collection of employer contributions, (82) 168-174
    collective bargaining, (82) 115-116, 186-188
    communication, (82) 460-461, 464-465
    Elser v. IAM National Pension Fund, (82) 188
    employer monitoring, (82) 190-191
    fiduciary liability, (82) 151-153, 175-180
      rights to documentation, (82) 153
      see also Insurance, liability
    Freeman v. IBEW, (82) 189
    investment manager evaluation, (82) 134
    Janowski v. Teamsters, (82) 189
    Lechner v. National Benefit Fund, (82) 189
    legislation's effect on, (82) 186-191
    McGinnis v. Joyce, (82) 189
    meeting agendas, (82) 234-235
    Miranda v. Audia, (82) 190
    participant as litigant, (82) 188-190
    personal liability *see* fiduciary liability
    Pierce v. NECA-IBEW Fund, (82) 189
    policy manuals, (82) 200
    Ponce v. Construction Laborers, (82) 189
    professional services, (82) 223-226
      evaluation, (82) 211-213, 216-218
      monitoring, (82) 211-213, 214-222, 227-229, 230-235
      sample engagement letter, (82) 221
      sample financial summary, (82) 222
      supervision, (82) 218-220
    Reuda v. Seafarers International, (82) 188
    self-assessment, (82) 230-231
    Taft-Hartley Act effect on, (82) 186-191

U

Unfunded pension liabilities *see under* Pension plans, vesting
United States
  economic conditions, (82) 343-346
  foreign relations, Canada, (82) 343-346, 347-351
  legislation, (82) 343-346, 347-351
  politics and government, (82) 343-346

V

Vesting *see* Pension plans, vesting

W

Welfare plans
  design, (82) 314-316
Withdrawal liability *see* Employer liability
Workers' compensation, (82) 159